MW00779870

LOOKING FOR INFORMATION

STUDIES IN INFORMATION

Recent Volumes

Fidelia Ibekwe
European Origins of Library and Information Science

Jack Andersen and Laura Skouvig
The Organization of Knowledge: Caught Between Global Structures and Local Meaning

Jack Andersen
Genre Theory in Information Studies

Dania Bilal and Jamshid Beheshti
New Directions in Children's and Adolescents' Information Behavior Research

Christine Bruce, Kate Davis, Hilary Hughes, Helen Partridge and Ian Stoodley
Information Experience: Approaches to Theory and Practice

Mark Hepworth and Geoff Walton
Developing People's Information Capabilities: Fostering Information Literacy in Educational, Workplace and Community Contexts

Jung-Ran Park and Lynne C. Howarth
New Directions in Information Organization

Amanda Spink and Jannica Heinström
Trends and Research: Europe

Gunilla Widén and Kim Holmberg
Social Information Research

Dirk Lewandowski
Web Search Engine Research

Donald O. Case and Lisa M. Given
Looking for Information, Fourth Edition

Amanda Spink and Diljit Singh
Trends and Research: Asia-Oceania

Amanda Spink and Jannica Heinstrom
New Directions in Information Behaviour

Eileen G. Abels and Deborah P. Klein
Business Information: Needs and Strategies

Leo Egghe
Power Laws in the Information Production Process: Lotkaian Informetrics

Mike Thelwall
Link Analysis: An Information Science Approach

Matthew Locke Saxton and John V. Richardson
Understanding Reference Transactions: Transforming Art Into a Science

Robert M. Hayes
Models for Library Management, Decision-Making, and Planning

Charles T. Meadow, Bert R. Boyce and Donald H. Kraft
Text Information Retrieval Systems, Second Edition

STUDIES IN INFORMATION

LOOKING FOR INFORMATION: EXAMINING RESEARCH ON HOW PEOPLE ENGAGE WITH INFORMATION

FIFTH EDITION

BY

LISA M. GIVEN
RMIT University, Australia

DONALD O. CASE
University of Kentucky, USA

And

REBEKAH WILLSON
McGill University, Canada

United Kingdom – North America – Japan
India – Malaysia – China

Emerald Publishing Limited
Howard House, Wagon Lane, Bingley BD16 1WA, UK

Fifth edition 2023

British Library Cataloguing in Publication Data
A catalogue record for this book is available from the British Library

ISBN: 978-1-80382-424-6 (Print)
ISBN: 978-1-80382-423-9 (Online)
ISBN: 978-1-80382-425-3 (Epub)

ISSN: 2055-5377 (Series)

Printed and bound by CPI Group (UK) Ltd, Croydon, CR0 4YY

CONTENTS

LIST OF FIGURES, TABLES AND SIDEBARS

Chapter 5 Research Design, Methodologies, and Methods

Chapter 6 Reviewing, Critiquing, Concluding, and Futuring

ABOUT THE AUTHORS

Lisa M. Given, PhD, FASSA, is Director of the Social Change Enabling Impact Platform, and Professor of Information Sciences, RMIT University (Melbourne, Australia). Her interdisciplinary research in human information behavior brings a critical, social research lens to studies of technology use and user-focused design. Her studies embed social change, focusing on diverse settings and populations, and methodological innovations. A former President of the Association for Information Science and Technology (ASIS&T), and the Canadian Association for Information Science (CAIS), Lisa is a Fellow of the Academy of the Social Sciences in Australia and has served on the Australian Research Council's (ARC's) College of Experts. In 2021 she received the ASIS&T *SIG-USE Award for Outstanding Contributions to Information Behavior Research* and was named a Fellow of the SIG-USE Academy. She has received funding from the ARC, Canadian Institutes for Health Research, and the Social Sciences and Humanities Research Council of Canada, working with university and community partners across disciplines. She is Editor-in-Chief of ASIS&T's *Annual Review of Information Science and Technology*. She completed her MLIS (1996) and PhD (2001) at The University of Western Ontario (Canada). You can follow her on Twitter @lisagiven and Mastodon @lisagiven@mastodon.social and read about her work at http://lisagiven.com/.

Donald O. Case, PhD, is Professor Emeritus at the University of Kentucky (Lexington, USA), where he was Professor in the College of Communication and Information for 21 years, serving as Director of the School of Information Science for three years. After completing his MLS at Syracuse University (1977) and PhD at Stanford (1984), he was a faculty member at the University of California, Los Angeles. During 1989 he received a four-month Fulbright Fellowship to lecture at the Universidade Nova de Lisboa, Portugal, and in 2011 a one-month Fulbright award to lecture at three universities in Finland. Case's research interests include information behavior, health-related information, and information policy. He is the author of over 50 academic articles on these and other topics. He authored the first edition of this book, *Looking for Information: A Survey of Research on Information Seeking, Needs, and Behavior* (2002), which was awarded the *Best Book of the Year Award* by the Association for Information Science & Technology (ASIS&T). He was President of ASIS&T during 2008–2009 and has been a member of the Editorial Board of the *Journal of the Association for Information Science and Technology* for 30 years.

Rebekah Willson, PhD, is Assistant Professor in the School of Information Studies, McGill University (Montreal, Canada). Her research focuses on information behavior and information practices, particularly with individuals and groups undergoing transitions and living with uncertainty, which has been funded by the Social Sciences and Humanities Research Council of Canada. She has served as Chair of the Association for Information Science & Technology's (ASIS&T) *Special Interest Group for Information Use, Seeking, and Needs (SIG-USE)* and as guest editor of two special issues of the *Journal of the Association of Information Science and Technology (JASIS&T)* on information behavior (*Special Issue on Information Behavior & Information Practices Theory* and *Retrospective Special Issue on Information Behavior*). She is a member of the Editorial Board for *JASIS&T* and President of the *Canadian Association for Information Science (2022–2023)*. She completed her MLIS at University of Alberta (Canada, 2008) and PhD at Charles Sturt University (Australia, 2016).

PREFACE

We are thrilled to introduce the fifth edition of *Looking for Information* – and with a revised subtitle: *Examining Research on How People Engage with Information*. This change in title reflects the overall broadening of focus across information behavior studies; just as the field has moved on from a primary focus on information *seeking* and *needs* to embrace concepts such as *use, creation,* and *embodiment*, so have we.

The book's first edition was published in 2002 and it was awarded the *Best Information Science Book* at that time by the Association for Information Science and Technology. New editions followed in 2007, 2012 and 2016, including translation of the fourth edition into Chinese and Greek. We are very proud of the large and loyal following we have gained, around the world, over these 20 years. For those of you reading this book for the first time – welcome! We are sure you will find some interesting insights within these pages and that you will be intrigued to learn more about the evolution of research on people's engagement with information. For returning readers – thank you! We have enjoyed discussing this book with you over the years and hope you enjoy the new approach we have taken with this new edition.

With this edition, we very purposely welcome readers from outside of information science who will benefit from reviewing key outcomes and trends in information behavior research. There is an increasing focus on interdisciplinarity as researchers (and society) grapple with the world's complex issues, including climate change, geopolitics, and adoption of new technologies. The COVID-19 pandemic provides a powerful case example in the need for health researchers to partner with experts in human information behavior, as misinformation and disinformation continue to shape global uptake of vaccinations and other public health interventions. There has never been a better, or more pressing, time for us to work together to address such complex questions in contemporary society.

THE BOOK'S SCOPE

Looking for Information provides an in-depth look at international research on people's engagement with information. It reviews a century of scholarship, providing examples of research approaches, models, and theories used in information behavior studies. The book is intended for researchers at all levels, from senior academics looking for an overview of key issues or theories, to graduate and undergraduate students who need an introduction to topics and approaches. The book is primarily focused on research conducted in the disciplinary *home* of information behavior research – information science. As information science is inherently interdisciplinary, the book also includes relevant citations from related fields, such as media and communication, sociology, psychology, digital humanities, education, business, management, medicine, nursing, and public health, among others. The studies cited in the book include a mix of quantitative, qualitative, and textual approaches used to investigate a wide variety of research problems.

Information behavior researchers have expanded their epistemological, methodological, and technological repertoires over the past 25 years. Since the previous (fourth) edition, the adoption of arts-based and mixed methods studies has continued, and with interdisciplinary projects expanding, globally. In this book, we present a detailed overview of the current state of information behavior research, including the new trends we see on the horizon. We cover the core topics explored in the discipline, including the populations, settings, contexts, and activities that researchers explore. We discuss key historic works alongside new innovations, providing readers with a solid overview of both landmark studies and cutting-edge trends. As with previous editions, we retain the book's core purpose – i.e., to outline the common and essential aspects of people's information behaviors by presenting robust examples of publications that demonstrate the contribution of this research area to information science and other disciplines.

A NEW LOOK AND FEEL

Readers familiar with the fourth edition of this book will note that the number of chapters is now reduced (to six) and the content is streamlined. The literature continues to grow at a fast pace, which makes the task of reviewing *all* new works published between editions that much more challenging! With this fifth edition, we include more than 1,200 publications, with the newest additions published in the last seven years (November 2015–2022). We removed at least 100 older references, replacing them with newer, contemporary examples. We also expanded our scope to include commentary on emergent areas (e.g., information creation) and those that received less attention, previously (e.g., information use).

Given the vast amount of literature published to date, we knew the book would either need to expand into two volumes or be refreshed as a single volume. We chose the latter, resulting in a significant remastering of the book's design. With this edition, we introduce new design features (such as sidebars and tables) that enable us to retain content within a smaller textual footprint. We carefully reviewed our use of appendices, tables, figures, and bulleted lists, to balance quick access to summaries and highlights, alongside long-form narratives. The result is a reformulated and streamlined approach to the layout of the book, while retaining the content and focus that our readers expect.

We constructed each chapter to serve as a stand-alone piece of writing, to make it easier to include select chapters on course syllabi, and to facilitate downloading of chapters on e-readers. Each chapter now has its own, complete reference list, as well as *Our Top 3 Must Read Recommendations*. We retained the full reference list to collate references from the entire book, and we have also retained detailed author and subject indices. We have also added DOIs to citations, where these were available. As a result of the streamlined chapter structure, we no longer group the chapters; however, we do retain a detailed table of contents for the chapters. All these features support findability of key concepts and cited authors, and we hope these will enhance your reading experience.

OUR APPROACH TO CITING EXAMPLES AND RELEVANT LITERATURE

As with previous editions, we portray both the depth and breadth of the information behavior literature by presenting selected studies that illustrate key topics. Choosing which studies to highlight for this volume has been challenging, and we have employed a few different approaches to make our selections. First, we retained the previous framework, which gathered studies by *roles* and *occupations* as part of our detailed overview of historic approaches to information behavior research. We then extended this framework to examine more *holistic* approaches to research, which account for *situations* and *contexts* that shape people's experiences. We have exercised judgment in choosing studies that we see as unique, well done or illustrative of a particular population or approach. We have also highlighted studies using innovative methodological or theoretical approaches, or those that reflect the ongoing shift towards interdisciplinarity.

Second, we omitted investigations focused exclusively on information retrieval and people's searching practices from channels, sources, or systems. Most of these excluded studies concern the use of the internet, social media, online databases, and library catalogs, and together these constitute a huge literature. The focus of these excluded works is on the *system or source*, rather than the *person* who is searching; for this reason, they fall outside the boundaries of our review.

Third, we focus primarily on recent publications, especially those from 2000 to 2022. In some cases, older items are portrayed to highlight the shifts in assumptions, methods, and findings that have taken place over several decades. We also cite earlier, landmark discussions and definitions of core concepts, to ensure proper credit and to provide a historical perspective. By focusing on works from recent decades, we aim to provide an efficient means for reviewing developments in the field, while keeping the book to a manageable size.

HOW TO READ THIS BOOK

Chapter 1 Information Behavior: An Introduction provides an overview of foundational concepts and key terms and definitions, including *information behavior, information practice, information experience, seeking, sharing, needs, use, creation,* and *encountering,* among others. The nature of *information* is also explored, including such topics as *truth* and *intentionality* in the information people seek, as well as common myths related to information use. The chapter examines the scope of information behavior research, including its focus on people's holistic and complex relationships with information.

Chapter 2 The Evolution of Information Behavior Research presents a brief, historical overview of information behavior research. The chapter discusses the traditional research focus on people's *roles* (e.g., academics; managers) and *activities* (e.g., seeking), as well as issues related to *motivation* and *gatekeeping* practices. This chapter introduces the history of information behavior research, expanding on the concepts introduced in Chapter 1, and setting the stage to explore contemporary, holistic studies in Chapter 3.

Chapter 3 The Complex Nature of Information Behavior examines contemporary approaches to information behavior research, focusing primarily on people's holistic experiences of information. This includes the shift towards approaches that embrace socio-cultural contexts, affect, and embodiment, among other topics. Misinformation and disinformation are explored in depth, and the chapter also provides a detailed snapshot of research on COVID-19.

Chapter 4 Metatheories, Theories, and Models examines the paradigmatic and theoretical influences that have shaped information behavior research, alongside detailed discussions of methodologies and methods. This chapter mentions the approaches used in empirical studies, but also explores conceptual and philosophical publications that address the critical concepts shaping information behavior, overall.

Chapter 5 Research Design, Methodologies, and Methods discusses how information behavior researchers have designed their studies, collected and analyzed data, and written about their findings, over time. This chapter maps the evolution from primarily descriptive, quantitative studies, through the adoption of qualitative and mixed methods approaches, to the use of arts-based and creative designs. The chapter also highlights the increasing shift towards the societal impact of research, globally.

Chapter 6 Reviewing, Critiquing, Concluding, and Futuring highlights critical reviews of information behavior research and explores emerging trends. The chapter examines global *megatrends* (e.g., climate change, sustainable development) and what the future may hold for information behavior scholars.

ACKNOWLEDGEMENTS

Over the last 20 years, countless individuals have provided advice, ideas and reflections on what to include in *Looking for Information*. We are grateful for the many people who have engaged with this book over the years, including those who have added it on course reading lists. We thank you for your ongoing support! This fifth edition has benefited greatly from the help of Dr Linus Tan, who assisted with graphics and referencing. Thanks also to the editors at Emerald, for their continued guidance and support.

Lisa M. Given
Donald O. Case
Rebekah Willson

Chapter 1

INFORMATION BEHAVIOR: AN INTRODUCTION

> Information has become like the air we breathe, so pervasive that we scarcely notice its existence and yet so essential that we cannot live without it. (Jean Tague-Sutcliffe, 1995, p. 1)

Chapter Outline

1.1 INTRODUCTION

Information behavior research has a long history within the discipline of information science. Although some would identify the publication of Dervin and Nilan's (1986) work as a turning point to a focus on people's information needs, and the uses they made of the information they found, the precursors of this focus date back over several decades. One of the complicating factors in this discussion is that the discipline of information science continues to debate what to call this area of research – whether information behavior, information practice, information experience, or similar terms. However, our research is connected by a common thread; our focus is on *people* and how their lives *intersect* with the information world. We care, for example, about how people perceive the world, how they locate and apply information in decision-making, and how technologies facilitate finding and using information. We explore the contexts, situations, feelings, physicality, and meanings of people's information landscapes, from *their* points of view. We are interested in people's active information seeking processes,

Looking for Information
Examining Research on How People Engage with Information, 1–21

ISSN: 2055-5377/doi:10.1108/S2055-53772023001

their serendipitous encountering of useful information, as well as their decisions not to look for information or to ignore the information they find. Information behavior researchers document, describe, explain, critique, and unravel the complexities of people's engagement with information. We follow people into all corners of their lives, to learn about preschoolers' use of mobile devices, to understand how pregnant women make vaccination decisions, and to document small business owners' social media practices. In short, we care about how people engage with information in all corners of their lives. We use "information behavior" as a broad overarching term that encompasses all types of information experiences, in diverse circumstances and settings, and across various personal activities and outcomes.

The sections that follow outline, briefly, the key concepts and research foci of studies that explore information behavior, and why this topic has attracted so much attention across several disciplines. We make the case that the nature of this research has changed over several decades, away from an emphasis on institutional sources of information and search strategies, toward a focus on how people encounter and make sense of their environment. This view considers people's information engagements as parts of broad, holistic ecosystems (Polkinghorne & Given, 2021). Information behaviors are intertwined with a person's culture, history, and situation and shaped by geography, gender, and numerous other contextual elements. Current approaches to information behavior research embrace these contexts and seek to represent people's information worlds *within* this complexity, rather than studying people, information sources, and tools in isolation.

In thinking about this holistic view of people's worlds, the internet itself serves as a microcosm of information behavior and the ways our research approaches have changed. If we think back to a time before the internet existed, information was available in individual books, journals, radio and TV programs, offices, filing cabinets, people's minds, and computers. However, because it was divided by source, by location, by person, and by channel, it was not always easily located or examined. Before the internet, when you wanted to plan a trip you would read about a destination in a travel guide, call hotels to make reservations, telephone an airline to learn departure times and fares, visit a travel agent to pick up a ticket, and so on. In terms of research, each of those needs and transactions needed to be conducted (and studied) separately. Now, it is possible to satisfy all travel-related requests on a single website, often with no direct interaction with other people. The many different sources of information, channels of communication, and interactions have merged.

Not only have many different information sources and channels of communication collapsed down to one, but less goal-oriented behaviors, such as browsing and monitoring various news feeds, also now play a larger role than ever before. Looking for information becomes more holistic, with more available choices and greater control on the part of the individual looking for information. At the same time, the contexts that shape that information are more complex; online hotel ads that are posted on an airline's site may not be comprehensive or complete but may be the result of formal sponsorship agreements between companies. The top sites listed in Google may be a mix of paid advertisements, companies who have paid to have their websites appear near the top of the page, or options that appear due to the previous browsing habits or geography of the person's computer, based on their cookies or IP address. These behind-the-scenes (often unseen) activities are part of the complex landscape people must navigate to find the information they need in today's world.

Today's information world is far more complex than it was 20 – or even 5 – years ago due to the rise in misinformation and disinformation, globally. The internet continues to be the go-to place to find the text of a government regulation, the date of an event, the author of a document; yet conflicting information, outdated information, and incorrect information remain prevalent. When combined with information created solely to mislead (such as deep fakes), people must now navigate information minefields in their quest for helpful, reliable information. As people have embraced information technologies to enable them to work and study from home during the COVID-19 pandemic, we have also faced a crisis of trustworthiness in the information presented in the mainstream media. While social media and videoconferencing enabled us to connect with family and friends under lockdown and despite border closures, these same technologies channeled "fake news" on the virus and vaccines into our living rooms. The need for information behavior research that embraces people's holistic experiences has never been greater.

1.2 THE LANGUAGE OF INFORMATION BEHAVIOR

Given the complexities of the various concepts and terms that are used in information science and other disciplines to represent the intersection of people and information, we start with a brief overview of the key concepts that identify the boundaries of information behavior. Although Section 1.3 explores and defines the concept of "information" in depth, let's first presume that there *are* such phenomena as "information sources" to be found and "information needs" that can be satisfied by "browsing" or "seeking," and that have some "use" or purpose in people's lives. All these concepts fall under an overarching concept that we call "information behavior." Over the past decade, many other terms have been used to represent overarching concepts that are similar to information behavior. Although some researchers may see these as equivalent terms, representing the same "umbrella" concept, others will argue each is unique. The diversity of language and scope of terms can be confusing for novice researchers in the field, and for scholars from other disciplines. However, there is a richness to these debates and explorations that speaks to the complexities of human experience. Rather than attempting to settle on a single term, with clear boundaries and inclusion/exclusion criteria for this domain, information behavior researchers engage in ongoing debate and exploration of what it means to study people's engagements with information across various life contexts. This is a strength of our research, as we continue to strive for inclusive and holistic approaches to how we understand information through a people-focused lens. While not an exhaustive list, Table 1.1 presents many of the key concepts that have

Table 1.1. Key Concepts Referred to in Information Behavior Research.

	Definition
Overarching Concepts	**These are top-level or "umbrella" concepts that are intended to encompass a broad range of actions, activities, feelings, experiences, etc.**
Information behavior	Encompasses information seeking and discovery, as well as the totality of *unintentional or serendipitous* behaviors (such as encountering information or sharing information with others). The concept includes purposive behaviors that do not involve seeking, such as actively *avoiding or ignoring* information. Information behavior also includes the broader context of how individuals *use* information in their lives, so accounts for situation, time, affect, culture, geography, and other contextual elements in understanding people's engagement with information
Information practice	Socially and culturally established sets of actions to identify, seek, encounter, use, and share information from a range of sources, which are often habitual, and that emphasize the social and situated nature of interacting with information
Information experience	Refers to engagement with information that is both complex and multidimensional, concerned with holistic experiences and deriving meaning from interacting with information during day-to-day life. The emphasis is on everyday learning, and what could be done to improve and support education and learning tools
Specific Elements	**These are specific examples or types that fall underneath or within the overarching concepts**
Seeking	A conscious effort to acquire information in response to a need or gap in one's knowledge, through reading, conversation, observing, or various other ways to locate information
Sharing	Exchanging information between people. It includes the giving and receiving of information that can be active and explicit or passive, implicit giving. Sharing involves communicating with others and is necessary for collaboration
Needs	A recognition that one's knowledge is inadequate to satisfy a goal that you have; there are also unconscious precursors to needs, such as curiosity
Use	How one engages with the information acquired through seeking, sharing, encountering, or other means. The concept of use includes applying – or ignoring – information to suit one's goals or personal context, as well as the effects or outcomes of information engagement on (for example) how one thinks or feels
Creation	Applying information to form or generate new information, which may include reuse and/or adaptation of existing information. Creation is related to information use but also includes the production of new information
Encountering	Serendipitous acquisition of information through unexpected discovery, which may be through unrelated information seeking, receiving information, or nongoal-oriented activities such as monitoring
Monitoring	Maintaining awareness by regularly observing what is happening with a particular source of information or at a particular geographic location
Browsing	Semi-directed information seeking or the casual examination of a source which is of potential interest
Avoidance	Deciding not to look for information or actively ignoring potential sources of information

informed these discussions and debates over many decades, which readers will encounter as they review research in the area.

Historically, the term *information seeking* was widely discussed in the literature and was used to represent the range of human experiences that we now call information behavior (or another of the overarching concepts listed in Table 1.1). Although the phrase "information seeking" continues to be used in other disciplines, information science researchers specializing in information behavior recognize that "seeking" is only one of many specific elements of a vast array of activities and other concepts. Information seeking is a behavior so commonplace that it is generally not an object of concern until time pressure makes it so. If we are making a major decision (e.g., buying a house) or completing a task by a deadline (e.g., writing a report), we might find ourselves in an earnest information seeking mode: talking to others, searching the internet, reading books and magazines, scrolling through social media, watching the news, and so on. We may do everything we can to satisfy our desire for input, until either our need is satisfied or we run out of time. More commonly, it is the latter, as the demand for "information" is usually elastic – there is always more information that one could gather. After our need is met (or we give up) we return to a more passive state of interest, at least as regards the object of our earlier curiosity.

However, this type of seeking (as an active state of looking for information) is only one part of an individual's approach to dealing with the information in their lives. They may choose *not* to seek, or information may simply find them (when they hear something on the news, or see something on Facebook), before a person even realizes they want to learn more. For this reason, the broader umbrella term of "information behavior" is often preferred by researchers, as it alerts us to the fact that there are many and varied behaviors and contexts that shape how we work with information in our lives.

We can also consider cases in which the acquisition of information does *not* concern an immediate task like purchasing something or writing. Our daily life is peppered with instances in which we become interested in learning more about a topic after accidently encountering some bit of information about it. This sort of curiosity, unmotivated by an immediate goal, is a common aspect of life – and of information behavior.

The situations described previously, no matter how familiar to all of us, are much more complex than they may appear on the surface. Information behavior often escapes observation. It is difficult to generalize about behaviors that vary so much across people, situations, and objects of interest, and which often take place inside a person's head. This book is about the many ways in which information behaviors have been defined, explicated, observed, described, and measured in studies of human thought and experience.

1.3 EXPLORING THE CONCEPT OF "INFORMATION"

Entire books have been written about the concept of "information," which remains a contested term in information science. "Information" is an old English word, making an early appearance in one of Chaucer's tales sometime between

1372 and 1386, where it was used to refer to an instruction or piece of advice (Schement, 1993a, p. 177). Capurro and Hjørland (2002) take its origins back to Latin and Greek terms of the pre-Christian era. Ordinarily, we both use and hear the word "information" without much concern for its definition; we know what we mean when we use the word. At first glance, the *Oxford Dictionary of English* definition of the term "information" seems adequate: "(1) facts provided or learned about something or someone: *a vital piece of information*; (2) what is conveyed or represented by a particular arrangement or sequence of things: *genetically transmitted information*" (Stevenson, 2015). Summarizing 30 years of commentary, Levitan (1980) declared that 29 different concepts had been associated with the term information. A review by Schement (1993b) includes a selection of 22 definitions written between 1968 and 1989. Frické (2009, p. 139) points out a dozen characterizations of information, while allowing that there are "many more." An essay by Mai (2013) addresses information quality, and in the process contrasts disagreements among various authors and viewpoints concerning definitions of information. The empirical work of Shenton and Hayter (2006) and Badia (2014) demonstrate that both scholars and laypeople exhibit diverse meanings for the term. How has the concept of information been used such that so many definitions have resulted?

> ***Must information be useful?*** If information does not have an effect (e.g., improving a task), why would we talk about it? One of the most cited definitions of information is "that which reduces uncertainty" (Bouazza, 1989, p. 145). Yet, some information *increases* uncertainty (e.g., a medical diagnosis). People claim *information is power*, but most information (e.g., the date Krakatoa exploded) gives us little or no power. If we knew what stocks would increase in value tomorrow, we could make money and use it in powerful ways. But, while having such specialized, *formal* knowledge may grant privileges, its power involves performance, competence, institutions and social relations. Some scholars consider all stimuli to be *informative*, including sounds (e.g., music), sights (e.g., videos), or touch (e.g., warm sunshine on skin). Each sensation *tells us* something, may impart useful information, and lead to knowledge; but knowledge must have agency to create power.

One would think that hundreds of years of usage would tend to settle a word and result in a consensus on its meaning. This has not been the case with the term "information." Especially in the last 70 years, as the various phenomena that people call information began to be objects of empirical study, meanings of the word have proliferated. Schrader (1983, p. 99), for example, complains about "the multiplicity of vague, contradictory, and sometimes bizarre notions of the nature of the term 'information'." There continue to be widespread disagreements about what would constitute a general definition of information, due to issues related to utility, intentionality, truth, physicality, and structure. The most common definitions that have emerged assume that information is something that either reduces uncertainty or changes one's image of reality. One of the classic definitions of "information" is where the term refers to any difference that makes a difference to a conscious, human mind (Bateson, 1972, p. 453). In other words, information is whatever appears significant to a human being, whether originating from an external environment or a (psychologically) internal world. Michael Buckland's (1991) widely cited article portrays uses of the term "information" as falling into one of three categories: information-as-process (referring to the act of informing, the communication of information, and how a person's state of knowledge is changed); information-as-knowledge (what is perceived or the knowledge communicated); and information-as-thing ("objects, such as data and documents ... are referred to as 'information' because they are regarded as being informative)" (p. 351). Other authors view the concept of information as linked to social context, noting that information cannot be easily separated from the practices, meanings, and actions that shape social activity (see Bates, 2010 for a discussion of key thinkers in this area, and Wilson, 2022, for examples of the social nature of information). In a recent review, Bosancic and Matijevic (2019) note, "It is entirely possible that we will never come to a satisfactory definition of information that would be acceptable to every scientist, and information will continue to be discussed in a metaphorical sense" (p. 622).

> ***Does information require intentions?*** Must information be *intentional* to communicate something? Must we explain information-related activities as *purposeful* activities that occurred *because* we needed to know something, or *to do* something else? When we think of *informing* others, we may think of *information exchange* (whether between people or via a system). Yet, we also can be informed by our environment. Whether we view nature (e.g., trees, animals) or human-made signs (e.g., what people are wearing), we take in stimuli that have *meaning*. A glance at dark storm clouds informs us rain is coming, but nature has no intentions. While some people may need to *intend to receive* to take in information, others will encounter information *serendipitously*, without expectation.

Over the decades there have been many arguments about distinctions between the words *data*, *information*, and *knowledge* (and sometimes *wisdom*), including the continued use of terminological hierarchies to represent these concepts. Frické (2009) and Rowley (2007) both criticize the commonly used DIKW (data-information-knowledge-wisdom) pyramid, in which wisdom appears at the top, with knowledge beneath, supported by information, and then data lying at the base. Frické (p. 140) favors making "... knowledge and information synonymous. Knowledge and information collapse into each other." Saab and Riss (2011) also demonstrate that different levels in the hierarchy are intertwined in the process of making meaning (or sense) of patterns of stimuli. Many information behavior scholars use the terms data, information, and knowledge synonymously, and with little attention paid to exploring wisdom. Knowledge and wisdom are strictly phenomena of the human mind, whereas data and information are often represented by tangible, physical objects. The idea that information usually has a physical manifestation has often been the key consideration in early studies of information seeking. The way that information behavior studies are typically approached now, is in the sense of knowledge gained – as something in someone's mind – and not primarily as a physical object.

In discussing constructivist views within information science, Bosancic and Matijevic (2019) map the evolution of constructivist answers to the question "What is Information?" from the 1940s to the present. They note the most prevalent view sees "information as a subjective, socially constructed entity which informs users' behaviour" (p. 626). We can see information as "an internal change of state, a self-produced aspect of communicative events" (Luhmann, 1990, p. 10), as "a plastic substance that can be shaped in many ways" (Talja et al., 2005, p. 83) or as "an invisible 'communication tool' between data and knowledge" (Bosancic, 2016, p. 952). As this means there is no single, universal definition of "information," it opens the possibility of variable interpretations that can satisfy different needs across disciplines, contexts, and experiences. As Belkin (1978) states, "we are not concerned with definitions of information, but rather with concepts of information. The distinction is that a definition presumably says what the phenomenon defined is, whereas a concept is a way of looking at, or interpreting, the phenomenon (p. 58)." A broad conceptualization of the concept of "information" is in keeping with the way the term has been employed in studies of information needs, uses, seeking, and sense-making. Understanding the variability in how we view "information" is a useful starting point for understanding the diversity of approaches to studying people's information behaviors.

Must information be true? Must we consider something *true* to call it *information*? If it is inaccurate, incomplete, or lacks evidence is it still information? If it is intended to deceive, demonstrably false, or untrue, is it *misinformation*? In distinguishing misinformation, information, and knowledge, some philosophers point to the idea of a *justified true belief* (or *strong knowledge*). Here, *justified* means there is sufficient, relevant evidence to call something *true*. Critiques of this idea refer to *weak knowledge*, or beliefs that are true but lack justification (Frické, 2009). Yet, we cannot always be sure something is true; even a *fact*, shown to be true now, may be proven false later. Buckland (1991) claims "the process of becoming informed is a matter of changing beliefs. Whether these beliefs are held or denied by others... need not detain us" (p. 43). Others claim a true–false distinction is essential, with false information and misinformation seen as distinct concepts.

1.4 THE SCOPE OF "INFORMATION BEHAVIOR"

Information behavior has been written about in thousands of documents from several distinct disciplines. Information behavior research explores active information seeking, unintentional or serendipitous activities, information avoidance, and other phenomena that focus on *people* and the *contexts* in which they use information. This research also examines people's affective responses to their information worlds, their embodied experiences of information, and how they process and consider information (in whatever form) to make decisions in their daily lives. Increasingly, it is almost impossible to separate people's information behaviors from the digital contexts that shape our worlds. We look for information on health websites, we stumble upon new information when scrolling social media, and we gain new insights during virtual tours of museums. Embodied information experiences may occur in virtual reality in similar ways to what we experience in "real" life. However, studies that focus on *system-oriented* search practices – such as log analyses that track online search behavior, or that document people's movement using their geolocations – and that do *not* address people's searching experiences and context, fall outside information behavior. These types of systems-oriented investigations are referred to as "information retrieval" studies. Similarly, recording uses of library materials or other research that focuses on a place or source *without* attending to people's perceptions, experiences, and/or their contexts do not fall under the information behavior umbrella. The following sections provide details on the scope of the concept of information behavior and how researchers specializing in this area draw boundaries around their work.

1.4.1 Emphasizing People (in Context) Rather Than Systems

Systematic research on information behavior – at least on the use of sources like books or newspapers – dates back more than a century (Case, 2014). In the initial three decades of the twentieth century, studies of information "channels" and "systems" – i.e., mainly libraries and the mass media – accumulated slowly. The 1940s saw the first published reviews of this literature. By the 1960s, such investigations, particularly of the specialized information needs and uses of scientists and engineers, were appearing regularly in a variety of journals and reports. However, much of this older literature was not about information seeking in the sense in which that concept is discussed in current research. Rather, most of the investigations focused on the *artifacts* (e.g., books, journals, newspapers, radio and television broadcasts) and *venues* (e.g., schools, universities, libraries, professional conferences) of information seeking. What was studied were the information *sources* and how they were used, rather than the individual users, their needs (as they saw them), where they went for information, how the information made them feel, or what kind of results they experienced. Surveys of individuals made such strong assumptions about people's needs, motivations, habits, and behaviors that the range of responses they could make was severely constrained; what mattered in these early investigations was how *formal information systems* served the serious (e.g., work, health, or political) information needs of the population studied. Typically, this literature was called "information needs and uses" research, or sometimes "user studies" or "audience research." Choo and Auster (1993) call this tradition "system-centered" research; Vakkari (1999) refers to it as "system oriented"; and Hartel (2019) calls this the "physical paradigm."

> ***Myth #1: Only "objective" information is valuable.*** People are not always rational; we do not always scan for new information to optimize our thinking, nor do we only access reliable, proven sources. People tend to use easily available sources of information, selecting quick, immediate answers, rather than the best information.

It was not until the 1970s that investigations began to branch out beyond the focus on formal channels and task-oriented needs. Brenda Dervin's (1976a, 1976b) early work challenged "dubious assumptions" on the nature of information she believed constrained information agencies and client services. Almost 50 years later many myths about information continue to circulate and must be challenged by information scientists and practitioners; we have highlighted 10 myths throughout this chapter (see sidebars labeled *Myths #1–10*). The emphasis shifted away from the structured "information system" and toward the person as a finder, creator, interpreter, and user of information. In research on the focus shifted to the "gratifications" that users experienced, rather than focusing on "effects" that messages had on people and how to persuade them to do things. Even studies of formal information systems began to consider a wider range of people, more general needs and problems, and the ways those systems often failed to serve their publics; this approach informed other work, for decades (e.g., Chatman, 1996). The term "information seeking" – and, later, "sense making" – began to be preferred in describing the kind of phenomena that interested a growing number of scholars. Information behavior scholars typically point to Dervin and Nilan's (1986) landmark review paper on "information needs and uses," as signaling the turning point towards a significant rise in user-centered research (see Fisher & Julien, 2009). This focus continues to grow and expand, more than three decades later, within information science (Julien et al., 2018; Tabak, 2014); now, researchers view people in holistic terms, where individuals are not easily disentangled from their history, culture, and social contexts. These *holistic* approaches embed people within the contexts of their lives and study the whole person and the social phenomena that shape their experiences (Ma, 2021; Polkinghorne & Given, 2021). Table 1.2 contrasts the system-oriented, person-oriented, and holistic approaches used in information behavior studies by presenting examples of research questions typical for each.

> ***Myth #2: More information is always better***. Too much information leads to cognitive overload, and we start to ignore or avoid information. People have plenty of information around them, yet they struggle to interpret and understand what they see, read, or hear. Having information is not the same as "being informed."

The left column in Table 1.2 reflects research questions that have motivated thousands of studies – typically institutionally sponsored evaluations of library use, selective dissemination of information programs, information retrieval systems, interface designs, information campaigns, advertising effectiveness, and the like. However, these studies focus on the system itself; people are included in these projects to test and tweak the systems being investigated. Study designs of this type are not the focus of information behavior research. The middle column reflects the shift to a person-focused perspective, where people's needs, beliefs, and activities are the central research focus. These types of studies form the core of historic (and much current) information behavior research in the discipline, including projects that take a human-centered approach to examining information technologies (see Allen et al., 2019; Fourie, 2020; Willson et al., 2022 for examples). The column on the right demonstrates how information behavior

Table 1.2. The Evolution of Information Behavior Research Questions, From System-Oriented to Holistic Approaches.

System-Oriented (Atomistic) Approach	Person-Oriented (Atomistic) Approach	Person-in-Context (Holistic) Approach
The task or situation is the primary focus of study (i.e., continued focus of information retrieval and human–computer interaction studies)	**The task or situation is studied in the context of the person's need(s) and how they use information** (i.e., continued focus of studies of information behavior)	**The task or situation is studied in the context of the person's need(s) and information uses, while accounting for sociocultural influences** (i.e., increasing focus of studies in information behavior)
What kinds of documents do engineers need for their work?	How do engineers make sense of their work tasks and the information needed to support those tasks?	How does the workplace context shape engineers' approaches to the information they need for their work?
How successful are student searches of a university library's web-based catalog?	How does a student learn about job-related information *outside of* formal organizational channels?	How do students' social circles influence how they look for and share information with their peers?
How effective are safety warnings on medication packages and advertisements aimed at seniors?	How do safety warnings on medication packages influence seniors' information-seeking behaviors?	What is the influence of families and healthcare support teams on managing seniors' safety and well-being?
What hashtags do casually employed academics use to discuss precarious employment on social media?	How do casually employed academics use social media to share information about precarious employment?	What do global increases in part-time employment mean for casually employed academics' use of social media to engage with colleagues?
What sources of information do home cooks use in planning family meals?	How do home cooks use YouTube videos to learn new cooking practices?	What is the embodied information experience of the home cook?

research has shifted again, particularly within the last decade. Researchers now contend not only with people and the contexts influencing their needs and uses of information but also with the sociocultural aspects that shape people's experiences (e.g., Birdi & Ford, 2018; Gallagher & Olsson, 2019).

Myth #3: Objective information can be transmitted out of context. People tend to ignore isolated facts. We want to understand how new information intersects with known facts, beliefs, and emotions.

Information behavior studies generally explore the broader contexts that influence individuals' experiences with information. Consider, for example, the artificial distinctions between "task" and "nontask," and between "work" and "leisure." Our personal life intrudes on our work life constantly, and vice versa. Take the context of working within a large organization (e.g., corporation, government agency, university): our mix of existing knowledge and current information sources reflects our prework education and experience and overlaps our personal life. We may, for example, learn relevant facts from a nonwork relationship that we could not find through our organization. Organizational culture may discourage certain kinds of information seeking (e.g., criticisms of a company) that are relevant to improving performance. The same is true of professionals: it took pediatricians decades to face the possibility that some parents intentionally harm their children – a conclusion reached by radiologists, years earlier.

Myth #4: Only formal sources, such as scientific journals or vetted institutions, are essential. Most people consult formal, vetted sources rarely. Instead, they rely on informal sources, often friends and family, or information they encounter serendipitously.

Social groups, whether a small family, a peer group, or a huge corporation, have biases in favor of certain kinds of information and activities, and against other ways of thinking and acting. Each group or situation will differ in the availability of external information, the norms for believing information, the degree of trust among the various actors, and the consequences of deviating from group or situational norms. Information behavior scholars have been particularly interested in the dynamics of isolated communities and individuals (e.g., rural residents, crime victims) and in social groups in which strong or unusual norms operate (e.g., teen peer groups, urban populations). These types of contextual constraints and opportunities deserve to be explored in a more holistic way, rather than through atomized types of questions that are narrow in scope and decontextualized to focus on the person, in isolation, from the broader world they inhabit.

Myth #5: There is relevant information for every need. Information alone cannot satisfy every need. While people want to learn, understand, and be entertained, we also need the physical and psychological necessities of daily life, such as food, shelter, clothing, respect, and love.

1.4.2 How Information Behavior Is Studied

Information behavior has been studied in many different settings, with a variety of people and exploring a broad array of motives, contexts, and goals. All people seek and use information, yet for some people and in some situations the stakes are much higher. We might all agree, for example, that treatments for heart disease that affect millions of lives is worthy of investigation. By studying the information needs of scientists working on heart disease, and how they go about satisfying their information needs, we just might be able to devise a tool or a service that would help them reach their research goals a little sooner. Or, by investigating women's information needs on the topics of heart attack and stroke, amid a sea of information geared towards men's symptoms, we may identify important gaps in available information. In such situations, the potential for

> ***Myth #6: Every problem has a solution.*** Institutions like libraries and medical clinics try to provide information to solve people's problems. Like search engines, they map requests onto the language and resources of their systems to produce a response. However, people are sometimes seeking empathy or reassurance (rather than information), which the system may not be able to provide.

public good is enormous. Additionally, information behavior researchers also explore and value the unique and relatively rare experiences of individuals and groups. Studying people's varied information behaviors (even those that may appear trivial or marginal when compared to others) contribute to our overall understanding of how people interact with their information worlds.

Many early studies took an atomistic view of information sources, ranging from the *formal* sources often noted in occupation studies (e.g., reports, journal articles, newspapers) to the *informal* sources that shaped many everyday experiences (e.g., friends, family). These studies also documented individuals' *intrapersonal* sources of information, including memories, prior skills, or other sources of knowledge arising from people's previous experiences that were relevant to the tasks and situations being explored. Today, the focus of information behavior research has shifted from an atomistic interest in information sources, alone (e.g., use of scholarly sources), to one that examines the influence of sociocultural, historical, political, and other contextual influences on people's lives. The way we study academics' information behaviors, for example, has shifted from an atomistic exploration of source use (e.g., selection of top-tier publishing venues) to one that contextualizes that use within the culture of academe (e.g., rankings culture; academic workloads; precarious employment) (see Willson & Given, 2020).

1.4.2.1 An Early Focus on Occupations

The potential for public good may be why many of the initial investigations of information behavior focused on high-stakes and high-status occupations, such as research scientists, medical doctors, aerospace engineers, lawyers, corporate managers, and the like. Occupations have been the most common type of social role investigated in information behavior studies; while the early studies took a more atomistic approach to studying resources and tasks, current research embraces a more contextually grounded approach to understanding workers within their various social contexts (see Table 1.2). Studying people's occupations provided the earliest structures for exploring information seeking, as can be seen from the many studies of scientists, engineers, scholars, and managers that populated the early reviews of information behavior research. Most of these works focused on the use of specific sources of information and/or particular information behaviors.

> ***Myth #7: It is always possible to make information available or accessible.*** Formal information systems cannot easily address vague, ambiguous, and constantly changing human needs. People often construct their own answers to unique, unpredictable questions without accessing formal information systems.

Julien and O'Brien's (2014) examination of the information behavior literature found 61% of all identifiable respondents in such studies were occupational: 20% scholars, 5% professionals, and 36% nonprofessional workers. In a later study, Julien et al. (2018) found 73% of all respondents were identified by type of occupation: professionals (71%) scholars (1%), and nonprofessional workers (1%). Across the two analyses then, about two-thirds of all studies had an occupational focus. In contrast, Lund's (2021) analysis of recent information behavior-themed dissertations shows only 18% of the 369 populations studied were occupational; while this finding may demonstrate a shift away from a focus on work, it was likely also influenced by the sample of dissertations, nearly half of which originated outside of the information studies discipline (e.g., from information systems, computer science, education, and communication).

> ***Myth #8: Material information, such as books or websites, will satisfy people's needs.*** Information systems rely on standardized "packages" of information and provide these on request (like a list of links returned by a search engine). Yet people may seek solutions, instructions, ideas, inspirations, and human contacts that do not match these standard packages and often cannot be provided by the system.

Most of the earliest chapters of the *Annual Review of Information Science and Technology* (1966–1974), along with other reviews, were concerned primarily with scientists and engineers, focusing on information seeking, information needs, and information use. Later, as researchers gained a firmer view of the pattern of behavior in science and engineering, attention turned first to the social sciences and later to the humanities (Bouazza, 1989, p. 159). As they did so, the academic world began to account for an even larger proportion of the studies than before (e.g., Ellis, 1993), as the latter groups were less likely to be found outside of the university. Marcia Bates (1996) summarized that progression of attention by researchers in this way:

> In the 1950s and 1960s – in part because of the availability of U.S. Federal grant money – the emphasis was on the needs of scientists and engineers.... Needs in the social sciences were attended to in the 1970s, especially with some major research studies that were performed in Great Britain.... attention turned to the arts and humanities in the 1980s and 1990s. (p. 155)

Both the accumulation of studies on some individual disciplines, and the impracticality of studying *all* disciplines in any depth, led to a tendency to aggregate results along the lines of *metadisciplines*, such as science, social science, and the humanities. There are some gray areas in these groupings (e.g., are historians chiefly humanities scholars, or are some of them social scientists?); however, these three basic categories seem to appeal to those attempting to summarize information behavior results.

1.4.2.2 A Shift to Studying Everyday Experiences

Despite the historic value placed on studies (and behaviors) that may lead to a large or significant impact on society, this does not discount the importance and impact of studies that investigate very local, personal, or (what many perceive to be) "small" impacts. The listening, watching, reading, and learning that take place in support of one's daily tasks has gained prominence in recent decades, in an area referred to as "everyday" information behavior. Studies of everyday information activities often explore information encountering, monitoring, browsing, and even avoiding information. These studies demonstrate that the experiences of one patient, in one hospital, in one country in the world is just as valuable and useful for societal change as large-scale studies of healthcare settings. The increasing focus on holistic, person-in-context studies (as noted in Table 1.2) requires an in-depth assessment of local context. For this reason, the shift from a systems-oriented approach to studying people's activities, in context, has necessitated a methodological shift from large-scale quantitative approaches (e.g., using national questionnaires or log analyses of online activities), to small-scale qualitative and mixed methods approaches (e.g., combining individual interviews with ethnographic observation and discourse analysis in a workplace). Such localized studies provide important knowledge about the ways that society excludes marginalized people or point to new trends that can develop into areas with broader impact, in future, as additional studies are conducted. Thus, many types of information behavior are worthy of study.

> ***Myth #9: Individual situations and contexts can be ignored.*** Typically, it is a person's experience of a situation or context that shapes their information needs and how they use information. When we face unpredictability and lack of control, we worry, and then the worry itself becomes a need.

As researchers embraced investigations of "everyday" life, they expanded the focus of a participant's occupation (e.g., lawyer, artist) to what can be seen as an equally atomistic approach that focused on a person's everyday role (e.g., voter, parent, consumer). An emphasis on the problems of everyday life is apparent in Savolainen's (1995) groundbreaking article. He equated "citizen information seeking" with any "nonwork" consumption of media, noting how the degree to which the study of "everyday life" has been "overshadowed by surveys of job-related information needs, seeking and use" (p. 259). Savolainen urged that greater attention be paid to how people encounter information while engaged in activities such as leisure and hobbies. His investigation of 22 Finnish citizens – half middle-class and half working class – involved 90-minute interviews on their jobs, consumption habits, leisure time, media use, and the values they attached to information and information seeking. Savolainen also had respondents choose a recent "problematic situation" and relate how they dealt with it (p. 270).

McKechnie et al. (2002) found that studies of "ordinary people" made up about 22% of the 1990s information behavior literature; and investigations of "students" (a role most people take on for a large portion of their lives) were the focus of another 19% of such studies. A later content analysis (Julien et al., 2011) of the 1999–2008 literature found the same percentage of students (19%) but only 7% of studies featured the general public; another 32% examined users of libraries and/or the web, while another 21% of people studied were unidentified. The breakdown of the 2009–2013 information behavior literature (Julien & O'Brien, 2014) found students comprised 14% of the studies, and the general public 15%; the corresponding figures in Julien et al. (2018) were students 12% and the public

14%. Lund (2021) shows 21% of study participants were students. So, the pattern is consistent over the last 30 years, with the roles of student and citizen each making up roughly one-seventh to one-fifth of all respondents.

Brenda Dervin says, in a 1989 article on "users as research inventions," that role categorizations of people (along with demographic groupings) are often a function of marketing segmentation and the consumer/user mentality that goes with it. Whether the goal is to sell someone something or to study his or her use of some "system" so that it may be improved, the result is not always positive for those studied. When people are "clustered" into groups and labeled, the resulting categories come to be *reified* – researchers, policymakers, and the public begin to believe that such categories are *real*, rather than just convenient fictions for the purpose of analysis and planning. The diverse individuals who make up these groups, and their perspectives, tend to be lost in the results. Unfortunately, it is not the case that such analyses of user categories lead automatically to improvements in services or systems. Indeed, Dervin claims that sometimes they reinforce inequities; finding, for example, that "the poor use the Internet less than the rich" does not suggest a solution to that inequity, but rather may lead to feelings of resignation and blame. Nevertheless, a common approach in information behavior literature has been to examine large populations in terms of the nonwork roles they play.

1.4.2.3 Studying People in Context

Currently, the examination of the person-in-context is common within studies of information behavior. Researchers now explore the specific activities and kinds of information people use alongside people's individual situations, motives for seeking information, and the surrounding environments and contexts shaping their experiences, among other points of focus. There is no nice, neat, logical delineation of these factors, as human behavior itself is not completely rational or uniform and is shaped by various social contexts. *Contexts* include the combinations of people and situations that frame an investigation. This may still begin with the *role* of the person under investigation – e.g., an *occupation* such as chemist, or a nonwork role like a patient – but the investigation is focused on that person within the broader contexts in which they live and work. These investigations also explore the intrapersonal experiences of the person *within* that context, to document their affective responses, the meaning they make of that context, their interactions with others, and their embodied experiences of various phenomena. Researchers also use other *demographic* groupings (e.g., by age, gender, race, ethnicity, and geography), to delineate the boundaries of a study. Although a respondent could easily represent an occupation, a role, and a demographic

> ***Myth #10: People make easy, conflict-free connections between external information and their internal reality***. People often struggle to make sense of situations and the world at large. Researchers need to ask more questions about why people think and act as they do, how they arrived at certain beliefs, and how they inform themselves.

Table 1.3. Moving From Atomistic to Holistic Approaches in Studies of Information Behavior.

Demographic/Role Focus	Situational Focus	Contextual Focus
Managers...	Purchasing new equipment...	To keep up with competitors
Parents...	Expecting a new baby...	Later in life
Architects...	Designing new buildings...	In earthquake zones
Patients...	Living with chronic disease...	In low-income countries
Voters...	Preparing for an election...	To address climate change
Seniors...	Moving to retirement homes...	Away from their families

group at the same time, as well as illustrating the use of any number of information sources, investigators often start by framing their research questions and respondent samples in one of these ways, while also attending to the broader contextual issues that may shape individuals' experiences. By studying people in context, the focus of research has once again expanded to include activities such as information sharing and information creation.

Table 1.3 presents examples of how studies can shift from a primary focus on the role or other demographic group as the focus (i.e., often leading to general studies of what sources they use, for what purpose), to a focus on the specific situation for that use (i.e., why information is needed to make a decision), and then shifting to account for broader, social experiences that shape the context for that group (i.e., where information from external contexts must also be taken into account). The addition of contextual and societal elements requires the researcher to gather data from participants about the worlds in which their information behaviors occur, to capture a more complete picture of what influences (for example) their choice of information sources, the use to which they put that information, and the affective or other intrapersonal elements bound up in that experience.

1.5 CONCLUSION

Studies of information behavior are becoming increasingly complex and rich as they attempt to understand people's experiences within local, national, and global contexts. Additionally, they are becoming increasingly interdisciplinary, and relying on various mixed methods to achieve a broader understanding of personal and societal influences on people's experiences. For example, to understand voters' information needs related to climate change ahead of an election, research exploring information behavior will also draw on relevant research in the science of climate change, the design of political campaigns, and mainstream media practices. In addition to relevant studies within information science, researchers may engage with the literature and colleagues from the disciplines of environmental studies, communication and media studies, and political science, among others, to design and implement robust studies of people's information behaviors.

What sets information behavior researchers apart is their focus on *people's* engagement with their information worlds. Whether we are exploring people's postings on social media, their knowledge management practices in organizations, or their reading preferences, we care about people's perceptions, experiences, and relationships with the information around them. We want to understand how they find information from the diverse sources available, what sources they use, how they use that information to make decisions, or when they ignore that information completely. We explore a wide range of personal and social contexts, technologies, feelings, and beliefs in exploring people's information worlds, with implications for technology design, organizational practices, personal choices, and policy creation. Information is everywhere; but *people* give meaning to that information and that, in turn, shapes what information means to the world.

1.6 OUR TOP 3 *MUST READ* RECOMMENDATIONS

Hartel, J. (2019). Turn, turn, turn. In *Proceedings of CoLIS, the Tenth International Conference on Conceptions of Library and Information Science*, Ljubljana, Slovenia, June 16–19, 2019. *Information Research, 24*(4). http://InformationR.net/ir/24-4/colis/colis1901.html
This well-crafted, fascinating essay describes seven shifts in attention among information science researchers over four decades of investigations.

Julien, H., McKechnie, L., Polkinghorne, S., & Chabot, R. (2018). The "user turn" in practice: Information behavior researchers' constructions of information users. *Information Research, 23*(4). http://InformationR.net/ir/23-4/isic2018/isic1804.html
An illustration of the degree to which information behavior research is changing its focus and study populations.

Polkinghorne, S., & Given, L. M. (2021). Holistic information research: From rhetoric to paradigm. *Journal of the Association for Information Science and Technology*, *72*(10), 1261–1271. https://doi.org/10.1002/asi.24450
An exploration of the rhetorical use of the concept of "holistic" research and what it would mean if researchers adopted substantively holistic approaches in their projects.

REFERENCES

Allen, D. K., Given, L. M., Burnett, G., & Karanasios, S. (2019). Information behaviour and information practices: A special issue for research on people's engagement with technology. *Journal of the Association for Information Science and Technology*, *70*(12), 1299–1301. https://doi.org/10.1002/asi.24303

Badia, A. (2014). Data, information, knowledge: An information science analysis. *Journal of the American Society for Information Science and Technology*, *65*(6), 1279–1287. https://doi.org/10.1002/asi.23043

Bates, M. J. (1996). Learning about the information seeking of interdisciplinary scholars and students. *Library Trends*, *45*(2), 155–164. https://hdl.handle.net/2142/8083

Bates, M. J. (2010). Information behavior. In M. J. Bates & M. N. Maack (Eds.), *Encyclopedia of library and information sciences* (3rd ed., pp. 2381–2391). CRC Press.

Bateson, G. (1972). *Steps to an ecology of mind*. Ballantine Books.

Belkin, N. J. (1978). Information concepts for information science. *Journal of Documentation*, *34*, 55–85. https://doi.org/10.1108/eb026653

Birdi, B., & Ford, N. (2018). Towards a new sociological model of fiction reading. *Journal of the Association for Information Science and Technology*, *69*(11), 1291–1303. https://doi.org/10.1002/asi.24053

Bosancic, B. (2016). Information in the knowledge acquisition process. *Journal of Documentation*, *72*(5), 930–960. https://doi.org/10.1108/JD-10-2015-0122

Bosancic, B., & Matijevic, M. (2019). Information as construction. *Journal of Librarianship and Information Science*, *52*(2), 620–630. https://doi.org/10.1177/0961000619841657

Bouazza, A. (1989). Information user studies. In *Encyclopedia of library and information science* (Vol. 44, Suppl. 9), pp. 144–164). M. Dekker.

Buckland, M. K. (1991). Information as thing. *Journal of the American Society for Information Science*, *42*, 351–360. https://doi.org/10.1002/1097-4571(199106)42:5%3C351::AID-ASI5%3E3.0.CO;2-3

Capurro, R., & Hjørland, B. (2002). The concept of information. In B. Cronin (Ed.), *Annual review of information science and technology* (Vol. 37, pp. 343–411). Information Today.

Case, D. O. (2014). Sixty years of measuring the use of information and its sources: From consultation to application. Presented at the *Libraries in the Digital Age (LIDA)*, Zadar, Croatia, June 16–20. https://slideplayer.com/slide/3956824/

Chatman, E. A. (1996). The impoverished life-world of outsiders. *Journal of the American Society for Information Science*, *47*, 193–206. https://doi.org/10.1002/1097-4571(199603)47:3%3C193::AID-ASI3%3E3.0.CO;2-T

Choo, C. W., & Auster, E. (1993). Environmental scanning: Acquisition and use of information by managers. In M. Williams (Ed.), *Annual review of information science and technology* (Vol. 28, pp. 279–314). Learned Information.

Dervin, B. (1976a). Strategies for dealing with human information needs: Information or communication? *Journal of Broadcasting*, *20*(3), 324–351. https://doi.org/10.1080/08838157609386402

Dervin, B. (1976b). The everyday information needs of the average citizen: A taxonomy for analysis. In M. Kochen & J. Donahue (Eds.), *Information for the community* (pp. 23–35). American Library Association.

Dervin, B. (1989). Users as research inventions: How research categories perpetuate inequities. *Journal of Communication*, *39*(3), 216–232. https://doi.org/10.1111/j.1460-2466.1989.tb01053.x

Dervin, B., & Nilan, M. (1986). Information needs and uses. In M. Williams (Ed.), *Annual review of information science and technology* (Vol. 21, pp. 1–25). Knowledge Industry.

Ellis, D. (1993). Modeling the information seeking patterns of academic researchers: A grounded theory approach. *The Library Quarterly*, *6*(3), 469–486. https://www.jstor.org/stable/4308867

Fisher, K. E., & Julien, H. (2009). Information behavior. In B. Cronin (Ed.), *Annual review of information science & technology* (Vol. 43). Information Today. https://doi.org/10.1002/aris.2009.1440430114

Fourie, I. (2020). Contextual information behaviour analysis of grief and bereavement: Temporal and spatial factors, multiplicity of contexts and person-in-progressive situation. *Information Research*, *25*(4). http://InformationR.net/ir/25-4/isic2020/isic2003.html

Frické, M. (2009). The knowledge pyramid: A critique of the DIKW hierarchy. *Journal of Information Science*, *35*(2), 131–142. https://doi.org/10.1177/0165551508094050

Gallagher, S., & Olsson, M. (2019). Reconciling doctor as clinician and doctor as entrepreneur: The information practices and identity work of early career surgeons. *Information Research*, *24*(3). http://www.informationr.nct/ir/24-3/rails/rails1810.html

Hartel, J. (2019). Turn, turn, turn. In *Proceedings of CoLIS, the Tenth International Conference on Conceptions of Library and Information Science*, Ljubljana, Slovenia, June 16–19, 2019. *Information Research, 24*(4). http://InformationR.net/ir/24-4/colis/colis1901.html

Julien, H., McKechnie, L., Polkinghorne, S., & Chabot, R. (2018). The "user turn" in practice: Information behaviour researchers' constructions of information users. *Information Research, 23*(4). http://www.informationr.net/ir/23-4/isic2018/isic1804.html

Julien, H., & O'Brien, M. (2014). Information behavior research: Where have we been, where are we going? *Canadian Journal of Information and Library Science*, *38*(4), 239–250.

Julien, H., Pecoskie, J. L., & Reed, K. (2011). Trends in information behavior research, 1999–2008: A content analysis. *Library & Information Science Research*, *33*(1), 19–24. https://doi.org/10.1016/j.lisr.2010.07.014

Levitan, K. B. (1980). Applying a holistic framework to synthesize information science research. In B. Dervin & M. Voigt (Eds.), *Progress in communication sciences* (Vol. 2, pp. 241–273). Ablex.

Luhmann, N. (1990). *Essays on self-reference*. Columbia University Press.

Lund, B. (2021). The structure of information behavior dissertations 2009–2018: Theories, methods, populations, disciplines. *Journal of Librarianship and Information Science*, *53*(2), 225–232. https://doi.org/10.1177/0961000620935499

Ma, Y. (2021). Understanding information: Adding a non-individualistic lens. *Journal of the Association of Information Science and Technology*, *72*, 1295–1305. https://doi.org/10.1002/asi.24441

Mai, J.-E. (2013). The quality and qualities of information. *Journal of the American Society for Information Science and Technology*, *64*(4), 675–688. https://doi.org/10.1002/asi.22783

McKechnie, L., Baker, L., Greenwood, M., & Julien, H. (2002). Research method trends in human information behaviour literature. *New Review of Information Behaviour Research*, *3*, 113–126.

Polkinghorne, S., & Given, L. M. (2021). Holistic information research: From rhetoric to paradigm. *Journal of the Association for Information Science and Technology*, *72*(10), 1261–1271. https://doi.org/10.1002/asi.24450

Rowley, J. (2007). The wisdom hierarchy: Representations of the DIKW hierarchy. *Journal of Information Science*, *33*(2), 163–180. https://doi.org/10.1177/0165551506070706

Saab, D. J., & Riss, U. V. (2011). Information as ontologization. *Journal of the American Society for Information Science and Technology*, *62*(11), 2236–2246. https://doi.org/10.1002/asi.21615

Savolainen, R. (1995). Everyday life information seeking: Approaching information seeking in the context of "way of life". *Library & Information Science Research*, *17*(3), 259–294. https://doi.org/10.1016/0740-8188(95)90048-9

Schement, J. R. (1993a). An etymological exploration of the links between information and communication. In J. R. Schement & B. Ruben (Eds.), *Information and behavior* (Vol. 4, pp. 173–187). Transaction Publishers.

Schement, J. R. (1993b). Communication and information. In J. R. Schement & B. Ruben (Eds.), *Information and behavior* (Vol. 4, pp. 3–33). Transaction Publishers.

Schrader, A. (1983). *Toward a theory of library and information science*. Indiana University.

Shenton, A. K., & Hayter, S. (2006). Terminology deconstructed: Phenomenographic approaches to investigating the term "information". *Library & Information Science Research*, *28*(4), 563–578. http://doi.org/10.1016/j.lisr.2006.10.003

Stevenson, A. (Ed.). (2015). *Oxford dictionary of English* (3rd ed.). OUP. http://10.1093/acref/9780199571123.001.0001

Tabak, E. (2014). Jumping between context and users: A difficulty in tracing information practices. *Journal of the American Society for Information Science and Technology*, *65*(11), 2223–2232. https://doi.org/10.1002/asi.23116

Tague-Sutcliffe, J. (1995). *Measuring information: An information services perspective*. Academic Press.

Talja, S., Tuominen, K., & Savolainen, R. (2005). "Isms" in information science: Constructivism, collectivism and constructionism. *Journal of Documentation*, *61*(1), 79–101. https://doi.org/10.1108/00220410510578023

Vakkari, P. (1999). Task complexity, problem structure and information actions. Integrating studies on information seeking and retrieval. *Information Processing & Management*, *35*(6), 819–837. https://doi.org/10.1016/S0306-4573(99)00028-X

Willson, R., & Given, L. M. (2020). 'I'm in sheer survival mode:' Information behaviour and affective experiences of early career academics. *Library & Information Science Research, 42*(2). https://doi.org/10.1016/j.lisr.2020.101014

Willson, R., Julien, H., & Burnett, G. (2022). JASIS&T special issue on information behavior and information practices theory [editorial]. *Journal of the Association for Information Science and Technology, 73*(4), 491–493. https://doi.org/10.1002/asi.24622

Wilson, T. D. (2022). *Exploring information behaviour: An introduction*. T.D. Wilson. http://informationr.net/ir/Exploring%20information%20behaviour.pdf

Chapter 2

THE EVOLUTION OF INFORMATION BEHAVIOR RESEARCH

Several thousand studies have appeared and, clearly, it is impossible to review *all* of this literature. (Thomas Wilson, 1994, p. 15)

Chapter Outline

2.1 THE ORIGINS OF INFORMATION BEHAVIOR RESEARCH

Research on information-related human practices dates back well over 100 years, beginning in the first two decades of the twentieth century. Yet we could also point to a much earlier, 1849 report to the British Parliament (see Wellard, 1935) as representing an initial theme of information behavior research: documenting the effects of libraries and reading on a particular audience. In the case of the Parliamentary report, the population in question was the English working class. However, this 1849 effort was far from a scholarly investigation; it was based on the testimony of experts (e.g.,

Looking for Information
Examining Research on How People Engage with Information, 23–70

Published under exclusive licence by Emerald Publishing Limited
ISSN: 2055-5377/doi:10.1108/S2055-53772023002

local educators, political leaders, or clergy), rather than interviews with the readers themselves; it is largely anecdotal, using evidence from just a few people in a few towns, without any systematic sampling. Yet, while lacking the consistency and rigor that we would today require of a scholarly study, it is at least an early example of an attempt to describe the effects of reading. In fact, its concern with "effects" presages an important development in much information behavior research: the importance of the *outcomes* of information.

Most scholars supply later dates for the start of the information behavior genre. According to Herbert Poole (1985), the first study of information needs and uses dates to 1902, when Charles Eliot wrote about the used and unused portions of a library's collection. In contrast Bouazza (1989, p. 144) says that "the history of user studies goes back to the 1920s," and Wilson (1994) credits a 1916 study by Ayres and McKinnie on reading habits in Cleveland public libraries as the beginning of this line of inquiry. Whichever claim is correct, the antecedents of information behavior research lie in these early investigations of library use and reading, with some attention paid in the latter study to user characteristics. A turning point in this vein was Berelson's (1949) report on "The library's public," which reviewed two decades' worth of research on the topic of public library use, and raised important questions about who used libraries, and why.

The fixation on venues or artifacts of information seeking remained in place until at least the 1970s (Dervin, 1976a). These investigations came to be called "user studies" (the term employed by Bouazza), that focused on those people who used some kind of service (e.g., a library) or source (e.g., books or magazines), usually with an eye toward improving institutional services (Burns, 1978; White, 1980). Gradually these early investigations moved beyond single channels (e.g., books, radio, or libraries), to consider multiple channels from among which an individual made active choices in pursuit of particular information. An example of this expansion of breadth and role is found in Westley and Barrow's (1959) study of student use of magazine, newspapers, radio, and television for news – among the first to describe "information seeking" by "information seekers." Westley and Barrow took a more holistic view than earlier studies, recognizing a basic need for "orienting information" about the world in which we live. The importance of consulting multiple channels within a complex information environment was later emphasized in investigations by Thomas Allen (Allen, 1965; Allen & Gerstberger, 1967).

The trickle of studies in the first decades of the twentieth century became a flood by midcentury. After World War II, with its great burst of energy into the endeavors of basic and applied sciences, attention (and funding) began to turn toward improving dissemination of information from research. Many investigations of "users" and "information needs and uses" were conducted during the 1950s and 1960s and, despite a temporary lull during the 1980s, continued to grow in number until the present day.

Yet, the focus and content of information behavior studies has continually evolved. The attention of researchers shifted from a dominant interest in the *use of channels and sources*, to an emphasis on the *encountering and seeking* of information, the *interpretation of meaning* from that information and other *outcomes* of receiving information. Investigators have recognized that information behavior does not always come down to the use of certain sources, an idea that is underscored in a commentary by Choo (2005):

> Our survey suggests that, over the years, information needs and uses studies have progressively broadened their research orientation and research focus [such that] studies have moved from an orientation that is primarily system-centered (in which information is objective, resides in a document or system, and where the main issue is how to get at this information) to an orientation that is also user-centered (in which information is subjective, resides in the users' minds, and is only useful when meaning has been created by the user). (p. 39)

The information behavior research has since shifted to embrace interdisciplinarity and extend its theoretical reach. Julien et al. (2011) noted this trend in their content analysis of the literature, while also highlighting the noticeable gap between studies produced by researchers and those coming from practice:

> Of special note in these results is the increasing interdisciplinarity reflected in the information behavior research literature. This suggests a maturing field and may encourage scholars in the area to expand their explorations of literature outside LIS for relevant work and theory. A less encouraging finding is the persistent gap between work produced by researchers and that published by practitioners. Effort is required to facilitate communication between these two groups, to reduce this gap, and to encourage stronger research by practitioners. (p. 23)

2.2 REVIEWS OF INFORMATION BEHAVIOR LITERATURE

With the publication of so many studies following World War II, several comprehensive reviews soon followed: Törnudd (1959), Menzel (1960), Davis and Bailey (1964), Auerbach (1965), Paisley (1965), North American Aviation (1966; updating Auerbach), and DeWeese (1967; an update of Davis & Bailey). With few exceptions (such as William Paisley's (1965) chapter on studies in the behavioral sciences), most of the reviews featured investigations of science and engineering personnel and materials.

Stand-alone bibliographies of information needs and uses research declined in number after 1966, when the *Annual Review of Information Science and Technology* (*ARIST*) included reviews of this body of publications. For the next 45 years, *ARIST* became the main vehicle by which interested scholars kept abreast of research on information behavior. *ARIST* chapters on information needs and uses appeared in 1966 (Menzel, 1966b), 1967 (Herner & Herner), 1968 (Paisley), 1969 (Allen), 1970 (Lipetz), 1971 (Crane), 1972 (Lin and Garvey), 1974 (Martyn), and 1978 (Crawford).

During the 1970s a few independent reviews also appeared, including Wood (1971), Waldhart and Waldhart (1975), and Ford (1977). These documents covered much of the same literature as the 1966–1974 *ARIST* chapters. Whether duc to an overabundance of reviews, or instead due to a decline in relevant investigations, few comprehensive reviews were published between 1978 and 1986. The most significant publication during this lull was Wilson's (1981) article on "user studies and information needs," in the *Journal of Documentation*, which was highly influential in encouraging qualitative research in information behavior.

Comprehensive *ARIST* chapters on information behavior reappeared in 1986 (Dervin & Nilan) and 1990 (Hewins). In the meantime, essays by Hogeweg de Haart (1981), Hernon (1984), and Slater (1988) together reviewed several hundred information behavior studies in the social sciences, Stone (1982) described investigations of the humanities, and Rohde (1986) discussed publications concerning information needs. Gradually, reviews of the information behavior literature grew more specialized and eventually lead to a temporary halt in attempts to review such publications in a comprehensive fashion, until the *ARIST* chapters of 2006 (Case) and 2009 (Fisher and Julien). After 2009 no more specialized reviews appeared before *ARIST* ceased publication in 2011; *ARIST* relaunched in 2022, so new reviews may appear, in future years.

Looking back over six decades of information behavior reviews, it is particularly puzzling to consider the patchwork nature of the *ARIST* chapters. The time periods covered in the general *ARIST* chapters varied from as little as one year's worth of new publications to more than eight years. Authors exercised considerable latitude in the scope of their reviews, based on their own interests, the amount of material to review and what earlier *ARIST* chapters had covered. For example, the 1966 and 1967 chapters reviewed only science and technology literature, and the 1990 review purposefully excluded any studies that used survey methods. Whatever the chosen period, each *ARIST* chapter cited earlier reviews and studies in the midst of reviewing recent material from their assigned period. The overlap among chapter references, coupled with the idiosyncratic choices of the authors, makes it difficult to say exactly how many unique publications were reviewed in *ARIST*, much less to come up with an estimate that includes other reviews of this literature. It is safe to conclude that several thousand unique information behavior investigations were conducted between 1950 and 2010.

2.3 INFORMATION NEEDS AND INFORMATION SEEKING

Not only has a definition of "information" proved difficult to establish, describing exactly how it influences human behavior has also been controversial. Historically, researchers studied people's information "needs" and the "seeking" strategies they used to satisfy those needs. Although this approach remains common (particularly in disciplines outside information science), information behavior researchers now take a more holistic approach to studying people's engagement with information and how they "use" what they find. Here, we address these historic approaches, leaving an exploration of contemporary approaches to Chapter 3.

2.3.1 What Is a "Need"?

It is fitting to begin with a definition of what we mean by a human "need" because it is upon this hook that most writers hang the motivations for information seeking. A "need" is typically characterized as an "inner motivational state" (Grunig, 1989, p. 209) that brings about thought and action. Other "inner states" may include, for example, wanting, believing, doubting, fearing, or expecting (Liebnau & Backhouse, 1990; Searle, 1983).

The distinctions made among varieties of "need" can be bewildering. An essay by Andrew Green (1990) describes debates over the nature of "needs" that have taken place among political philosophers and social policy advocates. Green identifies four general conclusions about the concept of need (pp. 65–67). First, a need is always *instrumental*: it involves reaching a desired goal. If I "need to know" the chemical composition of heroin, it is typically because I desire to accomplish something with that information. That "something" may be to answer a test question, to write about narcotics for a class assignment or simply to satisfy my curiosity. It is also the case that my need in those examples is based on some preexisting need: to pass a class, to get a degree, to be a knowledgeable person and so forth. The key factor is that knowing it will put me at, or closer to, an end state that I want to achieve.

Motivations for Information Seeking: Reducing Uncertainty

The idea that information reduces uncertainty goes back more than a century. It became very popular with the debut of *Information Theory* in the 1940s and with increased attention in communication studies in the 1970s. In information behavior, Robert Taylor (1968) addressed uncertainty in his approach to question negotiation, where a person's initial expressions of dissatisfaction in their knowledge might become a rambling statement of interest, leading to an articulated question needing new information. Belkin (2005) posited that an *Anomalous State of Knowledge* – i.e., when a person sees a gap or an uncertainty in their knowledge – was the basic motivator for information seeking. Kuhlthau (1993, 2005) positioned uncertainty as the start of a longer *Information Search Process*; she viewed the anxiety caused by uncertainty as a key motivator to either pursue information or to give up the search. Each of these scholars point to feelings of uncertainty, ambiguity, or uneasiness as leading to information needs.

Second, according to Green, "needs are usually contestable. In this they differ from wants." That is, if I say that I *want* to know the chemical formula for heroin, you could hardly argue with me about this odd desire. However, if I say I *need* to know what heroin consists of, you might ask me why; if I replied that I need it to write an essay on drug addiction for an English course, you could perhaps reasonably argue that I don't really "need" to know that fact to write a good essay on addiction (or to demonstrate writing skills, either). A good exploration of Green's first two points is found in Beautyman and Shenton (2009).

Third, need is related to the concept of *necessity* in such a way as to carry, at times, more moral weight. That is, we use phrases like "human need" or "basic need" to refer to goal states (e.g., to be safe or to be loved, in the view of Abraham Maslow, 1963) that everyone agrees are good. Doyal and Gough (1984) say that basic human needs include "health, autonomy, learning, production, reproduction, communication, and political authority"; Lederer et al.

(1980) suggest that hypothesizing any needs beyond "primary" ones like food and shelter is problematic. Distinctions among primary versus secondary needs have led some information seeking scholars (e.g., Wilson, 1981) to argue that information is clearly a secondary, rather than a basic, need.

On the other hand, for several decades, psychologists have treated "the need for cognition," as though it were a basic, rather than a secondary need (e.g., Cacioppo & Petty, 1982; Cohen et al., 1955; Henning & Vorderer, 2001). Experiments with sensory deprivation show that lack of stimuli can result in mental problems (Zubek 1969). Psychologists like Henry Murray (1938) and Abraham Maslow (1963), as well as economist Manfred Max-Neef (1992), believed that people have a need to understand, and perhaps even to share, what their senses tell them. For example, among the basic needs identified by Murray (1938) were three involving information: "exposition" (the need to provide information to, and educate, others); "harm avoidance" (the need to avoid pain, whether physical or mental); and "infavoidance" (the need to conceal weakness and failure). Max-Neef's (1992) needs include those for learning and curiosity, and for leisure and imagination.

To *deny* a life-sustaining need (e.g., for medical care) would be morally wrong. Yet even regarding such a basic need we might make distinctions; if I said to you that I *needed* narcotics, that statement may be true in the sense that drugs are *necessary* to accomplish my goal – to satisfy my addiction. But it would probably not motivate you to help me satisfy those needs. You might judge my felt need to imply such a "bad" purpose that, even while acknowledging the truth of my need, you would feel comfortable in denying me your help. Perhaps you would rationalize by saying that I really need something else, such as a drug treatment program.

This line of thinking leads to Green's (1990) fourth point: that need is not necessarily a state of mind, and it is possible to be unaware of one's *true* needs. For example, I may *think* I need to scan every psychology journal in the library to find information about recovered memory syndrome. But an experienced librarian might judge that what I *really* need to do is to search *Psychology Abstracts* on the internet. Thus, a need may be unrecognized or unacknowledged, undesired or simply misunderstood, by the individual who has it (Derr, 1983).

So, this leads us back to the distinction between needs and wants. Others have needs that we may judge to be "merely" desires, not needs. Obviously, it is more difficult to find evidence of needs than it is of wants, because wants more typically result in observable behaviors. We can also ask people what they want, but people may not be able to articulate their needs so easily – this is certainly true if they are not even aware of their needs.

Green (1990) suggests that, within the study of information behavior, most attempts to define "need" faded away after some initial attempts made during the 1960s and 1970s. According to his view, most subsequent writers have taken for granted whatever definitions had been proposed up to the 1970s, such as those discussed by Brittain (1970), Line (1974), Menzel (1966a), and Roberts (1975). One notable exception is Richard Derr (1983, 1985) who made worthwhile attempts to define both information and information need during the 1980s.

Charles Cole's (2012) book *Information Need* has brought new attention to the concept, as have the investigations of Lundh (2010) and Lu and Yuan (2011).

2.3.2 Needs vs. Demands

So, what then is an "information need"? Forsythe et al. (1992) point out that

> ...no explicit consensus exists in the literature regarding the meaning of the central concept of "information need."... In effect, "information need," has been defined according to the particular interests and expertise of various authors. (p. 182)

"Information need" is often described simply, and somewhat circularly, as a cause of information seeking. Ikoja-Odongo and Mostert (2006, p. 147), for example, say "an information need is a requirement that drives people into information seeking." Cole (2012, p. 3) says it is "the motivation people think and feel to seek information." It is problematic, however, to assume that one's actions are *solely* caused by an internal "need." Thus, the relationship between the initial need, and what we do about it (e.g., make a demand of an information source), is critical.

Brittain (1970) points out that most early information seeking research did not discuss need, but rather *demand* – the requests made of an information system, such as a library or database. Data regarding demands were readily available from (or at least easily collectible in) information agencies that studied their users. Demands are relatively easy to measure. Investigations of information demands supported the goals of libraries and vendors to improve their services. So, according to Brittain, "most studies which have purported to be of information needs have in fact been of information uses or, at best, demands" (1970, p. 3).

Another writer, John O'Connor (1968), has suggested three "possible meanings" of information need: (1) a "negotiated" (and thus, refined) version of an *initial* question or demand stated by an inquirer; (2) whatever information provided that actually "helps" the work of that person; or (3) giving the inquirer documents that she judges to be "pertinent" on the basis of a comparison with their internal need. O'Connor criticizes all these possible meanings as involving differing standards of judgment. That is, various people (e.g., the inquirer, the provider, groups of colleagues) use varying criteria, at different points in time (e.g., immediate versus long-term effects). O'Connor's concern with the relativity of judgment was echoed by Line (1974, p. 87), who ponders, "who is to say what is 'necessary' for himself or others?" Or, as Michael Ignatieff puts it "there are few presumptions in human relations more dangerous than the idea that one knows what another human being needs better than they do themselves" (1984, p. 11).

Few investigations of information seeking delve very deeply into the issue of what human "needs" really are. Not many even question the notion of "information needs." Rather, most writers assume that information needs exist and are unproblematic. When information behavior researchers *do* refer to fundamental discussions of how information needs arise, they typically cite one or more of four authors in doing so: Robert Taylor (1962, 1968), Nicholas Belkin (2005), Carol Kuhlthau (1993a), and Brenda Dervin (1983).

2.3.3 *The Trouble with Information Needs*

Wilson (1981, 1997) says that, while researchers fret over a definition of information *need*, much of the time they are really studying information seeking *behavior*. Belkin and Vickery (1985) point out that observing an information need is problematic because it exists inside someone's head and must be inferred by any interested observer while a search is in process, or after it has taken place:

> Less tractable is the issue of why people look for information at all; that is, what is the status of the concept or category of *information need*?... [I]s there such a thing as a need for information, which can be considered on its own ... or is information-seeking behaviour contingent upon the desire to satisfy other types of needs, or to resolve situations which are not in themselves information-dependent? (p. 6)

Indeed, other scholars (e.g., Poole, 1985; Wilson, 1981) believe that the notion of an information need is an unrealistic concept, as most information needs could be said to be accounted for by more general needs, and in any event, they cannot be observed. An example of their first type of objection would be that our need to know the prices of items (e.g., bread) might be driven by our need to eat (surely a more basic human need), or our need to conserve our resources (less basic, but compelling to most humans). That needs and motivations may be hierarchical in this way is also a central assumption of Terror Management Theory (Pyszczynksi et al., 1999). Others suggest that information may indeed be a basic human need but deny that needs are hierarchical (Max-Neef, 1992).

Bosman and Renckstorf (1996) point out the circular nature of assumptions about information needs as a distinct motivator:

> ...it is in fact an ad hoc notion created for practical purposes in order to predict information-seeking behaviour and information consumption. It is rather obvious that people who consume much

Motivations for Information Seeking: Making Sense

One alternative to defining information in mechanistic ways, for *uncertainty reduction*, is to see it in terms of producing *meaning* or *sense* from our experience of the world. Information behavior scholars have drawn heavily on Brenda Dervin's (1983) work, particularly for studies of everyday experiences. Dervin believes people struggle to *make sense* of a world full of discontinuities. A need means something is missing – i.e., a gap to be filled or bridged. People may have physical needs (e.g., food) or needs for expertise; gaps appear in the form of questions that can be address by information, or other forms of help to fill a gap. Sensemaking research often focuses on people struggling with problems, such as illness, unemployment or frustration in attaining life goals. In this view, people continually generate internal questions to make sense of situations; communication with others can *bridge the gap* and obtain the desired help. In sensemaking, looking for information is only *one* response to a gap; other responses include seeking reassurance, expressing feelings, or connecting with another person.

> information on a certain subject will also state that they have a certain need for this information. . .. However, if one wants to explain why some people do and others do not consume certain information, the information needs concept is as elucidating as, for instance, explaining criminal behaviour on the basis of hypothetical "criminality needs." (p. 43)

Similar critiques are voiced in other disciplines. For example, in discussing human motivations, Hirschman and Holbrook (1986) point out that "action theorists" (e.g., Goldman, 1970; Hampshire, 1982) argue that wants and desires – when coupled with beliefs about the relationship between means and ends – provide *reasons* for actions. However, these theorists stop short of claiming that such reasons *cause* actions.

In the case of information, Bosman and Renckstorf (1996) see three overlapping motivations that determine a need for it: "social utility (e.g., in order to have topics of conversation), instrumental utility (e.g., in order to decide whether to buy something) and intrinsic utility (e.g., the entertainment value of the information offered)" (p. 46).

The first (social) and last (intrinsic) of these "utilities" are not always counted as "real" information needs. Bryce Allen (1996) reinforces this view when he says

> . . .there may be a variety of gratifications that are provided by the information-seeking process that cannot be considered meeting a specific information need or solving a particular problem. Another way of looking at these information activities is that they meet needs (such as the need for entertainment or companionship) that are not classified as information needs. (p. 56)

Given the multidimensional nature of such needs, how are we to describe them? Harter (1992) argues that to talk about an individual's "information need" is virtually the same as describing his or her "current psychological state" because needs shift stochastically as each relevant piece of information is encountered. One bit of knowledge may raise questions, lead to another fact or to a new conclusion and so forth, which changes one's knowledge state and hence what one finds relevant and worth seeking. At least Wilson, Pool, Bosman and Renckstorf and Harter would agree that, however information needs are characterized, they are not something fixed and long-lasting. Kari's (2010) exploration of possible meanings of "information use" takes a similar view in that "use" may involve the construction of knowledge in response to an evolving need. Savolainen (2012a, 2012b, 2017) and Borlund and Pharo (2019) argue that needs can only be understood in the context of particular domains and purposes.

Most of what we have said (and quoted) thus far has downplayed the idea that having information is a "basic" human need. Some psychologists would disagree. George Miller (1983), for example, described information gathering in instinctual terms. Another psychologist, Abraham Maslow (1963), said "I am convinced that man *does* have a need to know," describing it as "instinct-like," even though he admitted that he couldn't prove its existence (p. 111). Wendell Garner, who wrote extensively on the role of information in forming cognitive structures, believed that "the search for structure is inherent in behavior. . .. People in any situation will search for meaningful relations between the variables existing in the situation" (1962, p. 339). Milton Rokeach's view was that "we are all motivated by the desire, which is sometimes strong and sometimes weak, to see reality as it actually is" (1960, p. 400). To "see reality," we *need* information about it.

2.3.4 Information Seeking

Information seeking is closely tied to the concept of "need." It is counterintuitive, but researchers have spent fewer words defining seeking (Savolainen, 2009a) than they have needs. Perhaps the meaning of "information seeking" is thought to be obvious. Most accounts of empirical investigations do not bother to provide a definition of information seeking, taking it for granted as what people do in response to a need for information. Instead, studies tend to rely on operational definitions of seeking, i.e., what actions are observed by investigators, or reported by the respondents in the study.

Authors who state an explicit definition of information seeking typically describe a process of either *discovering patterns* or *filling in gaps* in patterns previously recognized. Garner (1962), for example, implies that it is the search for relationships among stimuli. Likewise, Zerbinos (1990) says that

> ...information seeking takes place when a person has knowledge stored in long term memory that precipitates an interest in related information as well as the motivation to acquire it. It can also take place when a person recognizes a gap in their knowledge that may motivate that person to acquire new information. (p. 922)

The basic notions behind what Garner and Zerbinos describe date back to John Dewey's (1910/1933) characterizations; Dewey saw *inquiry* as motivated by recognition of a problem – of something lacking in a situation. Gary Marchionini's definition of information seeking is also problem oriented: "a process in which humans purposefully engage in order to change their state of knowledge" and which is "closely related to learning and problem solving" (1995, pp. 5–6). Brenda Dervin's (1983) definition of sensemaking is similar in terms of confronting problematic situations; indeed, for some investigators information seeking has come to be synonymous with sensemaking.

Johnson offers one of the more restrictive definitions: "Information seeking can be defined as the purposive acquisition of information from selected information carriers" (1997, p. 26) which does not identify the "purpose" itself, or what motivates a person to select a particular "carrier." Purpose is also presumed in other definitions of information seeking, such as Ford's (2015) description of seeking activities as "strategies a person devises in order to find information" (p. 14). More than three decades earlier, Krikelas (1983) described information seeking in like terms, saying that it starts with a "need-creating event/environment" – a characterization also echoed by Julien and Michels (2004, pp. 547–548) and Westbrook (2008, p. 24).

The word "purposive" in Johnson's definition is important as it underscores the idea that some information behaviors are passive, for example, serendipitous encounters with information that is recognized to be relevant, rather than something that is actively sought. However, as the term "information seeking" was not typically used to refer to *passive reception* of information, whether that information is *ignored*, or how it is *used*, a broader term was used – i.e., information behavior. Wilson (2022, p. 12) defines this term as:

> ...how we act towards information, how we seek it or discover it, how we use it, how we exchange it with others, how we may choose to ignore it, and, by extension, how we learn from it and act upon it.

In summary, information seeking is a taken-for-granted concept, a catchall phrase that encompasses a variety of behaviors seemingly motivated by the recognition of *missing* information. Although it is the most common term in use, information seeking is typically defined strictly in terms of active and intentional behavior, which limits its applicability to the broad range of research currently being conducted on human use of information.

> ***What Happened to Gatekeeping?***
>
> In all social research, some topics rise in popularity, only later to fade. Gatekeeping is one such topic. It appears far less in the information behavior research of the last 10 years than it did in the 30 years prior. The analogy of a gate that either stops or allows information flow was first discussed in 1943 around food choices. In libraries, in the 1980s and 1990s, specialist databases were not available for public use; many systems required expert searching skills, often with fee-for-service costs limiting access. The idea that a person or organization can be an information gatekeeper remains evident in mainstream media, with editors, publishers, and broadcasters controlling what (or how) information is shared with the public.
>
> Why does gatekeeping appear in so few recent studies? Perhaps it is because we now have many more sources of information, and many more ways for people to produce and share that information. Many people, globally, can access computers, phones, cameras, and digital platforms. In libraries, schools, workplaces, and homes, most people can search for new information, publish their observations, document their local worlds, and share what they find or create with others. Although Erizkova (2018) acknowledges that technological changes have reduced gatekeeping, she concludes that the concept remains highly relevant to digital networks. As algorithms shape our online experiences, gatekeeping may just now be less visible to the searcher than in the past. For example, Potnis and Tahamtan (2021) explore the gatekeeping function of social media hashtags. Perhaps, in time, we will see a resurgence in interest from information behavior scholars in exploring the power of gatekeeping on people's lives.

2.4 HISTORIC APPROACHES TO STUDYING NEEDS AND SEEKING

One of the most common approaches to studying people's information needs and seeking activities, historically, involved identifying and grouping people by their job roles and investigating the types of information needed to do that job. Over several decades, researchers studied a vast number of different roles including law enforcement personnel (Allen et al., 2008; Baker, 2004), teachers (Chang, 2006; Stefl-Mabry, 2005), sex workers (Baker et al., 2003; Stilwell, 2002), translators (White et al., 2008), financial professionals (Huvila, 2010; Miranda & Tarapanoff, 2008), securities analysts (Baldwin & Rice, 1997; Kuhlthau, 1999), government employees (Woudstra & van den Hooff, 2008), policymakers (Florio & DeMartini, 1993), architects (Makri & Warwick, 2010), musicians (Kostagiolas et al., 2015), army officers (Sonnenwald, 2006), aircraft pilots (von Thaden, 2008), directors of shelters for domestic abuse victims (Westbrook, 2009), managers of historic houses (Brine & Feather, 2010), and janitors (Chatman, 1990). Some studies of occupation are nonspecific: Agarwal et al. (2011), for example, studied the source preferences and usage of a variety of professional workers in Singapore, but did not identify the distribution of their job titles, saying only that they all use computers in their work.

In discussing some of the key types of role-related investigations, we proceed in the same fashion in which the research has developed: starting with studies of various types of academics and then discussing other occupations. Although research of this type is now considered far too limited in scope by most information behavior scholars (i.e., due to its lack of contextual framing and lack of attention of information "use"), it is useful to understand the evolution of information behavior given the broad range of studies that have explored workers' experiences.

That said, it is worth remembering that most of the studies discussed in the following sections exclude the sociocultural aspects of the work environment, as well as individuals' personal circumstances. These aspects (which are discussed in Chapter 3) are more prevalent in contemporary studies, as they reflect the complexity of human experience and implications for people's information behaviors. In early studies, the concept of "need" focused researchers' attention on the source material required (e.g., a preferred source, due to content or format) and the strategies used by the employee to "seek" resources that would satisfy that need. Figure 2.1 presents some of the digital "firsts" that have influenced people's behaviors. And, while qualitative and mixed methods studies are commonly used to attend to the complex environments shaping individuals' experience (as discussed in Chapter 5), most early studies used quantitative designs (e.g., questionnaires, structured interviews) to summarize the sources and ways of finding materials most common to specific groups.

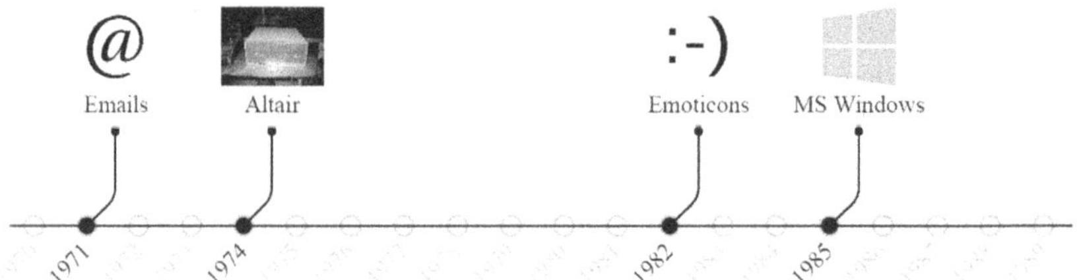

Fig. 2.1. A Timeline of Digital "Firsts" That Have Had a Significant Impact on People's Experiences With Information.
Image design by Dr Linus Tan. All images used with permission or available for use under creative commons licensing agreements.

2.4.1 Studies of Academics

Research on academics' information needs and seeking behaviors has often been aggregated by metadiscipline – i.e., science, social science, and the humanities. Wiberley and Jones (1994, p. 503), for example, declare "it is useful to look at all scholarship as a continuum from the physical sciences to the quantitative social sciences to the qualitative social sciences to the humanities." There are some gray areas in this typology. For example, are psychologists who are concerned with physiological influences on behavior chiefly scientists, or do they belong with the social scientists? And where do professions like education, or interdisciplinary fields like communication, belong? And do we consider the creative and fine arts part of the humanities? Or should a new metadiscipline represent these scholars?

Nevertheless, the three basic categories of science, social science, and humanities have appealed strongly to those completing reviews of information seeking results (e.g., the series edited by Constance Gould (1988), Gould and Handler (1989), and Gould and Pearce (1991)). For instance, many reviewers, historically, have concluded that the primary literature of science is found in journals, whereas that of humanities scholars is more likely found in books and archives. Many generalizations about disciplines and metadisciplines are problematic; however, the work of Bouazza (1989) provides helpful insight into the differences between fields, concluding that

> ...although physical scientists, social scientists, and humanists tend to rely more on formal sources of information than on informal ones, they do not behave in the same way as far as information use is concerned.... The factors that affect the information use [include]... (a) The availability, accessibility, quality, cost, and ease of use of information. (b) Seniority, experience, specialty, educational level, professional orientation, and the subjective impressions of the users. (c) The stage of a research project; and the physical, social, political, and economic environments surrounding the user. (p. 159)

Bouazza's research, on a sample of 240 scientists, social scientists and humanists from Carnegie-Mellon University, found that these three groups

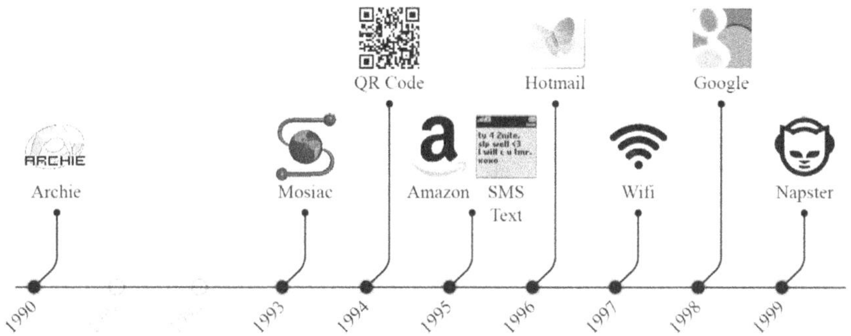

differed in the way that they used informal sources of information, especially in the data collection stage of research and in course preparation. In the following sections, we discuss some of the key, historic studies in each of the prevailing metadisciplines.

2.4.1.1 Scientists

It is fitting to start with a description of the information seeking of scientists because this is where information behavior research really expanded in the twentieth century. The "Big Science" (Price, 1963) investments sparked by World War II and the Cold War resulted in an explosion of research material. There were simply too many findings being published for individual scientists and engineers to monitor results effectively. The outcome was frustration and, sometimes, outright duplication of research efforts, because researchers did not always know that others were gathering or even publishing findings of interest to their work. As a result, money and attention became available to address problems in the dissemination of scientific information and to study communication among scientists and engineers.

Tom Wilson (1984) accurately characterizes the nature of the literature at that time, stating "the study of information-seeking behaviour can be said to be the study of *scientists*' information-seeking behaviour" (p. 199). From the 1940s through the 1970s, investigations of scientists (and to some extent, engineers) dominated all others. Comprehensive studies of scientists – i.e., of their overall information seeking and communication patterns – has declined since the 1980s. In part this may be because the phenomenon has been well documented and "played out," and so researchers moved on to less-studied groups; it may also reflect shifts in funding for such studies. Nevertheless, investigations of scientists continue to appear (e.g., Niu & Hemminger, 2012; Sahu & Singh, 2013; Wellings & Casselden, 2019). And, studies continue to explore scientists' citation practices (e.g., Borgman & Furner, 2002; Leydesdorff & Milojevic, 2015; Ma et al., 2022) and the social construction of

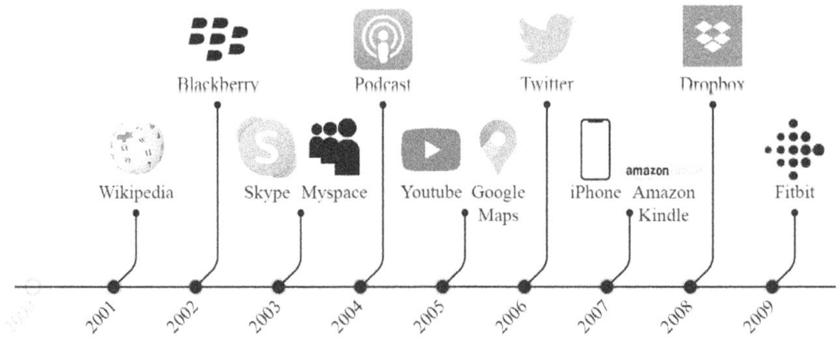

scientific problems and discourse communities (e.g., Latour, 2004; Touminen et al., 2005). What has changed is that investigations of scientists' use of *sources* are less common today than they were in past decades.

Generally, the research methods and samples have not changed much over the decades; studies of scientists have tended to employ questionnaires and interviews to study the reading and information gathering habits of those working in a single discipline, such as Flaxbart's (2001) interviews with university chemistry faculty, and studies by Sapa et al. (2014) and Gordon et al. (2020) of mathematicians. Each study documents use of print and interpersonal sources, while emphasizing the impact of digital content on the habits of people working in one discipline. Ward and Given (2019) explored agricultural scientists' use of information and communication technologies for information sharing within international, collaborative research teams. Their empirical work informed the development of an intercultural heuristic assessment tool that can be adapted by multinational research teams in various disciplines and global contexts.

Other typical studies retain the focus on sources of information, but cover multiple disciplines, usually for comparative purposes. Such studies of relying on journals, libraries, and the internet among diverse scientific groups include Ellis et al.'s (1993) interviews with physicists and chemists; Brown's (1999) email survey of astronomers, chemists, mathematicians, and physicists; Kuruppu and Gruber's (2006) interviews and focus groups with agricultural and biological scientists; Murphy's (2003) internet survey of toxicologists, biochemists, and other US Environmental Protection Agency scientists; Jamali and Nicholas' (2010) survey of physicists and astronomers; and Sahu and Singh's (2013) surveys and interviews with astronomists and astrophysicists. Whether sampling one discipline or several, few of these studies offer unexpected findings; yet, taken together, they illustrate scientists' continuing shift from print to digital sources over several decades.

The largest and most comprehensive multidisciplinary investigation of scientists involved surveys of 2,063 individuals across disciplines in five American

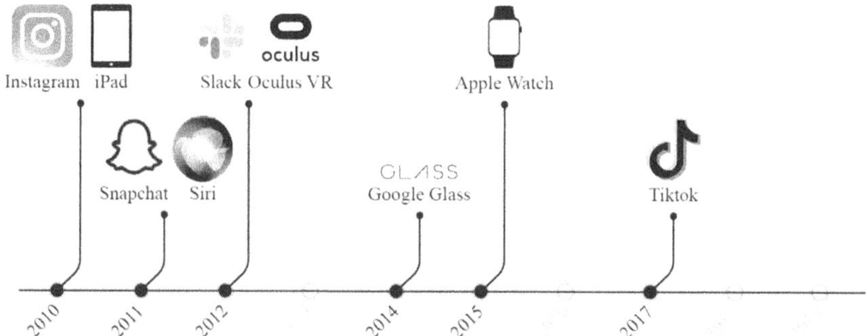

universities, conducted by Bradley Hemminger and colleagues (Hemminger et al., 2007; Niu & Hemminger, 2012; Niu et al., 2010). The analyses clarify the interactions among various factors (demographics, role/position, discipline) and respondents' habits of searching, collecting, and engaging with information. Many differences were found among various segments of the sample; however, in many cases these were inconsistent – as might be expected among such diverse populations. For example, there were not statistically significant interactions between disciplines or department types (natural sciences versus medical sciences versus engineering) in terms of time spent reading (all types of documents); overall most respondents were reading 15–20 hours per week. Yet it was clear that academic position was influential in determining reading habits, with doctoral students reading more than academics in other types of appointments. Types of publications varied by department type, with scientists spending more time with journals, while engineers read more conference proceedings. Overall, this large study documents scientists' transition away from print-based sources, including the increased reliance on databases and search engines to seek information, the decreased reliance on the physical library, and the shift to almost exclusive use of digital communications. Some more recent studies (e.g., Wellings & Casselden, 2019) continue to focus on sources (such as colleagues and journals), although with more emphasis on the use of search engines to locate digital texts.

Theory-guided investigations are more likely to reach beyond sources to consider the contexts and motivations of scientific labor. Kwon's (2017) and Chung et al.'s (2016) sensemaking interviews with laboratory scientists employed Activity Theory to document the importance of norms, culture, trust, interpersonal communication, and collaboration in the work practices of bio- and nanoscientists. As in Roos' (2012) study of scientists in molecular medicine, Activity Theory encourages the researcher to consider aspects beyond information searching and use, to consider the rules, community, roles, and objects (e.g., outcomes) of scientific research.

2.4.1.2 Social Scientists

The most comprehensive review of social science information needs and uses (with ample comparisons to those in science) is that by Hogeweg de Haart (1981). Emphasizing documentary sources of information, it does an excellent job of summarizing virtually all the studies conducted up to 1980. A larger but narrower review of social scientists, featuring historians and government publications, appeared in the United States a few years later (Hernon, 1984). Finally, Gould and Handler (1989) provided highlights from findings of social science studies, suggesting practical implications for libraries and communication systems.

One of the most ambitious and fundamental investigations of social scientists is by David Ellis (1989), focusing on the stages and processes in their information seeking activities. He interviewed 47 social scientists, resulting in the development of six characteristics of information seeking: starting, chaining, browsing, differentiating, monitoring, and extracting. Informal contacts were particularly important in the starting phases of projects and were also employed in monitoring developments in a field; the other activities mostly involved published literature. As the labels imply, browsing has to do with semidirected searches of publications or collections; chaining is the following of references from one document to another; differentiating concerns judgments made about the status, orientation, or quality of sources; and extracting is pulling out from sources specific information of interest. Meho and Tibbo (2003) used Ellis' (1989) model to study 65 faculty members from 14 countries, which confirmed the robustness of Ellis' model, while adding four new features: accessing, networking, verifying, and information managing.

Among other studies, Thivant (2005) used a questionnaire based on a qualitative approach called SICIA (Situation, Complexity, and Information Activity) to investigate the relationship between situations, professional contexts, and strategies in the work of a small sample of economists and financial analysts. He found similarity in information seeking and use strategies used by these two groups, with some differences stemming from the varying contexts of their work. Krampen et al. (2011) analyzed the information seeking of 298 psychologists, along with their demographics and several other factors affecting their work. The most unusual study of a social scientist may be Ruvane's (2005) two-year observation of a single geographer. Ruvane's sole informant was conducting a lengthy historical investigation of the influence of the Indian Trading Path on settlement patterns in the eighteenth century and on the subsequent growth of cities in North Carolina. The geographer created digital multimedia maps, based partly on land grant documents, to place otherwise isolated facts into a context in which they could be related.

Overall, there seems to have been a recent decline in the number of studies featuring samples of social science researchers, with most documents appearing between 1989 and 2011.

2.4.1.3 Humanities Scholars

Although Ellis and his colleagues took pains to say that the information behaviors of social scientists did not occur in a strict sequence, the existence of "stages" in research projects has long been suggested by various studies. For example, Jenny Bronstein (2007) applied Ellis' model in a qualitative interview study of 25 Jewish Studies scholars, which used a grounded theory approach to develop categories of activities. She found information seeking strategies (e.g., browsing, extracting, and citation tracking) varied with the stage or purpose of research, and proposed extensions to Ellis' model. Bronstein's informants developed close contacts with their colleagues, in contrast to the findings of Wiberley and Jones (1994) and others who found humanities scholars work alone.

Chu's (1999) survey of 31 Canadian literary scholars also focused on research stages. Using in-depth interviews and a lengthy questionnaire, Chu collected individual accounts of research projects and scholars' activities; these were used to create a descriptive model of the process of literary criticism, which was then subsequently tested by surveying 800 scholars. Chu confirmed a series of six stages typical of literary scholarship: idea generation, preparation, elaboration, analysis and writing, dissemination, and then "further writing and dissemination." Each of these stages was accompanied by specific activities such as searching for, reading and annotating materials in the preparation stage, and outlining and discussing ideas for a written work in the elaboration phase. In turn, each stage was seen as having "information functions," such as relating primary materials to different perspectives and themes in the preparation phase or determining central and peripheral focuses in the elaboration phase. Chu noted that these hypothesized stages do not necessarily occur in a strict sequential order; rather, their sequence is highly susceptible to the newness of the project, competing projects, and personal working style. Like Bronstein, Chu found that informal communication with colleagues is important among literary scholars.

A contrasting view of research stages is found in Foster (2004), who conducted interviews with 45 academics (faculty and graduate students), including humanities scholars. Foster identifies several activities that happen at initial, middle, and final stages; ultimately, he concludes that seeking is better described as dynamic and holistic rather than sequence-driven and consists of three nonlinear "core processes": opening, orientation, and consolidation. Tabak and Willson (2012) and Tabak (2014) suggest improvements on Foster's model, drawing upon Bruno Latour's actor–network theory.

In a replication of the Stieg (1981) study of historians' information sources, Dalton and Charnigo (2004) surveyed 278 historians. The pattern of preference for source material was like the older study, except for increased reliance on dissertations and digital sources, and decreased use of newspapers. Studies by Duff and Johnson (2002), Martin and Quan-Haase (2017), and Buchanan and Erdelez (2019) also included historians. Relatedly, Yakel (2005) argues in favor of paying more attention to archives (both physical and digital) as a place in which both scholars and students seek information. Twenty-five archeologists were the subjects in Huvila's (2008a, 2008b, 2009) investigation; using interviews and information horizon maps, Huvila depicted sources and interactions with information within seven work roles undertaken by these professionals. A later study (Huvila et al., 2021) examined how archeological field reports are created.

Brown (2001, 2002) conducted a series of studies of music scholars. Her 2001 publication focuses on communication patterns via email and electronic discussion groups used by such scholars in the United States and Canada to facilitate their research. Employing diffusion theory (Rogers, 2003) and using interviews and a survey, she found that music scholars rated email as more helpful than discussion groups. Overall, both modes of communication played marginal roles in music research. In a later work, Brown (2002) proposed a six-stage model of music research, based on interviews with 30 music scholars who described to her their recent research projects. Although focused more narrowly on library use, Liew and Ng's (2006) research on 14 ethnomusicologists adds to what we know about music scholarship. A literature review and subsequent investigation of creativity (Kostagiolas et al., 2017; Lavranos et al., 2016) included several music educators and academics, as well as performers; they found that higher self-efficacy and certain personality traits correlated with more active information seeking.

The worlds of art, architecture and design received scant attention in information behavior until Rose's (2003) study of the impact of new technologies on the research behaviors of art historians. More recently, several related studies have appeared. Larkin (2010) explored the information behavior of scholars in the visual arts, concluding that this group has needs unique from those of other humanities scholars. Designers of various types have been featured in some investigations. Pilerot (2013, 2014) and Pilerot and Limberg (2011) examined information sharing among Nordic design scholars, finding the building of trust to be a key element in successful exchanges. Harviainen et al. (2022) examine game designers, while Given and Kuys (2022) focus on coproduction of memorial designs, including an interdisciplinary team working across the disciplines of industrial design, history, and architecture.

Many investigations include samples of faculty from multiple disciplines, sometimes with the express purpose of studying the challenges of interdisciplinarity (see discussions by Caidi, 2001; Paisley, 1986, 1990, on this theme). An example is Palmer and Neumann's (2002) sample of 25 faculty members from 13 humanities and social sciences departments and who were affiliated with an interdisciplinary center several years earlier. The authors used semistructured interviews to explore a set of questions and analyzed the respondents' publications to determine sources they cited in writing those works. Palmer and Neumann (2002) identified three categories for which information sources were used: identifying, locating, or accessing and consulting or reading. For example, sources used to locate or access information included libraries, their own collections, colleagues' collections, or digital resources. They characterize the work of these scholars as composed of "exploration" and "translation," each of which has certain processes, activities, and sources associated with it.

Westbrook (2003) surveyed 215 scholars in women's studies – another group that could be placed in either the social sciences or the humanities. She found women's studies faculty face six types of information-resource problems: information is hard to find and use; information is of poor quality and coverage; information is of limited quantity; information on the internet is unsatisfactory; information's interdisciplinarity is difficult; and information is overabundant. These scholars reported three kinds of information-related problems with their own research: doing and keeping up with research; learning how to do and keep up with research; and managing information. The sources used fell into eight channels (or formats): books, journals, government documents, people, databases, the internet, other media, and gray/primary/archival material. Another heterogeneous population is that of Wiberley and Jones (1989) who studied 11 humanities scholars; their results, like Sievert and Sievert's (1989) interviews with 27 philosophers, emphasize the solitary nature of such scholarship, with most information acquired through reading. Wiberley and Jones (1994, 2000) revisited these scholars to assess the degree to which they had adopted information technology and found them somewhat slower to do so than social scientists.

New technologies may provide additional insights into the information behaviors of scholars of all types. Ross et al. (2011) used Twitter archives, as well as conventional questionnaires, to examine communication among attendees at a digital humanities conference. They detail the advantages and drawbacks of such "backchannel" communication, emphasizing how tweets may help attendees collaboratively create knowledge, document events, and feel more connected, even while it raises issues of etiquette and appropriateness that have become all too familiar with other forms of digital communication. Given and Willson's (2015, 2018) study of humanities scholars' collaborative information seeking also provides insights into the use of online tools for information sharing and other collaborative activities.

Reviews by Gould (1988), Bouazza (1989), and Watson-Boone (1994) remain good entry points into the pre-1990 humanities information seeking literature despite their age. Palmer and Neumann (2002) cover the relevant literature from the 1990s. There has not been a comprehensive review of more recent literature, nor very many new studies focusing on humanities scholars, exclusively.

2.4.2 Studies of Professionals

2.4.2.1 Engineers

In their comprehensive review of various information seeking literatures, Leckie et al. (1996) describe engineering as a highly specialized profession that includes the design, development, testing, and manufacturing of items, as well as research, management, consulting, and sales roles. Their work emphasizes the solving of technical problems rather than the production of general conclusions, which separates them from scientists, with whom engineering work is sometimes conflated in studies (e.g., Wellings & Casselden, 2019). Engineers are frequent consumers of information; a cross-national (India-United States) study by Allard et al. (2009) estimated engineers spend one-quarter of their time engaged in "information events," while Robinson's (2010) investigation suggests that approximately 56% of their time is spent on information behaviors.

One consistent finding in examinations of the information seeking of engineers (e.g., du Preez & Fourie, 2009; Holland & Powell, 1995; Pinelli, 1991; Tenopir & King, 2004) is that they rely on their own knowledge, their colleagues and within-organization sources of information more than they rely on the technical literature. What literature they *do* access from their trade – reports, catalogs, handbooks, and trade journals – more so than research publications. The most pertinent information is from clients and colleagues concerned with similar objectives, so they are perceived as the most accessible and familiar sources (Hertzum & Pejtersen, 2000).

Pinelli et al.'s (1991) study of more than 2000 aerospace engineers explored how aerospace knowledge diffuses among engineers and scientists. The study found the relevance of sources was the most compelling reason for their use, followed by accessibility and "technical quality or reliability"; the investigators concluded that "accessibility is simply not the issue that it apparently was 25 years ago" (p. 320) due to an increase in electronic channels of distribution and improved indexing, organization, and dissemination of information. Since then, the advent of online materials has made accessibility even less of an issue. Similarly, Fidel and Green (2004) studied the accessibility of information sources as perceived by engineers and found that saving time was the chief criterion for selecting among documents, while familiarity was the guiding factor in selecting between human sources of information.

Holland and Powell (1995) also documented the importance of interpersonal information seeking among engineers. They asked very detailed questions of 60 engineers regarding their information sources at work and the relative importance of those sources. The single most highly rated source was "word of mouth," just edging out engineers' own collections of documents and far exceeding any reliance on libraries or databases. Kwasitsu (2003) studied engineers working on the design and manufacturing of microprocessors, finding that the higher the level of education, the less likely engineers were dependent on memories, and the more likely they were to rely on libraries. du Preez and Fourie (2009) sampled 11 consulting engineers and discovered a high reliance on personal files and knowledge, and on other people. Another example of the importance of interpersonal communication is found in a study of computer hardware engineers (Sakai et al., 2012) as they talk about a production problem in their morning meeting. It is worth noting that studies of engineering faculty (e.g., Engel et al., 2011) and students (e.g., Basha et al., 2013; Kerins et al., 2004) show subtle differences from those investigations conducted in industry. Faculty face requirements to conduct studies and to publish, which shifts their orientation towards more formal, and often more digital, sources of information. Engineering students show a similar pattern (Qin et al., 2020).

As with other occupations, qualitative research techniques have been employed to capture a deeper level of detail in the work of engineers. Freund (2015), for example, employed both structured and unstructured interviews, and a focus group, to understand how context shapes selection of information sources by software engineers. The four key "contextual spheres" were person, project, work tasks, and information tasks, with each of these having subcomponents (e.g., expertise and role by person, and length and stage of completion for project). A different qualitative approach was taken in Sakai et al.'s (2012) study, which employed photos, audio and video recordings, observations, and field notes, to explore how computer hardware engineers discussed task-relevant information needs. Their ethnomethodology features analysis of the language used by the engineers, demonstrating how the group concluded what additional information was needed to address production problems. Borg et al. (2017) and Storer (2017) are additional studies that touch upon the information behaviors of computing engineers.

2.4.2.2 Lawyers

Lawyers have been among the most consistently studied professionals for almost three decades, perhaps due to the urgency and precision their work often requires. Attorneys need to stay current with published literature relevant to their work.

They cannot afford to miss any new ruling, decision, or regulation that concerns their practice, though some areas of the law (e.g., taxation, health, and safety regulation) require more research than others. Over two decades ago, Sutton (1994, p. 199) stated "there is little known empirically of the information seeking behavior of attorneys." The analysis of attorney information seeking by Leckie et al. (1996), for example, rests mainly on texts about the nature and practice of legal research. Those authors said the primary activities of attorneys – advocacy (with its accompanying legal research), drafting of legal documents, counseling of clients, negotiating outcomes, and managing their practice – all imply a great deal of information seeking of various types. Since those early commentaries, much more has been learned about the information behavior of attorneys.

Sutton's own analysis (1994) theorized about the "mental model" of legal reasoning held by attorneys, discussing the ways lawyers think about legal cases, and what this predicts about their search for relevant court decisions. According to Sutton, lawyers rely on their legal education to first identify key cases that define an area of law, then use "context-sensitive exploration" to find cases that apply legal principles to facts like those in the case at hand. Ultimately, the search may involve "tracking" citations from one legal decision to another. This can be a massive and frustrating task, with large numbers of potentially relevant cases, including those that have been overruled, criticized, or ignored by more recent decisions, with details not fully reflected in the indexing systems for case law. Since Sutton's groundbreaking work there have been many studies of lawyers and a few of judges. Cole and Kuhlthau's (2000) investigation of 15 attorneys at various career stages is one example. Drawing on psychological studies of problem-solving, Cole and Kuhlthau argued that part of what makes one "expert" in the law is an ability to link the recognition of a problem to potential solutions. Through interviews, they found lawyers with expertise can identify relevant information, construct and package that information, and then use it to persuade others. The Israeli attorney studies of Solomon and Bronstein (2015, 2022) and Bronstein and Solomon (2021) also emphasize problem-solving, but also social-networking and promotional goals of successful law practice.

Another investigation of attorneys by Kuhlthau and Tama (2001) concluded lawyers desire information services that are highly customized to their needs. Wilkinson (2001) conducted over 150 interviews with lawyers about how they solved problems in their practice, concluding that "legal research" is not synonymous with "information-seeking." Wilkinson's respondents identified other tasks, such as administration, as constituting both problem-solving and information-seeking activities. In general, they preferred informal and internal sources of information, especially those from larger firms. A three-nation investigation by Evans and Price (2017) of "managing information in law firms" reaches similar conclusions.

Choo et al. (2008) undertook a comparative study of three organizations: a law firm, an engineering firm, and a public health agency. One finding specific to the law firm was a higher reliance on informal sources, such as personal networks. The lawyers and engineers were less likely to share information with parties outside their firm than was the health agency. A contrasting comparison of different professionals was conducted by Russell-Rose et al. (2018), who surveyed lawyers, recruiters, healthcare professionals, and patent analysts in two related studies. The focus of the investigations is strictly on online searching, with a limited discussion of information-sharing or other nondigital sources.

2.4.2.3 Physicians, Nurses, and Other Healthcare Providers

There is ever more health-related information in existence and an increasing need to stay informed about medical and public health innovations, particularly for healthcare professionals (e.g., physicians, nurses, dentists, hospital administrators). As a result, there is interest in, and funding for, research related to health information. What is it that healthcare providers need to know, and how do they find it out? Most investigations – particularly the older ones – address these questions in terms of formal information sources and use mostly quantitative measures. Practitioners need to know, on the one hand, about the world of medical practice and research findings, and on the other, about their patients' conditions. Both aspects receive attention in the information seeking literature, but the overwhelming emphasis has been on how providers learn about treatment modalities, procedures, equipment, and medications.

Even in this era of ubiquitous online sources it is still worth reading some of the early literature on medical professionals. For example, the physician and psychologist team of Timpka and Arborlelius (1990) filmed physicians' consultations with patients and interviewed them in depth about problem-solving – including the social aspects of illnesses and their treatment. More typical investigations are cited in the comprehensive reviews of Paul Gorman (1995, 1999), who synthesized 16 years of physician studies. Gorman identified five types of information: patient data (from the patient's medical records, family, friends, and self-reports); population statistics (epidemiology); medical knowledge (generalizable research and practice); logistical information (policies, procedures, and forms); and social influences (local practice, as learned from colleagues).

Doctors who treat patients develop "questions" they need to answer; yet early studies varied widely in their estimates of how many questions and how often these were pursued. In the days before the internet and wireless access, more than two-thirds of doctors' questions were not followed up, according to Gorman and Helfand (1995). When doctors did pursue their questions, early metareviews (e.g., Haug, 1997) found these were typically satisfied by textbooks, drug texts, and people (colleagues, consultants, and nonphysicians), with a strong preference for highly familiar sources; at that time, relatively little use was made of library or internet resources.

As patient records became digital, and as medical information migrated to the internet, difficulties with access, convenience, and usability intensified (Bennett et al., 2006; Davies, 2007; Gorman et al., 2000; Younger, 2010). For nurses, fast access to digital information has remained an important goal (e.g., Fossum et al., 2022; Stokes & Urquhart, 2015). Recent reviews (e.g., Clarke et al., 2013; Daei et al., 2020; Fossum et al., 2022) continue to say that healthcare professionals' peers are the most used sources of information, although digital sources are very close in frequency of consultation. A higher percentage of patient-related questions are answered than in the 1990s, according to the review by Daei et al. (2020).

In the previous century, surveys, interviews, literature reviews, and meta-analyses of studies were common approaches to understanding physician information behaviors. Less often used were clinical case histories, or *vignettes* (Urquhart, 1999). Physicians were presented with several vignettes and asked questions about their confidence treating patients based on what they currently knew, and where they would go to seek additional information. If they had doubts, physicians preferred to consult specialists. Urquhart (1999) questioned whether vignettes were as valid for physicians as they have been in studies of other kinds of professionals.

While qualitative approaches are increasingly employed in studies of physicians and other healthcare workers, survey methods have continued to dominate the literature. The investigation by Grad et al. (2011) is notable for collecting responses at the point of information use, and for assessing *outcomes* (see Pluye et al., 2013). The investigators provided hand-held computers to 41 family doctors who were conducting clinical information searches. Physicians could immediately give yes-or-no responses to outcome statements like "I learned something new" or "I was reassured." Investigators were able to correlate the searches with subsequent patient treatments and health outcomes.

There are of course many other types of workers involved in healthcare, the most studied of which are nurses. Nurses are much more numerous than physicians but until the 1990s were less likely to be the subject of research. Even more so than doctors, nurses are focused on patient care. In addition to the literature described here, nursing journals contain many articles relevant to research in information behavior. Studies by Cogdill (2003), McKnight (2006, 2007), Stokes and Urquhart (2015), and Turner et al. (2008), among others, often emphasize that nurses consult primarily local sources of information in the context of caring for clients. These include patient records, laboratory results, and personal contacts with physicians, pharmacists, and other nurses. Stokes and Urquhart (2015) used the critical incident technique to elicit narratives, along with other interview questions. These were analyzed to model the interaction of learning styles and personality traits with information behaviors. A series of surveys by Stokes (Stokes et al., 2021; Stokes & Urquhart, 2011, 2015) sought to define similar profiles among student nurses.

Sundin (2002, 2003) and Sundin and Hedman (2005) conducted multiple interviews with Swedish nurses to explore the distinctions made between practical and theoretical knowledge and the relationship of that knowledge to the nurse's professional identity. Sundin argues persuasively for a sociocultural approach to studying information behavior as one aspect of professionalization. A related study (Johannisson & Sundin, 2007) analyzed the discourses of 56 nurses, finding a divide between science-oriented versus holistically oriented styles. Bonner and Lloyd (2011) interviewed six nurses in renal care units and explain how they couple knowledge gained from colleagues and bodily experience as well as documented sources, in support of caring for patients.

Other types of healthcare professionals studied include dentists (Landry, 2006), hospital social workers (Harrison et al., 2004), and midwives (Davies & McKenzie, 2004; McKenzie, 2004, 2009, 2010). Two other, more recent occupations sampled, are paramedics and psychiatrists. Sonnenwald et al. (2014) interviewed ambulance paramedics about collaborating with remote physicians via video. While the potential benefits are several, the barriers to success include lack of technology, delays in getting the attention of physicians, lack of understanding of paramedics' roles and constraints, as well as the lower status of paramedics in the medical hierarchy. López (2020) studied the information behavior of 92 psychiatrists, finding that they differed by institution, and highlighting the importance of communicating with colleagues to improve diagnosis and treatment.

Overall, investigations of physicians' information behavior have declined somewhat in recent years, although studies of nurses continue to appear frequently.

2.4.3 Studies of Business Owners and Managers

2.4.3.1 Farmers and Fishers

The information behavior of farmers was investigated rarely until 15 to 20 years ago, when a spate of studies in developing countries began to appear. Several investigations mention the increased importance of external (particularly business-related) information: Zhao et al.'s (2009) study of 167 dairy farmers in Inner Mongolia, and Elly and Silayo's (2013) simple survey of 120 Tanzanian farmers demonstrate that such external information is strategic, as it tells farmers what they should be doing (e.g., changing crops, rather than simply trying to increase yields of an existing crop) to meet market demands. Addressing the market, in turn, may increase profitability – although sometimes at an environmental or social cost.

Other investigations stress the importance of local and contextual information for farmers in developing countries (e.g., Ekoja, 2004; Meyer, 2003). Munyua and Stilwell (2013) show how farmers in Kenya blend local sources (e.g., their own experience and the advice of neighbors) with that of external sources to make decisions about their practices. They quote one farmer as saying, "External knowledge is more profitable but local knowledge is more sustainable and secure, hence the need to mix" (p. 329). In other cases, farmers directly took advice from external sources, e.g., changed to beekeeping or raising rabbits following training from extension agents. Given et al. (2017) used a mixed methods study design to examine the fit between a government horticulture website and the information needs of growers. Their findings point to the need for designers of web repositories to focus on accessibility, usefulness, and communication of available information to better align with growers' information experiences.

Starasts (2015) makes similar points about 16 farmers in Australia, noting that external information, however authoritative, must be personalized to be meaningful. Water availability and soil types, for example, may differ radically from place to place, making some practices harder to implement on a given farm, and rendering some external information inadequate. Growers often responded by seeking advice and "stories" from neighboring farmers, or from local associations of growers. Ultimately the farmer's own experience counted for a great deal. A more traditional study is that of Rui (2013), who describes the role of reading rooms and internet access for farmers outside Beijing. Rui concludes the government needs to take a more active role in addressing the information needs of farmers, not only improving and subsidizing electronic access but also encouraging the use of electronic sources and providing staff to facilitate that.

Two investigations focus on female farmers, in particular: Leckie (1996) and Inyang (2015). Leckie interviewed 32 female farmers from Canada about their experiences growing up on a farm and working in agriculture. She found the typical division of labor on farms tended to exclude women from learning important agricultural information. Inyang administered questionnaires to 193 female vegetable farmers in Nigeria, finding that consulting agricultural extension officers was more important for loan applications than for practical decisions about what to grow and how to grow it; the farmers tended to rely on other growers for the latter information. Inyang concludes the government should facilitate more entrepreneurial collaboration among vegetable farmers.

Ikoja-Odongo and Ocholla (2003, 2004) used the critical incident technique in two studies with people from varied occupations in Uganda. For the first study, they interviewed "artisan fisher folk," a group that includes a full range of different occupations involving the fishing industry: fish and equipment sales, processing, boat building, net making, fisheries research, government extension, and so forth. Ikoja-Odongo and Ocholla (2004) interviewed 602 entrepreneurs in various businesses in Uganda, including fishermen, metal fabricators, blacksmiths, quarry workers, brick makers, carpenters, builders, mechanics, craftsmen, and various others. Observations of the entrepreneurs' work environments and historical methods were also employed. Their results emphasize the importance of oral traditions and local knowledge in the trades they examined. Information behavior research, Ikoja-Odongo and Ocholla say, must be sensitive to the circumstances of poverty, illiteracy, and lack of infrastructure often found in developing areas, and in doing so could suggest ways of "repackaging" information for use by such entrepreneurs.

2.4.3.2 Managers

The heterogeneity of this group must be acknowledged right at the start: "managers" *could* be almost anybody from the person who directs the operations of a convenience store with four employees, to the chairperson of Toyota Motor Corporation. However, as studied in the information seeking literature, managers are typically higher-level employees of large organizations, often described as "executives" or "CEOs" and who are educated (having at least a bachelor's degree and perhaps a master's in business administration, or a comparable degree in another field). For our purposes, "managers" will be assumed to be individuals who have at least some university-level qualifications and who work in sizable organizations.

Reviews of managerial information seeking literature by Edwards et al. (2013) and de Alwis et al. (2006) are good places to start for this occupation. Edwards et al. (2013) examined the information seeking and use of healthcare managers in the United Kingdom; the results of this government study, including over 2,200 managers and librarians, are applicable to other contexts. Their results suggest that the pace and settings of managerial work often preclude thorough information gathering, due to overload and constraints on time and knowledge. Thus, managers tend to rely on interpersonal contacts and to make decisions collaboratively. In contrast, de Alwis, Majid, and Chaudhry (2006) present results of a more general survey focusing on source preferences. According to them, past studies have examined managerial responses to the accessibility, richness, and quality of information they encounter.

Choo and Auster (1993) focused on "environmental scanning" – a subset of the literature on managers' needs, uses, and seeking, primarily discussing information that is *external* to the organization (such as what competitors are doing), rather than internal. They highlight informal sources and ease of accessibility of information is of vital importance. To this they add that people and conversations are the primary ways that managers acquire information, and that a defining context of managerial work is the solving of immediate problems, meaning they rarely have the luxury of extended contemplation, and for that reason are much less likely to spend time reading.

Auster and Choo (1993) were interested in how managers acquire and use information about the external business environment finding, that CEOs see customers and technological trends as the most strategic portions of the environment to consider; however, those sectors are also the most uncertain for CEOs. Higher perceptions of uncertainty in the environment were associated with more scanning of the environment. To keep track of environmental change, CEOs relied on multiple sources, both internal and external, personal (e.g., company managers and staff), and impersonal (e.g., printed and broadcast media). A finding that contradicted some earlier studies was that the perceived quality of the source was a better predictor of use than either the accessibility of the source or even the perceived degree of uncertainty in the environment. The two sources that can most be relied upon are subordinate managers and company customers.

Auster and Choo suggest that an increasingly complex and fast-changing business environment prompts CEOs to stress the quality of information over ease of accessibility. Along with Auster and Choo, the studies by Culnan (1983) and Pinelli et al. (1991) argued that a more complex and turbulent environment places a premium on the reliability of information. In another environment, Babalhavaeji and Farhadpoor (2013) found that university library managers engage in a great deal of external seeking, due to the rapidly changing technological and fiscal environment of modern libraries. A thoughtful investigation by Steinarová (2019) of the goals and values of academic libraries argues that information behavior research could play a larger role in managing, promoting, and improving universities.

The related problem of information overload was addressed by Farhoom and Drury (2002). In their four-nation survey, 124 managers in companies and government were asked to define "information overload" and to identify its frequency, sources, effects, and the actions they take in response; over half experienced information overload frequently and typically responded by "filtering" information. Another study featuring government administrators is that of Saastamoinen and Kumpulainen (2014), who studied a small group of six administrators using pretask and posttask questionnaires. They found that the complexity of the 59 tasks examined, along with the type of information needed, tended to dictate which kinds of sources (e.g., internet versus human) were consulted. For example, the more complex the task, the more human sources were consulted; email, in contrast, tended to be used in simpler tasks.

Correia and Wilson (2001) interviewed 47 individuals in 19 Portuguese firms of differing sizes to discover factors that influence environmental scanning. Using a case-study approach, coupled with grounded theory, the factors revealed were partly individual: information consciousness (attitude towards information-related activities) and exposure to information (frequency of opportunities of contact with well-informed people and information-rich contexts); and partly organizational: information climate (conditions that determine access to and use of information in an organization) and "outwardness" (links to other organizations). They concluded that the more open the organization is to its environment, the more likely that individuals in the organization will be exposed to relevant information and to develop an information climate that supports the individual. In a related study, Maungwa and Fourie's (2018) interviews suggest that competitive intelligence is critical to organizations, and failures to develop and apply intelligence can be caused by many factors: relying too much on internal sources, lack of seeking skills, lack of verification and analysis of data, poor management, human error, and information overload.

Mackenzie (2003a) surveyed 50 business managers and 50 nonmanagers, finding significant differences between these two groups in terms of their information behavior and motivations. Managers tend to gather information they do not need to simplify their environment and to help make faster decisions, believing that gathering information gives them the reputation of being well connected and knowledgeable. In addition, Mackenzie's (2003b) interviews with 22 line managers reveal that in some cases they are drawn to a source that represents the best (e.g., most trusted or liked) relationship rather than the best information. Other studies by Mackenzie (2002, 2004, 2005) suggested that managers consciously cultivate other individuals as information sources.

In a study that encompasses both managers and engineers, Hirsh and Dinkelacker (2004) followed the information seeking of 180 researchers from Hewlett Packard Labs and Compaq Computers during the merger of those two companies. They found heavy use of internet sources, the corporate library, information from standards bodies, and from colleagues outside of the firm. Their results suggested that the factors most influencing selection of sources include timesavings, authoritativeness, and convenience, whereas currency, reliability, and familiarity were relatively less important. Another sample of both managers and engineers, this time in the oil and gas industry (Marcella et al., 2013) echoes the effect of time pressure on information seeking and discussed the validity of earlier models of seeking.

2.4.4 Studies of Workers in Creative Industries

2.4.4.1 Artists

The work of artists has drawn many commentaries in the professional literature (among whom Cowan, 2004; Layne, 1994; Stam, 1995, are very interesting pieces). Yet very few investigations have been published in scholarly journals, including Cobbledick (1996), Zach (2005), Hemmig (2009), Mason and Robinson (2011), and Gorichanaz (2017, 2019, 2020). Almost 30 years ago, Cobbledick (1996) made a startling point about how little artists' information needs and uses had been studied compared to other occupations, noting that in 1995, there were more artists in the United States than lawyers and social scientists, combined. Cobbledick argued this was partly because of a stereotype of artists as "self-contained individuals who create via inspiration" (p. 344), rather than needing information to fuel their work. Cobbledick (1996) conducted interviews with four artists working with different media and found artists have five types of information needs: inspiration (fulfilled in a variety of ways); "specific visual information" (visual elements which may come from printed pictures or their own experimental drawings); technical information ("The characteristics and properties of the various techniques and media used to create art" (p. 352), often found from other artists, or sometimes from books or experimentation); "current developments in the visual arts" (found mainly in fine arts journals but also popular magazines, art exhibits, and collages); and information about finding, exhibiting, and selling work (identified through art journals and personal contacts). Cobbledick discovered that the practices of these four artists were diverse yet included a common reliance on printed material and reading; the artists did not rely entirely on images to foster creativity, and some of the information they needed had nothing to do with "art" per se. Cobbledick also found that people, especially other artists, were very important sources in many contexts. She concludes the information needs of artists are as broad as human experience itself.

Hemmig's (2009) survey of 44 practicing artists built on some aspects of Cobbledick's work but employed a survey method focused on sources of information. The artists' top three sources of inspiration were forms occurring in nature, their own personal experience, and art works seen in person; art books and periodicals ranked fifth and sixth among 18 sources mentioned, and some of these apparently came from library usage. Sources of specific visual elements were widely varied and led by "qualities of the medium." Other types of sources examined concerned materials and techniques, and marketing. Hemmig concludes that artists' needs are idiosyncratic, that they like browsing, and that social contacts are important, especially for technical and marketing information. While most of the people in Hemmig's sample were over 40 years old, a larger survey (78 respondents) by Mason and Robinson (2011) concentrated on younger, "emerging" artists. Their responses show similarities to those of Hemmig and Cobbledick, except in a greater need for career advice.

More recently, Tim Gorichanaz (2017, 2019, 2020) has written several papers on the creative process of artists, including their information behaviors. In his 2020 paper, for example, he engaged with local artists using a phenomenology-of-practice study design. Artists documented their artistic practices through the creation of self-portraits, with semistructured interviews used to further interrogate their information experiences. This intersection of studying the creative process alongside people's engagement with information is gaining increasing interest among information behavior scholars. A special issue of *Library and Information Science Research* (Huvila et al., 2022), for example, presents current research studies that sit at this intersection. The issue crosses quite diverse contexts, ranging from people's experiences of tattooing (Campbell-Meyer & Krtalić, 2022), to the community-engagement process used to design a war memorial (Given & Kuys, 2022).

2.4.4.2 Journalists

In a very concrete way, journalism is *largely* information seeking, along with the prime job of sharing information with the public. Despite the large number of investigations of the audience for news (reader, viewer, or listener studies), until the late 1990s there were relatively few focused, empirical studies of what journalists do. One investigation stands out for its depth: Hannele Fabritius (1999) conducted a qualitative study of journalists using a variety of methods to document the work practices of reporters and their use of digital sources in that work. Fabritius observed and interviewed several journalists in a Finnish newspaper, including attending editorial meetings, collecting documents, employing talk-aloud protocols, in addition to observations and numerous other methods. Fabritius had 18 journalists complete "diary" forms after writing a news item, indicating the sources used and their importance; she coupled the resulting 250 diary entries to the actual published items in which they resulted, and in so doing linked process to outcome.

Fabritius' findings established the influence of the various "cultures" to which journalists belong. The concentric cultures of the profession, a particular medium (such as a newspaper), and the particular news beat within a medium (e.g., foreign news) are manifested in the values, norms, activities, and routines that make up work practice in that context. Together, these determine the criteria by which news is selected and produced, as well as the patterns of information seeking that accompany the processing of stories. Fabritius said that "continuous, proceeding stages" could be discerned in the production of news, "logical steps" that "do not follow each other in a strict chronological order" (p. 411). Searching for and evaluating information (facts and opinions) takes place in interaction with a wide variety of sources (e.g., people, documents, firsthand observation). Fabritius concluded that the way journalists learn to process news items, along with "situational factors such as lack of time," are the strongest constraints on the ways that information is sought in journalism (p. 411). Essays on journalistic work practice (e.g., Donsbach, 2004; Goren, 1989; Katz, 1989) support Fabritius' emphasis on the culture of journalism and the constraints of time and institutions; indeed, some of them (e.g., Stocking & Gross, 1989) see journalistic work as dominated strongly by predetermined frames of perception and labeling that tend to bias news.

There have been quite a few empirical studies that echo the findings of Fabritius. Attfield and Dowell (2003) and Attfield et al. (2003), for example, based their conclusions on interviews with reporters for the *London Times*. They examined the role of uncertainty in the work of newspaper reporters in Britain, looking at how they perceived newsworthiness, generated "angles" for stories, exercised creativity, and gathered information in the context of writing. The methods of Kuhlthau (see Kuhlthau & Tama, 2001) and Dervin (see Dervin & Nilan, 1986) figured prominently in this research. Bird-Meyer et al. (2019) interviewed 25 US newspaper journalists to explore the role of serendipity in developing story ideas, finding that journalists strive to put themselves in situations where potential stories are likely to appear.

Outside of Europe and North America, studies of journalist information behavior have been infrequent. However, they have been popular in the Indian subcontinent, where they reveal a digital divide separating developed from developing nations. Mahapatra and Panda (2001) found that lack of access to computers encouraged journalists in Orissa, India, to rely on libraries (particularly periodical and clippings files) as well as to use older means of communication like telephone, postal mail, and fax. While information technologies have become more available to journalists in recent years, even the 2013 study of Singh and Sharma in Delhi, India, found that "lack of modern communication gadgets [is] the major problem" (p. 234), inhibiting information seeking. Their results show that Indian journalists still rely on many print sources, such as biographical dictionaries, encyclopedias, book, clipping files, newspapers, and magazines. As usual, lack of time was also a major issue, as it was also among journalists in Bangladesh (Hossain & Islam, 2012), where the internet is now the major source of news and nearly half of those interviewed used library resources little or not at all. Two Pakistani studies, Anwar and Asghar (2009) and Ansari and Zuberi (2010), also focus on sources of information; however, the latter study contains some interesting comparisons of print with broadcast journalists. For example, according to Ansari and Zuberi, radio professionals do far less searching and reading than either newspaper or TV journalists; the latter group reported a great deal of usage of a broad variety of sources.

Many investigations in the more developed nations still tend to be source oriented but focused on how the internet has changed the practices of reporters. Nicholas and Williams (1999) and Nicholas et al. (2000), for example, raised the question of whether the internet was widely used as a source at that time. In a study of 150 journalists and news librarians in the United Kingdom, they concluded that fewer than 20% were making much use of the internet for finding information relevant to their reporting. Surprisingly, the heaviest users tended to be midcareer reporters rather than the very youngest (and supposedly most computer literate). Unsurprisingly, the most-used sites were those of online newspapers. Nicholas and Williams categorized the relationships that these news workers have with the internet as ranging from worship to complete disdain for it as an information source. Perhaps because of the earlier time frame, their study contrasts sharply with online surveys of journalists conducted in the United States (e.g., Dupagne & Garrison, 2006; Middleberg, 2001), which paint a much more enthusiastic picture of the use of online sources. While more focused on the convergence of print and electronic news gathering and reporting, Dupagne and Garrison (2006) considered the evolution of jobs and roles in the newsroom. The training of reporters and editors in online searching has resulted in less dependence on librarians and other news researchers.

In terms of methods, nearly all investigations of journalists are still relying on interviews and questionnaires; however, there are a few novel approaches among them. Chaudhry and Al-Sagheer (2011) say they are the first to use the critical incident technique to elicit examples of journalist information seeking. While this approach yields many interesting details it appears they asked only for a description of the most recent assignment, rather than a particularly revealing or challenging incident. Vergeer (2015), in an analysis of Twitter feeds from 2,152 journalists in the Netherlands, demonstrates how such flows result in multiple social networks, each with their own gatekeepers. Vergeer believes this can result in a homogenization of the news, as a group of tightly connected journalists all focus on the same news and frames of reference.

2.5 CONCLUSION

We began this chapter with a history of the information behavior genre, demonstrating the long evolution of such investigations. We discussed the initial focus of the literature through its key concepts of *needs* and *seeking*. We reviewed studies of occupations (e.g., academics, engineers, lawyers, managers, journalists) to show how these categories continue to persist and evolve in information behavior research, despite their lack of internal homogeneity. One example of change in these studies is an increased emphasis on social norms and networks, and hence, communication among colleagues.

We contend that the topics and themes of information behavior investigations have gradually moved beyond practical and professional considerations, into a broader range of topics and a more theoretical approach. Over time information behavior investigations have shifted away from an atomistic focus on sources, individuals, and occupations, and toward more holistic studies of roles, activities, and social contexts, as well as interdisciplinary concerns. Taken-for-granted concepts such as need, seeking, and use have been questioned, leading to recognition of additional distinctions and dimensions – such as other internal states of mind and body (believing, fearing, feeling, smelling) and additional ways of experiencing information (encountering, monitoring, deducing, creating). We continue our exploration of contemporary approaches to information behavior research in the following chapter.

2.6 OUR TOP 3 *MUST-READ* RECOMMENDATIONS

Case, D. O. (2014). Sixty years of measuring the use of information and its sources: From consultation to application. In *Proceedings of the Libraries in the Digital Age (LIDA) Conference*, Zadar, Croatia, June 16–20, 2014. http://ozk.unizd.hr/proceedings/index.php/lida/article/viewFile/174/220

This historical review characterizes the evolution of information behavior research as a gradual shift of samples and objectives.

Julien, H., & O'Brien, M. (2014). Information behavior research: Where have we been, where are we going? *Canadian Journal of Information and Library Science, 38*(4), 239–250.

A 30-year profile of the information behavior literature including research methods, types of groups studied, and uses of theory.

Kwon, N. (2017). How work positions affect the research activity and information behaviour of laboratory sciences in the research lifecycle: Applying activity theory. *Information Research, 22*(1). http://InformationR.net/ir/22-1/paper744.html

A thorough application of activity theory and sensemaking, showing how different kinds of evidence map onto theoretical concepts (e.g., norms, division of labor, research products) and resulting information behavior.

REFERENCES

Agarwal, N. K., Xu, Y., & Poo, D. (2011). A context-based investigation into source use by information seekers. *Journal of the American Society for Information Science and Technology, 62*(6), 1087–1104. https://doi.org/10.1002/asi.21513

Allard, S., Levine, K. J., & Tenopir, C. (2009). Design engineers and technical professionals at work: Observing information usage in the workplace. *Journal of the American Society for Information Science and Technology, 60*(3), 443–454. https://doi.org/10.1002/asi.21004

Allen, T. J. (1965). *Sources of ideas and their effectiveness in parallel R&D projects*. (Research Program on the Management of Science and Technology No. 130-65). Sloan School of Management, Massachusetts Institute of Technology.

Allen, T. J. (1969). Information needs and uses. In C. Cuadra (Ed.), *Annual review of information science and technology* (Vol. 4, pp. 3–29). Encyclopaedia Britannica.

Allen, B. L. (1996). *Information tasks: Toward a user-centered approach to information systems*. Academic Press.

Allen, T. J., & Gerstberger, P. G. (1967). *Criteria for selection of an information source*. Alfred P. Sloan School of Management, Massachusetts Institute of Technology. (Working Paper No. 284-67).

Allen, D. K., Wilson, T. D., Norman, A., & Knight, C. (2008). Information on the move: The use of mobile information systems by UK police forces. *Information Research, 13*(4). http://InformationR.net/ir/13-4/paper378.html

Ansari, M., & Zuberi, N. (2010). Information seeking behaviour of media professionals in Karachi. *Malaysian Journal of Library & Information Science, 15*(2), 71–84.

Anwar, M., & Asghar, M. (2009). Information seeking behavior of Pakistani newspaper journalists. *Pakistan Journal of Library and Information Science, 10*, 57–79.

Attfield, S., Blandford, A., & Dowell, J. (2003). Information seeking in the context of writing: A design psychology interpretation of the "problematic situation". *Journal of Documentation, 59*(4), 430–453. https://doi.org/10.1108/00220410310485712

Attfield, S., & Dowell, J. (2003). Information seeking and use by newspaper journalists. *Journal of Documentation, 59*(2), 187–204. https://doi.org/10.1108/00220410310463860

Auerbach. (1965). *DOD user needs study, Phase I*. Final technical report 1151-TR3. Auerbach Corporation.

Auster, E., & Choo, C. W. (1993). Environmental scanning by CEOs in two Canadian industries. *Journal of the American Society for Information Science*, *44*, 194–203. https://doi.org/10.1002/(SICI)1097-4571(199305)44:4%3C194::AID-ASI2%3E3.0.CO;2-1

Ayres, L. P., & McKinnie, A. (1916). *The public library and the public schools* (Vol. XXI). Survey Committee of the Cleveland Foundation.

Babalhavaeji, F., & Farhadpoor, M. (2013). Information source characteristics and environmental scanning by academic library managers. *Information Research*, *18*(1). http://informationr.net/ir/18-1/paper568.html

Baker, J. M. (2004). The information needs of female Police Officers involved in undercover prostitution work. *Information Research*, *10*(1). http://InformationR.net/ir/10-1/paper209.html

Baker, L. M., Case, P., & Policicchio, D. L. (2003). General health problems of inner-city sex workers: A pilot study. *Journal of the Medical Library Association*, *91*(1), 67–71.

Baldwin, N. S., & Rice, R. E. (1997). Information-seeking behavior of securities analysts: Individual and institutional influences, information sources and channels, and outcomes. *Journal of the American Society for Information Science*, *48*, 674–693.

Basha, I., Rani, P., Kannan, K., & Chinnasamy, K. (2013). Information seeking behaviour of engineering students in Tamil Nadu: A study. *International Journal of Library Science*, *7*(1). http://www.ceserpublications.com/index.php/IJLS/article/view/165

Beautyman, W., & Shenton, A. K. (2009). When does an academic information need stimulate a school-inspired information want? *Journal of Librarianship and Information Science*, *41*(2), 67–80. https://doi.org/10.1177/0961000609102821

Belkin, N. J. (2005). Anomalous state of knowledge. In K. E. Fisher, S. Erdelez, & E. F. McKechnie (Eds.), *Theories of information behavior* (pp. 44–48). Information Today, Inc.

Belkin, N. J., & Vickery, A. (1985). *Interaction in information systems: A review of research from document retrieval to knowledge-based systems*. British Library.

Bennett, N., Casebeer, L., Zheng, S., & Kristofco, R. (2006). Information-seeking behaviors and reflective practice. *Journal of Continuing Education in the Health Professions*, *26*(2), 120–127. https://doi.org/10.1002/chp.60

Berelson, B. (1949). *The library's public*. Columbia University Press.

Bird-Meyer, M., Erdelez, S., & Bossaller, J. (2019). The role of serendipity in the story ideation process of print media journalists. *Journal of Documentation*, *75*(5), 995–1012. https://doi.org/10.1108/JD-11-2018-0186

Bonner, A., & Lloyd, A. (2011). What information counts at the moment of practice? Information practices of renal nurses. *Journal of Advanced Nursing*, *67*(6). 1213–1221. https://doi.org/10.1111/j.1365-2648.2011.05613.x

Borg, M., Alégroth, E., & Runeson, P. (2017, May). Software engineers' information seeking behavior in change impact analysis-an interview study. In *2017 IEEE/ACM 25th International Conference on Program Comprehension (ICPC)* (pp. 12–22). IEEE.

Borgman, C. L., & Furner, J. (2002). Scholarly communication and bibliometrics. In B. Cronin (Ed.), *Annual review of information science and technology* (Vol. 36, pp. 3–72). Information Today, Inc. https://doi.org/10.1002/aris.1440360102

Borlund, P., & Pharo, N. (2019). A need for information on information needs. *Information Research*, 24(4). http://InformationR.net/ir/24-4/colis/colis1900.html

Bosman, J., & Renckstorf, K. (1996). Information needs: Problems, interests and consumption. In K. Renckstorf (Ed.), *Media use as social action* (pp. 43–52). John Libbey.

Bouazza, A. (1989). Information user studies. In *Encyclopedia of library and information science* (Vol. 44(Suppl. 9), pp. 144–164). M. Dekker.

Brine, A., & Feather, J. (2010). The information needs of UK historic houses: Mapping the ground. *Journal of Documentation*, *66*(1), 28–45. http://doi.org/10.1108/00220411011016353

Brittain, J. M. (1970). *Information and its users: A review with special reference to the social sciences*. Wiley-Interscience.

Bronstein, J. (2007). The role of the research phase in information seeking behaviour of Jewish studies scholars: A modification of Ellis's behavioural characteristics. *Information Research*, *12*(3). http://informationr.net/ir/12-3/paper318.html

Bronstein, J., & Solomon, Y. (2021). Exploring the information practices of lawyers. *Journal of Documentation*, *77*, 1003–1021. https://doi.org/10.1108/JD-10-2020-0165

Brown, C. D. (2001). The role of computer-mediated communication in the research process of music scholars: An exploratory investigation. *Information Research*, *6*(2). http://informationr.net/ir/6-2/paper99.html

Brown, C. D. (2002). Straddling the humanities and social sciences: The research process of music scholars. *Library & Information Science Research*, *24*(1), 73–94. https://doi.org/10.1016/S0740-8188(01)00105-0

Brown, C. M. (1999). Information seeking behavior of scientists in the electronic information age: Astronomers, chemists, mathematicians, and physicists. *Journal of the American Society for Information Science*, *50*, 929–943. https://doi.org/10.1002/(SICI)1097-4571(1999)50:10%3C929::AID-ASI8%3E3.0.CO;2-G

Buchanan, S. A., & Erdelez, S. (2019). Information encountering in the humanities: Embeddedness, temporality, and altruism. *Proceedings of the Association for Information Science and Technology*, *56*(1), 32–42. https://doi.org/https://doi.org/10.1002/pra2.58

Burns, R. W., Jr. (1978). Library use as a performance measure: Its background and rationale. *The Journal of Academic Librarianship*, *4*, 4–11.

Cacioppo, J. T., & Petty, R. E. (1982). The need for cognition. *Journal of Personality and Social Psychology*, *42*, 116–131.

Caidi, N. (2001). Interdisciplinarity: What is it and what are its implications for information seeking? *Humanities Collections*, *1*(4), 35–46. https://doi.org/10.1300/J139v01n04_04

Campbell-Meyer, J., & Krtalić, M. (2022). Tattoo information creation: Towards a holistic understanding of tattoo information experience. *Library & Information Science Research*, *44*(3). https://doi.org/10.1016/j.lisr.2022.101161

Case, D. O. (2006). Information behavior. In B. Cronin (Ed.), *Annual review of information science and technology* (Vol. 40, pp. 293–328). Information Today, Inc. https://doi.org/10.1002/aris.1440400114

Case, D. O. (2014). Sixty years of measuring the use of information and its sources: From consultation to application. Presented at the Libraries in the Digital Age (LIDA), Zadar, Croatia, June 16–20. https://slideplayer.com/slide/3956824/

Chang, S.-J. L. (2006). An investigation into information needs and information seeking behavior of elementary and middle school teachers teaching indigenous courses. *Journal of Library and Information Studies*, *4*(1/2), 49–76. https://www.oalib.com/paper/2817982

Chatman, E. A. (1990). Alienation theory: Application of a conceptual framework to a study of information among janitors. *RQ*, *29*, 355–368. https://www.jstor.org/stable/25828550

Chaudhry, A. S., & Al-Sagheer, L. (2011). Information behavior of journalists: Analysis of critical incidents of information finding and use. *The International Information & Library Review*, *43*(4), 178–184. https://doi.org/10.1016/j.iilr.2011.10.011

Choo, C. W. (2005). *The knowing organization: How organizations use information to construct meaning, create knowledge, and make decisions* (2nd ed.). Oxford University Press.

Choo, C. W., & Auster, E. (1993). Environmental scanning: Acquisition and use of information by managers. In M. Williams (Ed.), *Annual review of information science and technology* (Vol. 28, pp. 279–314). Learned Information.

Choo, C. W., Bergeron, P., Detlor, B., & Heaton, L. (2008). Information culture and information use: An exploratory study of three organizations. *Journal of the American Society for Information Science and Technology*, *59*(5), 792–804. https://doi.org/10.1002/asi.20797

Chu, C. M. (1999). Literary critics at work and their information needs: A research phases model. *Library & Information Science Research*, *21*(2), 247–273. https://doi.org/10.1016/S0740-8188(99)00002-X

Chung, E., Kwon, N., & Lee, J. (2016). Understanding scientific collaboration in the research life cycle: Bio-and nanoscientists' motivations, information-sharing and communication practices, and barriers to collaboration. *Journal of the Association for Information Science & Technology*, *67*(8), 1836–1848. https://doi.org/10.1002/asi.23520

Clarke, M. A., Belden, J. L., Koopman, R. J., Steege, L. M., Moore, J. L., Canfield, S. M., & Kim, M. S. (2013). Information needs and information-seeking behaviour analysis of primary care physicians and nurses: A literature review. *Health Information and Libraries Journal*, *30*(3), 178–190. https://doi.org/10.1111/hir.12036

Cobbledick, S. (1996). The information-seeking behavior of artists: Exploratory interviews. *The Library Quarterly*, *66*, 343–372. https://www.jstor.org/stable/4309154

Cogdill, K. W. (2003). Information needs and information seeking in primary care: A study of nurse practitioners. *Journal of the Medical Libraries Association*, *91*(2), 203–215.

Cohen, A. R., Stotland, E., & Wolfe, D. M. (1955). An experimental investigation of need for cognition. *Journal of Abnormal and Social Psychology*, *51*, 291–294.

Cole, C. (2012). *Information need: A theory connecting information search to knowledge formation*. Information Today Inc.

Cole, C., & Kuhlthau, C. C. (2000). Information and information seeking of novice versus expert lawyers: How experts add value. *New Review of Information Behaviour Research*, *1*, 103–116.

Correia, Z., & Wilson, T. D. (2001). Factors influencing environmental scanning in the organizational context. *Information Research*, *7*(1). http://informationr.net/ir/7-1/paper121.html

Cowan, S. (2004). Informing visual poetry: Information needs and sources of artists. *Art Documentation*, *23*(2), 14–20. https://www.jstor.org/stable/27949312

Crane, D. (1971). Information needs and uses. In C. A. Cuadra & A. W. Luke (Eds.), *Annual review of information science and technology* (Vol. 6, pp. 3–39). Encyclopaedia Britannica.

Crawford, S. (1978). Information needs and uses. In M. E. Williams (Ed.), *Annual review of information science and technology* (Vol. 13, pp. 61–81). Knowledge Industry.

Culnan, M. J. (1983). Environmental scanning: The effects of task complexity and sources accessibility on information gathering behavior. *Decision Sciences*, *14*(2), 194–206.

Daei, A., Soleymani, M., Ashrafi-rizi, H., Zargham-Boroujeni, A., & Kelishadi, R. (2020). Clinical information seeking behavior of physicians: A systematic review. *International Journal of Medical Informatics*, *139*. https://doi.org/10.1016/j.ijmedinf.2020.104144

Dalton, M. S., & Charnigo, L. (2004). Historians and their information sources. *College & Research Libraries*, *65*(5), 400–425. https://doi.org/10.5860/crl.65.5.400

Davies, K. (2007). The information-seeking behaviour of doctors: A review of the evidence. *Health Information and Libraries Journal*, *24*, 78–94. https://doi.org/10.1111/j.1471-1842.2007.00713.x

Davies, E., & McKenzie, P. J. (2004). Preparing for opening night: Temporal boundary objects in textually-mediated professional practice. *Information Research*, *10*(1). http://InformationR.net/ir/10-1/paper211.html

Davis, R., & Bailey, C. (1964). *Bibliography of use studies*. (No. Project No. 195) (p. 98). Drexel Institute of Technology.

de Alwis, G., Majid, S., & Chaudhry, A. S. (2006). Transformation in managers' information seeking behaviour: A review of the literature. *Journal of Information Science*, *32*(4), 362–377. http://doi.org/10.1177/0165551506065812

Derr, R. L. (1983). A conceptual analysis of information need. *Information Processing & Management*, *19*, 273–278.

Derr, R. L. (1985). The concept of information in ordinary discourse. *Information Processing & Management*, *21*(6), 489–499.

Dervin, B. (1976a). Strategies for dealing with human information needs: Information or communication? *Journal of Broadcasting*, *20*(3), 324–351. https://doi.org/10.1080/08838157609386402

Dervin, B. (1983). Information as a user construct: The relevance of perceived information needs to synthesis and interpretation. In S. A. Ward & L. J. Reed (Eds.), *Knowledge structure and use: Implications for synthesis and interpretation* (pp. 153–184). Temple University Press.

Dervin, B., & Nilan, M. (1986). Information needs and uses. In M. Williams (Ed.), *Annual review of information science and technology* (Vol. 21, pp. 1–25). Knowledge Industry.

DeWeese, L. (1967). *A bibliography of use studies: A supplement to Davis, R.A. and Bailey, C.A. "bibliography of use studies," Drexel Institute of technology, 1964*. Purdue University.

Dewey, J. (1933). *How we think*. D. C. Heath.

Donsbach, W. (2004). Psychology of news decisions: Factors behind journalists' professional behavior. *Journalism*, *5*(2), 131–157. https://doi.org/10.1177/146488490452002

Doyal, L., & Gough, I. (1984). A theory of human needs. *Critical Social Policy*, *11*, 147–150.

Duff, W. M., & Johnson, C. A. (2002). Accidently found on purpose: Information-seeking behavior of historians in archives. *The Library Quarterly*, *72*(4), 472–496. https://www.jstor.org/stable/40039793

Dupagne, M., & Garrison, B. (2006). The meaning and influence of convergence: A qualitative case study of newsroom work at the Tampa News center. *Journalism Studies*, *7*(2), 237–255. https://doi.org/10.1080/14616700500533569

Edwards, C., Fox, R., Gillard, S., Gourlay, S., Guven, P., Jackson, C., ... Drennan, V. (2013). *Explaining health managers' information seeking behaviour and use. Final report*. National Institute for Health Research, Service Delivery and Organisation programme.

Ekoja, I. I. (2004). Sensitising users for increased information use: The case of Nigerian farmers. *African Journal of Library, Archives and Information Science*, *14*(2), 193–204.

Ellis, D. (1989). A behavioural approach to information retrieval design. *Journal of Documentation*, *45*, 171–212. https://doi.org/10.1108/eb026843

Ellis, D., Cox, D., & Hall, K. (1993). A comparison of the information seeking patterns of researchers in the physical and social sciences. *Journal of Documentation*, *49*, 356–369. https://doi.org/10.1108/eb026919

Elly, T., & Silayo, E. (2013). Agricultural information needs and sources of the rural farmers in Tanzania: A case of Iringa rural district. *Library Review*, *62*(8/9), 547–566. https://doi.org/10.1108/LR-01-2013-0009

Engel, D., Robbins, S., & Kulp, C. (2011). The information-seeking habits of engineering faculty. *College & Research Libraries*, *72*(6), 548–567. https://doi.org/10.5860/crl-155

Erizkova, E. (2018). Gatekeeping. In *The international encyclopedia of strategic communication* (pp. 1–6). John Wiley & Sons. https://doi.org/10.1002/9781119010722.iesc0080

Evans, N., & Price, J. (2017). Managing information in law firms: Changes and challenges. *Information Research*, *22*(1). http://informationr.net/ir/22-1/paper736.html

Fabritius, H. (1999). Triangulation as a multi-perspective strategy in a qualitative study of information seeking behaviour of journalists. In T. D. Wilson & D. K. Allen (Eds.), *Information behaviour: Proceedings of the second international conference on research in information needs, seeking and use in different contexts*, 13/15 August 1998, Sheffield, UK (pp. 406–419). Taylor Graham.

Farhoom, A. F., & Drury, D. H. (2002). Managerial information overload. *Communications of the ACM*, *45*(10), 127–131. https://doi.org/10.1145/570907.570909

Fidel, R., & Green, M. (2004). The many faces of accessibility: Engineers' perception of information sources. *Information Processing & Management*, *40*(3), 563–581. https://doi.org/10.1016/S0306-4573(03)00003-7

Fisher, K. E., & Julien, H. (2009). Information behavior. In B. Cronin (Ed.), *Annual review of information science & technology* (Vol. 43). Information Today. https://doi.org/10.1002/aris.2009.1440430114

Flaxbart, D. (2001). Conversations with chemists: Information-seeking behavior of chemistry faculty in the electronic age. *Science & Technology Libraries*, *21*(3/4), 5–26. https://doi.org/10.1300/J122v21n03_02

Florio, E., & DeMartini, J. (1993). The use of information by policymakers at the local community level. *Knowledge: Creation, Diffusion, Utilization*, *15*(1), 106–123. https://doi.org/10.1177/107554709301500104

Ford, G. (1977). *User studies: An introductory guide and select bibliography*. (Occasional Paper No. 1). Centre for Research on User Studies, University of Sheffield.

Ford, N. (2015). *Introduction to information behaviour*. Facet. https://doi.org/10.29085/9781783301843

Forsythe, D., Buchanan, B., Osheroff, J., & Miller, R. (1992). Expanding the concept of medical information: An observational study of physicians' information needs. *Computers and Biomedical Research*, *25*, 181–200. https://doi.org/10.1016/0010-4809(92)90020-B

Fossum, M., Opsal, A., & Ehrenberg, A. (2022). Nurses' sources of information to inform clinical practice: An integrative review to guide evidence-based practice. *Worldviews on Evidence-Based Nursing*. https://doi.org/10.1111/wvn.12569

Foster, A. (2004). A nonlinear model of information-seeking behavior. *Journal of the American Society for Information Science and Technology*, *55*(3), 228–237. https://doi.org/10.1002/asi.10359

Freund, L. (2015). Contextualizing the information-seeking behavior of software engineers. *Journal of the Association for Information Science and Technology*, *66*(8), 1594–1605. https://doi.org/10.1002/asi.23278

Garner, W. R. (1962). *Uncertainty and structure as psychological concepts*. John Wiley.

Given, L. M., Hill, M., & Paschke, P. (2017). *Communicating online: An evaluation of the horticulture industry network website*. Swinburne University of Technology. http://apo.org.au/node/116971

Given, L. M., & Kuys, B. F. (2022). Memorial design as information creation: Honoring the past through co-production of an informing aesthetic. *Library & Information Science Research*, *44*. https://doi.org/10.1016/j.lisr.2022.101176

Given, L. M., & Willson, R. (2015). Collaborative information use with technology: A critical examination of humanities scholars' research activities. In *Collaborative information seeking best practices, new domains and new thoughts* (pp. 139–164). Springer-Verlag.

Given, L. M., & Willson, R. (2018). Information technology and the humanities scholar: Documenting digital research practices. *Journal of the Association for Information Science and Technology*, *69*(6), 807–819. https://doi.org/10.1002/asi.24008

Goldman, A. I. (1970). *A theory of human action*. Princeton University Press.

Gordon, I., Cameron, B., Chaves, D., & Hutchinson, R. (2020). Information seeking behaviors, attitudes, and choices of academic mathematicians. *Science & Technology Libraries*, *39*(3), 253–280. https://doi.org/10.1080/0194262X.2020.1758284

Goren, D. (1989). Journalists as scientists or prophets? Comments on Katz. *American Behavioral Scientist*, *33*, 251–254. https://doi.org/10.1177/0002764289033002024

Gorichanaz, T. (2017). Understanding art-making as documentation. *Art Documentation: Journal of the Art Libraries Society of North America*, *36*(2), 191–203. https://doi.org/10.1086/694239

Gorichanaz, T. (2019). Information creation and models of information behavior: Grounding synthesis and further research. *Journal of Librarianship and Information Science*, *51*(4), 998–1006. https://doi.org/10.1177/0961000618769968

Gorichanaz, T. (2020). Understanding and information in the work of visual artists. *Journal of the Association for Information Science and Technology*, *71*(6), 685–695. https://doi.org/10.1002/asi.24286

Gorman, P. (1995). Information needs of physicians. *Journal of the American Society for Information Science*, *46*, 729–736. https://doi.org/10.1002/(SICI)1097-4571(199512)46:10%3C729::AID-ASI3%3E3.0.CO;2-2

Gorman, P. (1999). Information seeking of primary care physicians: Conceptual models and empirical studies. In T. D. Wilson & D. K. Allen (Eds.), *Information behaviour: Proceedings of the second international conference on research in information needs, seeking and use in different contexts*, 13/15 August 1998, Sheffield, UK (pp. 226–240). Taylor Graham.

Gorman, P., Ash, J., Lavelle, M., Lyman, J., Delcambre, L., Maier, D., & Bowers, S. (2000). Bundles in the wild: Managing information to solve problems and maintain situation awareness. *Library Trends*, *49*(2), 266–289.

Gorman, P., & Helfand, M. (1995). Information seeking in primary care: How physicians choose which clinical questions to pursue and which to leave unanswered. *Medical Decision Making*, *15*, 113–119. https://doi.org/10.1177/0272989x9501500203

Gould, C. (1988). *Information needs in the humanities: An assessment*. Research Libraries Group.

Gould, C., & Handler, G. (1989). *Information needs in the social sciences: An assessment*. Research Libraries Group.

Gould, C., & Pearce, K. (1991). *Information needs in the sciences: An assessment*. Research Libraries Group.

Grad, R., Pluye, P., Granikov, V., Johnson-Lafleur, J., Shulha, M., Sridhar, S. B., ... Kloda, L. (2011/1999). Physicians' assessment of the value of clinical information: Operationalization of a theoretical model. *Journal of the American Society for Information Science and Technology*, *62*, 1884–1891. http://doi.org/10.1002/asi.21590

Green, A. (1990). What do we mean by user needs? *British Journal of Academic Librarianship*, *5*, 65–78.

Grunig, J. (1989). Publics, audience and market segments: Segmentation principles for campaigns. In C. Salmon (Ed.), *Information campaigns: Balancing social values and social change* (pp. 199–228). Sage.

Hampshire, S. (1982). *Thought and action*. University of Notre Dame Press.

Harrison, J., Hepworth, M., & De Chazal, P. (2004). NHS and social care interface: A study of social workers' library and information needs. *Journal of Librarianship and Information Science*, *36*(1), 27–35. https://doi.org/10.1177/0961000604042971

Harter, S. P. (1992). Psychological relevance and information science. *Journal of the American Society for Information Science, 43*, 602–615. https://doi.org/10.1002/(SICI)1097-4571(199210)43:9%3C602::AID-ASI3%3E3.0.CO;2-Q

Harviainen, J. T., Lehtonen, M. J., & Kock, S. (2022). Timeliness in information sharing within creative industries. Case: Finnish game design. *Journal of Documentation, 78*(1), 83–96. https://doi.org/10.1108/JD-12-2020-0207

Haug, J. D. (1997). Physicians' preferences for information sources: A meta analytic study. *Bulletin of the Medical Library Association, 85*(3), 223–232.

Hemmig, W. (2009). An empirical study of the information-seeking behavior of practicing visual artists. *Journal of Documentation, 65*(4), 682–703. http://doi.org/10.1108/00220410910970302

Hemminger, B. M., Lu, D., Vaughan, K. T. L., & Adams, S. J. (2007). Information seeking behavior of academic scientists. *Journal of the American Society for Information Science and Technology, 58*(14), 2205–2225. http://doi.org/10.1002/asi.20686

Henning, B., & Vorderer, P. (2001). Psychological escapism: Predicting the amount of television viewing by need for cognition. *Journal of Communication, 51*(1), 100–120. https://doi.org/10.1111/j.1460-2466.2001.tb02874.x

Herner, S., & Herner, M. (1967). Information needs and uses in science and technology. In C. A. Cuadra (Ed.), *Annual review of information science and technology* (Vol. 2, pp. 1–34). Encyclopaedia Britannica.

Hernon, P. (1984). Information needs and gathering patterns of academic social scientists, with special emphasis given to historians and their use of U.S. government publications. *Government Information Quarterly, 1*, 401–429. https://doi.org/10.1016/0740-624X(84)90005-4

Hertzum, M., & Pejtersen, A. M. (2000). The information-seeking practices of engineers: Searching for documents as well as people. *Information Processing & Management, 36*, 761–778. https://doi.org/10.1016/S0306-4573(00)00011-X

Hewins, E. T. (1990). Information need and use studies. In M. E. Williams (Ed.), *Annual review of information science and technology* (Vol. 25, pp. 145–172). Elsevier.

Hirschman, E. C., & Holbrook, M. B. (1986). Expanding the ontology and methdology of research on the consumption experience. In D. Brinberg & R. Lutz (Eds.), *Perspectives on methodology in consumer research* (pp. 213–252). Springer-Verlag.

Hirsh, S., & Dinkelacker, J. (2004). Seeking information in order to produce information: An empirical study at Hewlett Packard Labs. *Journal of the American Society for Information Science and Technology, 55*(9), 807–817. https://doi.org/10.1002/asi.20024

Hogeweg de Haart, H. P. (1981). *Characteristics of social science information*. Hungarian Academy of Sciences / International Federation for Documentation.

Holland, M. P., & Powell, C. K. (1995). A longitudinal survey of the information seeking and use habits of some engineers. *College & Research Libraries, 55*(1), 7–15. https://doi.org/10.5860/crl_56_01_7

Hossain, M. D., & Islam, M. S. (2012). Information-seeking by print media journalists in Rajshahi, Bangladesh. *IFLA Journal, 38*(4), 283–288. https://doi.org/10.1177/0340035212463137

Huvila, I. (2008a). Information work analysis: An approach to research on information interactions and information behaviour in context. *Information Research, 13*(3). http://InformationR.net/ir/13-3/paper349.html

Huvila, I. (2008b). The information condition: Information use by archaeologists in labour, work and action. *Information Research, 13*(4). http://informationr.net/ir/13-4/paper369.html

Huvila, I. (2009). Analytical information horizon maps. *Library & Information Science Research, 31*(1), 18–28. https://doi.org/10.1016/j.lisr.2008.06.005

Huvila, I. (2010). Information sources and perceived success in corporate finance. *Journal of the American Society for Information Science and Technology, 61*(11), 2219–2229. http://doi.org/10.1002/asi.21387

Huvila, I., Douglas, J., Gorichanaz, T., Koh, K., & Suorsa, A. (2022). Guest editorial: Advances in research on information creation. *Library & Information Science Research, 44*(3). https://doi.org/10.1016/j.lisr.2022.101178

Huvila, I., Sköld, O., & Börjesson, L. (2021). Documenting information making in archaeological field reports. *Journal of Documentation, 77*(5), 1107–1127. https://doi.org/10.1108/JD-11-2020-0188

Ignatieff, M. (1984). *The needs of strangers*. Chatto and Windus.

Ikoja-Odongo, R., & Mostert, J. (2006). Information seeking behaviour: A conceptual framework. *South African Journal of Library & Information Science*, *72*(3), 145–158.

Ikoja-Odongo, R., & Ocholla, D. N. (2003). Information needs and information-seeking behavior of artisan Fisher folk of Uganda. *Library & Information Science Research*, *25*, 89–105. https://doi.org/10.1016/S0740-8188(02)00167-6

Ikoja-Odongo, R., & Ocholla, D. N. (2004). Information seeking behaviour of the informal sector entrepreneurs: The Uganda experience. *Libri: International Journal of Libraries and Information Services*, *54*(1), 54–66. https://doi.org/10.1515/LIBR.2004.54

Inyang, O. G. (2015). The role of information and female vegetable farmers in Calabar municipal Council area, Nigeria. *Libri: International Journal of Libraries and Information Services*, *65*(2), 151–160. https://doi.org/10.1515/libri-2014-0036

Jamali, H. R., & Nicholas, D. (2010). Interdisciplinarity and the information-seeking behavior of scientists. *Information Processing & Management*, *46*(2), 233–243. http://doi.org/10.1016/j.ipm.2009.12.010

Johannisson, J., & Sundin, O. (2007). Putting discourse to work: Information practices and the professional project of nurses. *The Library Quarterly*, *77*(2), 199–218. https://doi.org/10.1086/517843

Johnson, J. D. (1997). *Cancer-related information seeking*. Hampton Press.

Julien, H., & Michels, D. (2004). Intra-individual information behaviour in daily life. *Information Processing & Management*, *40*(3), 547–562. https://doi.org/10.1016/S0306-4573(02)00093-6

Julien, H., & O'Brien, M. (2014). Information behavior research: Where have we been, where are we going? *Canadian Journal of Information and Library Science*, *38*(4), 239–250.

Julien, H., Pecoskie, J. L., & Reed, K. (2011). Trends in information behavior research, 1999–2008: A content analysis. *Library & Information Science Research*, *33*(1), 19–24. https://doi.org/10.1016/j.lisr.2010.07.014

Kari, J. (2010). Diversity in the conceptions of information use. *Proceedings of the Seventh International Conference on Conceptions of Library and Information Science— "Unity in Diversity"*, *15*(3). http://informationr.net/ir/15-3/colis7/colis709.html

Katz, E. (1989). Journalists as scientists: Notes towards an occupational classification. *American Behavioral Scientist*, *33*(2), 238–246. https://doi.org/10.1177/0002764289033002022

Kerins, G., Madden, R., & Fulton, C. (2004). Information seeking and students studying for professional careers: The cases of engineering and law students in Ireland. *Information Research*, *10*(1). http://InformationR.net/ir/10-1/paper208.html

Kostagiolas, P. A., Lavranos, C., Korfiatis, N., Papadatos, J., & Papavlasopoulos, S. (2015). Music, musicians and information seeking behaviour: A case study on a community concert band. *Journal of Documentation*, *71*(1), 3–24. https://doi.org/10.1108/JD-07-2013-0083

Kostagiolas, P., Lavranos, C., Martzoukou, K., & Papadatos, J. (2017). The role of personality in musicians' information seeking for creativity. *Information Research*, *22*(2). http://InformationR.net/ir/22-2/paper756.html

Krampen, G., Fell, C., & Schui, G. (2011). Psychologists' research activities and professional information-seeking behavior: Empirical analyses with reference to the theory of the intellectual and social organization of the sciences. *Journal of Information Science*, *37*(4), 439–450. https://doi.org/10.1177/0165551511412148

Krikelas, J. (1983). Information-seeking behavior: Patterns and concepts. *Drexel Library Quarterly*, *19*, 5–20.

Kuhlthau, C. C. (1993a). *Seeking meaning: A process approach to library and information services*. Ablex.

Kuhlthau, C. C. (1999). The role of experience in the information search process of an early career information worker: Perceptions of uncertainty, complexity, construction, and sources. *Journal of the American Society for Information Science*, *50*, 399–412. https://doi.org/10.1002/(SICI)1097-4571(1999)50:5%3C399::AID-ASI3%3E3.0.CO;2-L

Kuhlthau, C. C. (2005). Kuhlthau's information search process. In K. E. Fisher, S. Erdelez, & E. F. McKechnie (Eds.), *Theories of information behavior* (pp. 230–234). Information Today, Inc.

Kuhlthau, C. C., & Tama, S. L. (2001). Information search process of lawyers, a call for "just for me" information services. *Journal of Documentation*, *57*, 25–43. https://doi.org/10.1108/EUM0000000007076

Kuruppu, P. U., & Gruber, A. M. (2006). Understanding the information needs of academic scholars in agricultural and biological sciences. *The Journal of Academic Librarianship*, *32*(6), 609–623. https://doi.org/10.1016/j.acalib.2006.08.001

Kwasitsu, L. (2003). Information-seeking behavior of design, process, and manufacturing engineers. *Library & Information Science Research*, *25*(4), 459–476. https://doi.org/10.1016/S0740-8188(03)00054-9

Kwon, N. (2017). How work positions affect the research activity and information behaviour of laboratory scientists in the research lifecycle: Applying activity theory. *Information Research*, *22*(1). http://informationr.net/ir/22-1/paper744.html

Landry, C. F. (2006). Work roles, tasks, and the information behavior of dentists. *Journal of the American Society for Information Science and Technology*, *57*(14), 1896–1908. http://doi.org/10.1002/asi.20385

Larkin, C. (2010). Looking to the future while learning from the past: Information seeking in the visual arts. *Art Documentation*, *29*(1), 49–60. https://doi.org/10.1086/adx.29.1.27949539

Latour, B. (2004). *Politics of nature: How to bring the sciences into democracy*. Harvard University Press.

Lavranos, C., Kostagiolas, P., Korfiatis, N., & Papadatos, J. (2016). Information seeking for musical creativity: A systematic literature review. *Journal of the Association for Information Science and Technology*, *67*(9), 2105–2117. https://doi.org/10.1002/asi.23534

Layne, S. S. (1994). Artists, art historians, and visual art information. *The Reference Librarian*, *47*, 23–36. https://doi.org/10.1300/J120v22n47_03

Leckie, G. J. (1996). Female farmers and the social construction of access to agricultural information. *Library & Information Science Research*, *18*, 297–321. https://doi.org/10.1016/S0740-8188(96)90002-X

Leckie, G. J., Pettigrew, K. E., & Sylvain, C. (1996). Modeling the information seeking of professionals: A general model derived from research on engineers, health care professionals and lawyers. *The Library Quarterly*, *66*, 161–193. https://www.jstor.org/stable/4309109

Lederer, K., Galtung, J., & Antal, D. (Eds.), (1980). *Human needs, a contribution to the current debate*. Oelgeschlagen, Gunn & Hain.

Leydesdorff, L., & Milojevic, S. (2015). Scientometrics. In M. Lynch (Ed.), *International encyclopedia of social and behavioral sciences* (2nd ed., Vol. 21, pp. 322–327). Elsevier.

Liebnau, J., & Backhouse, J. (1990). *Understanding information*. Macmillan.

Liew, C. L., & Ng, S. N. (2006). Beyond the notes: A qualitative study of the information-seeking behavior of ethnomusicologists. *The Journal of Academic Librarianship*, *32*(1), 60–68. https://doi.org/10.1016/j.acalib.2005.10.003

Line, M. B. (1974). Draft definitions: Information and library needs, wants, demands and uses. *ASLIB Proceedings*, *27*(7), 87–97.

Lin, N., & Garvey, W. D. (1972). Information needs and uses. In C. Cuadra & A. W. Luke (Eds.). *Annual review of information science and technology* (Vol. 7, pp. 5–37). American Society for Information Science.

Lipetz, B.-A. (1970). Information needs and uses. In C. A. Cuadra & A. W. Luke (Eds.), *Annual review of information science and technology* (Vol. 5, pp. 3–32). Encyclopaedia Brittanica.

López, G. R. (2020). Information seeking patterns of psychiatrists during clinical practice. *Health Information and Libraries Journal*, *37*(1), 78–82. https://doi.org/10.1111/hir.12293

Lundh, A. (2010). Studying information needs as question-negotiations in an educational context: A methodological comment. *Information Research*, *15*(4). http://InformationR.net/ir/15-4/colis722.html

Lu, L., & Yuan, Y. (2011). Shall I Google it or ask the competent villain down the hall? The moderating role of information need in information source selection. *Journal of the American Society for Information Science and Technology*, *62*(1), 133–145. https://doi.org/10.1002/asi.21449

Mackenzie, M. L. (2002). Information gathering: The information behaviors of line-managers within a business environment. In *Proceedings of the 65th Annual Meeting of the American Society for Information Science and Technology*, Philadelphia, PA, November 18–21, 2002 (pp. 164–170).

Mackenzie, M. L. (2003a). An exploratory study investigating the information behaviour of line managers within a business environment. *New Review of Information Behaviour Research*, *4*(1), 63–78.

Mackenzie, M. L. (2003b). Information gathering: Revealed within the social network of line-managers. In R. Todd (Ed.), *Proceedings of the 66th Annual meeting of the American society for information science and technology*, long Beach, CA, October 19–22, 2003 (Vol. 40, pp. 85–94). Information Today.

Mackenzie, M. L. (2004). The cultural influences of information flow at work: Manager information behavior documented. In L. Schamber & C. Barry (Eds.), *Proceedings of the 67th Annual meeting of the American society for information science and technology*, providence, RI, November 12–17, 2004 (Vol. 41, pp. 184–190). Information Today.

Mackenzie, M. L. (2005). Managers look to the social network to seek information. *Information Research*, *10*(2). http://InformationR.net/ir/10-2/paper216.html

Mahapatra, R. K., & Panda, K. C. (2001). State of information seeking and searching behaviour of working journalists in Orissa: A study. *Annals of Library and Information Studies*, *48*(4), 133–138.

Makri, S., & Warwick, C. (2010). Information for inspiration: Understanding architects' information seeking and use behaviors to inform design. *Journal of the American Society for Information Science and Technology*, *61*(9), 1745–1770. http://doi.org/10.1002/asi.21338

Ma, T.-J., Lee, G.-G., Liu, J., Lan, R., & Weng, J.-H. (2022). Bibliographic coupling: A main path analysis from 1963 to 2020. *Information Research*, *27*(1). http://InformationR.net/ir/27-1/paper918.html

Marcella, R., Pirie, T., & Rowlands, H. (2013). The information seeking behaviour of oil and gas industry workers in the context of health, safety and emergency response: A discussion of the value of models of information behaviour. *Information Research*, *18*(3). http://informationr.net/ir/18-3/paper583.html

Marchionini, G. (1995). *Information seeking in electronic environments*. Cambridge University Press.

Martin, K., & Quan-Haase, A. (2017). "A process of controlled serendipity": An exploratory study of historians' and digital historians' experiences of serendipity in digital environments. *Proceedings of the Association for Information Science and Technology*, *54*(1), 289–297. https://doi.org/10.1002/pra2.2017.14505401032

Martyn, J. (1974). Information needs and uses. In M. Williams (Ed.), *Annual review of information science and technology* (Vol. 9, pp. 3–23). American Society for Information Science.

Maslow, A. H. (1963). The need to know and the fear of knowing. *The Journal of General Psychology*, *68*, 111–125.

Mason, H., & Robinson, L. (2011). The information-related behaviour of emerging artists and designers: Inspiration and guidance for new practitioners. *Journal of Documentation*, *67*(1), 159–180. http://doi.org/10.1108/00220411111105498

Maungwa, T., & Fourie, I. (2018). Exploring and understanding the causes of competitive intelligence failures: An information behaviour lens. *Information Research*, *23*(4). http://www.informationr.net/ir/23-4/isic2018/isic1813.html

Max-Neef, M. (1992). *From the outside looking in: Experiences in barefoot economics*. Dag Hammarskjöld Foundation.

McKenzie, P. J. (2004). Positioning theory and the negotiation of information needs in a clinical midwifery setting. *Journal of the American Society for Information Science and Technology*, *55*(8), 685–694. https://doi.org/10.1002/asi.20002

McKenzie, P. J. (2009). Informing choice: The organization of institutional interaction in clinical midwifery care. *Library & Information Science Research*, *31*(3), 163–173. https://doi.org/10.1016/j.lisr.2009.03.006

McKenzie, P. J. (2010). Informing relationships: Small talk, informing and relationship building in midwife-woman interaction. *Information Research*, *15*(1). http://InformationR.net/ir/15-1/paper423.html

McKnight, M. (2006). The information seeking of on-duty critical care nurses: Evidence from participant observation and in-context interviews RMP. *Journal of the Medical Library Association*, *94*(2), 145–151.

McKnight, M. (2007). A grounded theory model of on-duty critical care nurses' information behavior - the patient-chart cycle of informative interactions. *Journal of Documentation, 63*(1), 57–73. http://doi.org/10.1108/00220410710723885

Meho, L. I., & Tibbo, H. R. (2003). Modeling the information-seeking behavior of social scientists: Ellis's study revisited. *Journal of the American Society for Information Science and Technology, 54*(6), 570–587. https://doi.org/10.1002/asi.10244

Menzel, H. (1960). *Review of studies in the flow of information among scientists.* Columbia University Bureau of Applied Social Research.

Menzel, H. (1966a). Information needs and uses in science and technology. In C. A. Cuadra & A. W. Luke (Eds.), *Annual review of information science and technology* (Vol. 1, pp. 41–69). Encyclopaedia Britannica.

Menzel, H. (1966b). Can science information needs be ascertained empirically? In L. Thayer (Ed.), *Communications: Concepts and perspectives* (pp. 279–295). Spartan Books.

Meyer, H. W. J. (2003). Information use in rural development. *New Review of Information Behaviour Research, 4*(1), 109–125.

Middleberg, D. (2001). The seventh annual Middleberg/Ross survey of media in the wired world. www.writenews.com/2001/041301_journalists_internet.htm

Miller, G. A. (1983). Informavores. In F. Machlup & U. Mansfield (Eds.), *The study of information: Interdisciplinary messages* (pp. 111–113). John Wiley.

Miranda, S. V., & Tarapanoff, K. (2008). Information needs and information competencies: A case study of the off-site supervision of financial institutions in Brazil. *Information Research: An International Electronic Journal, 13*(2). http://InformationR.net/ir/13-2/paper344.html

Munyua, H. M., & Stilwell, C. (2013). Three ways of knowing: Agricultural knowledge systems of small-scale farmers in Africa with reference to Kenya. *Library & Information Science Research, 35*(4), 326–337. http://doi.org/10.1016/j.lisr.2013.04.005

Murphy, J. (2003). Information-seeking habits of environmental scientists: A study of interdisciplinary scientists at the environmental protection agency in research Triangle Park, North Carolina. *Issues in Science and Technology Librarianship.* http://www.istl.org/03-summer/refereed.html

Murray, H. A. (1938). *Explorations in personality.* Oxford University Press.

Nicholas, D., & Williams, P. (1999). The changing information environment: The impact of the Internet on information seeking behavior in the media. In T. D. Wilson & D. K. Allen (Eds.), *Information behaviour: Proceedings of the second international conference on research in information needs, seeking and use in different contexts*, 13/15 August 1998, Sheffield, UK (pp. 451–462). Taylor Graham.

Nicholas, D., Williams, P., Cole, P., & Martin, H. (2000). The impact of the internet on information seeking in the Medial. *ASLIB Proceedings, 52*(3), 98–114. https://doi.org/10.1108/EUM0000000007004

Niu, X., & Hemminger, B. M. (2012). A study of factors that affect the information-seeking behavior of academic scientists. *Journal of the American Society for Information Science and Technology, 63*(2), 336–353. http://doi.org/10.1002/asi.21669

Niu, X., Hemminger, B. M., Lown, C., Adams, S., Brown, C., Level, A., McLure, M., Powers, A., Tennant, M., & Cataldo, T. (2010). National study of information seeking behavior of academic researchers in the United States. *Journal of the American Society for Information Science and Technology, 61*(5), 869–890. https://doi.org/10.1002/asi.21307

North American Aviation. (1966). *Final report DOD user-needs study, Phase II; Flow of scientific and technical information within the defense industry. Volumes I-III.* North American Aviation, Autonetics Division.

O'Connor, J. (1968). Some questions concerning "information need". *American Documentation, 19*(2), 200–203.

Paisley, W. J. (1965). *The flow of (behavioral) science information: A review of the research literature.* Institute for Communication Research, Stanford University.

Paisley, W. J. (1968). Information needs and uses. In C. Cuadra (Ed.), *Annual review of information science and technology* (Vol. 3, pp. 1–30). Encyclopaedia Britannica.

Paisley, W. J. (1986). The convergence of communication and information science. In H. Edelman (Ed.), *Libraries and information science in the electronic age* (pp. 122–153). ISI Press.

Paisley, W. J. (1990). Information science as a multidiscipline. In J. Pemberton & A. Prentice (Eds.), *Information science: The interdisciplinary context* (pp. 3–24). Neal-Schuman Publishers.

Palmer, C. L., & Neumann, L. J. (2002). The information work of interdisciplinary humanities scholars: Exploration and translation. *The Library Quarterly*, *72*(1), 85–117. https://www.jstor.org/stable/4309582

Pilerot, O. (2013). A practice theoretical exploration of information sharing and trust in a dispersed community of design scholars. *Information Research*, *18*(4). http://informationr.net/ir/18-4/paper595.html

Pilerot, O. (2014). Making design researchers' information sharing visible through material objects. *Journal of the American Society for Information Science and Technology*, *65*(10), 2006–2016. http://doi.org/10.1002/asi.23108

Pilerot, O., & Limberg, L. (2011). Information sharing as a means to reach collective understanding: A study of design scholars' information practices. *Journal of Documentation*, *67*(2), 312–333. https://doi.org/10.1108/00220411111109494

Pinelli, T. E. (1991). The information-seeking habits and practices of engineers. *Science & Technology Libraries*, *11*(3), 5–25. https://doi.org/10.1300/J122v11n03_02

Pinelli, T. E., Barclay, R., Glassman, N., Kennedy, J., & Demerath, L. (1991). The relationship between seven variables and the use of U.S. government technical reports by U.S. aerospace engineers and scientists. In J. Griffiths (Ed.), *ASIS '91: Proceedings of the 54th ASIS Annual meeting*, Washington, DC, October 27–31, 1991 (Vol. 28, pp. 313–321). Learned Information.

Pluye, P., Grad, R., Repchinsky, C., Jovaisas, B., Johnson-Lafleur, J., Carrier, M.-E., … Légaré, F. (2013). Four levels of outcomes of information-seeking: A mixed methods study in primary health care. *Journal of the American Society for Information Science and Technology*, *64*(1), 108–125. http://doi.org/10.1002/asi.22793

Poole, H. (1985). *Theories of the middle range*. Ablex.

Potnis, D., & Tahamtan, I. (2021). Hashtags for gatekeeping of information on social media. *Journal of the Association for Information Science & Technology*, *72*(10), 1234–1246. https://doi.org/10.1002/asi.24467

du Preez, M., & Fourie, I. (2009). The information behaviour of consulting engineers in South Africa. *Mousaion*, *27*(1), 137–158.

Price, D. (1963). *Little science, big science*. Columbia University Press.

Pyszczynski, T., Greenberg, J., & Solomon, S. (1999). A dual-process model of defense against conscious and unconscious death-related thoughts: An extension of terror management theory. *Psychological Review*, *106*, 835–845. https://doi.org/10.1037/0033-295x.106.4.835

Qin, H., Wang, H., & Johnson, A. (2020). Understanding the information needs and information-seeking behaviours of new-generation engineering designers for effective knowledge management. *Aslib Journal of Information Management*, *72*(6), 853–868. https://doi.org/10.1108/AJIM-04-2020-0097

Roberts, N. (1975). Draft definitions: Information and library needs, wants, demands and uses: A comment. *ASLIB Proceedings*, *27*(7), 308–313.

Robinson, M. A. (2010). An empirical analysis of engineers' information behaviors. *Journal of the American Society for Information Science and Technology*, *61*(4), 640–658. http://doi.org/10.1002/asi.21290

Rogers, E. M. (2003). *Diffusion of innovations* (5th ed.). Free Press.

Rohde, N. F. (1986). Information needs. *Advances in Librarianship*, *14*, 49–73.

Rokeach, M. (1960). *The open and closed mind*. Basic Books.

Roos, A. (2012). Activity theory as a theoretical framework in the study of information practices in molecular medicine. *Information Research*, *17*(3). http://informationr.net/ir/17-3/paper526.html

Rose, T. (2003). Technology's impact on the information-seeking behavior of art historians. *Art Documentation*, *21*(2), 35–42. https://www.jstor.org/stable/27949206

Ross, C., Terras, M., Warwick, C., & Welsh, A. (2011). Enabled backchannel: Conference Twitter use by digital humanists. *Journal of Documentation*, *67*(2), 214–237. http://doi.org/10.1108/00220411111109449

Rui, T. (2013). Farmers' reading rooms and information and communications technology in rural areas of Beijing. *Library Trends*, *62*(1), 95–104. https://doi.org/10.1353/lib.2013.0030

Russell-Rose, T., Chamberlain, J., & Azzopardi, L. (2018). Information retrieval in the workplace: A comparison of professional search practices. *Information Processing & Management*, *54*(6), 1042–1057. https://doi.org/10.1016/j.ipm.2018.07.003

Ruvane, M. B. (2005). Annotation as process: A vital information seeking activity in historical geographic research. In A. Grove (Ed.), *ASIS&T '05: Proceedings of the Annual meeting of the American society for information science and technology* (Vol. 42, pp. 506–522). American Society for Information Science and Technology.

Saastamoinen, M., & Kumpulainen, S. (2014). Expected and materialised information source use by municipal officials: Intertwining with task complexity. *Information Research*, *19*(4). http://InformationR.net/ir/19-4/paper646.html

Sahu, H. K., & Singh, S. N. (2013). Information seeking behaviour of astronomy/astrophysics scientists. *ASLIB Proceedings*, *65*(2), 109–142. https://doi.org/10.1108/00012531311313961

Sakai, S., Awamura, N., & Ikeya, N. (2012). The practical management of information in a task management meeting: Taking "practice" seriously. *Information Research*, *17*(4). http://informationr.net/ir/17-4/paper537.html

Sapa, R., Krakowska, M., & Janiak, M. (2014). Information seeking behaviour of mathematicians: Scientists and students. *Information Research*, *19*(4). http://www.informationr.net/ir/19-4/paper644.html

Savolainen, R. (2009a). Information use and information processing: Comparison of conceptualizations. *Journal of Documentation*, *65*(2), 187–207. http://doi.org/10.1108/00220410910937570

Savolainen, R. (2012a). Conceptualizing information need in context. *Information Research*, *17*(4). http://InformationR.net/ir/17-4/paper534.html

Savolainen, R. (2012b). Elaborating the motivational attributes of information need and uncertainty. *Information Research*, *17*(2). http://InformationR.net/ir/17-2/paper516.html

Savolainen, R. (2017). Contributions to conceptual growth: The elaboration of Ellis's model for information-seeking behavior. *Journal of the Association for Information Science and Technology*, *68*(3), 594–608. https://doi.org/10.1002/asi.23680

Searle, J. (1983). *Intentionality. Essays in the philosophy of mind*. Cambridge University Press.

Sievert, D., & Sievert, M. (1989). Philosophical research: Report from the field. In *Humanists at work: Disciplinary perspectives and personal reflections* (pp. 95–99). University of Illinois at Chicago, Institute for the Humanities and the University Library.

Singh, G., & Sharma, M. (2013). Information seeking behavior of newspaper journalists. *International Journal of Library and Information Science*, *5*(7), 225–234.

Slater, M. (1988). Social scientists' information needs in the 1980's. *Journal of Documentation*, *44*, 226–237. https://doi.org/10.1108/eb026827

Solomon, Y., & Bronstein, J. (2015). Serendipity in legal information seeking behavior: Chance encounters of family-law advocates with court rulings. *Aslib Journal of Information Management*, *68*, 112–134. https://doi.org/10.1108/AJIM-04-2015-0056

Solomon, Y., & Bronstein, J. (2022). The information-gathering practice of liberal professionals in a workplace setting: More than just seeking information. *Journal of Librarianship and Information Science*, *54*(1), 54–68. https://doi.org/10.1177/0961000621992810

Sonnenwald, D. H. (2006). Challenges in sharing information effectively: Examples from command and control. *Information Research*, *11*(3). http://InformationR.net/ir/11-4/paper270.html

Sonnenwald, D. H., Söderholm, H. M., Welch, G. F., Cairns, B. A., Manning, J. E., & Fuchs, H. (2014). Illuminating collaboration in emergency healthcare situations: Paramedic-physician collaboration and 3D telepresence technology. *Information Research*, *19*(2). http://www.informationr.net/ir/19-2/paper618.html

Stam, D. C. (1995). Artists and art libraries. *Art Libraries Journal*, *20*(2), 21–24. https://doi.org/10.1017/S0307472200009329

Starasts, A. (2015). Unearthing farmers' information seeking contexts and challenges in digital, local and industry environments. *Library & Information Science Research*, *37*(2), 156–163. https://doi.org/10.1016/j.lisr.2015.02.004

Stefl-Mabry, J. (2005). The reality of media preferences: Do professional groups vary in awareness? *Journal of the American Society for Information Science and Technology*, *56*(13), 1419–1426. https://doi.org/10.1002/asi.20235

Steinerová, J. (2019). The societal impact of information behaviour research on developing models of academic information ecologies. In *Proceedings of CoLIS, the Tenth International Conference on Conceptions of Library and Information Science*, Ljubljana, Slovenia, June 16–19, 2019. Information Research, 24(4). http://InformationR.net/ir/24-4/colis/colis1905.html

Stieg, M. F. (1981). The information needs of historians. *College & Research Libraries*, *42*, 549–560.

Stilwell, C. (2002). The case for informationally based social inclusion for sex workers: A South African exploratory study. *Libri: International Journal of Libraries and Information Services*, *52*(2), 67–77. https://doi.org/10.1515/LIBR.2002.67

Stocking, S. H., & Gross, P. H. (1989). *How do journalists think? A proposal for the study of cognitive bias in newsmaking*. ERIC Clearinghouse on Reading and Communication Skills.

Stokes, P., Priharjo, R., & Urquhart, C. (2021). Validation of information-seeking behaviour of nursing students confirms most profiles but also indicates desirable changes for information literacy support. *Journal of Documentation*, *77*(3), 680–702. https://doi.org/10.1108/JD-09-2020-0158

Stokes, P., & Urquhart, C. (2011). Profiling information behaviour of nursing students: Part 1: Quantitative findings. *Journal of Documentation*, *67*(6), 908–932. https://doi.org/10.1108/00220411111183528

Stokes, P., & Urquhart, C. (2015). Profiling information behaviour of nursing students: Part 2: Derivation of profiles. *Journal of Documentation*, *71*(1), 52–79. https://doi.org/10.1108/JD-07-2013-0091

Stone, S. (1982). Humanities scholars: Information needs and uses. *Journal of Documentation*, *38*(4), 292–313. https://doi.org/10.1108/eb026734

Storer, T. (2017). Bridging the chasm: A survey of software engineering practice in scientific programming. *ACM Computing Surveys*, *50*(4), 47. https://doi.org/10.1145/3084225

Sundin, O. (2002). Nurses' information seeking and use as participation in occupational communities. *New Review of Information Behaviour Research*, *3*, 187–202.

Sundin, O. (2003). Towards an understanding of symbolic aspects of professional information: An analysis of the nursing knowledge domain. *Knowledge Organization*, *30*, 170–181.

Sundin, O., & Hedman, J. (2005). Professions and occupational identities. In K. E. Fisher, S. Erdelez, & E. F. McKechnie (Eds.), *Theories of information behavior* (pp. 293–297). Information Today, Inc.

Sutton, S. (1994). The role of attorney mental models of law in case relevance determinations: An exploratory analysis. *Journal of the American Society for Information Science*, *45*(3), 186–200. https://doi.org/10.1002/(SICI)1097-4571(199404)45:3%3C186::AID-ASI8%3E3.0.CO;2-F

Tabak, E. (2014). Jumping between context and users: A difficulty in tracing information practices. *Journal of the American Society for Information Science and Technology*, *65*(11), 2223–2232. https://doi.org/10.1002/asi.23116

Tabak, E., & Willson, M. (2012). A non-linear model of information sharing practices in academic communities. *Library & Information Science Research*, *34*(2), 110–116. http://doi.org/10.1016/j.lisr.2011.11.002

Taylor, R. S. (1962). The process of asking questions. *American Documentation*, *13*(4), 391–396.

Taylor, R. S. (1968). Question-negotiation and information seeking in libraries. *College & Research Libraries*, *29*, 178–194.

Tenopir, C., & King, D. W. (2004). *Communication patterns of engineers*. Wiley-Interscience.

Thivant, E. (2005). Information seeking and use behaviour of economists and business analysts. *Information Research*, *10*(4). http://informationr.net/ir/10-4/paper234.html

Timpka, T., & Arborlelius, E. (1990). The GP's dilemmas: A study of knowledge need and use during health care consultations. *Methods of Information in Medicine*, *29*, 23–29.

Törnudd, E. (1959). Study on the use of scientific literature and references services by scandinavian scientists and engineers engaged in research and development. In *Presented at the international conference on scientific information* (Vol. I). National Academy of Sciences - National Research Council.

Tuominen, K., Talja, S., & Savolainen, R. (2005). The social constructionist viewpoint on information practices. In K. E. Fisher, S. Erdelez, & E. F. McKechnie (Eds.), *Theories of information behavior* (pp. 328–333). Information Today, Inc.

Turner, A. M., Stavri, Z., Revere, D., & Altamore, R. (2008). From the ground up: Information needs of nurses in a rural public health department in Oregon. *Journal of the Medical Library Association*, *96*(4), 335–342. https://doi.org/10.3163/1536-5050.96.4.008

Urquhart, C. (1999). Using vignettes to diagnose information seeking strategies: Opportunities and possible problems for information use studies of health professionals. In T. D. Wilson & D. K. Allen (Eds.), *Information behaviour: Proceedings of the second international conference on research in information needs, seeking and use in different contexts*, 13/15 August 1998, Sheffield, UK (pp. 277–289). Taylor Graham.

Vergeer, M. (2015). Peers and sources as social capital in the production of news: Online social networks as communities of journalists. *Social Science Computer Review*, *33*(3), 277–297. https://doi.org/10.1177/0894439314539128

von Thaden, T. L. (2008). Distributed information behavior: A study of dynamic practice in a safety critical environment. *Journal of the American Society for Information Science and Technology*, *59*(10), 1555–1569. http://doi.org/10.1002/asi.20842

Waldhart, T. J., & Waldhart, E. S. (1975). *Communication research in library and information science: A bibliography on communication in the sciences, social sciences, and technology*. Libraries Unlimited, Inc.

Ward, W. S., & Given, L. M. (2019). Assessing intercultural communication: Testing technology tools for information sharing in multinational research teams. *Journal of the Association for Information Science and Technology*, *70*(4), 338–350. https://doi.org/10.1002/asi.24159

Watson-Boone, R. (1994). The information needs and habits of humanities scholars. *RQ*, *34*, 203–216. https://www.jstor.org/stable/20862645

Wellard, J. H. (1935). State of reading among the working classes of England during the first half of the nineteenth century. *The Library Quarterly*, *5*(1), 87–100.

Wellings, S., & Casselden, B. (2019). An exploration into the information-seeking behaviours of engineers and scientists. *Journal of Librarianship and Information Science*, *51*(3), 789–800. https://doi.org/10.1177/0961000617742466

Westbrook, L. (2003). Information needs and experiences of scholars in women's studies: Problems and solutions. *College & Research Libraries*, *64*(3), 192–209.

Westbrook, L. (2008). E-government support for people in crisis: An evaluation of police department website support for domestic violence survivors using "person-in-situation" information needs analysis. *Library & Information Science Research*, *30*(1), 22–38. https://doi.org/10.1016/j.lisr.2007.07.004

Westbrook, L. (2009). Crisis information concerns: Information needs of domestic violence survivors. *Information Processing & Management*, *45*(1), 98–114. http://doi.org/10.1016/j.ipm.2008.05.005

Westley, B. H., & Barrow, L. C. (1959). An investigation of news-seeking behavior. *Journalism Quarterly*, *36*, 431–438.

White, H. (1980). Library effectiveness—The elusive target. *American Libraries*, *11*(December), 682–683.

White, M. D., Matteson, M., & Abels, E. G. (2008). Beyond dictionaries - Understanding information behavior of professional translators. *Journal of Documentation*, *64*(4), 576–601. http://doi.org/10.1108/00220410810884084

Wiberley, S. E., & Jones, W. G. (1989). Patterns of information seeking in the humanities. *College & Research Libraries*, *50*, 638–645.

Wiberley, S. E., & Jones, W. G. (1994). Humanists revisited: A longitudinal look at the adoption of information technology. *College & Research Libraries*, *55*, 499–509.

Wiberley, S. E., & Jones, W. G. (2000). Time and technology: A decade-long look at humanists' use of electronic information technology. *College & Research Libraries*, *61*, 421–431.

Wilkinson, M. A. (2001). Information sources used by lawyers in problem solving: An empirical exploration. *Library & Information Science Research*, *23*(3), 257–276. https://doi.org/10.1016/S0740-8188(01)00082-2

Wilson, T. D. (1981). On user studies and information needs. *Journal of Documentation*, *37*, 3–15. https://doi.org/10.1108/eb026702

Wilson, T. D. (1984). The cognitive approach to information seeking behavior and information use. *Social Science Information Studies*, *4*, 197–204. https://doi.org/10.1016/0143-6236(84)90076-0

Wilson, T. D. (1994). Information needs and uses: Fifty years of progress? In B. Vickery (Ed.), *Fifty years of progress: A Journal of documentation review* (pp. 15–52). Aslib.

Wilson, T. D. (1997). Information behaviour: An interdisciplinary perspective. In P. Vakkari, R. Savolainen, & B. Dervin (Eds.), *Information seeking in context: Proceedings of a meeting in Finland 14–16 August 1996* (pp. 39–49). Taylor Graham.

Wilson, T. D. (2022). *Exploring information behaviour: An introduction*. T.D. Wilson. http://informationr.net/ir/Exploring%20information%20behaviour.pdf

Wood, D. N. (1971). User studies: A review of the literature from 1966–1970. *ASLIB Proceedings*, *23*(1), 11–23. https://doi.org/10.1108/eb050272

Woudstra, L., & van den Hooff, B. (2008). Inside the source selection process: Selection criteria for human information sources. *Information Processing & Management*, *44*(3), 1267–1278. https://doi.org/10.1016/j.ipm.2007.07.004

Yakel, E. (2005). Archival intelligence. In K. E. Fisher, S. Erdelez, & E. F. McKechnie (Eds.), *Theories of information behavior* (pp. 49–53). Information Today, Inc.

Younger, P. (2010). Internet-based information-seeking behaviour amongst doctors and nurses: A short review of the literature. *Health Information and Libraries Journal*, *27*(1), 2–10. https://doi.org/10.1111/j.1471-1842.2010.00883.x

Zach, L. (2005). When is "enough" enough? Modeling the information-seeking and stopping behavior of senior arts administrators. *Journal of the American Society for Information Science and Technology*, *56*(1), 23–35. https://doi.org/10.1002/asi.20092

Zerbinos, E. (1990). Information seeking and information processing: Newspapers versus videotext. *Journalism Quarterly*, *67*, 920–929. https://doi.org/10.1177/107769909006700446

Zhao, Y., Zhang, R., & Klein, K. K. (2009). Perceived information needs and availability: Results of a survey of small dairy farmers in Inner Mongolia. *Information Research*, *14*(3). http://InformationR.net/ir/14-3/paper411.html

Zubek, J. (Ed.). (1969). *Sensory deprivation: Fifteen years of research*. Appleton-Century-Crofts.

Chapter 3

THE COMPLEX NATURE OF INFORMATION BEHAVIOR

> We use the term complexity to refer to the inherently high level of organization among the constituent parts of information-related phenomena, including information systems, social information behavior, and individual information experiences. (Sarah Polkinghorne & Lisa M. Given, 2021, p. 1262)

Chapter Outline

3.1 MOVING TOWARD COMPLEXITY: EMBEDDING CONTEXT IN INFORMATION BEHAVIOR STUDIES

As information behavior studies have shifted towards understanding the complexity of people's lives, exploring the contexts that surround and shape people's experiences

Looking for Information
Examining Research on How People Engage with Information, 71–119

ISSN: 2055-5377/doi:10.1108/S2055-53772023003

is integral to that research. Where earlier studies typically adopted atomistic approaches, by examining specific resources used or reasons for using information, most contemporary studies embrace the whole person, including situational, affective, and other influences on their information-related experiences. This shift echoes Choo's (2005) distinction between studies that are investigating information channels (e.g., journals) or systems (e.g., libraries), compared to those that are studying *people*. Review authors have used varying terminology to reflect the latter type of investigations. For Choo and Auster (1993) they are studies of "work, organizational, and social settings of the users. . .users' membership in professional or social groups, their demographic backgrounds" (p. 284). Talja et al. (1999) speak of "socioeconomic conditions, work roles, tasks, problem situations, communities and organizations" (p. 752) as variables typically examined. Taylor (1991) talks about *information use environments* as consisting of four types: professions, entrepreneurs (including managers), special interest groups, and socioeconomic groups. Julien et al. (2011) refer to studies that are "broadly concerned with analysis of people's information seeking, both active and passive, and their information use" (p. 19). Olsson and Lloyd (2017, para 5) highlight the importance of understanding "dynamic, embodied and corporeal sense making processes [as critical for] understanding the relationship between people and information." Yet, many rhetorical claims of holistic approaches are not always evident in study designs. As Polkinghorne and Given (2021) note, studies designed to capture complexity must examine "the constituent parts of information-related phenomena, including information systems, social information behavior, and individual information experiences" (p. 1262).

3.1.1 From Resources to Roles

Given that the origins of information behavior research are found in nineteenth-century studies of library users, and studies only gradually expanded their horizons to include nonprint sources of information, it is not surprising that the use of books in libraries tended to be a common focus of the earliest research. From the 1940s onwards (as discussed in Chapter 2), attention shifted to the investigation of various occupational groups, especially scientists, engineers, and managers. This emphasis on work roles continued for several decades and gradually expanded to cover a wide variety of job roles. These studies tended toward the system-oriented and person-oriented atomistic approaches outlined in Chapter 1 (see Table 1.2).

Perhaps the only *nonwork* role to be widely studied in these early decades was that of *student*, of which there continue to be a great many investigations. Yet even student life has some resemblance to paid work; a significant development in the 1970s was the emergence of research questions concerning everyday life information needs (e.g., solving practical problems concerning food or shelter, or the pursuit of hobbies and political activities). Even so, *work-related*, and *nonwork-related* activities tended to be treated separately by investigators, as if activities outside the job did not matter. The subtle distinction between these categories corresponds to the notion of the "way of life as 'order of things'," as articulated by Reijo Savolainen (1995):

> … "things" stand for various activities taking place in the daily life world, including not only job but also necessary reproductive tasks such as household care and voluntary activities (hobbies) … in most cases order of things is a relatively well-established constellation of work and nonwork activities …. (pp. 262–263)

Beyond the categories of citizen, immigrant, consumer, hobbyist, patient, and student, other studies of roles tend to be based on narrowly defined groups. These other roles in the information behavior literature include newcomers (e.g., Lingel, 2015; Moring, 2017; Salzano et al., 2020), parent or mother (e.g., Barriage, 2015; Chávez & Sabelli, 2020; Loudon et al., 2016; Martinović & Stričević, 2016; Schlebbe, 2020), and victims of accidents, crime, discrimination, or violence (e.g., Burnett & Burnett, 2019; Fourie, 2020; Harr et al., 2016; Hong et al., 2018; Lee, 2018), as well as the ubiquitous *user*, the abstract object of thousands of studies (Julien et al., 2018).

Contemporary information behavior research has taken a more holistic approach, considering a wide range of overlapping interests, both paid and unpaid. Looking at information behavior more holistically, in terms of life projects and roles, represents a shift toward the perspective of the *person* (what was called during the 1970s and 1980s, *the user*), and away from the views of the system (e.g., use of the media, use of library materials, or use of the internet). Thus, the shifting *roles* one takes on – e.g., nurse (a paid occupation because of intentional preparation) or patient (unpaid, nonoccupational, and typically not the result of deliberate choice) – become overarching frameworks for studying all the sources one might encounter or consult, their effects, and how they are used.

There has also been a tendency in the literature to sample populations based on their demographics, such as age, gender, race, ethnicity, income, or education (which are among 10 examples of "demography" supplied by Dervin, 1989). Sometimes demographic-based research designs are dictated by administrative needs or social concerns, e.g., the well-being of the elderly, or the disadvantages affecting marginalized populations. At other times it is driven by a general lack of information about the information behavior of a particular population (e.g., gay men). Despite obvious limitations to such study designs – it is rare, for example, that any population is homogenous in its habits and attitudes – investigations of demographic groups continue to be conducted. Many studies still attempt to generalize about sources, groups of people, and the differences among them, despite long-standing skepticism that such generalization is possible. More than 25 years ago, for example, Talja (1997) noted

> … generalizations about differences between individuals or groups are often problematic. Firstly, the diversity of the individual's social roles, tasks and identities is not taken into account … Secondly, it is impossible to get unmediated knowledge about a person's cognitive skills or even information seeking behavior, because the ways in which they are accounted for are always mediated by culturally constructed interpretive repertoires. The explanations should not be taken as facts about the permanent attitudes or actual behavioural patterns of individuals or groups. (p. 74)

Talja and Hartel (2007), Tabak (2014) and Hartel (2019) have since revisited these and other disadvantages of focusing on individuals. Despite their reasonable concerns, there is some value in striving for well-evidenced quantitative generalizations or qualitative transferability of findings about individuals or groups; otherwise, there would be little point in ever investigating information practices. Such concerns also serve to emphasize the importance of attending to elements of *context*, particularly those social roles, tasks, and identities Talja (1997) mentioned, as a reminder about the dangers of making sweeping claims regarding large, diverse populations. This is particularly important when practitioners implement changes (e.g., new systems designs, changes in reference services) based on study results. Martzoukou (2005) and Saastamoinen and Järvelin (2018) make similar points in a critique of studies of online information seeking.

3.1.2 Contexts, Situations, and Emplacement

So, what constitutes a "context"? Brenda Dervin (1997) says that there "is no term more often used, less often defined, and when defined, defined so variously as context" (p. 14). She goes on to complain that "virtually every possible attribute of a person, culture, situation, behavior, organization, or structure has been defined as context." Dervin provides a few examples that help to narrow the definition. She quotes John Dewey (1960) as saying that "context is . . . a selective interest or bias which conditions the subject matter of thinking" (p. 90). To Gregory Bateson (1978) context is "the pattern that connects [as] without context there is no meaning" (p. 13). Tabak (2014) identifies context with the social and the collective, as contrasted with a focus on the cognitive and the individual. Talja et al. (1999), in an article devoted to how information behavior researchers have dealt with the study of context, characterize context as "a background for something the researcher wishes to understand and explain" (p. 752). They go on to describe context as

> . . . the site where a phenomenon is constituted as an object to us . . . any factors or variables that are seen to affect individuals' information-seeking behavior: socioeconomic conditions, work roles, tasks, problem situations, communities and organizations with their structures and cultures, etc. (p. 754)

A term related to context is *situation*. Talja and Nyce (2015) explain that while some view situation as synonymous with context, others view it as a smaller unit; that "within a context, a specific activity setting, or domain, various kinds of situations emerge, and different domains typically entail different kinds of typical situations" (p. 62). Investigators in the disciplines of both information science and communication have had much to say about the importance and influence of *situation* in relation to people's information behaviors. Dervin (1997) says when research is "focused on relationships between people, then factors describing the situation can become context" (p. 14). Savolainen (1993) holds that "the term situation refers to the time-space context in which sense is constructed" (p. 17). Vakkari (1997), in calling for closer attention to be paid to the influences of groups and society, notes that information seeking is "seen as embedded in the actions, tasks and situations they are supporting" (p. 457). Savolainen (2012a) identifies three major contexts affecting the formation and satisfaction of individuals' information needs: situation of action, task performance, and dialogue.

Cool (2001), Johnson (2003), Tabak (2014), and Huvila (2019) have described how context and situation have been defined. Johnson (2003) says context is commonly used in three, progressively complex, senses: as equivalent to the situation in which a process is immersed (a *positivist* orientation, specifying factors that moderate relationships); as contingency aspects of situations that have specific effects (a *postpositivist* view that emphasizes the prediction of outcomes); and as frameworks of meaning (a *postmodern* sense in which the individual is inseparable from the context). In contrast, Huvila (2019) discusses set theory, actor–network theory and agential realism as productive approaches to identifying context. Tabak (2014) also endorses actor–network theory as a means of clarifying foreground and background.

Another important aspect is related to the relationship between the mind, the body, and the situations people encounter, as they are embedded – or emplaced – within the context they experience. Since at least the color perception studies of the 1970s (see Rosch & Lloyd, 1978), it has been conjectured that bodily sensations greatly influence our thoughts, feelings, and decisions. It is no surprise that embodiment should come under scrutiny in the context of information behavior. Bonner and Lloyd (2011), for example, document how the sense of smell is used by renal care nurses in their work. Other studies that consider embodiment include Cox et al. (2017), Guzik (2018), Lloyd (2014, 2010), Lueg (2015), Olsson (2016), Olsson and Lloyd (2017), Polkinghorne (2021), and Veinot and Pierce (2019).

Context and situation are important concepts for information behavior research, even if they are ill defined. Information needs do not arise in a vacuum, but owe their existence to some history, purpose, and influence. The seeker – whether actively looking for information or receiving information through serendipity – exists in an environment that partially determines, constrains, and supports the types of needs and inquiries that arise. Seekers also have their own memories, predispositions, and motivations – i.e., internal environments of influence. Similar examples are offered by scholars who make arguments for *holism* in information behavior studies (e.g., Hartel, 2019; Polkinghorne & Given, 2021).

Such is the importance of context that it has given rise to a long-running series of conferences, the Information Seeking in Context (ISIC) meetings, which have taken place in even-numbered years since 1996. Many of the works cited in this volume were presented at that conference, with selected proceeding papers published in *Information Research*.

3.1.3 Information Sharing and Collaboration

Much of the early information behavior research adopted an individual perspective. Finding information, making sense of it, and applying it was typically examined as the work of one person at a time, while accounting rather weakly for the social world that the person inhabited. However, we know that people often

> ### *Misinformation vs. Disinformation – What's the Difference?*
>
> As sharing information online has increased exponentially, misinformation and disinformation have become increasingly important topics to consider. Søe (2018) distinguishes these concepts by intention: disinformation (e.g., a lie; a propaganda video) *intends to deceive*, while misinformation (i.e., inaccuracies – or *honest mistakes*) are *unintended*, arising from ignorance or bias. Most disinformation definitions exclude satires and parodies, as their intent is to entertain or spark critical thinking, presuming the audience knows the truth is being altered for effect, and not to deceive. While misinformation and disinformation are not new (see Fox, 1983), these terms are often conflated. Journalists mix many types together, including propaganda, hoax, rumors, clickbait, misleading images, false contexts, and altered videos (Cooke, 2022; Zannettou, Sirivianos, Blackburn & Kourtellis, 2019). Yet, by putting disinformation in a separate category, philosophers (e.g., Fallis, 2015) can tease out useful nuances. For example, simple lies are intended to directly mislead the audience from a particular truth, while elaborate disinformation campaigns (e.g., conspiracy theories) are intended to benefit their creators in many ways, often over longer timeframes.

work in groups, and that they actively share information among themselves, even when not working towards a common goal. For this reason, an exclusive focus on individuals is often inadequate (Hartel, 2019; Talja & Nyce, 2015). Researchers have increasingly gravitated toward theories (e.g., Situated Learning, Communities of Practice, Activity Theory) that account for social groups or cultures, and to examine how communities develop norms and practices around information gathering and dissemination.

Sharing information may be considered the broadest category of interpersonal information behavior. Sharing most commonly takes place between two individuals, as in a conversation or an email exchange. Sometimes these exchanges are *situational*; at other times sharing occurs arround joint *tasks*. As Talja and Nyce (2015) point out, personal situations are "more ambiguous and less predictable" (p. 62) than that of individuals performing well-defined tasks. So, it is not surprising that the latter form a distinct subgroup (sometimes called *collaboration*), among studies of sharing information.

As a number of studies demonstrate, networks of individuals operating outside of work environments may exchange information frequently; these are present, for example, in the communities that form around health problems (e.g., Chen, 2015; Chuang & Yang, 2014; Costello, 2017; Rothschild & Aharony, 2016; Veinot, 2010) and leisure pursuits (e.g., Bronstein & Lidor, 2021; Cox et al., 2017; Hartel, 2014a; Joseph, 2016; Mansourian, 2021; Skov, 2013). New technologies have provided additional insights into the information sharing activities of scholars, as well. Ross et al. (2011), for example, used Twitter archives and questionnaires to examine communication among attendees at a digital humanities conference. They detail how tweets help attendees collaboratively create knowledge, document events, and feel connected to others. Given and Willson's (2015) study of humanities scholars' collaborative information seeking also provides insights into the use of online tools for information sharing and other collaborative activities. Wilson

(2010a) charts the rapid growth in publications about "sharing information" as it became a popular topic about the year 2000. It is now commonly studied, with findings quite unique to the situation under examination. Some recent studies of ad hoc (mostly online) groups sharing information include: Harlan et al. (2014), Lee and Kang (2018), Lindau et al. (2022), Osatuyi (2013), Ryan et al. (2016), Savolainen (2015a, 2019), Ye et al. (2021), and Zhu et al. (2019).

However, much of the research concerning sharing focuses on work environments, and features collaboration in the pursuit of some common task or project. Indeed, Fidel et al. (2004) point out that information seeking by multiple persons should only be labeled *collaborative* if the individuals involved *do* share a common goal, whether work-related or not. Given and Willson (2015) note that the concept of *collaboration* (and the information tasks individuals pursue in collaborative work) must be viewed as a spectrum of solo and group activities, rather than a term that denotes a singular, shared definition.

Misinformation and Disinformation: Examples of Information Behavior Studies

Information behavior scholars use various classifications for these concepts. Ruokolainen and Widén's (2020) constructionist view contrasts *perceived* versus *normative* misinformation; the former represents the receiver's point of view, in a particular context, while the latter represents truth judgments of larger sets of receivers, often in very different contexts. These perceptions of truth are particularly relevant to studies of information behavior of people in vulnerable situations. Asylum seekers, for example, arrive as outsiders to a culture; they face barriers and uncertainties, and develop their own networks, to share and interpret information within their communities and contexts. Karlova and Fisher (2013) also make the case for considering subjective aspects of misinformation, disinformation, and truth. Wall et al.'s (2017) study of Syrian refugees showed interviewees' lived experiences under authoritarianism, along with repeated experiences with misinformation on Facebook, led them to mistrust most information on social media; they typically phoned trusted people to validate suspicious information.

Healthcare settings provide an interesting context for studying information sharing, particularly among practitioners. Isah and Byström (2015, 2017, 2020) applied Activity Theory in observing a university hospital, demonstrating how collective knowledge is constructed through interactions among doctors, patients, and case records. An ethnographic study of an emergency department patient care team identified seven types of patient information needs. These mainly concerned medical information, information about the medical team, and information about the hospital (Reddy & Spence, 2008). Searches for information were triggered by lack of expertise, lack of immediately accessible information, or complex needs (Reddy & Jansen, 2008). Scott et al.'s (2017) study of information behaviors related to pediatric emergency care demonstrated the importance of accepted treatments for common conditions, clinical pathways and practice guidelines, and professional development for information sharing across diverse teams. Hertzum and Hansen (2019) examine methodological challenges in undertaking studies of collaboration, including in medical settings, while Granikov et al. (2022) offer a framework for collaborative scanning. Gallagher and Olsson (2019) examine physician transitions from training to practice, including the formation of professional identities in the context of societal obligations.

Talja and Nyce (2015) and Shah (2014) show that collaboration has been studied in many work contexts. Their reviews emphasize that collaboration involves people interacting with a task or situation, and that this takes place within a social context, such as an organization. Prime locations for collaborative information sharing occur in knowledge-intensive work, such as healthcare (e.g., Granikov et al., 2022; Hertzum & Reddy, 2015; Isah & Byström, 2015, 2017, 2020; Johnson, 2019; Sonnenwald et al., 2014), scientific or academic research (e.g., Chung et al., 2016; Given & Willson, 2015; Pilerot, 2013, 2014), education (Shah & Leeder, 2016), software design (e.g., Harviainen et al., 2022), marketing (Du, 2014), or policing (e.g., Abrahamson & Goodman-Delahunty, 2013; Tian et al., 2021).

Several other labels are relevant to this category of studies. *Computer-Supported Cooperative Work* is a characterization long used by those involved in the design of information systems. Yet, because sharing information does not depend on using computers, other characterizations of it have come into use among information behavior researchers, including *collaborative information seeking*, *distributed cognition*, and *knowledge management*. Among other recent publications that discuss collaborative information sharing are Alshahrani and Rasmussen Pennington (2020), Burgess et al. (2022), Koh (2013), O'Connor (2013), Savolainen (2015a), Shah (2014), Sin and Kim (2013), Tabak and Willson (2012) and Worrall and Oh (2013).

3.1.4 Information Use

We come, at last, to the *use* of the information found through seeking. One would think that, given the frequency with which the word "use" occurs in the information behavior literature, that much has been done to define and measure it – yet this is true only in a limited sense. Savolainen (2009a) notes "Information use is a generic concept that is frequently referred to but rarely explicated" (p. 187). Evidence supporting Savolainen's statement is found in studies by Järvelin and Vakkari (1993), Tuomaala et al. (2014), Mishra et al. (2015) and Case and O'Connor (2016). Due to the ambiguity of the word *use*, there has been some confusion about what is being included under this label. Most commonly, information use has been characterized as the consolidation of particular sources or channels of information, even though the more important aspect is the outcomes that use provokes – an effect on the person receiving the information.

Over the years, scholars have noted that many studies measure needs, demands, seeking and/or gathering of information, but relatively few examine how retrieved information is used – i.e., the effects (Taylor, 1986), consequences (Paisley, 1968), impacts (Rich, 1997) or outcomes (Kari, 2007) of information seeking. Part of the problem is due to the vagueness of the word "use." Relatively early in the history of information behavior research, Brittain (1970) noted "ambiguity resides in the term 'use' . . . most frequently . . . it refers to the study of the gathering stage of use rather than the use to which information is put" (p. 1). Echoing Brittain, Taylor (1986) notes that

> The concept of "use" of information is quite ambiguous. Depending on context, it may mean the act of choosing a reference to a document . . . [or] receiving an answer to a question . . . [or] insertion of a chunk of information into a report or the direct input to a decision. (pp. 10–11)

This ambiguity is highlighted in Kari's (2010) examination of the literature, which found seven different conceptualizations of information use: as information practice, as information search, as information processing, as knowledge construction, as information production, as applying information, and as effects of information.

Even if we exclude the information *gathering* stage and focus on later stage definitions of use, we then encounter additional considerations. For example, Rich (1975) distinguished between *conceptual* and *instrumental* use of information: the former changes the way users know and/or think, while the latter results in observable changes in behavior, such as actions, enacted decisions, or explanations. Similarly, Taylor (1986) categorizes the purposes for information into two types: *tangible* and *intangible* functions. Tangible functions include "direct triggers for action and responses to questions," while the intangible include "informing, instructing, clarifying, and socializing" (p. 184). These distinctions parallel Ruthven's (2021) *arousal* versus *action* distinction in awareness of resonating information.

So, exposure to information can result in at least two kinds of results: changes in the knowledge of the recipient (conceptual or intangible), and application of the information to some task or decision (instrumental or tangible). Vakkari (1997, 1999, 2008) has repeatedly called attention to the neglect of information use in information behavior research, most pointedly in a section of his 1997 paper titled "information use is a seldom studied area" (p. 460). In a later publication, Vakkari (1999) explains that actions we label use are typically mere *consultations* of one or more channels of information – e.g., browsing the library or searching a database. Such actions tell us nothing about the *effect* of finding information, either how it changes people's thinking or how people subsequently apply it in a task or decision. Other scholars, including Giannini (1998), Todd (1999), Kirk (2002), Kari (2007), Tenopir (2011), Pluye et al. (2013), Ruthven (2021) and Granikov et al. (2022), make similar observations of this gap in the literature. For these authors, information use is defined as including both what a person *does with* information (*active* use) and the *effect of* information on a person's experiences (*passive* use). Thus, *using* information does not simply mean to become aware of it, but also encompasses its effects on people's thinking, feelings, bodies, and actions.

Postmodern, theoretical approaches to holistic understandings of information *use* have also emerged in the last few decades (e.g., Given, 2002b, 2005; Lloyd, 2007a, 2007b, 2009, 2017, 2021; Lloyd & Hicks, 2021; Lloyd & Olsson, 2019; McKenzie, 2009, 2010; Olsson 2010a, 2010b; Polkinghorne & Given, 2021; Savolainen, 2013, 2014; Talja, 2002, 2010). As Julien et al. (2011) note, many of these are represented not by the terms *information seeking* or *information behavior*; rather "other labels for the same general topic area include information practices, which is becoming more fashionable, particularly among social constructionists" (p. 19).

3.1.5 Information Creation

While the focus of information behavior is often on information that already exists, an important information activity is the process of information creation. Information creation has become an area of increased interest and research, though it remains relatively understudied. However, Gorichanaz (2019) makes the case that previous information behavior research has addressed information creation, though not necessarily using this term. For example, when studying the information behavior of academics, researchers have discussed writing (e.g., Chu, 1999; Palmer & Neumann, 2002; Palmer et al., 2009) – a fundamental information creation activity but one that has received little attention as such. For example, Chu (1999) identified six stages in the literary critics' research process. Information creation takes place during two of the stages – elaboration (ideas are sketched out, an outline is produced, ideas are discussed) and analysis and writing (the work is drafted and revised, help is acquired, more information is sought).

Gorichanaz (2019), in addressing information creation directly, has defined it as "when a person applies some information to create new information" (p. 999). From this definition, it can be viewed as related to or a type of information use – applying acquired information to accomplish something. Information creation can include both mental creation (e.g., coming up with new ideas) and physical manifestation of creation (e.g., new social media content). Some researchers have begun to address information creation directly in their studies. For example, Willson (2022) describes how academics "bounce ideas" with one another as a way of working on and expanding an idea. Bouncing ideas is a complex information practice, a process that is "active, iterative, and generative, resulting in the creation of new information that is then subject to further work or implementation" (p. 811). Koh (2013) describes the "information-creating behavior" of adolescents when using digital media, including remixing (reusing information in creative ways to produce new information) and tinkering (information production through evolving an idea by iteratively making modifications, using trial and error, and experimenting). Harlan et al. (2012) examine the information practices of teen content creators when creating and sharing digital content on social media. The creating practices – described as an "act of using a variety of information, both practical information regarding tools and inspirational information that is the genesis for creating" (p. 582) – include copying, modeling, and composing content.

3.2 SITUATIONAL AND CONTEXTUAL APPROACHES TO STUDYING INFORMATION BEHAVIOR COMPLEXITY

One of the most common strategies for studying information behavior complexity is to identify specific situations and contexts that shape how people engage with information. For example, being newly diagnosed with cancer places a person in a situation where they lack relevant and new information; studies can explore the person's individual information and affective needs, the organizational structures and systems that provide that information (e.g., hospitals, health technologies), and the ways the diagnosed person integrates this new life circumstance into their information worlds. Previously, researchers often sought to *limit* complexity by focusing their investigations on, for example, the types of resources accessed by newly diagnosed cancer patients. Today, many researchers seek to *embrace* complexity; they may still examine resource types, but they also focus on patients' interpretations of those resources, on how such materials help (or hinder) patients' interactions with health professionals, on how they share (or choose not to share) information with friends or other diagnosed individuals, and how those resources are used over time. The patients' other life circumstances (e.g., employment; family supports) are also considered, as are health policy (e.g., health insurance costs) and practice (e.g., hospital staffing shortages) contexts.

Contextual approaches also intersect with situational domains. Such approaches position people's information behavior within a broader frame of reference, which cannot easily be separated from the situational aspects of a topic or from the person. For example, studying first-in-family experiences of undergraduate education or gendered experiences of health-related information needs and contexts provide additional layers of complexity that help researchers to better understand people's information behaviors.

The sections that follow present examples of studies related to some of the most prevalent situations influencing contemporary information behavior research. While these sections are not a definitive list, nor do they include all types of studies (or situations, or contexts) examined to date, they demonstrate the shift away from atomistic and transactional views of information behavior towards studies that aim to account for the whole person situated within their broader sociocultural environment.

3.2.1 Health and Well-Being

Three factors have contributed to continued growth in the seeking of medical information by healthcare consumers: an increased concern with health, in general, and with preventive medicine in particular; a growing number of self-help texts; and the proliferation of consumer health information sites and online provider portals. Health and well-being, including managing emergent situations, are among the most prevalent topics for studies of information behavior scholars. The COVID-19 pandemic demonstrates the complex nature of such topics as prevention, vaccination, diagnosis, prognosis, and treatments and how these define individuals, families, and healthcare practitioners' diverse approaches to

The COVID-19 Pandemic as Context for People's Information Experiences

Writing this book during a global pandemic has highlighted the importance of studying people's engagement with information. While the virus is officially called severe acute respiratory syndrome coronavirus 2 (SARS-CoV-2), most people call it COVID-19. The pandemic began in November 2019; by late October 2022, confirmed cases exceeded 629 million and the number of "excess deaths" (i.e., those occurring earlier than expected) totaling more than 6.56 million, worldwide (https://covid19.who.int/).

The first few years of COVID-19 changed our lives significantly, affecting where we went, how we made a living, how we shopped, how we spent our leisure time, how we felt, and how we planned. Rolling lockdowns and new variants of the disease created anxiety, uncertainty, isolation, and work loss (Griffiths et al., 2022). The scope and variety of information behavior-related research questions has been vast, including: What do people want to know about COVID-19 – its effects, symptoms, spread, and prevention of infection? Where do they look for information? Has information seeking about COVID-19 changed over time? How and why does virus misinformation spread? Does belief in the virus and its treatments vary across populations and locations? How has the pandemic changed our habits? How has it affected our mental health? How do people use information to cope and adapt during a pandemic?

information seeking and use (see the *Sidebars* in this section for details on how information behavior researchers are studying COVID-19).

The growth and easy accessibility of health websites continues to shape individuals' behaviors. For those with adequate access and health literacy, using the internet to look for medical information is common, and often the "first source of consumer health information" (Pluye et al., 2019, p. 643). A recent review of international studies (Jia et al., 2021) concludes that between 70% and 86% of internet users search for health information, with usage highest in Asia. According to a five-nation qualitative study (Diviani et al., 2019), the purposes and consequences for searches appear to be similar across countries, at least the developed ones that constituted that sample. Kim (2015) found demographic and health status differences between searchers of medical information and those who were more likely to search general information, such as news; medical information seekers were more likely to have health problems and to have lower incomes. Estimates of the quality of information on medical websites vary widely (Zhang et al., 2015), but quality appears to be improving as better assessment methods are developed and as consumers grow more sophisticated.

Given the importance and popularity of health-related topics, the relevant literature is enormous and spread across many disciplines, including information studies, medical informatics, communication, public health, nursing, and medicine. As Greyson and Johnson (2016) note, the literature of public health and communication is more focused on changing health behaviors than on simply being informed.

Here we focus on emerging trends in research of the last two decades. Three types of health information have received more attention recently: that shared via *social media* (e.g., Facebook, Quora, Reddit, Blurtit, and discussion forums for specific health conditions or issues); that found in *personal medical records*, such as health histories, case notes, laboratory results, treatments, inoculations, and insurance records; and the *outcome* of receiving and using health information. Each of these three topics is explored in turn. A fourth, emerging research focus, information (and misinformation) about COVID-19, is addressed in Sidebars in this section.

Misinformation and Disinformation: A Particular Problem in the Pandemic

Misinformation and disinformation – and their origins – have been a special focus of COVID-19 investigations. Xie, He et al. (2020) believe the pandemic constitutes "an information crisis" in which scholars of information behavior should address misinformation and health literacy. Naeem et al. (2020) illustrate the types and sources of COVID-19 misinformation among 1,225 social media examples, calling it an "infodemic." Savolainen (2021) examined a Reddit discussion group to see how users assessed the credibility of postings on vaccines. He found users were sensitive to authors' competency, credibility, honesty, and the plausibility of their arguments.

Within examinations of misinformation, scholars have considered how the pandemic has become politicized in some nations. Lachlan et al. (2021) considered whether the notion of "echo chambers" – habitual selection of only those sources that conform to one's existing beliefs – applied to risk perceptions about COVID-19. Based on surveys of 5,000 adults, they concluded that perceptions of risk varied by one's political preferences, but this did not itself cause echo chambers. Instead, their results suggest that those with low information seeking in general tend to be more influenced by politicized sources. Romer and Jamieson (2020) found that belief in three specific political conspiracy theories predicted whether people used face masks and/or got vaccinated. Masks are very effective at reducing the spread of viruses to others, and yet misunderstood and underutilized by the public, according to van der Westhuizen, Kotze et al. (2020). Masks also have various meanings and differing levels of acceptance across cultures. The authors support the distribution and publicizing of masks, highlighting a creative Czech campaign that encouraged their use.

Many health conditions have appeared on social media, including discussions of pregnancy, diabetes, obesity, HIV, attention-deficit disorder, multiple sclerosis, Parkinson's disease, heart disease, depression, and various types of cancer. Literature reviews by Laukka et al. (2019), and Zhao and Zhang (2017) emphasize empowerment, emotional support, and interpersonal communication as reasons that patients and their caregivers participate in online discussion forums, while Zhao and Zhang (2017) note that lack of quality and authority in postings can discourage use. Librarians and nurses tend to be critical of the quality of answers on such forums and question/answer sites, according to Oh and Worrall (2013) and Chu et al. (2018). Other research concludes that health advice on forums is mostly sound (e.g., Cole et al., 2015), although communicable diseases and vaccinations (especially for COVID-19) have been a more recent and notable exception to such a generalization (Rolls & Massey, 2021).

It is also true that users apply multiple criteria for selecting health information, beyond accessibility and quality (Zhang, 2014); for example, those with stigmatic conditions, such as mental illness, may find online discussions more comfortable (Naslund et al., 2016; Rasmussen Pennington et al., 2013). Many studies of social media (e.g., Chen, 2015; Chuang & Yang, 2014; Godbold, 2013; Hamm et al., 2013; Kim & Syn, 2016; Pálsdóttir, 2014; Worrall & Oh, 2013) suggest that social interaction encourages proactive behavior change, as well as helping participants to cope with challenges. Oh et al. (2016) demonstrate that posters of cancer-related questions on *Yahoo! Answers* also reveal demographic, situational, emotional, and social background that may be of use to health professionals and systems designers. Unfortunately, some major search engines have discontinued their Q&A functions (e.g., *Google Answers* in 2006, and *Yahoo! Answers* in 2021); however, many condition-specific discussion sites have arisen to replace them.

Local hospital and clinic (and in some countries, nation-wide) portals now allow patients to read the results of their tests, procedures, and provider visits. Huvila et al. (2016) review the advantages (such as patient empowerment and engagement) and potential drawbacks (e.g., lack of health literacy, security and legal issues, increased work, and cost) of providing printed records to patients, within the context of structuration theory. Gerard et al. (2017) found many positive benefits from patients who read their after-visit notes, including positive feelings, the ability to share with care partners, correct errors, communicate with health professionals, and as an aid to memory. Huvila et al. (2016), Huvila et al. (2018), and Huvila et al. (2019) examined differences in experience and age cohorts among patients who read their medical records. Among their findings: many users say they understand their records; many would like to see additional information (referral letters, medications, vaccinations, test results); older adults (ages 55–70) were more likely to use the telephone to clarify their understanding, younger patients more likely to use the internet for an answer, while other patients may wait until their next visit to ask questions, or do not follow up at all. Some differences in whether and how patients use e-health are related to their attitudes toward digital records and perceptions of their potential utility (Huvila et al., 2015). Taking a Personal Information Management approach, Kim et al. (2020) examine a large sample of university students to understand why some were less active in managing their own health records. The less active students (who tended to be male) were more likely to rely on parents to keep track of their records, and more likely to search mass media and the internet for health information than to consult professionals.

Although the dissemination of health advice to the general public has always been important, a critical question is "why don't people act on the information they have?" Making useful (and potentially life-saving) information available to patients is the easier part of the equation; getting them to apply it is much more difficult. Pálsdóttir's (2014) research found that passivity may decrease when health information is encountered through social media, a finding also suggested in other studies (e.g., Chuang & Yang, 2014; Kim & Syn, 2016; Oh et al., 2016). Huisman et al. (2020) reminds us that sharing through face-to-face interaction increases circulation and acceptance of medical information just as social media does.

Another area of novel research concerns the actual application or *use* of health information, and its consequences of *outcomes*. Zimmerman and Shaw (2020) include outcomes in analyzing the concept of health information seeking behavior, dividing them into cognitive, behavioral, and affective. They identified 41 studies that mentioned outcomes, including increased knowledge about diseases and medical procedures, making treatment decisions, increasing self-care or vaccination, lower anxiety, increased self-efficacy, more positive feelings about one's health, and adhering to treatment plans. Pluye et al. (2019) derive a more elaborate outcome framework from analysis of 65 studies, including both patients and general consumers of health information, and both positive and negative health-related outcomes. Their contingent, four-level progression includes, first, determination of situational relevance (reading or skipping a webpage), then cognitive impacts (e.g., learning something, or change in attitude), followed by use of information (for decision-making, discussion, or social support), and finally health outcomes (e.g., prevention behavior, or problem management). The types of outcomes are many, including not just the effects of having medical treatment but also outcomes on satisfaction or personal relationships, and impacts on health professionals and their organizations.

In a different vein, Brown and Veinot (2020) offer examples of how family members can use health information to control patients through tactics like questioning their behavior, repeating certain messages, raising concerns, or prompting feelings of guilt. Wolf and Veinot (2015) explore a related theme, the use of biomedical information by the chronically ill to maintain autonomy and identity in contested interactions with family and friends. Veinot et al. (2011) show how collaborative information seeking between chronic disease patients and their family can create tensions among them.

While this review has covered mainly emerging topics of the most recent decade or so, there is a host of additional information behavior literature on disease-specific studies, including a large corpus of findings about the COVID-19 pandemic of recent years.

3.2.2 Education and Learning

Another situation that is widely studied in the information behavior literature is that of education, including formal (from kindergarten to university) and informal learning activities. There is a large body of work on students' in-classroom, online, and assignment-related activities, across ages, topic areas, and countries. Gross (2001) and Gross and Saxton (2001), for example, present reports of two investigations of "imposed" information seeking – queries developed by one person (usually a teacher) and given to someone else to resolve – in public and school libraries. Gross' first study took place in three elementary school libraries and found that between 32 and 43% of all circulation transactions involved imposed queries. The second survey, undertaken in 13 public libraries among 1,107 older users, also indicates that instructors' assignments are still a major source of imposed queries, along with requests from spouses and children of library users. Additional studies by Gross (2004a, 2004b) also concern imposed queries and information seeking in schools. Beautyman and Shenton (2009) examined the way that elementary school assignments sometimes lead to stimulation of students' curiosity and information seeking – a topic explored with adolescents by Bowler (2010). A related review by Hultgren and Limberg (2003) of the learning and information behavior literature suggested a strong relationship between the nature of school assignments and the ways in which students seek and use information.

Looking at student papers, Cole et al. (2013) coded 16 middle school student proposals for evidence of implicit knowledge and correlated that analysis with the score given by the instructor. Their investigation employed Kuhlthau's (1991) Information Search Process (ISP) model to demonstrate how students construct knowledge in the course of carrying out a school assignment. Sormunen and Lehtiö (2011) and Sormunen et al. (2012) show how close analysis of secondary school student papers can link the student's writing to the sources used and assess the degree to which source material was simply copied-and-pasted rather than synthesized and restated in the student's own words. Using the method described in the latter investigation enables assessment of a variety of other measures, such as accuracy of citing, types of claims (facts versus interpretations), and credibility of arguments. Hirvonen and Palmgren-Neuvonen (2019) examined how group projects can help secondary students to recognize cognitive authority in health-related sources.

University students have frequently been sampled in information behavior investigations. Whitmire (2003) examined the information seeking of 20 senior undergraduates as they researched a major paper, basing her investigation on Kuhlthau's ISP model and four other research models from educational psychology. She found students' epistemological beliefs (e.g., that right and wrong answers exist for everything, versus the idea that all knowledge is contextual) affected their choice of topic, the ways they looked for information, how they evaluated it, and their ability to recognize cognitive authority. In a similar vein, Willson and Given (2014) examined the self-concept and self-efficacy of 38 university students in a search task, finding that this shaped their interactions with information. The Willson and Given (2014) investigation, and that of Karlsson et al. (2012), were used to establish typologies of information seeking styles for research tasks. Clark (2017) reviews studies of imposed queries on the performance and self-efficacy of university students.

Foster and Ford (2003) examined the role of serendipity in the information behavior of 45 university students and faculty, particularly how they accidentally or incidentally acquired information of interest to them. Foster (2004) identifies three "core processes" (p. 232) and three levels of interaction with the context of the information – likening chosen behaviors to selections from an artist's "palette" (p. 235).

Given (2002a, 2002b) used Savolainen's (1995) everyday life information seeking framework to interview 25 mature university undergraduates, exploring how the academic and nonacademic information needs of these students relate to one another, including the role of social and cultural capital. Interviews and observations by Jeong (2004) revealed gaps in the knowledge of Korean graduate students in the United States regarding American culture; he documented language and financial barriers that inhibited these students from learning more about their surroundings. Sin and Kim (2013) found 97% of their sample of international students made use of social networking sites to find information useful to their everyday lives, particularly regarding health, finance, and news from their native lands. Another study of everyday information seeking by university students (Williamson et al., 2012) found widespread use of print and online newspapers, as well as social media. Matusiak et al. (2019) explored the use of images in the academic work of undergraduate and graduate students. They conclude that students lack skills in finding and evaluating images and tend to use them mainly in presentations rather than in academic papers.

Heinström (2003) tested the personality attributes of 305 master's degree students in a variety of disciplines, finding that five personality dimensions – neuroticism, extraversion, openness to experience, competitiveness, and conscientiousness – interact with contextual factors to affect students' information behavior. Toms and Duff (2002) used interviews and diaries of visits to archives to study 11 history students, mostly at the doctoral level. Toms and Duff note that diaries provide strong evidence that complements data gathered in interviews, yet which depends heavily on the commitment of respondents to complete the diary. Diaries were also used with Lee et al.'s (2012) large sample of undergraduates, finding that they used a wide variety of sources (one-third of them not online) to address their information needs.

Constance Mellon (1986) studied a large sample of university students to explore the role of anxiety in the search for information in libraries, a theme also explored in other studies of college (e.g., Jiao & Onwuegbuzie, 1997) and high school (Kuhlthau, 1988a, 1991) students. The information behavior of doctoral students was studied by Cole (1998), Mehra (2007), Seldén (2001), Bøyum and Aabø (2015), and Moore and Singley (2019). Additional studies of university students have been conducted by Cole et al. (2005), Hyldegård (2009), Kerins et al. (2004), and Barahmanda et al. (2019), among many others. Connaway et al. (2011) also include some students in their study of information source convenience, and Heinström's (2006) studies of incidental information acquisition included respondents ranging from grade six to master's degree level. Julien (1999) examined the information seeking of high-school age students, a group also featured in Lilley (2008) and Haras (2011), which focus more on the potential influence of ethnicity on information behaviors.

3.2.3 Leisure and Entertainment

Due perhaps to the influence of Savolainen's (1995) Everyday Life Information Seeking (ELIS) framework, along with Stebbins' (2001, 2009, 2018) Serious Leisure research agenda, more attention has been paid to nonwork information behavior, including such voluntary activities as engaging in hobbies, games, and sports. As highlighted by Borlund and Pharo (2019) leisure activities account for a large proportion of nonwork-related information seeking. These are preoccupations that go beyond a single experience or project, and are not paid work, yet may be work-like in the intensity and time frame in which they are pursued. Hartel's early (2003, 2005) and later works with other colleagues (Cox et al., 2017; Hartel et al., 2016) examine much of the literature on serious leisure. Hartel (2014a) contains a useful figure distilling serious leisure into three general categories: hobbyist (e.g., collecting stamps), volunteer (e.g., in a hospice) and amateur (e.g., playing in a community orchestra). A contrasting scheme is that of Mansourian (2020), who defines three groups (intellectual pursuits, creating or collecting physical objects, experiential activities) and three categories of activity (appreciators, producers/collectors, performers). Mansourian (2020) provides a comprehensive overview of research themes and publications. Hartel (2014a) also suggests that many types of sustained adult reading and learning (such as genealogy) fall into the category of "liberal arts hobby," and are worthy of further investigation. As Barriage (2015) establishes, children also practice hobbies. Many of the individual studies described below also contain reviews of research in a particular domain (e.g., genealogy, collecting, travel, cooking, games, or sports).

Genealogy has been a popular topic in the hobbyist genre of information behavior studies (Hartel, 2014a), perhaps because amateur genealogists are frequent users of libraries, archives, and the internet (Molto, 2010) and thus engage heavily with information. According to Bishop (2005) we could see genealogy as the collecting of people. Assembling family histories is one of the most popular hobbies in such countries as the United States, Canada, and Australia. Genealogy is a leisure pursuit with deep psychological motivations, particularly the quest for self-identity. Duff and Johnson's (2002) study was perhaps the first to focus on information behavior, examining patterns of use of libraries, archives, librarians, archivists, and other family historians. Yakel (2004) interviewed 29 genealogists and family historians, finding that the activity was a form of seeking meaning and led to the formation and use of strong social networks. In particular, information sharing via the internet and genealogical societies was very common, a theme also explored by Yakel and Torres (2007). Another prolific researcher on this topic has been Fulton (2005a, 2009a, 2009b). Her publications report interviews with 24 amateur genealogists from multiple nations, again with emphasis on the reciprocal sharing of information and the social and psychological benefits of this pastime. Friday (2014) presents a model of family history searching, based on nearly 4,000 survey responses, followed by smaller subsamples of diaries and shadowing sessions. Darby and Clough (2013) offer another model, emphasizing the stages of genealogical research. Case (2009b) explores the links between genealogy and health, suggesting that promoting family histories could be a way to increase awareness of healthy behaviors by focusing attention on ancestors' illnesses.

Traveling and tourism have attracted much recent attention in information behavior studies. An investigation of travelers' sharing of information online (Lueg, 2008) shows how their interactions create communities of knowledge production. Little et al. (2011) write about the historical evolution of information sources and habits of airline passengers. Chang (2009) turns her attention to the sport of backpacking, focusing on how those travelers gather information, finding that their use of sources varies by task, and tends to occur over three stages. A similar study is that by Hyatt (2017) of Pacific Crest Trail hikers. Exploring urban environments is the subject of Fulton (2017). Other investigations about travel and tourism include Feng and Agosto (2017), Oliveira and Baracho (2018), Ye (2019), Fardous et al. (2019), and Tan and Kuo (2019). Sharing of information, along with resulting information overload, are frequent themes among these newer studies.

Collecting is another example of a hobby. Perhaps 30% of the public collects *something*, yet it is not clear *why* they collect. Case (2009a) studied coin collectors, identifying four of the motivational themes developed by Formanek (1991): extension of the self, financial investment, addiction, and social. The fifth theme, preservation, appeared to have little relevance, perhaps because coins survive for millennia without human intervention. In a subsequent article, Case (2010) narrowed his focus to detecting counterfeit coins in online auctions. Music recordings are another object of collecting studies. Relevant studies include Lee and Downie (2004), Giles et al. (2007), Shuker (2010), Laplante and Downie (2011), Margree et al. (2014), and Vesga Vinchira (2019). Lee and Trace (2009) looked at collectors of rubber ducks. The investigators spotlight the importance of information sharing among members of a community, downplaying the importance of both individual seeking and of formal sources.

Cox et al. (2008) found photo-sharing website Flickr promoted the hobby of amateur photography without the complications of local photography clubs. Their interviews with 11 users suggest high satisfaction with the service, yet possible problems with reciprocal tagging, along with the potential for commercial colonization. Prigoda and McKenzie (2007) examined a group of knitters who meet in a public library, exploring this situation as a ground for both sharing of information and the development of caring and meaning. As examples of "performance," historical reenactments are the focus of Robinson and Yerbury (2015), while amateur music performance is discussed by Kostagiolas et al. (2015), and Hartel et al. (2016). More recently, Bronstein and Lidor (2021) examined a virtual community's motivations for seeking music information, while Price and Robinson (2017) explored the information behaviors of cult media fan communities. Forcier (2022) has also examined fan culture, as part of a large study of the *onlife practices* of fans.

Cooking is another popular hobbyist interest. Hartel's (2010, 2011) study of gourmet cooks shows the degree to which information is critical in support of this hobby; they are also good illustrations of the value of photography in conducting such studies. Polkinghorne's (2021) research also explored people's information practices around food, as part of a large study of people's everyday food experiences. Her findings address how people become informed about food practices, their ethical concerns, the role of food in families and culture, and people's embodied experiences of food practices.

Investing is a hobby for some people, particularly later in life. O'Connor (2011) characterized some of the 16 female investors she studied as hobbyists, examining their sources, motivations, cognitive biases, and interactions with one another. In a later study O'Connor (2013) analyzes the content of online investing forums to reveal the sources amateur investors cite, and the soundness of those. She finds extensive collaboration among investors, but also reliance on sources of questionable quality, including investor gurus, blogs, and commercially sponsored information. O'Connor and Dillingham (2014) analyzed other posts, demonstrating that descriptions of personal experience directly affected how much discussion was generated, and its quality. Another study of the information behavior of investors, although not explicitly hobby-oriented, is by Williamson and Smith (2010).

Games and sports are also common leisure activities that we could consider under this category. Adams (2009) investigates how players in virtual games find the information they need to succeed, and how they form meanings about their activities. Otto et al. (2011) review the information gathering of players of fantasy football and baseball. Hartel et al. (2016) and Gorichanaz (2015, 2017) discuss long-distance running. Horseback riding is studied by Nowé Hedvall et al. (2017). Motorsports clubs are investigated by Joseph (2016), and car restoration (also a potential collecting activity) by Olsson and Lloyd (2017). Players of board games are the focus of an investigation by Wylie Atmore (2017).

Finally, as Ross (1999) points out, reading for pleasure has many information dimensions and is a serious leisure pursuit. This is apparent in Mikkonen and Vakkari's (2016) study of readers' interests and criteria for fiction book selection as they search library catalogs, and in Greifeneder and Gäde's (2020) digital twin bookstore. A parallel situation is the search for videos on YouTube, as explored by Albassam and Ruthven (2020). How public libraries might respond is the subject of VanScoy et al. (2020); maker spaces in libraries, for arts and crafts hobbyists, have been one response (Williams & Willett, 2019).

3.2.4 Citizenship and Political Engagement

Investigations of the public (including citizens and voters), often aspire to improve community and democracy, but also cover other areas of general interest. This includes, for example, debate on specific political issues, activism, and identification of community problems that might benefit from governmental action. Most large-scale information behavior investigations of the general public are now quite dated; the most widely cited is Chen and Hernon's (1982) study of 2,400 US residents, living in New England. Among the more important findings of the study was the individual (and context-driven) nature of residents' information seeking activities. Fifty-two percent of the 3,548 information-seeking situations recounted by Chen and Hernon's informants were information needs about day-to-day problems; the rest were scattered across 18 different problem situations, with none accounting for more than 6% of the total. Typical problems fell into the following categories (in order of importance): work-related issues; consumer issues; home and housing issues; and issues related to education. In each case, interpersonal providers of information were ranked as much more important than institutions or the mass media.

Chen and Hernon's research, along with that by Durrance (1984) and Dervin et al. (1984), highlight a methodological shift in surveys of the public. These surveys asked more questions about basic human problems and situations and less about the usual institutions that were supposed to address them. Dervin et al. especially, probed deeper into the origins of, and solutions to, personal "gaps" in life. That investigation interviewed 1,040 Americans in California, who reported an average of 8.5 problem situations within the last month. These situations most commonly concerned (in order): family/friends, managing money, shopping/buying, or learning – all of which were reported by over two-thirds of the respondents. Other common gaps involved current events, recreation, health, jobs, children, transportation, or housing, each of which was mentioned by 40% or more of those questioned.

Savolainen (1995, 1999) describes a pattern of "passive monitoring" of everyday events that takes place when life moves along as we expect, versus "active seeking of practically effective information" that happens when the unexpected arises. A person may watch television absentmindedly to "keep an eye on life" and read the daily paper as an aspect of "belonging in the community" (1995, p. 273). Thus, some aspects of media use (and of information behavior, generally) are not purposeful; rather, they are simply a part of everyday life practices.

Conspiracy Theories: Complex Examples of Disinformation

This form of disinformation is complex, given the systematic and long-term nature of conspiracies. The pandemic offers many examples, including the 2020 films *Plandemic and Indoctornation.* Created by amateur filmmaker Mikki Willis, the films feature interviews with several anti-vaccination advocates. The films make many unsupported claims, which have since been debunked (see Nilsen, 2020), including: the COVID-19 pandemic was planned by elites to gain wealth and power; the virus originated in a Chinese lab funded by Americans; COVID-19 vaccines and face masks increase the likelihood of contracting and dying from the virus; and, the Gates Foundation's polio vaccination project in India paralyzed 490,000 children. Allen (2020) provides useful strategies for assessing the validity of such claims. While Willis' motivations for (and the reasons for viewers' acceptance of) these films are unclear, these may include to: resist vaccination and masking; protect certain civil liberties; promote alternative treatments; undermine faith in government and science; and enhance the reputations and goals of the films' contributors. Whatever the reasons, these conspiracy films operate on several levels – historical, political, medical, organizational, individual – and may continue to persuade viewers, for decades.

Where problem-oriented information seeking is concerned, Savolainen (1995) had similar findings to earlier, large-scale studies like Chen and Hernon (1982): types of everyday problems were diverse, with employment, health, and financial worries being mentioned most frequently. Which sources were pursued for problem-solving depended largely on availability and accessibility, with informal sources (e.g., acquaintances) being used much more commonly than formal sources. Interestingly, a study by Kalms (2008) suggests that some households, aided by the internet and various tools and practices, spend a great deal of effort managing information vital to their lives and households; these include information relevant to many of the "problems" descried in earlier studies (financial, medical, educational, political, legal, etc.), as well as about opportunities for improvement and enjoyment (advice, employment, entertainment, travel, social connections, etc.)

Few other large-sample community studies have been performed in recent decades. For example, Fisher et al. (2005) conducted a telephone survey of 612 urban residents to discover their "information grounds" – the places where they find useful knowledge in the pursuit of other activities. Among other results, they found the most common information grounds to be places of worship (mentioned by 24%), the workplace (22%), and club, sports team, play group, or hobby (nearly 11%); among nine other common places, libraries were ranked third to last at about a 2% incidence; by far the two strongest "habitual" information sources were individuals with whom they had a strong relationship and the internet, each identified by over 39% of the sample. From their sources, the respondents obtained general advice (34%) and information about hobbies or travel (22%) or healthcare (18%). Other large-sample surveys have tended to focus more narrowly on topics such as health (e.g., Pálsdóttir, 2008, 2010, 2011, 2014) or changing political opinions (Lee, 2017).

Another study (Pettigrew et al., 2002) employed a variety of approaches – surveys, observations, interviews, focus groups, and case studies – to assess the use of community information by the public. Libraries in the American states of Illinois, Pennsylvania, and Oregon were sampled to see how the internet and libraries disseminate local information, answer questions, provide access to governmental services, and connect citizens to one another. Audunson and Evjen (2017) consider the role of public library in encouraging policy discourse. A comprehensive review of information behavior in public libraries is found in the chapter by Leckie and Given (2005). Broader examinations, usually featuring the internet as a public sphere for political discourse, include Cruickshank and Hall (2020) and Cruickshank et al. (2020), on online platforms in Scotland for political information and discussion; and Taylor-Smith and Smith (2019) whose case studies of three community/activist groups compare a variety of online (e.g., social media, email and blogs) with paper and offline venues, concluding that they form Socio-Technical Interaction Networks with comparable characteristics.

Baxter et al. (2010) describe their interviews with representatives of 54 nongovernmental organizations that responded to requests by the Scottish government for consultation on policies. These were sampled out of a population of 4,168 who responded to issues such as medical care or the environment. Over half of these could be labeled *citizen groups* and the rest were mainly professional associations, business grips, or charities. Their external sources were evenly divided between the internet, subject experts, and "like-minded groups." Not surprisingly common complaints among respondents concerned lack of feedback about, and low effectiveness of, their input to the policy process. Other work by Baxter (2014) considers what the public knew about proposed Scottish property developments, while Baxter and Marcella (2014) examine how voters in the Scottish referendum on independence looked for relevant information online.

When citizens go beyond mere voting to attempt to influence others, we call them "activists." Savolainen (2008a, 2015a) examined citizens active in politics, in the first study environmental issues, and in the second, online discussions of immigration issues. Another study (Yerbury, 2015) compared Australian and Rwandan activists, showing that the African group were less likely to use the internet to reach people whom they did not already know; the Rwandans were more likely to stay inside their "small worlds," thus limiting their impact.

Susan Beer (2004) conducted interviews with representatives of over 100 community groups, businesses, and information providers in eight remote communities in Shetland and the Western Isles of Scotland. Beer discovered that strong personal ties within the communities enabled residents to find answers from other people. Her informants complained about the lack of relevance of some information from outside (e.g., "urban solutions"), and occasional withholding of information by local parties (sometimes due to journalistic sensitivity within such small communities). Difficulty of travel – even within the islands themselves – was judged to be a key barrier to finding information.

A dramatic change in the information seeking of the public is tied to the emergence of the internet as an omnibus channel that complements (and, in part, replicates) the usual array of interpersonal and mass media sources of information. Use of the internet, especially, is often discussed in information behavior research. For example, Case et al. (2004) argued that patterns of source preferences common in the past (e.g., a preference for information gained in face-to-face or telephone exchanges with friends and family members) have shifted in the light of the widespread availability of email and websites. They based their findings on data from a 2002 telephone survey of 882 adults regarding information seeking about the genetic basis of disease. Similarly, in the context of voting-related behavior, Kaye and Johnson (2003) used the results of an online survey of 442 respondents to demonstrate that the internet is gradually substituting for other media usage – particularly television, radio and magazines.

Investigations that consider internet use in the context of other sources (unlike those that only focused on the mechanics of information retrieval) have also been prevalent in information behavior research for at least two decades. For example, Hektor (2003) studied 10 Swedish residents, considering the place of internet sources among others available in the respondents' environment, including other people, television, and telephones. Based on interviews and diaries, Hektor noted that the internet was used broadly for both seeking and giving information, yet it was most often a complement or substitute for other sources, not a unique source in itself. Savolainen (2001, 2004), Kari and Savolainen (2003), and Savolainen and Kari (2004a, 2004b) also found the internet was one among many sources and channels used in people's daily lives. Kari and Savolainen (2003) made the case that internet-related searching needed to be considered within the larger contexts of other sources and the person's *life-world*, or everyday reality. A later article by Savolainen and Kari (2004a) extended this thesis by considering the "information source horizon" of the internet in the context of self-development. Source horizons place information sources and channels in an order of preference, based on attributes like accessibility and quality. Savolainen and Kari's sample of 18 internet users placed information sources into three categories, by degree of relevance to the respondents' interests and goals; human sources such as friends and colleagues were preferred, followed by print media such as newspapers and books; networked sources were ranked third among six source types. Savolainen and Kari's (2004b) interviews found that the informants conceptualized the internet as a space or place, and that they judged what they found there in terms of the quality of other information sources.

Contemporary studies have looked beyond the internet for sources of civic information. Hanlon (2021) looked at information communication within a European social democracy political party. Informal conversations were essential to the work of the party, including learning at individual and group levels. Smith and McMenemy (2017) examined the conceptions of political information of 14- and 15-year-olds in Northern England, including the sources they use to become politically informed and how they evaluate those sources on quality and authority. They used a wide range of sources and are aware of both passively encountering and actively engaging with sources. Their experiences with political information – including how actively they engaged with sources and the complexity of their interactions – varied substantially.

Rather than considering a broad array of information behavior, Yates and Partridge (2015) focused on use of social media by 25 Australian citizens, in the context of natural disasters (floods and a cyclone in Queensland during 2011). Through interviews, they found widespread and effective use of social media (Facebook and Twitter). Their analysis teased out eight themes of messages: connecting with others, reporting on one's well-being, emotional coping, asking for or offering help, brokering (finding, screening, and passing on) information, journalistic reporting of events, comparisons with other media, and descriptions of the experience of using social media during the disaster. They review and compare their findings with, similar studies of Australian (e.g., Taylor et al., 2012), Pakistani (Murthy & Longwell, 2013), and Japanese (e.g., Jung, 2012) disasters. Yates and Partridge conclude that social media can be extremely helpful during disasters and illustrate the value of research on information experience (Bruce et al., 2014).

3.2.5 Purchasing and Consuming

Marketing researchers have often studied individuals' information behaviors. While many of their investigations are proprietary, and thus unpublished, several studies of consumers, shoppers, and the like have appeared in scholarly journals. Consumer research has something interesting to say about information behavior, and according to an analysis by Jamali and Nabavi (2022) two consumer studies journals are among the top 10 noninformation science publications where information behavior research is found. Consumption has drawn the attention of sociologists (e.g., Stebbins, 2009) as well as marketers. Although it is true that most consumer studies are experiments, surveys, and descriptive focus groups aimed at marketing, the breadth of consumer research has widened greatly over the past four decades. More business studies have embraced qualitative methods and pursued more basic questions about human behavior. Many investigations now have less to do with sales and more to do with the concept of sensemaking.

Foxall (1983) argues for an emphasis on the way that situations influence the actions and choices of consumers (pp. 90–93). He identified the following as "situational characteristics": physical surroundings, social surroundings (other persons present, their characteristics, roles, and interpersonal interactions), temporal perspective (time of day, season of the year, time since/until other relevant action, deadlines, etc.), task definition (e.g., to obtain information about a purchase), and antecedent states and behaviors (such as momentary moods and conditions, as distinct from chronic individual traits). These characteristics have found their way into information behavior research. Xia (2010), for example, finds that both the characteristics of the individual consumer and the particular retail environment influence the degree of browsing that takes place, while Laplante and Downie (2011) discuss how information is gathered about potential purchases.

The notion of "situational variables" is discussed by Belk et al. (1988) who documented the *research process* of consumers browsing flea markets and swap meets. Case (2009a) used a similar approach for interactions at coin shows. At least two books (Belk, 1995; Bianchi, 1997) and many empirical investigations have been devoted to the intersections among consumption, collecting behavior, taste, flow, and self-concept. There are also theories of "consumer fun" (e.g., Oh & Pham, 2022). A relevant study from the information behavior tradition is Laplante and Downie's (2011) on music information seeking. Their investigation ties together themes of hedonic consumption, engagement, and taste. Xia (2010) and Laplante and Downie (2011) also found that browsing is only partly functional, but rather has strong recreational components. The latter study is echoed in Margree et al.'s (2014) investigation of music record buyers, who regularly browse the holdings of a wide variety of physical (e.g., music stores and charity shops) and online (eBay and Amazon) sellers.

Savolainen's (2009b, 2010) study of house buying is an example of consumer information behavior. Interviews with 16 prospective homebuyers resulted in the creation of information source horizon maps. These depictions allowed Savolainen to tease out the criteria used by these shoppers to screen possible homes for purchase. Internet listings were a prime source of information, yet buyers were particularly sensitive to the timeliness of the information on websites. Savolainen's 2009 article uses a content analysis of the shoppers' think-aloud responses to printed and internet house listings, as they identified those most relevant to their search. Grounded in earlier studies of information processing and consumer choice, his analysis examines the cognitive mechanisms used to interpret cues about dwelling places, including identification of key attributes of importance, specification of more particular details, comparison of attributes across houses, evaluations of dwellings, and explanations for their judgments. The liberal use of quotations from the respondents makes this study interesting reading.

The Rise of Fake News: A Major Research Focus

Fake news has received significant attention. Tandoc (2019) explores how biases and selective exposure make people prone to believing fake news. A focus group study (Duffy et al., 2019) also shed light on how fake news spreads (as unsuspecting readers share news with friends), including consequences (e.g., damaged relationships). Apuke and Omar (2021) found altruism fueled many people's desires to share interesting (yet fake) news – i.e., to share, inform, or connect with others. Loos et al.'s (2018) study of Netherlands children found only 7% identified a spoof website as unreliable. Rampersad and Althiyabi (2019) concluded that, except for older people (who are more trusting), demographics among Saudi Arabian residents had little influence on belief in fake news. Rather, cultural values (e.g., valuing community beliefs, strong leadership, and rules) had stronger influences on acceptance and use. Fake news can also lead to dangerous outcomes. Former US President's Donald Trump's tweets contributed to the invasion of the Capitol Building (Van Rickstal, 2021). Benetti and Gehrke's (2021) Brazilian study shows how ineffective drugs (e.g., ivermectin and hydroxychloroquine) were promoted by political figures, including then President Jair Bolsonaro, for treating COVID-19.

As the costliest purchase a consumer is likely to make, home buying has received more attention in information behavior studies than any other type of purchase. A recent collection is found in the book, *Where to live: Information studies on where to live in America*, edited by Ocepek and Aspray (2021). Among others, this includes essays on how emotion and time pressure affect buying decisions (Landry, 2021), the privacy issues of smart homes (Doty, 2021), the influence of decorating/remodeling videos on homeowners' taste and behaviors (Ocepek, 2021), and how people choose neighborhoods or communities in which to live (Aspray, 2021; Aspray & Ocepek, 2021).

3.2.6 Immigration and Asylum

Many information behavior studies examining immigrants and asylum seekers' experiences have appeared in the last two decades. Recent wars, civil unrest and climate change have caused unprecedented movements of human populations – which, in turn, have prompted many studies. Eskola et al. (2020) offer a review of relevant research in this area, with an emphasis on refugees.

It is clear from various investigations, including immigrants' personal accounts, that moving to a new land challenges people in many ways. Kennan et al. (2011), Lloyd et al. (2010, 2013), Qayyum et al. (2014) and Lloyd (2020) point to the significant problems immigrants (especially refugees) face, including social exclusion, prejudice, lack of employment, and lack of familiarity with local languages and customs. They characterize immigrants' attempts to acculturate as reflecting both information overload and information poverty. Their studies found that newcomers in Australia were often unaware of service providers (such as libraries) that could help them. Both governmental and private (e.g., church) organizations play a key role in the early stages of settlement (what Kennan, Lloyd et al. call "transitioning"); yet much more help is needed before immigrants feel truly *settled.* Relatedly Burnett and Lloyd (2019) invoke the concept of *desire lines* to explore how refugees create their own paths to information and solutions, outside of what is designed or intended for them by others.

Lloyd et al.'s (2017) investigation of Syrian resettlement in Sweden considered the role of social capital in making a place in a new society. Other views of immigrants to Sweden are those of Khan and Eskola (2020) and Kainat et al. (2022), who focused on women's experiences. Martzoukou and Burnett (2018) also examined Syrian resettlement, in this case to Scotland. Allard (2021) and Allard and Caidi (2018) have examined the information practices of Filipino migrants to Canada, focusing on sources of information and the process undertaken during the settlement process.

Bronstein (2017, 2019) looked at the information grounds of domestic migrant workers in Israel, examining the issues caused by their information poverty and language barriers, as well as the consequences for social inclusion within Israeli society. Mason and Lamain (2007) studied immigrants to New Zealand, where major barriers were language and discrimination, and information shortfalls concerned employment and local customs. However, in general, immigrants felt they were acculturating and were content with their choice of nation. In another New Zealand investigation, Sligo and Jameson (2000) focused on immigrants' need for health information, finding that language barriers and cultural beliefs could lead to medical problems. A case study of a Hmong population in the United States (Allen et al., 2004) found similar issues with translations between languages and belief systems (e.g., words and concepts that do not translate, and differing beliefs about causes of, and treatments for, disease). Both print and digital information need to be thoughtfully customized for specific populations of immigrants (Palmer et al., 2009).

Even when an immigrant language community is quite large, as with Spanish speakers in the United States (Courtright, 2005), the resulting social networks are not always adequate for providing reliable and accurate health information alone. Specialized formal channels (such as pamphlets and websites in the target language) remain important, although at the time of the Courtright study Mexican immigrants appeared to ignore the internet as a source of health information. An innovative experiment by Le Louvier and Innocenti (2021) used an information mapping board game to explore how refugees thought, felt, pictured, and strategized their information practices.

Fisher, Durrance et al. (2004) observed the use of American public library literacy programs by immigrants, while Fisher, Marcoux et al. (2004) interviewed 51 migrant Hispanic farm workers using two community technology centers in the United States. In the latter study respondents cited a wide variety of useful information found at the centers: employment, language, education, legal, and technology assistance. These immigrants still relied heavily on interpersonal sources they deemed credible, often finding these through work, school, or church. In both investigations the public programs and facilities were found to be helpful to the immigrant populations they served. Yeon and Lee (2021) considered similar issues among North Korean immigrants to South Korea, as they sought and experienced employment under a different economic system, pointing out the ways that public libraries could help in their adjustment.

Ruokolainen and Widén (2020) studied asylum seekers in Finland, most of whom were from the Middle East. They explain how *misinformation* can hamper resettlement, and how flawed information can take various forms (e.g., inaccurate, mistranslated, outdated, false hope, rumor) and involve many different topics (e.g., legal requirements, access to social benefits, health issues).

A cross-nation comparison of Canada and Australia by Caidi et al. (2020) of older Chinese migrants points out the special challenges that senior immigrants face, and the coping skills they develop. Another Australian study of Asian refugees is that of Khoir et al. (2015), which offers a model based on the pattern of information sources and strategies they documented. Also examining patterns of seeking is a clever study by Zimmerman (2018), who used information horizons mapping to represent the network of health information resources identified by immigrant women; the author suggests the results are predictive of health literacy.

Most studies of immigrants gravitate toward the more extreme cases, in which language and cultural barriers are quite high, due to refugee status and/or movement from a less-developed nation. One study that deals with immigrants moving between nations with strong ties and somewhat comparable standards of living is that of Shoham and Strauss (2007). They studied immigrants from Canada and the United States to Israel, finding that internet resources provided a great deal of the information needed until actual arrival, at which point interpersonal networks became much more important. In a study of skilled (healthcare) immigrants, Caidi et al. (2014) found a different set of problems facing foreign-trained health professionals who one would think would be readily integrated into the healthcare systems of Canada and the United States. Their content analysis of online forums show that nurses, doctors and others struggle to learn about immigration and certification requirements, as well as differing terminology and work practices.

As many other studies and commentaries point out (e.g., Audunson et al., 2011; Burke, 2008; Martzoukou & Burnett, 2018; Oduntan & Ruthven, 2019; Pilerot, 2018; Skøtt, 2019; Yeon & Lee, 2021) there is ample opportunity for libraries to play an important role in the lives of immigrants. Interventions can be as ambitious as multichannel outreach efforts partnered with other agencies (e.g., Allen et al., 2004), or as simple as providing appropriate reading material and advisory services (e.g., Dali, 2004, 2012, 2014). Yet, as virtually every investigation above indicates, print and digital documents will likely serve only as a supplement to the interpersonal sources central to immigrant communities.

3.3 CONCLUSION

This chapter began with the thesis that information behavior research has morphed over the decades by gradually shifting away from a focus on individuals, occupations, and sources, towards the incorporation of roles and social contexts. At the same time investigations have broadened their scope, considering the whole person, including their emotions, physical bodies, and senses. In this way information behavior research has grown more holistic and complex. Examples of this shift are found in the increased emphasis on how information is created, shared, and used.

We offered examples of recent research (especially over the last 20 years), under various categories. The area of *health*, for example, has grown steadily across many studies, including recent investigations of the COVID-19 pandemic. *Education and learning* is also a vast topic, sitting across many disciplines and with broad boundaries. We also considered *leisure*-related activities, such as hobbies, travel, and sports, which were hardly mentioned in information behavior studies over three decades ago. *Political engagement* (such as discussing and voting on community issues and candidates), *consumption* (seeking, browsing, and buying objects or experiences), and *immigration* (including being a newcomer to a community) rounded out our examples of context-driven situations.

In addition to these areas, we can also see potential for growth in new areas, such as studies related to the impacts of climate change. This one topic, for example, affects urban planning, migration, food security, border protection, and other issues, all with significant information behavior implications. We discuss potential information behavior research futures in more detail, in Chapter 6.

3.4 OUR TOP 3 *MUST READ* RECOMMENDATIONS

Johnson, J. D. (2003). On contexts of information seeking. ***Information Processing & Management, 39*****, 735–760.**
A painstaking analysis of what is meant by the term "context" and how the term has been used by various researchers.

Grad, R., Pluye, P., Granikov, V., Johnson-Lafleur, J., Shulha, M., Sridhar, S. B., Moscovici, J. L., Bartlett, G., Vandal, A. C., Marlow, B., & Kloda, L. (2011). Physicians' assessment of the value of clinical information: Operationalization of a theoretical model. ***Journal of the American Society for Information Science and Technology, 62*****(10), 1884–1891.**
An innovative study of the seeking and use of information for patient treatment by physicians and other medical staff, which sheds light on the fundamental question – does information make a difference?

Case, D. O., & O'Connor, L. G. (2016). What's the use? Measuring the frequency of studies of information outcomes. ***Journal of the Association for Information Science and Technology, 67*****(3), 649 661.**
An essay on the neglect of "use" within information behavior research, coupled with an attempt to measure how commonly this has been done, between 1950 and 2012.

REFERENCES

Abrahamson, D. E., & Goodman-Delahunty, J. (2013). The impact of organizational information culture on information use outcomes in policing: An exploratory study. *Information Research, 18*(4). http://informationr.net/ir/18-4/paper598.html

Adams, S. S. (2009). What games have to offer: Information behavior and meaning-making in virtual play spaces. *Library Trends, 57*(4), 676–693. https://doi.org/10.1353/lib.0.0058

Albassam, S., & Ruthven, I. (2020). Dynamic aspects of relevance: Differences in users' relevance criteria between selecting and viewing videos during leisure searches. *Information Research*, *25*(1). http://InformationR.net/ir/25-1/paper850.html

Allard, D. (2021). "So many things were new to us": Identifying the settlement information practices of newcomers to Canada across the settlement process. *Journal of Documentation*, *78*(2), 334–360. https://doi.org/10.1108/JD-02-2021-0024

Allard, D., & Caidi, N. (2018). Imagining Winnipeg: The translocal meaning making of Filipino migrants to Canada. *Journal of the Association for Information Science and Technology*, *69*(10), 1193–1204. https://doi.org/10.1002/asi.24038

Allen, M. (2020). I'm an investigative journalist. These are the questions I asked about the viral "Plandemic" video. ProPublica. https://www.propublica.org/article/im-an-investigative-journalist-these-are-the-questions-i-asked-about-the-viral-plandemic-video

Allen, M., Matthew, S., & Bolland, M. J. (2004). Working with immigrant and refugee populations: Issues and Hmong case study. *Library Trends*, *53*(2), 301–328.

Alshahrani, H., & Rasmussen Pennington, D. (2020). 'How to use it more?' Self-efficacy and its sources in the use of social media for knowledge sharing. *Journal of Documentation*, *76*(1), 231–257. https://doi.org/10.1108/JD-02-2019-0026

Apuke, O., & Omar, B. (2021). Fake news and COVID-19: Modelling the predictors of fake news sharing among social media users. *Telematics and Informatics*, *56*. https://doi.org/10.1016/j.tele.2020.101475

Aspray, W. (2021). Where to live in retirement: A complex information problem. In M. G. Ocepek & W. Aspray (Eds.), *Deciding where to live: Information studies on where to live in America* (pp. 281–308). Rowman & Littlefield.

Aspray, W., & Ocepek, M. G. (2021). Where to live as an information problem: Three contemporary examples. In M. G. Ocepek & W. Aspray (Eds.), *Deciding where to live: Information studies on where to live in America* (pp. 1–34). Rowman & Littlefield.

Audunson, R., Essmat, S., & Aabø, S. (2011). Public libraries: A meeting place for immigrant women? *Library & Information Science Research*, *33*(3), 220–227. https://doi.org/10.1016/j.lisr.2011.01.003

Audunson, R., & Evjen, S. (2017). The public library: An arena for an enlightened and rational public sphere? The case of Norway. *Information Research*, *22*(1). http://InformationR.net/ir/22-1/colis/colis1641.html

Barahmand, N., Nakhoda, M., Fahimnia, F., & Nazari, M. (2019). Understanding everyday life information seeking behavior in the context of coping with daily hassles: A grounded theory study of female students. *Library & Information Science Research*, *41*(4), 100980. https://doi.org/10.1016/j.lisr.2019.100980

Barriage, S. (2015). 'Talk, talk and more talk': Parental perceptions of young children's information practices related to their hobbies and interests. *Information Research*, *21*(3). http://InformationR.net/ir/21-3/paper721.html

Bateson, G. (1978). The pattern which connects. *CoEvolution Quarterly*, *18*, 4–15.

Baxter, G. (2014). Open for business? An historical, comparative study of public access to information about two controversial coastal developments in North-east Scotland. *Information Research*, *19*(1). http://InformationR.net/ir/19-1/paper603.html

Baxter, G., & Marcella, R. (2014). The 2014 Scottish independence referendum: A study of voters' online information behaviour. In *Proceedings of ISIC, the Information Behaviour Conference*, Leeds, 2–5 September, 2014. Part 1, 9. http://informationr.net/ir/19-4/isic/isicsp5.html

Baxter, G., Marcella, R., & Illingworth, L. (2010). Organizational information behaviour in the public consultation process in Scotland. *Information Research*, *15*(4). http://InformationR.net/ir/15-4/paper442.html

Beautyman, W., & Shenton, A. K. (2009). When does an academic information need stimulate a school-inspired information want? *Journal of Librarianship and Information Science*, *41*(2), 67–80. https://doi.org/10.1177/0961000609102821

Beer, S. (2004). Information flow and peripherality in remote island areas of Scotland. *Libri*, *54*(3), 148–157. https://doi.org/10.1515/LIBR.2004.148

Belk, R. W. (1995). *Collecting in a consumer society*. Routledge.

Belk, R. W., Sherry, J., Jr., & Wallendorf, M. (1988). Naturalistic inquiry into buyer-seller behavior at a swap meet. *Journal of Consumer Research*, *14*, 449–469. https://www.jstor.org/stable/2489153

Benetti, M., & Gehrke, M. (2021). Disinformation in Brazil during the Covid-19 pandemic: Topics, platforms, and actors. *Fronteiras*. https://doi.org/10.4013/fem.2021.232.02

Bianchi, M. (Ed.). (1997). *The active consumer. novelty and surprise in consumer choice*. Routledge.

Bishop, R. (2005). "The essential force of the clan": Developing a collecting-inspired ideology of genealogy through textual analysis. *The Journal of Popular Culture*, *8*, 990–1010. https://doi.org/10.1111/j.1540-5931.2005.00172.x

Bonner, A., & Lloyd, A. (2011). What information counts at the moment of practice? Information practices of renal nurses. *Journal of Advanced Nursing*, *67*(6), 1213–1221. https://doi.org/10.1111/j.1365-2648.2011.05613.x

Borlund, P., & Pharo, N. (2019). A need for information on information needs. *Information Research*, *24*(4). http://InformationR.net/ir/24-4/colis/colis1908.html

Bowler, L. (2010). The self-regulation of curiosity and interest during the information search process of adolescent students. *Journal of the American Society for Information Science and Technology*, *61*(7), 1332–1344. https://doi.org/10.1002/asi.21334

Bøyum, I., & Aabø, S. (2015). The information practices of Business PhD students. *New Library World*, *116*(3/4), 187–200. https://doi.org/10.1108/NLW-06-2014-0073

Brittain, J. M. (1970). *Information and its users: A review with special reference to the social sciences*. Wiley-Interscience.

Bronstein, J. (2017). An examination of social and informational support behavior codes on the Internet: The case of online health communities. *Library & Information Science Research*, *39*(1), 63–68. https://doi.org/10.1016/j.lisr.2017.01.006

Bronstein, J. (2019). A transitional approach to the study of the information behavior of domestic migrant workers: A narrative inquiry. *Journal of Documentation*, *75*(2), 314–333. https://doi.org/10.1108/JD-07-2018-0112

Bronstein, J., & Lidor, D. (2021). Motivations for music information seeking as serious leisure in a virtual community: Exploring a Eurovision fan club. *Journal of Information Management*, *73*(2), 271–287. https://doi.org/10.1108/AJIM-06-2020-0192

Brown, L. K., & Veinot, T. C. (2020). Information behavior and social control: Toward an understanding of conflictual information behavior in families managing chronic illness. *Journal of the Association for Information Science and Technology*, *72*(1), 66–82. https://doi.org/10.1002/asi.24362

Bruce, C. S., Davis, K., Hughes, H., Partridge, H., & Stoodley, I. (Eds.). (2014). *Information experience: Approaches to theory and practice*. Emerald Publishing Limited.

Burgess, E. R., Reddy, M. C., & Mohr, D. C. (2022). 'I just can't help but smile sometimes': Collaborative self-management of depression. *Proceedings of the ACM on Human-Computer Interaction*, *6*(CSCW1), 1–32. https://doi.org/10.1145/3512917

Burke, S. (2008). Public library resources used by immigrant households. *Public Libraries*, *47*(4), 32–41.

Burnett, K., & Burnett, G. (2019). Information domains, information ethics. In *Proceedings of the Tenth International Conference on Conceptions of Library and Information Science*, Ljubljana, Slovenia, June 16–19, 2019. http://InformationR.net/ir/24-4/colis/colis1942.html

Burnett, S., & Lloyd, A. (2019). The road not taken: Locating desire lines across information landscapes. *Information Research*, *24*(4). http://informationr.net/ir/24-4/colis/colis1911.html

Caidi, N., Du, J. T., Li, L., Shen, J. M., & Sun, Q. (2020). Immigrating after 60: Information experiences of older Chinese migrants to Australia and Canada. *Information Processing & Management*, *57*(3). https://doi.org/10.1016/j.ipm.2019.102111

Caidi, N., Komlodi, A., Abrao, A. L., & Martin-Hammond, A. (2014). Collectively figuring it out: Foreign-trained health professionals and labor market integration. *LIBRES*, *24*(2), 11. http://libres-ejournal.info/wp-content/uploads/2015/03/LIBRESv24i2p118-131.Caidi_.2014.pdf

Case, D. O. (2009a). Serial collecting as leisure, and coin collecting in particular. *Library Trends*, *57*(4), 729–752. https://doi.org/10.1353/lib.0.0063

Case, D. O. (2009b). Collection of family health histories: The link between genealogy and public health. *Journal of the American Society for Information Science and Technology*, *59*(14), 2312–2319. https://doi.org/10.1002/asi.20938

Case, D. O. (2010). A model of the information seeking and decision making of online coin buyers. *Information Research*, *15*(4). http://InformationR.net/ir/15-4/paper448.html

Case, D. O., Johnson, J. D., Andrews, J. E., Allard, S., & Kelly, K. M. (2004). From two-step flow to the Internet: The changing array of sources for genetics information seeking. *Journal of the American Society for Information Science and Technology*, *55*(8), 660–669. https://doi.org/10.1002/asi.20000

Case, D. O., & O'Connor, L. G. (2016). What's the use? Measuring the frequency of studies of information outcomes. *Journal of the American Society for Information Science and Technology*, *67*(3), 649–661. https://doi.org/10.1002/asi.23411

Chang, S.-J. L. (2009). Information research in leisure: Implications from an empirical study of backpackers. *Library Trends*, *57*(4), 711–768. https://doi.org/10.1353/lib.0.0062

Chávez, R., & Sabelli, M. (2020). Information behaviour of parents of children with autism spectrum disorder (ASD): A case study. In *Proceedings of ISIC, the Information Behaviour Conference*, Pretoria, South Africa, 28 September – 1 October, 2020. *Information Research*, *25*(4). http://InformationR.net/ir/25-4/isic2020/isic2014.html

Chen, A. T. (2015). Information use and illness representations: Understanding their connection in illness coping. *Journal of the Association for Information Science and Technology*, *66*(2), 340–353. https://doi.org/10.1002/asi.23173

Chen, C., & Hernon, P. (1982). *Information-seeking: Assessing and anticipating user needs.* Neal-Schuman.

Choo, C. W. (2005). *The knowing organization: How organizations use information to construct meaning, create knowledge, and make decisions* (2nd ed.). Oxford University Press.

Choo, C. W., & Auster, E. (1993). Environmental scanning: Acquisition and use of information by managers. In M. Williams (Ed.), *Annual review of information science and technology* (Vol. 28, pp. 279–314). Learned Information.

Chu, C. M. (1999). Literary critics at work and their information needs: A research-phases model. *Library & Information Science Research*, *21*(2), 247–273. https://doi.org/10.1016/S0740-8188(99)00002-X

Chu, S. K. W., Huang, H., Wong, W. N., van Ginneken, W. F., Wu, K. M., & Hung, M. Y. (2018). Quality and clarity of health information on Q&A sites. *Library & Information Science Research*, *40*(3–4), 237–244. https://doi.org/https://doi.org/10.1016/j.lisr.2018.09.005

Chuang, K., & Yang, C. (2014). Information support exchanges using different computer-mediated communication formats in a social media alcoholism community. *Journal of the American Society for Information Science and Technology*, *65*(1), 37–52. https://doi.org/10.1002/asi.22960

Chung, E., Kwon, N., & Lee, J. (2016). Understanding scientific collaboration in the research life cycle: Bio-and nanoscientists' motivations, information-sharing and communication practices, and barriers to collaboration. *Journal of the Association for Information Science & Technology*, *67*(8), 1836–1848. https://doi.org/10.1002/asi.23520

Clark, M. (2017). Imposed-inquiry information-seeking self-efficacy and performance of college students: A review of the literature. *The Journal of Academic Librarianship*, *43*(5), 417–422. https://doi.org/10.1016/j.acalib.2017.05.001

Cole, C. (1998). Information acquisition in history PhD students: Inferencing and the formation of knowledge structures. *The Library Quarterly*, *68*(1), 33–51. https://doi.org/10.1086/602934

Cole, C., Beheshti, J., Large, A., Lamoureux, I., Abuhimed, D., & AlGhamdi, M. (2013). Seeking information for a middle school history project: The concept of implicit knowledge in the students' transition from Kuhlthau's stage 3 to stage 4. *Journal of the American Society for Information Science and Technology*, *64*(3), 558–573. https://doi.org/10.1002/asi.22786

Cole, C., Leide, J., Beheshti, J., Large, A., & Brooks, M. (2005). Investigating the anomalous states of knowledge hypothesis in a real-life problem situation: A study of history and psychology undergraduates seeking information for a course essay. *Journal of the American Society for Information Science and Technology*, *56*, 1544–1554. https://doi.org/10.1002/asi.20248

Cole, J., Watkins, C., & Kleine, D. (2015). Health advice from Internet discussion forums: How bad Is dangerous? *Journal of Medical Internet Research*, *18*(1). https://www.jmir.org/2016/1/e4

Connaway, L. S., Dickey, T. J., & Radford, M. L. (2011). 'If it is too inconvenient I'm not going after it:' Convenience as a critical factor in information-seeking behaviors. *Library & Information Science Research*, *33*(3), 179–190. https://doi.org/10.1016/j.lisr.2010.12.002

Cooke, N. A. (2022). A right to be misinformed? Considering fake news as a form of information poverty. In *Advances in librarianship* (Vol. 50, pp. 15–60). Emerald Publishing Limited. https://doi.org/10.1108/S0065-283020210000050002

Cool, C. (2001). The concept of situation in information science. In M. E. Williams (Ed.), *Annual review of information science and technology* (Vol. 35, pp. 5–42). Information Today, Inc.

Costello, K. L. (2017). Social relevance assessments for virtual worlds: Interpersonal source selection in the context of chronic illness. *Journal of Documentation*, *73*(6), 1209–1227. https://doi.org/10.1108/JD-07-2016-0096

Courtright, C. (2005). Health information-seeking among Latino newcomers: An exploratory study. *Information Research*, *10*(2). http://InformationR.net/ir/10-2/paper224.html

Cox, A. M., Clough, P. D., & Marlow, J. (2008). Flickr: A first look at user behaviour in the context of photography as serious leisure. *Information Research*, *13*(1). http://InformationR.net/ir/13-1/paper336.html

Cox, A. M., Griffin, B., & Hartel, J. (2017). What everybody knows: Embodied information in serious leisure. *Journal of Documentation*, *73*(3), 386–406. https://doi-org.proxy3.library.mcgill.ca/10.1108/JD-06-2016-0073

Cruickshank, P., & Hall, H. (2020). Talking to imagined citizens? Information sharing practices and proxies for e-participation in hyperlocal democratic settings. *Information Research*, *24*(4). http://InformationR.net/ir/25-4/paper880.html

Cruickshank, P., Hall, H., & Ryan, B. (2020). Information literacy as a joint competence shaped by everyday life and workplace roles amongst Scottish community councillors. In *Proceedings of ISIC, the Information Behaviour Conference*, Pretoria, South Africa, 28 September – 1 October, 2020. *Information Research*, *25*(4). http://InformationR.net/ir/25-4/isic2020/isic2008.html

Dali, K. (2004). Reading by Russian-speaking immigrants in Toronto: Use of public libraries, bookstores, and home book collections. *The International Information & Library Review*, *36*(4), 341–377. https://doi.org/10.1080/10572317.2004.10762653

Dali, K. (2012). Reading their way through immigration: The leisure reading practices of Russian-speaking immigrants in Canada. *Library & Information Science Research*, *34*(3), 197–211. https://doi.org/10.1016/j.lisr.2012.02.004

Dali, K. (2014). From book appeal to reading appeal: Redefining the concept of appeal in readers' advisory. *The Library*, *84*(1), 22–48. https://doi.org/10.1086/674034

Darby, P., & Clough, P. (2013). Investigating the information-seeking behaviour of genealogists and family historians. *Journal of Information Science*, *39*(1), 73–84. https://doi.org/10.1177/0165551512469765

Dervin, B. (1989). Users as research inventions: How research categories perpetuate inequities. *Journal of Communication*, *39*(3), 216–232. https://doi.org/10.1111/j.1460-2466.1989.tb01053.x

Dervin, B. (1997). Given a context by any other name: Methodological tools for taming the unruly beast. In P. Vakkari, R. Savolainen, & B. Dervin (Eds.), *Information seeking in context: Proceedings of a meeting in Finland 14–16 August 1996* (pp. 13–38). Taylor Graham.

Dervin, B., Ellyson, S., Hawkes, G., Guagnano, G., & White, N. (1984). *Information needs of California—1984*. Institute of Governmental Affairs, University of California.

Dewey, J. (1960). *On experience, nature, and freedom*. The Liberal Arts Press.

Diviani, N., Fredriksen, E. H., Meppelink, C. S., Mullan, J., Rich, W., & Sudmann, T. T. (2019). Where else would I look for it? A five-country qualitative study on purposes, strategies, and consequences of online health information seeking. *Journal of Public Health Research*, *8*(1). https://doi.org/10.4081/jphr.2019.1518

Doty, P. (2021). Privacy, surveillance, and the "smart home". In M. G. Ocepek & W. Aspray (Eds.), *Deciding where to live: Information studies on where to live in America* (pp. 93–124). Rowman & Littlefield.

Du, J. T. (2014). The information journey of marketing professionals: Incorporating work task-driven information seeking, information judgments, information use, and information sharing.

Journal of the Association for Information Science and Technology, *65*(9), 1850–1869. https://doi.org/10.1002/asi.23085

Duff, W. M., & Johnson, C. A. (2002). Accidently found on purpose: Information-seeking behavior of historians in archives. *The Library Quarterly*, *72*(4), 472–496. https://www.jstor.org/stable/40039793

Duffy, A. M., Tandoc, E. C., & Ling, R. (2019). Too good to be true, too good not to share: The social utility of fake news. *Information, Communication & Society*, *23*, 1965–1979. https://doi.org/10.1080/1369118X.2019.1623904

Durrance, J. C. (1984). *Armed for action—Library response to citizen information needs*. Neal-Schuman Publishers.

Eskola, E.-L., Khan, K. S., & Widén, G. (2020). Adding the information literacy perspective to refugee integration research discourse: A scoping literature review. In *Proceedings of ISIC, the Information Behaviour Conference*, Pretoria, South Africa, 28–30 September, 2020. *Information Research, 25*(4). http://InformationR.net/ir/25-4/isic2020/isic2009.html

Fallis, D. (2015). What is disinformation? *Library Trends*, *63*(3), 401–426. https://doi.org/10.1353/lib.2015.0014

Fardous, J., Du, J. T., & Hansen, P. (2019). Collaborative information seeking during leisure travelling: Triggers and social media usage. *Information Research*, *24*(3). http://InformationR.net/ir/24-3/paper830.html

Feng, Y., & Agosto, D. E. (2017). The experience of mobile information overload: Struggling between needs and constraints. *Information Research*, *22*(2). http://informationr.net/ir/22-2/paper754.html

Fidel, R., Pejtersen, A. M., Cleal, B., & Bruce, H. (2004). A multidimensional approach to the study of human-information interaction: A case study of collaborative information retrieval. *Journal of the American Society for Information Science and Technology*, *55*, 939–953. https://doi.org/10.1002/asi.20041

Fisher, K. E., Durrance, J. C., & Hinton, M. B. (2004). Information grounds and the use of need-based services by immigrants in Queens, New York: A context-based, outcome evaluation approach. *Journal of the American Society for Information Science and Technology*, *55*(8), 754–766. https://doi.org/10.1002/asi.20019

Fisher, K. E., Marcoux, E., Miller, L. S., Sánchez, A., & Cunningham, E. R. (2004). Information behaviour of migrant Hispanic farm workers and their families in the Pacific Northwest. *Information Research*, *10*(1). http://InformationR.net/ir/10-1/paper199.html

Fisher, K., Naumer, C., Durrance, J., Stromski, L., & Christiansen, T. (2005). Something old, something new: Preliminary findings from an exploratory study about people's information habits and information grounds. *Information Research*, *10*(2). http://InformationR.net/ir/10-2/paper223.html

Forcier, E. (2022). *Everyday onlife practice and information behaviour: A study of media fans in a postdigital age*. Unpublished dissertation. Swinburne University of Technology. http://hdl.handle.net/1959.3/469057

Formanek, R. (1991). Why they collect: Collectors reveal their motivations. *Journal of Social Behavior & Personality*, *6*(6), 275–286.

Foster, A. (2004). A non-linear model of information-seeking behavior. *Journal of the American Society for Information Science and Technology*, *55*(3), 228–237. https://doi.org/10.1002/asi.10359

Foster, A., & Ford, N. (2003). Serendipity and information seeking: An empirical study. *Journal of Documentation*, *59*(3), 321–343. https://doi.org/10.1108/00220410310472518

Fourie, I. (2020). Contextual information behaviour analysis of grief and bereavement: Temporal and spatial factors, multiplicity of contexts and person-in-progressive situation. *Information Research*, *25*(4). http://InformationR.net/ir/25-4/isic2020/isic2003.html

Fox, C. J. (1983). *Information and misinformation*. Greenwood Press.

Foxall, G. R. (1983). *Consumer choice*. St. Martin's Press.

Friday, K. (2014). Learning from e-family history: A model of online family historian research behaviour. *Information Research*, *19*(4). http://informationr.net/ir/19-4/paper641.html

Fulton, C. (2005a). Finding pleasure in information seeking: Leisure and amateur genealogists exploring their Irish ancestry. In A. Grove (Ed.), *Proceedings of the American Society for Information Science and Technology* (Vol. 42, pp. 1292–1303). Information Today.

Fulton, C. (2009a). Quid pro quo: Information sharing in leisure activities. *Library Trends*, *57*(4), 753–768. https://doi.org/10.1353/lib.0.0056

Fulton, C. (2009b). The pleasure principle: The power of positive affect in information seeking. *ASLIB Proceedings*, *61*(3), 245–261. http://doi.org/10.1108/00012530910959808

Fulton, C. (2017). Urban exploration: Secrecy and information creation and sharing in a hobby context. *Library & Information Science Research*, *39*(3), 189–198. https://doi.org/10.1016/j.lisr.2017.07.003

Gallagher, S., & Olsson, M. (2019). Reconciling doctor as clinician and doctor as entrepreneur: The information practices and identity work of early career surgeons. *Information Research*, *24*(3). http://www.informationr.net/ir/24-3/rails/rails1810.html

Gerard, M., Fossa, A., Folcarelli, P. H., Walker, J., & Bell, S. K. (2017). What patients value about reading visit notes: A qualitative inquiry of patient experiences with their health information. *Journal of Medical Internet Research*, *19*(7). https://doi.org/10.2196/jmir.7212

Giannini, T. (1998). Information receiving: A primary mode of the information process. In *Proceedings of the 61st Annual Meeting of the American Society for Information Science* (pp. 362–371). Information Today.

Giles, D. C., Pietrzykowski, S., & Clark, K. E. (2007). The psychological meaning of personal record collections and the impact of changing technological forms. *Journal of Economic Psychology*, *28*(4), 429–443. https://doi.org/10.1016/j.joep.2006.08.002

Given, L. M. (2002a). Discursive constructions in the university context: Social positioning theory and mature undergraduates' information behaviours. *The New Review of Information Behaviour Research: Studies of Information Seeking in Context*, *3*, 127–142.

Given, L. M. (2002b). The academic and the everyday: Investigating the overlap in mature undergraduates' information–seeking behaviors. *Library & Information Science Research*, *24*(1), 17–29. https://doi.org/10.1016/S0740-8188(01)00102-5

Given, L. M. (2005). Social positioning. In K. E. Fisher, S. Erdelez, & E. F. McKechnie (Eds.), *Theories of information behavior* (pp. 334–338). Information Today, Inc.

Given, L. M., & Willson, R. (2015). Collaborative information use with technology: A critical examination of humanities scholars' research activities. In *Collaborative information seeking best practices, new domains and new thoughts* (pp. 139–164). Springer-Verlag. https://doi.org/10.1007/978-3-319-18988-8_8

Godbold, N. (2013). An information need for emotional cues: Unpacking the role of emotions in sense making. *Information Research*, *18*(1). http://informationr.net/ir/18-1/paper561.html

Gorichanaz, T. (2015). Information on the run: Experiencing information during an ultramarathon. *Information Research*, *20*(4). http://InformationR.net/ir/20-4/paper697.html

Gorichanaz, T. (2017). Understanding art-making as documentation. *Art Documentation: Journal of the Art Libraries Society of North America*, *36*(2), 191–203. https://doi.org/10.1086/694239

Gorichanaz, T. (2019). Information creation and models of information behavior: Grounding synthesis and further research. *Journal of Librarianship and Information Science*, *51*(4), 998–1006. https://doi.org/10.1177/0961000618769968

Grad, R., Pluye, P., Granikov, V., Johnson-Lafleur, J., Shulha, M., Sridhar, S. B., Moscovici, J. L., Bartlett, G., Vandal, A. C., Marlow, B., & Kloda, L. (2011). Physicians' assessment of the value of clinical information: Operationalization of a theoretical model. *Journal of the American Society for Information Science and Technology*, *62*(1999), 1884–1891. http://doi.org/10.1002/asi.21590

Granikov, V., El Sherif, R., Bouthillier, F., & Pluye, P. (2022). Factors and outcomes of collaborative information seeking: A mixed studies review with a framework synthesis. *Journal of the Association for Information Science and Technology*, *73*(4), 542–560. https://doi.org/10.1002/asi.24596

Greifeneder, E., & Gäde, M. (2020). Adventures in Winter Wonderland – Observing user behaviour in a digital twin bookstore. In *Proceedings of ISIC, the Information Behaviour Conference*,

Pretoria, South Africa, 28 September-01 October, 2020. *Information Research, 25*(4). http://InformationR.net/ir/25-4/isic2020/isic2028.html

Greyson, D., & Johnson, J. L. (2016). The role of information in health behavior: A scoping study and discussion of major public health models. *Journal of the Association for Information Science and Technology*, *67*(12), 2831–2841. https://doi.org/10.1002/asi.23392

Griffiths, D., Sheehan, L., Petrie, D., van Vreden, C., Whiteford, P., & Collie, A. (2022). The health impacts of a 4-month long community-wide COVID-19 lockdown: Findings from a prospective longitudinal study in the state of Victoria, Australia. *PLoS One*, *17*(4). https://doi.org/10.1371/journal.pone.0266650

Gross, M. (2001). Imposed information seeking in public libraries and school library media centers: A common behaviour? *Information Research*, *6*(2). http://informationr.net/ir/6-2/paper100.html

Gross, M. (2004a). Children's information seeking at school: Findings from a qualitative study. In M. K. Chelton & C. Cool (Eds.), *Youth information-seeking behavior: Theories, models and issues* (pp. 211–240). Scarecrow Press.

Gross, M. (2004b). *Children's questions: Information seeking behavior in school.* Scarecrow Press.

Gross, M., & Saxton, M. (2001). Who wants to know? Imposed queries in the public library. *Public Libraries*, *40*(3), 170–176. https://www.jstor.org/stable/20862879

Guzik, E. (2018). Information sharing as embodied practice in a context of conversion to Islam. *Library Trends*, *66*(3), 351–370. https://doi.org/10.1353/lib.2018.0007

Hamm, M. P., Chisholm, A., Shulhan, J., Milne, A., Scott, S. D., Given, L. M., & Hartling, L. (2013). Social media use among patients and caregivers: A scoping review. *British Medical Journal Open*, *3*(5). https://doi.org/10.1136/bmjopen-2013-002819

Hanlon, S. M. (2021). A dual lens approach to exploring informal communication's influence on learning in a political party. *Journal of Documentation*, *77*(4), 965–989. https://doi.org/10.1108/JD-08-2020-0128

Haras, C. (2011). Information behaviors of Latinos attending high school in East Los Angeles. *Library & Information Science Research*, *33*(1), 34–40. https://doi.org/10.1016/j.lisr.2010.05.001

Harlan, M. A., Bruce, C., & Lupton, M. (2012). Teen content creators: Experiences of using information to learn. *Library Trends*, *60*(3), 569–587. https://doi.org/10.1353/lib.2012.0001

Harlan, M. A., Bruce, C. S., & Lupton, M. (2014). Creating and sharing: Teens' information practices in digital communities. *Information Research*, *19*(1). http://informationr.net/ir/19-1/paper611.html

Harr, R., Nyberg, A., Berggren, M., Carlsson, R., & Källstedt, S. (2016). Friend or foe: Exploring master suppression techniques on Facebook. *Information Research*, *21*(2). http://InformationR.net/ir/21-2/SM4.html

Hartel, J. (2003). The serious leisure frontier in library and information science: Hobby domains. *Knowledge Organization*, *30*(3/4), 228–238.

Hartel, J. (2005). Serious leisure. In K. E. Fisher, S. Erdelez, & E. F. McKechnie (Eds.), *Theories of information behavior* (pp. 313–317). Information Today, Inc.

Hartel, J. (2010). Managing documents at home for serious leisure: A case study of the hobby of gourmet cooking. *Journal of Documentation*, *66*(6), 847–874. https://doi.org/10.1108/00220411011087841

Hartel, J. (2011). Information in the hobby of gourmet cooking: Four contexts. In W. Aspray & B. Hayes (Eds.), *Everyday information: The evolution of information seeking in America* (pp. 217–248). MIT Press.

Hartel, J. (2014a). An interdisciplinary platform for information behavior research in the liberal arts hobby. *Journal of Documentation*, *70*(5), 945–962. https://doi.org/10.1108/JD-08-2013-0110

Hartel, J. (2019). Turn, turn, turn. In *Proceedings of CoLIS, the Tenth International Conference on Conceptions of Library and Information Science*, Ljubljana, Slovenia, June 16–19, 2019. *Information Research, 24*(4). http://InformationR.net/ir/24-4/colis/colis1901.html

Hartel, J., Cox, A. M., & Griffin, B. L. (2016). Information activity in serious leisure. *Information Research*, *21*(4), 1–16. http://informationr.net/ir/21-4/paper728.html

Harviainen, J. T., Lehtonen, M. J., & Kock, S. (2022). Timeliness in information sharing within creative industries. Case: Finnish game design. *Journal of Documentation*, *78*(1), 83–96. https://doi.org/10.1108/JD-12-2020-0207

Heinström, J. (2003). Five personality dimensions and their influence on information behaviour. *Information Research*, *9*(1). http://informationr.net/ir/9-1/paper165.html

Heinström, J. (2006). Psychological factors behind incidental information acquisition. *Library & Information Science Research*, *28*(4), 579–594. http://doi.org/10.1016/j.lisr.2006.03.022

Hektor, A. (2003). Information activities on the Internet in everyday life. *The New Review of Information Behaviour Research*, *4*(1), 127–138.

Hertzum, M., & Hansen, P. (2019). Empirical studies of collaborative information seeking: A review of methodological issues. *Journal of Documentation*, *75*(1), 140–163. https://doi.org/10.1108/JD-05-2018-0072

Hertzum, M., & Reddy, M. C. (2015). Procedures and collaborative information seeking: A study of emergency departments. In *Collaborative information seeking: Best practices, new domains and new thoughts* (pp. 55–71). Springer. https://doi.org/10.1007/978-3-319-18988-8_4

Hirvonen, N., & Palmgren-Neuvonen, L. (2019). Cognitive authorities in health education classrooms: A nexus analysis on group-based learning tasks. *Library & Information Science Research*, *41*(3). https://doi.org/10.1016/j.lisr.2019.100964

Hong, J. Y. J., Kim, N., Lee, S., & Kim, J. H. (2018). Community disaster resilience and social solidarity on social media: A semantic network analysis on the Sewol ferry disaster. *Information Research*, *23*(3). http://InformationR.net/ir/23-3/paper798.html

Huisman, M., Biltereyst, D., & Joye, S. (2020). Sharing is caring: The everyday informal exchange of health information among adults aged fifty and over. *Information Research*, *25*(1). http://InformationR.net/ir/25-1/paper848.html

Hultgren, F., & Limberg, L. (2003). A study of research on children's information behaviour in a school context. *The New Review of Information Behaviour Research*, *4*(1), 1–15.

Huvila, I. (2019). Genres and situational appropriation of information: Explaining not-seeking of information. *Journal of Documentation*, *75*(6), 1503–1527. https://doi.org/10.1108/JD-03-2019-0044

Huvila, I., Cajander, A., Daniels, M., & Åhlfeldt, R. (2015). Patients' perceptions of their medical records from different subject positions. *Journal of the Association for Information Science and Technology*, *66*(12), 2456–2470. https://doi.org/10.1002/asi.23343

Huvila, I., Daniels, M., Cajander, A., & Åhlfeldt, R. (2016). Patients reading medical records: Differences in experiences and attitudes between regular and inexperienced readers. *Information Research*, *21*(1). http://informationr.net/ir/21-1/paper706.html#.Y28xg-xBwUo

Huvila, I., Enwald, H., Eriksson-Backa, M., Hirvonen, N., Nguyen, H., & Scandurra, I. (2018). Anticipating ageing: Older adults reading their medical records. *Information Processing &*, *54*(3), 394–407. https://doi.org/10.1016/j.ipm.2018.01.007

Huvila, I., Moll, J., Enwald, H., Åhlfeldt, R., & Cajander, Å. (2019). Age-related differences in seeking clarification to understand medical record information. *Information Research*, *24*(1). http://InformationR.net/ir/24-1/isic2018/isic1834.html

Hyatt, E. (2017). The information behaviour of Pacific crest Trail thru-hikers: An autoethnographic pilot study. In *Proceedings of ISIC, the Information Behaviour Conference*, Zadar, Croatia, 20–23 September, 2016. Part 2. *Information Research, 22*(1). http://InformationR.net/ir/22-1/isic/isics1607.html

Hyldegård, J. (2009). Beyond the search process – Exploring group members' information behavior in context. *Information Processing & Management*, *45*(1), 142–158. http://doi.org/10.1016/j.ipm.2008.05.007

Isah, E. E., & Byström, K. (2015). Physicians' learning at work through everyday access to information. *Journal of the Association for Information Science & Technology*, *66*, 318–332. https://doi.org/10.1002/asi.23378

Isah, E. E., & Byström, K. (2017). Enacting workplace information practices: The diverse roles of physicians in a health care team. In *Proceedings of the Ninth International Conference on Conceptions of Library and Information Science*, Uppsala, Sweden, June 27–29 2016. *Information Research, 22*(1). http://informationr.net/ir/22-1/colis/colis1650.html

Isah, E. E., & Byström, K. (2020). The mediating role of documents: Information sharing through medical records in healthcare. *Journal of Documentation*, *76*(6), 1171–1191. https://doi.org/10.1108/JD-11-2019-0227

Jamali, H. R., & Nabavi, M. (2022). The use of information behaviour research in human-computer interaction. *Information Research*, *27*(3). http://InformationR.net/ir/27-3/paper937.html

Järvelin, K., & Vakkari, P. (1993). The evolution of library and information science 1965–1985: A content analysis of journal articles. *Information Processing & Management*, *29*(1), 129–144. http://doi.org/10.1016/0306-4573(93)90028-C

Jeong, W. (2004). Unbreakable ethnic bonds: Information-seeking behavior of Korean graduate students in the United States. *Library & Information Science Research*, *26*(3), 384–400. https://doi.org/10.1016/j.lisr.2004.04.001

Jiao, Q., & Onwuegbuzie, A. J. (1997). Antecedents of library anxiety. *The Library Quarterly*, *67*, 372–389. https://www.jstor.org/stable/40039590

Jia, X., Pang, Y., & Liu, S. L. (2021). Online health information seeking behavior: A systematic review. *Healthcare*, *9*(12), 1740. https://doi.org/10.3390/healthcare9121740

Johnson, J. D. (2003). On contexts of information seeking. *Information Processing and Management*, *39*(5), 735–760. https://doi.org/10.1016/S0306-4573(02)00030-4

Johnson, J. D. (2019). Network analysis approaches to collaborative information seeking in inter-professional health care teams. *Information Research*, *24*(1). http://InformationR.net/ir/24-1/paper810.html

Joseph, P. (2016). Australian motor sport enthusiasts' leisure information behaviour. *Journal of Documentation*, *72*(6), 1078–1113. https://doi.org/10.1108/JD-12-2015-0150

Julien, H. (1999). Barriers to adolescent information seeking for career decision making. *Journal of the American Society for Information Science*, *50*, 38–48. https://doi.org/10.1002/(SICI)1097-4571(1999)50:1%3C38::AID-ASI6%3E3.0.CO;2-G

Julien, H., McKechnie, L., Polkinghorne, S., & Chabot, R. (2018). The "user turn" in practice: Information behaviour researchers' constructions of information users. *Information Research*, *23*(4). http://www.informationr.net/ir/23-4/isic2018/isic1804.html

Julien, H., Pecoskie, J. L., & Reed, K. (2011). Trends in information behavior research, 1999–2008: A content analysis. *Library & Information Science Research*, *33*(1), 19–24.

Jung, J.-Y. (2012). Social media use and goals after the Great East Japan earthquake. *First Monday*, *17*(8). http://firstmonday.org/ojs/index.php/fm/article/view/4071/3285

Kainat, K., Eskola, E.-L., & Widén, G. (2022). Sociocultural barriers to information and integration of women refugees. *Journal of Documentation*, *78*(5), 1131–1148. https://doi.org/10.1108/JD-05-2021-0107

Kalms, B. (2008). Household information practices: How and why householders process and manage information. *Information Research*, *13*(1). http://InformationR.net/ir/13-1/paper339.html

Kari, J. (2007). Conceptualizing the personal outcomes of information. *Information Research*, *12*(2). http://InformationR.net/ir/12-2/paper292.html

Kari, J. (2010). Diversity in the conceptions of information use. *Information Research*, *15*(3), 15-3. http://informationr.net/ir/15-3/colis7/colis709.html

Kari, J., & Savolainen, R. (2003). Towards a contextual model of information seeking on the Web. *The New Review of Information Behaviour Research*, *4*(1), 155–175.

Karlova, N. A., & Fisher, K. E. (2013). A social diffusion model of misinformation and disinformation for understanding human information behaviour. *Information Research*, *18*(1). http://InformationR.net/ir/18-1/paper573.html

Karlsson, L., Koivula, L., Ruokonen, I., Kajaani, P., Antikainen, L., & Ruismäki, H. (2012). From novice to expert: Information seeking processes of university students and researchers. *Procedia – Social and Behavioral Sciences*, *45*, 577–587. http://doi.org/10.1016/j.sbspro.2012.06.595

Kaye, B. K., & Johnson, T. J. (2003). From here to obscurity?: Media substitution theory and traditional media in an on-line world. *Journal of the American Society for Information Science and Technology*, *54*(3), 260–273. https://doi.org/10.1002/asi.10212

Kennan, M. A., Lloyd, A., Qayyum, A., & Thompson, K. M. (2011). Settling in: The relationship between information and social inclusion. *Australian Academic & Research Libraries*, *43*(2), 191–210. https://doi.org/10.1080/00048623.2011.10722232

Kerins, G., Madden, R., & Fulton, C. (2004). Information seeking and students studying for professional careers: The cases of engineering and law students in Ireland. *Information Research*, *10*(1). http://InformationR.net/ir/10-1/paper208.html

Khan, K. S., & Eskola, E.-L. (2020). The cultural landscape of women refugees in Sweden – A road to information and integration. In *Proceedings of ISIC, the Information Behaviour Conference*, Pretoria, South Africa, 28–30 September, 2020. *Information Research, 25*(4). http://InformationR.net/ir/25-4/isic2020/isic2033.html

Khoir, S., Du, J. T., & Koronios, A. (2015). Everyday information behaviour of Asian immigrants in South Australia: A mixed-methods exploration. *Information Research*, *20*(3). http://InformationR.net/ir/20-3/paper687.html

Kim, S., Sinn, D., & Syn, S. Y. S. (2020). Personal health information management by college students: Patterns of inaction. *Information Research*, *25*(1). http://InformationR.net/ir/25-1/paper851.html

Kim, S., & Syn, S. Y. S. (2016). Credibility and usefulness of health information on Facebook: A survey study with U.S. College students. *Information Research*, *21*(4). http://informationr.net/ir/21-4/paper727.html

Kim, Y.-M. (2015). Is seeking health information online different fromseeking general information online? *Journal of Information Science*, *4*(2), 228–241. https://doi.org/10.1177/0165551514561669

Kirk, J. (2002). *Theorising information use: Managers and their work*. (Unpublished doctoral dissertation). University of Technology, Sydney, Australia. https://opus.lib.uts.edu.au/bitstream/2100/309/2/02whole.pdf

Koh, K. (2013). Adolescents' information-creating behavior embedded in digital media practice using Scratch. *Journal of the American Society for Information Science and Technology*, *64*(9), 1826–1841. https://doi.org/10.1002/asi.22878

Kostagiolas, P. A., Lavranos, C., Korfiatis, N., Papadatos, J., & Papavlasopoulos, S. (2015). Music, musicians and information seeking behaviour: A case study on a community concert band. *Journal of Documentation*, *71*(1), 3–24. https://doi.org/10.1108/JD-07-2013-0083

Kuhlthau, C. C. (1988a). Developing a model of the library search process: Cognitive and affective aspects. *Reference Quarterly*, *28*, 232–242. https://www.jstor.org/stable/25828262

Kuhlthau, C. C. (1991). Inside the search process: Information seeking from the user's perspective. *Journal of the American Society for Information Science*, *42*, 361–371. https://doi.org/10.1002/(SICI)1097-4571(199106)42:5%3C361::AID-ASI6%3E3.0.CO;2-%23

Lachlan, K., Hutter, E., & Gilbert, C. (2021). COVID-19 echo chambers: Examining the impact of conservative and liberal news sources on risk perception and response. *Health Security*, *19*(1), 21–30. https://doi.org/10.1089/hs.2020.0176

Landry, C. F. (2021). Home buying in everyday life: How emotion and time pressure shape high-stakes deciders' information behavior. In M. G. Ocepek & W. Aspray (Eds.), *Deciding where to live: Information studies on where to live in America* (pp. 237–258). Rowman & Littlefield.

Laplante, A., & Downie, J. S. (2011). The utilitarian and hedonic outcomes of music information-seeking in everyday life. *Library & Information Science Research*, *33*(3), 202–210. http://doi.org/10.1016/j.lisr.2010.11.002

Laukka, E., Rantakokko, P., & Suhonen, M. (2019). Consumer-led health-related online sources and their impact on consumers: An integrative review of the literature. *Health Informatics Journal*, *25*(2), 247–266. https://doi.org/10.1177/1460458217704254

Le Louvier, K., & Innocenti, P. (2021). Heritage as an affective and meaningful information literacy practice: An interdisciplinary approach to the integration of asylum seekers and refugees. *Journal of the Association for Information Science and Technology*, *73*(5), 687–701. https://doi.org/10.1002/asi.24572

Leckie, G. J., & Given, L. M. (2005). Understanding information-seeking: The public library context. *Advances in Librarianship*, *29*(1). https://doi.org/10.1016/S0065-2830(05)29001-3

Lee, S. (2017). Implications of counter-attitudinal information exposure in further information-seeking and attitude change. *Information Research*, *22*(3). http://InformationR.net/ir/22-3/paper766.html

Lee, S. Y. (2018). Effects of relational characteristics of an answerer on perceived credibility of informational posts on social networking sites: The case of Facebook. *Information Research*, *23*(3). http://InformationR.net/ir/23-3/paper796.html

Lee, J. H., & Downie, J. S. (2004). *Survey of music information needs, uses, and seeking behaviours: Preliminary findings* (Vol. 2004, 5th ed.). ISMIR.

Lee, J., & Kang, J. H. (2018). Crying mothers mobilise for a collective action: Collaborative information behaviour in an online community. *Information Research*, *23*(2). http://InformationR.net/ir/23-2/paper792.html

Lee, J. Y., Paik, W., & Joo, S. (2012). Information resource selection of undergraduate students in academic search tasks. *Information Research*, *17*(1). http://InformationR.net/ir/17-1/paper511.html

Lee, C. P., & Trace, C. B. (2009). The role of information in a community of hobbyist collectors. *Journal of the American Society for Information Science and Technology*, *60*(3), 621–637. https://doi.org/10.1002/asi.20996

Lilley, S. C. (2008). Information barriers and Māori secondary school students. *Information Research*, *13*(4). http://InformationR.net/ir/13-4/paper373.html

Lindau, S. T., Makelarski, J. A., Abramsohn, E., Beiser, D., Boyd, K., Huang, E., Paradise, K., & Tung, E. (2022). Sharing information about health-related resources: Observations from a community resource referral intervention trial in a predominantly African American/Black community. *Journal of the Association for Information Science and Technology*, *73*(3), 438–448. https://doi.org/10.1002/asi.24560

Lingel, J. (2015). Information practices of urban newcomers: An analysis of habits and wandering. *Journal of the Association for Information Science & Technology*, *66*(6), 1239–1251. http://doi.org/10.1002/asi.23255

Little, R., Williams, C., & Yost, J. (2011). Airline travel: A history of information-seeking behavior by leisure and business passengers. In W. Aspray & B. Hayes (Eds.), *Everyday information: The evolution of information seeking in America* (pp. 121–156). MIT Press.

Lloyd, A. (2007a). Learning to put out the red stuff: Becoming information literate through discursive practice. *The Library Quarterly*, *77*(2), 181–198. https://doi.org/10.1086/517844

Lloyd, A. (2007b). Recasting information literacy as socio-cultural practice: Implications for library and information science researchers. *Information Research*, *12*(4). http://informationr.net/ir/12-4/colis/colis34.html

Lloyd, A. (2009). Informing practice: Information experiences of ambulance officers in training and on-road practice. *Journal of Documentation*, *65*(3), 396–419. http://doi.org/10.1108/00220410910952401

Lloyd, A. (2010). Corporeality and practice theory: Exploring emerging research agendas for information literacy. *Information Research*, *15*(3). http://InformationR.net/ir/15-3/colis7/colis704.html

Lloyd, A. (2014). Following the red thread of information in information literacy research: Recovering local knowledge through interview to the double. *Library & Information Science Research*, *36*(2), 99–105. https://doi.org/10.1016/j.lisr.2013.10.006

Lloyd, A. (2017). Researching fractured (information) landscapes: Implications for library and information science researchers undertaking research with refugees and forced migration studies. *Journal of Documentation*, *73*(1), 35–47. https://doi.org/10.1108/JD-03-2016-0032

Lloyd, A. (2020). Shaping the contours of fractured landscapes: Extending the layering of an information perspective on refugee resettlement. *Information Processing & Management*, *57*(3), 102062. https://doi.org/10.1016/j.ipm.2019.102062

Lloyd, A. (2021). *The qualitative landscape of information literacy research: Perspectives, methods and techniques*. Facet Publishing.

Lloyd, A., & Hicks, A. (2021). Contextualising risk: The unfolding information work and practices of people during the COVID-19 pandemic. *Journal of Documentation*, *77*(5), 1052–1072. https://doi.org/10.1108/JD-11-2020-0203

Lloyd, A., Kennan, M. A., Thompson, K. M., & Qayyum, A. (2013). Connecting with new information landscapes: Information literacy practices of refugees. *Journal of Documentation*, *69*(1), 121–144. http://doi.org/10.1108/00220411311295351

Lloyd, A., Lipu, S., & Kennan, M. A. (2010). On becoming citizens: Examining social inclusion from an information perspective. *Australian Academic and Research Libraries*, *41*(1), 42–53. https://doi.org/10.1080/00048623.2016.1256806

Lloyd, A., & Olsson, M. (2019). Untangling the knot: The information practices of enthusiast car restorers. *Journal of the Association for Information Science and Technology*, *70*(12), 1311–1323. https://doi.org/10.1002/asi.24284

Lloyd, A., Pilerot, O., & Hultgren, F. (2017). The remaking of fractured landscapes: Supporting refugees in transition (SpiRiT). *Information Research*, *22*(3). http://InformationR.net/ir/21-1/paper764.html

Loos, E., Ivan, L., & Leu, D. (2018). Save the Pacific Northwest tree octopus: A hoax revisited. Or: How vulnerable are school children to fake news? *Information and Learning Sciences*, *119*(9/10), 514–528. https://doi.org/10.1108/ILS-04-2018-0031

Loudon, K., Buchanan, S., & Ruthven, I. (2016). The everyday life information seeking behaviours of first-time mothers. *Journal of Documentation*, *72*(1), 24–46. https://doi.org/10.1108/JD-06-2014-0080

Lueg, C. P. (2008). Beyond FAQs: From information sharing to knowledge generation in online travel communities. In M.-L. Houtari & E. Davenport (Eds.), *Presented at from information provision to knowledge production* (pp. 105–120). Faculty of Humanities, University of Oulu.

Lueg, C. P. (2015). The missing link: Information behavior research and its estranged relationship with embodiment. *Journal of the Association for Information Science and Technology*, *66*(12), 2704–2707. https://doi.org/10.1002/asi.23441

Mansourian, Y. (2020). How passionate people seek and share various forms of information in their serious leisure. *Journal of the Australian Library and Information Association*, *69*(1), 17–30. https://doi.org/10.1080/24750158.2019.1686569

Mansourian, Y. (2021). Information activities in serious leisure as a catalyst for self-actualisation and social engagement. *Journal of Documentation*, *77*(4), 887–905. https://doi.org/10.1108/JD-08-2020-0134

Margree, P., Macfarlane, A., Price, L., & Robinson, L. (2014). Information behaviour of music record collectors. *Information Research*, *19*(4). http://informationr.net/ir/19-4/paper652.html

Martinović, I., & Stričević, I. (2016). Information needs and behaviour of parents of children with autism spectrum disorders: Parents' reports on their experiences and perceptions. In *Proceedings of ISIC, the Information Behaviour Conference*, Zadar, Croatia, 20–23 September, 2016. Part 1. *Information Research, 21*(4). http://InformationR.net/ir/21-4/isic/isic1609.html

Martzoukou, K. (2005). A review of web information seeking research: Considerations of method and foci of interest. *Information Research*, *10*(2). http://InformationR.net/ir/10-2/paper215.html

Martzoukou, K., & Burnett, S. (2018). Exploring the everyday life information needs and the socio-cultural adaption barriers of Syrian refugee in Scotland. *Journal of Documentation*, *74*(5), 1104–1132. https://doi.org/10.1108/JD-10-2017-0142

Mason, D., & Lamain, C. (2007). *Nau mai haere mai ki Aotearoa: Information seeking behaviour of New Zealand immigrants*. The Centre for Applied Cross-cultural Research, Victoria University of Wellington.

Matusiak, K. K., Heinbach, C., Harper, A., & Bovee, M. (2019). Visual literacy in practice: Use of images in students' academic work. *College & Research Libraries*, *80*(1), 123. https://doi.org/10.5860/crl.80.1.123

McKenzie, P. J. (2009). Informing choice: The organization of institutional interaction in clinical midwifery care. *Library & Information Science Research*, *31*(3), 163–173. https://doi.org/10.1016/j.lisr.2009.03.006

McKenzie, P. J. (2010). Informing relationships: Small talk, informing and relationship building in midwife-woman interaction. *Information Research*, *15*(1). http://InformationR.net/ir/15-1/paper423.html

Mehra, B. (2007). Affective factors in informtion seeking during the cross-cultural learning process of international doctoral students in library and information science education. In D. Nahl & D. Bilal (Eds.), *Information and emotion: The emergent affective paradigm in information behavior research and theory* (pp. 279–301). Information Today.

Mellon, C. (1986). Library anxiety: A grounded theory and its development. *College and Research Libraries*, *47*, 160–165.

Mikkonen, A., & Vakkari, P. (2016). Readers' interest criteria in fiction book search in library catalogs. *Journal of Documentation*, *72*(4), 696–715. https://doi.org/10.1108/JDOC-11-2015-0142

Mishra, J., Allen, D., & Pearman, A. (2015). Information seeking, use, and decision making. *Journal of the Association for Information Science and Technology*, *66*(4), 662–673. https://doi.org/10.1002/asi.23204

Molto, M. B. (2010). Genealogical literature and its users In *Encyclopedia of library and information science* (pp. 1–46). Taylor & Francis.

Moore, M., & Singley, E. (2019). Understanding the information behaviors of doctoral students: An exploratory study. *Portal: Libraries and the Academy*, *19*(2), 279–293. https://doi.org/10.1353/pla.2019.0016

Moring, C. (2017). Newcomer information seeking: The role of information seeking in newcomer socialization and learning in the workplace. *Information Research*, *22*(1), 1–21. http://www.informationr.net/ir/22-1/isic/isic1616.html

Murthy, D., & Longwell, S. A. (2013). Twitter and disasters: The uses of Twitter during the 2010 Pakistan floods. *Information, Communication & Society*, *16*(6), 837–855. https://doi.org/10.1080/1369118X.2012.696123

Naeem, S. B., Bhatti, R., & Khan, A. M. (2020). An exploration of how fake news is taking over social media and putting public health at risk. *Health Information and Libraries Journal*, *38*(2), 143–149. https://doi.org/10.1111/hir.12320

Naslund, J. A., Aschbrenner, K. A., Marsch, L. A., & Bartels, S. J. (2016). The future of mental health care: Peer-to-peer support and social media. *Epidemiology and Psychiatric Sciences*, *25*(2), 113–122. https://doi.org/10.1017/S2045796015001067

Nilsen, J. (2020). Distributed amplification: The plandemic documentary. *The Media Manipulation Case Book*. July 7, 2021. https://mediamanipulation.org/case-studies/distributed-amplification-plandemic-documentary

Nowé Hedvall, K., Gärdén, C., Ahlryd, S., Michnik, K., Carlén, U., & Byström, K. (2017). Social media in serious leisure: Themes of horse rider safety. *Information Research*, *22*(4). http://InformationR.net/ir/22-4/paper772.html

Ocepek, M. G. (2021). This *old house, fixer upper*, and *better Homes and gardens*: The housing crisis and media sources. In M. G. Ocepek & W. Aspray (Eds.), *Deciding where to live: Information studies on where to live in America* (pp. 125–150). Rowman & Littlefield.

Ocepek, M. G., & Aspray, W. (Eds.). (2021). *Deciding where to live: Information studies on where to live in America*. Rowman & Littlefield.

O'Connor, L. G. (2011). Duct tape and WD-40: The information worlds of female investors. *Library & Information Science Research*, *33*, 228–235. https://doi.org/10.1016/j.lisr.2010.09.009

O'Connor, L. G. (2013). Investors' information sharing and use in virtual communities. *Journal of the American Society for Information Science and Technology*, *64*(1), 36–47. http://doi.org/10.1002/asi.22791

O'Connor, L. G., & Dillingham, L. L. (2014). Personal experience as social capital in online investor forums. *Library & Information Science Research*, *36*(1), 27–35. http://doi.org/10.1016/j.lisr.2013.10.001

Oduntan, O., & Ruthven, I. (2019). The information needs matrix: A navigational guide for refugee integration. *Information Processing & Management*, *56*(3), 791–808. https://doi.org/10.1016/j.ipm.2018.12.001

Oh, T. T., & Pham, M. T. (2022). A liberating-engagement theory of consumer fun. *Journal of Consumer Research*, *49*(1), 46–73. https://doi.org/10.1093/jcr/ucab051

Oh, S., & Worrall, A. (2013). Health answer quality evaluation by librarians, nurses, and users in social Q&A. *Library & Information Science Research*, *35*(4), 288–298. https://doi.org/10.1016/j.lisr.2013.04.007

Oh, S., Zhang, Y., & Park, M. S. (2016). Cancer information seeking in social question and answer services: Identifying health-related topics in cancer questions on Yahoo! Answers. *Information Research*, *21*(3). http://informationr.net/ir/21-3/paper718.html#.Y3AV5exBwUo

Oliveira, R. A. de, & Baracho, R. M. A. (2018). The development of tourism indicators through the use of social media data: The case of Minas Gerais. *Brazil Information Research*, *23*(4). http://informationr.net/ir/23-4/paper805.html

Olsson, M. R. (2010a). All the world's a stage – The information practices and sense-making of theatre professionals. *Libri*, *60*(3), 241–252. http://doi.org/10.1515/libr.2010.021

Olsson, M. R. (2010b). Michel Foucault: Discourse, power/knowledge, and the battle for truth. In G. J. Leckie, L. M. Given, & J. E. Buschman (Eds.), *Critical theory for library and information science: Exploring the social from across the disciplines* (pp. 63–74). Libraries Unlimited.

Olsson, M. (2016). Making sense of the past: The embodied information practices of field archaeologists. *Journal of Information Science*, *42*(3), 410–419. https://doi.org/10.1177/0165551515621839

Olsson, M., & Lloyd, A. (2017). Being in place: Embodied information practices. *Information Research*, *22*(1). http://InformationR.net/ir/22-1/colis/colis1601.html

Osatuyi, B. (2013). Information sharing on social media sites. *Computers in Human Behavior*, *29*(6), 2622–2631. https://doi.org/10.1016/j.chb.2013.07.001

Otto, J., Metz, S., & Ensmenger, N. (2011). Sports fans and their information-gathering habits: How media technologies have brought fans closer to their teams over time. In W. Aspray & B. Hayes (Eds.), *Everyday information: The evolution of information seeking in America* (pp. 185–216). MIT Press.

Paisley, W. J. (1968). Information needs and uses. In C. Cuadra (Ed.), *Annual review of information science and technology* (Vol. 3, pp. 1–30). Encyclopaedia Britannica.

Palmer, R., Lemoh, C., Tham, R., Hakim, S., & Biggs, B. A. (2009). Sudanese women living in Victoria, Australia: Health-information-seeking behaviours and the availability, effectiveness and appropriateness of HIV/AIDS information. *Diversity in Health and Care*, *6*(2), 109–120.

Palmer, C. L., & Neumann, L. J. (2002). The information work of interdisciplinary humanities scholars: Exploration and translation. *The Library Quarterly*, *72*(1), 85–117. https://www.jstor.org/stable/4309582

Palmer, C. L., Teffeau, L. C., & Pirmann, C. M. (2009). *Scholarly information practices in the online environment: Themes from the literature and implications for library service development* (p. 59). OCLC. http://www.oclc.org/research/publications/library/2009/2009-02.pdf

Pálsdóttir, Á. (2008). Information behaviour, health self-efficacy beliefs and health behaviour in Icelanders' everyday life. *Information Research*, *13*(1). http://informationr.net/ir/13-1/paper334.html

Pálsdóttir, Á. (2010). The connection between purposive information seeking and information encountering: A study of Icelanders' health and lifestyle information seeking. *Journal of Documentation*, *66*(2), 224–244. http://doi.org/10.1108/00220411011023634

Pálsdóttir, Á. (2011). Opportunistic discovery of information by elderly Icelanders and their relatives. *Information Research*, *16*(3). http://informationr.net/ir/16-3/paper485.html

Pálsdóttir, Á. (2014). Preferences in the use of social media for seeking and communicating health and lifestyle information. *Information Research*, *19*(4). http://www.informationr.net/ir/19-4/paper642.html#.VN004FOUcqY

Pettigrew, K. E., Durrance, J. C., & Unruh, K. T. (2002). Facilitating community information seeking using the Internet: Findings from three public library-community network systems. *Journal of the American Society for Information Science and Technology*, *53*(11), 894–903. https://doi.org/10.1002/asi.10120

Pilerot, O. (2013). A practice theoretical exploration of information sharing and trust in a dispersed community of design scholars. *Information Research*, *18*(4). http://informationr.net/ir/18-4/paper595.html

Pilerot, O. (2014). Making design researchers' information sharing visible through material objects. *Journal of the American Society for Information Science & Technology*, *65*(10), 2006–2016. http://doi.org/10.1002/asi.23108

Pilerot, O. (2018). The practice of public library-work for newly arrived immigrants. *Information Research*, *23*(4). http://InformationR.net/ir/23-4/isic2018/isic1806.html

Pluye, P., El Sherif, R., Granikov, V., Hong, Q. N., Vedel, I., Galvao, M. C. B., Frati, F. E., Desroches, S., Repchinsky, C., Rihoux, B., Légaré, F., Burnand, B., Bujold, M., & Grad, R. (2019). Health outcomes of online consumer health information: A systematic mixed studies review with framework synthesis. *Journal of the Association for Information Science and Technology*, *70*(7), 643–659. https://doi.org/10.1002/asi.24178

Pluye, P., Grad, R., Repchinsky, C., Jovaisas, B., Johnson-Lafleur, J., Carrier, M.-E., ... Légaré, F. (2013). Four levels of outcomes of information-seeking: A mixed methods study in primary health care. *Journal of the American Society for Information Science and Technology*, *64*(1), 108–125. http://doi.org/10.1002/asi.22793

Polkinghorne, S. C. (2021). *Exploring everyday information practices: Embodied mutual constitution of people's complex relationships with food.* Unpublished dissertation, Swinburne University of Technology.

Polkinghorne, S., & Given, L. M. (2021). Holistic information research: From rhetoric to paradigm. *Journal of the Association for Information Science and Technology*, *72*(10), 1261–1271. https://doi.org/10.1002/asi.24450

Price, L., & Robinson, L. (2017). 'Being in a knowledge space': Information behaviour of cult media fan communities. *Journal of Information Science*, *43*(5), 649–664. https://doi.org/10.1177/0165551516658821

Prigoda, E., & McKenzie, P. J. (2007). Purls of wisdom: A collectivist study of human information behaviour in a public library knitting group. *Journal of Documentation*, *63*(1), 90–114. https://doi.org/10.1108/00220410710723902

Qayyum, A., Thompson, K. M., Kennan, M. A., & Lloyd, A. (2014). The provision and sharing of information between service providers and settling refugees. *Information Research*, *19*(2). http://informationr.net/ir/19-2/paper616.html

Rampersad, G., & Althiyabi, T. (2019). Fake news: Acceptance by demographics and culture on social media. *Journal of Information Technology & Politics*, *17*(1), 1–11. https://doi.org/10.1080/19331681.2019.1686676

Rasmussen Pennington, D., Richardson, G., Garinger, C., & Contursi, M. L. (2013). "I could be on Facebook by now": Insights from Canadian youth on online mental health information resources. *Canadian Journal of Information and Library Science*, *37*(3), 183–200.

Reddy, M. C., & Jansen, B. J. (2008). A model for understanding collaborative information behavior in context: A study of two healthcare teams. *Information Processing and Management*, *44*, 256–273. https://doi.org/10.1016/j.ipm.2006.12.010

Reddy, M. C., & Spence, P. R. (2008). Collaborative information seeking: A field study of a multidisciplinary patient care team. *Information Processing & Management*, *44*(1), 242–255. https://doi.org/10.1016/j.ipm.2006.12.003

Rich, R. F. (1975). Selective utilization of social science related information by federal policy-makers. *Inquiry: A Journal of Medical Care Organization, Provision and Financing*, *13*(3), 72–81.

Rich, R. F. (1997). Measuring knowledge utilization: Processes and outcomes. *Knowledge and Policy*, *10*(3), 11–24. https://doi.org/10.1007/BF02912504

Robinson, J., & Yerbury, H. (2015). Re-enactment and its information practices: Tensions between the individual and the collective. *Journal of Documentation*, *71*(3), 591–608. https://doi.org/10.1108/JD-03-2014-0051

Rolls, K., & Massey, D. (2021). Social media is a source of health-related misinformation. *Evidence-Based Nursing*, *24*(2), 46. http://dx.doi.org/10.1136/ebnurs-2019-103222

Romer, D., & Jamieson, K. H. (2020). Conspiracy theories as barriers to controlling the spread of COVID-19 in the U.S. *Social Science & Medicine*, *263*(113356). https://doi.org/10.1016/j.socscimed.2020.113356

Rosch, E., & Lloyd, B. (Eds.). (1978). *Cognition and categorization*. Lawrence Erlbaum Associates.

Ross, C. S. (1999). Finding without seeking: The information encounter in the context of reading for pleasure. *Information Processing & Management*, *35*, 783–799. https://doi.org/10.1016/S0306-4573(99)00026-6

Ross, C., Terras, M., Warwick, C., & Welsh, A. (2011). Enabled backchannel: Conference Twitter use by digital humanists. *Journal of Documentation*, *67*(2), 214–237. https://doi.org/10.1108/00220411111109449

Rothschild, N., & Aharony, N. (2016). Empathetic communication among discourse participants in virtual communities of people who suffer from mental illnesses. *Information Research*, *21*(1). http://InformationR.net/ir/21-1/paper701.html

Ruokolainen, H., & Widén, G. (2020). Conceptualising misinformation in the context of asylum seekers. *Information Processing & Management*, *57*(3). https://doi.org/10.1016/j.ipm.2019.102127

Ruthven, I. (2021). Resonance and the experience of relevance. *Journal of the Association for Information Science and Technology*, *72*(5), 554–569. https://doi.org/10.1002/asi.24424

Ryan, F. V. C., Cruickshank, P., Hall, H., & Lawson, A. (2016). Managing and evaluating personal reputations on the basis of information shared on social media: A generation X perspective. *Information Research*, *21*(4). http://informationr.net/ir/21-4/isic/isic1612.html

Saastamoinen, M., & Järvelin, K. (2018). Relationships between work task types, complexity and dwell time of information resources. *Journal of Information Science*, *44*(2), 265–284.

Salzano, R., Hall, H., & Webster, G. (2020). Investigating the 'why?' rather than the 'how?': Current research priorities on the influence of culture on newcomer populations' use of public libraries. In *Proceedings of ISIC, the Information Behaviour Conference*, Pretoria, South Africa, 28 September – 1 October, 2020. *Information Research, 25*(4). http://InformationR.net/ir/25-4/isic2020/isic2032.html

Savolainen, R. (1993). The sense-making theory: Reviewing the interests of a user-centered approach to information seeking and use. *Information Processing & Management*, *29*(1), 13–28. https://doi.org/10.1016/0306-4573(93)90020-E

Savolainen, R. (1995). Everyday life information seeking: Approaching information seeking in the context of "way of life". *Library & Information Science Research*, *17*(3), 259–294. https://doi.org/10.1016/0740-8188(95)90048-9

Savolainen, R. (1999). Seeking and using information for the internet: The context of non-work use. In T. D. Wilson & D. K. Allen (Eds.), *Information behaviour: Proceedings of the second international conference on research in information needs, seeking and use in different contexts, 13/15 August 1998, Sheffield, UK* (pp. 356–370). Taylor Graham.

Savolainen, R. (2001). "Living encyclopedia" or idle talk? Seeking and providing consumer information in an internet newsgroup. *Library & Information Science Research*, *23*(1), 67–90. https://doi.org/10.1016/S0740-8188(00)00068-2

Savolainen, R. (2004). Enthusiastic, realistic and critical: Discourses of internet use in the context of everyday life information seeking. *Information Research*, *10*(1). http://InformationR.net/ir/10-1/paper198.html

Savolainen, R. (2008a). Autonomous, controlled and half-hearted. Unemployed people's motivations to seek information about jobs. *Information Research*, *13*(4). http://informationr.net/ir/13-4/paper362.html

Savolainen, R. (2009a). Information use and information processing: Comparison of conceptualizations. *Journal of Documentation*, *65*(2), 187–207. http://doi.org/10.1108/00220410910937570

Savolainen, R. (2009b). Small world and information grounds as contexts of information seeking and sharing. *Library & Information Science Research*, *31*(1), 38–45. http://doi.org/10.1016/j.lisr.2008.10.007

Savolainen, R. (2010). Source preference criteria in the context of everyday projects: Relevance judgments made by prospective home buyers. *Journal of Documentation*, *66*(2), 70–92. http://doi.org/10.1108/00220411011016371

Savolainen, R. (2012a). Conceptualizing information need in context. *Information Research*, *17*(4). http://InformationR.net/ir/17-4/paper534.html

Savolainen, R. (2013). Approaching the motivators for information seeking: The viewpoint of attribution theories. *Library & Information Science Research*, *35*(1), 63–68. https://doi.org/10.1016/j.lisr.2012.07.004

Savolainen, R. (2014). Emotions as motivators for information seeking: A conceptual analysis. *Library & Information Science Research*, *36*(1), 59–65. http://doi.org/10.1016/j.lisr.2013.10.004

Savolainen, R. (2015a). Expressing emotions in information sharing: A study of online discussion about immigration. *Information Research*, *20*(1). http://InformationR.net/ir/20-1/paper662.html

Savolainen, R. (2019). Sharing information through book reviews in blogs: The viewpoint of Rosenblatt's reader-response theory. *Journal of Documentation*, *76*(2), 440–461. https://doi.org/10.1108/JD-08-2019-0161

Savolainen, R. (2021). Levels of critique in models and concepts of human information behaviour research. *Aslib Journal of Information Management*, *73*(5), 772–791. https://doi.org/10.1108/AJIM-01-2021-0028

Savolainen, R., & Kari, J. (2004a). Conceptions of the Internet in everyday life information seeking. *Journal of Information Science*, *30*(3), 219–226. https://doi.org/10.1177/0165551504044667

Savolainen, R., & Kari, J. (2004b). Placing the internet in information source horizons. A study of information seeking by internet users in the context of self-development. *Library & Information Science Research*, *26*(4), 415–433. https://doi.org/10.1016/j.lisr.2004.04.004

Schlebbe, K. (2020). Support versus restriction: Parents' influence on young children's information behaviour in connection with mobile devices. In *Proceedings of ISIC, the Information Behaviour Conference*, Pretoria, South Africa, 28 September – 1 October, 2020. *Information Research, 25*(4). http://InformationR.net/ir/25-4/isic2020/isic2006.html

Scott, S. D., Albrecht, L., Given, L. M., Hartling, L., Johnson, D. W., Jabbour, M., & Klassen, T. P. (2017). Pediatric information seeking behaviour, information needs, and information preferences of health care professionals in general emergency departments: Results from the Translating Emergency Knowledge for Kids (TREKK) needs assessment. *Canadian Journal of Emergency Medicine*, *20*(1), 89–99. http://dx.doi.org/10.1017/cem.2016.406

Seldén, L. (2001). Academic information seeking—Careers and capital types. *New Review of Information Behaviour Research*, *2*, 195–216.

Shah, C. (2014). Collaborative information seeking. *Journal of the American Society for Information Science and Technology*, *65*(2), 215–236. https://doi.org/10.1002/asi.22977

Shah, C., & Leeder, C. (2016). Exploring collaborative work among graduate students through the C5 model of collaboration: A diary study. *Journal of Information Science*, *42*(5), 609–629. https://doi.org/10.1177/0165551515603322

Shoham, S., & Strauss, S. (2007). Information needs of North American immigrants to Israel. *Journal of Information, Communication and Ethics in Society*, *5*(2/3), 185–205. https://doi.org/10.1108/14779960710837641

Shuker, R. (2010). *Wax trash and vinyl treasures: Record collecting as a social practice*. Ashgate.

Sin, S.-C. J., & Kim, K.-S. (2013). International students' everyday life information seeking: The informational value of social networking sites. *Library & Information Science Research*, *35*(2), 107–116. http://doi.org/10.1016/j.lisr.2012.11.006

Skøtt, B. (2019). Newcomers at the library: A library perspective on the integration of new citizens. In *Proceedings of the Tenth International Conference on Conceptions of Library and Information Science*, Ljubljana, Slovenia, June 16–19, 2019. *Information Research, 24*(4). http://InformationR.net/ir/24-4/colis/colis1947.html

Skov, M. (2013). Hobby-related information-seeking behaviour of highly dedicated online museum visitors. *Information Research*, *18*(4). http://www.informationr.net/ir/18-4/paper597.html

Sligo, F. X., & Jameson, A. M. (2000). The knowledge-behavior gap in use of health information. *Journal of the American Society for Information Science*, *51*(9), 858–869. https://doi.org/10.1002/(SICI)1097-4571(2000)51:9%3C858::AID-ASI80%3E3.0.CO;2-Q

Smith, L. N., & McMenemy, D. (2017). Young people's conceptions of political information: Insights into information experiences and implications for intervention. *Journal of Documentation*, *73*(5), 877–902. https://doi.org/10.1108/JD-03-2017-0041

Søe, S. O. (2018). Algorithmic detection of misinformation and disinformation: Gricean perspectives. *Journal of Documentation*, *75*(5), 1013–1034. https://doi.org/10.1108/JD-05-2017-0075

Sonnenwald, D. H., Söderholm, H. M., Welch, G. F., Cairns, B. A., Manning, J. E., & Fuchs, H. (2014). Illuminating collaboration in emergency healthcare situations: Paramedic-physician collaboration and 3D telepresence technology. *Information Research*, *19*(2). http://www.informationr.net/ir/19-2/paper618.html

Sormunen, E., Heinström, J., Romu, L., & Turunen, R. (2012). A method for the analysis of information use in source-based writing. *Information Research*, *17*(4). http://informationr.net/ir/17-4/paper535.html

Sormunen, E., & Lehtiö, L. (2011). Authoring Wikipedia articles as an information literacy assignment – copy-pasting or expressing new understanding in own words? *Information Research*, *16*(4). http://www.informationr.net/ir/16-4/paper503.html

Stebbins, R. A. (2001). *New directions in the theory and research of serious leisure*. The Edwin Mellen Press.

Stebbins, R. A. (2009). Leisure and its relationship to library and information science: Bridging the gap. *Library Trends*, *57*(4), 618–631. https://doi.org/10.1353/lib.0.0064

Stebbins, R. A. (2018). *Social worlds and the leisure experience*. Emerald Publishing Limited.

Tabak, E. (2014). Jumping between context and users: A difficulty in tracing information practices. *Journal of the American Society for Information Science and Technology*, *65*(11), 2223–2232. https://doi.org/10.1002/asi.23116

Tabak, E., & Willson, M. (2012). A non-linear model of information sharing practices in academic communities. *Library & Information Science Research*, *34*(2), 110–116. http://doi.org/10.1016/j.lisr.2011.11.002

Talja, S. (1997). Constituting "information" and "user" as research objects: A theory of knowledge formations as an alternative to the information man – Theory. In P. Vakkari, R. Savolainen, & B. Dervin (Eds.), *Information seeking in context: Proceedings of a meeting in Finland 14–16 August 1996* (pp. 67–80). Taylor Graham.

Talja, S. (2002). Information sharing in academic communities: Types and levels of collaboration in informaiton seeking and use. *The New Review of Information Behaviour Research: Studies of Information Seeking in Context*, *3*, 143–160.

Talja, S. (2010). Jean Lave's practice theory. In G. J. Leckie, L. M. Given, & J. E. Buschman (Eds.), *Critical theory for library and information science: Exploring the social from across the disciplines* (pp. 205–220). Libraries Unlimited.

Talja, S., & Hartel, J. (2007). Revisiting the user-centred turn in information science research: An intellectual history perspective. *Information Research*, *12*(4). http://InformationR.net/ir/12-4/colis/colis04.html

Talja, S., Keso, H., & Pietiläinen, T. (1999). The production of "context" in information seeking research: A metatheoretical view. *Information Processing & Management*, *35*(6), 751–763. https://doi.org/10.1016/S0306-4573(99)00024-2

Talja, S., & Nyce, J. M. (2015). The problem with problematic situations: Differences between practices, tasks, and situations as units of analysis. *Library & Information Science Research*, *37*(1), 61–67. https://doi.org/10.1016/j.lisr.2014.06.005

Tandoc, E. C. (2019). The facts of fake news: A research review. *Sociology Compass*, *13*(9). https://doi.org/10.1111/soc4.12724

Tan, W.-K., & Kuo, P.-C. (2019). The consequences of online information overload confusion in tourism. *Information Research*, *24*(2). http://InformationR.net/ir/24-2/paper826.html

Taylor, R. S. (1986). *Value-added processes in information systems*. Ablex.

Taylor, R. S. (1991). Information use environments. In B. Dervin & M. Voigt (Eds.), *Progress in communication sciences* (Vol. 10). Ablex.

Taylor-Smith, E., & Smith, C. (2019). Investigating the online and offline contexts of day-to-day democracy as participation spaces. *Information, Communication and Society*, *22*(13), 1853–1870. https://doi.org/10.1080/1369118x.2018.1469656

Taylor, M., Wells, G., Howell, G., & Raphael, B. (2012). The role of social media as psychological first aid as a support to community resilience building. *The Australian Journal of Emergency Management*, *27*(1), 20–26.

Tenopir, C. (2011). Beyond usage: Measuring library outcomes and value. *Library Management*, *33*(1/2), 5–13. https://doi.org/10.1108/01435121211203275

Tian, Y., Gomez, R., Cifor, M., Wilson, J., & Morgan, H. (2021). The information practices of law enforcement: Passive and active collaboration and its implication for sanctuary laws in Washington state. *Journal of the Association for Information Science and Technology*, *72*(11), 1354–1366. https://doi.org/10.1002/asi.24485

Todd, R. (1999). Back to our beginnings: Information utilization, Bertram Brookes and the fundamental equation of information science. *Information Processing & Management*, *35*(6), 851–870. https://doi.org/10.1016/S0306-4573(99)00030-8

Toms, E. G., & Duff, W. (2002). "I spent 1 1/2 hours sifting through one large box …". Diaries as information behavior of the archives user: Lessons learned. *Journal of the American Society for Information Science and Technology*, *53*(14), 1232–1238. https://doi.org/10.1002/asi.10165

Tuomaala, O., Järvelin, K., & Vakkari, P. (2014). Evolution of library and information science, 1965–2005: Content analysis of journal articles. *Journal of the American Society for Information Science and Technology*, *65*(7), 1446–1462. https://doi.org/10.1002/asi.23034

Vakkari, P. (1997). Information seeking in context: A challenging metatheory. In P. Vakkari, R. Savolainen, & B. Dervin (Eds.), *Information seeking in context: Proceedings of a meeting in Finland 14-16 August 1996* (pp. 451–463). Taylor Graham.

Vakkari, P. (1999). Task complexity, problem structure and information actions. Integrating studies on information seeking and retrieval. *Information Processing & Management, 35*(6), 819–837. https://doi.org/10.1016/S0306-4573(99)00028-X

Vakkari, P. (2008). Trends and approaches in information behaviour research. *Information Research, 13*(4). http://InformationR.net/ir/13-4/paper361.html

van der Westhuizen, H.-M., Kotze, K., Tonkin-Crine, S., Gobat, N., & Greenhalgh, T. (2020). Face coverings for Covid-19: From medical intervention to social practice. *British Medical Journal.* https://doi.org/10.1136/bmj.m3021

Van Rickstal, C. (2021). *American democracy under threat: Misinformation and disinformation on social media. A case study of Donald trump's mis- and disinformation tweets in the context of the 2021 Capitol siege.* (Unpublished master's thesis). Université de Liège, Liège, Belgique. https://matheo.uliege.be/handle/2268.2/12157

VanScoy, A., Thomson, L., & Hartel, J. (2020). Applying theory in practice: The serious leisure perspective and public library programming. *Library & Information Science Research, 42*(3), 101034. https://doi.org/10.1016/j.lisr.2020.101034

Veinot, T. C. (2010). A multilevel model of HIV/AIDS information/help network development. *Journal of Documentation, 66*(6), 875–905. https://doi.org/10.1108/00220411011087850

Veinot, T. C., Kim, Y.-M., & Meadowbrooke, C. C. (2011). Health information behavior in families: Supportive or irritating? *Proceedings of the Association for Information Science and Technology, 48*(1), 1–10. https://doi.org/10.1002/meet.2011.14504801070

Veinot, T. C., & Pierce, C. S. (2019). Materiality in information environments: Objects, spaces, and bodies in three outpatient hemodialysis facilities. *Journal of the Association for Information Science and Technology, 70*(12), 1324–1339. https://doi.org/10.1002/asi.24277

Vesga Vinchira, A. (2019). Modelling the information practices of music fans living in Medellín, Colombia. *Information Research, 24*(3). http://InformationR.net/ir/24-3/paper833.html

Wall, M., Otis Campbell, M., & Janbek, D. (2017). Syrian refugees and information precarity. *New Media & Society, 19*(2). https://doi.org/10.1177/1461444815591967

Whitmire, E. (2003). Epistemological beliefs and the information-seeking behavior of undergraduates. *Library & Information Science Research, 25*(2), 127–142. https://doi.org/10.1016/S0740-8188(03)00003-3

Williamson, K., Qayyum, A., Hider, P., & Liu, Y. H. (2012). Young adults and everyday-life information: The role of news media. *Library & Information Science Research, 34*(4), 258–264. http://doi.org/10.1016/j.lisr.2012.05.001

Williamson, K., & Smith, D. K. (2010). Empowered or vulnerable? The role of information for Australian online investors. *Canadian Journal of Information and Library Science, 34*(1), 39–81. https://doi.org/10.1353/ils.0.0004

Williams, R. D., & Willett, R. (2019). Makerspaces and boundary work: The role of librarians as educators in public library makerspaces. *Journal of Librarianship and Information Science, 51*(3), 801–813. https://doi.org/10.1177/0961000617742467

Willson, R. (2022). "Bouncing ideas" as a complex information practice: Information seeking, sharing, creation, and cooperation. *Journal of Documentation, 78*(4), 800–816. https://doi.org/10.1108/JD-03-2021-0047

Willson, R., & Given, L. M. (2014). Student search behaviour in an online public access catalogue: An examination of "searching mental models" and "searcher self-concept". *Information Research, 19*(3). http://informationr.net/ir/19-3/paper640.html

Wilson, T. D. (2010a). Information sharing: An exploration of the literature and some propositions. *Information Research, 15*(4). http://InformationR.net/ir/15-4/paper440.html

Wolf, C. T., & Veinot, T. C. (2015). Struggling for space and finding my place: An interactionist perspective on everyday use of biomedical information. *Journal of the Association for Information Science and Technology, 66*(2), 282–296. https://doi.org/10.1002/asi.23178

Worrall, A., & Oh, S. (2013). The place of health information and socio-emotional support in social questioning and answering. *Information Research, 18*(3). http://informationr.net/ir/18-3/paper587.html

Wylie Atmore, A. (2017). Just rol[l/e] with it: The sense-making practices of a tabletop roleplaying game community. In *Proceedings of RAILS – Research Applications, Information and Library*

Studies, 2016, School of Information Management, Victoria University of Wellington, New Zealand, 6–8 December, 2016. *Information Research, 22*(4). http://InformationR.net/ir/22-4/rails/rails1613.html

Xia, L. (2010). An examination of consumer browsing behaviors. *Qualitative Market Research: An International Journal, 13*(2), 154–173. https://doi.org/10.1108/13522751011032593

Xie, B., He, D., Mercer, T., Wang, Y., Wu, D., Fleischmann, K. R., Zhang, Y., Yoder, L. H., Stephens, K. K., Mackert, M., & Lee, M. K. (2020). Global health crises are also information crises: A call to action. *Journal of the Association for Information Science and Technology, 71*(12), 1419–1423. https://doi.org/10.1002/asi.24357

Yakel, E. (2004). Seeking information, seeking connections, seaking meaning: Genealogists and family historians. *Information Research, 10*(1). http://InformationR.net/ir/10-1/paper205.html

Yakel, E., & Torres, D. (2007). Genealogists as a "community of records". *American Archivist, 70*(1), 93–113. https://www.jstor.org/stable/40294451

Yates, C., & Partridge, H. (2015). Citizens and social media in times of natural disaster: Exploring information experience. *Information Research, 20*(1). http://InformationR.net/ir/20-1/paper659.html

Ye, M. (2019, March). Collaborative information seeking in tourism: A study of young Chinese leisure tourists visiting Australia. In *Proceedings of the 2019 Conference on Human Information Interaction and Retrieval* (pp. 441–444). https://doi.org/10.1145/3295750.3298979

Ye, E. M., Du, J. T., Hansen, P., Ashman, H., Sigala, M., & Huang, S. (2021). Understanding roles in collaborative information behaviour: A case of Chinese group travelling. *Information Processing & Management, 58*(4), 102581. https://doi.org/10.1016/j.ipm.2021.102581

Yeon, J., & Lee, J. Y. (2021). Employment information needs and information behaviour of North Korean refugees. *Information Research, 26*(4). https://doi.org/10.47989/irpaper914

Yerbury, H. (2015). Information practices of young activists in Rwanda. *Information Research, 20*(1). http://InformationR.net/ir/20-1/paper656.html

Zannettou, S., Sirivianos, M., Blackburn, J., & Kourtellis, N. (2019). The web of false information: Rumors, fake news, hoaxes, clickbait, and various other shenanigans. *Journal of Data and Information Quality, 11*(3), 1–37. https://doi.org/10.1145/3309699

Zhang, Y. (2014). Beyond quality and accessibility: Source selection in consumer health information searching. *Journal of the American Society for Information Science and Technology, 65*(5), 911–927. https://doi.org/10.1002/asi.23023

Zhang, Y., Sun, Y., & Xie, B. (2015). Quality of health information for consumers on the web: A systematic review of indicators, criteria, tools, and evaluation results. *Journal of the Association for Information Science and Technology, 66*(10), 2071–2084. https://doi.org/10.1002/asi.23311

Zhao, Y., & Zhang, J. (2017). Consumer health information seeking in social media: A literature review. *Health Information and Libraries Journal, 34*, 268–283. https://doi.org/10.1111/hir.12192

Zhu, C., Zeng, R., Zhang, W., Evans, R., & He, R. (2019). Pregnancy-related information seeking and sharing in the social media era among expectant mothers: Qualitative study. *Journal of Medical Internet Research, 21*(12), e13694. https://doi.org/10.1002/asi.23023

Zimmerman, M. S. (2018). Information horizons mapping to assess the health literacy of refugee and immigrant women in the USA. *Information Research, 23*(4). http://informationr.net/ir/23-4/paper802.html

Zimmerman, M. S., & Shaw, G. (2020). Health information seeking behaviour: A concept analysis. *Health Information & Libraries Journal, 37*(3), 173–191. https://doi.org/10.1111/hir.12287

Chapter 4

METATHEORIES, THEORIES, AND MODELS

> While there is a long and rich tradition of creating models and frameworks in information behaviour... this has not been the case with the development of theories. (Rebekah Willson et al., 2020, para. 1)

Chapter Outline

Looking for Information
Examining Research on How People Engage with Information, 121–178

ISSN: 2055-5377/doi:10.1108/S2055-53772023004

4.1 THE INTERSECTION OF PHILOSOPHY, THEORY, AND RESEARCH APPROACHES

A book like this one, focused as it is on information behavior research, cannot do justice to centuries of philosophical debate about reality, worldviews, and human knowledge. Instead, we identify some major questions and terms, and suggest several good sources that discuss the philosophies underlying our focus: the use of theory to guide investigations on the seeking, sharing, and use of information across contexts. We discuss some of the theories that are used by information behavior researchers, as well as some of the models that have been developed to explain human information behavior.

4.1.1 Metatheories

Metatheory is theory about theory. It addresses the philosophical assumptions about the nature of reality, and of knowledge, that stand behind specific theories and their related concepts. Metatheory concerns the assumptions that researchers hold about the world and how to investigate it. These include *ontology* (the nature of reality; what exists and how it might be categorized), *axiology* (the nature of values), *epistemology* (what we know, and how we can know), and *methodology* (how we can find out).

Metatheory is the usual name for such considerations, although there are overlapping terms used in the literature. For example, some argue that observable behavior should be the object of our studies, while others say we can be more objective by observing only the artifacts of human behavior (e.g., the traces or records that people leave behind). Yet, other researchers say that there is no true "objectivity" because the investigator is inextricably bound to the object of their study; they explain the best we can do is collect contextualized narratives or discourses in the domain of interest. Such diverse assumptions create a spectrum of research approaches, not only to "doing" research but also to the ways we see the world, how we view reality, and (therefore) how we choose what and how to study related to human information behavior.

A key issue regarding objectivity is the degree to which there is a reality separate from the human mind, such that we can study its contents as objects completely separate from mind and perception. The stance of *philosophical realism* is that what we perceive is *real*, and independent of thought. There is a continuum of positions regarding realism, from one maintaining that our own consciousness, experience and perceptions will have no effect on our ability to gain accurate knowledge of the world (including humans), to another extreme claiming that there is no reality "out there" at all, and that what we perceive of the world exists entirely in our own minds, meaning we cannot study the contents of the world as if

> ***Epistemology*** is a branch of philosophy concerned with the theory of knowledge. It explores the stances we take about the existence of reality and how we acquire knowledge. Epistemology encourages us to examine what we know, how we know it, and what justifies our belief that something is "true."

they were separate objects from one's consciousness. Obviously, there are many possible positions along this philosophical continuum regarding the nature of reality and the potential for knowledge.

A related issue has to do with the nature of "truth" – the degree to which it can be established, the criteria for doing so and whether there is one single truth or multiple "truths" in the world. There are competing philosophical theories regarding truth (i.e., correspondence, coherence, constructivist, consensus, and pragmatic), which are beyond the scope of this chapter; yet, they inform several of the theories and methodologies used by information behavior researchers.

4.1.2 The Research Spectrum and Dichotomies

Discussions of theory and metatheory sometimes refer to "positivist" (or "objectivist") versus "interpretivist" (or "subjectivist") assumptions in research. There are many alternative characterizations and labels for this dichotomy: "positivistic" versus "naturalistic" (Guba & Lincoln, 2005), "empirical" versus "interpretive" (Pavitt, 1999), "nomothetic" versus "idiographic" (Bates, 2005), or "objective" versus "subjective" (Ritzer, 2010). These dichotomies refer to a variety of differences in philosophical assumptions, goals, and research methods, and not simply the debate over objectivity described previously. The goals (and limits) of research are important as well: is our investigation intended to explain and predict behavior (objectivist), or rather to describe and understand human thoughts and actions (subjectivist) – including our own, as researchers? These issues are explored in a special issue of the *Journal of Documentation* edited by Hjørland (2005a, 2005b, 2005c), and in an article by Kelly (2021).

As Creswell and Clark (2017) suggest, dichotomies often conflate philosophical views with strategies of inquiry and research designs. For example, we might find a positivist researcher collecting "qualitative" data, but analyzing those data in a wholly positivist way (e.g., conducting frequency counts of key terms; reducing long passages of text to label data as "positive" or "negative"). Or an interpretivist may gather some "quantitative" data to provide context for a qualitative narrative inquiry; the analysis may focus on description or textual representations of those data, without the sample size required for advanced statistical analyses. The nature of the design and ways of knowing, as well as the research questions for the study, all affect the study design and the results that are presented. A key point to note is that the use of qualitative or quantitative *data* does not mean that a study is, by nature, a qualitative or quantitative research *design*. The researcher's paradigmatic worldview shapes the design, implementation, and analysis of the work, with a primary focus on data types that fit best with that paradigm (Given, 2016).

> ***Ontology*** is the philosophical theory of being. It examines objects, their structures, and their relationships. It encourages us to consider such concepts as existence, becoming, and the construction of reality, including how we classify objects.

4.1.3 Perspectives and Paradigms

In addition to calling them "metatheories," there are additional ways of characterizing groups of theories and their underlying assumptions. Giddens (1989), Dervin (1997), and Hjørland (2002a) choose the word "perspectives." Creswell and Clark (2017) prefer the term "worldview." Other authors (e.g., Bates, 2005; Tuominen, 2004) use the more popular term "paradigm" to mean much the same thing, although Bates also uses the word "approach."

One of the difficulties in discussing the concept of theory is that it has layers of meaning. That is, there are not only different levels of theory but there are also overarching concepts like "paradigm" that are sometimes conflated with theory. We will discuss paradigm and theory in the context of a hierarchy that places paradigm in the most global and encompassing position (followed by the concepts of grand theory, formal theory, and substantive theory), with "observations" at the bottom – the most limited and narrowest context of theory.

"Paradigm" is a term popularized by the work of science historian Thomas Kuhn, who wrote the influential book *The Structure of Scientific Revolutions* (1962). Over several decades the term became popular for describing the various points of view that researchers take in their search for explanations. Kuhn's most common characterization of a paradigm was that of a cluster of concepts, variables, and problems, along with related methodologies.

We might, for example, speak of a *conflict* paradigm, theorizing that conflicts among individuals or groups underlie much social interaction; many social theories, such as that of Karl Marx, share this view. Alternatively, the *exchange* paradigm says that much of life is based on individual calculations of the costs and benefits of undertaking a certain action, whether the action is speaking to a stranger or getting married. Or we might speak of a *sensemaking* paradigm that stresses how people create both meaning and social structure in their lives through interactions with others. Thus, asking another person for help in solving a personal issue may reveal a solution merely by sharing views of the problem; it might also encourage friendship, or dependency.

However vague the definition of a paradigm, it is an essential concept for describing research on information behavior. For one thing, it is difficult to talk about competing theories, or schools of theories, in the discipline. Information behavior is very diverse in its approaches, and formal theories are not always identified in individual investigations. Second, the notion of paradigm highlights the connections between research approaches and the purposes and beliefs of the investigator. For example, a distinction has been made between so-called "critical" and "administrative" research traditions (Livingstone, 2006) that parallel long-standing debates concerning the nature of both theory and research. Administrative research aims to support and improve existing systems of governance, while critical research tends to question those systems.

Consider two different investigators. The first believes that it is not up to her to question the nature of power relationships in the world, but rather to investigate practical problems that face the institution for which she works. Her focus is on why more people do not make use of a social service agency, with the goals of explaining such behavior and improving her employer's operations and services. In contrast, another investigator may feel compelled to challenge and expose what he judges to be an unfair social relationship – the failure of a government agency to provide the services that most people need – to raise public awareness of an injustice and to change the world. Although these two researchers might choose similar methodologies (and methods) to address the research problem as they have defined it, they would use dissimilar theories and operate under quite different paradigms. Livingstone quotes critical theorist Theodor Adorno as saying that his role was "to interpret phenomena – not to ascertain, sift, classify facts and make them available as information." For a comprehensive overview of the history of critical theory and implications for the field of information science, see Leckie and Buschman (2010).

> ***Axiology*** asks, how do we decide that something is "good"? Axiology examines the nature and varieties of value judgments relating to objects and concepts. Axiological questions include those related to *aesthetics* (or, how we regard beauty, in nature, art, music, and human-made objects), while *ethics* considers how people conduct ourselves in "right" and "good" ways.

4.2 THEORIES

4.2.1 What Is a Theory?

Theories are explanations. They are generalizations. Theories are statements that try to explain relationships among various phenomena (Baker, 1999) and from which one can make inferences and deductions. Theory results from interplay among ideas, evidence, and inference (Chaffee, 1991, p. 14). Bates (2005, p. 3) explains that models are a kind of proto-theory, a tentative proposed set of relationships, which sometimes guide research in a field for years, before the research matures to produce a formal theory.

Beyond these simple statements, more formal definitions of "theory" show wide variance in usage among researchers. Kerlinger (1973, p. 9), for example, defines theory as

> ... a set of interrelated constructs (concepts), definitions, and propositions that present a systematic view of phenomena by specifying relations among variables, with the purpose of explaining and predicting the phenomena.

Simon and Burstein (1985, p. 52) adhere to Kerlinger's complex definition when writing of disciplines like physics and economics, pointing out that "there is no theory unless it is a body of theory," a set of well-established definitions, assumptions, and systematically organized propositions. Nearly all explanations of theory invoke the idea that it must be systematic – relying on more than just a single, simple statement. Bates (2005, p. 3) notes that it is only "when we develop an explanation for a phenomenon can we properly say we have a theory." Along with their definition Simon and Burstein (1985, p. 52) also mention that theory "has a looser meaning; it often refers to a loosely organized collection of hypotheses . . . and sometimes is even used to refer to almost any speculative thinking offered as an explanation. . . ." Examples of this "looser" invocation of theory occur in everyday life, such as when a friend asks, "What's your theory about the origins of COVID-19?"

4.2.2 Levels of Theory

A theory is something more specific than a paradigm; the question is, *how* specific is it? The eminent sociologist Robert Merton (1968, p. 39) complained that the word "theory" was becoming "meaningless," as social scientists do not always define the term the same way, much less share the same goals about the kinds of theory to construct. Merton argued against attempts to create "grand" theories to explain human life in a universal way. In emulating major social theorists like Karl Marx, Herbert Spencer, and Talcott Parsons, other scholars tried (and failed) to predict actions and tendencies across all individuals, contexts, cultures, and societies (Merton, 1968, p. 44). Later, Skinner (1985) pointed to a "return of grand theory" in the work of Jürgen Habermas and Anthony Giddens, whose theories range widely across cultures, methods, and types of evidence. Other contemporary theorists, such as Theodore Schatzki, have also been described as explaining everything in a single theory (e.g., Schmidt, 2018). Schatzki (1996, p. 12) promotes practice theory as "a general conception of social life," and practices as "*the* fundamental social phenomenon." More recently, Polkinghorne and Given (2021) critique similar attempts by researchers to apply holism to their work, when the result often fails to realize the rhetorical promise of the approach.

> ***Practice Theory*** is associated with philosopher Theodore Schatzki (1996, 2019), who sees social organization as shaped by hierarchies of actions (e.g., doings, sayings, tasks, projects). *Practice Theory* emphasizes how language, discourse, institutions, roles, and social norms create the routines of shared practices that compose everyday life. Practice theory has frequently been cited within information science and was fundamental in the development of the concept of information practices.

Davis (1986) describes how "successful" social theories (i.e., those both famous and widely applied) addressed major problems (e.g., economic change) and overturned previous assumptions (e.g., that religion is largely unrelated to economic activity, a view challenged by Max Weber). Davis examined the theories of Karl Marx, Emile Durkheim, and Max Weber, among others, to show how broadly they were applied. For example, Durkheim's theory that the division of labor strongly influenced social organization has been used to study phenomena in government, law, religion, science, and the arts, as well as to explain human individuality. His notion that intermediate social groups, such as occupations, helped to hold society together in the face of declining community and family ties could be considered a "grand theory."

Rather than trying to reinvent or replace the broad theories that emerged during the nineteenth century, Merton argued that we should concentrate on the development of limited, "middle-range" theories; such theories function at a higher level than a testable hypothesis, but deal with limited settings, remain close to the level of observable phenomena and offer the potential for aggregating findings.

To illustrate the middle range we can consider Merton's reference group theory, the idea that individuals judge their situation by comparing themselves to significant people in their lives, rather than to some absolute criteria that apply to all humans. For example, we judge our own wealth by considering the wealth of our friends, relatives, coworkers, and acquaintances – rather than consulting government statistics on average annual incomes in the world or our own nation. Referential judgments can be seen in many social settings and across cultures, such that results can be compared and related to other concepts, such as class or education. Similar examples are found in Liehr and Smith's (1999, 2017) discussions of middle-range theories in nursing. For example, one theory considers several disruptive life transitions (e.g., becoming a parent, or becoming chronically ill), their challenges and indicators, and how nurses might improve outcomes for each type of transition.

In keeping with Merton's views, Glaser and Strauss (1967) argued that middle-range theories are best developed through induction. This involves building "upwards" from observations. Followed by a process of coding and analysis, leading to the identification of categories of phenomena from which propositions can be developed. In this way theory is "grounded" in observation rather than derived from abstract ideas. What they called grounded theory does not rely exclusively on induction (reasoning from particulars to generalizations), but rather moves back and forth from data gathering to deduction (reasoning from generalizations to particular cases) to test the theory. Glaser and Strauss (1967) make a distinction between "formal" and "substantive" middle-range theories. Formal theory is a typical social or psychological theory – conceptual statements applying to a general domain, like socialization or learning or deviance. Formal theory develops and marks the boundaries of a discipline; for example, certain theories of socialization are used widely in sociology, but little used in other disciplines. Substantive theory concerns a more limited domain, such as the nursing theories mentioned above, and is more focused on real-world applications.

Grounded theory itself has evolved since first being introduced in the late 1960s, including shifts in the approach introduced by Strauss and others. Strauss and Corbin's (1998) highly cited text (first published in 1990), for example, extends the procedures and practices originally outlined by Glaser and Strauss (1967). Kathy Charmaz's *Constructing Grounded Theory* (2014) reinterpreted grounded theory through a constructivist lens, providing a new way to apply this methodological approach. An example in information behavior research is Williamson and McGregor's (2006) exploration of secondary school students' information use, where a constructivist grounded theory approach was used to develop of model for understanding plagiarism.

A good example of grounded theory in information behavior is Kuhlthau's (1993a) model of the search process (discussed in detail in Section 4.6.2). Kuhlthau's model was developed through close observation of the ways information seekers construct knowledge by tying it to what they already know as they pass through various stages of uncertainty and understanding. Inspired by a psychological theory (Kelly, 1963), Kuhlthau's model could be expanded into a more general theory of information behavior through further observation and development. To see how these ideas evolve, we begin by looking at the foundations of information behavior theories.

4.3 SOURCES OF THEORY IN INFORMATION BEHAVIOR

A quarter-century ago Elfreda Chatman (1996, p. 193) lamented that information science researchers had no central theory (or body of interrelated theories) we could view as "middle range." Her view was that we remained focused on the application of conceptual frameworks rather than on the generation of specific theories for the discipline.

Much has changed since Chatman advocated for more use of theory. Many twentieth-century studies of information behavior made no explicit claims to theory. In its earliest days, information behavior research was more likely to be administrative in nature, collecting data to improve service in information agencies like libraries. In the last two decades investigators have shown a greater appreciation of the value of theory in information behavior research. In sharing a theory, individual researchers create communities where similar studies can be discussed, compared, and contrasted; these researchers share the same assumptions, vocabulary, and (often) methods to explore relevant phenomena.

Many academic disciplines have included theories relevant to the search for, and use of, information. Fifty years ago, theories about information seeking, sharing and use tended to come from either sociology, mass communication, or psychology (Zweizig, 1977). It is still the case today that sociology and psychology continue to inspire a significant amount of information behavior research.

Sociologists still account for much of the theory in information behavior research, particularly related to cultural theories rather than norm-based sociology (Reckwitz, 2002). The sociologists most cited in information behavior research include Alfred Schutz, Pierre Bourdieu, Anthony Giddens, Mark Granovetter, James Coleman, and Nan Lin. Other sociologists cited less frequently in recent years include Robert Merton, Erving Goffman, and Everett Rogers.

Among the psychologists cited in information behavior investigations, the most popular by far is Albert Bandura, for his social cognitive theory of learning, and his concept of self-efficacy. Also prominent are Aleksi Leont'ev, Lev Vygotsky, and Jonathon Potter. Other psychologists sometimes cited include George Kelly, Jean Piaget, Jerome Bruner, Martin Fishbein, Icek Ajzen, Peter Pirolli, Leon Festinger, Mihaly Csikszentmihalyi, Susan Folkman, Richard Lazrus, and Susan Miller.

> ***Discursive Positioning*** describes the cluster of theories and analytical techniques used in discourse analysis, discursive analysis, and positioning theory. There are many theorists in this space, including Foucault (1972, 1980), Harré (1994) and Potter (1996). Language (whether written, spoken, or signed) is viewed as a social interaction that creates power relationships. *Discourse Analysis* is used to study the role of language (or discourses) in social processes. In *Positioning Theory*, *positions* reflect individuals' beliefs about their rights, duties, and obligations, while *positioning* refers to how roles are taken, assigned, or denied. *Speech acts* and *narratives* are the mechanisms by which positioning takes place.

Some of the work of John Dewey (e.g., *How We Think*, 1933, and *On Experience*, 1960) could be counted among the psychologists, even though Dewey is more noted for his contributions to philosophy and education. Rom Harré (1984, 1994) taught psychology as well as in his primary discipline of philosophy. Similarly, Michel Foucault (1972, 1980) started his career as a psychologist, although his work is more concerned with language and cultural theory.

Other disciplines have also contributed theory to information behavior research: anthropology, education, communication, business (especially consumer research), and literature studies, to name the more prominent. Overall, many academic fields serve as sources of paradigms and theories for the study of information behavior and some of their theories have been actively used in such research.

4.3.1 Tracing the Theoretical Influences on Authors

Dozens of theories have been invoked in information behavior research, although some of them appear in only a few studies. Depending on what qualifies as theory, and how many citations of a theory must occur before we judge it to be recognized, there are many theories potentially relevant to information behavior. Fisher et al. (2005), Fleming-May (2014), González-Teruel, Araújo, and Sabelli (2022), Hartel (2019), Kankam (2019), Kelly (2021), and Wilson (2022) offer examples of relevant concepts, models, theories, and paradigms in their analyses of the literature, to name just a few.

Here we focus on formal theories, those that are more than a solitary concept, or a diagram of a model. Our examples encompass the following characteristics: a history of related work, definitions of concepts and their relationships, explanations of phenomena, kinds of problems to which the theory applies, and how one might gauge the theory's validity.

Table 4.1 highlights the 10 most popular theories invoked in studies of information behavior, for which we found at least 20 information behavior examples in journal articles over roughly two decades (2002–2022). The table is not exhaustive of citations to these theories. The examples are based solely on explicit citations (i.e., included in both the text and references) to works by particular theorists, appearing in four journals that have published much information behavior research (the *Journal of Documentation, Information Research*, the *Journal of the Association for Information Science and Technology (JASIS&T)*, and *Library & Information Science Research*); the first three of these journals were found by Pilerot et al. (2017) to contain the most citations to "practice theories." Adding additional journals or theorists might give a different sense of relative popularity. The table illustrates both the popularity of certain theories and sensitizing concepts, as well as the many influences on information behavior scholars. In this respect the table also indicates a theoretical sprawl that makes comparing investigations difficult, as they derive from distinct assumptions and methodologies (Pilerot et al., 2017).

The table lists theorists roughly in order of their relative citation rate in the four target journals – an indicator of their recent popularity. To the left are the names of theorists most often associated with the theory. In many cases citations to theorists

Table 4.1. Most-Cited Theorists and Formal Theories in Four Journals, 2002–2022.

Theorist	Theory/Concept	First Author/Year of Publication Citing the Theorist
Bandura 77, 86, 01	Social Cognitive (Learning) Theory, Self-Efficacy	Afifi 06; Albertson 16; Alshahrani 16,18; Bronstein 13, 15; Case 04; Choi 22; Ford 03; Greyson 18; Heinström 10; Hepworth 04; Hsiao 17; Huang 19; Hwang 11; Kim 15; Kostagiolas 17; Kurbanoglu 03,06; Kim 09, 10; Lindau 22; Lutz 17; Maceviciute 18; Meyer 16; Nel 20; Nikou 20; Pálsdóttir, 08,12; Park 20; Rosman 15; Ross 16; Sapa 14; Shen 19; Sin 15; Wang 20; Wei 08; Willson 14
Lave & Wenger 91, Wenger 98	Communities of Practice, Everyday Practice	Anderson 07; Bonner 11; Byström 17; Davenport 02; Davies 04; Durrance 06; Finholt 02; Gullbekk 16,19; Harris 10; Hemmig 09; Houston 11; Huizing 11; Isah 16,17,20; Joyce 05; Khazraee 19; Koh 19; Limberg 12; Lloyd 07,19; Lueg 08; Mansour 20; Mawby 15; Meyers 07; Moring 13; Multas 19; Nel 20; Nowé 08; Olsson 17; Pilerot 17; Poole 18; 17; Rubenstein 15; savolainen 07,08; Sundin 02; Talja 10; Wolf 15; Zhang 13
Schatzki 96, 02	Practice Theory	Caidi 10; Cavanagh 13; Cox 12; French 16; Gullbekk 16; Harviainen 14; Hicks 19 20 21; Huizing 11; Irvine-Smith 17; Jarrahi 17; Khazraee 19; Lloyd 06,07,08,09,10,13,14,19,21; Moring 13; Multas 19; Olsson 17; Pilerot 17; Savolainen 08,22; Tabak 12,14; Veinot 07; Yerbury 15,19
Giddens 84, 86, 91	Structuration Theory	Burnett 19; Byström 17; Eckerdal 11; French 16; Gibbons 19; Gullbekk 19; Hicks 21; Huvila 13,22; Huizing 11; Irvine-Smith 17; Jarrahi 17; LeLouvier 22; Lloyd 19,21; Miller 18; Moring 13; Nordsteien 17; Papen 13; Pham 19,20,21; Pilerot 17; Rosenbaum 10; Savolainen 07,08,09; Williamson 02; Yeh 08
Granovetter 73, 82	Social Network Theory, Theory of Weak Ties	Abbasi 14; Allard 18; Chen 14; Courtright 05; Desouza 06; Durrance 06; Fisher 07; Fransen-Taylor 16; Hersberger 03,05; Hultgren 13; Huotari 16; Huisman 20; JohnsonC 15; Lloyd 17; Lu 07; Mowbray 17,20; Morey 07; Olmeda-Gómez 08; Savolainen 08; Ujwary-Gil 19; Vårheim 17; Veinot 09,12; Webster 15; Worrall 13; Xie 08; Zhang 15
Bakhtin 81; Foucault 72, 80; Harré 84, 94	Discourse Analysis, Discursive Action, Positioning Theory	Dewey 16,20; Given 02; Gullbekk 16; Houston 11; Limberg 12; Ma 17; McKenzie 03a,04,05,06,10; Multas 19; Nahl 05,07; Olsson 05,10; Pilerot 17; Radford 15; Savolainen 08; Talja 05; Tuominen 05; Yerbury 19; Zhang 13
Bourdieu 77, 84, 86, 90	Theory of Taste/ Distinction/Practice, Cultural Capital, Symbolic Violence	Anderson 07; Chen 14; Choi 22; Cox 17; Dervin 03; Desrochers 15; Greyson 18; Gullbekk 19; Harviainen 14; Heinström 19; Houston 11; Huizing 11; Hussey 10; Irvine-Smith 17; Jarrahi 17; Kitzie 21,22; Laplante 11; Lloyd 19; Miller 18; Moring 13; Multas 19; Olsson 05; Papen 13; Savolainen 08,22; Wojciechowska 20
Lin 01; Coleman 88; Putnam 00	Social Capital	Chen 14; Hersberger 03,05; Houston 11; Johnson 05,07,12,15; Lloyd 17, Lu 07; O'Connor 14; Savolainen 08; Shuva 21; Tötterman 07; Vårheim 07,11; Veinot 09,10,12; Widén-Wulff 07; Wojciechowska 20; Yerbury 15
Vygotsky 78; Leont'ev 78; Engeström 87	Activity Theory	Allen 08, 11; Hasan 17; Huvila 22; Isah 16,17,20; Kane 07; Karanasios 13; Koh 19; Kwon 17; Meyers 07; Mishra 14,15; Mohammed 17; Multas 19; Nowé 08; Pang 20; Riley 22; Roos 12; Savolainen 08; Sonnenwald 06; von Thaden 08; Wang 13; Widén-Wulff 07; Wilson 06,08; Yu 12
Schutz 62, 64, 67, 70; Schutz & Luckmann 73	Phenomenology, Life World	Anderson 05,06,10; Cibangu 16; Hayter 07; Hultgren 13; Huvila 19; Kari 03; Knox 14; Miranda 07; Naveed 21; Ocepek 18; Riley 22; Savolainen 07,08 09; Sonnenwald 06; Suorsa 15; Wilson 02,16

> ***Social Network Theory*** focuses on how social relationships pass information, enable personal influence, and encourage changes in beliefs and practices. Networks can be *egocentric* (i.e., from a single person), *sociocentric* (i.e., the closed network of a formal group), or an *open-system* (e.g., a loose collective of activists). The most common general theory of networks cited in information behavior research is Granovetter's (1973, 1982) *strength of weak ties*. This is the tendency for distant or *weak* links in a network (e.g., a friend of a friend) to have special value not found within one's immediate network (e.g., knowledge of new job opportunities).

are so highly correlated that it is difficult to disentangle them. One example is social capital, a concept akin to cultural capital as described by Pierre Bourdieu, expanded by James Coleman, and articulated by Nan Lin. Further, social capital is dependent on social networks for its agency, so also overlaps with Granovetter's work on weak ties, and Bourdieu's ideas about the use of social assets to distinguish oneself. These formal theories are borrowed from other disciplines and share a long intellectual history, particularly among sociologists and psychologists. Albert Bandura's research on learning is somewhat distinct, as it does not connect directly to other theories in the table.

Most of the publications cited are empirical investigations; however, a few merely discuss how the theory might be applied to study information behavior. As shown by Rosenbaum (2010) and Dewey (2016), theories are often cited in a superficial manner. Rosenbaum examined 72 citations to Anthony Giddens' structuration theory across 13 information studies journals, finding that 54% appeared to be "ceremonial" rather than substantive. That is, in each case there were no quotations, explanations provided, or page numbers supplied, simply a citation to one of Giddens' works. This tendency for some citations to be perfunctory has been well studied (e.g., Cano, 1989; Case & Higgins, 2000; Polkinghorne & Given, 2021).

It would be helpful if theories and their paradigms could be sorted into neat typologies so that we can compare them. Some typologies have been devised, particularly in sociology – see, for example, Burrell and Morgan (1988), Littlejohn (1983), Ritzer (2010), and Rosengren (1974) – but without much agreement. Reckwitz (2002) offers a tidy explanation of three categories of sociological theory, and within the category of "cultural theory" four varieties (one of which is practice theory). Several philosophical examinations (Hacking, 1999; Slife & Williams, 1995) suggest that the assumptions and history of various metatheories (especially those explaining social action and social construction) are interwoven and difficult to tease apart.

Where information behavior is concerned, the sheer diversity of theoretical borrowings makes a single, comprehensive comparison difficult. In the next sections we outline the common distinction between the positivist (objectivist) ontological position and interpretivist (subjectivist) approaches. The latter is a term used by Pavitt (1999) and Kankam (2019), with somewhat different boundaries; we have adapted some of the categories used by Bates (2005) for this discussion. We recognize that these two broad groupings are open to dispute, but these will provide a useful starting point to understand the general principles that inform these approaches. For example, Trochim and Donnelly (2007) refer to constructivists as postpositivists (i.e., objectivists), and other scholars would place some critical theorists there as well.

4.4 POSITIVIST THEORIES

Among the older objectivist theorists and theories, several have been especially influential in information behavior research. Many of these originated in the disciplines of psychology and sociology during the 1970s and 1980s. In some cases, they may have since incorporated interpretivist elements; however, all of these have their roots in earlier theories.

Albert Bandura's evolving social cognitive theory (Bandura, 1977, 1986, 2001), and especially his central concept of self-efficacy, is increasingly cited in information behavior research, perhaps because of its relevance to health-related studies, which have also grown in number. Among the examples are a survey about seeking of genetics information (Case et al., 2004), Hepworth's (2004) study of informal information sources, Kurbanoglu's (2003) and Kurbanoglu et al.'s (2006) development of a self-efficacy scale for information literacy, Lim (2009) and Lim and Kwon's (2010) examination of student use of Wikipedia, Pálsdóttir's (2012) investigation of health information seeking in Iceland and her chapter in Wilson's (2013) edited book, Bronstein's (2014) study of Israeli library and information science students, Willson and Given's (2014) research on undergraduates' mental models and self-concepts while searching the library catalog, and a model proposed by Wiering (2005). More recent citations to Bandura's work include: Choi et al. (2022); Lindau et al. (2022); Greyson (2018); Hsiao et al. (2017); Huang et al. (2019); Nel (2020); Nikou et al. (2020); Park, Oh and You (2020); and Wang (2020).

The concepts of social capital and social networks are employed in several theories, including some of the interpretivist paradigms. Among traditional sociologists Coleman (1988) and Lin (2001) were among the first to focus on social capital. Putnam (2000) also drew on the concept for his popular book *Bowling Alone*. These various authors' work have been cited in studies and commentaries by: Chen et al. (2014), Hersberger (2003, 2005), Houston (2011), Johnson (2005, 2007, 2012, 2015), Lloyd et al. (2017); Lu (2007), O'Connor and Dillingham (2014), Savolainen (2008b), Shuva (2021), Tötterman and Widén-Wulff (2007), Vårheim (2007, 2011), Veinot (2009, 2010), Veinot and Williams (2012), Widén-Wulff (2007), Wojciechowska (2020), and Yerbury (2015).

Granovetter's (1973, 1982) related construct of the "strength of weak ties" (within general social network theory) is much more popular, cited by Abbasi et al. (2014), Allard and Caidi (2018), Courtright (2005), Desouza et al. (2006), Durrance et al. (2006), Dixon (2005), Fisher and Landry (2007), Fransen-Taylor and Narayan (2016), Hersberger (2003, 2005), Houston (2011), Hultgren (2013), Huotari et al. (2016), Huisman et al. (2020), Johnson (2015), Lloyd, Pilerot and Hultgren (2017), Lu (2007), Mowbray and Hall (2020), Mowbray, Hall, Raeside and Robertson (2017), Morey (2007), Olmeda-Gómez et al. (2008), Savolainen (2008c), Tsai (2012), Ujwary-Gil (2019), Vårheim (2017), Veinot (2009), Veinot and Williams (2012), Webster, Gollner and Nathan (2015), Worrall and Oh (2013), Xie (2008), Yerbury (2015), and Zhang and Jacob (2013). Granovetter's finding that secondary and tertiary contacts (those people whom our friends and their friends know well, yet whom we may not) is naturally relevant to those studying human sources of information.

Some information behavior researchers have advanced their own theoretical concepts. The most successful information behavior researcher in this regard was Elfreda Chatman, who is placed here due to her frequent reliance on mainstream sociological theory, such as Merton's (1968, 1972) reference group theory and his conception of insiders versus outsiders. Chatman referred to Merton's work in her various publications (1990, 1991, 1996), and in coauthored pieces: Burnett et al. (2001), Huotari and Chatman (2001), and Dawson and Chatman (2001). Chatman's theory of information poverty (see Hersberger, 2005) was based on her experience studying aging women in a retirement community (Chatman, 1992); and her concept of "life in the round" (Chatman, 1999; Fulton, 2005b) explores the influence of social norms and worldviews on information behavior.

Perhaps because of the origins of objectivist theory in the sciences, it is noteworthy that many of the investigations of information seeking in health contexts continue to use methods of observation and analysis (particularly multivariate statistical analysis), and sometimes theories, that originate in the objectivist tradition. We say "sometimes" because some of this research is atheoretical – focusing on variables like patient use of information sources. Examples of health research reflecting this tradition include: Afifi and Weiner (2006), Ankem (2007), Case (2009b), Harris et al. (2006), Kwon and Kim (2009), Pálsdóttir (2008), Park et al. (2020), Pluye et al. (2019), Stokes et al. (2021), and Wu and Li (2016).

Several theories examined in more depth in an earlier edition of this book (Case, 2012) have declined in popularity in information behavior research over the past two decades and so are not described here. These include the principle of least effort, optimal foraging theory, uses and gratifications, the diffusion of innovations, stress and coping theory, monitoring and blunting, flow theory, and the various uncertainty management theories.

4.5 INTERPRETIVIST THEORIES

Several clusters of contemporary theories often cited in information behavior investigations break from the earlier, *objectivist* traditions that attempt to follow research assumptions of the sciences. What these competing paradigms have in common is the belief that one cannot study the social world in the same way as the natural world, as the former contains agents who have intentions and make meanings. For inclusiveness we will call these *interpretivist* paradigms, even though the majority may also be considered "cultural theories." Interpretivist theories have become more popular over the last two decades, while positivist/objectivist theories have mostly declined in the degree to which they are cited.

The most popular interpretivist theories include these, which are discussed in the sections that follow:

- Social Constructionism: Practice Theories, Discourse Analysis, Positioning Theory
- Constructivism: Activity Theory, Personal Construct Theory, Sensemaking
- Phenomenology: The Everyday Life World
- Other Theories: Structuration, Face Theory, Critical Theory, Reader Response

4.5.1 Social Constructionism: Practice Theories, Discourse Analysis, Positioning Theory

Although the roots of "social constructionist" and "discourse-analytic" approaches stem from varying theorists and disciplines, the foundational theorists share a common emphasis on the importance of language and social interaction in knowledge formation and in establishing social/power relationships. Within the information behavior literature, these streams of thought are often cited together, so are discussed here together.

According to Tuominen et al. (2005) *constructionism* focuses on talk and language, as they emerge from interaction among members of a community. It is a "bundle of theoretical frameworks" (p. 329) with origins in sociology and in *structuralist* thinkers such as Bakhtin and Bourdieu (Lechte, 2007). Constructionism emphasizes the ways in which individuals construct understandings, meanings, and identities through discourse. It is a framework that emphasizes "what people do with their talk and writing and also with different sorts of cultural resources that people draw on" (Tuominen & Savolainen, 1997, p. 85). Among the functions that discourse serves is to define the nature of reality – what is real, what is true, who is responsible, and to explain one's motivations and behaviors.

Savolainen (2007b) sees constructionism as allied with the study of "practices" and standing in contrast to a "cognitive" (or "information processing") viewpoint that influences other information behavior research. Cox (2012, p. 182) also provides an overview of practice theories, discussing Schatzki, Wenger, and Gherardi, among others, while noting, "there is no one theorist to whom one can turn for a definitive account of the practice approach." Moring and Lloyd (2013), Pilerot et al. (2017), Savolainen (2008c), and Schmidt (2018) offer additional analyses of the roots and uses of practice theories. Through analysis of publications and citations, Pilerot, Hammarfelt and Moring (2017) provide evidence of strong growth in information behavior research using practice theories between 2005 and 2013. Our investigation of practice theory, noted in Table 4.1, points toward a continuation of that trend from 2013 to 2022.

Communities of practice (Lave & Wenger, 1991; Wenger, 1998, 2010) and practice theory (Schatzki, 1996, 2002) account for the strongest recent growth in citation among information behavior investigators. Generally, authors cite either Wenger or Schatzki, but not usually both together. Both theorists agree that practices

> ***Communities of Practice Theory*** presumes practices are a key feature of human society, arising from group-based (not individual) work, and are grounded in the human body. This approach places emphasis on the negotiation of meanings, and of identities, as outlined by Etienne Wenger (1998) and Jean Lave and Wenger (1991). This theory features in workplace studies where *competence* and *participation* are considered central to membership in a community of practice, and with a focus on learning in social situations. Moring and Lloyd (2013) and Huizing and Cavanagh (2011) differentiate Wenger's work from Schatzki's (1996, 2019) approach to the concept of practice.

are physical as well as mental and emotional, reflect the organized activities of many people, and that human life is best understood as grounded in the embodied activities of groups rather than individuals (Moring & Lloyd, 2013). Practices are routinized forms of behavior that include physical and mental activities, conversations, understandings, and often involve objects.

While their concerns and objects of research overlap, Wenger is more concerned with negotiation of meanings and participation, while learning to be a competent participant in a community organized around a practice. Identity and position within the community are important concerns. In contrast, Schatzki is less concerned with learning systems or community boundaries, instead focusing on how practices emerge and take place. The methods of the two practice approaches overlap, both taking a largely ethnographic approach (e.g., participant observation) in which conversation, stories, activities, knowledge, and objects are sources of evidence.

Schatzki (1996, 2002) guides the prolific research agenda of Annemaree Lloyd and her colleagues. Their writings on information literacy include Lloyd (2006, 2007a, 2007b), Lloyd and Williamson (2008), Lloyd et al. (2010), and Moring and Lloyd (2013), as well as studies of ambulance drivers (Lloyd, 2009), firefighters (Lloyd, 2014), car restorers (Lloyd & Olsson, 2019), nurses (Bonner & Lloyd, 2011), COVID-19 watchers (Lloyd & Hicks, 2021), refugees (Lloyd, 2014, 2015; Lloyd et al., 2013; Lloyd et al., 2017), and archeologists (Olsson & Lloyd, 2017). Schatzki's work influences research by an increasing number of other scholars, including: Caidi et al. (2010), Cavanagh (2013), Cox (2005, 2012), Davies and McKenzie (2004), French and Williamson (2016), Harviainen and Savolainen (2014), Irvine-Smith (2017), Jarrahi and Thomson (2017), Khazraee (2019); Multas and Hirvonen (2019), Savolainen (2008b), Savolainen and Thomson (2022), Tabak (2014), Tabak and Willson (2012), Veinot (2007), and Yerbury (2015).

In a related vein, Lave and Wenger (1991) and Wenger (1998) describe a "community of practice" as groups of people who share work or other interests, and thus knowledge. They share information, learn from one another, judge competence, and form meanings and identities. Lave and Wenger's works are cited by many information behavior scholars, including: Byström et al. (2017), Davenport and Hall (2002), Davies and McKenzie (2004), Finholt (2002), Gullbekk (2019), Harris et al. (2010), Hemmig (2009), Houston (2011), Isah and Byström (2016, 2017, 2020), Limberg, Sundin and Talja (2012), Lueg (2008), Mansour (2020), Mawby et al. (2015), Meyers (2007), Moring and Lloyd (2013),

Multas and Hirvonen (2019), Nel (2020), Nowé et al. (2008), Olsson and Lloyd (2017), Pilerot et al. (2017), Poole and Garwood (2018), Radford et al. (2017), Rubenstein (2015), Savolainen (2007a, 2008b), Sundin (2002), Talja (2010), Wolf and Veinot (2015), and Zhang and Jacob (2013).

The constructionist tradition also builds on the thinking of Bakhtin (1981) and Foucault (1972, 1980); other contributors have included Harré (1984, 1994), and Potter (1996) – and others (see Tuominen & Savolainen, 1997). Additional theorists sometimes cited in this vein include Berger and Luckmann (1967) on the social construction of reality, and Knorr-Cetina (1981) and Latour and Woolgar (1979) regarding the social construction of scientific knowledge. Constructionist investigations include Ma and Stahl's (2017) discourse analysis of anti-vaccination postings on Facebook; Multas and Hirvonen's (2019) demonstration of how "nexus analysis" incorporates various discursive theories and methodologies; Nahl (2007b), which applies "ecological constructionist" discourse analysis to three domains in education and psychology; and Zhang and Jacob's (2013) exploration of physical, epistemological, and virtual boundaries as impediments to the sharing of knowledge. A focus on Foucault's thoughts appears in studies of information literacy by Yerbury and Henninger (2019) and Limberg et al. (2012), and also in essays by Dewey (2016, 2020) about citations of Foucault in a broader selection of research.

Other varieties of constructionist information behavior studies rely on Harré's positioning theory, showing how discourse constructs identities for self and others. For example, Genuis (2013) applies the theory to patient information seeking and decision-making; Given (2002a, 2002b) investigates how undergraduates gave accounts of their information practices, emphasizing the ways in which the students' everyday information needs informed their academic work, and the role of cultural capital in information seeking. Julien and Given (2003) showed how academic librarians construct the identities of the faculty members with whom they work on information literacy activities. McKenzie has used this theoretical frame in her many publications (e.g., 2005, 2006, 2009, 2010). A short summary of social positioning theory is provided in Given (2005).

4.5.2 Constructivism: Activity Theory, Personal Construct Theory, Sensemaking

Included under this heading are various programs of research drawing their core ideas from theorists in psychology (Bruner, 1973; Kelly, 1963; Leont'ev, 1978; Vygotsky, 1978) and education (Dewey, 1933, 1960). The most heavily cited branch in recent years has been Activity Theory, originating with Vygotsky (1978) and Leont'ev (1978). It is concerned with human reasoning (internalization) and actions upon objects (externalization) that create new artifacts. Central to this theory are activities, which address needs, and actions, which work toward some transformation of reality. In this way activity has an important role in forming consciousness.

The theory made its way into information behavior research from studies of the workplace and computer usage. Nardi (1996) and Spasser (1999) were among the earlier writers to point out the relevance of Engeström's (1987, 1999) activity theory to information behavior, and Wilson (2006, 2008b) along with Allen et al. (2011) have explained how it might be used in that arena. The theory has been applied more in task analysis for information system development than in information behavior holistically, but see Hjørland and Christensen (2002), Widén-Wulff (2007), and Roos (2012) for counterexamples to that generalization. For example, Allen (2011), Allen et al. (2011), and Mishra et al. (2015) use activity theory to examine the relationship between information seeking and uncertainty in emergency response decision-making. Other studies include: Isah and Byström (2016, 2017, 2020), Kane (2007), Karanasios et al. (2013), Koh et al. (2019), Kwon (2017), Mohammed and Norman (2017), Multas and Hirvonen (2019), Pang et al. (2020), Roos (2012), Savolainen (2008c), Sonnenwald (2006), von Thaden (2008), Widén-Wulff and Davenport (2007), Wilson (2006, 2008a), and Yu (2012).

Another branch of constructivist thinking has been heavily cited across three decades, yet less so in recent years. Kelly's (1963) theory of personal construct formation (a component of his theory of personality) was the basis for Carol Kuhlthau's research program (1988, 1991, 1993a, 2005). Kelly saw a person's behavior as strongly shaped by his or her mental constructs of the world and how it operates; constructs are knowledge structures that "enable us to anticipate events and predict outcomes" (Kuhlthau, 1988, p. 233). Kelly's construction of knowledge also hypothesized five phases in thinking: encountering a new experience; initial feelings of confusion that result; the formation of a working hypothesis; taking actions that result in either reconstructing a (faulty) hypothesis or validating a (true) one; and, finally, assimilation of the findings with previous knowledge, resulting in changes of behavior.

Kelly's theory is not often directly cited in information behavior research, at least in the last decade. Kuhlthau continues to be among the top-cited authors in information science (Wilson, 2022), usually in the narrow context of literature searching by students. Kuhlthau's research is discussed in a review by Reynolds (2013). Other scholars who have drawn upon Kelly's theory include Beheshti et al. (2015), Julien (2004); Riley et al. (2022), Williamson (2005); and Wilson (2002).

It is awkward to incorporate sensemaking in our scheme, even though it springs from constructivist thought. Brenda Dervin, the primary proponent of this approach to information seeking and use, notes that "some people call sense making a theory, others a set of methods, others a methodology, others a body of findings" (Dervin, 1992, p. 61). Dervin (2005) describes her "sensemaking methodology" as a "theory for methodology" (p. 26) that builds a bridge between substantive theory (i.e., systematic propositional statements about phenomena) and metatheory ("assumptions about the phenomena and how to study it," p. 25). In contrast to these two senses of "theory," Dervin aims to create a third type of theory that connects the two. Due to this ambiguous relationship to formal theory, citations to Dervin are excluded from Table 4.1. However, it is obvious that including her citations might make it the largest set; over the last five years her work averaged five citations per year in *JASIS&T* research articles, which suggests her work continues to be cited dozens of times per year across multiple journals.

We consider sensemaking as a metatheory emphasizing naturalistic methods (Dervin & Nilan, 1986), having theoretical grounding in the constructivist learning theories of John Dewey and Jerome Bruner. Sensemaking also incorporates Kelly and Bruner's view of life as an encounter with problems and discontinuities in knowledge. Yet, Dervin acknowledges intellectual debts to many other scholars, including Carter (1965, 1973), Geertz (1973), Giddens (1984, 1986 1989), and Habermas (1979, 1984, 1987). Comprehensive overviews of her thinking are found in Dervin et al. (2003) and Dervin (2015).

A main tenet of sensemaking is that information is not "something that exists apart from human behavioral activity." Rather, information is "created at a specific moment in time-space by one or more humans" (Dervin, 1992, p. 63). Information is thus created through our interactions with obstacles in our progress through life. The result of this process – sense – is equated with knowledge, but also with opinions, intuitions, evaluations, and responses. Unlike a view of information as something "out there" that is transmitted to people (as Dervin says, an information "brick" that is put into a human "bucket"), sensemaking sees information as internally constructed to address discontinuities in life. This approach uncovers the problems that people experience in life and how they face those obstructions.

The sensemaking research agenda produces detailed evidence of the strategies by which individuals cope with problematic situations of all sorts. In doing so, sensemaking research places a high value on the insights gained by the persons under study, as they reconstruct their solutions to past problems. In contrast, the constructivist approach is more narrowly focused on learning in specific tasks, such as gathering evidence in a library for a term paper or testing a solution to a problem.

This constructivist metatheory continues to be used regularly in empirical investigations. Allard and Caidi (2018) apply sensemaking to immigrants, Turner (2010) employs it in her study of oral information transmission, as do Meyers et al. (2009) in their investigation of preteens, Olsson (2010a) in his study of theater professionals, and du Preez and Fourie (2009) in an investigation of engineers. In the health arena, McCaughan and McKenna (2007) apply sensemaking to the actions of newly diagnosed cancer patients while Genuis (2012) and Genuis and Bronstein (2016) explore it in the making of health decisions. More recent citations to Dervin's work include Chen (2022), Choi et al. (2022), Huvila (2022), Lee et al. (2022), Riley et al. (2022), and Savolainen and Thomson (2022).

4.5.3 Phenomenology: The Everyday Life World

Phenomenological approaches are paramount among information behavior researchers, yet it is difficult to separate this worldview from some others. Ritzer (2010) offers a three-part classification of social theory, one of which he calls "social definitionist." Included in the definitionist camp are action theory, symbolic interactionism, phenomenology, and existentialism. Manicas (1998, p. 267), on the other hand, refers to a divide between "objectivist" and "subjectivist" traditions, with the latter including phenomenology (the key figure being Alfred Schutz), ethnomethodology (pioneered by Harold Garfinkel), and "versions of hermeneutics and critical theory" (e.g., Gadamer, Habermas, and Ricoeur). Ritzer (2010) also describes Schutz, Garfinkel, and others as representing "sociologies of everyday life," overlapping in membership with the social constructionist thinkers. Schutz will be taken as an example of "phenomenology."

The philosophical roots of phenomenology lie in the work of Edmund Husserl. Schutz's focus is on intersubjectivity among human actors, and their subjective interpretations of meaning (including the behavior of others and self). Such interpretations – our definition of the situation – are among the intentional actions we take during our life "projects." The original explanations are found in Schutz (1962, 1964, 1967, 1970), while Wilson (2002, 2013) offers an introduction to the relevance of Schutz's work for research on information behavior.

One example of a project that applied Schutz's approach is Hultgren's (2013) use of "the stranger" concept to examine information seeking as an outsider activity. Phenomenology is also identified as the basis for investigations by Anderson (2006), Cibangu and Hepworth (2016), Hayter (2007), Kari and Savolainen (2003), Knox (2014), Marcella and Baxter (2005), Naveed, Batool and Anwar (2021), Ocepek (2018a, 2018b), Savolainen (2008b), and Suorsa and Huotari (2014). Schutz is also cited in reviews by Olsson (2005), Savolainen (2007c, 2008b, 2009c), Sonnenwald (2006), Suorsa (2015), and Wilson (2002, 2016).

4.5.4 Other Theories: Structuration, Face Theory, Critical Theory, Reader Response

Anthony Giddens' (1984) theorizing about the nature and evolution of social structures ("structuration") clarifies both the constraints under which human agents operate in society, and how this enables them to accomplish certain tasks, through an interaction of norms, meanings, practices, and power relations. Information behavior scholars citing Giddens include: Burnett and Lloyd (2019), Byström et al. (2017), Eckerdal (2011), French and Williamson (2016), Gibbons (2019), Gullbekk (2019), Hicks (2019), Huizing and Cavanagh (2011), Huvila (2013, 2022), Irvine-Smith, S. (2017), Jarrahi and Thomson (2017), Le Louvier and Innocenti (2021), Leckie (2005), Lloyd and Olsson (2019), Miller (2018), Moring and Lloyd (2013), Nordsteien (2017), Papen (2013), Pham and Williamson (2018), Pilerot et al. (2017), Rosenbaum (2010), Savolainen (2007c, 2008c, 2009c), Williamson and Manaszewicz (2002), and Yeh (2008).

An interesting application of structuration theory is found in Pham and Williamson (2018), who compared university libraries and faculties in Australia and Vietnam. Based on interviews, conversations, and documents that reflected collaboration and information sharing, they found differences in degrees of structure and trust between the two organizations. Individual actions (i.e., human agency) often compensated for structural barriers (such as stifling bureaucracy), in some cases using social media to share work information outside of formal channels.

While "critical theory" is sometimes mentioned in information behavior discourse as a source of theory, the only theorist regularly cited in that tradition is Jürgen Habermas. Critical theory was a later development of Marxism taken up by the Institute of Social Research in Frankfurt, from the 1920s through the 1970s. Affiliated with this "Frankfurt School" were the scholars Max Horkheimer, Theodor Adorno, Herbert Marcuse, and others (Ingram, 2014; Pyati, 2010). Their critiques of capitalism and culture, along with contributions to epistemology, are still influential. In the 1970s Habermas took up many of the same themes of these earlier scholars, but with some marked differences in assumptions, especially as regards the role of scientific research. Habermas' "Theory of Communicative Action" is usually identified as the most recent development in this long stream of thought. His notion of a "public sphere" is certainly relevant to many aspects of information exchange, especially to publishing and libraries. Habermas' theory has been regularly cited in relation to information seeking since the early 1980s, although often in passing and less employed in actual investigations. Among the scholars citing are: Benoit (2005), Burnett and Jaeger (2008), Cibangu (2013), Lee and Butler (2018), Mehra (2007), Pang et al. (2020), Savolainen (2008b), and Yerbury and Shahid (2017). Buschman (2010) presents an overview of Habermas' thinking, including a discussion of the potential value of his work for future research in information science.

Pierre Bourdieu (1984, 1986, 1990) is noted for his *theory of distinction* (or *taste*), along with the concept of *cultural capital.* His thinking has special relevance for studies of everyday life information seeking (ELIS, e.g., Savolainen, 2008b, 2022). Other information behavior scholars citing Bourdieu include Chen et al. (2014), Choi et al. (2022), Cox et al. (2017), Dervin (2003), Desrochers and Pecoskie (2015), Greyson (2018), Gullbekk (2019), Harviainen and Savolainen (2014), Heinström et al. (2019), Houston (2011), Hussey (2010), Huizing and Cavanagh (2011), Irvine-Smith (2017), Jarrahi and Thomson (2017), Joyce (2005), Kitzie et al. (2021), Kitzie et al. (2022), Laplante and Downie (2011), Leckie (2005), Lloyd and Olsson (2019), Miller (2018), Moring and Lloyd (2013), Multas and Hirvonen (2019), Olmeda-Gómez et al. (2008), Olsson (2005), Ujwary-Gil (2019), Vårheim (2017), Veinot (2009), Veinot and Williams (2012), Webster et al. (2015), Worrall and Oh (2013), Xie (2008), and Zhang and Sun (2015).

A theory not included in the table for lack of recent citations is Erving Goffman's (1959, 1963, 1974, 1983) presentation of self, or face theory. Face theory is still cited in information behavior investigations, although not often. Andersson (2017), for example, uses Goffman's notion of frontstage versus backstage in focus groups with students to explore what they might "hide" from teachers when writing an assignment (e.g., consulting Wikipedia, which was discouraged). How youth create and maintain their social media identity and evaluate those of other users was the concern of Ryan et al. (2016). Demasson et al. (2016) cite Goffman's (1963) work on stigma in an exploration of hobbyists researching their heritage. Goffman's observations about the importance of the human body in generating meaning are discussed in Olsson and Lloyd (2017). Other recent citations to Goffman include Brown and Veinot (2020), Wolf and Veinot (2015), and Zigron and Bronstein (2019).

Another less used theory is that of reader response, related to de Certeau's (1984) ideas about modifying our lived experience. The theory focuses on the way that readers actively experience and create meaning during the act of reading. This emphasis naturally aligns with other theories used in information behavior emphasizing the creation of meaning. Many scholars have been involved in building reader response theory, including Fish (1987), Iser (1978) and Rosenblatt (1994). Among the scholars who have cited the theory since 2002 are Birdi and Ford (2018), Latham (2014), Lindberg and Hedemark (2019), Massey et al. (2007), Massey et al. (2005), Reuter (2007), Ross (2005), Rothbauer (2009), and Savolainen (2008b, 2019).

4.6 MODELS

Models are flexible tools for guiding investigations and accumulating knowledge, and to build and test theories (Mershon & Shvetsova, 2019). They offer "a framework for thinking about the problem area" (Wilson, 2022, p. 23). According to Järvelin and Wilson (2003) models can identify the components to be studied and the relationships among them, as well as suggesting promising research goals and methods. Models are sometimes used to guide study designs, test theories, suggest hypotheses or research questions to be studied, and used during analysis to explain findings and depict relationships between the elements of a study.

As models are typically depicted in diagrams, they are somewhat easier to grasp than formal theories for those who are new to the subject matter under investigation. In the sections that follow we first discuss models in general, and then focus on a few specific models of information behavior. Most resemble flowcharts that suggest influences, sequences of events, and sometimes outcomes. They all aim to describe and explain circumstances that show how individuals or groups discover, assess, and apply information of some kind.

4.6.1 What Is a Model?

Models often focus on more specific problems than do theories. For example, a model might depict how research participants typically navigate through a series of website pages; the model may not address how *all* people find information on the internet (much less how people find information in multiple circumstances), and yet it might inspire a broader theory of searching. One instance of a limited model is Claude Shannon's (1949) depiction of signal transmission, which led to both explicit theories of the information content of messages and to vague theories about how mass media influenced viewers and readers.

Models are often discussed in relation to theories. Both theories and models are simplified versions of reality, yet models typically make their content more concrete through a visualization of some sort. By illustrating processes, models make it easier to see if what we believe about how people engage with information is consistent with what we observe in our research. Like a theory, a model describes relationships among concepts but is tied more closely to the real world: one changes a model only after first comparing it against an evidence base and confirming that modifications are warranted.

Models range from the purely pragmatic and descriptive (e.g., a flowchart of how a document moves through a bureaucratic process), to formal models that combine mathematical and pictorial logics (as found in statistical path analyses, such as that used by Sin (2011), to model the effect of sociostructural and individual factors on information behavior). Simulations, such as the use of algorithms in artificial intelligence to model certain behaviors (e.g., the perception of shapes in studies of computer vision), are also types of models. Some disciplines, such as psychology, make extensive use of complex models. An important function of a model is as a "testing device" (Bates, 2005, p. 2); that is, it should specify a way that the model can be validated, e.g., by suggesting hypotheses that can confirmed through observations.

Models can also be exploratory in their design, such as in qualitative studies where emergent findings lead to model development; these models may then evolve or change over time as new research data are gathered in later projects to further advance model development. Given's (2007) "Model of the Affective Information Behavior Ecology" (p. 166), for example, was developed based on empirical qualitative data of undergraduates' information-seeking activities. More recently, Given and Kuys (2022) developed the "Model of the Informing Aesthetic" to outline the interdisciplinary information creation process used to design a war memorial.

As a means of representing and organizing complex processes, models have strengths and weaknesses (Johnson, 1997, pp. 112–113). On the positive side, the depiction of key elements makes clear the investigator's approach and selection of explanatory factors. The strength of a model to simplify one phenomenon can become a weakness when it is overgeneralized to another, dissimilar phenomenon. Shannon's (1949) communication model is an apt example, as it has been applied much more broadly than was intended by its creator.

4.6.2 Modeling Information Behavior

Dozens of information behavior models have appeared over the past 60 years; early examples include that of Donohew and Tipton (1973) and Krikelas' (1983) models of information seeking. These models vary as to their assumptions, structure, purposes, scope and intended uses. An initial consideration is whether the model is intended to be general, or context specific. Table 4.2 presents the many models that have been reviewed in earlier editions of this book, some of which are mentioned in the sections that follow. This demonstrates the range and

Table 4.2. Information Behavior Models Profiled in Earlier Editions of *Looking for Information* (Case, 2002, 2007, 2012; Case & Given, 2016).

Model Name	*Looking for Information* Edition	Source Publication
Wilson Models	1st, 2nd, 3rd, 4th	Wilson (1999, 1997, 1994, 1981)
Krikelas Model	1st, 2nd, 3rd, 4th	Krikelas (1983)
Johnson Model	1st, 2nd, 3rd, 4th	Johnson (1997), Johnson and Meischke (1993)
Leckie Model	1st, 2nd, 3rd	Leckie et al. (1996)
Byström and Järvelin Model	2nd, 3rd, 4th	Byström and Järvelin (1995)
Savolainen Model	2nd, 3rd, 4th	Savolainen (2005), Savolainen (1995)
Ellis Model	3rd, 4th	Wilson (1999), Ellis (1989)
Kuhlthau Model	3rd, 4th	Kuhlthau (1993b)
Williamson Model	4th	Williamson (1998)
Foster Model	4th	Foster (2004)
Shenton and Hay-Gibson Model	4th	Shenton and Hay-Gibson (2011)
Robson and Robinson Model	4th	Robson and Robinson (2013)
Freund Model	4th	Freund (2015)

complexity of many (but not all) of the models that have informed information behavior studies over four decades.

An initial consideration of models is on what aspect of human life they take as their focus. Wilson (2022, p. 51) contrasts knowledge that supports *application* (i.e., in a task) versus *affect* (i.e., psychological support). Many models have been created around the role of information in performing a work task (e.g., Freund's 2015 model of information searches by software engineers). A lesser number have modeled nonwork aspects of life, such as solving personal problems and addressing emotional challenges (Dervin, 1992), or enjoying hobbies and maintaining health (Savolainen, 1995). Increasingly information behavior researchers aim to reflect all human experience, rejecting the suspect dichotomy of work/nonwork (Savolainen, 2021).

Another division among models is whether they emphasize *exposure* (typically to mass media or internet messages) rather than a proactive *seeking* of information (voluntary action based on an emerging situation or need). This is linked to the recurring nature of needs and uses: we always need good health (although we may not pay much attention to advice about maintaining it), and we often seek work-related facts, yet we infrequently need many other types of information (e.g., what's the right air pressure for a tire this size?). Thus, the models that emphasize exposure are typically those that have to do with health, workplaces, and sometimes shopping – i.e., topics in which other parties try to influence our behavior. An example is Longo's (2005) model of patient information seeking, which presents five scenarios in which a person passively receives information from a source of some kind, with various outcomes. The tendency to emphasize either exposure or seeking activities parallels the discussion by Robson and Robinson (2013) of the differences between models from information science versus those emerging from scholars of communication.

Another way that models vary is in their *structure*. Several of the most general models resemble flowcharts, and indeed some of them use flowcharting symbols, such as the yes-no decision diamond (e.g., Robson & Robinson, 2013). Flowchart models tend to be focused on information processing and decision-making, giving less attention to contextual and personal variables and types of sources and actions. They also tend to be unambiguous, with a deterministic sequence of actions from which any deviation is not depicted. As they deal with repeated comparisons, decisions, and actions, they may incorporate feedback loops to show the need to repeat certain sequences. A contrasting and more flexible approach can be found in models portrayed as boxes (e.g., Savolainen, 1995) or circles (e.g., Williamson, 1998), which include lists of variables and/or processes. Usually, arrows are used to indicate influences or sequences within or among the boxes or circles. There are also hybrid types that use both flowchart symbols and boxes to indicate sequences and variables.

The degree to which models specify *actions* and *sources* (or channels) used in information seeking, and *outcomes* that follow from that seeking (or avoiding) of information, is another dimension of variation. That is, some models simply "end" with a box or circle labeled "information seeking" or "search" (or "stop" if current information is considered adequate); many health-related models have such features (e.g., Afifi & Weiner, 2006; Kahlor, 2010). In contrast, other models suggest how that search might occur, or what kinds of sources it might involve (Longo, 2005; Niedzwiedzka, 2003). And some models go further to describe uses and outcomes, such as states of physical and psychological health (e.g., Czaja et al., 2003; Longo, 2005).

Another way that models differ is in their *specificity*. Like many models in other disciplines, information behavior models are often focused along some dimension – by occupation, academic discipline, task, or context. Many early information behavior models portrayed single occupations, such as those by Voigt (1961), Menzel (1964), Paisley (1968) and Orr (1970) for the information behavior of scientists. Hernon's (1984) model focused on social scientists. Some more recent models continue in that vein: Baldwin and Rice's (1997) for security analysts; Tabak and Willson's (2012) for information sharing among academics; Abrahamson and Goodman-Delahunty's (2013) for police officers; Stokes and Urquhart's (2015) for nurses; and Given and Willson's (2015) for humanities scholars. Likewise, there are many models focused on specific tasks, such as online or web searching (e.g., Awamura, 2006; Ingwersen, 1996; Marchionini, 1995; Marton, 2011), or Birdi and Ford's (2018) model of fiction reading selections. Other models examine a context such as health or the related role of "patient" (e.g., Longo's "Conceptual Model of Health Information Seeking" of

2005, and Kahlor's "Planned Risk Information Seeking Model" of 2010). Another context example is Lopatovska and Smiley's (2014) model of information behavior before and after a hurricane. So, there are many information behavior models for *specific* populations, contexts, and tasks.

Not surprisingly, the models that garner the most citations are *general*, in terms of the breadth of populations, roles, and tasks to which they are meant to apply. Wilson's (1999, 2022) various models have this level of generality, as does Robson and Robinson's (2013) and Niedzweidzka's (2003), and to a large degree Kuhlthau's (1991); even though Kuhlthau's model is more applicable to structured searches, its emphasis on feelings, thinking, and learning applies to a broader audience. It is, however, difficult to develop a general information behavior model without making it large and complicated – which works against the goal of parsimony. As Järvelin and Wilson (2003, p. 4) advise, "simpler is better other things being equal."

A final dividing point among the information seeking models is whether they are *assessable*, through either qualitative or quantitative research. How do we know that the model reflects reality for at least some people, and is not simply the idiosyncratic view of the author(s)? What evidence could we gather to decide whether the model is trustworthy? Some models are either vague or complicated, such that there is no way of knowing how closely they correspond to actual thoughts, feelings, and actions. Yeoman (2010, p. 165) observes that "few existing models are being tested and their role in ... theory generation is therefore restricted. Such models are frequently based on small studies that are context-bound."

The main point of this introduction is that models vary along several dimensions, not the least of which is the terminology they employ. Thus, it is often difficult to compare them. Later in this section, we feature five models in chronological order: Kuhlthau (1991, 2004), Savolainen and Thomson (2022), Robson and Robinson (2013) and Wilson (2022). Discussions of most of these models are found in Godbold (2006), Kundu (2017), Meyer (2016), Robson and Robinson (2013), Savolainen (1995, 2021), and Wilson (2022). Some of these models have been widely used while others are chosen to illustrate certain aspects of information behavior models. One criterion for inclusion here is that the model *attempts to depict and explain a sequence of cognition, emotion, and behavior* by referring to relevant variables, rather than merely indicating a sequence of events. For instance, the "flow model of information seeking, avoiding, and processing" by Donohew and Tipton (1973) – perhaps the earliest attempt to model information seeking – depicts sequences of events but does not identify important influences (e.g., task, contextual, psychological, or demographic differences). That is why Donohew and Tipton wrote that their model was not intended for designing investigations.

Models are *simplified* versions of reality and do not attempt to depict every possible influence or process. How theories (and models) become over-complicated has been called "nuance" (Healy, 2017) – the tendency to continue adding elements to theories because "theories are supposed to cover everything and offer multidimensional accounts, even at the expense of clarity" (Fuhse,

2022, p. 100). So, model designers are tempted to keep adding elements to reflect everything that might possibly be an influence on thoughts, feelings, and behaviors. According to Healy (p. 123) the result can be an "overpowered theoretical vocabulary that allows the researcher to evade refutation and say more or less anything." In other words, theories (and models) ought to be specific enough to offer us the possibility to judge how well they reflect reality; they cannot claim to flawlessly explain everything.

There are many examples of overly complex models, and these are often the result of attempts to combine and align earlier models – an awkward melding that mixes different levels of abstraction and varieties of observable concepts, sometimes ignoring the intent of the original authors. Shenton and Hay-Gibson (2012) present several integrated or "meta-models" in their review article. Examples of integrated models include those by Niedzweidzka (2003), Godbold (2006), Lakshminarayanan (2010) and Zhang and Soergel (2014). Each of these takes a somewhat different path in their modification of earlier models. Niedzweidzka builds on Wilson's early models by adding three contextual influences or "intervening variables" (personal, role-related, environmental), which act upon information behavior. Godbold's approach is to attempt to merge and extend various aspects of the Dervin, Wilson, Ellis, and Kuhlthau models. Lakshminarayanan (2010) based her model on exhaustive analyses of 34 diaries, each kept for 14 days, and accounting for 15 types of information behaviors. She integrates her findings into a complex, two-figure model of at least two-dozen elements. In each case the integration creates complicated figures that may be difficult to translate into a study design or explain how and why people act as they do.

Niedzwiedzka's (2003) recasting of one of Wilson's models to include "context" (in the form of personal, role-related, and environmental variables) cascading in from the top to influence the other 11 features of the model. Niedzwiedzka's is one of the better attempts to reflect "context" by placing it outside the rest of the model and indicating that it consists of certain intervening variables. Most other models do not fully specify what is meant by context, and how it affects the other processes and variables in the model; indeed, some (e.g., Agarwal, 2022) argue that context only emerges at the point that a person interacts with information – which suggests that contexts are ultimately unique and unclassifiable.

In a multi-year pursuit of his own integrated model, Agarwal (2022) has done researchers a great service by painstakingly comparing 29 information behavior models devised over four decades. The three spreadsheets included in his article demonstrate how difficult it is to compare the concepts and terminology of multiple authors over the 12 criteria he chose (five contextual aspects, plus need, seeking/searching, evaluation and processing of the information, use, sharing, behavior and/or practice, and metatheoretical approach). Each table includes between 8 and 12 models across the top and the 12 comparison points on the left side. Before reading the individual cells of these tables it is instructive to consider that 43% of the cells are blank, indicating that the cell is irrelevant to (or the vocabulary did not fit) the model in that column. No candidate has an entry for all 13 criteria, and only one fills all 12 cells in its column. This underscores how different the models are from one another in their vocabulary, specificity, and focus.

The following sections detail five examples of the many models that have been developed in studies of information behavior. Although this list is far from exhaustive, it includes several models that have been heavily cited, as well those that may be less well known but provide interesting perspectives to consider in future research.

4.6.2.1 The Kuhlthau Model

The model of "Information Search Process" by Carol Kuhlthau (1991) is applicable to any domain, but especially those in formal and/or structured learning contexts. Based on theories of learning, it depicts a series of cognitive and affective stages or behaviors through which people are thought to move as they find and evaluate information. As Wilson (1999, p. 254) points out, Kuhlthau's work attempts a different level of analysis than the other models in focus here. Her model does not consider some factors and variables usually featured in information behavior research (e.g., the type of need and what sort of information or other "help" might satisfy it), or the availability of sources and their characteristics. Originating in constructivist personality theory (Kelly, 1963), Kuhlthau's focus is on the feelings, thoughts, and actions that follow as a person becomes aware of uncertainty. Kuhlthau's model was among the first to bring attention to the importance of affect in information behavior, and her core publications have been cited over 8,000 times in the academic literature – evidence of its applicability, at least to formal learning.

The Kuhlthau model (Fig. 4.1) includes seven stages, moving from left to right as a time sequence. At the extreme left of the model (the beginning) is the stage of "initiation," in which a person becomes aware of uncertainty or lack of knowledge about something. This is the birth of an information need, as the person identifies what is missing in their knowledge. The stage that follows is "selection," in which we select the topic we are pursuing and how to approach it. At this point

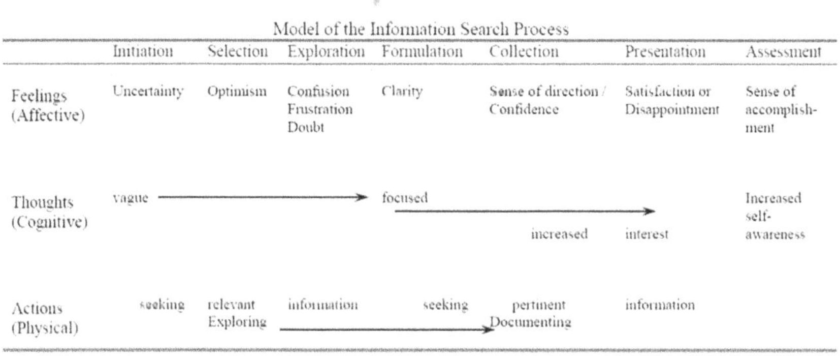

Model of the Information Search Process

	Initiation	Selection	Exploration	Formulation	Collection	Presentation	Assessment
Feelings (Affective)	Uncertainty	Optimism	Confusion Frustration Doubt	Clarity	Sense of direction / Confidence	Satisfaction or Disappointment	Sense of accomplishment
Thoughts (Cognitive)	vague →			focused →	increased	interest	Increased self-awareness
Actions (Physical)	seeking	relevant Exploring →	information	seeking	pertinent Documenting	information	

Fig. 4.1. The Kuhlthau Model. *Source:* Adapted from Kuhlthau (1993b).

one assesses one's own degree of interest, necessary tasks, and available resources (time, relevant information) and tends to be optimistic about the process and outcome. In the third stage, "exploration," feelings of doubt and confusion may arise, as sources are explored and the information search becomes difficult to frame or express to information systems or other persons. At this point some seekers may abandon their effort to expand their understanding. The fourth stage is "formulation," a time when focus is sharpened and clarity of purpose may be achieved. At this point the search may narrow and confidence in the outcome tends to return. Stage five is "collection," when effort is focused on gathering, digesting, and recording the most relevant information on the topic. At the sixth stage, "presentation," one can use the retrieved information to answer the initial question or complete the task (e.g., a report for school or work). Any further searching at this stage is likely to turn up redundant information. Finally, a seventh stage may be "assessment" of what one has accomplished, leading to improved self-awareness and esteem. Importantly, the stages are assumed to take place only in the sequence indicated.

Kuhlthau's model is based on many years of research, mainly with students. She identifies uncertainty as a key concept and emphasizes the role that emotions (such as frustration or doubt) play in motivating the search for information. It is distinct from the other models shown here in that it focuses on actions, cognitions, and emotions that take place during a search, while not offering a general explanation of the "before" and "after" of the sequence. That is, the model does not depict any contextual factors leading to the recognition of an information need (e.g., school or work or everyday life demands and curiosities), nor does it follow the actions out to their specifics (e.g., types of sources considered and pursued). While general in its statements, the model has been applied largely in education, and mostly with imposed queries (see Beheshti et al., 2015; Gross, 2001). Articles by Agarwal (2022), Kundu (2017), Meyer (2016), Robson and Robinson (2013), Savolainen (2015b), and Wilson (2022) offer further analyses of Kuhlthau's model.

4.6.2.2 The Savolainen and Thomson Model

Second for discussion, due to its long evolution, is Savolainen and Thomson's (2022) Expanded Model for Everyday Information Practices (EIP). Savolainen originally published his Model of Everyday Life Information Seeking (ELIS) in 1995, based on interviews with ordinary citizens pursuing "nonwork" activities. He argued that the traditional emphasis on work-related actions neglected the many actions that we all perform in our daily lives, such as shopping, taking care of our homes, and pursuing personal interests, such as hobbies, sports, and volunteer activities. As Savolainen (1995) pointed out, working and nonworking information practices are not exclusive of one another, but rather are often complementary. He saw Bourdieu's theory of *habitus* – our socially and culturally determined ways of thinking and acting – as an appropriate basis for a model of everyday life. Later, Savolainen (2008b) revised ELIS to be a Model for

Information Practices, dropping the concept of "Mastery of Life" and its four related orientations (e.g., Optimistic-Cognitive), among other changes.

Influenced by Thomson's (2018) model of information creation, the two authors (2022) have published their Expanded Model for Everyday Information Practices (Fig. 4.2). This model maintains the original emphasis on a phenomenological life-world of social, cultural, and economic factors as the background for everyday practices. The most significant change is a recognition of two modes of information practices: *acquiring* and *expressing*. Acquiring encompasses the usual concerns with active seeking and more passive monitoring, as well as *use* in the internal sense of information processing and decision-making. The second mode, expressing, includes creation of new information, sharing of information with others, and the acts of selecting and applying information (use in a sense that is more outcome-oriented). These two pathways and their constituent parts interact with one another. They are also subject to the influence of situational factors (such as urgency), social norms, and what the actor knows. Together all of these shape the goals and interests of the actor as they pursue their projects and tasks in life.

The model's potential is assessed in terms of conventional (e.g., positivist) and interpretive (e.g., social constructivist) criteria and thought to be "moderate" to

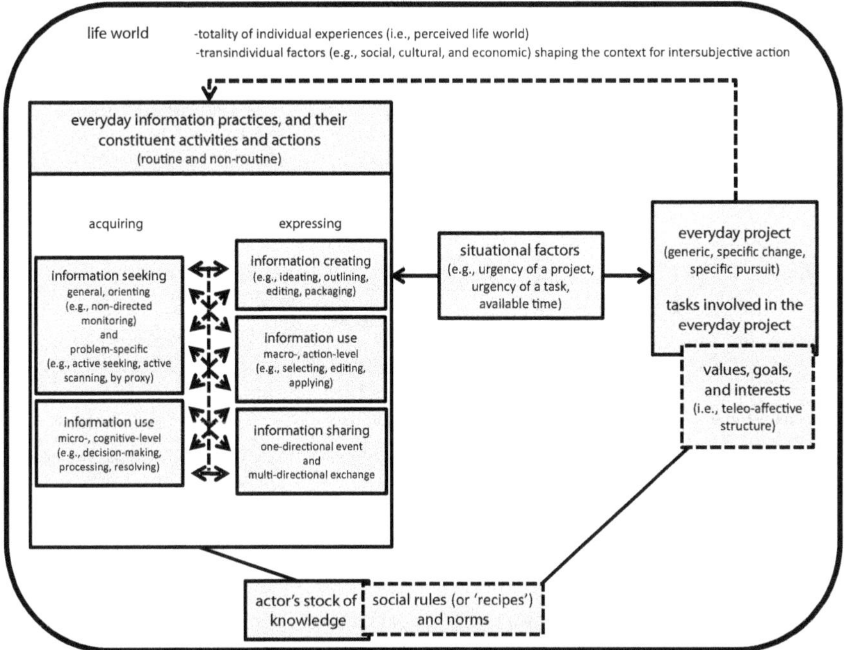

Fig. 4.2. The Savolainen and Thomson Model. *Source:* Adapted from Savolainen and Thomson (2022).

"high" in meeting most criteria. We will look forward to application of this new model in future research.

4.6.2.3 The Robson and Robinson Model

The Robson and Robinson model (Fig. 4.3) is the result of an analysis of other models, including those by Wilson, Ellis, Kuhlthau, Leckie et al., and Johnson. The other models that Robson and Robinson (2013) examined are more concerned with the source of information, i.e., a communicator, and the outcomes or effects of the information they provide. Distilling what these various models contain, Robson and Robinson identify nine factors affecting information behavior, noting that no single model reflects all of these:

(1) Context: The environment in which an information actor operates.
(2) Demographics: Age, sex, ethnicity, and so forth.
(3) Expertise: An actor's knowledge, education, training, experience, career stage, etc.
(4) Psychological factors: personality and mental processes, including self-efficacy, cognitive dissonance, coping abilities, emotions, and the like.
(5) The information recipient's needs, wants, and goals.

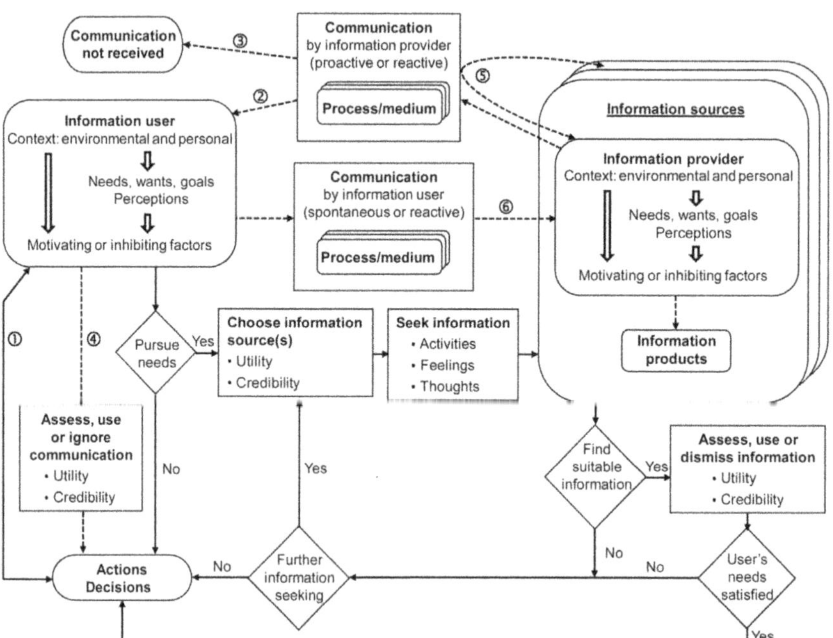

Fig. 4.3. The Robson and Robinson Model. *Source:* Adapted from Robson and Robinson (2013).

(6) The information provider's needs, wants, and goals.
(7) Motivating and inhibiting factors.
(8) Features of the information-seeking process, such as thoughts and feelings while searching.
(9) Characteristics of information and sources, such as its utility (e.g., relevance, timeliness, ease-of-use) and credibility (e.g., authority, reliability, lack of bias).

It is important to note that the Information Seeking and Communication Model (ISCM) that Robson and Robinson create from these factors is not a literal combination of the models they examined, but rather a new synthesis of elements they found occurring in various models. Their model is expressed as a flowchart and is accompanied by fuller definitions of what they mean when they refer to users, sources, providers, and products of information, including what is implied by environmental and personal contexts.

The process reflected in the ISCM could be said to begin at more than one point in the diagram; however, for the sake of simplicity one could say that a chain of events begins with an act of communication (e.g., information provided), which might not be received. Assuming that communicated information is noticed by a person, then environmental and personal contexts come into play, along with the needs/wants/goals of that person, and any factors that might inhibit or especially motivate the potential information user.

Once a communication has been received, several further actions are possible in the ISCM diagram. The information could be immediately used or evaluated or ignored. Needs could be invoked that lead to consultation of other sources. The user could react by communicating with the information provider.

There are a few details that are not fully addressed in Robson and Robinson's (2013) presentation of their model. A fundamental issue is introduced by the assumption of a communicator or provider of information, which leaves out some sources of information. For example, a geologist may seek information from the natural environment, and thus some of her observations, thoughts, actions, and decisions do not depend on intentional communication of information – even though journals and colleagues are surely important sources of information as well. Thus, sources of information could be defined more broadly.

A more specific issue has to do with definition and separation of the nine factors. For example, it is easier to imagine strong "inhibiting factors" (Lack of time? Wireless internet not available?) than effective "motivating factors" (Plenty of time? Wireless is available?). The latter do not seem to be "motivating" in and of themselves. So how are "motivating factors" distinct from the "needs/wants/goals" of the user, and from characteristics of the information/sources (e.g., ease-of-use)? Surely personal needs and goals are motivators. Perhaps "motivating factors" refer strictly to characteristics of the environment, but then it is difficult to see how these are distinct from factors that motivate the individual. Fuller definitions and examples would improve this model, along with demonstrations of its use in empirical research.

4.6.2.4 The Meyer Model

The Meyer model (Fig. 4.4) includes six components, connected by solid lines indicating interrelationships among them, and dotted lines depicting the flow of actions. Meyer aims to "provide novice researchers with a more holistic understanding of what information behavior entails and how it comes about." Her model is based on an extensive review of earlier models (especially Wilson, 1981 and 1999), the theories to which some models refer, as well as additional considerations identified in information behavior research.

Meyer's six components are: Personal (cognitive, affective, and sensorimotor – following Nahl, 2001), Needs (cognitive and affective), Information (facts, internal knowledge, people, objects, images, etc.), Context (roles, tasks, rules, regulations, events, situations, etc.), Technology (media, internet, mobile devices, social media, etc.), and Activities; this latter component is divided into three types of activity – Seeking (formal versus informal), Use (creating, collecting, applying, etc.), and Transfer (e.g., sharing). Context is the starting point for actions, which flow to the Personal component through Needs and then to Technology and the three Activities, via varying paths. As Meyer admits, prioritizing interrelationships is difficult, as nearly all components are closely related, and only Needs are unconnected by solid lines to the others in the diagram. Unlike many models that conflate forms of information with the source or technology that makes them available, Meyer's model indicates that any information (e.g., an image)

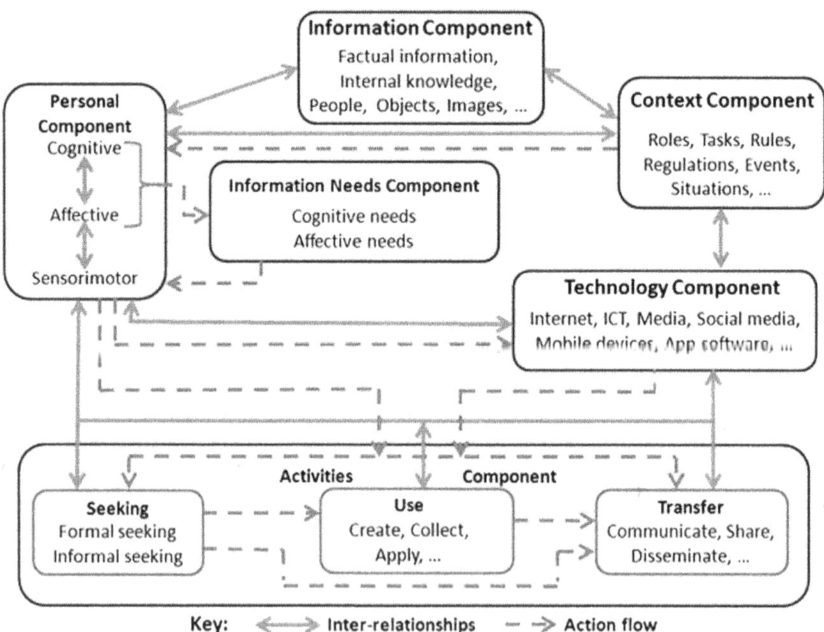

Fig. 4.4. The Meyer Model. *Source:* Adapted from Meyer (2016).

conveyed by a device (e.g., a tablet) is mediated by individual thoughts, feelings, and bodies.

Meyer's diagram depicts many concepts and examples in a compact way. It also discusses relevant features from earlier models. Among other prime influences are Dervin (1983), Kuhlthau (1991), Sonnenwald and Iivonen (1999), Nahl (2001), Wilson (2005), Cole (2013), Robson and Robinson (2013), Davies and Williams (2013), and Burford and Park (2014).

4.6.2.5 The Wilson Model

A series of models by Wilson (1981, 1994, 1997, 1999, 2022) reflects trends in the theory and practice of information behavior research. Their evolution makes them particularly interesting to analyze and compare with those of other researchers. The Wilson model examined here (2022, pp. 42–44) is based on his earlier diagrams, with this version adding distinctions between accidental and intentional discovery of information, and among types of searches. Some of these changes stem from an increasing appreciation of passive reception of information.

Over the years Wilson has identified relevant factors for his models from research in other disciplines, including decision-making, psychology, health communication, and consumer research. The current version (Fig. 4.5), including lengthy explanations, appears in his 2022 book, *Exploring Information Behavior*. Notably Wilson's model explicitly refers to theories to explain three aspects of information behavior:

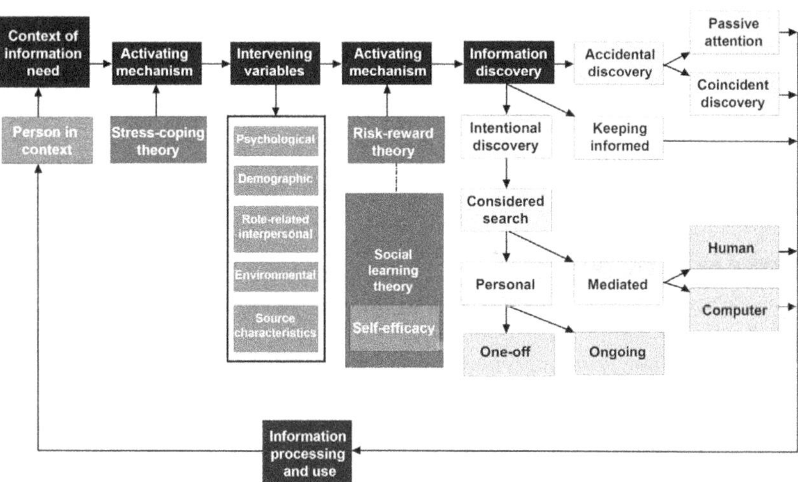

Fig. 4.5. The Wilson Model. *Source:* Adapted from Wilson, T. D. (2022).

- Why some needs prompt action more so than others (stress/coping theory, from psychology)
- Why some sources of information are used more than others (risk/reward theory, from consumer research), and
- Why we may, or may not, pursue a goal successfully, based on our perceptions of our own efficacy (social learning theory, from psychology).

We might think of Wilson's "activating mechanisms" as motivators: What motivates a person to search for information, and how and to what extent? These motivators are affected by intervening variables of five types: psychological predispositions (e.g., tending to be curious, or averse to risk); demographic background (e.g., age or education); factors related to one's social role (e.g., whether one is acting as a manager or a mother); environmental variables (e.g., the resources available); and characteristics of the sources (e.g., accessibility and credibility). The outer, "information processing and use" line in the model indicates that information is evaluated as to its effect on need and forms a feedback loop that may initiate further action if the need is not satisfied.

Having been around in various forms for more than 40 years, Wilson's models have drawn many commentaries. Niedwiedzka (2003), for example, analyzed Wilson's (1999) model, and proposed several modifications. Among other observations, she points out that Wilson's graphic separation of "the context" from the person, the intervening variables, and features of the information sources does not reflect how those factors form part of the context, and that the activating mechanisms are in operation not only at the point in which a decision is made to seek information but also at all the other stages. Perhaps, Niedwiedzka says, it would be better to give the activating mechanisms labels like "stress" or "perception of risk" rather than refer to theories about stress and risk. Robson and Robinson (2013, p. 181) criticized the same model for being too sequential, rather than representing the back-and-forth actions more typical in real searches. Yet, as with other models, it is difficult to depict such complexities in a two-dimensional drawing. Attempts to incorporate "context" into models are not always helpful, either.

4.6.2.6 Reviewing the Models

Given their differences in vocabulary, emphasis and focus, some of the five models are difficult to compare in detail. Kuhlthau's emphasis on process and its slant towards formal learning is distinct from the others. Kuhlthau's focus is on feelings, thoughts, and actions following recognition of uncertainty, rather than on contextual factors, characteristics of the seeker, or types of sources. Perhaps because of the huge number of studies conducted with students and/or about education, along with the age of her publications, Kuhlthau's (1991, 1993b) model has been the most heavily cited among these five.

Perhaps at the other end of a spectrum of formality, Savolainen's (1995) model of Everyday Life Information Seeking (including its most recent adaptation, in Savolainen & Thomson, 2022) applies to all sorts of people and settings. With a focus on "mastery of life," rather than learning, it considers a much longer time frame and thus pays more attention to social and material factors. Despite receiving over 1,500 citations, an analysis by González-Teruel and Pérez-Pulido (2020) of the source and contexts of citations to Savolainen's model concludes that it has not influenced research as much as its popularity would suggest – i.e., a "low adoption" pattern like that of other works in information science.

The other three models are newer and have been influenced by the models and commentaries that preceded them. Formative among them are Wilson's models, as they reflect four decades of his thinking and reaction to suggestions. Together the 1981 and 1999 versions have been cited over 6,000 times. The latest (2022) model identifies intervening variables and modes of discovery, and relevant theories of motivations behind search behaviors. It could apply to any person or content, and thus is very general. It does not attempt to specify types of contexts or information needs.

Robson and Robinson's (2013) model reflects the advantages and disadvantages inherent in melding together concepts from other models. In its use of decision points (see Wilson's, 2022, p. 34, discussion of these), it resembles early flowchart models of formal information seeking. Potential sources are also slanted towards the formal: "individuals, groups and organizations who produce, supply or communicate information, or who facilitate or control access to it" (p. 185), which may make it less applicable to studies of everyday information behavior.

Finally, Meyer's model likewise incorporates an analysis of several models and commentaries on them. For example, the author acknowledges the influence of Nahl (2001) on the personal component, Kuhlthau (1991) and Davies and Williams (2013) on needs, Sonnenwald and Iivonen (1999) on contexts, Wilson (1999, 2005) and Robson and Robinson (2013) on activities and Burford and Park (2014) on technologies, among many sources she considered. The six resulting components suggest variables that might be observed in an investigation, and what actions they influence.

4.6.2.7 Other Models

There are many other models of information behavior, sometimes meant to apply generally, but usually much more limited in their applicability. Among the often-cited models are those of Krikelas (1983), Ellis (1989), Byström and Järvelin (1995), Johnson and Meischke (1993), Leckie et al. (1996), Williamson (1998), McKenzie (2003b), Foster (2004), Shenton and Hay-Gibson (2011), Freund (2015), Nahl (2007a), Given (2007), Yeoman (2010), and Given and Willson (2015). Several of these are also discussed in articles by Agarwal (2022), Järvelin and Wilson (2003), Kundu (2017), and Savolainen (2015b, 2021).

A model by Zhang and Soergel (2014) lies near the periphery of the others discussed here, as their focus concept, "sensemaking," has broader meanings across several disciplines. Their model starts with a task or problem and charts how both data and the conceptual structure that "contains" it are identified iteratively and fitted, to update knowledge schemas. In this respect it seems closer to the computer science literature on problem-solving and task analysis (which are cited extensively), than the usual information behavior literature. Zhang and Soergel refer to Brenda Dervin's sensemaking research (which she describes as a perspective and methodology); Dervin has depicted gap-bridging as a person crossing a ravine; however, it is not obvious that this is meant to function as a model for research. Also very distinctive are the "information horizons" diagrams generated by respondents in Sonnenwald et al. (2001). These are sketches of information sources, with those less important or less used indicated at a further distance from the center of the drawing. As they are unique, they are not properly models, but suggest ways of modeling monitoring and active consultation (see the discussion by Savolainen, 2006).

Many information seeking models are found in the health domain. Examples include: Kahlor's (2010) "Planned Risk Information Seeking Model" (PRISM), the "Health Information Acquisition" model of Freimuth et al. (1989), Czaja et al.'s (2003) "Conceptual Model of Patient Information Seeking," Longo's (2005) "Expanded Conceptual Model of Information Seeking Behaviors," ter Huurne et al.'s (2009) "Risk Information Seeking and Processing" model, and the theory of motivated information management by Afifi and Weiner (2004). Many health-related models are less concerned about how or where seeking might take place (i.e., what sources of information will be monitored or consulted). That limits their applicability to the sorts of research questions typically explored by information behavior researchers. An exception is Veinot's (2010) "Multilevel Model of HIV/AIDS Information/Help Network Development," which considers information or advice as just one among several "resources" (or "helps" in Brenda Dervin's terms) that might be sought by a patient; other types of resources sought would include physical treatment and emotional support.

Where these health-related models most frequently overlap is in the concepts and theories they invoke. The concept of self-efficacy is frequently incorporated, and sometimes coping theory, or monitoring and blunting. Both self-efficacy and coping mechanisms feature in Wilson's (2022) model.

4.7 CONCLUSION

We began this chapter by discussing the nature of paradigms adopted by researchers. These are difficult to place in a single framework, both because they overlap and because they operate at different levels of generality. We noted that various words may be used to describe much the same thing regarding research: perspectives, traditions, or approaches. We use the word "paradigm" interchangeably with these.

We discussed the nature of theory, describing it as a generalized explanation of the relationships among various phenomena. We described the confusions that arise with varying usage of the term "theory." One implication of that confusion is that theories also vary in the degree to which they attempt to generalize; theorists and epistemologists refer to this as the issue of "levels of theory." For us, "theory" is assumed to be a closely related set of definitions and propositions, rather than a simple statement like "people seek information when they are uncertain." The latter declaration, though perhaps true, needs to have a supporting set of concepts and research questions or hypotheses to result in a useful series of investigations of which we can all make sense.

Next, we explored several theories that have been applied in information seeking research. These included social learning/cognitive theory, communities of practice, practice theory, structuration theory, positioning theory, theory of distinction, social network theory/strength of weak ties, social capital theory, phenomenology, and activity theory, among others.

Most of these theories have origins that are decades old. Some are likely to continue to attract adherents, especially the two theories of practice, which together form the most popular approach for the study of information behavior. Theories originating in sociology, psychology, and education continue to provide most of the theoretical bases for empirical work on information needs, sharing, uses, and related phenomena.

Finally, we pointed out that some citations of theory appear to be ceremonial or perfunctory, rather than deeply engaged in the design of investigations or the discussion of their results. This type of usage must decline if we are to make meaningful contributions to the communities of discourse that surround each of these theories. We also explored the development of models of information behavior, including a mix of those that are long-standing and heavily cited, as well as newer models that have emerged across research contexts.

4.8 OUR TOP 3 *MUST READ* RECOMMENDATIONS

Bates, M. J. (2005). An introduction to metatheories, theories, and models. In K. Fisher, S. Erdelez, & L. McKechnie (Eds.), *Theories of information behavior* (pp. 1–24). Information Today, Inc.
A good synopsis of the various paradigms for studying information behavior.

Robson, A., & Robinson, L. (2013). Building on models of information behavior: Linking information seeking and communication. *Journal of Documentation*, *69*(2), 169–193.
The authors compare models from communication with those generated in information science and then create their own "information-seeking and communication" model.

Wilson, T.D. (2022). *Exploring information behaviour: An introduction*. T.D. Wilson.
In addition to providing an overview of research on the topic, Wilson explains specific theories and models often used in investigations of information-related phenomena.

REFERENCES

Abbasi, A., Wigand, R. T., & Hossain, L. (2014). Measuring social capital through network analysis and its influence on individual performance. *Library & Information Science Research*, *36*(1), 66–73. https://doi.org/10.1016/j.lisr.2013.08.001

Abrahamson, D. E., & Goodman-Delahunty, J. (2013). The impact of organizational information culture on information use outcomes in policing: An exploratory study. *Information Research*, *18*(4). http://informationr.net/ir/18-4/paper598.html

Afifi, W. A., & Weiner, J. L. (2004). Toward a theory of motivated information management. *Communication Theory*, *14*(2), 167–190. https://doi.org/10.1111/j.1468-2885.2004.tb00310.x

Afifi, W. A., & Weiner, J. L. (2006). Seeking information about sexual health: Applying the theory of motivated information management. *Human Communication Research*, *32*, 35–57. https://doi.org/10.1111/j.1468-2958.2006.00002.x

Agarwal, N. K. (2022). Integrating models and integrated models: Towards a unified model of information seeking behaviour. *Information Research*, *27*(1). http://InformationR.net/ir/27-1/paper922.html

Allard, D., & Caidi, N. (2018). Imagining Winnipeg: The translocal meaning making of Filipino migrants to Canada. *Journal of the Association for Information Science and Technology*, *69*(10), 1193–1204. https://doi.org/10.1002/asi.24038

Allen, D. K. (2011). Information behavior and decision making in time-constrained practice: A dual-processing perspective. *Journal of the American Society for Information Science and Technology*, *62*(11), 2165–2181. https://doi.org/10.1002/asi.21601

Allen, D., Karanasios, S., & Slavova, M. (2011). Working with activity theory: Context, technology, and information behavior. *Journal of the American Society for Information Science and Technology*, *62*(4), 776–788. https://doi.org/10.1002/asi.21441

Anderson, T. D. (2006). Uncertainty in action: Observing information seeking within the creative processes of scholarly research. *Information Research*, *12*(1). http://InformationR.net/ir/12-1/paper283.html

Andersson, C. (2017). The front and backstage: Pupils' information activities in secondary school. *Information Research*, *22*(1). http://InformationR.net/ir/22-1/colis/colis1604.html

Ankem, K. (2007). Information-seeking behavior of women in their path to an innovative alternate treatment for symptomatic uterine fibroids. *Journal of the Medical Library Association*, *95*(2), 164–172. https://www.ncbi.nlm.nih.gov/pmc/articles/PMC1852624/

Awamura, N. (2006). Rethinking the information behavior model of information encountering: An analysis of the interviews on information encountering on the web. *Library and Information Science*, *55*, 47–69.

Baker, T. L. (1999). *Doing social research* (3rd ed.). McGraw-Hill.

Bakhtin, M. M. (1981). *The dialogic imagination*. University of Texas Press.

Baldwin, N. S., & Rice, R. E. (1997). Information-seeking behavior of securities analysts: Individual and institutional influences, information sources and channels, and outcomes. *Journal of the American Society for Information Science*, *48*, 674–693.

Bandura, A. (1977). *Social learning theory*. Prentice-Hall.

Bandura, A. (1986). *Social foundations of thought and action*. Prentice-Hall.

Bandura, A. (2001). Social cognitive theory: An agentic perspective. In *Annual review of psychology* (Vol. 52, pp. 1–26). Annual Reviews.

Bates, M. J. (2005). An introduction to metatheories, theories, and models. In K. E. Fisher, S. Erdelez, & E. F. McKechnie (Eds.), *Theories of information behavior* (pp. 1–24). Information Today, Inc.

Beheshti, J., Cole, C., Abuhimed, D., & Lamoureux, I. (2015). Tracking middle school students' information behavior via Kuhlthau's ISP Model: Temporality. *Journal of the Association for Information Science and Technology*, *66*(5), 943–960. https://doi.org/10.1002/asi.23230

Benoit, G. (2005). Communicative action. In K. E. Fisher, S. Erdelez, & E. F. McKechnie (Eds.), *Theories of information behavior* (pp. 99–103). Information Today, Inc.

Berger, P., & Luckmann, T. (1967). *The social construction of reality*. Doubleday.

Birdi, B., & Ford, N. (2018). Towards a new sociological model of fiction reading. *Journal of the Association for Information Science and Technology*, *69*(11), 1291–1303. https://doi.org/10.1002/asi.24053

Bonner, A., & Lloyd, A. (2011). What information counts at the moment of practice? Information practices of renal nurses. *Journal of Advanced Nursing*, *67*(6), 1213–1221. https://doi.org/10.1111/j.1365-2648.2011.05613.x

Bourdieu, P. (1977). *Outline of a theory of practice*. Cambridge University Press.

Bourdieu, P. (1984). *Distinction: A social critique of the judgement of taste* (R. Nice, Trans.). Routledge.

Bourdieu, P. (1986). The forms of capital. In *The handbook of theory and research for the sociology of education* (pp. 241–258). Greenwood Press.

Bourdieu, P. (1990). *The logic of practice* (R. Nice, Trans.). Polity Press.

Bronstein, J. (2014). The role of perceived self-efficacy in the information seeking behavior of library and information science students. *The Journal of Academic Librarianship*, *40*(2), 101–106. https://doi.org/10.1016/j.acalib.2014.01.010

Brown, L. K., & Veinot, T. C. (2020). Information behavior and social control: Toward an understanding of conflictual information behavior in families managing chronic illness. *Journal of the Association for Information Science and Technology*, *72*. https://doi.org/10.1002/asi.24362

Bruner, J. S. (1973). *Beyond the information given: Studies in the psychology of knowing*. Norton.

Burford, S., & Park, S. (2014). The impact of mobile tablet devices on human information behaviour. *Journal of Documentation*, *70*(4), 622–639. https://doi.org/10.1108/JD-09-2012-0123

Burnett, G., Besant, M., & Chatman, E. A. (2001). Small worlds: Normative behavior in virtual communities and feminist bookselling. *Journal of the American Society for Information Science and Technology*, *52*(7), 536–547. https://doi.org/10.1002/asi.1102

Burnett, G., & Jaeger, P. T. (2008). Small worlds, lifeworlds, and information: The ramifications of the information behaviour of social groups in public policy and the public sphere. *Information Research*, *13*(2). http://InformationR.net/ir/13-2/paper346.html

Burnett, S., & Lloyd, A. (2019). The road not taken: Locating desire lines across information landscapes. *Information Research*, *24*(4). http://informationr.net/ir/24-4/colis/colis1911.html

Burrell, G., & Morgan, G. (1988). *Sociological paradigms and organizational analysis*. Heinemann.

Buschman, J. E. (2010). The social as fundamental and a source of the critical: Jurgen Habermas. In *Critical theory for library and information science: Exploring the social from across the disciplines* (pp. 161–172). Libraries Unlimited.

Byström, K., & Järvelin, K. (1995). Task complexity affects information seeking and use. *Information Processing & Management*, *31*, 191–213. https://doi.org/10.1016/0306-4573(95)80035-R

Byström, K., Ruthven, I., & Heinström, J. (2017). Work and information: Which workplace models still work in modern digital workplaces? *Information Research*, *22*(1). http://InformationR.net/ir/22-1/colis/colis1651.html

Caidi, N., Allard, D., & Quirke, L. (2010). The information practices of immigrants. In B. Cronin (Ed.), *Annual review of information science and technology* (Vol. 44, pp. 493–531). Information Today. https://doi.org/10.1002/aris.2010.1440440118

Cano, V. (1989). Citation behavior: Classification, utility, and location. *Journal of the American Society for Information Science*, *40*, 284–290. https://doi.org/10.1002/(SICI)1097-4571(198907)40:4%3C284::AID-ASI10%3E3.0.CO;2-Z

Carter, R. (1965). Communication and affective relations. *Journalism Quarterly*, *42*, 203–212.

Carter, R. (1973). Communication as behavior. Presented at the *Annual Meeting of the Association for Education in Journalism.*

Case, D. O. (2002). *Looking for information: A survey of research on information seeking, needs, and behavior*. Elsevier/Academic Press.

Case, D. O. (2007). *Looking for information: A survey of research on information seeking, needs, and behavior* (2nd ed.). Elsevier/Academic Press.

Case, D. O. (2009b). Collection of family health histories: The link between genealogy and public health. *Journal of the American Society for Information Science and Technology*, *59*(14), 2312–2319. https://doi.org/10.1002/asi.20938

Case, D. O. (2012). *Looking for information: A survey of research on information seeking, needs, and behavior* (3rd ed.). Emerald Publishing Limited.

Case, D. O., & Given, L. M. (2016). *Looking for information: A survey of research on information seeking, needs, and behavior* (4th ed.). Emerald Publishing Limited.

Case, D. O., & Higgins, G. M. (2000). How can we investigate citation behavior? A study of reasons for citing literature in communication. *Journal of the American Society for Information Science*, *51*(7), 635–645. https://doi.org/10.1002/asi.20000

Case, D. O., Johnson, J. D., Andrews, J. E., Allard, S., & Kelly, K. M. (2004). From two-step flow to the Internet: The changing array of sources for genetics information seeking. *Journal of the American Society for Information Science and Technology*, *55*(8), 660–669.

Cavanagh, M. F. (2013). Interpreting reference work with contemporary practice theory. *Journal of Documentation*, *69*(2), 214–242. https://doi.org/10.1108/00220411311300057

Chaffee, S. (1991). *Communication concepts 1: Explication*. Sage Publications.

Charmaz, K. (2014). *Constructing grounded theory: A practical guide through qualitative analysis* (2nd ed.). SAGE Publications Ltd.

Chatman, E. A. (1990). Alienation theory: Application of a conceptual framework to a study of information among janitors. *RQ*, *29*, 355–368. https://www.jstor.org/stable/25828550

Chatman, E. A. (1991). Life in a small world: Applicability of gratification theory to information-seeking behavior. *Journal of the American Society for Information Science*, *42*, 438–449. https://doi.org/10.1002/(SICI)1097-4571(199107)42:6%3C438::AID-ASI6%3E3.0.CO;2-B

Chatman, E. A. (1992). *The information world of retired women*. Greenwood Press.

Chatman, E. A. (1996). The impoverished life-world of outsiders. *Journal of the American Society for Information Science*, *47*, 193–206. https://doi.org/10.1002/(SICI)1097-4571(199603)47:3%3C193::AID-ASI3%3E3.0.CO;2-T

Chatman, E. A. (1999). A theory of life in the round. *Journal of the American Society for Information Science*, *50*, 207–217. https://doi.org/10.1002/(SICI)1097-4571(1999)50:3%3C207::AID-ASI3%3E3.0.CO;2-8

Chen, A. T. (2022). Interactions between affect cognition, and information behavior in the context of fibromyalgia. *Journal of the Association for Information Science and Technology*, *73*(1), 31–44. https://doi.org/10.1002/asi.24538

Chen, W., Lee, K.-H., Straubhaar, J. D., & Spence, J. (2014). Getting a second opinion: Social capital, digital inequalities, and health information repertoires. *Journal of the American Society for Information Science and Technology*, *65*(12), 2552–2563. http://doi.org/10.1002/asi.23130

Choi, W., Park, M. S., & Lee, Y. (2022). Associations between mastery of life and everyday life information-seeking behavior among older adults: Analysis of the Pew Research Center's information engaged and information wary survey data. *Journal of the Association for Information Science and Technology*, *73*(3), 393–406. https://doi.org/10.1002/asi.24556

Cibangu, S. K. (2013). A memo of qualitative research for information science: Toward theory construction. *Journal of Documentation*, *69*(2), 194–213. https://doi.org/10.1108/00220411311300048

Cibangu, S. K., & Hepworth, M. (2016). The uses of phenomenology and phenomenography: A critical review. *Library & Information Science Research*, *38*(2), 148–160. https://doi.org/10.1016/j.lisr.2016.05.001

Cole, C. (2013). Concepts, propositions, models and theories in information behavior research. In *The information behavior of a new generation: Children and teens in the 21st century* (pp. 1–22). Scarecrow Press.

Coleman, J. (1988). Social capital in the creation of human capital. *American Journal of Sociology*, *94*(Suppl.), 95–120.

Courtright, C. (2005). Health information-seeking among Latino newcomers: An exploratory study. *Information Research*, *10*(2). http://InformationR.net/ir/10-2/paper224.html

Cox, A. M. (2005). What are communities of practice? A comparative review of four seminal works. *Journal of Information Science*, *31*(6), 527–540. https://doi.org/10.1177/0165551505057016

Cox, A. M. (2012). An exploration of the practice approach and its place in information science. *Journal of Information Science*, *38*, 176–188. http://doi.org/10.1177/0165551511435881

Cox, A. M., Griffin, B., & Hartel, J. (2017). What everybody knows: Embodied information in serious leisure. *Journal of Documentation*, *73*(3), 386–406. https://doi.org/10.1108/JD-06-2016-0073

Creswell, J. W., & Clark, V. L. P. (2017). *Designing and conducting mixed methods research* (3rd ed.). Sage Publications.

Czaja, R., Manfredi, C., & Price, J. (2003). The determinants and consequences of information seeking among cancer patients. *Journal of Health Communication*, *8*, 529–562. https://doi.org/10.1080/716100418

Davenport, E., & Hall, H. (2002). Organizational knowledge and communities of practice. In B. Cronin (Ed.), *Annual review of information science and technology* (Vol. 36, pp. 171–219). Information Today. https://doi.org/10.1002/aris.1440360105

Davies, E., & McKenzie, P. J. (2004). Preparing for opening night: Temporal boundary objects in textually-mediated professional practice. *Information Research*, *10*(1). http://InformationR.net/ir/10-1/paper211.html

Davies, R., & Williams, D. (2013). Towards a conceptual framework for provider information behaviour. *Journal of Documentation*, *69*(4), 545–566. https://doi.org/10.1108/JD-01-2012-0001

Davis, M. (1986). That's classic! The phenomenology and rhetoric of successful social theories. *Philosophy of the Social Sciences*, *16*, 285–301.

Dawson, M., & Chatman, E. A. (2001). Reference group theory with implications for information studies: A theoretical essay. *Information Research*, *6*(3). http://informationr.net/ir/6-3/paper105.html

de Certeau, M. (1984). *The practice of everyday life*. University of California Press.

Demasson, A., Partridge, H., & Bruce, C. (2016). Information literacy and the serious leisure participant: Variation in the experience of using information to learn. *Information Research*, *21*(2). http://InformationR.net/ir/21-2/paper711.html

Dervin, B. (1983). Information as a user construct: The relevance of perceived information needs to synthesis and interpretation. In S. A. Ward & L. J. Reed (Eds.), *Knowledge structure and use: Implications for synthesis and interpretation* (pp. 153–184). Temple University Press.

Dervin, B. (1992). From the mind's eye of the user: The sense-making qualitative-quantitative methodology. In J. Glazier & R. Powell (Eds.), *Qualitative research in information management* (pp. 61–84). Libraries Unlimited.

Dervin, B. (1997). Given a context by any other name: Methodological tools for taming the unruly beast. In P. Vakkari, R. Savolainen, & B. Dervin (Eds.), *Information seeking in context: Proceedings of a meeting in Finland 14–16 August 1996* (pp. 13–38). Taylor Graham.

Dervin, B. (2003). Human studies and user studies: A call for methodological interdisciplinarity. *Information Research*, *9*(1). http://informationr.net/ir/9-1/paper166.html

Dervin, B. (2005). What methodology does to theory: Sense-making methodology as exemplar. In K. E. Fisher, S. Erdelez, & E. F. McKechnie (Eds.), *Theories of information behavior* (pp. 25–30). Information Today, Inc.

Dervin, B. (2015). Dervin's sense-making theory. In M. Al-Suqri & A. Al-Aufi (Eds.), *Information seeking behavior and technology adoption: Theories and trends* (pp. 59–80). IGI Global.

Dervin, B., Foreman-Wernet, L., & Lauterbach, E. (Eds.). (2003). *Sense-making methodology reader: Selected writings of Brenda Dervin*. Hampton Press.

Dervin, B., & Nilan, M. (1986). Information needs and uses. In M. Williams (Ed.), *Annual review of information science and technology* (Vol. 21, pp. 1–25). Knowledge Industry.

Desouza, K., Awazu, Y., & Wan, Y. (2006). Factors governing the consumption of explicit knowledge. *Journal of the American Society for Information Science and Technology*, *57*(1), 36–43. https://doi.org/10.1002/asi.20250

Desrochers, N., & Pecoskie, J. (2015). Studying a boundary-defying group: An analytical review of the literature surrounding the information habits of writers. *Library & Information Science Research*, *37*(4), 311–322. https://doi.org/10.1016/j.lisr.2015.11.004

Dewey, J. (1933). *How we think*. D. C. Heath.

Dewey, J. (1960). *On experience, nature, and freedom*. The Liberal Arts Press.

Dewey, S. H. (2016). (Non-)use of Foucault's archaeology of knowledge and order of things in LIS journal literature, 1990–2015. *Journal of Documentation*, *72*(3), 454–489. https://doi.org/10.1108/JD-08-2015-0096

Dewey, S. H. (2020). Foucault's toolbox: Use of Foucault's writings in LIS journal literature, 1990–2016. *Journal of Documentation*, *76*(3), 689–707. https://doi.org/10.1108/JD-08-2019-0162

Dixon, C. M. (2005). Strength of weak ties. In K. E. Fisher, S. Erdelez, & E. F. McKechnie (Eds.), *Theories of information behavior* (pp. 344–348). Information Today, Inc.

Donohew, L., & Tipton, L. (1973). A conceptual model of information seeking, avoiding and processing. In P. Clarke (Ed.), *New models for mass communication research* (pp. 243–269). Sage Publications.

du Preez, M., & Fourie, I. (2009). The information behaviour of consulting engineers in South Africa. *Mousaion*, *27*(1), 137–158.

Durrance, J. C., Souden, M., Walker, D., & Fisher, K. E. (2006). Community problem-solving framed as a distributed information use environment: Bridging research and practice. *Information Research*, *11*(4). http://InformationR.net/ir/11-4/paper262.html

Eckerdal, J. R. (2011). To jointly negotiate a personal decision: A qualitative study on information literacy practices in midwifery counselling about contraceptives at youth centres in Southern Sweden. *Information Research*, *16*(1). http://InformationR.net/ir/16-1/paper466.html

Ellis, D. (1989). A behavioural approach to information retrieval design. *Journal of Documentation*, *45*, 171–212. https://doi.org/10.1108/eb026843

Engeström, Y. (1987). *Learning by expanding: An activity-theoretical approach to developmental research*. Orienta-Konsultit.

Engeström, Y. (1999). Activity theory and individual and social transformation. In Y. Engeström, R. Miettinen, & R.-L. Punamäki (Eds.), *Perspectives on activity theory* (pp. 19–38). Cambridge University Press. https://doi.org/10.1017/CBO9780511812774.003

Finholt, T. A. (2002). Collaboratories. In B. Cronin (Ed.), *Annual review of information science and technology* (Vol. 36, pp. 73–107). Information Today. https://doi.org/10.1002/aris.1440360103

Fish, S. (1987). *Is there a text in this class? The authority of interpretive communities* (2nd ed.). Harvard University Press.

Fisher, K. E., & Landry, C. F. (2007). Understanding the information behavior of stay-at-home mothers through affect. In D. Nahl & D. Bilal (Eds.), *Information and emotion: The emergent affective paradigm in information behavior research and theory* (pp. 211–233). Information Today.

Fisher, K., Naumer, C., Durrance, J., Stromski, L., & Christiansen, T. (2005). Something old, something new: Preliminary findings from an exploratory study about people's information habits and information grounds. *Information Research*, *10*(2). http://InformationR.net/ir/10-2/paper223.html

Fleming-May, A. (2014). Concept analysis for library and information science: Exploring usage. *Library & Information Science Research*, *36*(3–4), 203–210. https://doi.org/10.1016/j.lisr.2014.05.001

Foster, A. (2004). A non-linear model of information-seeking behavior. *Journal of the American Society for Information Science and Technology*, *55*(3), 228–237. https://doi.org/10.1002/asi.10359

Foucault, M. (1972). *The order of things: An archaeology of the human sciences*. Tavistock.

Foucault, M. (1980). *Power/knowledge: Selected interviews and writings, 1972–1977*. Harvester Press.

Fransen-Taylor, P., & Narayan, B. (2016). #Homeless but at home in cyberspace. *Information Research*, *21*(4). http://InformationR.net/ir/21-4/isic/isic1610.html

Freimuth, V., Stein, J., & Kean, T. (1989). *Searching for health information: The cancer information service model*. University of Pennsylvania Press.

French, R., & Williamson, K. (2016). Conceptualising welfare workers as information bricoleurs: Theory building using literature analysis, organisational ethnography and grounded theory analysis. *Information Research*, *21*(4). http://InformationR.net/ir/21-4/isic/isic1605.html

Freund, L. (2015). Contextualizing the information-seeking behavior of software engineers. *Journal of the Association for Information Science and Technology*, *66*(8), 1594–1605. https://doi.org/10.1002/asi.23278

Fuhse, B. (2022). *Social networks of meaning and communication*. Oxford University Press.

Fulton, C. (2005b). Chatman's life in the round. In K. E. Fisher, S. Erdelez, & E. F. McKechnie (Eds.), *Theories of information behavior* (pp. 79–82). Information Today, Inc.

Geertz, C. (1973). *The interpretation of culture*. Basic Books.

Genuis, S. K. (2012). Constructing "sense" from evolving health information: A qualitative investigation of information seeking and sense making across sources. *Journal of the American Society for Information Science and Technology*, *63*(8), 1553–1566. http://doi.org/10.1002/asi.22691

Genuis, S. K. (2013). Social positioning theory as a lens for exploring health information seeking and decision making. *Qualitative Health Research*, *23*(4), 555–567. https://doi.org/10.1177/1049732312470029

Genuis, S. K., & Bronstein, J. (2016). Looking for 'normal': Sense making in the context of health disruption. *Journal of the Association for Information Science and Technology*, *68*(3), 750–761. https://doi.org/10.1002/asi.23715

Gibbons, L. (2019). Connecting personal and community memory-making: Facebook Groups as emergent community archives. In *Proceedings of RAILS - Research Applications Information and Library Studies,* 2018, 28–30 November 2018. Faculty of Information Technology, Monash University. *Information Research, 24*(3). http://InformationR.net/ir/24-3/rails/rails1804.html

Giddens, A. (1984). *The constitution of society: Outline of the theory of structuration.* Polity Press.

Giddens, A. (1986). *The constitution of society. Outline of a theory of structuration.* University of California Press.

Giddens, A. (1989). The orthodox consensus and the emerging synthesis. In B. Dervin, L. Grossberg, B. O'Keefe, & E. Wartella (Eds.), *Rethinking communication: Paradigm issues* (Vol. 1, pp. 53–65). Sage Publications.

Giddens, A. (1991). *Modernity and self-identity: Self and society in the late modern age.* Stanford University Press.

Given, L. M. (2002a). Discursive constructions in the university context: Social positioning theory and mature undergraduates' information behaviours. *The New Review of Information Behaviour Research: Studies of Information Seeking in Context, 3,* 127–142.

Given, L. M. (2002b). The academic and the everyday: Investigating the overlap in mature undergraduates' information–seeking behaviors. *Library & Information Science Research, 24*(1), 17–29. https://doi.org/10.1016/S0740-8188(01)00102-5

Given, L. M. (2005). Social positioning. In K. E. Fisher, S. Erdelez, & E. F. McKechnie (Eds.), *Theories of information behavior* (pp. 334–338). Information Today, Inc.

Given, L. M. (2007). Emotional entanglements on the university campus: The role of affect in undergraduates' information behaviors. In D. Nahl & D. Bilal (Eds.), *Information and emotion: The emergent affective paradigm in information behavior research and theory* (pp. 161–175).

Given, L. M. (2016). *100 questions (and answers) about qualitative research.* Sage Publications, Inc.

Given, L. M., & Kuys, B. F. (2022). Memorial design as information creation: Honoring the past through co-production of an informing aesthetic. *Library & Information Science Research, 44.* https://doi.org/10.1016/j.lisr.2022.101176

Given, L. M., & Willson, R. (2015). Collaborative information use with technology: A critical examination of humanities scholars' research activities. In *Collaborative information seeking best practices, new domains and new thoughts* (pp. 139–164). Springer-Verlag. https://doi.org/10.1007/978-3-319-18988-8_8

Glaser, B., & Strauss, A. (1967). *The discovery of grounded theory: Strategies for qualitative research.* Aldine Publishing.

Godbold, N. (2006). Beyond information seeking: Towards a general model of information behaviour. *Information Research, 11*(4). http://InformationR.net/ir/11-4/paper269.html

Goffman, E. (1959). *The presentation of self in everyday life.* Doubleday.

Goffman, E. (1963). *Stigma: Notes on the management of spoiled identity.* Prentice-Hall.

Goffman, E. (1974). *Frame analysis: An essay on the organization of experience.* Macmillan.

Goffman, E. (1983). Interaction order. *American Sociological Review, 48,* 1–17.

González-Teruel, A., Araújo, C.-A.-A., & Sabelli, M. (2022). Diffusion of theories and theoretical models in the Ibero-American research on information behavior. *Journal of the Association for Information Science and Technology, 73*(4), 561–578. https://doi.org/10.1002/asi.24598

González-Teruel, A., & Pérez-Pulido, M. (2020). The diffusion and influence of theoretical models of information behaviour. The case of Savolainen's ELIS model. *Journal of Documentation, 76*(5), 1069–1089. https://doi.org/10.1108/JD-10-2019-0197

Granovetter, M. S. (1973). The strength of weak ties. *American Journal of Sociology, 78,* 1360–1380.

Granovetter, M. S. (1982). The strength of weak ties: A network theory revisited. In P. Marsden & N. Lin (Eds.), *Social structure and network analysis* (pp. 105–130). Sage Publications.

Greyson, D. (2018). Information triangulation: A complex and agentic everyday information practice. *Journal of the Association for Information Science and Technology, 69*(7), 869–878. https://doi.org/10.1002/asi.24012

Gross, M. (2001). Imposed information seeking in public libraries and school library media centers: A common behaviour? *Information Research, 6*(2). http://informationr.net/ir/6-2/paper100.html

Guba, E. G., & Lincoln, Y. S. (2005). Paradigmatic controversies, contradictions, and emerging confluences. In N. Denzin & Y. Lincoln (Eds.), *The Sage handbook of qualitative research* (pp. 191–215). Sage Publications.

Gullbekk, E. (2019). What can we make of our interview data? From interdisciplinary to intra-disciplinary research. In *Proceedings of the Tenth International Conference on Conceptions of Library and Information Science,* Ljubljana, Slovenia, June 16–19, 2019. *Information Research, 24*(2). http://informationr.net/ir/24-4/colis/colis1934.html

Habermas, J. (1979). *Communication and the evolution of society* (T. McCarthy, Trans.). Beacon Press.

Habermas, J. (1984). *Theory of communicative action. Reason and rationalization of society* (T. McCarthy, Trans.) (Vol. 1). Beacon Press.

Habermas, J. (1987). *Theory of communicative action. Lifeworld and system: A critique of functionalist reason* (Vol. 2). Polity Press.

Hacking, I. (1999). *The social construction of what?* Harvard University Press.

Harré, R. (1984). *Personal being: A theory for individual psychology*. Harvard University Press.

Harré, R. (1994). *The discursive mind.* Sage.

Harris, R. M., Veinot, T. C., & Bella, L. (2010). A relational perspective on HIV/AIDS information behaviour in rural Canada. *Libri: International Journal of Libraries and Information Services, 60*(2), 129–141. https://doi.org/10.1515/libr.2010.012

Harris, R. M., Wathen, C. N., & Fear, J. M. (2006). Searching for health information in rural Canada. Where do residents look for health information and what do they do when they find it? *Information Research, 12*(1). http://InformationR.net/ir/12-1/paper274.html

Hartel, J. (2019). Turn, turn, turn. In *Proceedings of CoLIS, the Tenth International Conference on Conceptions of Library and Information Science,* Ljubljana, Slovenia, June 16–19, 2019. *Information Research, 24*(4). http://InformationR.net/ir/24-4/colis/colis1901.html

Harviainen, J. T., & Savolainen, R. (2014). Information as capability for action and capital in synthetic worlds. In *Proceedings of ISIC, the Information Behaviour Conference, Leeds, 2–5 September, 2014 (Vol. 19*). Part 1. http://informationr.net/ir/19-4/isic/isic12.html#.Y27iTOxBw6A

Hayter, S. (2007). The affective dimensions of information behaviour: A small world perspective. In D. Nahl & D. Bilal (Eds.), *Information and emotion: The emergent affective paradigm in information behavior research and theory* (pp. 255–266). Information Today.

Healy, K. (2017). Fuck nuance. *Sociological Theory*, *35*(2), 118–127. https://doi.org/10.1177/0735275117709046

Heinström, J., Sormunen, E., Savolainen, R., & Ek, S. (2019). Developing an empirical measure of everyday information mastering. *Journal of the Association for Information Science and Technology*, *71*(7), 729–741. https://doi.org/10.1002/asi.24305

Hemmig, W. (2009). An empirical study of the information-seeking behavior of practicing visual artists. *Journal of Documentation*, *65*(4), 682–703. http://doi.org/10.1108/00220410910970302

Hepworth, M. (2004). A framework for understanding user requirements for an information service: Defining the needs of informal carers. *Journal of the American Society for Information Science and Technology*, *55*(8), 695–708. https://doi.org/10.1002/asi.20015

Hernon, P. (1984). Information needs and gathering patterns of academic social scientists, with special emphasis given to historians and their use of U.S. government publications. *Government Information Quarterly*, *1*, 401–429. https://doi.org/10.1016/0740-624X(84)90005-4

Hersberger, J. (2003). A qualitative approach to examining information transfer via social networks among homeless populations. *New Review of Information Behaviour Research*, *4*(1), 95–108.

Hersberger, J. (2005). Chatman's information poverty. In K. E. Fisher, S. Erdelez, & E. F McKechnie (Eds.), *Theories of information behavior* (pp. 75–78). Information Today, Inc.

Hicks, A. (2019). Moving beyond the descriptive: The grounded theory of mitigating risk and the theorisation of information literacy. *Journal of Documentation*, *76*(1), 126–144. https://doi.org/10.1108/JD-07-2019-0126

Hjørland, B. (2002a). Domain analysis in information science. Eleven approaches – traditional as well as innovative. *Journal of Documentation*, *58*(4), 422–462.

Hjørland, B. (2005a). Introduction to the special issue: Library and information science and the philosophy of science. *Journal of Documentation*, *61*, 5–10. https://doi.org/10.1108/00220410510577970

Hjørland, B. (2005b). Empiricism, rationalism and positivism in library and information science. *Journal of Documentation*, *61*, 130–155. https://doi.org/10.1108/00220410510578050

Hjørland, B. (2005c). Afterword: Comments on the articles and proposals for further work. *Journal of Documentation*, *61*, 5–10. https://doi.org/10.1108/00220410510578069

Hjørland, B., & Christensen, F. S. (2002). Work tasks and socio-cognitive relevance: A specific example. *Journal of the American Society for Information Science and Technology*, *53*(11), 960–965. https://doi.org/10.1002/asi.10132

Houston, R. (2011). CNI: Compelled nonuse of information. *Information Processing & Management*, *47*(3), 363–375. https://doi.org/10.1016/j.ipm.2010.08.002

Hsiao, B., Zhu, Y.-Q., & Chen, L.-Y. (2017). Untangling the relationship between internet anxiety and internet identification in students: The role of internet self-efficacy. *Information Research*, *22*(2). http://InformationR.net/ir/22-2/paper753.html

Huang, H., Tse, S.-k., Chu, S. K.-W., Xiao, X.-Y., Lam, J. W.-Y., Ng, R. H.-W., & Hui, S.-Y. (2019). The correlation between out-of-school and in-school reading resources with primary school students' reading attainment. *Information Research*, *24*(3). http://InformationR.net/ir/24-3/paper834.html

Huisman, M., Biltereyst, D., & Joye, S. (2020). Sharing is caring: The everyday informal exchange of health information among adults aged fifty and over. *Information Research*, *25*(1). http://InformationR.net/ir/25-1/paper848.html

Huizing, A., & Cavanagh, M. (2011). Planting contemporary practice theory in the garden of information science. *Information Research*, *16*(4). http://InformationR.net/ir/16-4/paper497.html

Hultgren, F. (2013). The stranger's tale: Information seeking as an outsider activity. *Journal of Documentation*, *69*(2), 275–294. http://doi.org/10.1108/00220411311300075

Huotari, M.-L., & Chatman, E. A. (2001). Using everyday life information seeking to explain organizational behavior. *Library & Information Science Research*, *23*(4), 351–366. https://doi.org/10.1016/S0740-8188(01)00093-7

Huotari, M.-L., Suorsa, A., Ikonen, K., & Innanen, K. (2016). Knowledge creation in an R&D project. A multiple case study in the context of clean energy markets in Finland. In *Proceedings of ISIC, the Information Behaviour Conference,* Zadar, Croatia, 20–23 September, 2016. Part 1, *Information Research, 21*(4). http://InformationR.net/ir/21-4/isic/isics1602.html

Hussey, L. (2010). Social capital, symbolic violence, and fields of cultural production: Pierre Bourdieu and Library and Information Science. In G. J. Leckie, L. M. Given, & J. E. Buschman (Eds.), *Critical theory for library and information science: Exploring the social from across the disciplines* (pp. 41–52). Libraries Unlimited.

Huvila, I. (2013). "Library users come to a library to find books": The structuration of the library as a soft information system. *Journal of Documentation*, *69*(5), 715–735. http://doi.org/10.1108/JD-06-2012-0080

Huvila, I. (2022). Making and taking information. *Journal of the Association for Information Science and Technology*, *73*(4), 528–541. https://doi.org/10.1002/asi.24599

Ingram, D. (2014). *Critical theory to structuralism: Philosophy, politics and the human sciences* (Vol. 5). Routledge.

Ingwersen, P. (1996). Cognitive perspectives of information retrieval interaction: Elements of a cognitive IR theory. *Journal of Documentation*, *52*, 3–50. https://doi.org/10.1108/eb026960

Irvine-Smith, S. (2017). Information through the lens: Information research and the dynamics of practice. In *Proceedings of the Ninth International Conference on Conceptions of Library and Information Science,* Uppsala, Sweden, June 27–29, 2016. *Information Research, 22*(1). http://InformationR.net/ir/22-1/colis/colis1603.html

Isah, E. E., & Byström, K. (2016). Physicians' learning at work through everyday access to information. *Journal of the American Society for Information Science and Technology*, *67*(2), 318–332. https://doi.org/10.1002/asi.23378

Isah, E. E., & Byström, K. (2017). Enacting workplace information practices: The diverse roles of physicians in a health care team. In *Proceedings of the Ninth International Conference on Conceptions of Library and Information Science,* Uppsala, Sweden, June 27–29 2016. *Information Research, 22*(1). http://informationr.net/ir/22-1/colis/colis1650.html

Isah, E. E., & Byström, K. (2020). The mediating role of documents: Information sharing through medical records in healthcare. *Journal of Documentation*, *76*(6), 1171–1191. https://doi.org/10.1108/JD-11-2019-0227

Iser, W. (1978). *The act of reading*. Johns Hopkins University.

Jarrahi, M. H., & Thomson, L. (2017). The interplay between information practices and information context: The case of mobile knowledge workers. *Journal of the Association for Information Science and Technology*, *68*(5), 1073–1089. https://doi.org/10.1002/asi.23773

Järvelin, K., & Wilson, T. D. (2003). On conceptual models for information seeking and retrieval research. *Information Research*, *9*(1). http://informationr.net/ir/9-1/paper163.html

Johnson, C. A. (2005). Nan Lin's theory of social capital. In K. E. Fisher, S. Erdelez, & E. F. McKechnie (Eds.), *Theories of information behavior* (pp. 323–327). Information Today, Inc.

Johnson, C. A. (2007). Social capital and the search for information: Examining the role of social capital in information seeking behavior in Mongolia. *Journal of the American Society for Information Science and Technology*, *58*(6), 883–894. http://doi.org/10.1002/asi.20561

Johnson, C. A. (2012). How do public libraries create social capital? An analysis of interactions between library staff and patrons. *Library & Information Science Research*, *34*(1), 52–62. https://doi.org/10.1016/j.lisr.2011.07.009

Johnson, C. A. (2015). Social capital and library and information science research: Definitional chaos or coherent research enterprise? *Information Research*, *20*(4). http://InformationR.net/ir/20-4/paper690.html

Johnson, J. D. (1997). *Cancer-related information seeking*. Hampton Press.

Johnson, J. D., & Meischke, H. (1993). A comprehensive model of cancer-related information seeking applied to magazines. *Human Communication Research*, *19*, 343–367. https://doi.org/10.1111/j.1468-2958.1993.tb00305.x

Joyce, S. (2005). Symbolic violence. In K. E. Fisher, S. Erdelez, & E. F. McKechnie (Eds.), *Theories of information behavior* (pp. 349–353). Information Today, Inc.

Julien, H. (2004). Adolescent decision-making for careers: An exploration of information behavior. In M. Chelton & C. Cool (Eds.), *Youth information-seeking behavior: Theories, models and issues* (pp. 321–352). Scarecrow Press.

Julien, H., & Given, L. M. (2003). Faculty-librarian relationship in the information literacy context: A content analysis of librarians' expressed attitudes and experiences. *Canadian Journal of Information and Library Science*, *27*, 65–87. https://doi.org/10.29173/cais526

Kahlor, L. (2010). PRISM: A planned risk information seeking model. *Health Communication*, *25*(4), 345–356. https://doi.org/10.1080/10410231003775172

Kane, S. K. (2007). Everyday inclusive web design: An activity perspective. *Information Research*, *12*(1). http://InformationR.net/ir/12-3/paper309.html

Kankam, P. K. (2019). The use of paradigms in information research. *Library & Information Science Research*, *41*(2), 85–92. https://doi.org/10.1016/j.lisr.2019.04.003

Karanasios, S., Thakker, D., Lau, L., Allen, D., Dimitravo, V., & Norman, A. (2013). Making sense of digital traces: An activity theory driven ontological approach. *Journal of the American Society for Information Science and Technology*, *64*(12), 2452–2467. https://doi.org/10.1002/asi.22935

Kari, J., & Savolainen, R. (2003). Towards a contextual model of information seeking on the Web. *New Review of Information Behaviour Research*, *4*(1), 155–175.

Kelly, G. (1963). *A theory of personality: The psychology of personal constructs*. Norton.

Kelly, M. (2021). Epistemology, epistemic belief, personal epistemology, and epistemics: A review of concepts as they impact information behavior research. *Journal of the Association for Information Science and Technology*, *72*(4), 507–519. https://doi.org/10.1002/asi.24422

Kerlinger, F. (1973). *Foundations of behavioral research*. Holt Rinehart & Winston.

Khazraee, E. (2019). Assembling narratives: Tensions in collaborative construction of knowledge. *Journal of the Association for Information Science and Technology*, *70*(4), 325–337. https://doi.org/10.1002/asi.24133

Kitzie, V. L., Wagner, T. L., Lookingbill, V., & Vera, N. (2022). Advancing information practices theoretical discourses centered on marginality, community, and embodiment: Learning from the experiences of lesbian, gay, bisexual, transgender, queer, intersex, and asexual

(LGBTQIA+) communities. *Journal of the Association for Information Science and Technology*, *73*(4), 495–510. https://doi.org/10.1002/asi.24594

Kitzie, V., Wagner, T., & Vera, A. N. (2021). Discursive power and resistance in the information world maps of lesbian, gay, bisexual, transgender, queer, intersex and asexual community leaders. *Journal of Documentation*, *77*(3), 638–662. https://doi.org/10.1108/JD-08-2020-0138

Knorr-Cetina, K. D. (1981). *The manufacture of knowledge: A essay on the constructivist and contextual nature of science*. Pergamon Press.

Knox, E. J. M. (2014). Society, institutions, and common sense: Themes in the discourse of book challengers in 21st century United States. *Library & Information Science Research*, *36*(3–4), 171–178. https://doi.org/10.1016/j.lisr.2014.06.003

Koh, K., Snead, J. T., & Lu, K. (2019). The processes of maker learning and information behavior in a technology-rich high school class. *Journal of the Association for Information Science and Technology*, *70*(12), 1395–1412. https://doi.org/10.1002/asi.24197

Krikelas, J. (1983). Information-seeking behavior: Patterns and concepts. *Drexel Library Quarterly*, *19*, 5–20.

Kuhlthau, C. C. (1988). Developing a model of the library search process: Cognitive and affective aspects. *Reference Quarterly*, *28*, 232–242. https://www.jstor.org/stable/25828262

Kuhlthau, C. C. (1991). Inside the search process: Information seeking from the user's perspective. *Journal of the American Society for Information Science*, *42*, 361–371. https://doi.org/10.1002/(SICI)1097-4571(199106)42:5%3C361::AID-ASI6%3E3.0.CO;2-%23

Kuhlthau, C. C. (1993a). *Seeking meaning: A process approach to library and information services*. Ablex.

Kuhlthau, C. C. (1993b). A principle of uncertainty for information seeking. *Journal of Documentation*, *49*, 339–355. https://doi.org/10.1108/eb026918

Kuhlthau, C. C. (2004). *Seeking meaning: A process approach to library and information services* (Second). Libraries Unlimited.

Kuhlthau, C. C. (2005). Kuhlthau's information search process. In K. E. Fisher, S. Erdelez, & E. F. McKechnie (Eds.), *Theories of information behavior* (pp. 230–234). Information Today, Inc.

Kuhn, T. (1962). *The structure of scientific revolutions*. U. of Chicago Press.

Kundu, D. K. (2017). Models of information seeking behaviour: A comparative study. *International Journal of Library and Information Studies*, *7*(4), 393–405.

Kurbanoglu, S. S. (2003). Self-efficacy: A concept closely linked to information literacy and lifelong learning. *Journal of Documentation*, *59*(6), 635–646. https://doi.org/10.1108/00220410310506295

Kurbanoglu, S. S., Akkoyunlu, B., & Umay, A. (2006). Developing the information literacy self-efficacy scale. *Journal of Documentation*, *62*(6), 730–743. https://doi.org/10.1108/00220410610714949

Kwon, N. (2017). How work positions affect the research activity and information behaviour of laboratory scientists in the research lifecycle: Applying activity theory. *Information Research*, *22*(1). http://informationr.net/ir/22-1/paper744.html

Kwon, N., & Kim, K. (2009). Who goes to a library for cancer information in the e-health era? A secondary data analysis of the health information National trends survey (HINTS). *Library & Information Science Research*, *31*(3), 192–200. https://doi.org/10.1016/j.lisr.2009.01.006

Lakshminarayanan, B. (2010). *Towards developing an integrated model of information behaviour*. Ph.D. Queensland University of Technology.

Laplante, A., & Downie, J. S. (2011). The utilitarian and hedonic outcomes of music information-seeking in everyday life. *Library & Information Science Research*, *33*(3), 202–210. http://doi.org/10.1016/j.lisr.2010.11.002

Latham, K. F. (2014). Experiencing documents. *Journal of Documentation*, *70*(4), 3. http://doi.org/10.1108/JD-01-2013-0013

Latour, B., & Woolgar, S. (1979). *Laboratory life: The social construction of scientific facts*. Sage Publications.

Lave, J., & Wenger, E. (1991). *Situated learning: Legitimate peripheral participation*. Cambridge University Press.

Le Louvier, K., & Innocenti, P. (2021). Heritage as an affective and meaningful information literacy practice: An interdisciplinary approach to the integration of asylum seekers and refugees.

Journal of the Association for Information Science and Technology, *73*(5), 687–701. https://doi.org/10.1002/asi.24572

Lechte, J. (2007). *Fifty key contemporary thinkers: From structuralism to post-humanism* (2nd ed.). Routledge.

Leckie, G. J. (2005). General model of the information seeking of professionals. In K. E. Fisher, S. Erdelez, & E. F. McKechnie (Eds.), *Theories of information behavior* (pp. 158–163). Information Today, Inc.

Leckie, G. J., & Buschman, J. E. (2010). Introduction: The necessity for theoretically informed critique in library and information science (LIS). In *Critical theory for library and information science: Exploring the social from across the disciplines* (pp. vii–xxii). Libraries Unlimited.

Leckie, G. J., Pettigrew, K. E., & Sylvain, C. (1996). Modeling the information seeking of professionals: A general model derived from research on engineers, health care professionals and lawyers. *The Library Quarterly*, *66*, 161–193. https://www.jstor.org/stable/4309109

Lee, M., & Butler, B. S. (2018). How are information deserts created? A theory of local information landscapes. *Journal of the Association for Information Science and Technology*, *70*(2), 101–116. https://doi.org/10.1002/asi.24114

Lee, L., Ocepek, M. G., & Makri, S. (2022). Information behavior patterns: A new theoretical perspective from an empirical study of naturalistic information acquisition. *Journal of the Association for Information Science and Technology*, *73*(4), 594–608. https://doi.org/10.1002/asi.24595

Leont'ev, A. N. (1978). *Activity, consciousness and personality*. Prentice-Hall.

Liehr, P., & Smith, M. J. (1999). Middle range theory: Spinning research and practice to create knowledge for the new millennium. *Advances in Nursing Science*, *21*(4), 81–91.

Liehr, P., & Smith, M. J. (2017). Middle range theory. *Advances in Nursing Science*, *40*(1), 51–63. https://doi.org/10.1097/00012272-199906000-00011

Lim, S. (2009). How and why do college students use Wikipedia? *Journal of the American Society for Information Science and Technology*, *60*(11), 2189–2202. https://doi.org/10.1002/asi.21142

Limberg, L., Sundin, O., & Talja, S. (2012). Three theoretical perspectives on information literacy. *Journal for Information Technology Studies as a Human Science*, *11*(2), 93–110.

Lim, S., & Kwon, N. (2010). Gender differences in information behavior concerning Wikipedia: An unorthodox information source? *Library & Information Science Research*, *32*(3), 212–220. https://doi.org/10.1016/j.lisr.2010.01.003

Lin, N. (2001). *Social capital: A theory of social structure and action*. Cambridge University Press.

Lindau, S. T., Makelarski, J. A., Abramsohn, E., Beiser, D., Boyd, K., Huang, E., Paradise, K., & Tung, E. (2022). Sharing information about health-related resources: Observations from a community resource referral intervention trial in a predominantly African American/Black community. *Journal of the Association for Information Science and Technology*, *73*(3), 438–448. https://doi.org/10.1002/asi.24560

Lindberg, J., & Hedemark, A. (2019). Meaningful reading experiences among elderly: Some insights from a small-scale study of Swedish library outreach services. In *Proceedings of ISIC, The Information Behaviour Conference,* Krakow, Poland, 9–11 October. Part 2. *Information Research, 24*(1). http://InformationR.net/ir/24-1/isic2018/isic1836.html

Littlejohn, S. W. (1983). *Theories of human communication*. Wadsworth.

Livingstone, S. (2006). The influence of Personal Influence on the study of audiences. *The Annals of the American Academy of Political and Social Science*, *608*(1), 233–250. https://doi.org/10.1177/0002716206292325

Lloyd, A. (2006). Information literacy landscapes: An emerging picture. *Journal of Documentation*, *62*(5), 570–583. https://doi.org/10.1108/00220410610688723

Lloyd, A. (2007a). Learning to put out the red stuff: Becoming information literate through discursive practice. *The Library Quarterly*, *77*(2), 181–198. https://doi.org/10.1086/517844

Lloyd, A. (2007b). Recasting information literacy as socio-cultural practice: Implications for library and information science researchers. *Information Research*, *12*(4). http://informationr.net/ir/12-4/colis/colis34.html

Lloyd, A. (2009). Informing practice: Information experiences of ambulance officers in training and on-road practice. *Journal of Documentation*, *65*(3), 396–419. http://doi.org/10.1108/00220410910952401

Lloyd, A. (2014). Following the red thread of information in information literacy research: Recovering local knowledge through interview to the double. *Library & Information Science Research*, *36*(2), 99–105. https://doi.org/10.1016/j.lisr.2013.10.006

Lloyd, A. (2015). Stranger in a strange land: Enabling information resilience in the resettlement landscape. *Journal of Documentation*, *71*(5), 1029–1042. https://doi.org/10.1108/JD-04-2014-0065

Lloyd, A., & Hicks, A. (2021). Contextualising risk: The unfolding information work and practices of people during the COVID-19 pandemic. *Journal of Documentation*, *77*(5), 1052–1072. https://doi.org/10.1108/JD-11-2020-0203

Lloyd, A., Kennan, M. A., Thompson, K. M., & Qayyum, A. (2013). Connecting with new information landscapes: Information literacy practices of refugees. *Journal of Documentation*, *69*(1), 121–144. http://doi.org/10.1108/00220411311295351

Lloyd, A., Lipu, S., & Kennan, M. A. (2010). On becoming citizens: Examining social inclusion from an information perspective. *Australian Academic and Research Libraries*, *41*(1), 42–53. https://doi.org/10.1080/00048623.2016.1256806

Lloyd, A., & Olsson, M. (2019). Untangling the knot: The information practices of enthusiast car restorers. *Journal of the Association for Information Science and Technology*, *70*(12), 1311–1323. https://doi.org/10.1002/asi.24284

Lloyd, A., Pilerot, O., & Hultgren, F. (2017). The remaking of fractured landscapes: Supporting refugees in transition (SpiRiT). *Information Research*, *22*(3). http://informationr.net/ir/22-3/paper764.html

Lloyd, A., & Williamson, K. (2008). Towards an understanding of information literacy in context. *Journal of Librarianship and Information Science*, *40*(1), 3–12. https://doi.org/10.1177/0961000607086616

Longo, D. R. (2005). Understanding health information, communication, and information seeking of patients and consumers: A comprehensive and integrated model. *Health Expectations*, *8*, 189–194. https://doi.org/10.1111%2Fj.1369-7625.2005.00339.x

Lopatovska, I., & Smiley, B. (2014). Proposed model of information behaviour in crisis: The case of hurricane Sandy. *Information Research*, *19*(1). http://informationr.net/ir/19-1/paper610.html

Lu, Y. (2007). The human in human information acquisition: Understanding gatekeeping and proposing new directions in scholarship. *Library & Information Science Research*, *29*(1), 103–123. https://doi.org/10.1016/j.lisr.2006.10.007

Lueg, C. P. (2008). Beyond FAQs: From information sharing to knowledge generation in online travel communities. In M.-L. Houtari & E. Davenport (Eds.), *Presented at from information provision to knowledge production* (pp. 105–120). Faculty of Humanities, University of Oulu.

Manicas, P. T. (1998). *A history and philosophy of the social sciences*. Basil Blackwell.

Mansour, A. (2020). Shared information practices on Facebook: The formation and development of a sustainable online community. *Journal of Documentation*, *76*(3), 625–646. https://doi.org/10.1108/JD-10-2018-0160

Marcella, R., & Baxter, G. (2005). Information interchange. In K. E. Fisher, S. Erdelez, & E. F. McKechnie (Eds.), *Theories of information behavior* (pp. 204–209). Information Today, Inc.

Marchionini, G. (1995). *Information seeking in electronic environments*. Cambridge University Press.

Marton, C. (2011). *Understanding how women seek health information on the web*. PhD thesis. University of Toronto. http://hdl.handle.net/1807/29808

Massey, S., Druin, A., & Weeks, A. (2007). Emotion, response, and recommendation: The role of affect in children's book reviews in a digital library. In D. Nahl & D. Bilal (Eds.), *Information and emotion: The emergent affective paradigm in information behavior research and theory* (pp. 135–160). Information Today.

Massey, S., Weeks, A., & Druin, A. (2005). Initial findings from a three-year international case study exploring children's responses to literature in a digital library. *Library Trends*, *54*(3), 245–265. https://doi.org/10.1353/lib.2006.0018

Ma, J., & Stahl, L. (2017). A multimodal critical discourse analysis of anti-vaccination information on Facebook. *Library & Information Science Research*, *39*(4), 303–310. https://doi.org/10.1016/j.lisr.2017.11.005

Mawby, J., Foster, A., & Ellis, D. (2015). Everyday life information seeking behaviour in relation to the environment. *Library Review*, *64*(6/7), 468–479. http://doi.org/10.1108/LR-10-2014-0120

McCaughan, E., & McKenna, H. (2007). Never-ending making sense: Towards a substantive theory of the information-seeking behaviour of newly diagnosed cancer patients. *Journal of Clinical Nursing*, *16*, 2096–2104. https://doi.org/10.1111/j.1365-2702.2006.01817.x

McKenzie, P. J. (2003a). Justifying cognitive authority decisions: Discursive strategies of information seekers. *The Library Quarterly*, *73*(3), 261–288. https://www.jstor.org/stable/4309663

McKenzie, P. J. (2003b). A model of information practices in accounts of everyday-life information seeking. *Journal of Documentation*, *59*, 19–40. https://doi.org/10.1108/00220410310457993

McKenzie, P. J. (2005). Interpretive repertoires. In K. E. Fisher, S. Erdelez, & E. F. McKechnie (Eds.), *Theories of information behavior* (pp. 221–224). Information Today, Inc.

McKenzie, P. J. (2006). The seeking of baby-feeding information by Canadian women pregnant with twins. *Midwifery*, *22*(3), 218–227. https://doi.org/10.1016/j.midw.2005.03.006

McKenzie, P. J. (2009). Informing choice: The organization of institutional interaction in clinical midwifery care. *Library & Information Science Research*, *31*(3), 163–173. https://doi.org/10.1016/j.lisr.2009.03.006

McKenzie, P. J. (2010). Informing relationships: Small talk, informing and relationship building in midwife-woman interaction. *Information Research*, *15*(1). http://InformationR.net/ir/15-1/paper423.html

Mehra, B. (2007). Affective factors in information seeking during the cross-cultural learning process of international doctoral students in library and information science education. In D. Nahl & D. Bilal (Eds.), *Information and emotion: The emergent affective paradigm in information behavior research and theory* (pp. 279–301). Information Today.

Menzel, H. (1964). The information needs of current scientific research. *The Library Quarterly*, *34*, 4–19.

Mershon, C., & Shvetova, O. (2019). *Formal modeling in social science*. University of Michigan Press.

Merton, R. K. (1968). *Social theory and social structure* (2nd ed.). Free Press.

Merton, R. K. (1972). Insiders and outsiders: A chapter in the sociology of knowledge. *American Journal of Sociology*, *78*, 9–47.

Meyer, H. W. J. (2016). Untangling the building blocks: A generic model to explain information behaviour to novice researchers. *Information Research*, *21*(4). http://InformationR.net/ir/21-4/isic/isic1602.html

Meyers, E. M. (2007). From activity to learning: Using cultural historical activity theory to model school library programmes and practices. *Information Research*, *12*(3). http://InformationR.net/ir/12-3/paper313.html

Meyers, E. M., Fisher, K. E., & Marcoux, E. (2009). Making sense of an information world: The everyday-life information behavior of preteens. *The Library Quarterly*, *79*(3), 301–341. https://doi.org/10.1086/599125

Miller, H. (2018). Veblen online: Information and the risk of commandeering the conspicuous self. *Information Research*, *23*(2). http://informationr.net/ir/23-3/paper797.html

Mishra, J., Allen, D., & Pearman, A. (2015). Information seeking, use, and decision making. *Journal of the Association for Information Science and Technology*, *66*(4), 662–673. https://doi.org/10.1002/asi.23204

Mohammed, F., & Norman, A. (2017). Understanding information sharing behaviour of millennials in large multinational organizations: Research in progress. In *Proceedings of ISIC, the Information Behaviour Conference,* Zadar, Croatia, 20–23 September, 2016. Part 2. *Information Research, 22*(1). http://informationr.net/ir/22-1/isic/isics1605.html

Morey, O. (2007). Health information ties: Preliminary findings on the health information seeking behaviour of an African-American community. *Information Research*, *12*(2). http://informationr.net/ir/12-2/paper297.html

Moring, C., & Lloyd, A. (2013). Analytical implications of using practice theory in workplace information literacy research. *Information Research, 18*(3). http://www.informationr.net/ir/18-3/colis/paperC35.html#.Vc0V_lOqqko

Mowbray, J., & Hall, H. (2020). Networking as an information behaviour during job search: A study of active jobseekers in the Scottish youth labour market. *Journal of Documentation, 76*(2), 424–439. https://doi.org/10.1108/JD-05-2019-0086

Mowbray, J., Hall, H., Raeside, R., & Robertson, P. (2017). The role of networking and social media tools during job search: An information behaviour perspective. *Information Research, 22*(1). http://InformationR.net/ir/22-1/colis/colis1615.html

Multas, A. M., & Hirvonen, N. (2019). Employing nexus analysis in investigating information literacy. In *Proceedings of the Tenth International Conference on Conceptions of Library and Information Science,* Ljubljana, Slovenia, June 16–19, 2019. *Information Research, 24*(4). http://InformationR.net/ir/24-4/colis/colis1944.html

Nahl, D. (2001). Conceptual framework for defining information behavior. *Studies in Media and Information Literacy Education, 1*(2), 1–15.

Nahl, D. (2005). Affective load. In K. E. Fisher, S. Erdelez, & E. F. McKechnie (Eds.), *Theories of information behavior* (pp. 39–44). Information Today, Inc.

Nahl, D. (2007a). The centrality of the affective in information behavior. In *Information and emotion: The emergent affective paradigm in information behavior research and theory* (pp. 3–37). Information Today.

Nahl, D. (2007b). Social-biological information technology: An integrated conceptual framework. *Journal of the American Society for Information Science and Technology, 58*(13), 2021–2046. https://doi.org/10.1002/asi.20690

Nardi, B. (Ed.). (1996). *Context and consciousness: Activity theory and human-computer interaction.* MIT Press.

Naveed, M. A., Batool, S. H., & Anwar, M. A. (2021). Resident university students' everyday life information seeking behaviour in Pakistan. *Information Research, 26*(2). http://InformationR.net/ir/26-2/paper901.html

Nel, M. A. (2020). Information behaviour and information practices of academic librarians: A scoping review to guide studies on their learning in practice. In *Proceedings of ISIC, the Information Behaviour Conference,* Pretoria, South Africa, 28 September 2020 – 1 October, 2020. *Information Research, 25*(4). http://InformationR.net/ir/25-4/isic2020/isic2020.html

Niedwiedzka, B. (2003). A proposed general model of information behaviour. *Information Research, 9*(1). http://informationr.net/ir/9-1/paper164.html

Nikou, S., Molinari, A., & Widén, G. (2020). The interplay between literacy and digital technology: A fuzzy-set qualitative comparative analysis approach. In *Proceedings of ISIC, the Information Behaviour Conference,* Pretoria, South Africa, 28 September – 1 October, 2020. *Information Research, 25*(4). http://InformationR.net/ir/25-4/isic2020/isic2016.html

Nordsteien, A. (2017). Handling inconsistencies between information modalities - workplace learning of newly qualified nurses. *Information Research, 22*(1). http://InformationR.net/ir/22-1/colis/colis1652.html

Nowé, K., Macevičiūtė, E., & Wilson, T. D. (2008). Tensions and contradictions in the information behaviour of Board members of a voluntary organization. *Information Research, 13*(4). http://InformationR.net/ir/13-4/paper363.html

Ocepek, M. G. (2018a). Bringing out the everyday in everyday information behavior. *Journal of Documentation, 74*(2), 398–411. https://doi.org/10.1108/JD-10-2016-0119

Ocepek, M. G. (2018b). Sensible shopping: A sensory exploration of the information environment of the grocery store. *Library Trends, 66*(3), 371–394. https://doi.org/10.1353/lib.2018.0008

O'Connor, L. G., & Dillingham, L. L. (2014). Personal experience as social capital in online investor forums. *Library & Information Science Research, 36*(1), 27–35. http://doi.org/10.1016/j.lisr.2013.10.001

Olmeda-Gómez, C., Perianes-Rodríguez, A., Ovalle-Perandones, M. A., & Moya-Anegón, F. (2008). Comparative analysis of university-government-enterprise co-authorship networks in three scientific domains in the region of Madrid, 1995–2003. *Information Research, 13*(3). http://InformationR.net/ir/13-3/paper352.html

Olsson, M. (2005). Beyond "needy" individuals: Conceptualizing information behavior. In A. Grove (Ed.), *ASIS&T '05: Proceedings of the annual meeting of the American society for information science and technology* (Vol. 42, pp. 43–55). American Society for Information Science and Technology.

Olsson, M. R. (2010a). All the world's a stage – The information practices and sense-making of theatre professionals. *Libri: International Journal of Libraries and Information Services*, *60*(3), 241–252. http://doi.org/10.1515/libr.2010.021

Olsson, M., & Lloyd, A. (2017). Being in place: Embodied information practices. *Information Research*, *22*(1). http://InformationR.net/ir/22-1/colis/colis1601.html

Orr, R. (1970). The scientist as information processor: A conceptual model illustrated with data on variables related to library utilization. In C. Nelson & D. Pollock (Eds.), *Communication among scientists and engineers* (pp. 143–189). D. C. Heath.

Paisley, W. J. (1968). Information needs and uses. In C. Cuadra (Ed.), *Annual review of information science and technology* (Vol. 3, pp. 1–30). Encyclopaedia Britannica.

Pálsdóttir, A. (2008). Information behaviour, health self-efficacy beliefs and health behaviour in Icelanders' everyday life. *Information Research*, *13*(1). http://informationr.net/ir/13-1/paper334.html

Pálsdóttir, A. (2012). Relatives as supporters of elderly peoples' information behavior. *Information Research*, *17*(4). http://InformationR.net/ir/17-4/paper546.html

Pang, N., Karanasios, S., & Anwar, M. (2020). Exploring the information worlds of older persons during disasters. *Journal of the Association for Information Science and Technology*, *71*(6), 619–631. https://doi.org/10.1002/asi.24294

Papen, U. (2013). Conceptualising information literacy as social practice: A study of pregnant women's information practices. *Information Research*, *18*(2). http://informationr.net/ir/18-2/paper580.html#.Y3AZjexBwUo

Park, M. S., Oh, H., & You, S. (2020). Health information seeking among people with multiple chronic conditions: Contextual factors and their associations mined from questions in social media. *Library & Information Science Research*, *42*(3). https://doi.org/10.1016/j.lisr.2020.101030

Pavitt, C. (1999). The third way: Scientific realism and communication theory. *Communication Theory*, *9*, 162–188. https://doi.org/10.1111/j.1468-2885.1999.tb00356.x

Pham, H. T. (2019). The application of structuration theory in studying collaboration between librarians and academic staff in universities in Australia and Vietnam. *Information Research*, *24*(3). http://InformationR.net/ir/24-3/paper829.html

Pham, H. T., & Williamson, K. (2018). A two-way street: Collaboration and information sharing in academia. A theoretically-based, comparative Australian/Vietnamese study. *Information Research*, *23*(4). http://www.informationr.net/ir/23-4/isic2018/isic1810.html

Pilerot, O., Hammarfelt, B., & Moring, C. (2017). The many faces of practice theory in library and information studies. *Information Research*, *22*(1). http://InformationR.net/ir/22-1/colis/colis1602.html

Pluye, P., El Sherif, R., Granikov, V., Hong, Q. N., Vedel, I., Galvao, M. C. B., Frati, F. E., Desroches, S., Repchinsky, C., Rihoux, B., Légaré, F., Burnand, B., Bujold, M., & Grad, R. (2019). Health outcomes of online consumer health information: A systematic mixed studies review with framework synthesis. *Journal of the Association for Information Science and Technology*, *70*(7), 643–659. https://doi.org/10.1002/asi.24178

Polkinghorne, S., & Given, L. M. (2021). Holistic information research: From rhetoric to paradigm. *Journal of the Association for Information Science and Technology*, *72*(10), 1261–1271. https://doi.org/10.1002/asi.24450

Poole, A. H., & Garwood, D. A. (2018). Interdisciplinary scholarly collaboration in data-intensive, public-funded, international digital humanities project work. *Library & Information Science Research*, *40*(3–4), 184–193. https://doi.org/10.1016/j.lisr.2018.08.003

Potter, J. (1996). *Representing reality: Discourse, rhetoric and social construction*. Sage.

Putnam, R. D. (2000). *Bowling alone: The collapse and revival of American community*. Simon & Schuster.

Pyati, A. (2010). Herbert Marcuse: Liberation, Utopia, and revolution. In G. J. Leckie, L. M. Given, & J. E. Buschman (Eds.), *Critical theory for library and information science: Exploring the social from across the disciplines* (pp. 237–248). Libraries Unlimited.

Radford, M. L., Connaway, L. S., Mikitish, S., Alpert, M., Shah, C., & Cooke, N. A. (2017). Shared values, new vision: Collaboration and communities of practice in virtual reference and SQA. *Journal of the Association for Information Science and Technology*, *68*(2), 438–449. https://doi.org/10.1002/asi.23668

Reckwitz, A. (2002). Toward a theory of social practices: A development in culturalist theorizing. *European Journal of Social Theory*, *5*(2), 243–263. https://doi.org/10.1177/13684310222225432

Reuter, K. (2007). Assessing aesthetic relevance: Children's book selection behavior in a digital library. *Journal of the American Society for Information Science and Technology*, *58*(12), 1745–1763. https://doi.org/10.1002/asi.20657

Reynolds, R. (2013). Personal construct theory. In T. Wilson (Ed.), *Theory in information behaviour research* (pp. 68–82). Eiconics.

Riley, F., Allen, D. K., & Wilson, T. D. (2022). When politicians and the experts collide: Organization and the creation of information spheres. *Journal of the American Society for Information Science and Technology*, *73*(8), 1127–1139. https://doi.org/10.1002/asi.24618

Ritzer, G. (2010). *Classical sociological theory* (6th ed.). McGraw-Hill.

Robson, A., & Robinson, L. (2013). Building on models of information behaviour: Linking information seeking and communication. *Journal of Documentation*, *69*(2), 169–193. http://doi.org/10.1108/00220411311300039

Roos, A. (2012). Activity theory as a theoretical framework in the study of information practices in molecular medicine. *Information Research*, *17*(3). http://informationr.net/ir/17-3/paper526.html

Rosenbaum, H. (2010). Anthony Giddens' influence on library and information science. In G. J. Leckie, L. M. Given, & J. E. Buschman (Eds.), *Critical theory for library and information science: Exploring the social from across the disciplines* (pp. 119–130). Libraries Unlimited.

Rosenblatt, L. (1994). *The reader, the text, the poem: The transactional theory of the literary work* (2nd ed.). Southern Illinois Press.

Rosengren, K. (1974). Uses and gratifications: A paradigm outlined. In J. Blumler & E. Katz (Eds.), *The uses of mass communication: Current perspectives on uses and gratifications research* (pp. 269–286). Sage Publications.

Ross, C. S. (2005). Reader response theory. In K. E. Fisher, S. Erdelez, & E. F. McKechnie (Eds.), *Theories of information behavior* (pp. 303–307). Information Today, Inc.

Rothbauer, P. (2009). Exploring the placelessness of reading among older teens in a Canadian rural municipality. *The Library Quarterly*, *79*(4), 465–483. https://doi.org/10.1086/605384

Rubenstein, E. L. (2015). "They are always there for me": The convergence of social support and information in an online breast cancer community: "They are always there for me". *Journal of the Association for Information Science and Technology*, *66*(7), 1418–1430. https://doi.org/10.1002/asi.23263

Ryan, F. V. C., Cruickshank, P., Hall, H., & Lawson, A. (2016). Managing and evaluating personal reputations on the basis of information shared on social media: A Generation X perspective. In *Proceedings of ISIC, the Information Behaviour Conference,* Zadar, Croatia, 20–23 September, 2016. Part 1. *Information Research, 21*(4). http://InformationR.net/ir/21-4/isic/isic1612.html

Savolainen, R. (1995). Everyday life information seeking: Approaching information seeking in the context of "way of life". *Library & Information Science Research*, *17*(3), 259–294. https://doi.org/10.1016/0740-8188(95)90048-9

Savolainen, R. (2005). Everyday life information seeking. In K. E. Fisher, S. Erdelez, & E. F. McKechnie (Eds.), *Theories of information behavior* (pp. 143–148). Information Today, Inc.

Savolainen, R. (2006). Spatial factors as contextual qualifiers of information seeking. *Information Research*, *11*(4). http://InformationR.net/ir/11-4/paper261.html

Savolainen, R. (2007a). Information behavior and information practice: Reviewing the "umbrella concepts" of information-seeking studies. *The Library Quarterly*, *77*(2), 109–132. https://doi.org/10.1086/517840

Savolainen, R. (2007b). Filtering and withdrawing: Strategies for coping with information overload in everyday contexts. *Journal of Information Science*, *33*(5), 611–621. https://doi.org./10.1177/0165551506077418

Savolainen, R. (2007c). Information source horizons and source preferences of environmental activists: A social phenomenological approach. *Journal of the American Society for Information Science and Technology*, *58*(12), 1709–1719. http://doi.org/10.1002/asi.20644

Savolainen, R. (2008b). *Everyday information practices: A social phenomenological perspective*. Scarecrow Press.

Savolainen, R. (2008c). Source preferences in the context of seeking problem-specific information. *Information Processing & Management*, *44*(1), 274–293. http://doi.org/10.1016/j.ipm.2007.02.008

Savolainen, R. (2009c). Epistemic work and knowing in practice as conceptualizations of information use. *Information Research*, *14*(1). http://InformationR.net/ir/14-1/paper392.html

Savolainen, R. (2015b). The interplay of affective and cognitive factors in information seeking and use: Comparing Kuhlthau's and Nahl's models. *Journal of Documentation*, *71*(1), 175–197. http://doi.org/10.1108/JD-10-2013-0134

Savolainen, R. (2019). Sharing information through book reviews in blogs: The viewpoint of Rosenblatt's reader-response theory. *Journal of Documentation*, *76*(2), 440–461. https://doi.org/10.1108/JD-08-2019-0161

Savolainen, R. (2021). Levels of critique in models and concepts of human information behaviour research. *Aslib Journal of Information Management*, *73*(5), 772–791. https://doi.org/10.1108/AJIM-01-2021-0028

Savolainen, R., & Thomson, L. (2022). Assessing the theoretical potential of an expanded model for everyday information practices. *Journal of the Association for Information Science and Technology*, *73*(4), 511–527. https://doi.org/10.1002/asi.24589

Schatzki, T. R. (1996). *Social practices: A Wittgensteinian approach to human activity and the social*. Cambridge University Press.

Schatzki, T. R. (2002). *The site of the social: A philosophical account of the constitution of social life and change*. University of Pennsylvania Press.

Schatzki, T. R. (2019). *Social change in a material world*. Routledge.

Schmidt, K. (2018). 'Practice theory': A critique. In V. Wulf, V. Pipek, D. Randall, M. Rohde, K. Schmidt, & G. Stevens (Eds.), *Socio-informatics: A practice-based perspective on the design and use of IT artifacts* (pp. 105–137). Oxford University Press.

Schutz, A. (1962). *Collected papers, I: The problem of social reality*. Martinus Nijhoff.

Schutz, A. (1964). *Collected papers, II: Studies in social theory*. Martinus Nijhoff.

Schutz, A. (1967). *The phenomenology of the social world*. Northwestern University.

Schutz, A. (1970). *Alfred Schutz on phenomenology and social relations* (Vol. 360). University of Chicago Press.

Schutz, A., & Luckmann, T. (1973). *The structures of the life-world*. Northwestern University Press.

Shannon, C. (1949). The mathematical theory of communication. In C. Shannon & W. Weaver (Eds.), *The mathematical theory of communication* (pp. 31–125). University of Illinois Press.

Shenton, A. K., & Hay-Gibson, N. V. (2011). Modelling the information-seeking behaviour of children and young people: Inspiration from beyond LIS. *ASLIB Proceedings*, *63*(1), 57–75. https://doi.org/10.1108/00012531111103786

Shenton, A. K., & Hay-Gibson, N. V. (2012). Information behaviour meta-models. *Library Review*, *61*(2), 92–109. https://doi.org/10.1108/00242531211220735

Shuva, N. Z. (2021). Information experiences of Bangladeshi immigrants in Canada. *Journal of Documentation*, *77*(2), 479–500. https://doi.org/10.1108/JD-08-2020-0137

Simon, J., & Burstein, P. (1985). *Basic research methods in social science* (3rd ed.). Random House.

Sin, S.-C. J. (2011). Towards agency–structure integration: A person-in-environment (PIE) framework for modelling individual-level information behaviours and outcomes. In A. Spink & J. Heinström (Eds.), *New directions in information behaviour* (Vol. 1, pp. 181–209). Emerald Publishing Limited.

Skinner, Q. (Ed.). (1985). *The return of grand theory in the human sciences*. Cambridge University Press.

Slife, B., & Williams, R. N. (1995). *What's behind the research?: Discovering hidden assumptions in the behavioral sciences*. Sage Publications, Inc.

Sonnenwald, D. H. (2006). Challenges in sharing information effectively: Examples from command and control. *Information Research*, *11*(3). http://InformationR.net/ir/11-4/paper270.html

Sonnenwald, D. H., & Iivonen, M. (1999). An integrated human information behavior research framework for information studies. *Library & Information Science Research*, *21*(4), 429–457. https://doi.org/10.1016/S0740-8188(99)00023-7

Sonnenwald, D. H., Wildemuth, B. M., & Harmon, G. L. (2001). A research method to investigate information seeking using the concept of information horizons: An example from a study of lower socio-economic student's information seeking behaviour. *New Review of Information Behaviour Research*, *2*, 65–86.

Spasser, M. A. (1999). Informing information science: The case for activity theory. *Journal of the American Society for Information Science*, *50*(12), 1136–1138. https://doi.org/10.1002/(SICI)1097-4571(1999)50:12%3C1136::AID-ASI17%3E3.0.CO;2-0

Stokes, P., Priharjo, R., & Urquhart, C. (2021). Validation of information-seeking behaviour of nursing students confirms most profiles but also indicates desirable changes for information literacy support. *Journal of Documentation*, *77*(3), 680–702. https://doi.org/10.1108/JD-09-2020-0158

Stokes, P., & Urquhart, C. (2015). Profiling information behaviour of nursing students: Part 2: Derivation of profiles. *Journal of Documentation*, *71*(1), 52–79. https://doi.org/10.1108/JD-07-2013-0091

Strauss, A., & Corbin, J. (1998). *Basics of qualitative research: Grounded theory procedures and techniques* (2nd ed.). Sage.

Sundin, O. (2002). Nurses' information seeking and use as participation in occupational communities. *New Review of Information Behaviour Research*, *3*, 187–202.

Suorsa, A. (2015). Knowledge creation and play – A phenomenological approach. *Journal of Documentation*, *71*(3), 503–525. https://doi.org/10.1108/JD-11-2013-0152

Suorsa, A., & Huotari, M.-L. (2014). Knowledge creation and the concept of a human being: A phenomenological approach. *Journal of the American Society for Information Science and Technology*, *65*(5), 1042–1057. https://doi.org/10.1002/asi.23035

Tabak, E. (2014). Jumping between context and users: A difficulty in tracing information practices. *Journal of the American Society for Information Science and Technology*, *65*(11), 2223–2232. https://doi.org/10.1002/asi.23116

Tabak, E., & Willson, M. (2012). A non-linear model of information sharing practices in academic communities. *Library & Information Science Research*, *34*(2), 110–116. http://doi.org/10.1016/j.lisr.2011.11.002

Talja, S. (2010). Jean Lave's practice theory. In G. J. Leckie, L. M. Given, & J. E. Buschman (Eds.), *Critical theory for library and information science: Exploring the social from across the disciplines* (pp. 205–220). Libraries Unlimited.

ter Huurne, E. F. J., Griffen, R. J., & Gutteling, J. M. (2009). Risk information seeking among U.S. And Dutch residents: An application of the model of risk information seeking and processing. *Science Communication*, *31*(2), 215–237. http://doi.org/10.1177/1075547009332653

Thomson, L. (2018). *"'Doing' YouTube": Information creating in the context of serious beauty and lifestyle YouTube*. PhD thesis. The University of North Carolina.

Tötterman, A., & Widén-Wulff, G. (2007). What a social capital perspective can bring to the understanding of information sharing in a university context. *Information Research*, *12*(4). http://Inform ationR.net/ir/12-4/colis/colis19.html

Trochim, W., & Donnelly, J. (2007). *The research methods knowledge base* (3rd ed.). Atomic Dog Publishing.

Tsai, T.-I. (2012). Social networks in the information horizons of undergraduate students. *Journal of Library and Information Studies*, *10*(1), 19–45.

Tuominen, K. (2004). "Whoever increases his knowledge merely increases his heartache." Moral tensions in heart surgery patients' and their spouses' talk about information seeking. *Information Research*, *10*(1). http://InformationR.net/ir/10-1/paper202.html

Tuominen, K., & Savolainen, R. (1997). A social constructionist approach to the study of information use as discursive action. In P. Vakkari, R. Savolainen, & B. Dervin (Eds.), *Information seeking in context: Proceedings of a meeting in Finland 14–16 August 1996* (pp. 81–96). Taylor Graham.

Tuominen, K., Talja, S., & Savolainen, R. (2005). The social constructionist viewpoint on information practices. In K. E. Fisher, S. Erdelez, & E. F. McKechnie (Eds.), *Theories of information behavior* (pp. 328–333). Information Today, Inc.

Turner, D. (2010). Orally-based information. *Journal of Documentation*, *66*(3), 370–383. http://doi.org/10.1108/00220411011038458

Ujwary-Gil, A. (2019). Organizational network analysis: A study of a university library from a network efficiency perspective. *Library & Information Science Research*, *41*(1), 48–57. https://doi.org/10.1016/j.lisr.2019.02.007

Vårheim, A. (2007). Social capital and public libraries: The need for research. *Library & Information Science Research*, *29*(3), 416–428. https://doi.org/10.1016/j.lisr.2007.04.009

Vårheim, A. (2011). Gracious space: Library programming strategies towards immigrants as tools in the creation of social capital. *Library & Information Science Research*, *33*(1), 12–18. https://doi.org/10.1016/j.lisr.2010.04.005

Vårheim, A. (2017). Public libraries, community resilience, and social capital. *Information Research*, *22*(1). http://InformationR.net/ir/22-1/colis/colis1642.html

Veinot, T. C. (2007). The eyes of the power company: Workplace information practices of a vault inspector. *The Library Quarterly*, *77*(2), 157–179. https://doi.org/10.1086/517842

Veinot, T. C. (2009). Interactive acquisition and sharing: Understanding the dynamics of HIV/AIDS information networks. *Journal of the American Society for Information Science and Technology*, *60*(11), 2313–2332. http://doi.org/10.1002/asi.21151

Veinot, T. C. (2010). A multilevel model of HIV/AIDS information/help network development. *Journal of Documentation*, *66*(6), 875–905. https://doi.org/10.1108/00220411011087850

Veinot, T. C., & Williams, K. (2012). Following the "community" thread from sociology to information behavior and informatics: Uncovering theoretical continuities and research opportunities. *Journal of the American Society for Information Science and Technology*, *63*(5), 847–864. https://doi.org/10.1002/asi.21653

Voigt, M. (1961). *Scientists' approaches to information*. American Library Association.

von Thaden, T. L. (2008). Distributed information behavior: A study of dynamic practice in a safety critical environment. *Journal of the American Society for Information Science and Technology*, *59*(10), 1555–1569. http://doi.org/10.1002/asi.20842

Vygotsky, L. (1978). *Mind in society: The development of higher psychological processes*. Harvard University Press.

Wang, H.-J. (2020). Adoption of open government data: Perspectives of user innovators. *Information Research*, *25*(1). http://InformationR.net/ir/25-1/paper849.html

Webster, T., Gollner, K., & Nathan, L. (2015). Neighbourhood book exchanges: Localising information practices. *Information Research*, *20*(1). http://InformationR.net/ir/20-3/paper684.html

Wenger, E. (1998). *Communities of practice: Learning, meaning, and identity*. Cambridge University Press.

Wenger, E. (2010). Communities of practice and social learning systems: The career of a concept. In *Social learning systems and communities of practice* (pp. 179–198). Springer.

Widén-Wulff, G. (2007). *Challenges of knowledge sharing in practice: A social approach*. Chandos.

Widén-Wulff, G., & Davenport, E. (2007). Activity systems, information sharing and the development of organizational knowledge in two Finnish firms: An exploratory study using Activity Theory. *Information Research*, *12*(3). http://InformationR.net/ir/12-3/paper310.html

Wiering, L. (2005). Uncertainty in the face of illness: Factors influencing patients' knowledge-related confidence. In S. Rubinelli & J. Haes (Eds.), *Presented at the Tailoring health messages: Bridging the gap between social and humanistic perspectives on health communication* (pp. 20–25). University of Lugano.

Williamson, K. (1998). Discovered by chance: The role of incidental information acquisition in an ecological model of information use. *Library & Information Science Research*, *20*, 23–40. https://doi.org/10.1016/S0740-8188(98)90004-4

Williamson, K. (2005). Ecological theory of human information behavior. In K. E. Fisher, S. Erdelez, & E. F. McKechnie (Eds.), *Theories of information behavior* (pp. 128–132). Information Today, Inc.

Williamson, K., & Manaszewicz, R. (2002). Breast cancer information needs and seeking: Towards an intelligent, user sensitive portal to breast cancer knowledge online. *New Review of Information Behaviour Research*, *3*, 203–219.

Williamson, K., & McGregor, J. (2006). Information use and secondary school students: A model for understanding plagiarism. *Information Research*, *12*(1). http://InformationR.net/ir/12-1/paper288.html

Willson, R., Allen, D., Julien, H., & Burnett, K. (2020). JASIS&T special issue on information behaviour & information practices theory: Call for papers. *Association for Information Science and Technology*. https://www.asist.org/2020/02/25/jasist-special-issue-on-information-behaviour-information-practices-theory-call-for-papers/

Willson, R., & Given, L. M. (2014). Student search behaviour in an online public access catalogue: An examination of "searching mental models" and "searcher self-concept". *Information Research*, *19*(3). http://informationr.net/ir/19-3/paper640.html

Wilson, T. D. (1981). On user studies and information needs. *Journal of Documentation*, *37*, 3–15. https://doi.org/10.1108/eb026702

Wilson, T. D. (1994). Information needs and uses: Fifty years of progress? In B. Vickery (Ed.), *Fifty years of progress: A journal of documentation review* (pp. 15–52). Aslib.

Wilson, T. D. (1997). Information behaviour: An interdisciplinary perspective. In P. Vakkari, R. Savolainen, & B. Dervin (Eds.), *Information seeking in context: Proceedings of a meeting in Finland 14–16 August 1996* (pp. 39–49). Taylor Graham.

Wilson, T. D. (1999). Models in information behaviour research. *Journal of Documentation*, *55*(3), 249–270. https://doi.org/10.1108/EUM0000000007145

Wilson, T. D. (2002). Alfred Schutz, phenomenology and research methodology for information behaviour research. *New Review of Information Behaviour Research*, *3*, 71–81. http://informationr.net/tdw/publ/papers/schutz02.html

Wilson, T. D. (2005). Evolution in information behavior modeling: Wilson's model. In K. E. Fisher, S. Erdelez, & L. E. F. McKechnie (Eds.), *Theories of information behavior* (pp. 31–36). Information Today, Inc.

Wilson, T. D. (2006). A re-examination of information seeking behaviour in the context of activity theory. *Information Research*, *11*(4). http://InformationR.net/ir/11-4/paper260.html

Wilson, T. D. (2008a). The information user: Past, present and future. *Journal of Information Science*, *34*(4), 457–464. https://doi.org/10.1177/0165551508091309

Wilson, T. D. (2008b). Activity theory and information seeking. *Annual Review of Information Science & Technology*, *42*(1), 119–161. https://doi.org/10.1002/aris.2008.1440420111

Wilson, T. D. (Ed.). (2013). *Theory in information behaviour research*. Eiconics Ltd.

Wilson, T. D. (2016). A general theory of human information behaviour. In *Proceedings of ISIC, the Information Behaviour Conference,* Zadar, Croatia, 20–23 September, 2016. Part 1. *Information Research, 21*(4). http://InformationR.net/ir/21-4/isic/isic1601.html

Wilson, T. D. (2022). *Exploring information behaviour: An introduction*. T.D. Wilson. http://informationr.net/ir/Exploring%20information%20behaviour.pdf

Wojciechowska, M. (2020). Social capital, trust and social activity among librarians: Results of research conducted in 20 countries across the world. *Library & Information Science Research*, *42*(4). https://doi.org/10.1016/j.lisr.2020.101049

Wolf, C. T., & Veinot, T. C. (2015). Struggling for space and finding my place: An interactionist perspective on everyday use of biomedical information. *Journal of the Association for Information Science and Technology*, *66*(2), 282–296. https://doi.org/10.1002/asi.23178

Worrall, A., & Oh, S. (2013). The place of health information and socio-emotional support in social questioning and answering. *Information Research*, *18*(3). http://informationr.net/ir/18-3/paper587.html

Wu, D., & Li, Y. (2016). Online health information seeking behaviors among Chinese elderly. *Library & Information Science Research*, *38*(3), 272–279. https://doi.org/10.1016/j.lisr.2016.08.011

Xie, B. (2008). The mutual shaping of online and offline social relationships. *Information Research, 13*(3). http://informationr.net/ir/13-3/paper350.html

Yeh, N.-C. (2008). The social constructionist viewpoint on gays and lesbians, and their information behaviour. *Information Research, 13*(4). http://InformationR.net/ir/13-4/paper364.html

Yeoman, A. (2010). Applying McKenzie's model of information practices in everyday life information seeking in the context of menopause transition. *Information Research, 15*(4). http://InformationR.net/ir/15-4/paper444.html

Yerbury, H. (2015). Information practices of young activists in Rwanda. *Information Research, 20*(1). http://InformationR.net/ir/20-1/paper656.html

Yerbury, H., & Henninger, M. (2019). Information literacy and regimes of truth: Continuity and disruption. In *Proceedings of RAILS - Research Applications, Information and Library Studies, 2018,* Australia, 28–30 November 2018. Faculty of Information Technology, Monash University. *Information Research, 24*(3). http://InformationR.net/ir/24-3/rails/rails1801.html

Yerbury, H., & Shahid, A. (2017). Social media activism in Maldives; information practices and civil society. *Information Research, 22*(1). http://InformationR.net/ir/22-1/colis/colis1614.html

Yu, X. (2012). Exploring visual perception and children's interpretations of picture books. *Library & Information Science Research, 34*(4), 292–299. https://doi.org/10.1016/j.lisr.2012.06.004

Zhang, G., & Jacob, E. K. (2013). Understanding boundaries: Physical, epistemological and virtual dimensions. *Information Research, 18*(3). http://InformationR.net/ir/18-3/colis/paperC21.html

Zhang, P., & Soergel, D. (2014). Towards a comprehensive model of the cognitive process and mechanisms of individual sensemaking. *Journal of the American Society for Information Science and Technology, 65*(9), 1733–1756. https://doi.org/10.1002/asi.23125

Zhang, Y., & Sun, Y. (2015). Users' link sharing behaviour in an online health community. In *Proceedings of ISIC, the Information Behaviour Conference,* Leeds, 2–5 September, 2014. Part 2. *Information Research, 20*(1). http://InformationR.net/ir/20-1/isic2/isic35.html

Zigron, S., & Bronstein, J. (2019). "Help is where you find it": The role of weak ties networks as sources of information and support in virtual health communities. *Journal of the Association for Information Science and Technology, 70*(2), 130–139. https://doi.org/10.1002/asi.24106

Zweizig, D. (1977). Measuring library use. *Drexel Library Quarterly, 13*, 2–15.

Chapter 5

RESEARCH DESIGN, METHODOLOGIES, AND METHODS

> What do I want to know in this study? This is a critical beginning point. Regardless of point of view, and quite often because of our point of view, we construct and frame a question for inquiry. After this question is clear, we select the most appropriate methodology to proceed with the research project. (Valerie Janesick, 1998, p. 37)

Chapter Outline

Looking for Information
Examining Research on How People Engage with Information, 179–235

Published under exclusive licence by Emerald Publishing Limited
ISSN: 2055-5377/doi:10.1108/S2055-53772023005

5.1 RELATING THEORY TO RESEARCH DESIGN

It is important to recognize that paradigms and theories are intertwined with one another, as well as with the research methodologies and methods chosen by investigators. As Poole and McPhee (1994) explain, the *domains* of theory and methodology overlap in significant ways; what theories we use indicate what methods are available to us. The overlap occurs because *both* theory and method must be concerned with our type of *explanation* (e.g., is our goal to demonstrate that one variable influences another?) and our approach to *inquiry* (e.g., whether we use a theory to guide observation, or whether we start making observations to build a theory). These points are also explored by Dervin (2005) and Given (2016).

Yet, it is also important to understand where theory and methodology do *not* overlap. Methodology is *not* concerned with *substantive assumptions* about what is being studied, which is a matter for theory (or, more specifically, for metatheory). Only theory addresses the basic assumptions that we make about the nature of reality – whether, for instance, we can ever be objective in our observations of other people. It is the theory that assumes, for example, that the *meaning* of a word is a matter of *agreement* between people (i.e., socially constructed), rather than an objective reality. This, in turn, informs methodological decisions.

Likewise, our *techniques of data collection and analysis* are *not* a part of theory but rather are of prime concern in research design and methods selection. These techniques and tools inform the process of designing and implementing research. Our choices of research design, methodology and method have profound implications for what we can know about the phenomena we study.

The following sections highlight general considerations in *designing* research projects and reference methodologies and methods commonly used for studying people's information behaviors. We must consider *how* information behavior has been studied to assess what we know about it. This is where methodology enters the picture.

5.1.1 Why We Need Sound Research Design

Methodology concerns how we can *find out*. What kind of principles, logic, and evidence would best advance our goal of learning (and most likely, recording) new knowledge about an area or object of study? Whether using a descriptive or survey methodology in a quantitative study, or a grounded theory or phenomenological methodology in a qualitative study, it is one's methodology that shapes the overall research design and the choice of methods – i.e., the specific ways, tools, and techniques of observation and measurement that will be used to gather data. As Poole and McPhee emphasize (1994, p. 43), "method is one's point of contact with the world." We need to have systematic approaches in research design to control for human error, which is always present when we are thinking, exploring, and making observations about the world (see sidebar for seven *Common Sources of Human Error*). By agreeing to guidelines for identifying research problems and gathering and interpreting evidence, researchers establish communities of discourse and of practice regarding their approaches to investigation. The point of epistemology and methodology is to provide a basis of agreement for debating and assessing knowledge claims in given areas. The resulting research communities are loosely coupled and often disagree about the appropriateness of assumptions or techniques – but that is also the nature of research.

Research designs are conscious attempts to (collectively) overcome some human failings, while promoting dialogue among researchers. To that end we employ techniques that guard us against common mistakes. For instance, we might use instruments (notes, photographs, video recordings, computer logs) to be more certain that we do not "miss" any information. We make lots of observations to have plenty of evidence on which to base our findings. To keep ourselves honest, we decide in advance which specific things we are going to observe. We state, again in advance, what we think our conclusions are likely to be, when testing hypotheses – or we set out a detailed plan to uncover new knowledge in the field, when conducting exploratory studies. As scholars, we make a professional commitment to be methodical and rigorous in our studies and to be open to criticisms from our colleagues. We agree to a continuing dialogue about our research and agree not to cling so strongly to our conclusions that no one can persuade us with compelling counterevidence. We also agree that certain criteria must be met for findings to be widely accepted: they must be grounded in evidence gathered through a systematic approach to research design, even when our chosen methodology allows for varied perspectives on what we perceive to be happening in the world.

Common Sources of Human Error[1]

(1) *People are poor observers.* When observing, we make errors of omission (not seeing what is there) and admission (seeing things that are not there)

(2) *People overgeneralize.* We tend to take small samples of evidence or opinion and apply them in broad ways

(3) *People perceive selectively.* We tend to notice those things that support our beliefs and ignore evidence that does not

(4) *People invent supportive information.* We sometimes make up information that supports our beliefs

(5) *People are defensive.* We are prone to being defensive when others challenge our point of view because our egos are often involved in what we "know" and profess to be true

(6) *People are prejudiced.* We sometimes close our minds to any new evidence about an issue, due to our prejudices

(7) *People mystify what they do not understand.* We sometimes take the easy way out when faced with complex issues by saying they simply cannot be understood

[1]See Schutt (2022), Babbie (2020), Given (2016).

Finally, there must be an alignment between the paradigms, theories, research questions, methodologies, and methods used in a research study. Each aspect, separately, is important to the creation of a sound research design but there must also be an internal logic to the decisions made. Paradigms and theories offer ways of viewing the world, which should determine the types of research problems and topics that researchers explore, as well as the types of questions they ask of the

> ***Methodology*** is the framework that underpins and informs the research strategies and methods used in research designs. Methodology helps us to understand how investigations might be conducted, including how evidence may be gathered and analyzed to address research questions. As human-centered research approaches are diverse, and informed by varied assumptions about reality and knowledge, different methodologies enable different approaches to studying human experience.

world around them. In turn, hypotheses or research questions should determine the methodologies and methods used to collect and analyze the data used as evidence about the world around us. There are choices made about research on these multiple levels.

5.1.2 Qualitative, Quantitative, and Mixed Research Designs

Research exploring people's information behaviors is often described as being qualitative (i.e., inductive), quantitative (i.e., deductive), or of a mixed research design. These studies may involve human participants (e.g., with data gathered via questionnaires or interviews), or they may explore the artifacts of human experience (e.g., social media posts). The common feature is their positioning of *people's experiences* as central to the investigation, rather than the primary focus being (for example) the information system (e.g., a database) or setting (e.g., a hospital) where the information behavior occurred. These other aspects are important *contextual* elements that may be considered in the study, but they are not the primary focus for information behavior investigations.

Most investigators have previously established assumptions and preferences that lead them to choose certain designs and techniques. A key consideration is whether they are proceeding inductively or deductively in their research design. Taking an inductive approach (typically aligned with qualitative designs) means that the research will examine particular instances and reason toward transferability of results. That is, a researcher is gathering, analyzing, and interpreting data in such a way that it may lead to general principles, such as theories. *Grounded theory* is a research methodology that builds theory from concrete observations; any findings are discussed within the contexts in which they originated, rather than attempting to build an abstract theory that strives (and typically fails) to apply in all situations. Most qualitative methods and methodologies are inductive in nature, mainly because they assume that transferability of results across contexts is difficult to achieve when one is studying people or their creations.

The deductive approach (typically aligned with quantitative designs) proceeds in the opposite fashion, reasoning from the general to the particular. This is typically the way the natural sciences are portrayed, as applying a theory to a particular case to test the theory. Presumably the theory is either supported or revised based on the results. However, the number of formal tests of theory is relatively sparse when it comes to studying people's information behaviors. Rather, much of the research has been merely descriptive of a unique situation (i.e., a given information user or organization), or an inductive attempt to transfer results across certain types of persons, sources, or situations. Early information behavior research often used quantitative methods to collect data on the information sources used by (and information-seeking behaviors of) specific groups.

> ***Methods*** are the tools, techniques, and strategies used to gather research evidence. Method selection is informed by a study's chosen epistemological, theoretical, and methodological *paradigm*. A study may reflect a single paradigm, using one or more methods; or, a study may embrace multiple paradigms, with methods aligned to each to demonstrate paradigmatic "fit."

Few investigators stick solely to induction or deduction, although a particular project might focus on one approach or the other to make the project manageable. Rather, researchers tend to move back and forth between these modes: collecting information that allows the researcher to state a principle or tendency, then testing that finding through further research, in an endless chain of logic. That said, because of the influence of one's epistemological worldview on the design of research, researchers may focus all their work in one paradigmatic mode – i.e., choosing primarily qualitative or primarily quantitative designs, which best suit their beliefs about the nature of reality and ways of knowing. Research teams that involve people with a mix of views can design elaborate mixed paradigm studies, drawing on both inductive and deductive approaches (see Keith et al., 2022). These approaches are key considerations when choosing methodologies and methods.

5.1.3 Methodologies and Methods

Choices of methodology are intertwined with choices of method. Due to this interdependence, we often refer to investigations as if they were solely the methodological approach: experiments, surveys, case studies, and so forth. However, it is important to remember that there are distinct differences between the "methodologies" that inform our research designs and the "methods" we use to gather and analyze data. As Crotty (1998, p. 3) notes, methodology sets out "the strategy, plan of action, process or design lying behind the choice and use of methods to the desired outcomes," whereas methods are "the techniques or procedures used to gather and analyze data related to some research question or hypothesis." Methods often refer to two types of techniques – data collection and data analysis. Methods of collection and analysis may be multiple or singular. Some methodologies and data require certain kinds of analysis; for example, experiments that gather quantitative data necessitate statistical analysis. For other approaches, there may be a choice of analysis; for example, collections of diaries may use thematic analysis or qualitative content analysis of the entries. In other cases, multiple types of analyses might be used with one type of evidence; for example, a study of book circulation records might use both statistical analysis and thematic analysis. Table 5.1 is a primer for the types of investigations discussed in later sections, to provide examples of how such research designs have been used to study information behavior.

Studies may also use mixed designs – employing quantitative and qualitative data collection methods. One of the significant challenges in mixing approaches is

Table 5.1. Methodologies and Methods for Data Collection and Analysis.

Examples of Methodologies (i.e., the Overall Strategy or Plan of Action)	**Examples of Data Collection Methods** (i.e., Techniques for Gathering Data)	**Examples of Data Analysis Methods** (i.e., Techniques to Describe and Interpret Data)
• Experimental research • Survey research • Grounded theory • Phenomenology • Case study research • Action research • Content analysis • Ethnography • Discourse analysis • Network analysis • Heuristic analysis • Oral history • Narrative inquiry • Meta-analysis	• Observation • Interviews • Questionnaires • Focus groups • Participant observation • Data mining • Photovoice • Diaries • Concept mapping	• Thematic analysis • Statistical analysis • Exploratory analysis • Comparative analysis • Descriptive analysis • Explanatory analysis

ensuring that research incorporating both quantitative and qualitative data also reflects an appropriate mix of paradigmatic approach. A study that includes (for example) questionnaires and interviews may not necessarily be one that mixes quantitative and qualitative *paradigms*. If the data gathered are only analyzed through a quantitative lens (e.g., by running descriptive statistics on the qualitative dataset), rather than a qualitative one (e.g., the use of thematic coding and rich analytic descriptions), a study cannot be said to be truly a mixed-methods design. The mixing of paradigms allows researchers to gather strength from both approaches. In practice, this requires both quantitative and qualitative expertise in the research team to ensure that the project is designed – and that data are analyzed – using the different research perspectives that inform each paradigmatic approach. See Given's (2016) qualitative research text for an overview of the paradigm vs. data focus in mixed-methods studies.

5.2 GENERAL CONSIDERATIONS IN RESEARCH DESIGN

The classic view of the research process is often portrayed in five stages. These include: (1) developing a research problem and research questions, (2) designing a research study, (3) designing and implementing data collection practices, (4) analyzing and interpreting data, and (5) writing up the study. In practice, it is rarely as simple (or as linear) as these five stages suggest, but it is worth briefly considering these typical steps in the research process. Then we will consider some of the issues that lead researchers to choose one type of research approach over another.

5.2.1 Stage One: Conceptualization and Problem Development

The first stage is the one in which an investigation is conceptualized. Investigators may be working with a particular theory or may be drawn to a particular topic, issue or problem for some reason. The researcher may have some personal connection to the topic of investigation, or they may be collaborating with research colleagues, community groups, government agencies, or other non-research partners who have helped to define the problem to be investigated. Perhaps a scholar is drawn to research on workplace information sharing because she sees a need for improvement in the place she works, or because she feels some aspect of workplaces offers a concrete place to study an abstract concept (e.g., boundary objects). As a result, research problems are formed and then examined. In projects involving participants as coinvestigators (e.g., community-based participatory research), researchers work closely with their community partners to conceptualize, design, and implement all elements of the research. Although some organizations and partners may wish to remain "hands-off" in terms of the project design (e.g., where an organization provides access to participants but leaves decision-making to the researchers), others may expect close involvement in all stages of the work (e.g., as is the case with Indigenous research).

5.2.1.1 Exploring, Describing or Explaining – What Is the Purpose of the Research?

Research may vary regarding its purpose. For topics that have not yet been widely studied, the goal is simply to *explore* the phenomenon to gain an initial understanding of it. For example, when new media (such as social media platforms) appear, the first research questions that emerge may be: "What functionality do these platforms have?" and "How do people use them?" When the object of study is novel, some aspects of it may not yet be defined well enough for further investigation. As new information sources and new variations on existing channels emerge with some frequency, exploratory studies are common in information behavior research. Often, researchers may use qualitative approaches for exploratory studies, as the methodologies and methods allow researchers to tap into people's minds to examine a new idea, tool, or experience. If a phenomenon is very new, and we do not yet know the key issues or variables involved, an exploratory qualitative study may be needed to provide some data and begin to generate theory. Once a theory is generated it can be explored in more depth – using additional qualitative designs (in new settings or with new populations) to extend the theory, or with a quantitative design, to formally test the theory.

When a phenomenon is well established, the focus of investigation is likely to be on documenting its characteristics. *Descriptive* studies are intended to measure well-defined variables regarding the people or objects involved with the phenomenon. To use the internet as an example, descriptive research might explore: "How many searches are being conducted on the web about COVID-19?" "Which are the most popular sites?" "How many people are using these sites, and with what frequency?" and "What are the demographic characteristics of people searching for this information?" Much of the information behavior literature, particularly the early studies that focused on channels, sources, and audiences for information, are chiefly descriptive in nature.

Other types of investigations offer *explanations* for the phenomena. An explanatory study attempts to answer "why" questions, particularly regarding people's motives and actions. Where the internet is concerned, such questions might include "Why do people use the internet, rather than other sources of information?" "Why are companies spending so much money on website development and advertising?" and "Why is free speech such an issue for internet content?" As studying and measuring human intentions is difficult, fewer investigations have attempted to offer explanations for information behavior. Constructing explanations for events brings into play the concept of causation: when does one thing cause another to happen? This in turn requires rigorous evidence and logic to establish robust results.

5.2.1.2 Research Questions and Hypotheses

During this stage, the research problem is identified, along with the research questions (in qualitative designs) to be explored or the hypotheses to be tested (in quantitative designs). A research problem "describes the point of focus for the project, including the rationale and need for the study itself" (Given, 2016, p. 54). A problem might be stated as "What are teenagers' experiences sharing health information via social media?" Or a problem statement might be stated as "What effect does an increase in the number of available information sources have upon the use of an individual source?" Problem statements typically express relationships between *variables* and suggest ways in which they might be tested or explored empirically. However, the diversity of assumptions and methods in social research means that there are also many ways to describe research problems.

For research problems that generate new theory, *research questions* are identified. In many qualitative studies, five or six questions (often with subquestions) are outlined to guide the design of the specific instruments (e.g., interview questions) that will be used with participants. For example, a researcher might ask, "What are teenagers' perspectives on the value of social media use among their friends and family? In what situations will teens choose to share, or not share, health information through social networks?" These research designs are very common in contemporary studies of people's information behaviors, as they enable researchers to explore many contextual elements alongside people's individual experiences.

For research problems that test a preexisting theory, *hypotheses* are derived. A hypothesis is a conjectural statement about the relationship between two or more variables. Often, this approach to knowledge is used in experimental studies in which the researcher can manipulate (or at least anticipate) a change in the environment that might produce a measurable effect among the people present; however, experimental designs are not commonly used by information behavior researchers. Typically, hypothesis testing occurs with descriptive and survey methodologies. For example, a researcher might hypothesize that "as people get older, the likelihood they will read graphic novels decreases" and design a questionnaire to test this hypothesis.

5.2.2 Stage Two: Designing the Study

In the second stage, a specific study about people's information behaviors is designed. This could explore an activity (e.g., information sharing), in a specific venue or setting (e.g., a nonprofit organization), with specific elements (e.g., using Microsoft Teams). A plan is derived for what goal is to be achieved in the study and how to go about it. Again, a theory (if employed) may dictate the goal of the research project and what kinds of designs and data are necessary to achieve it. Or, a specific methodology may require certain ways of working, which also affects the choice of methods. Other key considerations, such as the resources available in terms of time, money, and personnel, will also affect the overall project design.

Early in the research process, the object(s) of examination must be identified and defined for data collection. This process is called *operationalization* and informs the choice of research methods. After explicating a concept of interest, we must lay out the procedures or operations we will use to collect data about that concept. We must specify the conditions under which an instance of the concept might be produced and observed. For example, where would we look on Microsoft Teams to find an instance of "information sharing"? How will we recognize it when we see it? What would indicate that "information sharing" is present? How will we measure an instance of "information sharing" once it is observed? The resulting *operational definition* guides the methods and analysis we use to examine the phenomena.

We discover ways to classify the things we observe: *attributes* (characteristics or qualities) of people (e.g., junior vs senior employees) or their behavior (e.g., asking a question), which are grouped together in logical groupings (e.g., job status = junior or senior). We develop a strategy for examining those elements in a particular context. Our method might involve watching people while they work, or interviewing people; we might examine artifacts people create (e.g., task lists in Microsoft Teams), or how people discuss information sharing via Teams in online forum discussions. There are any number of different possibilities, which can be quantitative, qualitative, or a mix of study designs.

Then, specific methods and procedures are chosen to collect data for the study. The methods selected must provide the data needed to address the research questions or test the hypotheses. Multiple sources of evidence may contribute to more compelling conclusions and often preferred in some designs – see, for example, Creswell and Clark (2017) and Fidel (2008) on the advantages of mixed methods. When designing a study, there must be alignment between the approach to research, the methodology, and the methods selected. In qualitative studies, triangulation of sites, data sources, and participants may enrich a single study or inform analysis across subsequent designs (see Given, 2016, pp. 71–72).

5.2.3 Stage Three: Planning and Implementing Data Collection

The third step is to design specific procedures for data collection in the study, and to carry them out. When designing a study, we must be clear about the primary *unit of analysis*. Studies of information behavior, by definition, involve humans; therefore, individual *people* are most commonly observed and analyzed in these studies. We may also investigate those people within a broad context – such as their workplace or the grocery store, where they may interact with friends, colleagues, computers, animals, etc. Yet there are also cases in which our focus is on aggregates of individuals, as in a comparative study of organizations (e.g., companies or universities); in such cases our unit of analysis is a group, rather than an individual. In addition, any kind of human artifact – *objects*, such as books or podcasts or social *events*, such as a conference or conversation – may also be a unit of analysis. In other words, the design of a study is partly determined by what kind of thing we wish to discuss in our findings. Are we trying to reach a conclusion about the opinions of individuals, for example, or about the usage of a book? Deciding what we are observing and reasoning about, will determine how our measures are developed and implemented.

When methods have been selected, this is still a long way from the detailed planning needed to implement the study. Researchers must decide who will be participating in the research (or where artifacts will be derived), the data gathering instruments to be used, where and how the methods will be implemented, among other details. When thinking about research participants, researchers must outline sampling procedures and create recruitment materials, such as text to be used in emails or social media posts. Researchers must also develop or adopt the research instruments they will use to collect data, such as questionnaires or interview guides. Once the participants and research instruments are identified, there must be a plan for how data collection will proceed, including procedures for interacting with participants, storing data, and timelines for project completion. Ethics applications must also be completed to seek approval for project implementation prior to data collection. The more detailed and realistic the planning done at this stage, the smoother the actual data collection process. However, even with the best advance planning, data collection will always include challenges and require contingency plans to deal with unforeseen circumstances.

The *time* dimension of the investigation is especially important, particularly when we wish to reason about causes and effects. Time is also important because people and their environments change constantly, so we are always faced with the issue of whether results from a decade ago are still applicable to the world of today. A typical distinction made in methodology is between studies that are conducted solely at *one point in time*, versus those in which multiple measures are taken over *several points in time*. These two approaches are called, respectively, *cross-sectional* versus *longitudinal* studies.

One could look at the time dimension as a question of sampling, just as we must do when we consider human populations: is it enough to sample one person/time, or should we sample many people/times? The considerable increase in effort required to study phenomenon over time has meant that relatively few studies in information behavior have incorporated a long timeframe in their design. However, it is not uncommon for some survey designs to ask the same questions several months or years apart to address the question of change over time. Kim et al. (2021), for example, used online, quantitative questionnaires to look at how undergraduates evaluate information from social media; the questionnaire was administered in 2013 and repeated, in 2019, to compare findings. Qualitative designs may also involve interviews conducted over several months to investigate changes in people's thinking about specific phenomenon. For example, Rousi et al. (2019) collected data in phases over 3–5 months; they used follow-up qualitative interviews (alongside quantitative questionnaires) to explore situational relevance during information seeking.

5.2.3.1 Rigor and Trustworthiness

Well-designed studies are conducted in (quantitatively) *rigorous* or (qualitatively) *trustworthy* ways to ensure that the quality of the data, and the resulting analyses, are the best they can be. In qualitative studies, elements of trustworthiness are necessary to ensure the transferability of results; in quantitative projects, the goal is generalizability, which requires rigor in the project design. Mixed-methods studies can also offer the "best of both worlds" when they combine appropriate qualitative and quantitative designs. This will be explored further in the discussions of methods and the examples that follow in later sections. Here, we explore the key elements of rigor or trustworthiness that affect the overall quality of a study's findings.

5.2.3.2 Rigorous Quantitative Designs

The twin concepts of validity and reliability determine how compelling the results of a quantitative study will be, so they are important considerations in the choice of methods and implementation of procedures in the study design. *Validity* is the extent that the measurement procedures accurately reflect the concept we are studying. Asking someone if she "knows a lot about world events" is not a particularly valid way of studying "news consumption." Asking the respondent if she subscribes to a newspaper would be more valid, as it gets closer to the heart of the matter. However, an answer to that question does not tell you whether she actually *reads* the newspaper; questions about her newspaper *reading habits* would have even more validity. Perhaps the most valid measures might be some questions – whether administered through an interview or a questionnaire – that would tell us if she can identify the top news stories of the day or week, and so forth.

Reliability is demonstrated when measures are *repeated under the same conditions* and yield highly similar results each time. We expect a bathroom scale to give us the same weight from one minute to the next, because we have not had enough time to gain or lose significant weight in such a short period. We would not necessarily expect the scale to register the same weight 20 years later, because the conditions have changed, and we may have gained weight. In contrast, asking several observers to *guess* our weight (and then taking the average of their guesses) would likely be an unreliable measure, as human perceptions vary considerably across observers and even within the same person across time.

There can be a trade-off between validity and reliability. Measures that are highly reliable may not be high on validity, whereas highly valid measures sometimes have problems with reliability. Although it is easily possible to develop measures that are both invalid and unreliable (asking "is the sky blue today?" would not be a valid measure of color perception, as is likely to draw unreliable answers as well), it is difficult to come up with measures that are both highly valid and highly reliable.

Consider a situation in which we wish to study the use of materials in a library. One question would be how many people actually have an opportunity to use the library materials – by entering the building. To answer that simple question, we could station an observer at the door and have him or her count people. However, such a measurement will not be completely reliable; a second observer watching the crowd enter the library might come up with a slightly different count. A superior method would be to install a turnstile in the entrance; we could then assume that one "rotation" of the turnstile equals one "user" of the library. Now we have a reliable count of the persons entering the building.

But what does that simple count tell us about the actual use of the informational materials or services found in the library – the kinds of activities that people more commonly think of as constituting "use"? Virtually nothing: people might have entered merely to use the bathroom or to ask for directions to another building.

To capture a more valid measure of the use of materials and services we could distribute a questionnaire at the doorway with specific questions about such uses. Users would fill them out and we would have data about the use of materials by many users. However, we would find that the more questions we ask, and the more detail we require, the fewer the users who will complete the questionnaire. The fewer the number of respondents, the less confident we are that we can generalize from our results to the entire population of users. In other words, we might encounter a trade-off between the depth and the breadth of the information we gather.

One way to ensure rigor in design is to use measures or instruments that have been developed and tested by other researchers. One example is the "scales for information-seeking behavior" questionnaire described by Timmers and Glas (2010), which was later used by Leeder (2019) to examine college students' evaluation and sharing of fake news stories. While these apply mainly to information literacy studies, they are good examples of how standardized instruments may be developed to improve reliability of responses and allow for comparisons across studies.

5.2.3.3 Trustworthy Qualitative Designs

In qualitative research, rather than validity, we use the term credibility, and rather than reliability, we use the term dependability. *Credibility* refers to data being represented fairly and accurately. Many activities can help increase credibility such as citing negative cases (discussing instances in the data that disagree with main findings) and member checking (confirming findings with participants). *Dependability* refers to whether similar participants in a similar study would generally lead to similar results, including that other researchers would interpret the data in similar ways. One way to increase dependability is to have multiple researchers coding the data to see if they find similar codes and themes. In addition to credibility and dependability, transparency and reflexivity are important in trustworthiness. *Transparency* is thoroughly describing all the steps in the research process, essentially leaving an audit trail. *Reflexivity* is the researcher discussing her/his own role in the research and the findings; as bias cannot be removed it is accounting for how the researcher may have influenced the study (Saumure & Given, 2008).

So, if we are searching for a highly detailed picture of information usage, we might consider close observations of a small number of users. Perhaps we could follow them around the library (with their consent, of course) and they could talk to us in detail about their internal experience of searching and finding information. Making these detailed observations and hearing from the individuals themselves, we would get closer to the phenomenon of concern: what people actually *do* when they use the library. These data potentially have a great deal of credibility (as we gain access to participants' personal views of their reality) and dependability (as the data are the result of the individuals' views, rather than the researcher's own beliefs about what people do). With a large enough sample size these data can also be *transferable* across similar contexts, populations, or personal circumstances. If the data are gathered over many weeks or months, or if the same participants remain involved in the study and return for multiple interviews, the findings are also dependable, despite the normal variations and changes that one would expect to see over time. In qualitative studies the goal is not to eliminate variability in the data gathered, but to be able to track and explain that variability, embracing anomalies or elements that may seem to challenge typical views.

Another key element of qualitative designs is that a researcher's own perspective may be embedded in the design and become a key part of the analytic approach. In ethnographic studies, for example, the researcher may engage with a community over a long period of time, gathering data from various people and using many sources of evidence. Triangulation is a multimethod approach to collecting and analyzing data to better understand a phenomenon through a variety of perspectives (Rothbauer, 2008). It can include numerous sites, data sources, and/or participants that may enrich a single study or inform analysis across subsequent designs (see Given, 2016, pp. 71–72). An ethnographic study in a library may take several weeks or months, with a researcher triangulating data sources to gather various perspectives – and then analyzing those data in the context of his or her own areas of expertise. In these studies, researchers acknowledge that people's thoughts and behaviors can change over time as people remember things once forgotten or as they change their personal views. If we ask three witnesses to a crime what they saw and remember, do they say the same things? Due to both selective perception and variability of memory, typically the witnesses do not say *exactly* the same things; but multiple accounts are often close enough to draw some conclusions. Although a quantitative researcher (in aiming for reliable data) would find this scenario problematic, a qualitative researcher would embrace these differences and attempt to gain insight on each person's view. In this way, qualitative researchers can account for variability in participants' experiences and conduct analyses that reflect multiple realities, varied situational contexts, and results that change over time.

5.2.4 Stage Four: Analyzing and Interpreting Data

Once data are gathered, they are analyzed and interpreted. In many cases, data are being interpreted *while* they are generated or captured. In qualitative studies, the analysis and writing processes are linked, resulting in integrated approaches to analyzing findings and presenting a discussion of those findings. In quantitative studies, generating the results of the study and discussing the meaning of those results are often separate activities. Classification, categorization, and counting activities are central to many analytical approaches. In survey research, for example, the measurement and analysis may be primarily quantitative, yet data gathering involves some degree of interpretation and classification. Consider the common practice of allowing survey respondents to supply an "other" response not anticipated on the questionnaire – all these responses must be categorized and coded in some way for convenient summary and interpretation. These types of qualitative data can provide insights on participants' views to enhance the quantitative analyses; however, as Given (2016, p. 13) notes, these data "are limited in scope and do not provide the same depth of analysis as found in studies designed with a qualitative paradigm" as the overarching research approach. Computer software packages have made it increasingly easy to record, interpret, and analyze both qualitative (e.g., NVivo; Atlas.ti) and quantitative (e.g., SPSS, R) data; there are also specialized programs for specific analyses, such as those available for social network analysis (see Camacho et al., 2020).

5.2.5 Stage Five: Writing Up and Sharing Results

In the final stage, researchers write up their results to share with academic colleagues, businesses, government, and the public (to name a few). Although this may occur at the end of a project (e.g., to prepare a research report for an industry partner), many researchers publish multiple works at various stages of project completion. They also write for varied audiences, by publishing in a range of academic (e.g., journal articles; book chapters; art exhibitions) and nonacademic (e.g., blogs; social media posts; professional conferences) venues. Much of this work involves the oftenunder-emphasized work of drawing conclusions. This involves the intellectual work involved in summarizing and considering the results to draw findings and conclusions, and to generate theory. Beyond stating the results of the analysis, this work includes taking the larger context into consideration to discuss the contributions to scholarship and to practice, including what the findings mean. It is about answering the "so what?" question about the research. Ideally, this step leads to a reconceptualization of the research – whether it "worked," contributed to theory, was worth the effort, or how the approach might be improved. Researchers write and talk about what they have found and share their conclusions with those who may benefit from this knowledge – such as other researchers, practitioners, governments, as well as people who participated in the study.

Information behavior researchers also use a diverse set of representation styles for writing up and sharing research results. For example, it remains common to see traditional styles of scholarly writing in journal articles and book chapters. Quantitative reports of empirical findings are highly structured, including summary tables and graphs, with research findings and discussions sections presented separately. Qualitative reports will include lengthy narratives of participants' views, with the findings and discussions sections combined to explore the theoretical and contextual meaning of the data as they are presented. As research methods have involved to include visual sources of data, research publications also present excerpts and examples drawn from these sources. For example, Given and Kuys (2022) present photographs, architectural drawings, and other visual artifacts alongside a theoretical model of an informing esthetic for a war memorial. Forcier (2022) includes screenshots of Twitter postings in his study of transmedia fans' information practices. Barriage (2021) and Greyson et al. (2017) include photographs of some of the materials generated by their participants during data collection.

5.2.6 Ethical Practice

Given human failings and motivations, it should come as no surprise that ethical considerations loom large in social research, including information behavior studies. Researchers are people, people have values and attitudes, and those predispositions inevitably creep into their investigations of other people. Investigators also have a strong desire to achieve interesting results. Competent researchers strive to keep their values from unduly or inappropriately influencing the results of their studies – a difficult thing to do when one cares deeply about the topic – and to be candid with themselves and others regarding their own potential biases. In studies where research participants serve as coinvestigators, or where the researcher is embedded in the situation under study, the ethical issues may be complex and may change over time. In specific contexts where research is conducted (e.g., on social media platforms, in hospitals) researchers may also need to follow specific plans and protocols unique to these contexts. Research with and for Indigenous communities also requires specific designs and protocols, with implications for codesign practices, data stewardship, publication of results, and many other considerations in research design and implementation.

Ethics reflect our beliefs about what constitutes just and right behavior versus what we judge to be unjust and wrong. Individuals often disagree about the ultimate bases for judgments of right and wrong, so ethics tend to be based on consensual group norms, sometimes called "standards of conduct." Social researchers have worked out several such standards through years of challenging experiences with investigations that have crossed into gray areas of behavior. Several general ethical guidelines have evolved that are commonly followed in investigations involving humans, including not harming people, ensuring consent is free and informed and managing data confidentially and with care. In many public agencies, entities sometimes called "institutional review boards" or "research ethics committees" or "human participant committees" provide oversight of research activities in their organizations to ensure appropriate, ethical conduct. The following sections outline some of the key principles and issues that information behavior researchers must address in planning and implementing their studies.

5.2.6.1 Researchers Must Manage Potential Risks in Study Designs

Although it may seem obvious that the risk of *physical* harm to an information behavior study participant is extremely unlikely (due to the nature of our study designs), a more challenging issue is preventing potential *psychological* discomfort. Who can say for certain when and how mental or emotional discomforts might occur? Such harm could be something as subtle as embarrassment that might occur when certain information is revealed about an individual or an identifiable group of persons – say, where they shared personal information on social media, or made controversial statements at a political rally. Many study methods (e.g., questionnaires, library circulation records) can be designed to capture data anonymously, to protect participants data from being linked to them, personally. With other methods (e.g., interviews, focus groups) – including those where participants choose to be identified as part of an informed consent process – the research team may withhold some details from publication and agree to treat some data as "off the record" to capture participants' stories without compromising confidentiality. Where data are being gathered from people indirectly (e.g., analyzing public online postings) researchers should follow established guidelines for use of those data (e.g., franzke et al., 2020). Researchers must also provide details on how to withdraw from a study, so that participants can manage their own comfort levels once the project gets underway. Researchers must understand the potential for harm within their studies and design their work to manage risks to participants. Although information behavior studies may often be considered as presenting low or minimal risk – i.e., no more than an individual or group would encounter in their everyday lives – a researcher must consider the potential risk and take steps to ensure that participants are not harmed in the process of doing the research and in sharing study results.

5.2.6.2 Researchers Must Not Deceive or Mislead Study Participants

Participants should be fully informed about the purpose of the research and the nature of data collection, analysis, and publishing as part of the study's informed consent process. Although some studies may require partial disclosure (e.g., sharing the nature of the questions to be asked, but not the full question set), so as not to bias the results and/or due to the emergent nature of data collection, researchers must be as clear as possible about the intentions of the project. In most investigations of information behaviors, providing clear direction of the research project's purpose is straightforward. Questionnaire respondents who answer an ad for people to share what sources they look to for consumer purchasing decisions might fully understand that they are going to be asked about what sources of information they turn to, and how they perceive the value of those sources. However, there can be more difficulty in explaining the intention of a study when what the investigator is interested in is something deeper and more personal than a simple, factual question. For example, if one was to say bluntly to a participating journalist "I'm going to ask you questions about how you report the news, so that I can see whether you perceive events according to stereotypical formulas," that would lead to self-consciousness on the part of the participant and may diminish honesty or completeness of their answers. In many cases, especially in exploratory studies, the researcher may not know in advance what themes and findings may be drawn from the answers, so they cannot disclose their possible interpretations of what they have not yet heard from the participants. Researchers must tread a fine line between sharing the study's intentions with potential participants and ensuring that the integrity of study design is maintained.

5.2.6.3 Researchers Must Ensure Participant Consent Is Informed and Voluntary

In the early days of social research and even up to the mid-twentieth century, it was not unusual for institutions (e.g., schools, government agencies, the military) to require that certain individuals participate in studies and/or provide personal information to investigators. For several decades now, the norm in countries with formalized ethics review processes has been that individuals have the right to refuse to be involved in research, even if little harm could come from participating in it. The standard is that, before participating, *free and informed consent* must be given; participants must be informed of the study's purpose, how their data will be used and stored, how their data will be shared with others, and the risks and benefits involved in participating. Generally, information about the study is provided in an information sheet given to participants. Consent is often documented by asking participants to sign a form, click a consent statement online, or by providing verbal consent to researchers at the start of data collection. If the individual is under the legal age and, therefore, cannot legally sign a consent form, the parent or guardian may be required to give consent and the child or young adult must give *assent* (agree to take part). Even if participants are adults, investigators must take special care with any who are in a power relationship with the researchers (e.g., students) and with those in vulnerable situations (e.g., prisoners).

Consent is also recognized as an ongoing process, with researchers expected to enable participants to (for example) refuse to answer specific questions, decide not to participate in all activities or even to withdraw entirely during or immediately following data collection. The general idea is that participants should understand what they are being asked to do before they agree to participate and be given agency to manage (or end) their participation as the project proceeds. Participants must not be obliged or induced to participate; where participants are going to be compensated for their time (e.g., a small remuneration or other benefit, such as a gift card or food), the compensation should not be so large as to unduly influence people to participate.

5.2.6.4 Researchers Must Treat Data Confidentially and Respectfully

Different jurisdictions have guidelines and regulations about long-term storage of data and archiving (or destruction) protocols that researchers must follow. However, the question of whether and when to identify participants varies with the study design and context. In some studies, data are gathered anonymously from participants, with no names or other identifiable information collected (e.g., when people complete a questionnaire that does not track their identity). In other cases, data gathered from participants are held confidentially; information such as names or email addresses that are collected from individuals (e.g., when a person agrees to be interviewed) is not included with the dataset, and participants are only identified in publications by a pseudonym. In some cases, identifying people and using their names in publications is entirely appropriate – and expected – but participants must give their consent to be identified. Thus, in reporting the results of a study, care should be taken to see that individual responses are not identifiable, unless the participant has agreed to be named.

Even when people are named, their data can be treated in confidence; for example, a participant may tell a story that they wish to be "off the record" and not shared – but they tell the story so that the researcher understands their context or point of view. In some investigations of small communities or organizations, or where a participant has a unique role, it is sometimes possible for a reader of a publication to make informed guesses about the origin of some quotations or opinions, if they know the group being studied. In such cases the investigator must exercise caution in reporting any expression that might be controversial or sensitive so that it cannot come back to haunt the participant. Choosing whether (or if) a participant will be anonymized in a project report can be a very challenging issue; researchers should seek advice and consult specialist ethics guidelines, alongside national ethics policies, to guide appropriate and ethical project design.

5.2.6.5 Ethics as an Evolving Practice

Ethical guidelines and practices change as our understandings of people's needs, new technologies, and social contexts evolve. The ubiquity of information exchange on the internet, for example, has led to ongoing discussion among researchers regarding the ethics of collecting public submissions to social media, mailing lists, discussion boards, and websites (e.g., Buchanan & Ess, 2009; Markham, 2012). Although chat rooms and individual e-mail exchanges are considered "private," some researchers maintain that postings to public websites and open mailing lists are fair game for analysis and reporting (Zimmer, 2010). Many studies use postings to public websites, including data logs of search terms or Twitter feeds, as sources of data for analysis. Often, publicly available material is treated in similar ways to letters to the editors of newspapers, or to personal letters that appear in public archives – i.e., available for analysis without the need for ethics review. However, when researchers wish to engage with potential participants (e.g., by posting questions via Twitter to gauge people's responses to an issue), ethics review is typically required, with the expectation that participants will be informed about the study and choose to participate – or not. This is a very complex issue, with rapid changes to technology requiring researchers to examine the ethical implications of their work on an ongoing basis. Given (2016) provides a detailed overview of these issues in the context of qualitative research, while the Association of Internet Researchers publishes detailed ethical guidelines (see franzke et al., 2020).

As digital technologies provide increased monitoring capability of people's behaviors, we can expect more challenges to the boundaries of acceptable research. Witness the increased awareness of privacy brought about by use of the internet. Many users are now aware that commercial entities are not only tracking the most obvious data – their demographic background (such as they were willing to supply voluntarily) and online purchases – but use cookies to record their visits to websites in which transactions were *not* conducted. The pervasive use of tracking cookies and of online forms and questionnaires, coupled with the ability to aggregate and cross-reference data by individual computer user, has led to massive collections of data of people's behaviors and preferences. That much of this has been collected without the full consent and understanding of internet users is an example of how far things can go if ethical data-collection principles are not observed. However, there are also several studies that point to a shift in people's understanding and expectations of the concept of privacy, particularly for younger generations of computer users. While previous research found that teens who use social media were not overly concerned with privacy (e.g., Madden et al., 2013), newer research has found a more nuanced picture. Adorjan and Ricciardelli (2019) found a "privacy paradox," where teens express significant concern about privacy yet do not engage in privacy management practices online. Researchers examining digital information behavior will continue to be challenged by the various ethical issues that emerge and change with the advent of new technologies and new modes of communication.

Projects involving Indigenous peoples also require researchers to be led by Indigenous communities in the design and implementation of all phases of the project. For example, Indigenous protocols may expect that elders are named and compensated for their study contributions. Communities may require that results are shared openly and that the research data will be controlled by Indigenous project partners. Researchers' roles may comprise stewardship, rather than co-ownership, with implications for study design and ethical practices in keeping with community expectations. Du and Haines (2019) present several insightful reflections on engaging with Indigenous communities in their information behavior studies. Researchers designing projects with Indigenous peoples should review relevant published guidelines for study design and ethical practices (e.g., Australian Institute of Aboriginal and Torres Strait Islander Studies, 2020; Government of Canada, 2018). Researchers must codesign projects with

Indigenous communities to ensure that study designs and implementation practices are ethical and appropriate for those communities.

5.2.7 Academic and Societal Impact of Research

Information behavior researchers have often worked with communities, businesses, and other people and groups outside of universities who can benefit from the results of research projects. The potential to contribute to societal impact (i.e., where research leads to demonstrable change in the economy, culture, society, the environment, etc.), alongside contributions to academic impact (i.e., through publications, grants, citations, etc.) is a growing area of focus for researchers, globally. As such, it is worthwhile to explore the different meanings of research impact, how impact is connected to research design and methods, and how information behavior researchers have demonstrated both academic and societal impact.

Scholarly or academic research impact is what many people think of when they hear the phrase "research impact." Academic impact is when researchers have conducted original research that contributes to the knowledge of a discipline, advancing or benefitting a research community, discipline, field, topic, or theory. While it can take years for findings to have an impact, disciplinary norms of citing papers helps to demonstrate how an idea or researcher has influenced a field. Scholarly impact is typically measured through bibliometrics, the field that looks at mathematical and statistical measures of usage of published materials at the publication, author, or item level. Bibliometric measures include citation counts, journal impact factors, and altmetrics (alternative metrics that look at nontraditional item-level measures such as views, shares, and downloads). While often considered a proxy measure for impact, bibliometrics can demonstrate how research findings have been used by the scholarly community and influenced subsequent work.

Bibliometric studies of information behavior research are not common; however, bibliometric studies across information science demonstrate that information behavior is one of the main areas of research focus in the last 30 years (e.g., Li et al., 2019; Zhao & Strotmann, 2022). One study that examined information behavior citations directly was Lund (2019), who looked at the citation impact of theories in the academic literature. Lund used Fisher et al.'s (2005) book *Theories of Information Behavior* to identify theories cited in Google Scholar. The 10 most cited theories, in order, were: Kuhlthau's (1991) information search process; Bates' (1989) berrypicking; Taylor's (1968) question-negotiation; Ingwerson and Järvelin's (2005) integrative framework; Ellis' (1989) information-seeking model; Dervin's (1976a) sense-making; Csikszentmihalyi's (1990) flow theory; Savolainen's (1995) everyday life information seeking; Hjørland's (2002b) sociocognitive theory of users; and Leckie et al.'s (1996) information seeking of professionals.

The societal impact of research has more recently been a topic of discussion, as there have been increasing calls by governments, funding bodies, and universities to ensure that research outcomes contribute to both disciplinary knowledge and to society at large. This impact – an "effect on, change or benefit to the economy, society, culture, public policy or services, health, the environment or quality of life, beyond academia" (Research Excellence Framework, 2011, p. 48) can consist of benefits, harm reduction, and harm prevention, including changing or benefiting an "activity, attitude, awareness, behaviour, capacity, opportunity, performance, policy, practice, process or understanding" (Research Excellence Framework, 2011, p. 48). As the broad definition of societal impact implies, there are many ways for researchers to create change in the world.

Societal impact may take many years to manifest; it may also be intangible, indirect, or unexpected. In some disciplines (e.g., medicine, engineering, education, sociology) solving practical problems and thinking about societal benefits are naturally an integral part of research designs. In these areas, demonstrating benefits to society may be quite straightforward (e.g., a new vaccine saves lives, or CO_2 levels from engine exhaust are reduced). In other disciplines (e.g., philosophy, history, mathematics, physics), demonstrating societal impact may be more challenging. Current research impact measures only report on *academic* impacts, leaving researchers to find ways to demonstrate the influence of their research beyond academe. Although tracking engagement activities (e.g., giving workshops to practitioners or being interviewed by media) can demonstrate potential pathways to societal impact, tracking the actual change that has occurred (e.g., a librarian changing how they conduct a reference interview based on research advice) is much more challenging. For example, a project may include working with healthcare practitioners to determine better ways to share treatment information with patients for improved decision-making. How would societal impact be determined? How could a researcher track those practitioners, in the short and long term, to show that they changed their practices? And, if they did, is there a way to show that patients' decision making was improved? These types of questions can be considered in study design (e.g., to track adoption of practices longitudinally); but the ability to do so may be limited by time and funding, and by practitioners leaving the organization or not responding to follow-up requests for interviews.

Another challenge is that many publications do not report societal impacts of research. While some details may be shared at conferences (e.g., Willson et al., 2020), particularly those targeting nonacademic delegates, many impacts occur long after the project has ended. Researchers often translate that work directly for local communities and groups, without writing about the outcomes of that work. More work is needed to capture the societal impact of information behavior research, worldwide. However, this requires funding and time, as the decision to change a practice resides with the practice community and (in the long term) must be tracked independently of the original research project. Qualitative research methods offer flexible approaches to document societal research impact (Given et al., 2015); however, these should be built into the research design from the outset. Du and Chu (2022) present one of the first models for building community engagement into information behavior designs. Kelly's (2019) dissertation used an information behavior lens to assess social scientist and humanities scholars' success strategies for community engagement. Although researchers can share the results of their work with potential beneficiaries, and advise on strategies for potential adoption, the decision to implement a change is often well beyond the researcher's control. Societal impact must also be addressed in dissemination plans, including specific plans for how to apply research findings in practice (which is often labeled as knowledge translation, knowledge transfer, knowledge exchange, or knowledge mobilization); this is an important part of one's research design.

5.3 AN OVERVIEW OF METHODOLOGIES AND METHODS USED IN INFORMATION BEHAVIOR RESEARCH

Now that we have explored general research design principles, we present some examples from the information behavior literature. The approaches discussed here are not exhaustive of all possible approaches, or all examples of their use, but reflect those that have been *used* with some regularity – in some cases frequently, in other cases rarely. Many of the studies described could be categorized in more than one section (e.g., ethnographic studies that use interviews, observations, and visual methods), but the descriptions that follow provide an overview of the wide variety of methods used in information behavior research.

One methodological approach is very common: surveys. Whether the data are collected on a paper questionnaire, through a website or by way of a personal interview, methods associated with survey research have been the dominant means of investigation in information behavior research, as they have been in most of the human sciences. An analysis completed two decades ago by McKechnie et al. (2002) showed that over a third of all information behavior investigations use survey methodology. They conducted a content analysis of information behavior articles published during 1993–2000 in seven major information studies journals and conference proceedings and identified 14% (247 of 1,739 articles) as being information behavior research. Over half of these studies used more than one method (although this was not always well described): 35% were interviews, 20% were questionnaires, 14% observations, 11.6% content or document analysis, and 4.5% diaries; all other methods were in less than 4% of the studies, and most accounted for only 1% of the sample. These results have remained consistent over time. In an update to the McKechnie et al. (2002) study, Julien et al. (2011, p. 21) found that in the published information behavior literature, the methods employed between 1999 and 2008 "remain consistent with those reported earlier," with the largest proportion being methods used in survey research (i.e., questionnaires and interviews), which account for 44.7% of all methods. Looking at the methods used in information behavior dissertations between 2009 and 2018, Lund (2021) found that the top five methods used were interviews (61%), questionnaires (38%), experiments (18%), observation (13%), and ethnographic methods (13%) – some of which were used in combination.

Some methods are used sparingly in investigations of information behavior, such as experimentation and discourse analysis (each used in about 1% of the studies examined by McKechnie et al., 2002), although the latter is gaining in popularity. Other methods that were not so common 30 years ago, such as ethnography, have become increasingly popular for studying information behavior. With the rise in new technologies, researchers are also investigating a host of new methods – from ways to analyze social media feeds to tracking people's engagement with internet sources through user experience studies. Despite these new innovations, the tried-and-true methods of questionnaires, interviews, and focus groups continue to hold sway in the field. What follows is only a small sample of the range of research approaches that are now used in the field.

5.3.1 Survey Methods: Questionnaires, Interviews, Focus Groups, and Diaries

Survey methodology is a type of research used to systematically gather information that provides an overview of a topic; it is research in which a sample of individuals is asked to respond to questions. As a research strategy the survey approach encompasses a variety of methods of data collection, including the distribution of questionnaires (online, by email, or in paper form), individual interviews (in person, by phone, or over videoconference), the interviewing of people (individually, or together in small groups), and diaries (paper, online, or through mobile phone apps). Survey research uses various question types and techniques, such as asking the respondent to relate a "critical incident" that illustrates an important type of event or change in the life of the respondent or an organization (see Davenport, 2010; Urquhart et al., 2003, for reviews of this technique).

The questionnaire (often used in quantitative studies) is an exemplar of the survey approach, but interviews are more difficult to categorize. The strength of the survey approach is gathering responses from large numbers of individuals – data that can easily be quantified; phone interviews are often verbal questionnaires, with many yes/no or multiple-choice questions, so can be analyzed using quantitative methods. As interviews become longer and more intensive, we enter a different realm of data collection and research strategy. That is, interviews that require lengthy, unrestricted responses (such as critical incident questions) or that involve more than one respondent (e.g., focus group interviews) are qualitative approaches that allow for more in-depth, narrative investigations of the topic at hand. Diaries provide a first-hand, chronological account of daily activities and experiences; these may also include self-reflective writing, often referred to as journaling.

This section focuses on both quantifiable examples of survey research, such as large-scale studies using highly structured questionnaires and interview schedules, as well as qualitative designs. However, it is important to note that qualitative survey methods may also be designed using other methodological approaches – such as grounded theory, phenomenology, or ethnography. The choice of methodology shapes the analytical approach to be used in the design, which also affects how data are gathered during data collection.

Online Questionnaires: A Mainstay for Gathering Descriptive Data in the Pandemic

Online questionnaires are often used to document information sources, attitudes, and practices; these have been useful during the pandemic, particularly to reach people living under lockdown conditions. One nuanced view of COVID-19 information sources emerged from a questionnaire of almost 5,000 Chinese adults, by Zhou et al. (2020). The top sources included experts, television, newspapers, and social media (text or videos); relatively few respondents consulted friends or relied on their own past experiences. Other questions revealed misinformation (e.g., on alternative treatments) on social media, with older respondents more likely to be misled by these. Hornik et al. (2020) surveyed 1,000 people to see whether belief in COVID-19 misinformation was correlated with mask wearing and social distancing. They found believing certain misinformation is not as predictive as beliefs about how well masks and distancing work. They suggest publicizing the latter, rather than trying to stamp out false claims.

5.3.1.1 Questionnaires

Questionnaires gather data using a series of questions to collect reported understandings, attitudes, feelings, or behaviors on a topic. Many different types of questions can be used, including multiple choice, yes/no, rankings, Likert ratings, and short answer. An example of a large-scale postal survey is Pálsdóttir's (2008, 2010) study of health-related behaviors and beliefs among residents of Iceland. In 2002 and 2007, questionnaires were mailed to a random sample of 1,000 residents, about half of whom responded each time. The method resulted in sufficient responses to run a range of statistical tests, including cluster analysis, that resulted in discovering that 38% of respondents are passive in their learning about health issues and practices, due to the degree to which they felt they could effectively adopt and maintain healthy behaviors. To examine problems encountered during purposive information seeking, Ek (2017) sent out 1,486 postal questionnaires to a cross section of Finnish citizens (purchasing names and addresses through the Finnish Population Register Centre) and received 687 responses. The response rate may have been helped by sending a mail reminder to complete the questionnaire. Paper questionnaires can be distributed by other means than postal mail, although this is not often done, due to both logistical and sampling issues. Agarwal et al. (2011) collected a large (346 responses) convenience sample of office workers in Singapore by distributing questionnaires in food courts where they ate their lunch. The token payment they offered undoubtedly helped to improve the return rate.

A more common application of the survey methodology is the distribution of questionnaires online, whether as digital forms circulated through email, or via web links to online systems (e.g., SurveyMonkey, Qualtrics, Google Forms), which are advertised on social media or discussion lists. While web-based surveys have been a boon to researchers in most senses, it is worth remembering that response rates are often extremely low (affecting the quality of the data) or impossible to calculate (as it may not be possible to determine how many people received the link). Given the amount of email traffic (including spam) that people deal with every day, the use of online questionnaires is challenging to implement. However, systems like SurveyMonkey (where data are automatically coded, with descriptive statistics available at the click of a button) make these tools very attractive to researchers.

While online questionnaires can lead to low response rates, these can be useful to gather large numbers of responses that would be difficult to reach using other formats. To explore how undergraduates use social media for information seeking, Kim and Sin (2015) distributed online questionnaires to all undergraduate students at a public university (N = 26,528), offering an opportunity to win a bookstore gift card to those who completed the questionnaire. The questionnaire received 1,355 responses, a response rate of approximately 5% that, while low, was enough to run ANOVAs to determine the effects of sex and problem-solving style. To explore health information seeking using smartphones, Wang et al. (2022) used an online survey company to recruit 9,086 participants in 10 Asian countries. While this allowed the researchers to run multilevel regression models, this is a small percentage of the total population. To recruit enough participants, a variety of recruitment strategies may be necessary. Nelissen et al. (2017) recruited 2008 respondents to answer questions about information seeking about cancer, including 1,387 members of the Belgian public who had not received a cancer diagnosis (recruited online through adult education centers) and 621 who had received a cancer diagnosis (recruited through links posted to cancer forums, links, and paper questionnaires spread through self-help groups, and by approaching patients in an oncology hospital consultation room).

Information behavior researchers use online questionnaires to gather data from many different groups of people in many different circumstances. Some of the work continues the tradition of examining the information behavior of students and researchers, such as: Wellings and Casselden (2019), who examined the information seeking and resources use of engineers and scientists in the United Kingdom; Donkor and Nwagwu (2019), who looked at the information creation, information organization and information storage activities of academics in Ghana; Lopatovska and Sessions (2016), who examined the connection between information seeking and reading of graduate students in the United States; and Sin (2016), who explored American undergraduates' experiences using social media in everyday life information seeking. Other questionnaires explore the information behavior of new or relatively unexplored groups, including: Kuwaiti judges (Mansour & Ghuloum, 2017); motor sport enthusiasts (Joseph, 2016); Belgian speech language pathologists (Durieux et al., 2016); Greek musicians (Kostagiolas et al., 2017); and Canadian police officers (Abrahamson & Goodman-Delahunty, 2013).

As online questionnaires are quick to design and easy to implement, this method can be useful when studying phenomena as they happen, such as with COVID-19. Several recent studies looked at the information behavior of different

Qualitative Studies of COVID-19: An Emerging Research Focus

Qualitative approaches have been used to study individuals' experiences of the pandemic, mainly via individual and small group interviews. Montesi's (2021) review concludes that more qualitative research is needed to understand specific contexts and marginalized populations. One deep examination is by Lloyd and Hicks (2021), who documented everyday experiences and adaptations to the evolving, long-term risk of the virus. The investigators' interviewed 17 residents of the United Kingdom, showing how they interpreted and mitigated pandemic-related uncertainties (e.g., health, financial, and legal concerns). They suggest these informants conceptualized risk along dimensions of cultural discourse (e.g., narratives and norms of public health), material-economic terms (e.g., the need to social distance or work from home), and a communal dimension (e.g., sharing of information and responses). Tandoc and Lee's (2020) focus groups with 89 young adults highlight the importance of regulating uncertainty and emotional responses. Most informants found COVID-19 information impossible to avoid, although some tried; sharing information among friends had a calming effect, while some young people reduced their anxiety by viewing the virus as a threat mostly to older individuals. Wang (2020) employed parent diaries among nine families to examine parents' information behaviors and emotional responses during school closures.

groups during the pandemic and gathered responses from relatively large numbers of participants. This is the case with Soroya et al.'s (2021) study of the health information behavior of Finnish adults (N = 321), Huang et al.'s (2021) examination of the information needs and seeking behaviors of Chinese university students (N = 400), and Song et al.'s (2021) study of information avoidance by Chinese consumers (N = 721).

Although questionnaires have strengths, they also have weaknesses, especially superficiality. Questionnaires cannot easily capture the complexity of people's information behaviors, nor can they observe the influence of context (e.g., place, time, and situation) in the actual use of information. For this reason, other approaches – including in-depth interviews, participant observation or other methods – are needed, to provide a more complete picture of people's experiences.

5.3.1.2 Interviews

The interview is a very flexible method, as it can last a short or long time, and it can be conducted in person, over the phone, or online (e.g., via Zoom). Interview questions can be asked just once or repeated over time with the same respondent. The format of the interview can be structured (asking the same questions in the same way to every participant, as with a quantitative questionnaire), semistructured (asking similar questions to participants but allowing the interview to branch off to explore individual experiences), or unstructured (allowing participants to talk freely on a topic without set questions). The interviewer can take the formal role of a neutral investigator, or the role of a coparticipant in the same activities as the respondent. This section discusses information behavior studies that have used different types of interviews; however, interviewing is so commonly used that we cite only a few examples from many studies that use this method.

Although they are rather rare in the context of information behavior studies, door-to-door (or "doorstep") interviews are still conducted in other fields. A familiar example is a visit from a census worker. The main advantage of doorstep interviews is that they can gather data from hundreds of respondents and obtain answers of reasonable depth and reliability. In a doorstep survey concerning information needs in the United Kingdom, Marcella and Baxter (2000, 2001) discussed the methodology of a random sample of almost 900 members of the public. The Citizenship Information research project was funded by the British Library from 1997 to 1999 to investigate the needs and acquisition of information by or about the government that "may be of value to the citizen either as a part of everyday life or in the participation by the citizen in government" (p. 2). The first stage of the project was a questionnaire survey of almost 1,300 citizens, conducted through public libraries and other agencies; however, it oversampled library users and thus was complemented with a large sample of doorstep interviews. The interview method could probe more deeply and reach individuals less likely to use the library, such as those lacking in literacy, education or mobility, than could the distribution of questionnaires. In this study, use of the random walk method was found to reach greater proportions of women, elderly, retired, homemakers, and lower social classes, in most cases forming a more representative sample than the questionnaire method (Marcella & Baxter, 2000, 2001, 2005).

Interviews can also take place over the phone or online, using videoconferencing technologies; they may be brief and structured (i.e., to gather facts, such as demographic details) or in depth and less structured (i.e., to gather opinions, in people's own words). An example of a study using an in-depth, less structured phone interview is Mansourian (2021), which examined information activities involved in serious leisure. Recruitment was done through the community directory published by the city council of a small Australian city to identify serious leisure associations and societies. Recruitment materials were distributed to associations and societies. Participants were given the option of face-to-face or telephone interviews; 17 of the 20 participants interviewed opted for the telephone, as it was easier to organize that meeting in person. Other examples of phone interview studies include those by Abrahamson et al. (2008), Baxter et al. (2010), Cox et al. (2008), Dankasa (2016), Fulton (2005a, 2009a, 2009b), Harris et al. (2006), Kelly et al. (2009), Morey (2007), Scarton et al. (2018), and Williamson and Roberts (2010).

When interviews strive for in-depth information on a person's feelings, experiences, and perceptions, qualitative interview techniques are used. The explanations that result may be specific to those individuals, contexts, places, and times being studied; but, depending on the design of the project, the findings may be transferable to similar people, places, and situations. Often, in-depth, intensive interviews are used with a small sample of a large social group to understand an entire subculture, or with a few individuals to understand their personal viewpoints. Elfreda Chatman (1990) used in-depth interviews, along with observation, to "discover the social and information worlds of a poor population" (p. 357). We could consider this an example of participant observation or ethnography.

Chatman studied a group of 52 janitors – a sample of "the working poor" – over a two-year period; her goal was to document the meanings, feelings, and language that reflected the social reality of this group, and to examine this evidence in the light of theories of social alienation. On repeated occasions, over many months, Chatman followed these workers around during their jobs, talking with them and observing their actions. Most of Chatman's evidence is in the form of verbatim comments, recorded in her field notes. In her report of the research, representative samples of respondent comments are categorized by what theme they represent, such as "media channels to the outside world." The most compelling evidence is listed under the five headings – normlessness, powerlessness, meaninglessness, isolation, and self-estrangement – which are indicators of "alienation." The strengths of the intensive interview lie in the detail that is provided regarding the people studied. This study, which sampled a fairly large number of people over a long period of time, gives us a good idea of the trade-offs between this type of design and a large-scale survey conducted at one point in time. Chatman could not interview the larger numbers of respondents that are typically sampled in quantitative survey research, but she sampled a smaller number over more points in time. It is a group that would be difficult to study by other means, because of the very alienation she highlighted in her investigation. The data she collected are rich in detail; some of her evidence could be summarized, but most could not, and had to be sampled as it was reported.

For many people, their information activities are not front of mind. To help participants express and/or remember their experiences with information, researchers may use different techniques in their interviews. One way to do this is through a critical incident technique – a retrospective self-report technique that asks participants to remember a specific event that is related to the interview and is explored in depth to help gain concrete detail. Makri et al. (2019) used this technique when interviewing game designers, asking participants for examples of finding online information to support creative design idea generation and development. The site of interviews can be important when asking about participants' information behaviors occurring in a specific location. Thus, interviews frequently take place where people spend their time – at work, school, or home. Many information behavior investigations have interviewed respondents, entirely or predominantly, in their place of employment (e.g., Attfield & Dowell, 2003; Brine & Feather, 2010; Huvila, 2008a, 2008b, 2009; Isah & Byström, 2015; Lambert, 2010; McCaughan & McKenna, 2007; Nicholas et al., 2005; Pilerot, 2013). When looking at the information behavior of students, interviews frequently take place in schools (e.g., Chang, 2006; Diehm & Lupton, 2014; Lu, 2010; O'Brien et al., 2014; Seldén, 2001; Walker, 2009). Studies of the information behavior of children, family, and parents, as well as everyday information behaviors, often take place in the home, (e.g., Johnson, 2007; Margree et al., 2014; Ooi, 2011; Savolainen, 2010; Xie, 2008). These interviews often provide particularly rich data, but special considerations (e.g., related to privacy and safety) must be considered when carrying out interviews in private or remote locations.

Interviews are a ubiquitous method often used in conjunction with other data gathering techniques, or with certain analytic approaches. For example, Woudstra and van den Hooff (2008) used a "think-aloud" technique to elicit thoughts about the selection of human information sources, to better understand why a particular person was chosen (i.e., this usually had to do with the quality of their knowledge). Other researchers using the think-aloud technique include Makri and Buckley (2020), Everhart and Escobar (2018), and Pontis and Blandford (2015). Huvila (2008a, 2008b, 2009), Sonnenwald et al. (2001), and Chandler (2019) use a technique called "information horizon maps," in which respondents sketch out their sources on paper, with distance representing less importance or less usage. Another approach, called *domain analysis* (see Berrío-Zapata et al., 2021; Hjørland, 2002b, 2005d; Hjørland & Albrechtsen, 1995; Roos & Hedlund, 2016; Talja, 2005), uses interviews with members of a discourse community (e.g., scholars in a particular discipline, or practitioners of a certain hobby) to understand their culture and knowledge, as well as examine their documents and databases to gather additional information. Talja and Maula's (2003) and Fry's (2006) respective interviews with scholars, Sundin's with nurses (2003) and Hartel's (2003) with hobbyist cooks, are examples of this.

5.3.1.3 Focus Groups

Like in-depth individual interviews, focus group interviews are primarily qualitative in their design, as the goal is to capture spontaneous, verbatim responses from participants, complemented by group observations, research notes, and recordings. However, unlike individual interviews, the point of the focus group is to have discussion and interaction between group members to get a variety of perspectives or to understand points of contention (see Davenport, 2010; Lunt & Livingstone, 1996, for histories and critiques of the method). Focus groups are particularly useful for uncovering the underlying reasons for opinions, and motivations for actions; emotions and feelings (sometimes captured by facial expressions and body movements as much as spoken words) can also be important data to gather as group members engage with one another. In addition to the interviewer(s), it is not uncommon to have one or more additional researchers observing the action; in market research, where focus groups are heavily used to evaluate product advertising, it is common to hide the observers behind a one-way mirror, so that their presence does not influence people's responses.

Focus group size can vary widely, but most commonly involves approximately eight participants. Groups smaller than eight may not generate the diversity and critical mass typically needed by the investigators. Groups larger than 12 present difficulties in participation (individuals talk less in larger groups) and observation (it is difficult to observe many individuals at once). A single facilitator typically conducts focus group interviews, with the assistance of one or more helpers. The participants usually sit around a table or in a circle of chairs in a room that offers as little distraction as possible; or, the group may engage with one another online, using videoconferencing software. Often, specially prepared materials are used to provoke response: printed texts, photographs or videorecordings, for example. Flip charts or online whiteboards (e.g., Miro) are sometimes used to record responses so that group members can respond, in writing, to questions or visual prompts. For example, focus groups – without additional materials – were used to examine the information behavior of prisoners in Nigeria (Eze, 2016) and in Malawi (Gama et al., 2020), focusing on the information needed by prisoners and available resources (including the prison library). Other studies utilizing focus groups include Al-Muomen et al. (2012), Haras (2011), Kassim (2021), Kuruppu and Gruber (2006), Lloyd et al. (2013), Meyers et al. (2009), Miranda and Tarapanoff (2008), Prabha et al. (2007), Shenton and Dixon (2003, 2004), Silvio (2006), Solis (2018), and White et al. (2008).

5.3.1.4 Diaries

Diaries are another self-reporting option for gathering participant data. Diary methods enable researchers to capture activities and reflections in real time, while people engage in an experience, which are more difficult to capture with questionnaires, interviews, or other retrospective methods. The *diary* method takes its name from the common type of daily journal in which we record our personal reflections, but with several variations. A key difference lies in whether the respondent chooses when to fill out the diary (as we do when we keep a personal journal), or if the investigator chooses the time (a far more common use of the technique). Another difference is in the form required for reporting, which could be completely "open," or which could involve the use of precoded forms or prompting questions of varying degree of complexity. Although earlier studies relied on print diaries or tape-recordings, researchers also now use online forms, digital audio and video recordings, blogs, social media posts, and other techniques to capture participants' views in a real-time diary format. Julien et al. (2013), for example, gave cameras to students to document their information behaviors as part of a broader photovoice method. Similarly, Shankar et al. (2018) had participants use their smartphones to capture photo diaries of mobile information-seeking practices.

An early example of the use of respondent-controlled diaries is found in Maxine Reneker's (1993) study of "information-seeking among members of an academic community." Reneker recruited 31 informants on the Stanford University campus, giving them tape-recorders on which to note incidents of information seeking. The informants were directed to make a recording "whenever they had a question they could not answer "out of their own heads" over two one-week time periods. Respondents recorded how they went about addressing their information need and whether they were satisfied with the answer they obtained (p. 491). In this way Reneker collected 2,050 information-seeking incidents, which she transcribed and reviewed with the informants. This proved to be an extremely effective way to collect data about salient information-seeking experiences.

Diaries are frequently used in conjunction with other methods, such as with Hertzum and Hyldegård (2019) who used group interviews, individual interviews, and weekly diaries to collect longitudinal data about the academic and everyday information seeking of international students. For 10 consecutive weeks participants were emailed a link to an online diary, which consisted of a brief questionnaire. The questionnaire included general questions about the past week and concrete questions about an instance when information was needed. This allowed Hertzum and Hyldegård to sample participants' experiences and provide rich data about participants over an extended period. Other recent examples of the diary method include Colosimo and Badia's (2021) study of the information behavior of older adults, Du's (2014) study of the information behaviors of marketing professionals, Huvila's (2013) study of library professionals, Elsweiler et al.'s (2011) study of leisure information needs and television viewing, Lakshminarayan's (2010) dissertation, sampling two weeks of the experiences of 34 participants in six countries, Shah and Leeder's (2016) study of master's students' collaborative work, and Tan and Goh's (2015) examination of information seeking of tourists.

Time-sampling methods have also gotten more sophisticated over the years. As a scientific tool, this version of the diary method originated in "work sampling" studies of employees and their tasks. Whereas early "time and motion" studies of factory workers relied upon observations by investigators, white-collar tasks were more amenable to self-recording by the worker. In its earlier uses, investigators asked respondents to carry with them a notebook or precoded form and to record what they were doing during certain moments or periods of time. For instance, on a certain day they might be asked to record, at the top and bottom of each hour, what they were doing. To make the method more reliable, investigators also sampled recording times randomly; a pager or some other kind of alarm mechanism was used to prompt the respondents, at random times, to record what they had been doing. The random selection of times got around the problem of respondents having to watch the clock, and their tendency to "anticipate" what they would be writing about in their diary entry. Since the 1970s, the random-alarm method has shifted to include what people are *thinking and feeling* (the internal dimension of experience) as well as what they are doing (the external dimension). Given and Leckie (2003) used a timed approach to data collection in their "seating sweeps" method, documenting library users' information activities in the library space across various times of the day and days of the week.

Depending on the purpose and context of the study, respondents might be asked to record their thoughts and/or behaviors from 3 to 10 times per day, in periods ranging from a few days up to several months. Earlier studies of this type used pagers with both audio and vibrating signals, e-mails, or phone calls to prompt participants to record their data. One example of this technique is Robinson's (2010) survey of 78 design engineers, in which each of them carried a personal digital assistant for a 20-day period. Once per hour they were prompted to enter information about their current work task into this handheld computer. This enabled Robinson to draw some conclusions about the amount of time the engineers spent with various sources, and other patterns in their use of information. Morrison (2012) describes a series of studies that used a program called

Pocket Interview to prompt participants via their smartphones when it was time to complete a diary task. Today, researchers use smartphone apps that enable participants to provide their thoughts and feelings directly into their personal devices; and wearable devices (e.g., FitBit; iWatch) can be used to track participant data (e.g., heart rates) and also be used to prompt diary reflections.

5.3.2 Visual Methods: Observation and Visual Analysis

While observational methods have a long history in studying people's information behaviors, the range of visual methods used by researchers (and by their participants) continues to expand. Smartphone technologies enable researchers and participants to capture high-quality video and audio recordings during data collection, while studies of information creation and production techniques continue to grow. Often, these techniques are combined with survey methods, providing a mix of textual and visual data that can enrich data analysis and sharing of research results. This section discusses examples of some of the long-standing and more recent approaches to the capture of visual data.

5.3.2.1 Observation

Watching what people actually do (whether covertly or overtly) in libraries, workplaces, classrooms, or even in their homes, provides insight into the ways people gather and use various types of information sources and technological tools. Two of the earliest studies to use unobtrusive observation are Eugene Rawdin's (1975) study of industrial users of science and technology libraries and Johanna Ross' (1983) research on users' browsing activities in the academic library. Given and Leckie (2003) developed the unobtrusive "seating sweeps" method as a strategy to document users' information behaviors in the library space, including their possessions (e.g., pens, paper, laptops) and activities (e.g., writing, searching online). This technique for gathering data in a physical space has since been used in a range of other settings by Mandel (2010), May and Black (2010), and Given and Archibald (2015). Unobtrusive observation has also been used to explore patrons' information-seeking encounters at the public library reference desk (Cavanagh, 2013; Curry, 2005), to document (using videos recorded by parents) preschool children's use of technology in the home (Given et al., 2014), to examine the reading habits of older teens (Rothbauer, 2009), to determine the browsing behavior of children looking for informational picture books in a public library (Larkin-Lieffers, 2001), to understand how archeologists make use of information (Huvila, 2019), and to examine the use of an academic library's information commons (Archambault & Justice, 2017).

Unobtrusive observation has also been used to gather data on what people actually do online or when using a particular computer program. Some of this observation is indirect, such as analyzing transaction logs (e.g., Spink et al., 2004; Wu et al., 2019) and clickstreams (e.g., Jiang et al., 2017) to document people's searching activities. Other observation is direct, such as using screen-capture software (e.g., Camtasia) to track how people navigate websites (e.g., Abdullah

& Basar, 2019; Birru et al., 2004) or eye-tracking studies that follow people's gaze and visual attention, including where they look on a screen (e.g., Gwizdka et al., 2019; Jiang et al., 2022; Lee & Pang, 2017; Lorigo et al., 2006; Urban, 2020). Many studies also document users' engagement with websites, computer programs, and other digital tools, including as part of broader explorations of online information behavior. Skov and Ingwersen (2014), for example, explored visitors' engagement with a museum website through a series of observed search tasks completed in participants' homes.

Overt, or obtrusive, approaches for observing people's behaviors are also used to examine what people do in a range of social and private contexts. Researchers may observe participants as they engage in a task, while simultaneously asking them questions about their information-seeking decisions. This was the case with McKay et al. (2019), where library patrons who approached bookshelves were asked if they would consent to being observed and questioned about their activities and information-seeking goals. In other studies, researchers may ask participants to undertake activities "as they normally would," with researchers quietly observing in real time, followed by other methods (e.g., postactivity interviews) to understand what they had done. This approach was used by Lee et al. (2022) in their study of arts and crafts hobbyists; participants were asked to engage in exploration either in craft stores or on Pinterest and were observed, followed by semistructured interviews. Ocepek (2018b) recruited participants to two studies to explore sensory-based information sources used by grocery shoppers. Makri and Buckley (2020) used "think-aloud observations" to understand participants' web-based information encountering.

Participant observation (a method commonly used in ethnographic studies) is an approach where the researcher takes part in a group's activities to understand a particular topic or situation. Lynne McKechnie's (2000) research of preschool children's use of the public library is an example of one of the earliest studies of this type. Since then, several projects have used different types of observational methods to explore people engaging with information in various contexts. Examples include Wolf and Veinot's (2015) study of the everyday use of biomedical information; Brown and Kasper's (2013) participation observation study of a library's video game club; McKechnie's (2006) study of baby storytime; Prigoda and McKenzie's (2007) study of the information behavior of public library knitting groups; Olsson's (2016) study of the information practices of field archeologists; O'Brien et al.'s (2018) study of the information practices of young parents feeding their children; Lloyd and Olsson's (2019) study of the information practices of enthusiast car restorers; Veinot and Pierce's (2019) study of the materiality of information environments of patients on hemodialysis; Vardell et al.'s (2022) study of the information practices of an online cosplay community; and, Barriage's (2022) study of the information-seeking practices of young children in center-based childcare. Participant observation is typically paired with other data collection methods, particularly interviews.

5.3.2.2 Visual Analysis

An increasing number of studies in information behavior also make use of various visual analysis methods (including those involving digital technologies), although this continues to be an emerging area of research development. Polkinghorne's (2021) dissertation exploring people's food-related information practices used visual methods to document participants' real-time engagement in cooking, shopping, and other food-related activities. Hartel (2014b) describes the visual "iSquares" method, where she asked participants to respond to the question "What is Information?" by drawing on a 4 × 4 piece of paper. Crow (2009) used a participant-generated drawing activity to analyze elementary school children's information-seeking activities. Participant-generated drawings were also used by Greyson et al. (2017) in information world mapping, a draw and talk data-elicitation method to depict participants' social information world, including their information practices. Greyson et al. (2020) detail four methods for analyzing information world maps, describing what each one entails. This approach has since been used by Kitzie et al. (2021) to look at the health information practices of LGBTQ+ community leaders, and McKenzie and Dalmer (2020) to look at invisible information work.

Several studies also use visual approaches to explore individuals' information behaviors in the context of online information activities. Although many computer-based studies focus solely on information retrieval activities (such as query-term matching), information behavior scholars examine search practices within the broader context of an individual's information needs and preferences, and the reasons information is being sought. Given and Willson's (2015, 2018) examination of humanities scholars' collaborative information behaviors, for example, used an in-depth interview method in combination with a guided exploration of online tools designed for research engagement. In an earlier study, Given et al. (2007) used a prototype image-browsing technique to explore seniors' online health information behaviors. Kitalong et al. (2008) used card-sorting and affinity mapping to explore university researchers' information-seeking processes when using an academic library website. Somerville and Brar (2009) advocate for using various methods, including paper prototypes, in user-centered studies of digital library designs.

Participant-generated visuals are increasingly being analyzed by information behavior researchers. Hartel's (2006) study of information activities related to gourmet cooking analyzed photo inventories of participants' home cooking spaces. Agosto and Hughes-Hassell (2006) analyzed digital photographs generated by urban teens to document the places where they typically sought information. Julien et al. (2013) used photovoice to engage university students by asking them to take photographs representing their information behaviors. Li (2021) used photovoice (as well as observation, interviews, and focus groups) to explore the information practices of young people in library makerspaces. Barriage (2021) used a combination of several visual methods – including creating a poster, creating PixStories (combination of photo and audio recording using an app), photo-elicitation conversation and photo categorization – to capture the information practices of young children. Hartel and Thomson's (2011) review paper outlines the possibilities for integrating photographic techniques into studies of people's activities in information spaces. Everhart and Escobar (2018) used wearable video cameras and think-aloud protocols to capture the information-seeking experiences of a student with autism spectrum disorder and a neurotypical student in an academic library. These methods demonstrate how new techniques and technologies can be used to explore information behavior in new ways.

5.3.3 Textual Methods: Content Analysis and Discourse Analysis

Textual approaches are commonly used by information behavior scholars. Here, we refer to two of the most common approaches – content analysis and discourse analysis. Although these are distinct methodologies, they are sometimes conflated, which can be confusing for readers. Some publications also refer to these as methods or analytic techniques, rather than methodologies that shape the overall study design. We discuss these as a suite of approaches used to analyze various textual documents, such as policies, social media posts or books; however, interview transcripts, open-ended questionnaire responses, and other artifacts of participant-focused data collection practices can also be analyzed using content and discourse analysis techniques.

5.3.3.1 Content Analysis

A prominent text on content analysis (Krippendorff, 1980) explains how any artifact of communication – newspapers, journal articles, books, speeches, letters, songs, paintings – might be analyzed to understand themes and orientations. Either the *manifest* content (i.e., surface features such as words) or the *latent* content (underlying themes and meanings) of such artifacts may be recorded and analyzed. Both types of content may be analyzed in the same investigation. While historically a quantitative method, content analysis is flexible and methodologists have detailed how it can be used either quantitatively or qualitatively. An example of quantitative content analysis, White (2000) used content analysis to study questions on colon cancer that were submitted to a consumer health mailing list. She wanted to know what kinds of questions were being asked in a digital environment, what aspects of disease questioners were most concerned about, how the context of questions were portrayed, and what kind of patterns were manifest in the exchanges (e.g., if there were one or many questions per message). White sampled 1,000 messages gathered from 3,000 submitted over nearly three months. Messages to the list came from 152 people (about half of the list) and 58% of these participants asked questions, an average of four per "questioner." The 365 questions that were asked were coded for type, subject, and context using coding schemes developed by other researchers. By far the most popular type (comprising 41% of all questions) were those asking for *verification* of information (e.g., "Do you have to make a special trip just to do gene testing?"), while the remaining 59% were scattered over 17 other categories of

> ### *Big Data and COVID-19: A Common Analytic Approach*
>
> The most common approach to studying information behaviors under COVID-19 has been through analyses of large datasets of internet searches or social media posts. Shen et al. (2020), for example, examined Google searches and found people wanted to know how the virus spread, the signs and symptoms of infection, and what they could do to stay safe. In most cases, reputable sources (e.g., World Health Organization), were chosen. Benis et al. (2021) studied "infodemiology," where individuals were the sources of COVID-19 information, on Twitter. The authors clustered almost 3 billion tweets from over 420,000 users into term/topic folksonomies, illustrating changes in numbers and topics of tweets over 17 months. They identified three major themes: Health/Medicine (e.g., illness, deaths), Protection/Responsibility (e.g., vaccination, social distancing), and Politics (e.g., policies, leaders).
>
> Similarly, Afzal (2020) used content analysis to examine news dissemination by organizations (via broadcasts and websites), focusing on three large agencies (BBC, CNN, and ABC). Identifying eight categories of relevant news, Afzal found some variance in categories, yet similar dates of beginning and increasing coverage. More importantly, he detected signs of "information failures," where important facts were missing or obscured among an avalanche of less crucial information (e.g., changes to sporting events). Misinformation was also a major category of network news coverage.

question type. By looking at the categories of questions, the information needed becomes apparent.

Many information behavior researchers have used content analysis to examine online posts from question and answer (Q&A) boards and social media posts. Yerbury and Shahid (2017) examined tweets and Facebook posts from a campaign in the Maldives for the information practices of human rights activists; Westbrook and Zhang (2015) examined posts about cervical cancer from a Q&A site to determine the information needs of those posting on the forum; Lee and Kang (2018) examined online posts for collaborative information behavior after a South Korean maritime disaster; Bronstein and Lidor (2021) examined the information seeking of music fans of the Eurovision Song contest; Costello et al. (2017) examined posts on Reddit about illicit drug use to study information disclosure in online forums; and Ma et al. (2021) examined online posts in a Chinese online health community for the information needs of the family members of cancer patients.

Other studies use content analysis to examine documents created by different organizations or published in the literature. Looking at government records obtained through a freedom on information request, Tian et al. (2021) studied the information practices of law enforcement, looking at the ways "federal and local agents seek, share and use information for immigration enforcement" (p. 1358). Researchers have also examined trends in the body of published literature of information behavior research, including Julien (1996), Julien and Duggan (2000), Julien et al. (2011), Julien and O'Brien (2014), Tuomaala et al. (2014), Desrochers and Pecoskie (2015), and Hertzum (2017). Content analysis can also be used to provide a deeper understanding of interview transcripts, as in studies by Mokros et al. (1995) of interactions between librarians and patrons; O'Brien et al. (2014)

of motivations for choosing online news items; Yeon and Lee (2021) of information needs and behavior of North Korean refugees; and Solomon and Bronstein (2022) of information gathering practices of lawyers in Israel.

5.3.3.2 Discourse Analysis

Discourse analysis explores conversation and writing for clues to how people envision their world and how it works; it offers a collection of techniques to study how language is used and the role it plays in shaping society. There is a wide array of styles using this method and works using this approach range from short to book-length. Given the extensive use of quotations from the material studied, however, most accounts are rather lengthy. Budd and Raber (1996) is a good introduction to this style of research, and Olsson (2009, 2010b) has also written relevant explanations of its utility and theoretical connections. Some early examples of its practice in studies of information behavior are those by Given (2002a), Savolainen (2004), and McKenzie (2002, 2003a, 2003b).

Given (2002a), explored student discourses on the university campus to examine the influence of these on mature students' information behaviors. She interviewed mature students and completed a discourse analysis of university texts, including student newspapers, websites, admissions procedures, and other documents that shape students' experiences. An analysis of Canadian Census materials provided a macrolevel view of the ways that students are positioned in society, with implications for those who return to study later in life.

Savolainen (2004) was interested in how people talked about the internet among their other choices of information sources; he wanted to see what kind of accounts individuals gave of their preferences. He interviewed 18 individuals about their everyday-life information seeking, looking for evidence of their "subject positions" as regards the internet. In his analysis Savolainen identifies three "interpretative repertoires" in what his informants said; he calls them enthusiastic, realistic, and critical. The enthusiastic repertoire sees the internet as a wonderful tool that enables freedom and a first-choice source of information. In contrast, the realistic position sees one's choice of sources as strongly dependent on situations and contexts. Finally, the critical repertoire points out the low amount of relevant information available online and its poor organization, which make effective information seeking difficult. The informants did not inhabit these positions absolutely, but rather tended to shift from one repertoire to another within the same conversation.

McKenzie (2002, 2003a, 2003b) conducted a long-term study of 19 pregnant women. After initial interviews, she telephoned them twice a week to record recent incidents of everyday-life information seeking. Based on their detailed accounts, she identified four modes of information practices: active seeking; active scanning of the environment; everyday (nondirected) monitoring of the environment; and by proxy (i.e., via other people seeking on one's behalf). McKenzie's work contains long quotes from informants recounting their information practices. McKenzie (2004, 2009, 2010) and Davies and McKenzie (2004) use a similar approach in analyzing the responses of midwives.

More recently, Ma and Stahl (2017) used critical discourse analysis to examine posts in a public antivaccine Facebook group to help understand parental information seeking and sharing. Schreiber (2013) explored the discourse of information literacy in Scandinavian web tutorials. Schindel and Given (2013) used discourse analysis to explore the information shared about pharmacists' prescribing rights in Canadian news media. Abrahamson and Rubin (2012) examined discourse structures between consumers and physicians related to questions about diabetes in a health information website. Gaston et al. (2015) used discourse analysis to examine spirituality and everyday information behavior in Laos, focusing on the role of context in information behavior. Thatcher et al. (2015) used discourse and content analysis to examine reports on the Fukushima nuclear power disaster, looking at the role of information behavior on information failure.

5.3.4 Using Multiple Methods to Enrich Research Designs

Although many studies of information behavior rely on one type of data and data-gathering method, the use of multiple methods is becoming more commonplace, particularly in large-scale and mixed paradigm studies. Investigations that employ multiple types of methods and data are not uncommon, but many of these rely on predictable combinations of methods (e.g., questionnaires and individual interviews). Creswell and Clark (2017) and Fidel (2008) offer practical advice for going beyond those usual patterns, to "triangulate" the evidence, making up for the inadequacies or limitations caused by use of a single method. An explanation of how a mixed-methods approach connects to epistemology can be found in Onwuegbuzie et al. (2009) and in several sections of Given's *Sage Encyclopedia of Qualitative Research Methods* (2008).

Commonly, a multimethods approach takes the form of using two or three sources of data drawn from some mix of individual interviews, focus groups, visual methods, questionnaires, and textual analysis. These have been the dominant designs in a growing number of mixed-methods investigations. However, other investigations use many types of data. For example, a study by Miranda and Tarapanoff (2008) of Brazilian financial managers employs participant observation, individual interviews, focus groups, document analysis, and work process analysis. Other examples of mixed-methods studies that include several methods include Pluye et al.'s (2013) study of healthcare practitioners' information seeking, Elsweiler and Harvey's (2015) study of Twitter users, Mowbray and Hall's (2020) study of young people's networking while searching for a job, and Hyatt et al.'s (2021) study of long-distance backpacker's technology use.

One older study of note for its use of a wide variety of evidence types is Solomon's (1997a, 1997b) three-year study of sensemaking and information behavior in the annual work-planning phase of a public agency, using what he described as an "ethnography of communication." The agency provided technical assistance on natural resource conservation to external groups and had been recently merged with a larger agency – a situation featuring a great deal of change and uncertainty. As Solomon (1997b) describes it, "his interest was in discovering how the individuals separately and in consort made sense of their situation and in making sense how they defined, sought, and used information" (p. 1097). Among the data collected and analyzed in this study included first-hand observation and participation in meetings, field notes and tape-recordings of meetings, taped interviews with participants in the meetings, special logs kept by the participants regarding their related activities, and documents pertinent to the work-planning (e.g., memos and reports). Thus, Solomon's research design combines aspects of several methods, mainly interviews, content analysis, and participant observation. The latter refers to Solomon's participation to some degree in the activities of the group, rather than merely observing. His multimethod approach allowed him to examine information behavior from many different angles and to paint a rich portrait with detail and examples. The results of this extensive, multimethod study – which are reported in three journal articles consisting of 42 pages of fine print – provide in-depth understanding and unique insight into the information behavior of the public agency's employees.

Certain methodologies are also associated with the use of multiple sources of data and data collection methods, such as case studies, action research, grounded theory, and ethnography. Lundh and Alexandersson (2012) used multiple methods in their ethnographic study, for example, where they examined the information seeking of primary school children looking for pictures, using field notes, observations, informal conversations, and examining booklets produced by the children. Pilerot (2014) studied design researchers' information sharing using participant observation, including recorded conversations, field notes, photographs, and documents produced by participants. Rubenstein (2015) conducted a two-year ethnographic study of the exchange of information and social support in online breast cancer communities using archival analysis, participant observation, and interviews. Guzik (2018) studied the information-sharing practices of people converting to Islam using participant observation, semistructured interviews, and timeline drawings. Li et al.'s (2019) study of the information-seeking behavior of strategic planners in a pharmaceutical company in China, used participant observation, unstructured interviews, researcher journals, and project reports.

Grounded theory is another methodology that remains popular in information behavior research, and where the use of multiple methods is common. Costello (2017), for example, examined the interpersonal source selection of those with chronic illness using in-depth interviews and posts in online support groups. Willson (2018) explored the information behavior of early career academics using semistructured interviews, check-ins, and document analysis. Floegel (2020) examined fanfiction for queer information worlds using semistructured interviews and content analysis of online fanfiction platforms. Ye et al. (2021) examined roles within collaborative information seeking of a group traveling using demographic questionnaires, pre- and posttrip interviews, and diaries. Forcier (2022) used a constructivist grounded theory approach to explore the onlife information behaviors experiences of transmedia fans.

One of the significant challenges in mixing methods is ensuring that research incorporating both quantitative and qualitative data also reflect an appropriate mix of paradigmatic approach. A study that includes (for example) questionnaires and interviews may not necessarily be one that mixes quantitative and qualitative *paradigms*. If the data gathered are only analyzed through a quantitative lens (e.g., by running descriptive statistics on the qualitative dataset), rather than a qualitative one (e.g., the use of thematic coding and rich analytic descriptions), a study cannot be said to be truly a mixed-methods design. The mixing of paradigms allows researchers to gather strength from both approaches. In practice, this requires both quantitative and qualitative expertise in the research team to ensure that the project is designed – and that data are analyzed – using the different research perspectives that inform each paradigmatic approach. Given's (2016) qualitative research text provides a useful overview of the paradigm versus data focus in studies using multiple methods. Keith et al.'s (2022) toolkit provides guidance for study designs within interdisciplinary collaborative teams, working across paradigms.

5.3.5 Review Methods: Meta-Analyses and Systematic Reviews

As the prefix "meta" implies, meta-analysis takes us one level of abstractness above the methods discussed in previous sections. Meta-analyses have been used for several years in the health sciences and, to a lesser degree, in the social sciences. In brief, meta-analysis is a procedure for synthesizing and interpreting the findings of several studies at once, systematically, and with predefined processes for gathering and assessing literature on a given topic. Such systematic reviews offer methods to comprehensively examine the literature on a subject to provide a summary of research in an area. Recent examples include Lavranos et al.'s (2016) review of the literature from 1973 to 2015 on information seeking for musical creativity; Hertzum and Hansen's (2019) examination of empirical research on methodological issues in collaborative information seeking; Pian et al.'s (2020) review of measures of consumer health information needs; Petersen et al.'s (2021) analysis of information seeking when coping with cancer; and Jia et al.'s (2022) review of the characteristics of health information-seeking behavior of LGBTQ+ individuals.

Systematic review approaches go far beyond what might constitute a *literature review* (of the type appearing in students' doctoral dissertations, for example). By combining and reanalyzing comparable data from related investigations, systematic analyses extend what we can learn from individual studies. By combining results from different investigations, meta-analyses can expand the size and scope of the samples of human subjects and increase the generalizability of the findings (Cook & Leviton, 1980; Wolf, 1986). Systematic reviews do not just involve thorough searching; they require expert searching practices to find everything on a topic. Research questions are developed along with a set of criteria that help to identify relevant work. Once systematic searching has taken place and relevant studies are identified, they are critically appraised and measured against the criteria. Studies that are included in a systematic review are then examined; their data are extracted, analyzed, and synthesized to answer the research question. The results of a systematic review contribute to knowledge and can also be used for decision-making.

One of the challenges with meta-analyses and systematic reviews is that the processes for conducting such reviews (and the standards used to gauge the value of evidence presented) have been designed based on the *gold standard of evidence* that has been crafted in the medical sciences – i.e., a standard that privileges randomized-control trials over other research designs. While it is possible to conduct meta-analyses and systematic reviews of quantitative research, most information behavior studies are qualitative in nature or combine multiple methods. This means that the mechanisms for conducting systematic reviews do not always align themselves to the types of research designs – or the questions beings explored – in these studies. Given (2016) explores this issue in more depth in her discussion of the fit between qualitative research and evidence-based practice within the discipline of information science. Sandelowski and Barroso's (2006) *Handbook for Synthesizing Qualitative Research* provides useful guidance for reviewing these types of studies.

Ankem's studies (2005, 2006a, 2006b) are examples of meta-analysis, exploring the factors affecting information needs and sources among cancer patients. Yet, as Ankem (2005) notes, meta-analysis has been used rarely in research on information behavior. Haug (1997) is one of the earliest investigators to use this approach, analyzing 12 studies of physicians' preferences for information sources published between 1978 and 1992. All 12 investigations recorded quantitative data about the frequency of use and/or preferential ranking of various channels and sources of medical information. As in many such analyses, comparisons among the investigations were limited by dissimilar research questions, instruments, and reports and by the typically small samples. Meta-analyses often combine results of tests of statistical significance, but such a procedure was not possible with these studies due to the differing nature of their data. However, Haug was able to identify nine comparable information sources and, by reinterpreting some of the data, rank the first and second choices of sources of medical information among the many physicians surveyed in the 12 investigations. In addition, Haug's meta-analysis exposed the problems of validity that face quantitative research using questionnaires, as these may be self-reports of idealized behavior, rather than reporting of real actions.

There are several other examples, more recently, of authors using systematic approaches to review information behavior literature in particular areas. These include Yang et al.'s (2014) meta-analysis of the risk information-seeking and processing model; Kauer et al.'s (2014) review of help-seeking for mental health issues; Jordan's (2013) metastudy on the information behavior of graduate students; Chang and Huang's (2020) review of the antecedents that predict health information seeking; and Wang et al.'s (2021) examination of the process of data reusc. However, readers must be cautious when considering authors' approaches, as not all publications labeled as "systematic" reviews may follow the *gold standard* methods used by clinicians or apply appropriate review styles for qualitative and multiple methods studies.

5.4 CONCLUSION

The examples of investigations presented throughout this chapter reflect a variety of designs and research intentions. In most of the studies the unit of analysis is individuals – their characteristics (e.g., age or education), their orientations (e.g., attitudes or opinions), and most of all, their actions (e.g., the use of a particular information source). Some of the studies have taken multiple measures over time, while in other cases the time dimension is ignored. Together they represent a fair sampling of the types of research designs and methods common to information behavior research. However, there are some emergent trends. For example, while information behavior scholars have been working with communities, organizations, and governments for several decades, there is a growing and intentional focus on how we engage outside of academe and the impact of our work. This includes considerations of ethical practices, engagement with marginalized groups, and interdisciplinary approaches to research design. There is a continuing expansion beyond the tried-and-true survey methods (i.e., questionnaires and interviews) that we have embraced for decades, with researchers incorporating new and multiple methods (e.g., arts-based and creative practices) into their work. Information behavior scholars also continue to integrate new technologies in their work, whether as sites for data collection and analysis (e.g., analysis of social media) or as tools for data collection (e.g., smartphone apps). We hope readers will recognize that there is no single way to approach studies of people's information behaviors and therefore no "perfect" study design by which to judge the overall quality of all studies. The people and contexts explored in information behavior studies are diverse and, therefore, so too are the methodologies and methods used in these investigations.

5.5 OUR TOP 3 *MUST-READ* RECOMMENDATIONS

Fabritius, H. (1999). Triangulation as a multiperspective strategy in a qualitative study of information seeking behaviour of journalists. In T. D. Wilson & D. K. Allen (Eds.), *Information behaviour: Proceedings of the second international conference on research in information needs, seeking and use in different contexts*, 13–15 August 1998, Sheffield, UK (pp. 406–419). Taylor Graham.
An example of the use of multiple methods and sources of data in studying a single population: participant observation, interviews, participant and researcher diaries, talk-alouds, video-recordings, and photography.

Charmaz, K. (2014). *Constructing grounded theory: A practical guide through qualitative analysis* (2nd ed.). SAGE Publications.
This reinterpretation of the classic grounded theory methodology provides new perspectives for investigating information behavior using a social constructionist lens.

Kelly, W. (Ed.). (2022). *The impactful academic: Building a research career that makes a difference*. Emerald Publishing Limited.
A collection of articles written by researchers who foster societal impact, and by impact professionals who support researchers' impact-related activities, across disciplines.

REFERENCES

Abdullah, N., & Basar, S. K. R. (2019). How children gauge information trustworthiness in online search: Credible or convenience searcher? *Pakistan Journal of Information Management and Libraries*, *21*, 1–19. https://doi.org/10.47657/2019211468

Abrahamson, J. A., Fisher, K. E., Turner, A. G., Durrance, J. C., & Turner, T. C. (2008). Lay information mediary behavior uncovered: Exploring how nonprofessionals seek health information for themselves and others online. *Journal of the Medical Library Association*, *96*(4), 310–323. https://doi.org/10.3163/1536-5050.96.4.006

Abrahamson, D. E., & Goodman-Delahunty, J. (2013). The impact of organizational information culture on information use outcomes in policing: An exploratory study. *Information Research*, *18*(4). http://informationr.net/ir/18-4/paper598.html

Abrahamson, J. A., & Rubin, V. L. (2012). Discourse structure differences in lay and professional health communication. *Journal of Documentation*, *68*(6), 826–851. https://doi.org/10.1108/00220411211277064

Adorjan, M., & Ricciardelli, R. (2019). A new privacy paradox? Youth agentic practices of privacy management despite "nothing to hide" online. *Canadian Review of Sociology*, *56*(1), 8–29. https://doi.org/10.1111/cars.12227

Afzal, W. (2020). What we can learn from information flows about COVID-19: Implications for research and practice. *Proceedings of the Association for Information Science and Technology*, *57*(1). https://doi.org/10.1002/pra2.245

Agarwal, N. K., Xu, Y., & Poo, D. (2011). A context-based investigation into source use by information seekers. *Journal of the American Society for Information Science and Technology*, *62*(6), 1087–1104. https://doi.org/10.1002/asi.21513

Agosto, D. E., & Hughes-Hassell, S. (2006). Toward a model of the everyday life information needs of urban teenagers, part 2: Empirical model. *Journal of the American Society for Information Science and Technology*, *57*(11), 1418–1426. http://doi.org/10.1002/asi.20452

Al-Muomen, N., Morris, A., & Maynard, S. (2012). Modelling information-seeking behaviour of graduate students at Kuwait University. *Journal of Documentation*, *68*(4), 430–459. http://doi.org/10.1108/00220411211239057

Ankem, K. (2005). Approaches to meta-analysis: A guide for LIS researchers. *Library & Information Science Research*, *27*(2), 164–176. https://doi.org/10.1016/j.lisr.2005.01.003

Ankem, K. (2006a). Factors influencing information needs among cancer patients: A meta-analysis. *Library & Information Science Research*, *28*(1), 7–23. https://doi.org/10.1016/j.lisr.2005.11.003

Ankem, K. (2006b). Use of information sources by cancer patients: Results of a systematic review of the research literature. *Information Research*, *11*(3). http://informationr.net/ir/11-3/paper254.html

Archambault, S. G., & Justice, A. (2017). Student use of the information commons: An exploration through mixed methods. *Evidence Based Library and Information Practice*, *12*(4), 13. https://doi.org/10.18438/B8VD45

Attfield, S., & Dowell, J. (2003). Information seeking and use by newspaper journalists. *Journal of Documentation*, *59*(2), 187–204. https://doi.org/10.1108/00220410310463860

Australian Institute of Aboriginal and Torres Strait Islander Studies (AIATSIS). (2020). *A guide to applying the AIATSIS code of ethics for Aboriginal and Torres Strait Islander research*. AIATSIS. https://aiatsis.gov.au/sites/default/files/2020-10/aiatsis-guide-applying-code-ethics_0.pdf

Babbie, E. (2020). *The practice of social research* (15th ed.). Cengage Learning.

Barriage, S. (2021). Examining young children's information practices and experiences: A child-centered methodological approach. *Library & Information Science Research*, *43*(3), 101106. https://doi.org/10.1016/j.lisr.2021.101106

Barriage, S. (2022). Young children's information-seeking practices in center-based childcare. *Journal of Librarianship and Information Science*, *54*(1), 144–158. https://doi.org/10.1177/0961000620962164

Bates, M. J. (1989). The design of browsing and berrypicking techniques for the online search interface. *Online Review*, *13*(5), 407–424. https://doi.org/10.1108/eb024320

Baxter, G., Marcella, R., & Illingworth, L. (2010). Organizational information behaviour in the public consultation process in Scotland. *Information Research*, *15*(4). http://InformationR.net/ir/15-4/paper442.html

Benis, A., Chatsubi, A., Levner, E., & Ashkenazi, S. (2021). Change in threads on Twitter regarding influenza, vaccines, and vaccination during the COVID-19 pandemic: Artificial Intelligence–based infodemiology study. *JMIR Infordemiology*, *1*(1), e31983. https://doi.org/10.2196/31983

Berrío-Zapata, C., da Silva, E. F., & Teles Condurú, M. (2021). The technological informavore: Information behavior and digital sustainability in the global platform ecosystem. *First Monday*, *26*(11), 1. https://doi.org/10.5210/fm.v26i11.12354

Birru, M. S., Monaco, V. M., Charles, L., Drew, H., Njie, V., Bierria, T., Detlefsen, E., & Steinman, R. (2004). Internet usage by low-literacy adults seeking health information: An observational analysis. *Journal of Medical Internet Research*, *6*(3). https://doi.org/10.2196/jmir.6.3.e25

Brine, A., & Feather, J. (2010). The information needs of UK historic houses: Mapping the ground. *Journal of Documentation*, *66*(1), 28–45. http://doi.org/10.1108/00220411011016353

Bronstein, J., & Lidor, D. (2021). Motivations for music information seeking as serious leisure in a virtual community: Exploring a Eurovision fan club. *Aslib Journal of Information Management*, *73*(2), 271–287. https://doi.org/10.1108/AJIM-06-2020-0192

Brown, R. T., & Kasper, T. (2013). The fusion of literacy and games: A case study in assessing the goals of a library video game program. *Library Trends*, *61*(4), 755–778. https://doi.org/10.1353/lib.2013.0012

Buchanan, E., & Ess, C. (2009). Internet research ethics and the institutional review board: Current practices and issues. *Computers and Society*, *39*(3), 43–49. https://doi.org/10.1145/1713066.1713069

Budd, J. M., & Raber, D. (1996). Discourse analysis: Method and application in the study of information. *Information Processing & Management*, *32*, 217–226. https://doi.org/10.1016/S0306-4573(96)85007-2

Camacho, D., Panizo-LLedot, Á., Bello-Orgaz, G., Gonzalez-Pardo, A., & Cambria, E. (2020). The four dimensions of social network analysis: An overview of research methods, applications, and software tools. *Information Fusion*, *63*, 88–120. https://doi.org/10.1016/j.inffus.2020.05.009

Cavanagh, M. F. (2013). Interpreting reference work with contemporary practice theory. *Journal of Documentation*, *69*(2), 214–242. https://doi.org/10.1108/00220411311300057

Chandler, M. (2019). The information searching behaviour of music directors. *Evidence Based Library and Information Practice*, *14*(2), 85–99. https://doi.org/10.18438/eblip29515

Chang, S.-J. L. (2006). An investigation into information needs and information seeking behavior of elementary and middle school teachers teaching indigenous courses. *Journal of Library and Information Studies*, *4*(1/2), 49–76. https://www.oalib.com/paper/2817982

Chang, C.-C., & Huang, M.-H. (2020). Antecedents predicting health information seeking: A systematic review and meta-analysis. *International Journal of Information Management*, *54*, 102115. https://doi.org/10.1016/j.ijinfomgt.2020.102115

Charmaz, K. (2014). *Constructing grounded theory: A practical guide through qualitative analysis* (2nd ed.). SAGE Publications Ltd.

Chatman, E. A. (1990). Alienation theory: Application of a conceptual framework to a study of information among janitors. *RQ*, *29*, 355–368. https://www.jstor.org/stable/25828550

Colosimo, A. L., & Badia, G. (2021). Diaries of lifelong learners: Information seeking behaviors of older adults in peer-learning study groups at an academic institution. *Library & Information Science Research*, *43*(3), 101102. https://doi.org/10.1016/j.lisr.2021.101102

Cook, T., & Leviton, L. (1980). Reviewing the literature: A comparison of traditional methods with meta-analysis. *Journal of Personality*, *48*, 449–472.

Costello, K. L. (2017). Social relevance assessments for virtual worlds: Interpersonal source selection in the context of chronic illness. *Journal of Documentation*, *73*(6), 1209–1227. https://doi.org/10.1108/JD-07-2016-0096

Costello, K. L., Martin, J. D., & Edwards Brinegar, A. (2017). Online disclosure of illicit information: Information behaviors in two drug forums. *Journal of the Association for Information Science and Technology*, *68*(10), 2439–2448. https://doi.org/10.1002/asi.23880

Cox, A. M., Clough, P. D., & Marlow, J. (2008). Flickr: A first look at user behaviour in the context of photography as serious leisure. *Information Research*, *13*(1). http://InformationR.net/ir/13-1/paper336.html

Creswell, J. W., & Clark, V. L. P. (2017). *Designing and conducting mixed methods research* (3rd ed.). Sage Publications.

Crotty, M. (1998). *The foundations of social research: Meaning and perspective in the research process*. Sage Publications, Inc.

Crow, S. (2009). Relationships that foster intrinsic motivation for information seeking. *School Libraries Worldwide*, *15*(2), 91–112. https://doi.org/10.29173/slw6794

Csikszentmihalyi, M. (1990). *Flow: The psychology of optimal experience*. Harper & Row.

Curry, A. (2005). If I ask, will they answer? Evaluating public library reference service to gay and lesbian youth. *Reference and User Services Quarterly*, *45*(1), 65–75. https://www.jstor.org/stable/20864443

Dankasa, J. (2016). Mapping the everyday life information needs of Catholic clergy: Savolainen's ELIS model revisited. *Journal of Documentation*, *72*(3), 549–568. https://doi.org/10.1108/JD-08-2015-0097

Davenport, E. (2010). Confessional methods and everyday life information seeking. In B. Cronin (Ed.), *Annual review of information science and technology* (Vol. 44, pp. 533–562). Information Today.

Davies, E., & McKenzie, P. J. (2004). Preparing for opening night: Temporal boundary objects in textually-mediated professional practice. *Information Research*, *10*(1). http://InformationR.net/ir/10-1/paper211.html

Dervin, B. (1976a). Strategies for dealing with human information needs: Information or communication? *Journal of Broadcasting*, *20*(3), 324–351. https://doi.org/10.1080/08838157609386402

Dervin, B. (2005). What methodology does to theory: Sense-making methodology as exemplar. In K. E. Fisher, S. Erdelez, & E. F. McKechnie (Eds.), *Theories of information behavior* (pp. 25–30). Information Today, Inc.

Desrochers, N., & Pecoskie, J. (2015). Studying a boundary-defying group: An analytical review of the literature surrounding the information habits of writers. *Library & Information Science Research*, *37*(4), 311–322. https://doi.org/10.1016/j.lisr.2015.11.004

Diehm, R., & Lupton, M. (2014). Learning information literacy. *Information Research*, *19*(1). http://InformationR.net/ir/19-1/paper607.html

Donkor, A. B., & Nwagwu, W. E. (2019). Personal factors and personal information activities behaviors of faculty in selected universities in Ghana. *Library & Information Science Research*, *41*(4). https://doi.org/10.1016/j.lisr.2019.100985

Du, J. T. (2014). The information journey of marketing professionals: Incorporating work task-driven information seeking, information judgments, information use, and information sharing. *Journal of the Association for Information Science and Technology*, *65*(9), 1850–1869. https://doi.org/10.1002/asi.23085

Du, J. T., & Chu, C. M. (2022). Toward community-engaged information behavior research: A methodological framework. *Library & Information Science Research*. https://doi.org/10.1016/j.lisr.2022.101189

Du, J. T., & Haines, J. (2019). Working with Indigenous communities: Reflections on ethical information research with Ngarrindjeri people in South Australia. In L. Freund (Ed.), *Proceedings of the 81st association for information science & technology annual meeting* (pp. 794–796). https://doi.org/10.1002/pra2.2018.14505501120

Durieux, N., Pasleau, F., Piazza, A., Donneau, A., Vandenput, S., & Maillart, C. (2016). Information behaviour of French-speaking speech-language therapists in Belgium: Results of a questionnaire survey. *Health Information and Libraries Journal*, *33*(1), 61–76. https://doi.org/10.1111/hir.12118

Ek, S. (2017). Factors relating to problems experienced in information seeking and use: Findings from a cross-sectional population study in Finland. *Information Research*, *22*(4). http://InformationR.net/ir/22-4/paper775.html

Ellis, D. (1989). A behavioural approach to information retrieval design. *Journal of Documentation*, *45*, 171–212. https://doi.org/10.1108/eb026843

Elsweiler, D., & Harvey, M. (2015). Engaging and maintaining a sense of being informed: Understanding the tasks motivating twitter search. *Journal of the Association for Information Science and Technology*, *66*(2), 264–281. https://doi.org/10.1002/asi.23182

Elsweiler, D., Wilson, M. L., & Lunn, B. K. (2011). Understanding casual-leisure information behaviour. In A. Spink & J. Heinström (Eds.). *New directions in information behaviour* (Vol. 1, pp. 211–241). Emerald Publishing Limited.

Everhart, N., & Escobar, K. L. (2018). Conceptualizing the information seeking of college students on the autism spectrum through participant viewpoint ethnography. *Library & Information Science Research*, *40*(3–4), 269–276. https://doi.org/10.1016/j.lisr.2018.09.009

Eze, J. U. (2016). Information needs of prisoners in Southeast Nigerian prisons. *Information Development*, *32*(3), 243–253. https://doi.org/10.1177/0266666914538042

Fabritius, H. (1999). Triangulation as a multi-perspective strategy in a qualitative study of information seeking behaviour of journalists. In T. D. Wilson & D. K. Allen (Eds.), *Information behaviour: Proceedings of the second international conference on research in information needs, seeking and use in different contexts, 13–15 August 1998, Sheffield, UK* (pp. 406–419). Taylor Graham.

Fidel, R. (2008). Are we there yet?: Mixed methods research in library and information science. *Library & Information Science Research*, *30*(4), 265–272. https://doi.org/10.1016/j.lisr.2008.04.001

Fisher, K. E., Erdelez, S., & McKechnie, E. F. (Eds.). (2005). *Theories of information behavior*. Information Today, Inc.

Fisher, K., Naumer, C., Durrance, J., Stromski, L., & Christiansen, T. (2005). Something old, something new: Preliminary findings from an exploratory study about people's information habits and information grounds. *Information Research*, *10*(2). http://InformationR.net/ir/10-2/paper223.html

Floegel, D. (2020). "Write the story you want to read": World-queering through slash fanfiction creation. *Journal of Documentation*, *76*(4), 785–805. https://doi.org/10.1108/JD-11-2019-0217

Forcier, E. (2022). *Everyday onlife practice and information behaviour: A study of media fans in a postdigital age*. Unpublished dissertation, Swinburne University of Technology. http://hdl.handle.net/1959.3/469057

franzke, a. s., Bechmann, A., Zimmer, M., & Ess, C., & the Association of Internet Researchers. (2020). *Internet research: Ethical guidelines 3.0*. https://aoir.org/reports/ethics3.pdf

Fry, J. (2006). Scholarly research and information practices: A domain analytic approach. *Information Processing & Management*, *42*(1), 299–316. https://doi.org/10.1016/j.ipm.2004.09.004

Fulton, C. (2005). Finding pleasure in information seeking: Leisure and amateur genealogists exploring their Irish ancestry. In A. Grove (Ed.), *Proceedings of the American Society for Information Science and Technology* (Vol. 42, pp. 1292–1303). https://doi.org/10.1002/meet.14504201228

Fulton, C. (2009a). Quid pro quo: Information sharing in leisure activities. *Library Trends*, *57*(4), 753–768. https://doi.org/10.1353/lib.0.0056

Fulton, C. (2009b). The pleasure principle: The power of positive affect in information seeking. *ASLIB Proceedings*, *61*(3), 245–261. http://doi.org/10.1108/00012530910959808

Gama, L. C., Chipeta, G. T., Phiri, A., & Chawinga, W. D. (2020). Information behaviour of prison inmates in Malawi. *Journal of Librarianship and Information Science*, *52*(4), 1224–1236. https://doi.org/10.1177/0961000620908655

Gaston, N. M., Dorner, D. G., & Johnstone, D. (2015). Spirituality and everyday information behaviour in a non-Western context: Sense-making in Buddhist Laos. *Information Research*, *20*(2). http://InformationR.net/ir/20-2/paper665.html

Given, L. M. (2002a). Discursive constructions in the university context: Social positioning theory and mature undergraduates' information behaviours. *The New Review of Information Behaviour Research: Studies of Information Seeking in Context*, *3*, 127–142.

Given, L. M. (Ed.). (2008). *The Sage encyclopedia of qualitative research methods*. Sage.

Given, L. M. (2016). *100 questions (and answers) about qualitative research*. Sage Publications, Inc.

Given, L. M., & Archibald, H. (2015). Visual traffic sweeps (VTS): A research method for mapping user activities in the library space. *Library & Information Science Research*, *37*(2), 100–108. https://doi.org/10.1016/j.lisr.2015.02.005

Given, L. M., Kelly, W., & Willson, R. (2015). Bracing for impact: The role of information science in supporting societal research impact. *Proceedings of the Association for Information Science and Technology*, *52*(1), 1–10. https://doi.org/10.1002/pra2.2015.145052010048

Given, L. M., & Kuys, B. F. (2022). Memorial design as information creation: Honoring the past through co-production of an informing aesthetic. *Library & Information Science Research, 44*(3). https://doi.org/10.1016/j.lisr.2022.101176

Given, L. M., & Leckie, G. J. (2003). "Sweeping" the library: Mapping the social activity space of the public library. *Library & Information Science Research, 25*(4), 365–385. https://doi.org/10.1016/S0740-8188(03)00049-5

Given, L. M., Ruecker, S., Simpson, H., Sadler, E. B., & Ruskin, A. (2007). Inclusive interface design for seniors: Image-browsing for a health information context. *Journal of the American Society for Information Science and Technology, 58*(11), 1610–1617. https://doi.org/10.1002/asi.20645

Given, L. M., & Willson, R. (2015). Collaborative information use with technology: A critical examination of humanities scholars' research activities. In *Collaborative information seeking best practices, new domains and new thoughts* (pp. 139–164). Springer-Verlag. https://doi.org/10.1007/978-3-319-18988-8_8

Given, L. M., & Willson, R. (2018). Information technology and the humanities scholar: Documenting digital research practices. *Journal of the Association for Information Science and Technology, 69*(6), 807–819. https://doi.org/10.1002/asi.24008

Given, L. M., Winkler, D. C., Willson, R., Davidson, C., Danby, S., & Thorpe, K. (2014). Documenting young children's technology use: Observations in the home. In *Proceedings of the Association for Information Science and Technology* (Vol. 51). https://doi.org/10.1002/meet.2014.14505101028

Government of Canada. (2018). *Tri-council policy statement (TCPS) 2: Chapter 9 – Research involving the first nations, Inuit and Métis peoples of Canada*. Panel on Research Ethics. https://ethics.gc.ca/eng/tcps2-eptc2_2018_chapter9-chapitre9.html

Greyson, D., O'Brien, H., & Shankar, S. (2020). Visual analysis of information world maps: An exploration of four methods. *Journal of Information Science, 46*(3), 361–377. https://doi.org/10.1177/0165551519837174

Greyson, D., O'Brien, H., & Shoveller, J. (2017). Information world mapping: A participatory arts-based elicitation method for information behavior interviews. *Library & Information Science Research, 39*(2), 149–157. https://doi.org/10.1016/j.lisr.2017.03.003

Guzik, E. (2018). Information sharing as embodied practice in a context of conversion to Islam. *Library Trends, 66*(3), 351–370. https://doi.org/10.1353/lib.2018.0007

Gwizdka, J., Zhang, Y., & Dillon, A. (2019). Using the eye-tracking method to study consumer online health information search behaviour. *Aslib Journal of Information Management, 71*(6), 739–754. https://doi.org/10.1108/AJIM-02-2019-0050

Haras, C. (2011). Information behaviors of Latinos attending high school in East Los Angeles. *Library & Information Science Research, 33*(1), 34–40. https://doi.org/10.1016/j.lisr.2010.05.001

Harris, R. M., Wathen, C. N., & Fear, J. M. (2006). Searching for health information in rural Canada. Where do residents look for health information and what do they do when they find it? *Information Research, 12*(1). http://InformationR.net/ir/12-1/paper274.html

Hartel, J. (2003). The serious leisure frontier in library and information science: Hobby domains. *Knowledge Organization, 30*(3/4), 228–238.

Hartel, J. (2006). Information activities and resources in an episode of gourmet cooking. *Information Research, 12*(1). http://informationr.net/ir/12-1/paper282.html

Hartel, J. (2014b). An arts-informed study of information using the draw-and-write technique. *Journal of the American Society for Information Science and Technology, 65*(7), 1349–1367. http://doi.org/10.1002/asi.23121

Hartel, J., & Thomson, L. (2011). Visual approaches and photography for the study of immediate information space. *Journal of the American Society for Information Science and Technology, 62*(11), 2214–2224. https://doi.org/10.1002/asi.21618

Haug, J. D. (1997). Physicians' preferences for information sources: A meta analytic study. *Bulletin of the Medical Library Association, 85*(3), 223–232.

Hertzum, M. (2017). Collaborative information seeking and expertise seeking: Different discourses about similar issues. *Journal of Documentation, 73*(5), 858–876. https://doi.org/10.1108/JD-04-2016-0053

Hertzum, M., & Hansen, P. (2019). Empirical studies of collaborative information seeking: A review of methodological issues. *Journal of Documentation*, *75*(1), 140–163. https://doi.org/10.1108/JD-05-2018-0072

Hertzum, M., & Hyldegård, J. S. (2019). Information seeking abroad: An everyday-life study of international students. *Journal of Documentation*, *75*(6), 1298–1316. https://doi.org/10.1108/JD-11-2018-0183

Hjørland, B. (2002b). Epistemology and the socio-cognitive perspective in information science. *Journal of the American Society for Information Science and Technology*, *53*(4), 257–270. https://doi.org/10.1002/asi.10042

Hjørland, B. (2005d). The socio-cognitive theory of users situated in specific contexts and domains. In K. E. Fisher, S. Erdelez, & E. F. McKechnie (Eds.), *Theories of information behavior* (pp. 339–343). Information Today, Inc.

Hjørland, B., & Albrechtsen, H. (1995). Toward a new horizon in information science: Domain analysis. *Journal of the American Society for Information Science*, *46*, 400–425. https://doi.org/10.1002/(SICI)1097-4571(199507)46:6%3C400::AID-ASI2%3E3.0.CO;2-Y

Hornik, R., Kikut, A., Jesch, E., Woko, C., Siegel, L., & Kim, K. (2020). Association of COVID-19 misinformation with face mask wearing and social distancing in a nationally representative US sample. *Health Communication*, *36*(1), 6–14. https://doi.org/10.1080/10410236.2020.1847437

Huang, K., Hao, X., Guo, M., Deng, J., & Li, L. (2021). A study of Chinese college students' COVID-19-related information needs and seeking behavior. *Aslib Journal of Information Management*, *73*(5), 679–698. https://doi.org/10.1108/AJIM-10-2020-0307

Huvila, I. (2008a). Information work analysis: An approach to research on information interactions and information behaviour in context. *Information Research*, *13*(3). http://InformationR.net/ir/13-3/paper349.html

Huvila, I. (2008b). The information condition: Information use by archaeologists in labour, work and action. *Information Research*, *13*(4). http://informationr.net/ir/13-4/paper369.html

Huvila, I. (2009). Analytical information horizon maps. *Library & Information Science Research*, *31*(1), 18–28. https://doi.org/10.1016/j.lisr.2008.06.005

Huvila, I. (2013). "Library users come to a library to find books": The structuration of the library as a soft information system. *Journal of Documentation*, *69*(5), 715–735. http://doi.org/10.1108/JD-06-2012-0080

Huvila, I. (2019). Genres and situational appropriation of information: Explaining not-seeking of information. *Journal of Documentation*, *75*(6), 1503–1527. https://doi.org/10.1108/JD-03-2019-0044

Hyatt, E., Harvey, M., Pointon, M., & Innocenti, P. (2021). Whither wilderness? An investigation of technology use by long-distance backpackers. *Journal of the Association for Information Science and Technology*, *72*(6), 683–698. https://doi.org/10.1002/asi.24437

Ingwersen, P., & Järvelin, K. (2005). *The turn: Integration of information seeking and retrieval in context*. Springer.

Isah, E. E., & Byström, K. (2015). Physicians' learning at work through everyday access to information. *Journal of the Association for Information Science & Technology*, *67*(2), 318–332. https://doi.org/10.1002/asi.23378

Janesick, V. J. (1998). The dance of qualitative research design: Metaphor, methodolatry, and meaning. In N. Denzin & Y. Lincoln (Eds.), *Strategies of qualitative inquiry* (pp. 35–55). Sage Publications, Inc.

Jia, R. M., Du, J. T., & Zhao, Y. C. (2022). Characteristics of the health information seeking behavior of LGBTQ+ individuals: A systematic review on information types, information sources and influencing factors. *Journal of Documentation*, *78*(2), 361–388. https://doi.org/10.1108/JD-03-2021-0069

Jiang, T., Chi, Y., & Gao, H. (2017). A clickstream data analysis of Chinese academic library OPAC users' information behavior. *Library & Information Science Research*, *39*(3), 213–223. https://doi.org/10.1016/j.lisr.2017.07.004

Jiang, T., Fu, S., Erdelez, S., & Guo, Q. (2022). Understanding the seeking-encountering tension: Roles of foreground and background task urgency. *Information Processing & Management*, *59*(3), 102910. https://doi.org/10.1016/j.ipm.2022.102910

Johnson, C. A. (2007). Social capital and the search for information: Examining the role of social capital in information seeking behavior in Mongolia. *Journal of the American Society for Information Science and Technology*, *58*(6), 883–894. https://doi.org/10.1002/asi.20561

Jordan, J. L. (2013). Meta-synthesis of the research on information seeking behaviour of graduate students highlights different library resource needs across disciplines and cultures. *Evidence Based Library and Information Practice*, *8*(4), 132–135. https://doi.org/10.18438/B8MK7V

Joseph, P. (2016). Australian motor sport enthusiasts' leisure information behaviour. *Journal of Documentation*, *72*(6), 1078–1113. https://doi.org/10.1108/JD-12-2015-0150

Julien, H. (1996). A content analysis of the recent information needs and uses literature. *Library & Information Science Research*, *18*, 53–65. https://doi.org/10.1016/S0740-8188(96)90030-4

Julien, H., & Duggan, L. (2000). A longitudinal analysis of the information needs and uses literature. *Library & Information Science Research*, *22*, 291–309. https://doi.org/10.1016/S0740-8188(99)00057-2

Julien, H., Given, L. M., & Opryshko, A. (2013). Photovoice: A promising method for studies of individuals' information practices. *Library & Information Science Research*, *35*(4), 257–263. http://doi.org/10.1016/j.lisr.2013.04.004

Julien, H., & O'Brien, M. (2014). Information behavior research: Where have we been, where are we going? *Canadian Journal of Information and Library Science*, *38*(4), 239–250.

Julien, H., Pecoskie, J. L., & Reed, K. (2011). Trends in information behavior research, 1999–2008: A content analysis. *Library & Information Science Research*, *33*(1), 19–24. https://doi.org/10.1016/j.lisr.2010.07.014

Kassim, M. (2021). A qualitative study of the maternal health information-seeking behaviour of women of reproductive age in Mpwapwa district, Tanzania. *Health Information and Libraries Journal*, *38*(3), 182–193. https://doi.org/10.1111/hir.12329

Kauer, S. D., Mangan, C., & Sanci, L. (2014). Do online mental health services improve help-seeking for young people? A systematic review. *Journal of Medical Internet Research*, *16*(3). https://doi.org/10.2196/jmir.3103

Keith, R. J., Given, L. M., Martin, J. M., & Hochuli, D. F. (2022). Collaborating with qualitative researchers to co-design social-ecological studies. *Austral Ecology*, *47*(4), 880–888. https://doi.org/10.1111/aec.13172

Kelly, W. (2019). *Navigating pathways to community: Exploring the experiences of community-engaged humanities and social sciences academics*. Unpublished dissertation. Swinburne University of Technology.

Kelly, W. (Ed.). (2022). *The impactful academic: Building a research career that makes a difference*. Emerald Publishing Limited.

Kelly, K. M., Sturm, A., Kemp, K., Holland, J., & Ferketich, A. (2009). How can we reach them? Information seeking and preferences for a cancer family history campaign in underserved communities. *Journal of Health Communication*, *14*(6), 573–589. https://doi.org/10.1080/10810730903089580

Kim, K.-S., & Sin, S.-C. J. (2015). Use of social media in different contexts of information seeking: Effects of sex and problem-solving style. *Information Research*, *20*(1). http://InformationR.net/ir/20-1/isic2/isic24.html

Kim, K.-S., Sin, S.-C. J., & Yoo-Lee, E. (2021). Use and evaluation of information from social media: A longitudinal cohort study. *Library & Information Science Research*, *43*(3). N.PAG. https://doi.org/10.1016/j.lisr.2021.101104

Kitalong, K. S., Hoeppner, A., & Scharf, M. (2008). Making sense of an academic library web site: Toward a more useable interface for university researchers. *Journal of Web Librarianship*, *2*(2–3), 177–204. https://doi.org/10.1080/19322900802205742

Kitzie, V., Wagner, T., & Vera, A. N. (2021). Discursive power and resistance in the information world maps of lesbian, gay, bisexual, transgender, queer, intersex and asexual community leaders. *Journal of Documentation*, *77*(3), 638–662. https://doi.org/10.1108/JD-08-2020-0138

Kostagiolas, P., Lavranos, C., Martzoukou, K., & Papadatos, J. (2017). The role of personality in musicians' information seeking for creativity. *Information Research*, *22*(2). http://InformationR.net/ir/22-2/paper756.html

Krippendorff, K. (1980). *Content analysis: An introduction to its methodology*. Sage.

Kuhlthau, C. C. (1991). Inside the search process: Information seeking from the user's perspective. *Journal of the American Society for Information Science*, *42*, 361–371. https://doi.org/10.1002/(SICI)1097-4571(199106)42:5%3C361::AID-ASI6%3E3.0.CO;2-%23

Kuruppu, P. U., & Gruber, A. M. (2006). Understanding the information needs of academic scholars in agricultural and biological sciences. *The Journal of Academic Librarianship*, *32*(6), 609–623. https://doi.org/10.1016/j.acalib.2006.08.001

Lakshminarayanan, B. (2010). *Towards developing an integrated model of information behaviour*. Ph.D. Queensland University of Technology.

Lambert, J. D. (2010). The information-seeking habits of Baptist ministers. *Journal of Religious & Theological Information*, *9*(1/2), 1–19. http://doi.org/10.1080/10477845.2010.508449

Larkin-Lieffers, P. A. (2001). Informational picture books in the library: Do young children find them? *Public Library Quarterly*, *20*(3), 3–28. https://doi.org/10.1300/J118v20n03_02

Lavranos, C., Kostagiolas, P., Korfiatis, N., & Papadatos, J. (2016). Information seeking for musical creativity: A systematic literature review. *Journal of the Association for Information Science and Technology*, *67*(9), 2105–2117. https://doi.org/10.1002/asi.23534

Leckie, G. J., Pettigrew, K. E., & Sylvain, C. (1996). Modeling the information seeking of professionals: A general model derived from research on engineers, health care professionals and lawyers. *The Library Quarterly*, *66*, 161–193. https://www.jstor.org/stable/4309109

Lee, J., & Kang, J. H. (2018). Crying mothers mobilise for a collective action: Collaborative information behaviour in an online community. *Information Research*, *23*(2). http://InformationR.net/ir/23-2/paper792.html

Lee, L., Ocepek, M. G., & Makri, S. (2022). Information behavior patterns: A new theoretical perspective from an empirical study of naturalistic information acquisition. *Journal of the Association for Information Science and Technology*, *73*(4), 594–608. https://doi.org/10.1002/asi.24595

Lee, H., & Pang, N. (2017). Information scent – Credibility and gaze interactions: An eye-tracking analysis in information behaviour. In *Proceedings of ISIC, the Information Behaviour Conference*, Zadar, Croatia, 20–23 September, 2016. Part 2, *22*(1). http://InformationR.net/ir/22-1/isic/isic1613.html

Leeder, C. (2019). How college students evaluate and share "fake news" stories. *Library & Information Science Research*, *41*(3). https://doi.org/10.1016/j.lisr.2019.100967

Li, X. (2021). Young people's information practices in library makerspaces. *Journal of the Association for Information Science and Technology*, *72*(6), 744–758. https://doi.org/10.1002/asi.24442

Li, Y., Li, Y., Pan, Y., & Han, H. (2019). Work-task types, stages, and information-seeking behavior of strategic planners. *Journal of Documentation*, *75*(1), 2–23. https://doi.org/10.1108/JD-01-2018-0015

Li, P., Yang, G., & Wang, C. (2019). Visual topical analysis of library and information science. *Scientometrics*, *121*(3), 1753–1791. https://doi.org/10.1007/s11192-019-03239-0

Lloyd, A., & Hicks, A. (2021). Contextualising risk: The unfolding information work and practices of people during the COVID-19 pandemic. *Journal of Documentation*, *77*(5), 1052–1072. https://doi.org/10.1108/JD-11-2020-0203

Lloyd, A., Kennan, M. A., Thompson, K. M., & Qayyum, A. (2013). Connecting with new information landscapes: Information literacy practices of refugees. *Journal of Documentation*, *69*(1), 121–144. http://doi.org/10.1108/00220411311295351

Lloyd, A., & Olsson, M. (2019). Untangling the knot: The information practices of enthusiast car restorers. *Journal of the Association for Information Science and Technology*, *70*(12), 1311–1323. https://doi.org/10.1002/asi.24284

Lopatovska, I., & Sessions, D. (2016). Understanding academic reading in the context of information-seeking. *Library Review*, *65*(8/9), 502–518. https://doi.org/10.1108/LR-03-2016-0026

Lorigo, L., Pan, B., Hembrooke, H., Joachims, T., Granka, L., & Granka, G. (2006). The influence of task and gender on search and evaluation behavior using Google. *Information Processing & Management*, *42*(4), 1123–1131. https://doi.org/10.1016/j.ipm.2005.10.001

Lu, Y.-L. (2010). Children's information seeking in coping with daily-life problems: An investigation of fifth- and sixth-grade students. *Library & Information Science Research*, *32*(1), 77–88. https://doi.org/10.1016/j.lisr.2009.09.004

Lund, B. D. (2019). The citation impact of information behavior theories in scholarly literature. *Library & Information Science Research*, *41*(4). https://doi.org/10.1016/j.lisr.2019.100981

Lund, B. (2021). The structure of information behavior dissertations 2009–2018: Theories, methods, populations, disciplines. *Journal of Librarianship and Information Science*, *53*(2), 225–232. https://doi.org/10.1177/0961000620935499

Lundh, A., & Alexandersson, M. (2012). Collecting and compiling: The activity of seeking pictures in primary school. *Journal of Documentation*, *68*(2), 238–253. https://doi.org/10.1108/00220411211209212

Lunt, P., & Livingstone, S. (1996). Rethinking the focus group in media and communications research. *Journal of Communication*, *46*(2), 79–98. https://doi.org/10.1111/j.1460-2466.1996.tb01475.x

Madden, M., Lenhart, A., Cortesi, S., Gasser, U., Duggan, M., Smith, A., & Beaton, M. (2013). *Teens, social media, and privacy*. Pew Research Center. https://www.pewresearch.org/internet/2013/05/21/teens-social-media-and-privacy/

Makri, S., & Buckley, L. (2020). Down the rabbit hole: Investigating disruption of the information encountering process. *Journal of the Association for Information Science and Technology*, *71*(2), 127–142. https://doi.org/10.1002/asi.24233

Makri, S., Hsueh, T., & Jones, S. (2019). Ideation as an intellectual information acquisition and use context: Investigating game designers' information-based ideation behavior. *Journal of the Association for Information Science & Technology*, *70*(8), 775–787. https://doi.org/10.1002/asi.24169

Mandel, L. H. (2010). Geographic information systems: Tools for displaying in-library use data. *Information Technology and Libraries*, *29*(1), 47–52. https://doi.org/10.6017/ital.v29i1.3158

Mansour, E., & Ghuloum, H. (2017). The information-seeking behaviour of Kuwaiti judges. *Journal of Librarianship and Information Science*, *49*(4), 468–485. https://doi.org/10.1177/0961000616654749

Mansourian, Y. (2021). Information activities in serious leisure as a catalyst for self-actualisation and social engagement. *Journal of Documentation*, *77*(4), 887–905. https://doi.org/10.1108/JD-08-2020-0134

Marcella, R., & Baxter, G. (2000). Information need, information seeking behaviour and participation, with special reference to needs related to citizenship: Results of a national survey. *Journal of Documentation*, *56*, 136–160. https://doi.org/10.1108/EUM0000000007112

Marcella, R., & Baxter, G. (2001). A random walk around Britain: A critical assessment of the random walk sample as a method of collecting data on the public's citizenship information needs. *New Review of Information Behaviour Research*, *2*, 87–103.

Marcella, R., & Baxter, G. (2005). Information interchange. In K. E. Fisher, S. Erdelez, & E. F. McKechnie (Eds.), *Theories of information behavior* (pp. 204–209). Information Today, Inc.

Margree, P., Macfarlane, A., Price, L., & Robinson, L. (2014). Information behaviour of music record collectors. *Information Research*, *19*(4). http://informationr.net/ir/19-4/paper652.html

Markham, A. (2012). Fabrication as ethical practice: Qualitative inquiry in ambiguous internet contexts. *Information, Communication & Society*, *5*(3), 334–353. https://doi.org/10.1080/1369118X.2011.641993

Ma, J., & Stahl, L. (2017). A multimodal critical discourse analysis of anti-vaccination information on Facebook. *Library & Information Science Research*, *39*(4), 303–310. https://doi.org/10.1016/j.lisr.2017.11.005

May, F., & Black, F. (2010). The life of the space: Evidence from Nova Scotia public libraries. *Evidence Based Library and Information Practice*, *5*(2), 5–34. https://doi.org/10.18438/B8MS6J

Ma, D., Zuo, M., & Liu, L. (2021). The information needs of Chinese family members of cancer patients in the online health community: What and why? *Information Processing & Management*, *58*(3), 102517. https://doi.org/10.1016/j.ipm.2021.102517

McCaughan, E., & McKenna, H. (2007). Never-ending making sense: Towards a substantive theory of the information-seeking behaviour of newly diagnosed cancer patients. *Journal of Clinical Nursing*, *16*, 2096–2104. https://doi.org/10.1111/j.1365-2702.2006.01817.x

McKay, D., Chang, S., Smith, W., & Buchanan, G. (2019). The things we talk about when we talk about browsing: An empirical typology of library browsing behavior. *Journal of the Association for Information Science and Technology*, *70*(12), 1383–1394. https://doi.org/10.1002/asi.24200

McKechnie, E. F. (2000). Ethnographic observation of preschool children. *Library & Information Science Research*, *22*(1), 61–76. https://doi.org/10.1016/S0740-8188(99)00040-7

McKechnie, L. (2006). Observations of babies and toddlers in library settings. *Library Trends*, *55*(1), 190–201.

McKechnie, L., Baker, L., Greenwood, M., & Julien, H. (2002). Research method trends in human information behaviour literature. *New Review of Information Behaviour Research*, *3*, 113–126.

McKenzie, P. J. (2002). Connecting with information sources: How accounts of information seeking take discursive action. *New Review of Information Behaviour Research*, *3*, 161–174.

McKenzie, P. J. (2003a). Justifying cognitive authority decisions: Discursive strategies of information seekers. *The Library Quarterly*, *73*(3), 261–288. https://www.jstor.org/stable/4309663

McKenzie, P. J. (2003b). A model of information practices in accounts of everyday-life information seeking. *Journal of Documentation*, *59*, 19–40. https://doi.org/10.1108/00220410310457993

McKenzie, P. J. (2004). Positioning theory and the negotiation of information needs in a clinical midwifery setting. *Journal of the American Society for Information Science and Technology*, *55*(8), 685–694. https://doi.org/10.1002/asi.20002

McKenzie, P. J. (2009). Informing choice: The organization of institutional interaction in clinical midwifery care. *Library & Information Science Research*, *31*(3), 163–173. https://doi.org/10.1016/j.lisr.2009.03.006

McKenzie, P. J. (2010). Informing relationships: Small talk, informing and relationship building in midwife-woman interaction. *Information Research*, *15*(1). http://InformationR.net/ir/15-1/paper423.html

McKenzie, P. J., & Dalmer, N. K. (2020). "This is really interesting. I never even though about this." Methodological strategies for studying invisible information work. *Nordic Journal of Library and Information Studies*, *1*(2), 1–17. https://doi.org/10.7146/njlis.v1i2.120437

Meyers, E. M., Fisher, K. E., & Marcoux, E. (2009). Making sense of an information world: The everyday-life information behavior of preteens. *The Library Quarterly*, *79*(3), 301–341. https://doi.org/10.1086/599125

Miranda, S. V., & Tarapanoff, K. (2008). Information needs and information competencies: A case study of the off-site supervision of financial institutions in Brazil. *Information Research: An International Electronic Journal*, *13*(2). http://InformationR.net/ir/13-2/paper344.html

Mokros, H., Mullins, L., & Saracevic, T. (1995). Practice and personhood in professional interaction: Social identities and information needs. *Library & Information Science Research*, *17*, 237–257. https://doi.org/10.1016/0740-8188(95)90047-0

Montesi, M. (2021). Human information behavior during the Covid-19 health crisis. *Library & Information Science Research*. https://doi.org/10.1016/j.lisr.2021.101122

Morey, O. (2007). Health information ties: Preliminary findings on the health information seeking behaviour of an African-American community. *Information Research*, *12*(2). http://informationr.net/ir/12-2/paper297.html

Morrison, K. (2012). Guided sampling using mobile electronic diaries. *International Journal of Mobile Human Computer Interaction*, *4*(1), 1–24. http://dx.doi.org/10.4018/jmhci.2012010101

Mowbray, J., & Hall, H. (2020). Networking as an information behaviour during job search: A study of active jobseekers in the Scottish youth labour market. *Journal of Documentation*, *76*(2), 424–439. https://doi.org/10.1108/JD-05-2019-0086

Nelissen, S., Van den Bulck, J., & Beullens, K. (2017). A typology of cancer information seeking, scanning and avoiding: Results from an exploratory cluster analysis. *Information Research*, *22*(2). http://InformationR.net/ir/22-2/paper747.html

Nicholas, D., Williams, P., Smith, A., & Longbottom, P. (2005). The information needs of perioperative staff: A preparatory study for a proposed specialist library for theatres (NeLH). *Health Information and Libraries Journal*, *22*(1), 35–43. https://doi.org/10.1111/j.1471-1842.2005.00535.x

O'Brien, H., Freund, L., & Westman, S. (2014). What motivates the online news browser? News item selection in a social information seeking scenario. *Information Research*, *19*(3). http://informationr.net/ir/19-3/paper634.html

O'Brien, H., Greyson, D., Chabot, C., & Shoveller, J. (2018). Young parents' personal and social information contexts for child feeding practices: An ethnographic study in British Columbia, Canada. *Journal of Documentation*, *74*(3), 608–623. https://doi.org/10.1108/JD-09-2017-0127

Ocepek, M. G. (2018b). Sensible shopping: A sensory exploration of the information environment of the grocery store. *Library Trends*, *66*(3), 371–394. https://doi.org/10.1353/lib.2018.0008

Olsson, M. R. (2009). Re-thinking our concept of users. *Australian Academic and Research Libraries*, *40*(1), 22–35. https://doi.org/10.1080/00048623.2016.1253426

Olsson, M. R. (2010b). Michel Foucault: Discourse, power/knowledge, and the battle for truth. In G. J. Leckie, L. M. Given, & J. E. Buschman (Eds.), *Critical theory for library and information science: Exploring the social from across the disciplines* (pp. 63–74). Libraries Unlimited.

Olsson, M. (2016). Making sense of the past: The embodied information practices of field archaeologists. *Journal of Information Science*, *42*(3), 410–419. https://doi.org/10.1177/0165551515621839

Onwuegbuzie, A. J., Johnson, R. B., & Collins, K. (2009). Call for mixed analysis: A philosophical framework for combining qualitative and quantitative approaches. *International Journal of Multiple Research Approaches*, *3*(2), 114–139. https://doi.org/10.5172/mra.3.2.114

Ooi, K. (2011). Selecting fiction as part of everyday life information seeking. *Journal of Documentation*, *67*(5), 748–772. https://doi.org/10.1108/00220411111164655

Pálsdóttir, A. (2008). Information behaviour, health self-efficacy beliefs and health behaviour in Icelanders' everyday life. *Information Research*, *13*(1). http://informationr.net/ir/13-1/paper334.html

Pálsdóttir, A. (2010). The connection between purposive information seeking and information encountering: A study of Icelanders' health and lifestyle information seeking. *Journal of Documentation*, *66*(2), 224–244. http://doi.org/10.1108/00220411011023634

Petersen, E., Jensen, J. G., & Frandsen, T. F. (2021). Information seeking for coping with cancer: A systematic review. *Aslib Journal of Information Management*, *73*(6), 885–903. https://doi.org/10.1108/AJIM-01-2021-0004

Pian, W., Song, S., & Zhang, Y. (2020). Consumer health information needs: A systematic review of measures. *Information Processing & Management*, *57*(2), 102077. https://doi.org/10.1016/j.ipm.2019.102077

Pilerot, O. (2013). A practice theoretical exploration of information sharing and trust in a dispersed community of design scholars. *Information Research*, *18*(4). http://informationr.net/ir/18-4/paper595.html

Pilerot, O. (2014). Making design researchers' information sharing visible through material objects. *Journal of the American Society for Information Science and Technology*, *65*(10), 2006–2016. http://doi.org/10.1002/asi.23108

Pluye, P., Grad, R., Repchinsky, C., Jovaisas, B., Johnson-Lafleur, J., Carrier, M.-E., Granikov, V., Farrell, B., Rodriguez, C., Bartlett, G., Loiselle, C., & Légaré, F. (2013). Four levels of outcomes of information-seeking: A mixed methods study in primary health care. *Journal of the American Society for Information Science and Technology*, *64*(1), 108–125. http://doi.org/10.1002/asi.22793

Polkinghorne, S. C. (2021). *Exploring everyday information practices: Embodied mutual constitution of people's complex relationships with food.* Unpublished dissertation. Swinburne University of Technology.

Pontis, S., & Blandford, A. (2015). Understanding "influence:" an exploratory study of academics' processes of knowledge construction through iterative and interactive information seeking. *Journal of the Association for Information Science & Technology*, *66*(8), 1576–1593. https://doi.org/10.1002/asi.23277

Poole, M. S., & McPhee, R. D. (1994). Methodology in interpersonal communication research. In M. L. Knapp & G. R. Miller (Eds.), *Handbook of interpersonal communication* (2nd ed., pp. 42–99). Sage Publications.

Prabha, C., Connaway, L. S., Olszewski, L., & Jenkins, L. R. (2007). What is enough? Satisficing information needs. *Journal of Documentation*, *63*(1), 74–89. http://doi.org/10.1108/00220410710723894

Prigoda, E., & McKenzie, P. J. (2007). Purls of wisdom: A collectivist study of human information behaviour in a public library knitting group. *Journal of Documentation*, *63*(1), 90–114. https://doi.org/10.1108/00220410710723902

Rawdin, E. (1975). Field survey of information needs of industry sci/tech library users. In *Information Revolution: Proceedings of the Eighth ASIS Annual Meeting*. Washington (DC), American Society for Information Science, Boston, Massachusetts, October 26–30, 1975, *12*, 41–42.

Reneker, M. (1993). A qualitative study of information seeking among members of an academic community: Methodological issues and problems. *The Library Quarterly*, *63*, 487–507. https://www.jstor.org/stable/4308868

Research Excellence Framework. (2011). Assessment framework and guidance on submissions. https://www.ref.ac.uk/2014/media/ref/content/pub/assessmentframeworkandguidanceonsubmissions/GOS%20including%20addendum.pdf

Robinson, M. A. (2010). An empirical analysis of engineers' information behaviors. *Journal of the American Society for Information Science and Technology*, *61*(4), 640–658. http://doi.org/10.1002/asi.21290

Roos, A., & Hedlund, T. (2016). Using the domain analytical approach in the study of information practices in biomedicine. *Journal of Documentation*, *72*(5), 961–986. https://doi.org/10.1108/JD-11-2015-0139

Ross, J. (1983). Observations of browsing behaviour in an academic library. *College & Research Libraries*, *44*(4).

Rothbauer, P. M. (2008). Triangulation. In L. M. Given (Ed.), *The SAGE encyclopedia of qualitative research methods* (pp. 893–894). SAGE Publications, Inc.

Rothbauer, P. (2009). Exploring the placelessness of reading among older teens in a Canadian rural municipality. *The Library Quarterly*, *79*(4), 465–483. https://doi.org/10.1086/605384

Rousi, A. M., Savolainen, R., & Vakkari, P. (2019). Adopting situationally relevant modes of music information at different stages of information-seeking processes: A longitudinal investigation among music students. *Journal of Documentation*, *75*(6), 1230–1257. https://doi.org/10.1108/JD-12-2018-0210

Rubenstein, E. L. (2015). "They are always there for me": The convergence of social support and information in an online breast cancer community: "They are always there for me". *Journal of the Association for Information Science and Technology*, *66*(7), 1418–1430. https://doi.org/10.1002/asi.23263

Sandelowski, M., & Barroso, J. (2006). *Handbook for synthesizing qualitative research*. Springer Publishing.

Saumure, K., & Given, L. M. (2008). Rigor in qualitative research. In L. M. Given (Ed.), *The SAGE encyclopedia of qualitative research methods* (pp. 796–797). SAGE Publications, Inc.

Savolainen, R. (1995). Everyday life information seeking: Approaching information seeking in the context of "way of life". *Library & Information Science Research*, *17*(3), 259–294. https://doi.org/10.1016/0740-8188(95)90048-9

Savolainen, R. (2004). Enthusiastic, realistic and critical: Discourses of internet use in the context of everyday life information seeking. *Information Research*, *10*(1). http://InformationR.net/ir/10-1/paper198.html

Savolainen, R. (2010). Source preference criteria in the context of everyday projects. Relevance judgments made by prospective home buyers. *Journal of Documentation*, *66*(2), 70–92. http://doi.org/10.1108/00220411011016371

Scarton, L. A., Fiol, G. D., Oakley-Girvan, I., Gibson, B., Logan, R., & Workman, T. E. (2018). Understanding cancer survivors' information needs and information-seeking behaviors for complementary and alternative medicine from short- to long-term survival: A mixed-methods study. *Journal of the Medical Library Association*, *106*(1), 87–97. https://doi.org/10.5195/jmla.2018.200

Schindel, T. J., & Given, L. M. (2013). The pharmacist as prescriber: A discourse analysis of Canadian newspaper media. *Research in Social and Administrative Pharmacy*, *9*(4), 384–395. https://doi.org/10.1016/j.sapharm.2012.05.014

Schreiber, T. (2013). Questioning a discourse of information literacy practice in web-based tutorials. *Information Research*, *18*(3). http://InformationR.net/ir/18-3/colis/paperC36.html

Schutt, R. K. (2022). *Investigating the social world: The process and practice of research* (10th ed.). Sage Publications.

Seldén, L. (2001). Academic information seeking – careers and capital types. *New Review of Information Behaviour Research*, *2*, 195–215.

Shah, C., & Leeder, C. (2016). Exploring collaborative work among graduate students through the C5 model of collaboration: A diary study. *Journal of Information Science*, *42*(5), 609–629. https://doi.org/10.1177/0165551515603322

Shankar, S., O'Brien, H. L., & Absar, R. (2018). Rhythms of everyday life in mobile information seeking: Reflections on a photo-diary study. *Library Trends*, *66*(4), 535–567. https://doi.org/10.1353/lib.2018.0016

Shen, T. S., Chen, A. Z., Bovonratwet, P., Shen, C. L., & Su, E. P. (2020). COVID-19-Related Internet search patterns among people in the United States: Exploratory analysis. *Journal of Medical Internet Research*, *22*(11), e22407. https://doi.org/10.2196/22407

Shenton, A. K., & Dixon, P. (2003). Youngsters' use of other people as an information-seeking method. *Journal of Librarianship and Information Science*, *35*(4), 219–233. https://doi.org/10.1177/0961000603035004002

Shenton, A. K., & Dixon, P. (2004). Issues arising from youngsters' information-seeking behavior. *Library & Information Science Research*, *26*(2), 177–200. https://doi.org/10.1016/j.lisr.2003.12.003

Silvio, D. H. (2006). The information needs and information seeking behaviour of immigrant southern Sudanese youth in the city of London, Ontario: An exploratory study. *Library Review*, *55*(4), 259–266. https://doi.org/10.1108/00242530610660807

Sin, S.-C. J. (2016). Social media and problematic everyday life information-seeking outcomes: Differences across use frequency, gender, and problem-solving styles. *Journal of the Association for Information Science and Technology*, *67*(8), 1793–1807. https://doi.org/10.1002/asi.23509

Skov, M., & Ingwersen, P. (2014). Museum Web search behavior of special interest visitors. *Library & Information Science Research*, *36*(2), 91–98. https://doi.org/10.1016/j.lisr.2013.11.004

Solis, E. (2018). Information-seeking behavior of economics graduate students: If you buy it, will they come? *Journal of Business & Finance Librarianship*, *23*(1), 11–25. https://doi.org/10.1080/08963568.2018.1431866

Solomon, P. (1997a). Conversation in information-seeking contexts: A test of an analytical framework. *Library & Information Science Research*, *19*, 217–248. https://doi.org/10.1016/S0740-8188(97)90014-1

Solomon, P. (1997b). Discovering information behavior in sense making: I. Time and timing; II. The social; III. The person. *Journal of the American Society for Information Science*, *48*(12), 1097–1138. https://doi.org/10.1002/(SICI)1097-4571(199712)48:12%3C1097::AID-ASI4%3E3.0.CO;2-P

Solomon, Y., & Bronstein, J. (2022). The information-gathering practice of liberal professionals in a workplace setting: More than just seeking information. *Journal of Librarianship and Information Science*, *54*(1), 54–68. https://doi.org/10.1177/0961000621992810

Somerville, M. M., & Brar, N. (2009). A user-centered and evidence-based approach for digital library projects. *The Electronic Library*, *27*(3), 409–425. https://doi.org/10.1108/02640470910966862

Song, S., Yao, X., & Wen, N. (2021). What motivates Chinese consumers to avoid information about the COVID-19 pandemic?: The perspective of the stimulus-organism-response model. *Information Processing & Management*, *58*(1), 102407. https://doi.org/10.1016/j.ipm.2020.102407

Sonnenwald, D. H., Wildemuth, B. M., & Harmon, G. (2001). A research method to investigate information seeking using the concept of information horizons: An example from a study of lower socio-economic student's information seeking behaviour. *New Review of Information Behaviour Research*, *2*, 65–86.

Soroya, S. H., Farooq, A., Mahmood, K., Isoaho, J., & Zara, S. (2021). From information seeking to information avoidance: Understanding the health information behavior during a global health crisis. *Information Processing & Management*, *58*(2), 102440. https://doi.org/10.1016/j.ipm.2020.102440

Spink, A., Ozmutlu, H. C., & Lorence, D. P. (2004). Web searching for sexual information: An exploratory study. *Information Processing & Management*, *40*(1), 113–133. https://doi.org/10.1016/S0306-4573(02)00082-1

Sundin, O. (2003). Towards an understanding of symbolic aspects of professional information: An analysis of the nursing knowledge domain. *Knowledge Organization*, *30*, 170–181.

Talja, S. (2005). The domain analytic approach to scholars' information practices. In K. E. Fisher, S. Erdelez, & E. F. McKechnie (Eds.), *Theories of information behavior* (pp. 123–127). Information Today, Inc.

Talja, S., & Maula, H. (2003). Reasons for the use and non-use of electronic journals and databases: A domain analytic study in four scholarly disciplines. *Journal of Documentation*, *59*(6), 673–691. https://doi.org/10.1108/00220410310506312

Tan, E. M.-Y., & Goh, D. H.-L. (2015). A study of social interaction during mobile information seeking: A study of social interaction during mobile information seeking. *Journal of the Association for Information Science and Technology*, *66*(10), 2031–2044. https://doi.org/10.1002/asi.23310

Tandoc, E. C., & Lee, J. C. B. (2020). When viruses and misinformation spread: How young Singaporeans navigated uncertainty in the early stages of the COVID-19 outbreak. *New Media & Society*, *24*(3), 778–796. https://doi.org/10.1177/1461444820968212

Taylor, R. S. (1968). Question-negotiation and information seeking in libraries. *College & Research Libraries*, *29*, 178–194.

Thatcher, A., Vasconcelos, A. C., & Ellis, D. (2015). An investigation into the impact of information behaviour on information failure: The Fukushima Daiichi nuclear power disaster. *International Journal of Information Management*, *35*(1), 57–63. https://doi.org/10.1016/j.ijinfomgt.2014.10.002

Tian, Y., Gomez, R., Cifor, M., Wilson, J., & Morgan, H. (2021). The information practices of law enforcement: Passive and active collaboration and its implication for sanctuary laws in Washington state. *Journal of the Association for Information Science and Technology*, *72*(11), 1354–1366. https://doi.org/10.1002/asi.24485

Timmers, C. F., & Glas, C. A. W. (2010). Developing scales for information-seeking behaviour. *Journal of Documentation*, *66*(1), 44–69. https://doi.org/10.1108/00220411011016362

Tuomaala, O., Järvelin, K., & Vakkari, P. (2014). Evolution of library and information science, 1965–2005: Content analysis of journal articles. *Journal of the American Society for Information Science and Technology*, *65*(7), 1446–1462. https://doi.org/10.1002/asi.23034

Urban, A. C. (2020). Narrative ephemera: Documents in storytelling worlds. *Journal of Documentation*, *77*(1), 107–127. https://doi.org/10.1108/JD-04-2020-0058

Urquhart, C., Light, A., Thomas, R., Barker, A., Yeoman, A., Cooper, J., Armstrong, C., Fenton, R., Lonsdale, R., & Spink, S. (2003). Critical incident technique and explication interviewing in studies of information behavior. *Library & Information Science Research*, *25*(1), 63–88. https://doi.org/10.1016/S0740-8188(02)00166-4

Vardell, E., Wang, T., & Thomas, P. A. (2022). "I found what I needed, which was a supportive community": An ethnographic study of shared information practices in an online cosplay community. *Journal of Documentation*, *78*(3), 564–579. https://doi.org/10.1108/JD-02-2021-0034

Veinot, T. C., & Pierce, C. S. (2019). Materiality in information environments: Objects, spaces, and bodies in three outpatient hemodialysis facilities. *Journal of the Association for Information Science and Technology*, *70*(12), 1324–1339. https://doi.org/10.1002/asi.24277

Walker, C. G. (2009). Seeking information: A study of the use and understanding of information by parents of young children. *Journal of Information Literacy*, *3*(2), 53–63. https://doi.org/10.11645/3.2.214

Wang, K. (2020). Information behavior of parents during COVID-19 in relation to their young school-age children's education. *The Serials Librarian*, *79*, 1–16. https://doi.org/10.1080/0361526X.2020.1806179

Wang, X., Duan, Q., & Liang, M. (2021). Understanding the process of data reuse: An extensive review. *Journal of the Association for Information Science and Technology*, *72*(9), 1161–1182. https://doi.org/10.1002/asi.24483

Wang, X., Shi, J., & Lee, K. M. (2022). The digital divide and seeking health information on smartphones in Asia: Survey study of ten countries. *Journal of Medical Internet Research*, *24*(1), e24086. https://doi.org/10.2196/24086

Wellings, S., & Casselden, B. (2019). An exploration into the information-seeking behaviours of engineers and scientists. *Journal of Librarianship and Information Science*, *51*(3), 789–800. https://doi.org/10.1177/0961000617742466

Westbrook, L., & Zhang, Y. (2015). Questioning strangers about critical medical decisions: 'What happens if you have sex between the HPV shots?'. *Information Research*, *20*(2). http://InformationR.net/ir/20-2/paper667.html

White, M. D. (2000). Questioning behavior on a consumer health electronic list. *The Library Quarterly*, *70*, 302–334. https://www.jstor.org/stable/4309440

White, M. D., Matteson, M., & Abels, E. G. (2008). Beyond dictionaries – Understanding information behavior of professional translators. *Journal of Documentation*, *64*(4), 576–601. http://doi.org/10.1108/00220410810884084

Williamson, K., & Roberts, J. (2010). Developing and sustaining a sense of place: The role of social information. *Library & Information Science Research*, *32*(4), 281–287. https://doi.org/10.1016/j.lisr.2010.07.012

Willson, R. (2018). "Systemic managerial constraints": How universities influence the information behaviour of HSS early career academics. *Journal of Documentation*, *74*(4), 862–879. https://doi.org/10.1108/JD-07-2017-0111

Willson, R., Greyson, D., Gibson, A. N., & Bronstein, J. (2020). Pulling back the curtain on conducting social impact research. *Proceedings of the Association for Information Science and Technology*, *57*(1). https://doi.org/10.1002/pra2.427

Wolf, C. T., & Veinot, T. C. (2015). Struggling for space and finding my place: An interactionist perspective on everyday use of biomedical information. *Journal of the Association for Information Science and Technology*, *66*(2), 282–296. https://doi.org/10.1002/asi.23178

Wolf, F. M. (1986). *Meta-analysis: Quantitative methods for research scientists*. Sage Publications.

Woudstra, L., & van den Hooff, B. (2008). Inside the source selection process: Selection criteria for human information sources. *Information Processing & Management*, *44*(3), 1267–1278. https://doi.org/10.1016/j.ipm.2007.07.004

Wu, D., Dong, J., & Liu, C. (2019). Exploratory study of cross-device search tasks. *Information Processing & Management*, *56*(6), 102073. https://doi.org/10.1016/j.ipm.2019.102073

Xie, B. (2008). The mutual shaping of online and offline social relationships. *Information Research*, *13*(3). http://informationr.net/ir/13-3/paper350.html

Yang, Z. J., Aloe, A. M., & Feeley, T. H. (2014). Risk information seeking and processing model: A meta-analysis. *Journal of Communication*, *64*(1), 20–41. https://doi.org/10.1111/jcom.12071

Ye, E. M., Du, J. T., Hansen, P., Ashman, H., Sigala, M., & Huang, S. (S.) (2021). Understanding roles in collaborative information behaviour: A case of Chinese group travelling. *Information Processing & Management*, *58*(4), 102581. https://doi.org/10.1016/j.ipm.2021.102581

Yeon, J., & Lee, J. Y. (2021). Employment information needs and information behaviour of North Korean refugees. *Information Research*, *26*(4). https://doi.org/10.47989/irpaper914

Yerbury, H., & Shahid, A. (2017). Social media activism in Maldives; information practices and civil society. *Information Research*, *22*(1). http://InformationR.net/ir/22-1/colis/colis1614.html

Zhao, D., & Strotmann, A. (2022). Intellectual structure of information science 2011–2020: An author co-citation analysis. *Journal of Documentation*, *78*(3), 728–744. https://doi.org/10.1108/JD-06-2021-0119

Zhou, J., Ghose, B., Wang, R., Wu, R., Li, Z., Huang, R., Feng, D., Feng, Z., & Tang, S. (2020). Health perceptions and misconceptions regarding COVID-19 in China: Online survey study. *Journal of Medical Internet Research*, *22*(11), e21099. https://doi.org/doi:10.2196/21099

Zimmer, M. (2010). But the data is already public: On the ethics of research in Facebook. *Ethics and Information Technology*, *12*(4), 313–325. https://doi.org/10.1007/s10676-010-9227-5

Chapter 6

REVIEWING, CRITIQUING, CONCLUDING, AND FUTURING

> Information behaviour is central to all aspects of our lives – intellectual, emotional and social. It is therefore unsurprising that a wide range of disciplines have developed an interest in it. This trend is likely to continue, offering the prospect of our developing a multifaceted understanding of the ways in which we go about acquiring information and transforming it into knowledge, the contexts in which we do this, the effects of a range of factors influencing this behaviour, and how we might be able to develop improved skills and systems to enhance the effectiveness with which we go about learning, decision making and problem solving. (Nigel Ford, 2015, p. 242)

Chapter Outline

6.1 REVIEWING

This book has described the many ways people experience information and how those experiences have been studied. We will first review, briefly, some key highlights and then comment on the changing emphasis of information behavior research. We will end by discussing some recent and future trends.

Chapter 1 defined the overarching concepts of behavior, practices and experiences, and their underlying elements (such as seeking, needs, use, and encountering). We contrasted older, system- and person-oriented approaches to research

Looking for Information
Examining Research on How People Engage with Information, 237–255

Published under exclusive licence by Emerald Publishing Limited
ISSN: 2055-5377/doi:10.1108/S2055-53772023006

with the "person-in-context" frame for studying information behavior that has become ubiquitous in contemporary scholarship. Our purpose as information behavior scholars now is to emphasize the holistic and context-driven nature of people's information experiences.

In *Chapter 2* we briefly considered the history and scope of information behavior, emphasizing the changing nature of research conducted over more than a century. We discussed how an increasingly research-based literature accumulated, and how it was debated and reviewed. Key debates involved the nature of information needs and what constituted "seeking" to answer those needs.

Early investigations emphasized occupations (e.g., scientists, engineers, managers) and formal sources (e.g., publications and libraries), with some attention paid to interpersonal exchanges. As digital sources evolved (initially descriptions of documents, and later their full texts) these became a key focus of study. Over time the scope of studies expanded to include different types of social roles (e.g., gatekeepers or hobbyists) and demographic groups (e.g., older people; those living in poverty).

In *Chapter 3* we detailed how the assumptions and emphases in investigations have shifted towards holism, to reflect the more complex and social nature of information behavior. Only in this way can we attempt to explain phenomena like information sharing, collaborative work, and leisure pursuits. We also discussed the spread of misinformation, fake news and conspiracy theories that continue to shape contemporary information experiences.

Models and theories were the focus of *Chapter 4*, with five representative models chosen that reflect interactions of motivations, thoughts, feelings, decisions, and actions involving information. A discussion of various philosophical assumptions underlying research preceded an exploration of theories used in information behavior. Ten theories popular in recent years were given particular attention.

In *Chapter 5* we examined methodologies, methods, and research designs as they have been applied to information behavior investigations. We also highlighted the global shift towards a focus on societal impact. Our goal in this chapter is to guide novice researchers in designing their own projects, as well as providing key reflections on the variety and limitations of research approaches that scholars at any career stage will find useful.

Now, in *Chapter 6*, we take a brief look back at the history of scholarly critique of information behavior studies, before embarking on a discussion of future trends. We aim to provide critical insights to guide researchers who are planning future studies, given some of the social imperatives that arise from climate change, the COVID-19 pandemic, and other critical moments that will continue to shape people's information experiences in the coming years.

6.2 CRITIQUING

6.2.1 A History of Criticism

In 1966, Herbert Menzel of New York University published what was to become the first among a series of *Annual Review of Information Science and Technology (ARIST)* chapters on *information needs and uses*. Menzel, whose concern was strictly limited to reviewing the burgeoning number of studies on scientists and engineers, opined that "all is not well with the quality of work performed in the field during the past few years [as] sometimes excellent ideas lead to results that are either of dubious reliability and validity, or else of a barren superficiality" (1966a, p. 42). Menzel described "poorly designed opinion polls," "primitive data-gathering instruments," and "categories too much tied to specific situations to make generalizations and extrapolations plausible" in his list of the faults of studies of "communication gathering behavior" (1966a, pp. 42–44). Menzel's suggested corrective was that researchers should draw upon "methods and techniques ... in communication behavior research and other branches of sociology and psychology," among other disciplines (p. 42).

Thus began a series of critiques and remedies directed at the study of information needs and seeking. A year after Menzel's review, Herner and Herner (1967) identified seven faults of such studies: using a narrow range of research techniques, studying too many disparate groups of users, failing to use consistent language, failing to innovate, failing to build on past findings, failing to learn from mistakes, and not using experimental designs.

In 1968 William Paisley pointed out the "defective methodology" and "shallow conceptualization" apparent in this research, expressing his "concern over the field's failure to adopt the sound methods of its own best work. Mistakes of the 1950s are repeated in the 1960s. Inconclusive studies are conducted to fill gaps left by previous inconclusive studies" (p. 2). Paisley also regretted that "the field has almost no theory" (p. 26), yet was able to conclude that it was "growing in size and maturing in quality [and that] adequate theories of information-processing behavior will follow" (p. 23). Similarly, Tom Allen griped about "the sort of trivia that many authors submit as research reports," particularly those "so involved with local circumstances that any generalization is questionable"; still, Allen thought there was "a strong corpus of good research in the field" (1969, p. 3).

6.2.1.1 A Long History of Negative Reviews and Calls for Change

This pattern of criticism – i.e., the presentation of disparaging remarks about the state of findings and methodology, coupled with optimistic comments about recent and future improvements – has persisted for more than five decades. In 1970, Lipetz's *ARIST* chapter observed that "the study of information needs and uses is still in its infancy, yet it exhibits considerable vigor" (p. 25). Diana Crane (1971) of Johns Hopkins University praised advances in methodology while acknowledging weaknesses in theory. Lin and Garvey (1972) declared that the literature lacked a conceptual framework.

John Martyn's 1974 *ARIST* chapter spoke of a literature "cluttered with the results of an enormous number of surveys of indifferent quality ... what this reviewer classes as 'Gee Whiz' research" (p. 4). Martyn suggested that progress could be made by focusing more on "communication" and less on "information" (p. 21), a point Brenda Dervin (1976a) reinforced and that Tom Wilson later argued had yet to be fully realized even by 1994.

The fault-finding intensified in the 1980s. The problem was not so much with a general definition for information, wrote Tom Wilson in 1981, "as with a failure to use a definition appropriate to the . . .investigation" (p. 3). Four years later, Wersig and Windel (1985) objected to a lack of "empirically supported theoretical basis", particularly that which would explain "the subjective and nonrational aspects of information behavior" (p. 12). Dervin and Nilan's (1986) *ARIST* review cited several of the complaints mentioned previously, characterizing them as a "concern for conceptual impoverishment" that had impeded the development of definitions and theories. And yet they still concluded that "a quantum and revolutionary conceptual leap in this area has been made since 1978" (p. 24).

Eight years later, a 50-year perspective by Tom Wilson (1994) agreed with Dervin and Nilan about those "leaps" forward. Wilson believed there *had* been discernible progress accomplished in five decades of research on information needs and uses, although "much time has been wasted." Wilson concluded that "a firmer theoretical base now exists than was the case 50 (or even 20) years ago" (p. 43).

While criticism of information behavior research may have lessened in recent years, its alleged lack of theory and small-scale focus continues to be mentioned in the context of the human side of information science, generally. For example, Nigel Ford (2015, p. 238) observes that

> . . . despite an increasing volume of information behaviour-related research, we still arguably lack robust applicable models and theories. Relevant to this issue is a criticism that has for some time been levelled at research into human aspects of information science, that much of it has been small-scale and fragmented, providing a snapshot view of phenomena . . . There is arguably a need for more co-ordinated, long-term, large-scale research programmes which focus on information behaviour with both breadth and depth.

There are also allegations that information behavior findings (and those across information science) lack any influence or effect outside of the communities of researchers who produce them. While it is commonplace for publications to include a closing statement like "practitioners may find these results useful in improving information services," there is little evidence that information behavior findings have strong impacts on the design of services or technologies. Although practitioners may well apply the results of information behavior studies (particularly in user-focused areas of practice, such as reference services, information literacy, and web usability), practitioners do not often publish about the influence of research on practice change, nor do they contact researchers to share details of such innovations.

6.2.1.2 A Call for Action – To Highlight Outcomes and Impact in Information Behavior Research

Ford (2015) calls for greater collaborations between researchers and practitioners and a focus on outcomes – i.e., "whether and how information is used, and what impact it has on the user and others" (p. 240). Researchers in the field do not typically track or publish about the impact of their work beyond academe. However, Given et al. (2015) point to the potential for information science to take a lead in documenting and supporting impact in practice; this concept was explored, more fully, in Kelly's (2019) doctoral research. They note that despite the global interest in formalized measures of societal impact, more work is needed to link research and practice in productive ways. Researchers must work together to ensure that information behavior research informs other investigations in information science (and vice versa), as well as in other disciplines. In judging that many studies are neither influenced nor influential outside of their niche, Sylvain Cibangu (2013, p. 204) complains of "research silos" that result in "little to no (intra-)collaboration between subfields of information science. What is published in information indexing, for example, is simply ignored and un-quoted in other subfields [such as] information behavior. . . ." On a positive note, it is evident that information behavior research has increased its use of theory and produced greater depth of results than a few decades ago. Trends in the field also indicate that information behavior researchers are beginning to address other criticisms, as well. This demonstrates a strong level of maturity and growth in research on people's experiences of information, which we expect to continue well into the future.

6.2.2 Changes in Methodology, Theory, and Impact

Are we making progress toward better understanding people's information behaviors? Or does "progress" in information behavior research remain illusory?

Over several decades, information behavior research has been criticized for focusing on a limited range of activities (e.g., needs, demands, seeking, searching), a tendency to focus on individuals rather than social learning and interactions, privileging cognition to the detriment of emotions and embodiment, sparse (and sometimes shallow) use of theory, and rarely going beyond finding and encountering to explore how relevant information is used to achieve some effect. On a disciplinary level there are also concerns that the corpus of our research has little influence outside of information science and may also fail to make a difference in the larger world.

There is now sufficient evidence that critiques of the range of activities studied, the focus on individuals, lack of attention to emotions or embodiment, little use of theory, and few outcomes have been addressed. The range of concerns that so dominated early information behavior research before 1980 (e.g., browsing and searching of formal information sources like libraries and databases) has expanded greatly over the last four decades. Not only has the range of sources increased (facilitated by advances in technology), but most of these new channels connect us to other people: email, texts, shared online documents, social media, videoconferencing, gaming, and so forth. These, in turn, have invoked new styles of interaction – i.e., discovery, encountering, sharing, collaboration, emotion, affect, embodiment, literacy, and others – all aspects of information experiences that are now mainstream topics of investigation.

6.2.2.1 The Rise of Theory in Information Behavior Research

Most investigations conducted before the 1980s were atheoretical, in keeping with the practical ends many studies intended (e.g., learning who was consulting certain resources to inform library collection practices). Since that time that it has been common to cite one or more among several dozen theorists and their theories. Since earlier editions of this book appeared, information behavior researchers have coalesced around a smaller number of theories than in the past, and now apply them in a more meaningful fashion. Some of the most prominent among these theories are two streams of *practice*: Schatzki's (1996) *practice theory* and Wenger's (1998) *communities of practice*. An analysis of information science research by Limberg (2017) illustrates the strong influence of practice theories. Albert Bandura's (2001) *social cognitive theory of learning*, and his concept of *self-efficacy* also remain popular, as does Anthony Giddens' (1984) *structuration theory* and Mark Granovetter's (1982) *social network theory* and the concept of *weak ties*.

This greater use of theory, more focused on a smaller number of theories than in the past, is a positive development. Yet we still face some degree of fragmentation. Undoubtedly, the wide range of theory employed is partly due to the diversity of the investigators themselves, who bring a mixture of scholarly backgrounds in the humanities, arts, social sciences, and sciences. We tend to cite literature we first encounter, early in our education, and weave this knowledge into our study designs. Colleagues educated in humanities traditions may lack common ground with those whose background lies in the social sciences or sciences. Exposure to philosophical traditions and methodological texts, as well as understanding the paradigmatic approaches that shape research designs, is critical for scholars to collaborate. Working *across disciplines* is as much an issue within our field as it is with researchers outside of information science. Theories form communities of discourse, around which individual investigations are discussed and compared.

As Pilerot et al. (2017) point out, the wide variety of theories used in information behavior investigations makes it difficult to compare results, as they derive from distinct assumptions and methodologies. A more focused set of common theories might bring increased coherence to information behavior research. We might develop a more meaningful dialogue about our research results and their importance for each theory, as well as the potential impact of our study findings beyond academe. We might influence scholars in other disciplines, from which those theories originated, by contributing to the broader dialogue of the evolution of those theories. We might develop a better explanation for our research agenda and, thereby, influence others to embrace our approaches to studying human-focused information experiences.

6.2.2.2 Information Behavior Research Is Making a Difference

While earlier writers alleged information behavior findings, and those from information science generally, have little influence or effect beyond our own research communities, Wilson (2020) presents evidence to the contrary. He shows that the disciplines of computer science and education, along with the more amorphous research areas of information systems and health, have regularly drawn on work in information behavior. Wilson highlights the many citations to his own work, alongside that of Carol Kuhlthau, Brenda Dervin, and Reijo Savolainen. In addition, Gorichanaz (2020) shows strong connections between information behavior and research in human–computer interaction. Examining journals in sociology or health, such as the *Journal of Leisure Research, Leisure Sciences*, the *Journal of Medical Internet Research*, or *Health Communication*, one will find reports of information behavior research like what is found in the pages of the *Journal of the Association of Information Science and Technology (JASIS&T)* or the *Journal of Documentation*.

On a structural level there has been a multidecade movement, globally, for academic departments of information science to merge with units with overlapping interests – communication, media studies, journalism, education, information systems or computer science, to name a few. This physical proximity has exposed other academics to research on information behavior. Although scholars may be concerned with the lack of *presence* to be found in a stand-alone department or school, being situated alongside colleagues in cognate disciplines also raises new opportunities for collaboration and interdisciplinary design. As information behavior scholars move toward a focus on outcomes and societal impact, new academic alliances may also open doors to a broader range of communities that may benefit from that work.

6.3 CONCLUDING

In addition to moving beyond past concerns about an overuse of some research designs, and a lack of theory, information behavior research has matured in several other ways. More research on people's experiences of information is being conducted than ever before, with scholars embracing various new paradigms, methodologies, and methods. The research community is also very international now, compared to 50 years ago. In the 1970s, most of the research was conducted in the United Kingdom, United States, and Canada. Today, the research community is global, with leading investigators found in other parts of Europe (especially the Nordic nations), and across Australia, Asia, and Africa.

The field has many talented scholars, some of them highly influential and productive even in the early stages of their careers. This development is largely due to the success of the biennial *Information Seeking in Context* (ISIC) conferences, the 14th of which took place in Berlin in September 2022; these meetings have provided a fertile ground for the exchange of ideas and findings about information behavior. Other conferences, such as the triennial *International Conference on Conceptions of Library and Information Science (CoLIS)*, the 11th of which was held in Oslo in 2022, and the iConference series, which met online in 2022, have also showcased information behavior research. The Association of Information Science and Technology (ASIS&T) continues to highlight information behavior research at its *Annual Meeting* (the latest of which was held in October 2022), and information behavior research is published regularly in

JASIS&T and the (recently relaunched) *Annual Review of Information Science and Technology (ARIST)*. In recent years, *JASIS&T* has also published two special issues on information behavior research – the first, edited by Allen et al. (2019), explored people's engagement with technology; the second, edited by Willson et al. (2020), focused on theory development in the field. ASIS&T is also home to the largest special interest group, globally, for information behavior researchers – SIG-USE, which sponsored Fisher et al.'s (2005) landmark work *Theories of Information Behavior*.

6.3.1 A Focus on the Whole Person

Information behavior research now brings *the whole person* into focus, paying attention not only to the search process they use or the sources they encounter but also to their emotions, the body, and how they experience information across a wide spectrum of situations and contexts. The role of affect in information behavior has received particular attention (e.g., Heinström, 2010; Nahl & Bilal, 2007; Savolainen, 2014, 2015), while embodiment has become another focus (e.g., Given, 2007; Guzik, 2018; Lloyd, 2010, 2014; Lueg, 2015; Olsson & Lloyd, 2017; Polkinghorne, 2021). Progress has been made towards clarifying what constitutes *use* and its outcomes or effects, as well as the impact of information behavior research itself (Case & O'Connor, 2016; Granikov, El Sherif et al., 2022; Pluye, El Sherif et al., 2019). These developments have addressed long-standing deficiencies in the collective information behavior research agenda. Today addressing the dynamic, personal, and context-laden nature of information behavior seems to be taken as an expectation by all investigators. This paradigmatic shift has resulted in greater use of theory, as well as more diversity in methods. While the resulting research has not always been rigorous, or as holistic in its approach as one might expect (see Polkinghorne & Given, 2021), the rest has added a new dimension to what was once merely a collection of shallow surveys of large, heterogeneous populations (like engineers).

Information behavior research has embraced new perspectives, theories, and methods that would have been considered highly unusual in 1970. The vigor it has shown over the last five decades – and with contributions of many productive researchers across all career stages – bodes well for the future. Outside of the domain of research, what developments might offer new topics or the means of studying them? Wilson (2022, pp. 97–98) points to expected developments in computing and machine learning. These might offer both additional ways of learning and communicating, as well as tools for analyzing records of human interactions. As can be seen from the evolution of social media (as only one example), people will continue to follow changes in these types of technologies, offering both new research questions and sources of data of interest to scholars. At the same time, as COVID-19 has taught us, the future will also present new and unforeseen contexts that will continue to shape people's information experiences. In the following sections, we explore potential research futures that are likely to shape information behavior research in the years to come.

6.3.2 Ten Lessons Learned of People's Experiences With Information

In *Chapter 1* we detailed *Ten Myths* about information. We now revisit these myths to discuss what is currently happening in studies of people's experiences with information, and the lessons we can take from the research literature to date.

Lesson #1: Searching for formal sources is only one small part of information behavior. Empirical research tells us that many people use formal sources (e.g., reference books) rarely, relying instead on informal sources such as friends, family, peers, collaborative tools (e.g., social media), and what they see in their environment, among other sources. Often, informal sources (e.g., seeing an advertisement on the subway) and informal networks (e.g., chatting in the lunchroom at work) give us useful information, directly. Although some librarians (and researchers) may believe that *least effort seeking* is too common, leading one to overlook the *best* source of information, this approach is efficient and effective for most people. For instance, searching the first page of returned hits in Google is quick to produce, on average, a satisfactory result. Although this approach may not seem rational to expert searchers, such behavior can be both satisfying and successful for most people.

Lesson #2: More information is not always better. We have seen that people spend a lot of time filtering, interpreting, and managing the overwhelming amount of information they experience each day. People must consciously ignore or filter out both irrelevant – and even, at times, very relevant – information when there is not enough time or energy to consider it all. Ignoring or avoiding information is a reasonable strategy to employ across all aspects of one's life, especially when doing so promotes psychological well-being. The ever-evolving number of channels and sources bombarding us with information only makes this point more obvious with the passage of time and with advances in new technologies.

Lesson #3: Context is central to information behavior. Information behavior research demonstrates that people strive for a holistic view of their world. Sometimes they do not connect external information to their internal reality because of anxiety, or because they do not see the relevance of it to their circumstances. People are prone to ignoring isolated bits of information, sometimes at great cost to their daily needs or long-term goals. Contextual factors also have significant influence over the ways information is sought, shared, used, and created. An individual's *perception* of a situation will shape their needs as much as the situation itself; this means different people approach similar situations in different ways, requiring different information, at different points, through various channels. Much of what we bring to bear in creating meaning from information is not only related to the *form or content* of the information but also related to our personal experience, history, culture, language, and our general understanding of the world.

Lesson #4. Information behavior is dynamic. Information needs may arise quickly, and either be satisfied or fade away. The nature of one's *question* may change at various points; so, satisfying one information need may simply give rise to yet another question or problem. The challenge in studying such shifting scenarios leads to a tendency to consider an information seeking episode as something simple, linear and bounded. A classic script for this type of analysis assumes that a need arises, then a person conducts a search of a single source, using a particular channel, and they find an answer – i.e., the end of search! Research tells us that people's information behaviors are not this straightforward or as easily resolved. Information behavior is like a series of interruptions, punctuated by more interruptions. People's information needs evolve; they ask questions of their world; they learn something, which leads to more questions; they find out they were relying on inaccurate information; they become frightened by new information they find; they stop searching; someone posts something on Twitter that sparks their curiosity to read more... and so on. The dynamic, iterative nature of information behavior, within context, must be considered in studying people's experiences.

Lesson #5: Sometimes information does not help. Information cannot satisfy all needs. People want to *understand,* but they also need to pursue more basic needs such as food, shelter, and human contact. It is not clear that there is a basic *need for information,* although some scholars believe this to be true. People facing problems are often looking for a customized, personal solution, rather than the standardized, one-size-fits-all response of an information system or agency. Even when individuals do *need* information, the pieces of information represented in books, articles, and websites may not provide all the answers people need. This is one reason that other people (intermediaries) continue to play a vital role in information behavior. Additionally, information cannot always help in situations that are unstable and changing. During a natural disaster, for example, information about future government assistance programs will not necessarily help you to find immediate advice to fix your roof. However, even during unstable and changing times, it is useful to understand what information people need, how they will seek that information, and how it can be usefully applied during a crisis.

Lesson #6: Sometimes information cannot be made available or accessible. Institutions and their formal information systems cannot keep up with the unique and unpredictable demands they face. Formal systems can never satisfy all information needs, whether due to resource limitations, privacy regulations, embargoes, preservation requirements, or the many other reasons some information cannot be shared. Yet, people often act as if they expect all information to be readily accessible and available for their use. The continuing exploration of issues of access, equity, and bridging the *digital divide* illustrates the critical role of information in addressing basic human needs. This highlights the importance of taking a broad perspective on the potential reach of information behavior studies, to explore the social contexts surrounding people's needs, as well as the systemic constraints and limitations that can inhibit access to information for some people, at some points in time.

Lesson #7: Information behavior is not always about a "problem" or a "gap." Not all information behaviors are driven by the need to respond to a situation. In fact, some behaviors are purely creative, while others arise from curiosity, or boredom. Much of the classic information behavior research, and even some contemporary studies, assume that people only seek information as a reaction to a problem state. In many cases, this is true enough: people often *do* seek information to solve problems or to find explicit answers to specific questions. Yet, the inadequacies of many early, historic studies of people's information behavior stem, in part, from starting with such a simplistic view of *why* people looked for information. Researchers now know that information behavior is about much more than solving problems, finding facts, or making decisions. Sometimes it is a quest for entertainment or distraction; sometimes it is an act of serendipity. Additionally, the *problem* perspective is often linked to a *deficit view* of people's information needs, rather than seeing the complex and dynamic reasons behind people's desire for new knowledge, skills, and understandings, bounded by social contexts and situations.

Lesson #8. Information behavior is not always about making sense. Historic studies of information behavior focused heavily on channels and sources (e.g., finding medical articles in a database), often with the goal of helping the searcher (e.g., a patient) to *make sense* of the problem they faced (e.g., a new diagnosis). Advances in digital technologies and online media have increased the range of channels and sources to study, encouraging both investigation and speculation on people's reasons and desires for information, entertainment, and exchanges with others. Yet, life is not entirely about uncertainty, gaps, or discontinuities. Approaching the design of information behavior research by focusing primarily on how people make sense of their world risks limiting what we can learn, significantly. Taking a more holistic approach, by positioning the whole person at the center of our investigations, will provide a more nuanced understanding of people's complex information behaviors.

Lesson #9: People's experiences of information are intertwined with emotional and bodily experiences. We know that individuals can feel overwhelmed, anxious, intimidated or even fearful of information, including the sources and platforms they use to access that information. A positive interpersonal encounter (e.g., with a helpful librarian) can leave a person feeling supported, acknowledged, and content, even when the information they receive is limited or inappropriate for their needs. Similarly, a personal's ability to hold a computer mouse or navigate a library space, or the memories sparked by the smell of an old book, can affect people's experiences with information, significantly. Emotion, affect, and embodied experiences must be considered in designing information behavior studies and in analyzing people's experiences.

Lesson #10. Better system design will not eliminate the need for human connection. There are limits to technology's ability to satisfy (and anticipate) our information needs. Although the design of voice recognition, text interpretation, recommender systems, virtual assistants, and robots are improving, rapidly, these systems cannot yet fully replace the people we rely on to help us in our quest for information. Human connection, emotion, and embodied experiences are just as central to information seeking as the need to have a system receive, understand, and retrieve relevant materials at our request. Maintaining a connection to other people, while fulfilling our need for content, continues to shape people's information behaviors. Technology is not a panacea, nor a replacement, for people.

6.4 FUTURING

It is a dangerous thing to try to predict the future. Significant unseen, or unknown, trends may swamp our immediate concerns; consider, for example, the COVID-19 pandemic, which has affected every aspect of our lives, globally. As we write this final chapter, waves of infection continue to disrupt people's lives, and hospitals are overflowing; some parts of the world remain in lockdown, while others have yet to return to prepandemic levels of travel, nightlife, or work patterns. At present, there is no clear end in sight. At the same time, many parts of the world are suffering from protracted conflicts, leading to rising refugee numbers. The planet continues to face extreme weather patterns due to climate change. Higher education is undergoing fundamental shifts in its goals and economic models; increased workforce casualization, the ongoing shift to hybrid learning and tensions between traditional publishing and open research practices, are changing academic work, significantly. An increased focus on the societal impact of research, alongside a continued focus on international university rankings, is reshaping the research questions, populations, and contexts researchers (and granting agencies) choose to explore. Yet, our focus on people's holistic experiences of information, accounting for the person *in context*, means information behavior scholars are ideally positioned to tackle all these issues in our work.

More than a decade ago, Tom Wilson (2010b) made several predictions informed by his long career in information behavior research. He predicted, for example, that technological developments, particularly around social media, would continue to drive research. He believed the digital divide would continue to persist within and between nations, attracting policy-related research efforts. He also expected that negative effects of the internet on children, and its positive use in education, would open opportunities for applied and policy-based research. Wilson also predicted that the focus on small-scale studies would decline, in favor of large-scale, policy-focused work. Over the past decade, many of Wilson's predictions have been realized. Ongoing technological advances (including social media) continue to affect the behaviors and habits of people, which (in turn) affects their information seeking and use activities. The negative effects of the internet on children and teens (e.g., bullying; grooming) remain, while internet access issues (e.g., low bandwidth; slow speeds; high mobile device costs) continue to create inequities.

Yet, knowing how to resolve these issues requires us to design research that ensures people's information experiences are central to the creation of new technologies, policy changes, and government funding priorities. What purpose do new technologies serve without people to *use* them? How can climate change be mitigated without changes to *people's* behaviors? Where will refugees turn for support without *people* to help, who understand their needs? The challenges of tomorrow remain *human* challenges; the question is, what are these challenges – and how can information behavior researchers provide the evidence needed to effect positive change? The following sections explore what we see as some of the significant future trends that all information behavior scholars should consider.

6.4.1 Global Trends: Information Behavior Research at Scale

There are many broad areas of research that influence all people, in all settings, worldwide – and where information behavior researchers can contribute, significantly. Research on people's health and well-being is one example, with significant information-related angles to pursue to better understand people's experiences. Although health-related topics have been explored for decades among information behavior scholars, it is perhaps more challenging to predict the specific *subtopics* related to health and well-being where we should put our energies in the coming years.

One significant source of guidance in recent years have been the United Nation's *Sustainable Development Goals (SDGs)*. All 17 goals, including *Quality Education, Reduced Inequalities,* and *Peace, Justice, and Strong Institutions*, align well to information behavior researchers' focus on people's information experiences. The SDGs also inform the *Times Higher Education's* international *Impact Rankings* of universities. Many universities have aligned their missions, as well as internal research schemes, to the SDGs, which may open avenues of potential funding for information behavior scholars.

Another useful resource for guiding the potential focus of information

Source: https://sdgs.un.org/

behavior research in the next decade (or more) is *Our Future World: Global Megatrends Impacting the Way We Live Over Coming Decades* (Naughtin et al., 2022). This report outlines seven significant trends that will affect all people, globally, with implications for information behavior research (see Fig. 6.1). The following sections provide a brief snapshot of just some of the questions and contexts that should be considered in future research designs.

Global Megatrend #1: Adapting to a Changing Climate. What information will people need to adapt their lives to a changing climate? How do people decide whether to relocate (e.g., moving away from floodplains) or to stay and adapt to extreme events? Do government policies reflect people's climate mitigation knowledge needs? Can people access reliable emergency information systems during extreme weather events? "This megatrend speaks to the new ways of operating that organisations and communities will need to adapt to in the face of a changing climate" (Naughtin et al., 2022, p. 4).

Global Megatrend #2: Leaner, Cleaner and Greener. What information strategies are needed to educate communities on the value of adopting renewable technologies? How can consumers inform themselves about retailers' environmental practices? "This megatrend explores the opportunities pushing us towards a more sustainable horizon and the importance of science, technology and innovation in helping organisations to operate within much tighter envelopes" (Naughtin et al., 2022, p. 4).

Global Megatrend #3: The Escalating Health Imperative. How are people with *long COVID* (i.e., with long-lasting and often debilitating symptoms) finding information to support their emergent and uncertain health situations? Can new technologies enable aging adults to remain in their homes, longer, before requiring institutionalized care? How can healthcare providers better inform communities about strategies for living healthier, longer? "This megatrend highlights the opportunities provided by preventative health and precision health in supporting better health outcomes for all" (Naughtin et al., 2022, p. 4).

Global Megatrend #4: Geopolitical Shifts. How can public libraries better support refugees and asylum seekers as they settle into their communities? What new knowledge management practices can small businesses adopt to mitigate against supply chain disruptions? How can researchers manage security of information and data while working across borders? "This megatrend explores the implications of emerging geopolitical shifts relating to science, technology, trade, supply chains and defence strategy" (Naughtin et al., 2022, p. 4).

Global Megatrend #5: Diving into Digital. How are granting agencies' open access mandates changing authors' scholarly communication practices? Can telehealth enhance health information access in remote communities? How has

Fig. 6.1. Seven Global Megatrends © Copyright CSIRO Australia, *Our Future World*, July 2022. Used With Permission.

working from home changed people's information interactions in their local communities? "This megatrend details the next wave of digitisation for organisations and the opportunities enabled by digital and data technologies" (Naughtin et al., 2022, p. 5).

Global Megatrend #6: Increasingly Autonomous. Do recommendation algorithms reinforce social biases by limiting access to information? What are the privacy implications of *big data* capture and analysis? How do social media algorithms affect people's ability to critically assess information? "This megatrend unpacks how AI and related science, research and technology capabilities are helping to boost productivity and solve humanity's greatest challenges and the socio-economic considerations of these technology developments" (Naughtin et al., 2022, p. 5).

Global Megatrend #7: Unlocking the Human Dimension. Can citizen science enable governments to be better informed about local environmental concerns?

What information and communication strategies are needed to shift consumers' buying habits away from unsustainable products? How can researchers ensure that they continue to be viewed as trusted sources of information in a world of fake news and disinformation campaigns? "This megatrend highlights the social drivers influencing future consumer, citizen and employee behaviours" (Naughtin et al., 2022, p. 5).

6.4.2 Interdisciplinary and Cross-Sectoral Research

These global trends point to the ongoing need for information behavior scholars to further embrace interdisciplinary research practices. As with information science, generally, information behavior research is inherently interdisciplinary in its focus, which positions us well to explore large-scale issues such as climate change, health, and digital innovations, among others. We employ theories, models, concepts, and methods from many other fields in the sciences, humanities, and social sciences. Information behavior researchers are skilled at examining an innovation or an issue itself (such as the design of a technology or a policy), alongside conducting a focused investigation of the implications of people *interacting with* or *being affected by* that innovation or issue. Our scholars often have academic qualifications from various disciplines that inform their research approaches and provide access to diverse networks of people from which we can develop collaborative partnerships.

In addition, information behavior researchers are well connected to their communities. Many scholars have formal, professional training and experience in the information professions (e.g., libraries, archives, galleries, museums, knowledge management organizations), as well as specialist expertise (e.g., health, education, computing science, law). Information behavior scholars are therefore well positioned to engage with practitioners, government officials, businesses, and community organizations across various sectors. With the increasing focus on societal impact, we can develop cross-sectoral partnerships to foster adoption of research innovations, beyond academe.

Although no one can predict the future, fully, we expect the coming years to be shaped by complex, global issues and problems that require larger teams, more interdisciplinarity, more diverse methodologies and methods of investigation, and collaborative partnerships with external stakeholders. Funding schemes will remain highly competitive, and increasingly focused in areas that present the most significant challenges to our governments, communities, and institutions. If we use COVID-19, once again, as an example – the impact of ongoing waves of infections on workplaces, hospitals, schools, and in the home will continue for the foreseeable future. The flow-on effect of stretched healthcare resources will likely continue to delay other health interventions (e.g., elective procedures), which will affect people's quality of life, and lead to more complex health needs. This one disease, coupled with ongoing efforts to make healthcare more efficient, to address the needs of an aging population, and to do so with continuing shortages of health professionals, will only continue to increase the pressures on individuals to find and navigate relevant health information. The renewed attention

COVID-19 has brought to the topics of misinformation, disinformation, fake news, conspiracies, denial, and avoidance, will all need to continue to be investigated in various settings.

Whatever the future holds, information behavior research has developed along multiple lines and maintained its relevance and importance within information science. The field retains appropriate themes, theories, and methodologies from half a century past, and it continues to evolve and embrace new approaches. While there is an increasing emphasis on social contexts, it is important to recognize that for some research problems (e.g., the information behavior of understudied or marginalized people, or of specific health-related conditions) focusing on individual experiences remains an important endeavor. Through its mature approach to interdisciplinarity, and its increasing focus on team-based research, information behavior is also having an impact in society at large. All of this bodes well for a productive future, where we can continue to document, understand, and give voice to the varied and complex ways that people engage with the information around them.

6.5 OUR TOP 3 *MUST READ* RECOMMENDATIONS

Limberg, L. (2017). Synthesizing or diversifying library and information science: Sketching past achievements, current happenings and future prospects, with an interest in including or excluding approaches. *Information Research*, *22*(1). http://informationr.net/ir/22-1/colis/colis1600.html
A keynote address for the 2016 Conceptions of Library and Information Science (CoLIS) conference by one of the field's leading scholars, reflecting on the evolution of the discipline and its focus on studies of information seeking, information literacy, and related topics.

Savolainen, R. (2021). Levels of critique in models and concepts of human information behaviour research. *Aslib Journal of Information Management*, *73*(5), 772–791. https://doi.org/10.1108/AJIM-01-2021-0028
Provides a conceptual analysis of 58 key studies that critique core concepts and models in human information behavior research.

Naughtin, C., Hajkowicz, S., Schleiger, E., Bratanova, A., Cameron, A., Zamin, T., & Dutta, A. (2022). *Our future world: Global megatrends impacting the way we live over coming decades*. CSIRO. https://www.csiro.au/en/research/technology-space/data/Our-Future-World
Provides a twenty-year horizon of global megatrends, or the trajectories of change expected to influence investment, strategy, and policy direction (including for research) from government, industry, nonprofits, and the community.

REFERENCES

Allen, T. J. (1969). Information needs and uses. In C. Cuadra (Ed.), *Annual review of information science and technology* (Vol. 4, pp. 3–29). Encyclopaedia Britannica.

Allen, D. K., Given, L. M., Burnett, G., & Karanasios, S. (2019). Information behaviour and information practices: A special issue for research on people's engagement with technology. *Journal of the Association for Information Science and Technology*, *70*(12), 1299–1301. https://doi.org/10.1002/asi.24303

Bandura, A. (2001). Social cognitive theory: An agentic perspective. *Annual review of psychology* (Vol. 52, pp. 1–26). Annual Reviews.

Case, D. O., & O'Connor, L. G. (2016). What's the use? Measuring the frequency of studies of information outcomes. *Journal of the American Society for Information Science and Technology*, *67*(3), 649–661. https://doi.org/10.1002/asi.23411

Cibangu, S. K. (2013). A memo of qualitative research for information science: Toward theory construction. *Journal of Documentation*, *69*(2), 194–213. https://doi.org/10.1108/00220411311300048

Crane, D. (1971). Information needs and uses. In C. A. Cuadra & A. W. Luke (Eds.), *Annual review of information science and technology* (Vol. 6, pp. 3–39). Encyclopaedia Britannica.

Dervin, B. (1976a). Strategies for dealing with human information needs: Information or communication? *Journal of Broadcasting*, *20*(3), 324–351. https://doi.org/10.1080/08838157609386402

Dervin, B., & Nilan, M. (1986). Information needs and uses. In M. Williams (Ed.). *Annual review of information science and technology* (Vol. 21, pp. 1–25). Knowledge Industry.

Fisher, K. E., Erdelez, S., & McKechnie, E. F. (Eds.). (2005). *Theories of information behavior*: Information Today, Inc.

Ford, N. (2015). *Introduction to information behaviour* (1st ed.). Facet. https://doi.org/10.29085/9781783301843

Giddens, A. (1984). *The constitution of society: Outline of the theory of structuration*. Polity Press.

Given, L. M. (2007). Emotional entanglements on the university campus: The role of affect in undergraduates' information behaviors. In D. Nahl & D. Bilal (Eds.), *Information and emotion: The emergent affective paradigm in information behavior research and theory* (pp. 161–175).

Given, L. M., Kelly, W., & Willson, R. (2015). Bracing for impact: The role of information science in supporting societal research impact. *Proceedings of the Association for Information Science and Technology*, *52*(1), 1–10. https://doi.org/10.1002/pra2.2015.145052010048

Gorichanaz, T. (2020). Understanding and information in the work of visual artists. *Journal of the Association for Information Science and Technology*, *71*(6), 685–695. https://doi.org/10.1002/asi.24286

Granikov, V., El Sherif, R., Bouthillier, F., & Pluye, P. (2022). Factors and outcomes of collaborative information seeking: A mixed studies review with a framework synthesis. *Journal of the Association for Information Science and Technology*, *73*(4), 542–560. https://doi.org/10.1002/asi.24596

Granovetter, M. S. (1982). The strength of weak ties: A network theory revisited. In P. Marsden & N. Lin (Eds.), *Social structure and network analysis* (pp. 105–130). Sage Publications.

Guzik, E. (2018). Information sharing as embodied practice in a context of conversion to Islam. *Library Trends*, *66*(3), 351–370. https://doi.org/10.1353/lib.2018.0007

Heinström, J. (2010). *From fear to flow: Personality and information interaction*. Chandos Publishing.

Herner, S., & Herner, M. (1967). Information needs and uses in science and technology. In C. A. Cuadra (Ed.), *Annual review of information science and technology* (Vol. 2, pp. 1–34). Encyclopaedia Britannica.

Kelly, W. (2019). *Navigating pathways to community: Exploring the experiences of community-engaged humanities and social sciences academics*. Unpublished dissertation. Swinburne University of Technology.

Limberg, L. (2017). Synthesizing or diversifying library and information science: Sketching past achievements, current happenings and future prospects, with an interest in including or excluding approaches. *Information Research*, *22*(1). http://InformationR.net/ir/22-1/colis/colis1600.html

Lin, N., & Garvey, W. D. (1972). Information needs and uses. In C. Cuadra & A. W. Luke (Eds.), *Annual review of information science and technology* (Vol. 7, pp. 5–37). American Society for Information Science.

Lipetz, B.-A. (1970). Information needs and uses. In C. A. Cuadra & A. W. Luke (Eds.), *Annual review of information science and technology* (Vol. 5, pp. 3–32). Encyclopaedia Brittanica.

Lloyd, A. (2010). Corporeality and practice theory: Exploring emerging research agendas for information literacy. *Information Research*, *15*(3). http://InformationR.net/ir/15-3/colis7/colis704.html

Lloyd, A. (2014). Following the red thread of information in information literacy research: Recovering local knowledge through interview to the double. *Library & Information Science Research*, *36*(2), 99–105. https://doi.org/10.1016/j.lisr.2013.10.006

Lueg, C. P. (2015). The missing link: Information behavior research and its estranged relationship with embodiment. *Journal of the Association for Information Science and Technology*, *66*(12), 2704–2707. https://doi.org/10.1002/asi.23441

Martyn, J. (1974). Information needs and uses. In M. Williams (Ed.). *Annual review of information science and technology* (Vol. 9, pp. 3–23). American Society for Information Science.

Menzel, H. (1966a). Information needs and uses in science and technology. In C. A. Cuadra & A. W. Luke (Eds.), *Annual review of information science and technology* (Vol. 1, pp. 41–69).

Nahl, D., & Bilal, D. (2007). *Information and emotion: The emergent affective paradigm in information behavior research and theory*. Information Today.

Naughtin, C., Hajkowicz, S., Schleiger, E., Bratanova, A., Cameron, A., Zamin, T., & Dutta, A. (2022). *Our future world: Global megatrends impacting the way we live over coming decades*. CSIRO. https://www.csiro.au/en/research/technology-space/data/Our-Future-World

Olsson, M., & Lloyd, A. (2017). Being in place: Embodied information practices. *Information Research*, *22*(1). http://InformationR.net/ir/22-1/colis/colis1601.html

Paisley, W. J. (1968). Information needs and uses. In C. Cuadra (Ed.), *Annual review of information science and technology* (Vol. 3, pp. 1–30). Encyclopaedia Britannica.

Pilerot, O., Hammarfelt, B., & Moring, C. (2017). The many faces of practice theory in library and information studies. *Information Research*, *22*(1). http://InformationR.net/ir/22-1/colis/colis1602.html

Pluye, P., El Sherif, R., Granikov, V., Hong, Q. N., Vedel, I., Galvao, M. C. B., Frati, F. E., Desroches, S., Repchinsky, C., Rihoux, B., Légaré, F., Burnand, B., Bujold, M., & Grad, R. (2019). Health outcomes of online consumer health information: A systematic mixed studies review with framework synthesis. *Journal of the Association for Information Science and Technology*, *70*(7), 643–659. https://doi.org/10.1002/asi.24178

Polkinghorne, S. C. (2021). *Exploring everyday information practices: Embodied mutual constitution of people's complex relationships with food*. Unpublished dissertation. Swinburne University of Technology.

Polkinghorne, S., & Given, L. M. (2021). Holistic information research: From rhetoric to paradigm. *Journal of the Association for Information Science and Technology*, *72*(10), 1261–1271. https://doi.org/10.1002/asi.24450

Savolainen, R. (2014). Emotions as motivators for information seeking: A conceptual analysis. *Library & Information Science Research*, *36*(1), 59–65. http://doi.org/10.1016/j.lisr.2013.10.004

Savolainen, R. (2015). Expressing emotions in information sharing: A study of online discussion about immigration. *Information Research*, *20*(1). http://InformationR.net/ir/20-1/paper662.html

Savolainen, R. (2021). Levels of critique in models and concepts of human information behaviour research. *Aslib Journal of Information Management*, *73*(5), 772–791. https://doi.org/10.1108/AJIM-01-2021-0028

Schatzki, T. R. (1996). *Social practices: A Wittgensteinian approach to human activity and the social*. Cambridge University Press.

Wenger, E. (1998). *Communities of practice: Learning, meaning, and identity*. Cambridge University Press.

Wersig, G., & Windel, G. (1985). Information science needs a theory of 'information actions'. *Social Science Information Studies*, *5*, 11–23. https://doi.org/10.1016/0143-6236(85)90003-1

Willson, R., Allen, D., Julien, H., & Burnett, K. (2020). JASIS&T special issue on information behaviour & information practices theory: Call for papers. *Association for Information Science and Technology*. https://www.asist.org/2020/02/25/jasist-special-issue-on-information-behaviour-information-practices-theory-call-for-papers/

Wilson, T. D. (1981). On user studies and information needs. *Journal of Documentation*, *37*, 3–15. https://doi.org/10.1108/eb026702

Wilson, T. D. (1994). Information needs and uses: Fifty years of progress? In B. Vickery (Ed.), *Fifty years of progress: A journal of documentation review* (pp. 15–52). Aslib.

Wilson, T. D. (2010b). Fifty years of information behavior research. *Bulletin of the American Society for Information Science and Technology*, *36*(3), 27–34. https://doi.org/10.1002/bult.2010.1720360308

Wilson, T. D. (2020). The transfer of theories and models from information behaviour research into other disciplines. *Information Research*, *25*(3). https://doi.org/10.47989/irpaper873

Wilson, T. D. (2022). *Exploring information behaviour: An introduction*. T.D. Wilson. http://informationr.net/ir/Exploring%20information%20behaviour.pdf

REFERENCES

Abbasi, A., Wigand, R. T., & Hossain, L. (2014). Measuring social capital through network analysis and its influence on individual performance. *Library & Information Science Research*, *36*(1), 66–73. https://doi.org/10.1016/j.lisr.2013.08.001

Abdullah, N., & Basar, S. K. R. (2019). How children gauge information trustworthiness in online search: Credible or convenience searcher? *Pakistan Journal of Information Management and Libraries*, *21*, 1–19. https://doi.org/10.47657/2019211468

Abrahamson, J. A., Fisher, K. E., Turner, A. G., Durrance, J. C., & Turner, T. C. (2008). Lay information mediary behavior uncovered: Exploring how nonprofessionals seek health information for themselves and others online. *Journal of the Medical Library Association*, *96*(4), 310–323. https://doi.org/10.3163/1536-5050.96.4.006

Abrahamson, D. E., & Goodman-Delahunty, J. (2013). The impact of organizational information culture on information use outcomes in policing: An exploratory study. *Information Research*, *18*(4). http://informationr.net/ir/18-4/paper598.html

Abrahamson, J. A., & Rubin, V. L. (2012). Discourse structure differences in lay and professional health communication. *Journal of Documentation*, *68*(6), 826–851. https://doi.org/10.1108/00220411211277064

Adams, S. S. (2009). What games have to offer: Information behavior and meaning-making in virtual play spaces. *Library Trends*, *57*(4), 676–693. https://doi.org/10.1353/lib.0.0058

Adorjan, M., & Ricciardelli, R. (2019). A new privacy paradox? Youth agentic practices of privacy management despite "nothing to hide" online. *Canadian Review of Sociology*, *56*(1), 8–29. https://doi.org/10.1111/cars.12227

Afifi, W. A., & Weiner, J. L. (2004). Toward a theory of motivated information management. *Communication Theory*, *14*(2), 167–190. https://doi.org/10.1111/j.1468-2885.2004.tb00310.x

Afifi, W. A., & Weiner, J. L. (2006). Seeking information about sexual health: Applying the theory of motivated information management. *Human Communication Research*, *32*, 35–57. https://doi.org/10.1111/j.1468-2958.2006.00002.x

Afzal, W. (2020). What we can learn from information flows about COVID-19: Implications for research and practice. *Proceedings of the Association for Information Science and Technology*, *57*(1). https://doi.org/10.1002/pra2.245

Agarwal, N. K. (2022). Integrating models and integrated models: Towards a unified model of information seeking behaviour. *Information Research*, *27*(1). Paper 922. http://InformationR.net/ir/27-1/paper922.html

Agarwal, N. K., Xu, Y., & Poo, D. (2011). A context-based investigation into source use by information seekers. *Journal of the American Society for Information Science and Technology*, *62*(6), 1087–1104. https://doi.org/10.1002/asi.21513

Agosto, D. E., & Hughes-Hassell, S. (2006). Toward a model of the everyday life information needs of urban teenagers, part 2: Empirical model. *Journal of the American Society for Information Science and Technology*, *57*(11), 1418–1426. http://doi.org/10.1002/asi.20452

Al-Muomen, N., Morris, A., & Maynard, S. (2012). Modelling information-seeking behaviour of graduate students at Kuwait University. *Journal of Documentation*, *68*(4), 430–459. http://doi.org/10.1108/00220411211239057

Albassam, S., & Ruthven, I. (2020). Dynamic aspects of relevance: Differences in users' relevance criteria between selecting and viewing videos during leisure searches. *Information Research*, *25*(1). http://InformationR.net/ir/25-1/paper850.html

Allard, D. (2021). "So many things were new to us": Identifying the settlement information practices of newcomers to Canada across the settlement process. *Journal of Documentation*, *78*(2), 334–360. https://doi.org/10.1108/JD-02-2021-0024

Allard, D., & Caidi, N. (2018). Imagining Winnipeg: The translocal meaning making of Filipino migrants to Canada. *Journal of the Association for Information Science and Technology*, *69*(10), 1193–1204. https://doi.org/10.1002/asi.24038

Allard, S., Levine, K. J., & Tenopir, C. (2009). Design engineers and technical professionals at work: Observing information usage in the workplace. *Journal of the American Society for Information Science and Technology*, *60*(3), 443–454. https://doi.org/10.1002/asi.21004

Allen, T. J. (1965). *Sources of ideas and their effectiveness in parallel R&D projects (Research Program on the Management of Science and Technology No. 130-65)*. Sloan School of Management, Massachusetts Institute of Technology.

Allen, T. J. (1969). Information needs and uses. In C. Cuadra (Ed.), *Annual review of information science and technology* (Vol. 4, pp. 3–29). Encyclopaedia Britannica.

Allen, B. L. (1996). *Information tasks: Toward a user-centered approach to information systems*. Academic Press.

Allen, D. K. (2011). Information behavior and decision making in time-constrained practice: A dual-processing perspective. *Journal of the American Society for Information Science and Technology*, *62*(11), 2165–2181. https://doi.org/10.1002/asi.21601

Allen, M. (2020). I'm an investigative journalist. These are the questions I asked about the viral "Plandemic" video. ProPublica. https://www.propublica.org/article/im-an-investigative-journalist-these-are-the-questions-i-asked-about-the-viral-plandemic-video

Allen, T. J., & Gerstberger, P. G. (1967). *Criteria for selection of an information source*. (Working Paper No. 284-67). Alfred P. Sloan School of Management, Massachusetts Institute of Technology.

Allen, D. K., Given, L. M., Burnett, G., & Karanasios, S. (2019). Information behaviour and information practices: A special issue for research on people's engagement with technology. *Journal of the Association for Information Science and Technology*, *70*(12), 1299–1301. https://doi.org/10.1002/asi.24303

Allen, D., Karanasios, S., & Slavova, M. (2011). Working with activity theory: Context, technology, and information behavior. *Journal of the American Society for Information Science and Technology*, *62*(4), 776–788. https://doi.org/10.1002/asi.21441

Allen, M., Matthew, S., & Bolland, M. J. (2004). Working with immigrant and refugee populations: Issues and Hmong case study. *Library Trends*, *53*(2), 301–328.

Allen, D. K., Wilson, T. D., Norman, A., & Knight, C. (2008). Information on the move: The use of mobile information systems by UK police forces. *Information Research*, *13*(4). http://InformationR.net/ir/13-4/paper378.html

Alshahrani, H., & Rasmussen Pennington, D. (2020). 'How to use it more?' Self-efficacy and its sources in the use of social media for knowledge sharing. *Journal of Documentation*, *76*(1), 231–257. https://doi.org/10.1108/JD-02-2019-0026

de Alwis, G., Majid, S., & Chaudhry, A. S. (2006). Transformation in managers' information seeking behaviour: A review of the literature. *Journal of Information Science*, *32*(4), 362–377. http://doi.org/10.1177/0165551506065812

Anderson, T. D. (2006). Uncertainty in action: Observing information seeking within the creative processes of scholarly research. *Information Research*, *12*(1). Paper 283. http://InformationR.net/ir/12-1/paper283.html

Andersson, C. (2017). The front and backstage: Pupils' information activities in secondary school. *Information Research*, *22*(1). http://InformationR.net/ir/22-1/colis/colis1604.html

Ankem, K. (2005). Approaches to meta-analysis: A guide for LIS researchers. *Library & Information Science Research*, *27*(2), 164–176. https://doi.org/10.1016/j.lisr.2005.01.003

Ankem, K. (2006a). Factors influencing information needs among cancer patients: A meta-analysis. *Library & Information Science Research*, *28*(1), 7–23. https://doi.org/10.1016/j.lisr.2005.11.003

Ankem, K. (2006b). Use of information sources by cancer patients: Results of a systematic review of the research literature. *Information Research*, *11*(3). http://informationr.net/ir/11-3/paper254.html

Ankem, K. (2007). Information-seeking behavior of women in their path to an innovative alternate treatment for symptomatic uterine fibroids. *Journal of the Medical Library Association*, *95*(2), 164–172. https://www.ncbi.nlm.nih.gov/pmc/articles/PMC1852624/

Ansari, M., & Zuberi, N. (2010). Information seeking behaviour of media professionals in Karachi. *Malaysian Journal of Library & Information Science*, *15*(2), 71–84.

Anwar, M., & Asghar, M. (2009). Information seeking behavior of Pakistani newspaper journalists. *Pakistan Journal of Library and Information Science*, *10*, 57–79.

Apuke, O., & Omar, B. (2021). Fake news and COVID-19: Modelling the predictors of fake news sharing among social media users. *Telematics and Informatics*, *56*. https://doi.org/10.1016/j.tele.2020.101475

Archambault, S. G., & Justice, A. (2017). Student use of the information commons: An exploration through mixed methods. *Evidence Based Library and Information Practice*, *12*(4), 13. https://doi.org/10.18438/B8VD45

Aspray, W. (2021). Where to live in retirement: A complex information problem. In M. G. Ocepek & W. Aspray (Eds.), *Deciding where to live: Information studies on where to live in America* (pp. 281–308). Rowman & Littlefield.

Aspray, W., & Ocepek, M. G. (2021). Where to live as an information problem: Three contemporary examples. In M. G. Ocepek & W. Aspray (Eds.), *Deciding where to live: Information studies on where to live in America* (pp. 1–34). Rowman & Littlefield.

Attfield, S., Blandford, A., & Dowell, J. (2003). Information seeking in the context of writing: A design psychology interpretation of the "problematic situation". *Journal of Documentation*, *59*(4), 430–453. https://doi.org/10.1108/00220410310485712

Attfield, S., & Dowell, J. (2003). Information seeking and use by newspaper journalists. *Journal of Documentation*, *59*(2), 187–204. https://doi.org/10.1108/00220410310463860

Audunson, R., Essmat, S., & Aabø, S. (2011). Public libraries: A meeting place for immigrant women? *Library & Information Science Research*, *33*(3), 220–227. https://doi.org/10.1016/j.lisr.2011.01.003

Audunson, R., & Evjen, S. (2017). The public library: An arena for an enlightened and rational public sphere? The case of Norway. *Information Research*, *22*(1). http://InformationR.net/ir/22-1/colis/colis1641.html

Auerbach. (1965). *DOD user needs study, Phase I. Final technical report 1151-TR3*. Auerbach Corporation.

Auster, E., & Choo, C. W. (1993). Environmental scanning by CEOs in two Canadian industries. *Journal of the American Society for Information Science*, *44*, 194–203. https://doi.org/10.1002/(SICI)1097-4571(199305)44:4%3C194::AID-ASI2%3E3.0.CO;2-1

Australian Institute of Aboriginal and Torres Strait Islander Studies (AIATSIS). (2020). *A guide to applying the AIATSIS code of ethics for Aboriginal and Torres Strait Islander research*. AIATSIS. https://aiatsis.gov.au/sites/default/files/2020-10/aiatsis-guide-applying-code-ethics_0.pdf

Awamura, N. (2006). Rethinking the information behavior model of information encountering: An analysis of the interviews on information encountering on the web. *Library and Information Science*, *55*, 47–69.

Ayres, L. P., & McKinnie, A. (1916). *The public library and the public schools* (No. Volume XXI). Survey Committee of the Cleveland Foundation.

Babalhavaeji, F., & Farhadpoor, M. (2013). Information source characteristics and environmental scanning by academic library managers. *Information Research*, *18*(1). http://informationr.net/ir/18-1/paper568.html

Babbie, E. (2020). *The practice of social research* (15th ed.). Cengage Learning.

Badia, A. (2014). Data, information, knowledge: An information science analysis. *Journal of the American Society for Information Science and Technology*, *65*(6), 1279–1287. https://doi.org/10.1002/asi.23043

Baker, T. L. (1999). *Doing social research* (3rd ed.). McGraw-Hill.

Baker, J. M. (2004). The information needs of female Police Officers involved in undercover prostitution work. *Information Research*, *10*(1). http://InformationR.net/ir/10-1/paper209.html

Baker, L. M., Case, P., & Policicchio, D. L. (2003). General health problems of inner-city sex workers: A pilot study. *Journal of the Medical Library Association*, *91*(1), 67–71.

Bakhtin, M. M. (1981). *The dialogic imagination*. University of Texas Press.

Baldwin, N. S., & Rice, R. E. (1997). Information-seeking behavior of securities analysts: Individual and institutional influences, information sources and channels, and outcomes. *Journal of the American Society for Information Science*, *48*, 674–693.

Bandura, A. (1977). *Social learning theory*. Prentice-Hall.

Bandura, A. (1986). *Social foundations of thought and action*. Prentice-Hall.

Bandura, A. (2001). Social cognitive theory: An agentic perspective. In *Annual review of psychology* (Vol. 52, pp. 1–26). Annual Reviews.

Barahmand, N., Nakhoda, M., Fahimnia, F., & Nazari, M. (2019). Understanding everyday life information seeking behavior in the context of coping with daily hassles: A grounded theory study of female students. *Library & Information Science Research*, *41*(4), 100980. https://doi.org/10.1016/j.lisr.2019.100980

Barriage, S. (2015). 'Talk, talk and more talk': Parental perceptions of young children's information practices related to their hobbies and interests. *Information Research*, *21*(3). http://InformationR.net/ir/21-3/paper721.html

Barriage, S. (2021). Examining young children's information practices and experiences: A child-centered methodological approach. *Library & Information Science Research*, *43*(3), 101106. https://doi.org/10.1016/j.lisr.2021.101106

Barriage, S. (2022). Young children's information-seeking practices in center-based childcare. *Journal of Librarianship and Information Science*, *54*(1), 144–158. https://doi.org/10.1177/0961000620962164

Basha, I., Rani, P., Kannan, K., & Chinnasamy, K. (2013). Information seeking behaviour of engineering students in Tamil Nadu: A study. *International Journal of Library Science*, *7*(1). http://www.ceserpublications.com/index.php/IJLS/article/view/165

Bates, M. J. (1989). The design of browsing and berrypicking techniques for the online search interface. *Online Review*, *13*(5), 407–424. https://doi.org/10.1108/eb024320

Bates, M. J. (1996). Learning about the information seeking of interdisciplinary scholars and students. *Library Trends*, *45*(2), 155–164. https://hdl.handle.net/2142/8083

Bates, M. J. (2005). An introduction to metatheories, theories, and models. In K. E. Fisher, S. Erdelez, & E. F. McKechnie (Eds.), *Theories of information behavior* (pp. 1–24). Information Today, Inc.

Bates, M. J. (2010). Information behavior. In M. J. Bates & M. N. Maack (Eds.), *Encyclopedia of Library and information sciences* (3rd ed., pp. 2381–2391). CRC Press.

Bateson, G. (1972). *Steps to an ecology of mind*. Ballantine Books.

Bateson, G. (1978). The pattern which connects. *CoEvolution Quarterly*, *18*, 4–15.

Baxter, G. (2014). Open for business? An historical, comparative study of public access to information about two controversial coastal developments in North-east Scotland. *Information Research*, *19*(1). http://InformationR.net/ir/19-1/paper603.html

Baxter, G., & Marcella, R. (2014). The 2014 Scottish independence referendum: A study of voters' online information behaviour. In *Proceedings of ISIC, the Information Behaviour Conference*, Leeds, 2–5 September, 2014: Part 1, 19. http://informationr.net/ir/19-4/isic/isicsp5.html

Baxter, G., Marcella, R., & Illingworth, L. (2010). Organizational information behaviour in the public consultation process in Scotland. *Information Research*, *15*(1). http://InformationR.net/ir/15-1/paper442.html

Beautyman, W., & Shenton, A. K. (2009). When does an academic information need stimulate a school-inspired information want? *Journal of Librarianship and Information Science*, *41*(2), 67–80. https://doi.org/10.1177/0961000609102821

Beer, S. (2004). Information flow and peripherality in remote island areas of Scotland. *Libri – International Journal of Libraries and Information Services*, *54*(3), 148–157. https://doi.org/10.1515/LIBR.2004.148

Beheshti, J., Cole, C., Abuhimed, D., & Lamoureux, I. (2015). Tracking middle school students' information behavior via Kuhlthau's ISP model: Temporality. *Journal of the Association for Information Science and Technology*, *66*(5), 943–960. https://doi.org/10.1002/asi.23230

Belk, R. W. (1995). *Collecting in a consumer society*. Routledge.

Belkin, N. J. (1978). Information concepts for information science. *Journal of Documentation*, *34*, 55–85. https://doi.org/10.1108/eb026653

Belkin, N. J. (2005). Anomalous state of knowledge. In K. E. Fisher, S. Erdelez, & E. F. McKechnie (Eds.), *Theories of information behavior* (pp. 44–48). Information Today, Inc.

Belkin, N. J., & Vickery, A. (1985). *Interaction in information systems: A review of research from document retrieval to knowledge-based systems*. British Library.

Belk, R. W., Sherry, J., Jr., & Wallendorf, M. (1988). Naturalistic inquiry into buyer-seller behavior at a swap meet. *Journal of Consumer Research, 14*, 449–469. https://www.jstor.org/stable/2489153

Benetti, M., & Gehrke, M. (2021). Disinformation in Brazil during the Covid-19 pandemic: Topics, platforms, and actors. *Fronteiras*. https://doi.org/10.4013/fem.2021.232.02

Benis, A., Chatsubi, A., Levner, E., & Ashkenazi, S. (2021). Change in threads on Twitter regarding influenza, vaccines, and vaccination during the COVID-19 pandemic: Artificial Intelligence–based infodemiology study. *JMIR Infordemiology, 1*(1), e31983. https://doi.org/10.2196/31983

Bennett, N., Casebeer, L., Zheng, S., & Kristofco, R. (2006). Information-seeking behaviors and reflective practice. *Journal of Continuing Education in the Health Professions, 26*(2), 120–127. https://doi.org/10.1002/chp.60

Benoit, G. (2005). Communicative action. In K. E. Fisher, S. Erdelez, & L. E. F. McKechnie (Eds.), *Theories of information behavior* (pp. 99–103). Information Today, Inc.

Berelson, B. (1949). *The library's public*. Columbia University Press.

Berger, P., & Luckmann. (1967). *The social construction of reality*. Doubleday.

Berrío-Zapata, C., da Silva, E. F., & Teles Condurú, M. (2021). The technological informavore: Information behavior and digital sustainability in the global platform ecosystem. *First Monday, 26*(11), 1. https://doi.org/10.5210/fm.v26i11.12354

Bianchi, M. (Ed.). (1997). *The active consumer: Novelty and surprise in consumer choice*. Routledge.

Bird-Meyer, M., Erdelez, S., & Bossaller, J. (2019). The role of serendipity in the story ideation process of print media journalists. *Journal of Documentation, 75*(5), 995–1012. https://doi.org/10.1108/JD-11-2018-0186

Birdi, B., & Ford, N. (2018). Towards a new sociological model of fiction reading. *Journal of the Association for Information Science and Technology, 69*(11), 1291–1303. https://doi.org/10.1002/asi.24053

Birru, M. S., Monaco, V. M., Charles, L., Drew, H., Njie, V., Bierria, T., Detlefsen, E., & Steinman, R. (2004). Internet usage by low-literacy adults seeking health information: An observational analysis. *Journal of Medical Internet Research, 6*(3). https://doi.org/10.2196/jmir.6.3.e25

Bishop, R. (2005). "The essential force of the clan": Developing a collecting-inspired ideology of genealogy through textual analysis. *Journal of Popular Culture, 8*, 990–1010. https://doi.org/10.1111/j.1540-5931.2005.00172.x

Bonner, A., & Lloyd, A. (2011). What information counts at the moment of practice? Information practices of renal nurses. *Journal of Advanced Nursing, 67*(6). 1213–1221. https://doi.org/10.1111/j.1365-2648.2011.05613.x

Borg, M., Alégroth, E., & Runeson, P. (2017, May). Software engineers' information seeking behavior in change impact analysis-an interview study. In *2017 IEEE/ACM 25th International Conference on Program Comprehension (ICPC)* (pp. 12–22). IEEE.

Borgman, C. L., & Furner, J. (2002). Scholarly communication and bibliometrics. In B. Cronin (Ed.), *Annual review of information science and technology* (Vol. 36, pp. 3–72). Information Today, Inc. https://doi.org/10.1002/aris.1440360102

Borlund, P., & Pharo, N. (2019). A need for information on information needs. *Information Research, 24*(4). http://InformationR.net/ir/24-4/colis/colis1908.html

Bosancic, B. (2016). Information in the knowledge acquisition process. *Journal of Documentation, 72*(5), 930–960. https://doi.org/10.1108/JD-10-2015-0122

Bosancic, B., & Matijevic, M. (2019). Information as construction. *Journal of Librarianship and Information Science, 52*(2), 620–630. https://doi.org/10.1177/0961000619841657

Bosman, J., & Renckstorf, K. (1996). Information needs: Problems, interests and consumption. In K. Renckstorf (Ed.), *Media use as social action* (pp. 43–52). John Libbey.

Bouazza, A. (1989). Information user studies. In *Encyclopedia of library and information science* (Vol. 44(Suppl. 9), pp. 144–164). M. Dekker.

Bourdieu, P. (1977). *Outline of a theory of practice*. Cambridge University Press.

Bourdieu, P. (1984). *Distinction: A social critique of the judgement of taste* (R. Nice, Trans.). Routledge.

Bourdieu, P. (1986). The forms of capital. In *The handbook of theory and research for the sociology of education* (pp. 241–258). Greenwood Press.

Bourdieu, P. (1990). *The logic of practice* (R. Nice, Trans.). Polity Press.

Bowler, L. (2010). The self-regulation of curiosity and interest during the information search process of adolescent students. *Journal of the American Society for Information Science and Technology*, *61*(7), 1332–1344. https://doi.org/10.1002/asi.21334

Bøyum, I., & Aabø, S. (2015). The information practices of Business PhD students. *New Library World*, *116*(3/4), 187–200. https://doi.org/10.1108/NLW-06-2014-0073

Brine, A., & Feather, J. (2010). The information needs of UK historic houses: Mapping the ground. *Journal of Documentation*, *66*(1), 28–45. http://doi.org/10.1108/00220411011016353

Brittain, J. M. (1970). *Information and its users: A review with special reference to the social sciences.* Wiley-Interscience.

Bronstein, J. (2007). The role of the research phase in information seeking behaviour of Jewish studies scholars: A modification of Ellis's behavioural characteristics. *Information Research*, *12*(3). http://informationr.net/ir/12-3/paper318.html

Bronstein, J. (2014). The role of perceived self-efficacy in the information seeking behavior of library and information science students. *The Journal of Academic Librarianship*, *40*(2), 101–106. https://doi.org/10.1016/j.acalib.2014.01.010

Bronstein, J. (2017). An examination of social and informational support behavior codes on the Internet: The case of online health communities. *Library & Information Science Research*, *39*(1), 63–68. https://doi.org/10.1016/j.lisr.2017.01.006

Bronstein, J. (2019). A transitional approach to the study of the information behavior of domestic migrant workers: A narrative inquiry. *Journal of Documentation*, *75*(2), 314–333. https://doi.org/10.1108/JD-07-2018-0112

Bronstein, J., & Lidor, D. (2021). Motivations for music information seeking as serious leisure in a virtual community: Exploring a Eurovision fan club. *Journal of Information Management*, *73*(2), 271–287. https://doi.org/10.1108/AJIM-06-2020-0192

Bronstein, J., & Solomon, Y. (2021). Exploring the information practices of lawyers. *Journal of Documentation*, *77*, 1003–1021. https://doi.org/10.1108/JD-10-2020-0165

Brown, C. D. (2001). The role of computer-mediated communication in the research process of music scholars: An exploratory investigation. *Information Research*, *6*(2). http://informationr.net/ir/6-2/paper99.html

Brown, C. D. (2002). Straddling the humanities and social sciences: The research process of music scholars. *Library & Information Science Research*, *24*(1), 73–94. https://doi.org/10.1016/S0740-8188(01)00105-0

Brown, C. M. (1999). Information seeking behavior of scientists in the electronic information age: Astronomers, chemists, mathematicians, and physicists. *Journal of the American Society for Information Science*, *50*, 929–943. https://doi.org/10.1002/(SICI)1097-4571(1999)50:10%3C929::AID-ASI8%3E3.0.CO;2-G

Brown, R. T., & Kasper, T. (2013). The fusion of literacy and games: A case study in assessing the goals of a library video game program. *Library Trends*, *61*(4), 755–778. https://doi.org/10.1353/lib.2013.0012

Brown, L. K., & Veinot, T. C. (2020). Information behavior and social control: Toward an understanding of conflictual information behavior in families managing chronic illness. *Journal of the Association for Information Science and Technology*, *72*. https://doi.org/10.1002/asi.24362

Bruce, C. S., Davis, K., Hughes, H., Partridge, H., & Stoodley, I. (Eds.). (2014). *Information experience: Approaches to theory and practice.* Emerald Publishing Limited.

Bruner, J. S. (1973). *Beyond the information given: Studies in the psychology of knowing.* Norton.

Buchanan, S. A., & Erdelez, S. (2019). Information encountering in the humanities: Embeddedness, temporality, and altruism. *Proceedings of the Association for Information Science and Technology*, *56*(1), 32–42. https://doi.org/https://doi.org/10.1002/pra2.58

Buchanan, E., & Ess, C. (2009). Internet research ethics and the institutional review board: Current practices and issues. *Computers and Society*, *39*(3), 43–49. https://doi.org/10.1145/1713066.1713069

Buckland, M. K. (1991). Information as thing. *Journal of the American Society for Information Science, 42*, 351–360. https://doi.org/10.1002/(SICI)1097-4571(199106)42:5%3C351::AID-ASI5%3E3.0.CO;2-3

Budd, J. M., & Raber, D. (1996). Discourse analysis: Method and application in the study of information. *Information Processing & Management, 32*, 217–226. https://doi.org/10.1016/S0306-4573(96)85007-2

Burford, S., & Park, S. (2014). The impact of mobile tablet devices on human information behaviour. *Journal of Documentation, 70*(4), 622–639. https://doi.org/10.1108/JD-09-2012-0123

Burgess, E. R., Reddy, M. C., & Mohr, D. C. (2022). 'I just can't help but smile sometimes': Collaborative self-management of depression. *Proceedings of the ACM on Human-Computer Interaction, 6*(CSCW1), 1–32. https://doi.org/10.1145/3512917

Burke, S. (2008). Public library resources used by immigrant households. *Public Libraries, 47*(4), 32–41.

Burnett, G., Besant, M., & Chatman, E. A. (2001). Small worlds: Normative behavior in virtual communities and feminist bookselling. *Journal of the American Society for Information Science and Technology, 52*(7), 536–547. https://doi.org/10.1002/asi.1102

Burnett, K., & Burnett, G. (2019). Information domains, information ethics. In *Proceedings of the Tenth International Conference on Conceptions of Library and Information Science*, Ljubljana, Slovenia, June 16–19, 2019. *Information Research, 24*(4). http://InformationR.net/ir/24-4/colis/colis1942.html.

Burnett, G., & Jaeger, P. T. (2008). Small worlds, lifeworlds, and information: The ramifications of the information behaviour of social groups in public policy and the public sphere. *Information Research, 13*(2). http://InformationR.net/ir/13-2/paper346.html

Burnett, S., & Lloyd, A. (2019). The road not taken: Locating desire lines across information landscapes. *Information Research, 24*(4). http://informationr.net/ir/24-4/colis/colis1911.html

Burns, R. W., Jr. (1978). Library use as a performance measure: Its background and rationale. *The Journal of Academic Librarianship, 4*, 4–11.

Burrell, G., & Morgan, G. (1988). *Sociological paradigms and organizational analysis*. Heinemann.

Buschman, J. E. (2010). The social as fundamental and a source of the critical: Jurgen Habermas. In *Critical theory for library and information science: Exploring the social from across the disciplines* (pp. 161–172). Libraries Unlimited.

Byström, K., & Järvelin, K. (1995). Task complexity affects information seeking and use. *Information Processing & Management, 31*, 191–213. https://doi.org/10.1016/0306-4573(95)80035-R

Byström, K., Ruthven, I., & Heinström, J. (2017). Work and information: Which workplace models still work in modern digital workplaces? *Information Research, 22*(1). CoLIS paper 1651. http://InformationR.net/ir/22-1/colis/colis1651.html

Cacioppo, J. T., & Petty, R. E. (1982). The need for cognition. *Journal of Personality and Social Psychology, 42*, 116–131.

Caidi, N. (2001). Interdisciplinarity: What is it and what are its implications for information seeking? *Humanities Collections, 1*(4), 35–46. https://doi.org/10.1300/J139v01n04_04

Caidi, N., Allard, D., & Quirke, L. (2010). The information practices of immigrants. In B. Cronin (Ed.). *Annual review of information science and technology* (Vol. 44, pp. 493–531). Information Today. https://doi.org/10.1002/aris.2010.1440440118

Caidi, N., Du, J. T., Li, L., Shen, J. M., & Sun, Q. (2020). Immigrating after 60: Information experiences of older Chinese migrants to Australia and Canada. *Information Processing & Management, 57*(3). https://doi.org/10.1016/j.ipm.2019.102111

Caidi, N., Komlodi, A., Abrao, A. L., & Martin-Hammond, A. (2014). Collectively figuring it out: Foreign-trained health professionals and labor market integration. *LIBRES, 24*(2), 11. http://libres-ejournal.info/wp-content/uploads/2015/03/LIBRESv24i2p118-131.Caidi_.2014.pdf.

Camacho, D., Panizo-LLedot, Á., Bello-Orgaz, G., Gonzalez-Pardo, A., & Cambria, E. (2020). The four dimensions of social network analysis: An overview of research methods, applications, and software tools. *Information Fusion, 63*, 88–120. https://doi.org/10.1016/j.inffus.2020.05.009

Campbell-Meyer, J., & Krtalić, M. (2022). Tattoo information creation: Towards a holistic understanding of tattoo information experience. *Library & Information Science Research, 44*(3). https://doi.org/10.1016/j.lisr.2022.101161

Cano, V. (1989). Citation behavior: Classification, utility, and location. *Journal of the American Society for Information Science*, *40*, 284–290. https://doi.org/10.1002/(SICI)1097-4571(198907)40:4%3C284::AID-ASI10%3E3.0.CO;2-Z

Capurro, R., & Hjørland, B. (2002). The concept of information. In B. Cronin (Ed.), *Annual review of information science and technology* (Vol. 37, pp. 343–411). Information Today.

Carter, R. (1965). Communication and affective relations. *Journalism Quarterly*, *42*, 203–212.

Carter, R. (1973). Communication as behavior. Presented at *the Annual Meeting of the Association for Education in Journalism*.

Case, D. O. (2002). *Looking for information: A survey of research on information seeking, needs, and behavior*. Elsevier/Academic Press.

Case, D. O. (2006). Information behavior. In B. Cronin (Ed.), *Annual review of information science and technology* (Vol. 40, pp. 293–328). Information Today, Inc. https://doi.org/10.1002/aris.1440400114

Case, D. O. (2007). *Looking for information: A survey of research on information seeking, needs, and behavior* (2nd ed.). Elsevier/Academic Press.

Case, D. O. (2009a). Serial collecting as leisure, and coin collecting in particular. *Library Trends*, *57*(4), 729–752. https://doi.org/10.1353/lib.0.0063

Case, D. O. (2009b). Collection of family health histories: The link between genealogy and public health. *Journal of the American Society for Information Science and Technology*, *59*(14), 2312–2319. https://doi.org/10.1002/asi.20938

Case, D. O. (2010). A model of the information seeking and decision making of online coin buyers. *Information Research*, *15*(4). http://InformationR.net/ir/15-4/paper448.html

Case, D. O. (2012). *Looking for information: A survey of research on information seeking, needs, and behavior* (3rd ed.). Emerald Publishing Limited.

Case, D. O. (2014). Sixty years of measuring the use of information and its sources: From consultation to application. Presented at *the Libraries in the Digital Age (LIDA)*, Zadar, Croatia, June 16–20. https://slideplayer.com/slide/3956824/

Case, D. O., & Given, L. M. (2016). *Looking for information: A survey of research on information seeking, needs, and behavior* (4th ed.). Emerald Publishing Limited.

Case, D. O., & Higgins, G. M. (2000). How can we investigate citation behavior? A study of reasons for citing literature in communication. *Journal of the American Society for Information Science*, *51*(7), 635–645. https://doi.org/10.1002/(SICI)1097-4571(2000)51:7%3C635::AID-ASI6%3E3.0.CO;2-H

Case, D. O., Johnson, J. D., Andrews, J. E., Allard, S., & Kelly, K. M. (2004). From two-step flow to the Internet: The changing array of sources for genetics information seeking. *Journal of the American Society for Information Science and Technology*, *55*(8), 660–669. https://doi.org/10.1002/asi.20000

Case, D. O., & O'Connor, L. G. (2016). What's the use? Measuring the frequency of studies of information outcomes. *Journal of the American Society for Information Science and Technology*, *67*(3), 649–661. https://doi.org/10.1002/asi.23411

Cavanagh, M. F. (2013). Interpreting reference work with contemporary practice theory. *Journal of Documentation*, *69*(2), 214–242. https://doi.org/10.1108/00220411311300057

de Certeau, M. (1984). *The practice of everyday life*. University of California Press.

Chaffee, S. (1991). *Communication concepts 1: Explication*. Sage Publications.

Chandler, M. (2019). The information searching behaviour of music directors. *Evidence Based Library and Information Practice*, *14*(2), 85–99. https://doi.org/10.18438/eblip29515

Chang, S.-J. L. (2006). An investigation into information needs and information seeking behavior of elementary and middle school teachers teaching indigenous courses. *Journal of Library and Information Studies*, *4*(1/2), 49–76. https://www.oalib.com/paper/2817982

Chang, S.-J. L. (2009). Information research in leisure: Implications from an empirical study of backpackers. *Library Trends*, *57*(4), 711–768. https://doi.org/10.1353/lib.0.0062

Chang, C.-C., & Huang, M.-H. (2020). Antecedents predicting health information seeking: A systematic review and meta-analysis. *International Journal of Information Management*, *54*, 102115. https://doi.org/10.1016/j.ijinfomgt.2020.102115

Charmaz, K. (2014). *Constructing grounded theory: A practical guide through qualitative analysis* (2nd ed.). SAGE Publications Ltd.

Chatman, E. A. (1990). Alienation theory: Application of a conceptual framework to a study of information among janitors. *RQ*, *29*, 355–368. https://www.jstor.org/stable/25828550

Chatman, E. A. (1991). Life in a small world: Applicability of gratification theory to information-seeking behavior. *Journal of the American Society for Information Science*, *42*, 438–449. https://doi.org/10.1002/(SICI)1097-4571(199107)42:6%3C438::AID-ASI6%3E3.0.CO;2-B

Chatman, E. A. (1992). *The information world of retired women*. Greenwood Press.

Chatman, E. A. (1996). The impoverished life-world of outsiders. *Journal of the American Society for Information Science*, *47*, 193–206. https://doi.org/10.1002/(SICI)1097-4571(199603)47:3%3C193::AID-ASI3%3E3.0.CO;2-T

Chatman, E. A. (1999). A theory of life in the round. *Journal of the American Society for Information Science*, *50*, 207–217. https://doi.org/10.1002/(SICI)1097-4571(1999)50:3%3C207::AID-ASI3%3E3.0.CO;2-8

Chaudhry, A. S., & Al-Sagheer, L. (2011). Information behavior of journalists: Analysis of critical incidents of information finding and use. *The International Information & Library Review*, *43*(4), 178–184. https://doi.org/10.1016/j.iilr.2011.10.011

Chávez, R., & Sabelli, M. (2020). Information behaviour of parents of children with autism spectrum disorder (ASD): A case study. In *Proceedings of ISIC, the Information Behaviour Conference*, Pretoria, South Africa, 28 September – 1 October, 2020. *Information Research*, *25*(4). http://InformationR.net/ir/25-4/isic2020/isic2014.html

Chen, A. T. (2015). Information use and illness representations: Understanding their connection in illness coping. *Journal of the Association for Information Science and Technology*, *66*(2), 340–353. https://doi.org/10.1002/asi.23173

Chen, A. T. (2022). Interactions between affect cognition, and information behavior in the context of fibromyalgia. *Journal of the Association for Information Science and Technology*, *73*(1), 31–44. https://doi.org/10.1002/asi.24538

Chen, C., & Hernon, P. (1982). *Information-seeking: Assessing and anticipating user needs*. Neal-Schuman.

Chen, W., Lee, K.-H., Straubhaar, J. D., & Spence, J. (2014). Getting a second opinion: Social capital, digital inequalities, and health information repertoires. *Journal of the American Society for Information Science and Technology*, *65*(12), 2552–2563. http://doi.org/10.1002/asi.23130

Choi, W., Park, M. S., & Lee, Y. (2022). Associations between mastery of life and everyday life information-seeking behavior among older adults: Analysis of the Pew Research Center's information engaged and information wary survey data. *Journal of the Association for Information Science and Technology*, *73*(3), 393–406. https://doi.org/10.1002/asi.24556

Choo, C. W. (2005). *The knowing organization: How organizations use information to construct meaning, create knowledge, and make decisions* (2nd ed.). Oxford University Press.

Choo, C. W., & Auster, E. (1993). Environmental scanning: Acquisition and use of information by managers. In M. Williams (Ed.), *Annual review of information science and technology* (Vol. 28, pp. 279–314). Learned Information.

Choo, C. W., Bergeron, P., Detlor, B., & Heaton, L. (2008). Information culture and information use: An exploratory study of three organizations. *Journal of the American Society for Information Science and Technology*, *59*(5), 792–804. https://doi.org/10.1002/asi.20797

Chu, C. M. (1999). Literary critics at work and their information needs: A research phases model. *Library & Information Science Research*, *21*(2), 247–273. https://doi.org/10.1016/S0740-8188(99)00002-X

Chu, S. K. W., Huang, H., Wong, W. N., van Ginneken, W. F., Wu, K. M., & Hung, M. Y. (2018). Quality and clarity of health information on Q&A sites. *Library & Information Science Research*, *40*(3–4), 237–244. https://doi.org/10.1016/j.lisr.2018.09.005

Chuang, K., & Yang, C. (2014). Information support exchanges using different computer-mediated communication formats in a social media alcoholism community. *Journal of the American Society for Information Science and Technology*, *65*(1), 37–52. https://doi.org/10.1002/asi.22960

Chung, E., Kwon, N., & Lee, J. (2016). Understanding scientific collaboration in the research life cycle: Bio-and nanoscientists' motivations, information-sharing and communication practices, and barriers to collaboration. *Journal of the Association for Information Science & Technology*, *67*(8), 1836–1848. https://doi.org/10.1002/asi.23520

Cibangu, S. K. (2013). A memo of qualitative research for information science: Toward theory construction. *Journal of Documentation*, *69*(2), 194–213. https://doi.org/10.1108/00220411311300048

Cibangu, S. K., & Hepworth, M. (2016). The uses of phenomenology and phenomenography: A critical review. *Library & Information Science Research*, *38*(2), 148–160. https://doi.org/10.1016/j.lisr.2016.05.001

Clark, M. (2017). Imposed-inquiry information-seeking self-efficacy and performance of college students: A review of the literature. *The Journal of Academic Librarianship*, *43*(5), 417–422. https://doi.org/10.1016/j.acalib.2017.05.001

Clarke, M. A., Belden, J. L., Koopman, R. J., Steege, L. M., Moore, J. L., Canfield, S. M., & Kim, M. S. (2013). Information needs and information-seeking behaviour analysis of primary care physicians and nurses: A literature review. *Health Information and Libraries Journal*, *30*(3), 178–190. https://doi.org/10.1111/hir.12036

Cobbledick, S. (1996). The information-seeking behavior of artists: Exploratory interviews. *The Library Quarterly*, *66*, 343–372. https://www.jstor.org/stable/4309154

Cogdill, K. W. (2003). Information needs and information seeking in primary care: A study of nurse practitioners. *Journal of the Medical Library Association*, *91*(2), 203–215.

Cohen, A. R., Stotland, E., & Wolfe, D. M. (1955). An experimental investigation of need for cognition. *Journal of Abnormal and Social Psychology*, *51*, 291–294.

Cole, C. (1998). Information acquisition in history Ph.D. students: Inferencing and the formation of knowledge structures. *The Library Quarterly*, *68*(1), 33–54. https://doi.org/10.1086/602934

Cole, C. (2012). *Information need: A theory connecting information search to knowledge formation.* Information Today Inc.

Cole, C. (2013). Concepts, propositions, models and theories in information behavior research. In *The information behavior of a new generation: Children and teens in the 21st century* (pp. 1–22). Scarecrow Press.

Cole, C., Beheshti, J., Large, A., Lamoureux, I., Abuhimed, D., & AlGhamdi, M. (2013). Seeking information for a middle school history project: The concept of implicit knowledge in the students' transition from Kuhlthau's stage 3 to stage 4. *Journal of the American Society for Information Science and Technology*, *64*(3), 558–573. https://doi.org/10.1002/asi.22786

Cole, C., & Kuhlthau, C. C. (2000). Information and information seeking of novice versus expert lawyers: How experts add value. *New Review of Information Behaviour Research*, *1*, 103–116.

Cole, C., Leide, J., Beheshti, J., Large, A., & Brooks, M. (2005). Investigating the anomalous states of knowledge hypothesis in a real-life problem situation: A study of history and psychology undergraduates seeking information for a course essay. *Journal of the American Society for Information Science and Technology*, *56*, 1544–1554. https://doi.org/10.1002/asi.20248

Cole, J., Watkins, C., & Kleine, D. (2015). Health advice from Internet discussion forums: How bad is dangerous? *Journal of Medical Internet Research*, *18*(1). https://www.jmir.org/2016/1/e4

Coleman, J. (1988). Social capital in the creation of human capital. *American Journal of Sociology*, *94*(Suppl.), 95–120.

Colosimo, A. L., & Badia, G. (2021). Diaries of lifelong learners: Information seeking behaviors of older adults in peer-learning study groups at an academic institution. *Library & Information Science Research*, *43*(3), 101102. https://doi.org/10.1016/j.lisr.2021.101102

Connaway, L. S., Dickey, T. J., & Radford, M. L. (2011). "If it is too inconvenient I'm not going after it:" Convenience as a critical factor in information-seeking behaviors. *Library & Information Science Research*, *33*(3), 179–190. https://doi.org/10.1016/j.lisr.2010.12.002

Cook, T., & Leviton, L. (1980). Reviewing the literature: A comparison of traditional methods with meta-analysis. *Journal of Personality*, *48*, 449–472.

Cooke, N. A. (2022). A right to be misinformed? Considering fake news as a form of information poverty. *Advances in Librarianship*, *50*, 15–60. Emerald Publishing Limited. https://doi.org/10.1108/S0065-283020210000050002

Cool, C. (2001). The concept of situation in information science. In M. E. Williams (Ed.), *Annual review of information science and technology* (Vol. 35, pp. 5–42). Information Today, Inc.

Correia, Z., & Wilson, T. D. (2001). Factors influencing environmental scanning in the organizational context. *Information Research*, *7*(1). http://informationr.net/ir/7-1/paper121.html

Costello, K. L. (2017). Social relevance assessments for virtual worlds: Interpersonal source selection in the context of chronic illness. *Journal of Documentation*, *73*(6), 1209–1227. https://doi.org/10.1108/JD-07-2016-0096

Costello, K. L., Martin, J. D., & Edwards Brinegar, A. (2017). Online disclosure of illicit information: Information behaviors in two drug forums. *Journal of the Association for Information Science and Technology*, *68*(10), 2439–2448. https://doi.org/10.1002/asi.23880

Courtright, C. (2005). Health information-seeking among Latino newcomers: An exploratory study. *Information Research*, *10*(2). http://InformationR.net/ir/10-2/paper224.html

Cowan, S. (2004). Informing visual poetry: Information needs and sources of artists. *Art Documentation*, *23*(2), 14–20. https://www.jstor.org/stable/27949312

Cox, A. M. (2005). What are communities of practice? A comparative review of four seminal works. *Journal of Information Science*, *31*(6), 527–540. https://doi.org/10.1177/0165551505057016

Cox, A. M. (2012). An exploration of the practice approach and its place in information science. *Journal of Information Science*, *38*, 176–188. http://doi.org/10.1177/0165551511435881

Cox, A. M., Clough, P. D., & Marlow, J. (2008). Flickr: A first look at user behaviour in the context of photography as serious leisure. *Information Research*, *13*(1). http://InformationR.net/ir/13-1/paper336.html

Cox, A. M., Griffin, B., & Hartel, J. (2017). What everybody knows: Embodied information in serious leisure. *Journal of Documentation*, *73*(3), 386–406. https://doi.org/10.1108/JD-06-2016-0073

Crane, D. (1971). Information needs and uses. In C. A. Cuadra & A. W. Luke (Eds.), *Annual review of information science and technology* (Vol. 6, pp. 3–39). Encyclopaedia Britannica.

Crawford, S. (1978). Information needs and uses. In M. E. Williams (Ed.), *Annual review of information science and technology* (Vol. 13, pp. 61–81). Knowledge Industry.

Creswell, J. W., & Clark, V. L. P. (2017). *Designing and conducting mixed methods research* (3rd ed.). Sage Publications.

Crow, S. (2009). Relationships that Foster Intrinsic motivation for information seeking. *School Libraries Worldwide*, *15*(2), 91–112. https://doi.org/10.29173/slw6794

Cruickshank, P., & Hall, H. (2020). Talking to imagined citizens? Information sharing practices and proxies for e-participation in hyperlocal democratic settings. *Information Research*, *24*(4). http://InformationR.net/ir/25-4/paper880.html

Cruickshank, P., Hall, H., & Ryan, B. (2020). Information literacy as a joint competence shaped by everyday life and workplace roles amongst Scottish community councillors. In *Proceedings of ISIC, the Information Behaviour Conference*, Pretoria, South Africa, 28 September – 1 October, 2020. Information Research, 25(4). http://InformationR.net/ir/25-4/isic2020/isic2008.html

Csikszentmihalyi, M. (1990). *Flow: The psychology of optimal experience*. Harper & Row.

Culnan, M. J. (1983). Environmental scanning: The effects of task complexity and sources accessibility on information gathering behavior. *Decision Sciences*, *14*(2), 194–206.

Curry, A. (2005). If I ask, will they answer? Evaluating public library reference service to gay and lesbian youth. *Reference and User Services Quarterly*, *45*(1), 65–75. https://www.jstor.org/stable/20864443

Czaja, R., Manfredi, C., & Price, J. (2003). The determinants and consequences of information seeking among cancer patients. *Journal of Health Communication*, *8*, 529–562. https://doi.org/10.1080/716100418

Daei, A., Soleymani, M., Ashrafi-rizi, H., Zargham-Boroujeni, A., & Kelishadi, R. (2020). Clinical information seeking behavior of physicians: A systematic review. *International Journal of Medical Informatics*, *139*. https://doi.org/10.1016/j.ijmedinf.2020.104144

Dali, K. (2004). Reading by Russian-speaking immigrants in Toronto: Use of public libraries, bookstores, and home book collections. *The International Information & Library Review*, *36*(4), 341–377. https://doi.org/10.1080/10572317.2004.10762653

Dali, K. (2012). Reading their way through immigration: The leisure reading practices of Russian-speaking immigrants in Canada. *Library & Information Science Research*, *34*(3), 197–211. https://doi.org/10.1016/j.lisr.2012.02.004

Dali, K. (2014). From book appeal to reading appeal: Redefining the concept of appeal in readers' advisory. *Library*, *84*(1), 22–48. https://doi.org/10.1086/674034

Dalton, M. S., & Charnigo, L. (2004). Historians and their information sources. *College & Research Libraries*, *65*(5), 400–425. https://doi.org/10.5860/crl.65.5.400

Dankasa, J. (2016). Mapping the everyday life information needs of Catholic clergy: Savolainen's ELIS model revisited. *Journal of Documentation*, *72*(3), 549–568. https://doi.org/10.1108/JD-08-2015-0097

Darby, P., & Clough, P. (2013). Investigating the information-seeking behaviour of genealogists and family historians. *Journal of Information Science*, *39*(1), 73–84. https://doi.org/10.1177/0165551512469765

Davenport, E. (2010). Confessional methods and everyday life information seeking. In B. Cronin (Ed.), *Annual review of information science and technology* (Vol. 44, pp. 533–562). Information Today. https://doi.org/10.1002/aris.2010.1440440119

Davenport, E., & Hall, H. (2002). Organizational knowledge and communities of practice. In B. Cronin (Ed.), *Annual review of information science and technology* (Vol. 36, pp. 171–219). Information Today. https://doi.org/10.1002/aris.1440360105

Davies, K. (2007). The information-seeking behaviour of doctors: A review of the evidence. *Health Information and Libraries Journal*, *24*, 78–94. https://doi.org/10.1111/j.1471-1842.2007.00713.x

Davies, E., & McKenzie, P. J. (2004). Preparing for opening night: Temporal boundary objects in textually-mediated professional practice. *Information Research*, *10*(1). http://InformationR.net/ir/10-1/paper211.html

Davies, R., & Williams, D. (2013). Towards a conceptual framework for provider information behaviour. *Journal of Documentation*, *69*(4), 545–566. https://doi.org/10.1108/JD-01-2012-0001

Davis, M. (1986). That's classic! The phenomenology and rhetoric of successful social theories. *Philosophy of the Social Sciences*, *16*, 285–301.

Davis, R., & Bailey, C. (1964). *Bibliography of use studies (No. Project No. 195)* (p. 98). Drexel Institute of Technology.

Dawson, M., & Chatman, E. A. (2001). Reference group theory with implications for information studies: A theoretical essay. *Information Research*, *6*(3). http://informationr.net/ir/6-3/paper105.html

Demasson, A., Partridge, H., & Bruce, C. (2016). Information literacy and the serious leisure participant: Variation in the experience of using information to learn. *Information Research*, *21*(2). http://InformationR.net/ir/21-2/paper711.html

Derr, R. L. (1983). A conceptual analysis of information need. *Information Processing & Management*, *19*, 273–278.

Derr, R. L. (1985). The concept of information in ordinary discourse. *Information Processing & Management*, *21*(6), 489–499.

Dervin, B. (1976a). Strategies for dealing with human information needs: Information or communication? *Journal of Broadcasting*, *20*(3), 324–351. https://doi.org/10.1080/08838157609386402

Dervin, B. (1976b). The everyday information needs of the average citizen: A taxonomy for analysis. In M. Kochen & J. Donahue (Eds.), *Information for the community* (pp. 23–35). American Library Association.

Dervin, B. (1983). Information as a user construct: The relevance of perceived information needs to synthesis and interpretation. In S. A. Ward & L. J. Reed (Eds.), *Knowledge structure and use: Implications for synthesis and interpretation* (pp. 153–184). Temple University Press.

Dervin, B. (1989). Users as research inventions: How research categories perpetuate inequities. *Journal of Communication*, *39*(3), 216–232. https://doi.org/10.1111/j.1460-2466.1989.tb01053.x

Dervin, B. (1992). From the mind's eye of the user: The sense-making qualitative-quantitative methodology. In J. Glazier & R. Powell (Eds.), *Qualitative research in information management* (pp. 61–84). Libraries Unlimited.

Dervin, B. (1997). Given a context by any other name: Methodological tools for taming the unruly beast. In P. Vakkari, R. Savolainen, & B. Dervin (Eds.), *Information seeking in context: Proceedings of a meeting in Finland 14–16 August 1996* (pp. 13–38). Taylor Graham.

Dervin, B. (2003). Human studies and user studies: A call for methodological interdisciplinarity. *Information Research*, *9*(1). http://informationr.net/ir/9-1/paper166.html

Dervin, B. (2005). What methodology does to theory: Sense-making methodology as exemplar. In K. E. Fisher, S. Erdelez, & E. F. McKechnie (Eds.), *Theories of information behavior* (pp. 25–30). Information Today, Inc.

Dervin, B. (2015). Dervin's sense-making theory. In M. Al-Suqri & A. Al-Aufi (Eds.), *Information seeking behavior and technology adoption: Theories and trends* (pp. 59–80). IGI Global.

Dervin, B., Ellyson, S., Hawkes, G., Guagnano, G., & White, N. (1984). *Information needs of California–1984*. Institute of Governmental Affairs, University of California.

Dervin, B., Foreman-Wernet, L., & Lauterbach, E. (Eds.). (2003). *Sense-making methodology reader: Selected writings of Brenda Dervin*. Hampton Press.

Dervin, B., & Nilan, M. (1986). Information needs and uses. In M. Williams (Ed.), *Annual review of information science and technology* (Vol. 21, pp. 1–25). Knowledge Industry.

Desouza, K., Awazu, Y., & Wan, Y. (2006). Factors governing the consumption of explicit knowledge. *Journal of the American Society for Information Science and Technology*, *57*(1), 36–43. https://doi.org/10.1002/asi.20250

Desrochers, N., & Pecoskie, J. (2015). Studying a boundary-defying group: An analytical review of the literature surrounding the information habits of writers. *Library & Information Science Research*, *37*(4), 311–322. https://doi.org/10.1016/j.lisr.2015.11.004

DeWeese, L. (1967). *A bibliography of use studies: A supplement to Davis, R.A. and Bailey, C.A. "Bibliography of use studies"*. Drexel Institute of Technology, 1964. Purdue University.

Dewey, J. (1933). *How we think*. Heath.

Dewey, J. (1960). *On experience, nature, and freedom*. The Liberal Arts Press.

Dewey, S. H. (2016). (Non-)use of Foucault's archaeology of knowledge and order of things in LIS journal literature, 1990–2015. *Journal of Documentation*, *72*(3), 454–489. https://doi.org/10.1108/JD-08-2015-0096

Dewey, S. H. (2020). Foucault's toolbox: Use of Foucault's writings in LIS journal literature, 1990–2016. *Journal of Documentation*, *76*(3), 689–707. https://doi.org/10.1108/JD-08-2019-0162

Diehm, R., & Lupton, M. (2014). Learning information literacy. *Information Research*, *19*(1). http://InformationR.net/ir/19-1/paper607.html

Diviani, N., Fredriksen, E. H., Meppelink, C. S., Mullan, J., Rich, W., & Sudmann, T. T. (2019). Where else would I look for it? A five-country qualitative study on purposes, strategies, and consequences of online health information seeking. *Journal of Public Health Research*, *8*(1). https://doi.org/10.4081/jphr.2019.1518

Dixon, C. M. (2005). Strength of weak ties. In K. E. Fisher, S. Erdelez, & E. F. McKechnie (Eds.), *Theories of information behavior* (pp. 344–348). Information Today, Inc.

Donkor, A. B., & Nwagwu, W. E. (2019). Personal factors and personal information activities behaviors of faculty in selected universities in Ghana. *Library & Information Science Research*, *41*(4). https://doi.org/10.1016/j.lisr.2019.100985

Donohew, L., & Tipton, L. (1973). A conceptual model of information seeking, avoiding and processing. In P. Clarke (Ed.), *New models for mass communication research* (pp. 243–269). Sage Publications.

Donsbach, W. (2004). Psychology of news decisions: Factors behind journalists' professional behavior. *Journalism*, *5*(2), 131–157. https://doi.org/10.1177/146488490452002

Doty, P. (2021). Privacy, surveillance, and the "smart home". In M. G. Ocepek & W. Aspray (Eds.), *Deciding where to live: Information studies on where to live in America* (pp. 93–124). Rowman & Littlefield.

Doyal, L., & Gough, I. (1984). A theory of human needs. *Critical Social Policy*, *11*, 147–150.

Du, J. T. (2014). The information journey of marketing professionals: Incorporating work task-driven information seeking, information judgments, information use, and information sharing. *Journal of the Association for Information Science and Technology*, *65*(9), 1850–1869. https://doi.org/10.1002/asi.23085

Du, J. T., & Chu, C. M. (2022). Toward community-engaged information behavior research: A methodological framework. *Library & Information Science Research*. https://doi.org/10.1016/j.lisr.2022.101189

Duff, W. M., & Johnson, C. A. (2002). Accidently found on purpose: Information-seeking behavior of historians in archives. *The Library Quarterly*, *72*(4), 472–496. https://www.jstor.org/stable/40039793

Duffy, A. M., Tandoc, E. C., & Ling, R. (2019). Too good to be true, too good not to share: The social utility of fake news. *Information, Communication & Society*, *23*, 1965–1979. https://doi.org/10.1080/1369118X.2019.1623904

Du, J. T., & Haines, J. (2019). Working with Indigenous communities: Reflections on ethical information research with Ngarrindjeri people in South Australia. In L. Freund (Ed.), *Proceedings of the 81st Association for information science & technology annual meeting* (pp. 794–796). https://doi.org/10.1002/pra2.2018.14505501120.

Dupagne, M., & Garrison, B. (2006). The meaning and influence of convergence: A qualitative case study of newsroom work at the Tampa News Center. *Journalism Studies*, *7*(2), 237–255. https://doi.org/10.1080/14616700500533569

Durieux, N., Pasleau, F., Piazza, A., Donneau, A., Vandenput, S., & Maillart, C. (2016). Information behaviour of French-speaking speech-language therapists in Belgium: Results of a questionnaire survey. *Health Information and Libraries Journal*, *33*(1), 61–76. https://doi.org/10.1111/hir.12118

Durrance, J. C. (1984). *Armed for action – library response to citizen information needs*. Neal-Schuman Publishers.

Durrance, J. C., Souden, M., Walker, D., & Fisher, K. E. (2006). Community problem-solving framed as a distributed information use environment: Bridging research and practice. *Information Research*, *11*(4). http://InformationR.net/ir/11-4/paper262.html

Eckerdal, J. R. (2011). To jointly negotiate a personal decision: A qualitative study on information literacy practices in midwifery counselling about contraceptives at youth centres in southern Sweden. *Information Research*, *16*(1). http://InformationR.net/ir/16-1/paper466.html

Edwards, C., Fox, R., Gillard, S., Gourlay, S., Guven, P., Jackson, C., ... Drennan, V. (2013). *Explaining health managers' information seeking behaviour and use. Final report*. National Institute for Health Research, Service Delivery and Organisation programme.

Ek, S. (2017). Factors relating to problems experienced in information seeking and use: Findings from a cross-sectional population study in Finland. *Information Research*, *22*(4). http://InformationR.net/ir/22-4/paper775.html

Ekoja, I. I. (2004). Sensitising users for increased information use: The case of Nigerian farmers. *African Journal of Library, Archives and Information Science*, *14*(2), 193–204.

Ellis, D. (1989). A behavioural approach to information retrieval design. *Journal of Documentation*, *45*, 171–212. https://doi.org/10.1108/eb026843

Ellis, D. (1993). Modeling the information seeking patterns of academic researchers: A grounded theory approach. *The Library Quarterly*, *6*(3), 469–486. https://www.jstor.org/stable/4308867

Ellis, D., Cox, D., & Hall, K. (1993). A comparison of the information seeking patterns of researchers in the physical and social sciences. *Journal of Documentation*, *49*, 356–369. https://doi.org/10.1108/eb026919

Elly, T., & Silayo, E. (2013). Agricultural information needs and sources of the rural farmers in Tanzania: A case of Iringa rural district. *Library Review*, *62*(8/9), 547–566. https://doi.org/10.1108/LR-01-2013-0009

Elsweiler, D., & Harvey, M. (2015). Engaging and maintaining a sense of being informed: Understanding the tasks motivating twitter search. *Journal of the Association for Information Science and Technology*, *66*(2), 264–281. https://doi.org/10.1002/asi.23182

Elsweiler, D., Wilson, M. L., & Lunn, B. K. (2011). Understanding casual-leisure information behaviour. In A. Spink & J. Heinström (Eds.), *New directions in information behaviour* (Vol. 1, pp. 211–241). Emerald Publishing Limited.

Engel, D., Robbins, S., & Kulp, C. (2011). The information-seeking habits of engineering faculty. *College & Research Libraries*, *72*(6), 548–567. https://doi.org/10.5860/crl-155

Engeström, Y. (1987). *Learning by expanding: An activity-theoretical approach to developmental research*. Orienta-Konsultit.

Engeström, Y. (1999). Activity theory and individual and social transformation. In Y. Engeström, R. Miettinen, & R.-L. Punamäki (Eds.), *Perspectives on activity theory* (pp. 19–38). Cambridge University Press. https://doi.org/10.1017/CBO9780511812774.003

Erizkova, E. (2018). Gatekeeping. In *The international encyclopedia of strategic communication* (pp. 1–6). John Wiley & Sons. https://doi.org/10.1002/9781119010722.iesc0080

Eskola, E.-L., Khan, K. S., & Widén, G. (2020). Adding the information literacy perspective to refugee integration research discourse: A scoping literature review. In *Proceedings of ISIC, the Information Behaviour Conference*, Pretoria, South Africa, 28–30 September, 2020. Information Research, *25*(4). http://InformationR.net/ir/25-4/isic2020/isic2009.html

Evans, N., & Price, J. (2017). Managing information in law firms: Changes and challenges. *Information Research, 22*(1). http://informationr.net/ir/22-1/paper736.html

Everhart, N., & Escobar, K. L. (2018). Conceptualizing the information seeking of college students on the autism spectrum through participant viewpoint ethnography. *Library & Information Science Research, 40*(3–4), 269–276. https://doi.org/10.1016/j.lisr.2018.09.009

Eze, J. U. (2016). Information needs of prisoners in Southeast Nigerian prisons. *Information Development, 32*(3), 243–253. https://doi.org/10.1177/0266666914538042

Fabritius, H. (1999). Triangulation as a multi-perspective strategy in a qualitative study of information seeking behaviour of journalists. In T. D. Wilson & D. K. Allen (Eds.), *Information behaviour: Proceedings of the second international conference on research in information needs, seeking and use in different contexts, 13/15 August 1998, Sheffield, UK* (pp. 406–419). Taylor Graham.

Fallis, D. (2015). What is disinformation? *Library Trends, 63*(3), 401–426. https://doi.org/10.1353/lib.2015.0014

Fardous, J., Du, J. T., & Hansen, P. (2019). Collaborative information seeking during leisure travelling: Triggers and social media usage. *Information Research, 24*(3). http://InformationR.net/ir/24-3/paper830.html

Farhoom, A. F., & Drury, D. H. (2002). Managerial information overload. *Communications of the ACM, 45*(10), 127–131. https://doi.org/10.1145/570907.570909

Feng, Y., & Agosto, D. E. (2017). The experience of mobile information overload: Struggling between needs and constraints. *Information Research, 22*(2). http://informationr.net/ir/22-2/paper754.html

Fidel, R. (2008). Are we there yet?: Mixed methods research in library and information science. *Library & Information Science Research, 30*(4), 265–272. https://doi.org/10.1016/j.lisr.2008.04.001

Fidel, R., & Green, M. (2004). The many faces of accessibility: Engineers' perception of information sources. *Information Processing & Management, 40*(3), 563–581. https://doi.org/10.1016/S0306-4573(03)00003-7

Fidel, R., Pejtersen, A. M., Cleal, B., & Bruce, H. (2004). A multidimensional approach to the study of human-information interaction: A case study of collaborative information retrieval. *Journal of the American Society for Information Science and Technology, 55*, 939–953. https://doi.org/10.1002/asi.20041

Finholt, T. A. (2002). Collaboratories. In B. Cronin (Ed.), *Annual review of information science and technology* (Vol. 36, pp. 73–107). Information Today. https://doi.org/10.1002/aris.1440360103

Fish, S. (1987). *Is there a text in this class? The authority of interpretive communities* (2nd ed.). Harvard University Press.

Fisher, K., Naumer, C., Durrance, J., Stromski, L., & Christiansen, T. (2005). Something old, something new: Preliminary findings from an exploratory study about people's information habits and information grounds. *Information Research, 10*(2). http://InformationR.net/ir/10-2/paper223.html

Fisher, K. E., Durrance, J. C., & Hinton, M. B. (2004). Information grounds and the use of need-based services by immigrants in Queens, New York: A context-based, outcome evaluation approach. *Journal of the American Society for Information Science and Technology, 55*(8), 754–766. https://doi.org/10.1002/asi.20019

Fisher, K. E., Erdelez, S., & McKechnie, E. F. (Eds.). (2005). *Theories of information behavior*. Information Today, Inc.

Fisher, K. E., & Julien, H. (2009). Information behavior. In B. Cronin (Ed.), *Annual review of information science & technology* (Vol. 43). Information Today. https://doi.org/10.1002/aris.2009.1440430114

Fisher, K. E., & Landry, C. F. (2007). Understanding the information behavior of stay-at-home mothers through affect. In D. Nahl & D. Bilal (Eds.), *Information and emotion: The emergent affective paradigm in information behavior research and theory* (pp. 211–233). Information Today.

Fisher, K. E., Marcoux, E., Miller, L. S., Sánchez, A., & Cunningham, E. R. (2004). Information behaviour of migrant Hispanic farm workers and their families in the Pacific Northwest. *Information Research, 10*(1). http://InformationR.net/ir/10-1/paper199.html

Flaxbart, D. (2001). Conversations with chemists: Information-seeking behavior of chemistry faculty in the electronic age. *Science & Technology Libraries, 21*(3/4), 5–26. https://doi.org/10.1300/J122v21n03_02

Fleming-May, A. (2014). Concept analysis for library and information science: Exploring usage. *Library & Information Science Research, 36*(3–4), 203–210. https://doi.org/10.1016/j.lisr.2014.05.001

Floegel, D. (2020). "Write the story you want to read": World-queering through slash fanfiction creation. *Journal of Documentation, 76*(4), 785–805. https://doi.org/10.1108/JD-11-2019-0217

Florio, E., & DeMartini, J. (1993). The use of information by policymakers at the local community level. *Knowledge: Creation, Diffusion, Utilization, 15*(1), 106–123. https://doi.org/10.1177/107554709301500104

Forcier, E. (2022). *Everyday onlife practice and information behaviour: A study of media fans in a postdigital age.* Unpublished dissertation. Swinburne University of Technology. http://hdl.handle.net/1959.3/469057

Ford, G. (1977). *User studies: An introductory guide and select bibliography.* (Occasional Paper No. 1). Centre for Research on User Studies, University of Sheffield.

Ford, N. (2015). *Introduction to information behaviour.* Facet. https://doi.org/10.29085/9781783301843

Formanek, R. (1991). Why they collect: Collectors reveal their motivations. *Journal of Social Behavior & Personality, 6*(6), 275–286.

Forsythe, D., Buchanan, B., Osheroff, J., & Miller, R. (1992). Expanding the concept of medical information: An observational study of physicians' information needs. *Computers and Biomedical Research, 25*, 181–200. https://doi.org/10.1016/0010-4809(92)90020-B

Fossum, M., Opsal, A., & Ehrenberg, A. (2022). Nurses' sources of information to inform clinical practice: An integrative review to guide evidence-based practice. *Worldviews on Evidence-Based Nursing.* https://doi.org/10.1111/wvn.12569

Foster, A. (2004). A non-linear model of information-seeking behavior. *Journal of the American Society for Information Science and Technology, 55*(3), 228–237. https://doi.org/10.1002/asi.10359

Foster, A., & Ford, N. (2003). Serendipity and information seeking: An empirical study. *Journal of Documentation, 59*(3), 321–343. https://doi.org/10.1108/00220410310472518

Foucault, M. (1972). *The order of things. An archaeology of the human sciences.* Tavistock.

Foucault, M. (1980). *Power/knowledge: Selected interviews and writings, 1972–1977.* Harvester Press.

Fourie, I. (2020). Contextual information behaviour analysis of grief and bereavement: Temporal and spatial factors, multiplicity of contexts and person-in-progressive situation. *Information Research, 25*(4). http://InformationR.net/ir/25-4/isic2020/isic2003.html

Fox, C. J. (1983). *Information and misinformation.* Greenwood Press.

Foxall, G. R. (1983). *Consumer choice.* St. Martin's Press.

Fransen-Taylor, P., & Narayan, B. (2016). #Homeless but at home in cyberspace. *Information Research, 21*(4). Paper isic1610. http://InformationR.net/ir/21-4/isic/isic1610.html

franzke, a. s., Bechmann, A., Zimmer, M., Ess, C., & and the Association of Internet Researchers. (2020). *Internet research: Ethical guidelines 3.0.* https://aoir.org/reports/ethics3.pdf

Freimuth, V., Stein, J., & Kean, T. (1989). *Searching for health information: The cancer information service model.* University of Pennsylvania Press.

French, R., & Williamson, K. (2016). Conceptualising welfare workers as information bricoleurs: Theory building using literature analysis, organisational ethnography and grounded theory analysis. *Information Research, 21*(4). http://InformationR.net/ir/21-4/isic/isic1605.html

Freund, L. (2015). Contextualizing the information-seeking behavior of software engineers. *Journal of the Association for Information Science and Technology, 66*(8), 1594–1605. https://doi.org/10.1002/asi.23278

Frické, M. (2009). The knowledge pyramid: A critique of the DIKW hierarchy. *Journal of Information Science, 35*(2), 131–142. https://doi.org/10.1177/0165551508094050

Friday, K. (2014). Learning from e-family history: A model of online family historian research behaviour. *Information Research, 19*(4). http://informationr.net/ir/19-4/paper641.html

Fry, J. (2006). Scholarly research and information practices: A domain analytic approach. *Information Processing & Management, 42*(1), 299–316. https://doi.org/10.1016/j.ipm.2004.09.004

Fuhse, B. (2022). *Social networks of meaning and communication.* Oxford University Press.

Fulton, C. (2005a). Finding pleasure in information seeking: Leisure and amateur genealogists exploring their Irish ancestry. In A. Grove (Ed.), *Proceedings of the American Society for Information Science and Technology* (Vol. 42, pp. 1292–1303). Information Today. https://doi.org/10.1002/meet.14504201228

Fulton, C. (2005b). Chatman's life in the round. In K. E. Fisher, S. Erdelez, & E. F. McKechnie (Eds.), *Theories of information behavior* (pp. 79–82). Information Today, Inc.

Fulton, C. (2009a). Quid pro quo: Information sharing in leisure activities. *Library Trends, 57*(4), 753–768. https://doi.org/10.1353/lib.0.0056

Fulton, C. (2009b). The pleasure principle: The power of positive affect in information seeking. *ASLIB Proceedings, 61*(3), 245–261. http://doi.org/10.1108/00012530910959808

Fulton, C. (2017). Urban exploration: Secrecy and information creation and sharing in a hobby context. *Library & Information Science Research, 39*(3), 189–198. https://doi.org/10.1016/j.lisr.2017.07.003

Gallagher, S., & Olsson, M. (2019). Reconciling doctor as clinician and doctor as entrepreneur: The information practices and identity work of early career surgeons. *Information Research, 24*(3). http://www.informationr.net/ir/24-3/rails/rails1810.html

Gama, L. C., Chipeta, G. T., Phiri, A., & Chawinga, W. D. (2020). Information behaviour of prison inmates in Malawi. *Journal of Librarianship and Information Science, 52*(4), 1224–1236. https://doi.org/10.1177/0961000620908655

Garner, W. R. (1962). *Uncertainty and structure as psychological concepts.* John Wiley.

Gaston, N. M., Dorner, D. G., & Johnstone, D. (2015). Spirituality and everyday information behaviour in a non-Western context: Sense-making in Buddhist Laos. *Information Research, 20*(2). Paper 665. http://InformationR.net/ir/20-2/paper665.html

Geertz, C. (1973). *The interpretation of culture.* Basic Books.

Genuis, S. K. (2012). Constructing "sense" from evolving health information: A qualitative investigation of information seeking and sense making across sources. *Journal of the American Society for Information Science and Technology, 63*(8), 1553–1566. http://doi.org/10.1002/asi.22691

Genuis, S. K. (2013). Social positioning theory as a lens for exploring health information seeking and decision making. *Qualitative Health Research, 23*(4), 555–567. https://doi.org/10.1177/1049732312470029

Genuis, S. K., & Bronstein, J. (2016). Looking for 'normal': Sense making in the context of health disruption. *Journal of the Association for Information Science and Technology, 68*(3), 750–761. https://doi.org/10.1002/asi.23715

Gerard, M., Fossa, A., Folcarelli, P. H., Walker, J., & Bell, S. K. (2017). What patients value about reading visit notes: A qualitative inquiry of patient experiences with their health information. *Journal of Medical Internet Research, 19*(7). https://doi.org/10.2196/jmir.7212

Giannini, T. (1998). Information receiving: A primary mode of the information process. In *Proceedings of the 61st annual meeting of the American society for information science* (pp. 362–371). Information Today.

Gibbons, L. (2019). Connecting personal and community memory-making: Facebook Groups as emergent community archives. In *Proceedings of RAILS - Research Applications Information and Library Studies*, 2018, Faculty of Information Technology, 28–30 November 2018. Monash University. *Information Research, 24*(3). http://InformationR.net/ir/24-3/rails/rails1804.html

Giddens, A. (1984). *The constitution of society: Outline of the theory of structuration*. Polity Press.

Giddens, A. (1986). *The constitution of society. Outline of a theory of structuration*. University of California Press.

Giddens, A. (1989). The orthodox consensus and the emerging synthesis. In B. Dervin, L. Grossberg, B. O'Keefe, & E. Wartella (Eds.), *Rethinking communication: Paradigm issues* (Vol. 1, pp. 53–65). Sage Publications.

Giddens, A. (1991). *Modernity and self-identity: Self and society in the late modern age*. Stanford University Press.

Giles, D. C., Pietrzykowski, S., & Clark, K. E. (2007). The psychological meaning of personal record collections and the impact of changing technological forms. *Journal of Economic Psychology*, *28*(4), 429–443. https://doi.org/10.1016/j.joep.2006.08.002

Given, L. M. (2002a). Discursive constructions in the university context: Social positioning theory and mature undergraduates' information behaviours. *The New Review of Information Behaviour Research: Studies of Information Seeking in Context*, *3*, 127–142.

Given, L. M. (2002b). The academic and the everyday: Investigating the overlap in mature undergraduates' information–seeking behaviors. *Library & Information Science Research*, *24*(1), 17–29. https://doi.org/10.1016/S0740-8188(01)00102-5

Given, L. M. (2005). Social positioning. In K. E. Fisher, S. Erdelez, & E. F. McKechnie (Eds.), *Theories of information behavior* (pp. 334–338). Information Today, Inc.

Given, L. M. (2007). Emotional entanglements on the university campus: The role of affect in undergraduates' information behaviors. In D. Nahl & D. Bilal (Eds.), *Information and emotion: The emergent affective paradigm in information behavior research and theory* (pp. 161–175).

Given, L. M. (Ed.). (2008). *The Sage encyclopedia of qualitative research methods*. Sage.

Given, L. M. (2016). *100 questions (and answers) about qualitative research*. Sage Publications, Inc.

Given, L. M., & Archibald, H. (2015). Visual traffic sweeps (VTS): A research method for mapping user activities in the library space. *Library & Information Science Research*, *37*(2), 100–108. https://doi.org/10.1016/j.lisr.2015.02.005

Given, L. M., Hill, M., & Paschke, P. (2017). *Communicating online: An evaluation of the Horticulture Industry Network Website*. Swinburne University of Technology. http://apo.org.au/node/116971

Given, L. M., Kelly, W., & Willson, R. (2015). Bracing for impact: The role of information science in supporting societal research impact. *Proceedings of the Association for Information Science and Technology*, *52*(1), 1–10. https://doi.org/10.1002/pra2.2015.145052010048

Given, L. M., & Kuys, B. F. (2022). Memorial design as information creation: Honoring the past through co-production of an informing aesthetic. *Library & Information Science Research*, *44*. https://doi.org/10.1016/j.lisr.2022.101176

Given, L. M., & Leckie, G. J. (2003). "Sweeping" the library: Mapping the social activity space of the public library. *Library & Information Science Research*, *25*(4), 365–385. https://doi.org/10.1016/S0740-8188(03)00049-5

Given, L. M., Ruecker, S., Simpson, H., Sadler, E., (Bess), & Ruskin, A. (2007). Inclusive interface design for seniors: Image-browsing for a health information context. *Journal of the American Society for Information Science and Technology*, *58*(11), 1610–1617. https://doi.org/10.1002/asi.20645

Given, L. M., & Willson, R. (2015). Collaborative information use with technology: A critical examination of humanities scholars' research activities. In *Collaborative information seeking best practices, new domains and new thoughts* (pp. 139–164). Springer-Verlag. https://doi.org/10.1007/978-3-319-18988-8_8

Given, L. M., & Willson, R. (2018). Information technology and the humanities scholar: Documenting digital research practices. *Journal of the Association for Information Science and Technology*, *69*(6), 807–819. https://doi.org/10.1002/asi.24008

Given, L. M., Winkler, D. C., Willson, R., Davidson, C., Danby, S., & Thorpe, K. (2014). Documenting young children's technology use: Observations in the home. *Proceedings of the Association for Information Science and Technology*, *51*. https://doi.org/10.1002/meet.2014.14505101028

Glaser, B., & Strauss, A. (1967). *The discovery of grounded theory: Strategies for qualitative research*. Aldine Publishing.

Godbold, N. (2006). Beyond information seeking: Towards a general model of information behaviour. *Information Research*, *11*(4). http://InformationR.net/ir/11-4/paper269.html

Godbold, N. (2013). An information need for emotional cues: Unpacking the role of emotions in sense making. *Information Research*, *18*(1). http://informationr.net/ir/18-1/paper561.html

Goffman, E. (1959). *The presentation of self in everyday life*. Doubleday.

Goffman, E. (1963). *Stigma: Notes on the management of spoiled identity*. Prentice-Hall.

Goffman, E. (1974). *Frame analysis: An essay on the organization of experience*. Macmillan.

Goffman, E. (1983). Interaction order. *American Sociological Review*, *48*, 1–17.

Goldman, A. I. (1970). *A theory of human action*. Princeton University Press.

González-Teruel, A., Araújo, C.-A.-A., & Sabelli, M. (2022). Diffusion of theories and theoretical models in the Ibero-American research on information behavior. *Journal of the Association for Information Science and Technology*, *73*(4), 561–578. https://doi.org/10.1002/asi.24598

González-Teruel, A., & Pérez-Pulido, M. (2020). The diffusion and influence of theoretical models of information behaviour. The case of Savolainen's ELIS model. *Journal of Documentation*, *76*(5), 1069–1089. https://doi.org/10.1108/JD-10-2019-0197

Gordon, I., Cameron, B., Chaves, D., & Hutchinson, R. (2020). Information seeking behaviors, attitudes, and choices of academic mathematicians. *Science & Technology Libraries*, *39*(3), 253–280. https://doi.org/10.1080/0194262X.2020.1758284

Goren, D. (1989). Journalists as scientists or prophets? Comments on Katz. *American Behavioral Scientist*, *33*, 251–254. https://doi.org/10.1177/0002764289033002024

Gorichanaz, T. (2015). Information on the run: Experiencing information during an ultramarathon. *Information Research*, *20*(4). http://InformationR.net/ir/20-4/paper697.html

Gorichanaz, T. (2017). Understanding art-making as documentation. *Art Documentation: Journal of the Art Libraries Society of North America*, *36*(2), 191–203. https://doi.org/10.1086/694239

Gorichanaz, T. (2019). Information creation and models of information behavior: Grounding synthesis and further research. *Journal of Librarianship and Information Science*, *51*(4), 998–1006. https://doi.org/10.1177/0961000618769968

Gorichanaz, T. (2020). Understanding and information in the work of visual artists. *Journal of the Association for Information Science and Technology*, *71*(6), 685–695. https://doi.org/10.1002/asi.24286

Gorman, P. (1995). Information needs of physicians. *Journal of the American Society for Information Science*, *46*, 729–736. https://doi.org/10.1002/(SICI)1097-4571(199512)46:10%3C729::AID-ASI3%3E3.0.CO;2-2

Gorman, P. (1999). Information seeking of primary care physicians: Conceptual models and empirical studies. In T. D. Wilson & D. K. Allen (Eds.), *Information behaviour: Proceedings of the second international conference on research in information needs, seeking and use in different contexts, 13/15 August 1998, Sheffield, UK* (pp. 226–240). Taylor Graham.

Gorman, P., Ash, J., Lavelle, M., Lyman, J., Delcambre, L., Maier, D., & Bowers, S. (2000). Bundles in the wild: Managing information to solve problems and maintain situation awareness. *Library Trends*, *49*(2), 266–289.

Gorman, P., & Helfand, M. (1995). Information seeking in primary care: How physicians choose which clinical questions to pursue and which to leave unanswered. *Medical Decision Making*, *15*, 113–119. https://doi.org/10.1177/0272989x9501500203

Gould, C. (1988). *Information needs in the humanities: An assessment*. Research Libraries Group.

Gould, C., & Handler, G. (1989). *Information needs in the social sciences: An assessment*. Research Libraries Group.

Gould, C., & Pearce, K. (1991). *Information needs in the sciences: An assessment*. Research Libraries Group.

Government of Canada. (2018). *Tri-council policy statement (TCPS) 2: Chapter 9 – Research involving the first nations, Inuit and Métis peoples of Canada*. Ottawa: Panel on Research Ethics. https://ethics.gc.ca/eng/tcps2-eptc2_2018_chapter9-chapitre9.html

Grad, R., Pluye, P., Granikov, V., Johnson-Lafleur, J., Shulha, M., Sridhar, S. B., Moscovici, J. L., Bartlett, G., Vandal, A. C., Marlow, B., & Kloda, L. (2011). Physicians' assessment of the value of clinical information: Operationalization of a theoretical model. *Journal of the American Society for Information Science and Technology*, *62*(1999), 1884–1891. http://doi.org/10.1002/asi.21590

Granikov, V., El Sherif, R., Bouthillier, F., & Pluye, P. (2022). Factors and outcomes of collaborative information seeking: A mixed studies review with a framework synthesis. *Journal of the Association for Information Science and Technology*, *73*(4), 542–560. https://doi.org/10.1002/asi.24596

Granovetter, M. S. (1973). The strength of weak ties. *American Journal of Sociology*, *78*, 1360–1380.

Granovetter, M. S. (1982). The strength of weak ties: A network theory revisited. In P. Marsden & N. Lin (Eds.), *Social structure and network analysis* (pp. 105–130). Sage Publications.

Green, A. (1990). What do we mean by user needs? *British Journal of Academic Librarianship*, *5*, 65–78.

Greifeneder, E., & Gäde, M. (2020). Adventures in Winter Wonderland - observing user behaviour in a digital twin bookstore. In *Proceedings of ISIC, the Information Behaviour Conference*, Pretoria, South Africa, 28 September–01 October, 2020. *Information Research, 25*(4). http://InformationR.net/ir/25-4/isic2020/isic2028.html

Greyson, D. (2018). Information triangulation: A complex and agentic everyday information practice. *Journal of the Association for Information Science and Technology*, *69*(7), 869–878. https://doi.org/10.1002/asi.24012

Greyson, D., & Johnson, J. L. (2016). The role of information in health behavior: A scoping study and discussion of major public health models. *Journal of the Association for Information Science and Technology*, *67*(12), 2831–2841. https://doi.org/10.1002/asi.23392

Greyson, D., O'Brien, H., & Shankar, S. (2020). Visual analysis of information world maps: An exploration of four methods. *Journal of Information Science*, *46*(3), 361–377. https://doi.org/10.1177/0165551519837174

Greyson, D., O'Brien, H., & Shoveller, J. (2017). Information world mapping: A participatory arts-based elicitation method for information behavior interviews. *Library & Information Science Research*, *39*(2), 149–157. https://doi.org/10.1016/j.lisr.2017.03.003

Griffiths, D., Sheehan, L., Petrie, D., van Vreden, C., Whiteford, P., & Collie, A. (2022). The health impacts of a 4-month long community-wide COVID-19 lockdown: Findings from a prospective longitudinal study in the state of Victoria, Australia. *PLoS One*, *17*(4). https://doi.org/10.1371/journal.pone.0266650

Gross, M. (2001). Imposed information seeking in public libraries and school library media centers: A common behaviour? *Information Research*, *6*(2). http://informationr.net/ir/6-2/paper100.html

Gross, M. (2004a). Children's information seeking at school: Findings from a qualitative study. In M. K. Chelton & C. Cool (Eds.), *Youth information-seeking behavior: Theories, models and issues* (pp. 211–240). Scarecrow Press.

Gross, M. (2004b). *Children's questions: Information seeking behavior in school*. Scarecrow Press.

Gross, M., & Saxton, M. (2001). Who wants to know? Imposed queries in the public library. *Public Libraries*, *40*(3), 170–176. https://www.jstor.org/stable/20862879

Grunig, J. (1989). Publics, audience and market segments: Segmentation principles for campaigns. In C. Salmon (Ed.), *Information campaigns: Balancing social values and social change* (pp. 199–228). Sage.

Guba, E. G., & Lincoln, Y. S. (2005). Paradigmatic controversies, contradictions, and emerging confluences. In N. Denzin & Y. Lincoln (Eds.), *The Sage handbook of qualitative research* (pp. 191–215). Sage Publications.

Gullbekk, E. (2019). What can we make of our interview data? From interdisciplinary to intra-disciplinary research. In *Proceedings of the Tenth International Conference on Conceptions of Library and Information Science*, Ljubljana, Slovenia, June 16–19, 2019. *Information Research, 24*(2). http://informationr.net/ir/24-4/colis/colis1934.html

Guzik, E. (2018). Information sharing as embodied practice in a context of conversion to Islam. *Library Trends*, *66*(3), 351–370. https://doi.org/10.1353/lib.2018.0007

Gwizdka, J., Zhang, Y., & Dillon, A. (2019). Using the eye-tracking method to study consumer online health information search behaviour. *Aslib Journal of Information Management*, *71*(6), 739–754. https://doi.org/10.1108/AJIM-02-2019-0050

Habermas, J. (1979). *Communication and the evolution of society* (T. McCarthy, Trans.). Beacon Press.

Habermas, J. (1984). *Theory of communicative action. Reason and rationalization of society* (T. McCarthy, Trans.) (Vol. 1). Beacon Press.

Habermas, J. (1987). *Theory of communicative action. Lifeworld and system: A critique of functionalist reason* (Vol. 2). Polity Press.

Hacking, I. (1999). *The social construction of what?* Harvard University Press.

Hamm, M. P., Chisholm, A., Shulhan, J., Milne, A., Scott, S. D., Given, L. M., & Hartling, L. (2013). Social media use among patients and caregivers: A scoping review. *British Medical Journal Open*, *3*(5). https://doi.org/10.1136/bmjopen-2013-002819

Hampshire, S. (1982). *Thought and action*. University of Notre Dame Press.

Hanlon, S. M. (2021). A dual lens approach to exploring informal communication's influence on learning in a political party. *Journal of Documentation*, *77*(4), 965–989. https://doi.org/10.1108/JD-08-2020-0128

Haras, C. (2011). Information behaviors of Latinos attending high school in east Los Angeles. *Library & Information Science Research*, *33*(1), 34–40. https://doi.org/10.1016/j.lisr.2010.05.001

Harlan, M. A., Bruce, C., & Lupton, M. (2012). Teen content creators: Experiences of using information to learn. *Library Trends*, *60*(3), 569–587. https://doi.org/10.1353/lib.2012.0001

Harlan, M. A., Bruce, C. S., & Lupton, M. (2014). Creating and sharing: Teens' information practices in digital communities. *Information Research*, *19*(1). http://informationr.net/ir/19-1/paper611.html

Harré, R. (1984). *Personal being: A theory for individual psychology*. Harvard University Press.

Harré, R. (1994). *The discursive mind*. Sage.

Harrison, J., Hepworth, M., & De Chazal, P. (2004). NHS and social care interface: A study of social workers' library and information needs. *Journal of Librarianship and Information Science*, *36*(1), 27–35. https://doi.org/10.1177/0961000604042971

Harris, R. M., Veinot, T. C., & Bella, L. (2010). A relational perspective on HIV/AIDS information behaviour in rural Canada. *Libri - International Journal of Libraries and Information Services*, *60*(2), 129–141. https://doi.org/10.1515/libr.2010.012

Harris, R. M., Wathen, C. N., & Fear, J. M. (2006). Searching for health information in rural Canada. Where do residents look for health information and what do they do when they find it? *Information Research*, *12*(1). http://InformationR.net/ir/12-1/paper274.html

Harr, R., Nyberg, A., Berggren, M., Carlsson, R., & Källstedt, S. (2016). Friend or foe: Exploring master suppression techniques on Facebook. *Information Research*, *21*(2). http://InformationR.net/ir/21-2/SM4.html

Hartel, J. (2003). The serious leisure frontier in library and information science: Hobby domains. *Knowledge Organization*, *30*(3/4), 228–238.

Hartel, J. (2005). Serious leisure. In K. E. Fisher, S. Erdelez, & E. F. McKechnie (Eds.), *Theories of information behavior* (pp. 313–317). Information Today, Inc.

Hartel, J. (2006). Information activities and resources in an episode of gourmet cooking. *Information Research*, *12*(1). http://informationr.net/ir/12-1/paper282.html

Hartel, J. (2010). Managing documents at home for serious leisure: A case study of the hobby of gourmet cooking. *Journal of Documentation*, *66*(6), 847–874. https://doi.org/10.1108/00220411011087841

Hartel, J. (2011). Information in the hobby of gourmet cooking: Four contexts. In W. Aspray & B. Hayes (Eds.), *Everyday information: The evolution of information seeking in America* (pp. 217–248). MIT Press.

Hartel, J. (2014a). An interdisciplinary platform for information behavior research in the liberal arts hobby. *Journal of Documentation*, *70*(5), 945–962. https://doi.org/10.1108/JD-08-2013-0110

Hartel, J. (2014b). An arts-informed study of information using the draw-and-write technique. *Journal of the American Society for Information Science and Technology*, *65*(7), 1349–1367. http://doi.org/10.1002/asi.23121

Hartel, J. (2019). Turn, turn, turn. In *Proceedings of CoLIS, the Tenth International Conference on Conceptions of Library and Information Science*, Ljubljana, Slovenia, June 16–19, 2019. *Information Research, 24*(4). http://InformationR.net/ir/24-4/colis/colis1901.html

Hartel, J., Cox, A. M., & Griffin, B. L. (2016). Information activity in serious leisure. *Information Research*, *21*(4), 1–16. http://informationr.net/ir/21-4/paper728.html

Hartel, J., & Thomson, L. (2011). Visual approaches and photography for the study of immediate information space. *Journal of the American Society for Information Science and Technology*, *62*(11), 2214–2224. https://doi.org/10.1002/asi.21618

Harter, S. P. (1992). Psychological relevance and information science. *Journal of the American Society for Information Science*, *43*, 602–615. https://doi.org/10.1002/(SICI)1097-4571(199210)43:9%3C602::AID-ASI3%3E3.0.CO;2-Q

Harviainen, J. T., Lehtonen, M. J., & Kock, S. (2022). Timeliness in information sharing within creative industries. Case: Finnish game design. *Journal of Documentation*, *78*(1), 83–96. https://doi.org/10.1108/JD-12-2020-0207

Harviainen, J. T., & Savolainen, R. (2014). Information as capability for action and capital in synthetic worlds. In *Proceedings of ISIC, the Information Behaviour Conference*, Leeds, 2–5 September, 2014: Part 1 (Vol. 19). http://informationr.net/ir/19-4/isic/isic12.html#.Y27iTOxBw6A

Haug, J. D. (1997). Physicians' preferences for information sources: A meta analytic study. *Bulletin of the Medical Library Association*, *85*(3), 223–232.

Hayter, S. (2007). The affective dimensions of information behaviour: A small world perspective. In D. Nahl & D. Bilal (Eds.), *Information and emotion: The emergent affective paradigm in information behavior research and theory* (pp. 255–266). Information Today.

Healy, K. (2017). Fuck nuance. *Sociological Theory*, *35*(2), 118–127. https://doi.org/10.1177/0735275117709046

Heinström, J. (2003). Five personality dimensions and their influence on information behaviour. *Information Research*, *9*(1). http://informationr.net/ir/9-1/paper165.html

Heinström, J. (2006). Psychological factors behind incidental information acquisition. *Library & Information Science Research*, *28*(4), 579–594. http://doi.org/10.1016/j.lisr.2006.03.022

Heinström, J. (2010). *From fear to flow: Personality and information interaction*. Chandos Publishing.

Heinström, J., Sormunen, E., Savolainen, R., & Ek, S. (2019). Developing an empirical measure of everyday information mastering. *Journal of the Association for Information Science and Technology*, *71*(7), 729–741. https://doi.org/10.1002/asi.24305

Hektor, A. (2003). Information activities on the Internet in everyday life. *New Review of Information Behaviour Research*, *4*(1), 127–138.

Hemmig, W. (2009). An empirical study of the information-seeking behavior of practicing visual artists. *Journal of Documentation*, *65*(4), 682–703. http://doi.org/10.1108/00220410910970302

Hemminger, B. M., Lu, D., Vaughan, K. T. L., & Adams, S. J. (2007). Information seeking behavior of academic scientists. *Journal of the American Society for Information Science and Technology*, *58*(14), 2205–2225. http://doi.org/10.1002/asi.20686

Henning, B., & Vorderer, P. (2001). Psychological escapism: Predicting the amount of television viewing by need for cognition. *Journal of Communication*, *51*(1), 100–120. https://doi.org/10.1111/j.1460-2466.2001.tb02874.x

Hepworth, M. (2004). A framework for understanding user requirements for an information service: Defining the needs of informal carers. *Journal of the American Society for Information Science and Technology*, *55*(8), 695–708. https://doi.org/10.1002/asi.20015

Herner, S., & Herner, M. (1967). Information needs and uses in science and technology. In C. A. Cuadra (Ed.), *Annual review of information science and technology* (Vol. 2, pp. 1–34). Encyclopaedia Britannica.

Hernon, P. (1984). Information needs and gathering patterns of academic social scientists, with special emphasis given to historians and their use of U.S. government publications. *Government Information Quarterly*, *1*, 401–429. https://doi.org/10.1016/0740-624X(84)90005-4

Hersberger, J. (2003). A qualitative approach to examining information transfer via social networks among homeless populations. *New Review of Information Behaviour Research*, *4*(1), 95–108.

Hersberger, J. (2005). Chatman's information proverty. In K. E. Fisher, S. Erdelez, & E. F. McKechnie (Eds.), *Theories of information behavior* (pp. 75–78). Information Today, Inc.

Hertzum, M. (2017). Collaborative information seeking and expertise seeking: Different discourses about similar issues. *Journal of Documentation*, *73*(5), 858–876. https://doi.org/10.1108/JD-04-2016-0053

Hertzum, M., & Hansen, P. (2019). Empirical studies of collaborative information seeking: A review of methodological issues. *Journal of Documentation*, *75*(1), 140–163. https://doi.org/10.1108/JD-05-2018-0072

Hertzum, M., & Hyldegård, J. S. (2019). Information seeking abroad: An everyday-life study of international students. *Journal of Documentation*, *75*(6), 1298–1316. https://doi.org/10.1108/JD-11-2018-0183

Hertzum, M., & Pejtersen, A. M. (2000). The information-seeking practices of engineers: Searching for documents as well as people. *Information Processing & Management*, *36*, 761–778. https://doi.org/10.1016/S0306-4573(00)00011-X

Hertzum, M., & Reddy, M. C. (2015). Procedures and collaborative information seeking: A study of emergency departments. In *Collaborative information seeking: Best practices, new domains and new thoughts* (pp. 55–71). Springer. https://doi.org/10.1007/978-3-319-18988-8_4

Hewins, E. T. (1990). Information need and use studies. In M. E. Williams (Ed.), *Annual review of information science and technology* (Vol. 25, pp. 145–172). Elsevier.

Hicks, A. (2019). Moving beyond the descriptive: The grounded theory of mitigating risk and the theorisation of information literacy. *Journal of Documentation*, *76*(1), 126–144. https://doi.org/10.1108/JD-07-2019-0126

Hirschman, E. C., & Holbrook, M. B. (1986). Expanding the ontology and methdology of research on the consumption experience. In D. Brinberg & R. Lutz (Eds.), *Perspectives on methodology in consumer research* (pp. 213–252). Springer-Verlag.

Hirsh, S., & Dinkelacker, J. (2004). Seeking information in order to produce information: An empirical study at Hewlett Packard Labs. *Journal of the American Society for Information Science and Technology*, *55*(9), 807–817. https://doi.org/10.1002/asi.20024

Hirvonen, N., & Palmgren-Neuvonen, L. (2019). Cognitive authorities in health education classrooms: A nexus analysis on group-based learning tasks. *Library & Information Science Research*, *41*(3). https://doi.org/10.1016/j.lisr.2019.100964

Hjørland, B. (2002a). Domain analysis in information science. Eleven approaches – traditional as well as innovative. *Journal of Documentation*, *58*(4), 422–462.

Hjørland, B. (2002b). Epistemology and the socio-cognitive perspective in information science. *Journal of the American Society for Information Science and Technology*, *53*(4), 257–270. https://doi.org/10.1002/asi.10042

Hjørland, B. (2005a). Introduction to the special issue: Library and information science and the philosophy of science. *Journal of Documentation*, *61*, 5–10. https://doi.org/10.1108/00220410510577970

Hjørland, B. (2005b). Empiricism, rationalism and positivism in library and information science. *Journal of Documentation*, *61*, 130–155. https://doi.org/10.1108/00220410510578050

Hjørland, B. (2005c). Afterword: Comments on the articles and proposals for further work. *Journal of Documentation*, *61*, 5–10. https://doi.org/10.1108/00220410510578069

Hjørland, B. (2005d). The socio-cognitive theory of users situated in specific contexts and domains. In K. E. Fisher, S. Erdelez, & E. F. McKechnie (Eds.), *Theories of information behavior* (pp. 339–343). Information Today, Inc.

Hjørland, B., & Albrechtsen, H. (1995). Toward a new horizon in information science: Domain analysis. *Journal of the American Society for Information Science*, *46*, 400–425. https://doi.org/10.1002/(SICI)1097-4571(199507)46:6%3C400::AID-ASI2%3E3.0.CO;2-Y

Hjørland, B., & Christensen, F. S. (2002). Work tasks and socio-cognitive relevance: A specific example. *Journal of the American Society for Information Science and Technology*, *53*(11), 960–965. https://doi.org/10.1002/asi.10132

Hogeweg de Haart, H. P. (1981). *Characteristics of social science information*. Hungarian Academy of Sciences / International Federation for Documentation.

Holland, M. P., & Powell, C. K. (1995). A longitudinal survey of the information seeking and use habits of some engineers. *College & Research Libraries*, *55*(1), 7–15. https://doi.org/10.5860/crl_56_01_7

Hong, J. Y. J., Kim, N., Lee, S., & Kim, J. H. (2018). Community disaster resilience and social solidarity on social media: A semantic network analysis on the Sewol ferry disaster. *Information Research*, *23*(3). http://InformationR.net/ir/23-3/paper798.html

Hornik, R., Kikut, A., Jesch, E., Woko, C., Siegel, L., & Kim, K. (2020). Association of COVID-19 misinformation with face mask wearing and social distancing in a nationally representative US sample. *Health Communication*, *36*(1), 6–14. https://doi.org/10.1080/10410236.2020.1847437

Hossain, M. D., & Islam, M. S. (2012). Information-seeking by print media journalists in Rajshahi, Bangladesh. *IFLA Journal*, *38*(4), 283–288. https://doi.org/10.1177/0340035212463137

Houston, R. (2011). CNI: Compelled nonuse of information. *Information Processing & Management*, *47*(3), 363–375. https://doi.org/10.1016/j.ipm.2010.08.002

Hsiao, B., Zhu, Y.-Q., & Chen, L.-Y. (2017). Untangling the relationship between Internet anxiety and Internet identification in students: The role of Internet self-efficacy. *Information Research*, *22*(2). http://InformationR.net/ir/22-2/paper753.html

Huang, H., Tse, S.-k., Chu, S. K.-W., Xiao, X.-Y., Lam, J. W.-Y., Ng, R. H.-W., & Hui, S.-Y. (2019). The correlation between out-of-school and in-school reading resources with primary school students' reading attainment. *Information Research*, *24*(3). http://InformationR.net/ir/24-3/paper834.html

Huang, K., Hao, X., Guo, M., Deng, J., & Li, L. (2021). A study of Chinese college students' COVID-19-related information needs and seeking behavior. *Aslib Journal of Information Management*, *73*(5), 679–698. https://doi.org/10.1108/AJIM-10-2020-0307

Huisman, M., Biltereyst, D., & Joye, S. (2020). Sharing is caring: The everyday informal exchange of health information among adults aged fifty and over. *Information Research*, *25*(1). http://InformationR.net/ir/25-1/paper848.html

Huizing, A., & Cavanagh, M. (2011). Planting contemporary practice theory in the garden of information science. *Information Research*, *16*(4). http://InformationR.net/ir/16-4/paper497.html

Hultgren, F. (2013). The stranger's tale: Information seeking as an outsider activity. *Journal of Documentation*, *69*(2), 275–294. http://doi.org/10.1108/00220411311300075

Hultgren, F., & Limberg, L. (2003). A study of research on children's information behaviour in a school context. *New Review of Information Behaviour Research*, *4*(1), 1–15.

Huotari, M.-L., & Chatman, E. A. (2001). Using everyday life information seeking to explain organizational behavior. *Library & Information Science Research*, *23*(4), 351–366. https://doi.org/10.1016/S0740-8188(01)00093-7

Huotari, M.-L., Suorsa, A., Ikonen, K., & Innanen, K. (2016). Knowledge creation in an R&D project. A multiple case study in the context of clean energy markets in Finland. In *Proceedings of ISIC, the Information Behaviour Conference*, Zadar, Croatia, 20–23 September, 2016: Part 1. *Information Research, 21*(4). http://InformationR.net/ir/21-4/isic/isics1602.html

Hussey, L. (2010). Social capital, symbolic violence, and fields of cultural production: Pierre Bourdieu and Library and Information Science. In G. J. Leckie, L. M. Given, & J. E. Buschman (Eds.), *Critical theory for library and information science: Exploring the social from across the disciplines* (pp. 41–52). Libraries Unlimited.

Huvila, I. (2008a). Information work analysis: An approach to research on information interactions and information behaviour in context. *Information Research*, *13*(3). http://InformationR.net/ir/13-3/paper349.html

Huvila, I. (2008b). The information condition: Information use by archaeologists in labour, work and action. *Information Research*, *13*(4). http://informationr.net/ir/13-4/paper369.html

Huvila, I. (2009). Analytical information horizon maps. *Library & Information Science Research*, *31*(1), 18–28. https://doi.org/10.1016/j.lisr.2008.06.005

Huvila, I. (2010). Information sources and perceived success in corporate finance. *Journal of the American Society for Information Science and Technology*, *61*(11), 2219–2229. http://doi.org/10.1002/asi.21387

Huvila, I. (2013). "Library users come to a library to find books": The structuration of the library as a soft information system. *Journal of Documentation*, *69*(5), 715–735. http://doi.org/10.1108/JD-06-2012-0080

Huvila, I. (2019). Genres and situational appropriation of information: Explaining not-seeking of information. *Journal of Documentation*, *75*(6), 1503–1527. https://doi.org/10.1108/JD-03-2019-0044

Huvila, I. (2022). Making and taking information. *Journal of the Association for Information Science and Technology*, *73*(4), 528–541. https://doi.org/10.1002/asi.24599

Huvila, I., Cajander, A., Daniels, M., & Åhlfeldt, R. (2015). Patients' perceptions of their medical records from different subject positions. *Journal of the Association for Information Science and Technology*, *66*(12), 2456–2470. https://doi.org/10.1002/asi.23343

Huvila, I., Daniels, M., Cajander, A., & Åhlfeldt, R. (2016). Patients reading medical records: Differences in experiences and attitudes between regular and inexperienced readers. *Information Research*, *21*(1). http://informationr.net/ir/21-1/paper706.html#.Y28xg-xBwUo

Huvila, I., Douglas, J., Gorichanaz, T., Koh, K., & Suorsa, A. (2022). Guest editorial: Advances in research on information creation. *Library & Information Science Research*, *44*(3). https://doi.org/10.1016/j.lisr.2022.101178

Huvila, I., Enwald, H., Eriksson-Backa, M., Hirvonen, N., Nguyen, H., & Scandurra, I. (2018). Anticipating ageing: Older adults reading their medical records. *Information Processing &*, *54*(3), 394–407. https://doi.org/10.1016/j.ipm.2018.01.007

Huvila, I., Moll, J., Enwald, H., Åhlfeldt, R., & Cajander, Å. (2019). Age-related differences in seeking clarification to understand medical record information. *Information Research*, *24*(1). http://InformationR.net/ir/24-1/isic2018/isic1834.html

Huvila, I., Sköld, O., & Börjesson, L. (2021). Documenting information making in archaeological field reports. *Journal of Documentation*, *77*(5), 1107–1127. https://doi.org/10.1108/JD-11-2020-0188

Hyatt, E. (2017). The information behaviour of Pacific crest Trail thru-hikers: An autoethnographic pilot study. In *Proceedings of ISIC, the Information Behaviour Conference*, Zadar, Croatia, 20–23 September, 2016: Part 2. *Information Research, 22*(1). http://InformationR.net/ir/22-1/isic/isics1607.html

Hyatt, E., Harvey, M., Pointon, M., & Innocenti, P. (2021). Whither wilderness? An investigation of technology use by long-distance backpackers. *Journal of the Association for Information Science and Technology*, *72*(6), 683–698. https://doi.org/10.1002/asi.24437

Hyldegård, J. (2009). Beyond the search process – Exploring group members' information behavior in context. *Information Processing & Management*, *45*(1), 142–158. http://doi.org/10.1016/j.ipm.2008.05.007

Ignatieff, M. (1984). *The needs of strangers*. Chatto and Windus.

Ikoja-Odongo, R., & Mostert, J. (2006). Information seeking behaviour: A conceptual framework. *South African Journal of Library & Information Science*, *72*(3), 145–158.

Ikoja-Odongo, R., & Ocholla, D. N. (2003). Information needs and information-seeking behavior of artisan fisher folk of Uganda. *Library & Information Science Research*, *25*, 89–105. https://doi.org/10.1016/S0740-8188(02)00167-6

Ikoja-Odongo, R., & Ocholla, D. N. (2004). Information seeking behaviour of the informal sector entrepreneurs: The Uganda experience. *Libri – International Journal of Libraries and Information Services*, *54*(1), 54–66. https://doi.org/10.1515/LIBR.2004.54

Ingram, D. (2014). *Critical theory to structuralism: Philosophy, politics and the human sciences* (Vol. 5). Routledge.

Ingwersen, P. (1996). Cognitive perspectives of information retrieval interaction: Elements of a cognitive IR theory. *Journal of Documentation*, *52*, 3–50. https://doi.org/10.1108/eb026960

Ingwersen, P., & Järvelin, K. (2005). *The turn: Integration of information seeking and retrieval in context*. Springer.

Inyang, O. G. (2015). The role of information and female vegetable farmers in Calabar municipal Council area, Nigeria. *Libri – International Journal of Libraries and Information Services*, *65*(2), 151–160. https://doi.org/10.1515/libri-2014-0036

Irvine-Smith, S. (2017). Information through the lens: Information research and the dynamics of practice. In *Proceedings of the Ninth International Conference on Conceptions of Library and Information Science*, Uppsala, Sweden, June 27–29, 2016. *Information Research, 22*(1). http://InformationR.net/ir/22-1/colis/colis1603.html

Isah, E. E., & Byström, K. (2015). Physicians' learning at work through everyday access to information. *Journal of the Association for Information Science & Technology*, *67*(2), 318–332. https://doi.org/10.1002/asi.23378

Isah, E. E., & Byström, K. (2017). Enacting workplace information practices: The diverse roles of physicians in a health care team. In *Proceedings of the Ninth International Conference on Conceptions of Library and Information Science*, Uppsala, Sweden, June 27–29, 2016. *Information Research, 22*(1). http://informationr.net/ir/22-1/colis/colis1650.html

Isah, E. E., & Byström, K. (2020). The mediating role of documents: Information sharing through medical records in healthcare. *Journal of Documentation*, *76*(6), 1171–1191. https://doi.org/10.1108/JD-11-2019-0227

Iser, W. (1978). *The act of reading*. Johns Hopkins University.

Jamali, H. R., & Nabavi, M. (2022). The use of information behaviour research in human-computer interaction. *Information Research*, *27*(3). http://InformationR.net/ir/27-3/paper937.html

Jamali, H. R., & Nicholas, D. (2010). Interdisciplinarity and the information-seeking behavior of scientists. *Information Processing & Management*, *46*(2), 233–243. http://doi.org/10.1016/j.ipm.2009.12.010

Janesick, V. J. (1998). The dance of qualitative research design: Metaphor, methodolatry, and meaning. In N. Denzin & Y. Lincoln (Eds.), *Strategies of qualitative inquiry* (pp. 35–55). Sage Publications, Inc.

Jarrahi, M. H., & Thomson, L. (2017). The interplay between information practices and information context: The case of mobile knowledge workers. *Journal of the Association for Information Science and Technology*, *68*(5), 1073–1089. https://doi.org/10.1002/asi.23773

Järvelin, K., & Vakkari, P. (1993). The evolution of library and information science 1965–1985: A content analysis of journal articles. *Information Processing & Management*, *29*(1), 129–144. http://doi.org/10.1016/0306-4573(93)90028-C

Järvelin, K., & Wilson, T. D. (2003). On conceptual models for information seeking and retrieval research. *Information Research*, *9*(1). http://informationr.net/ir/9-1/paper163.html

Jeong, W. (2004). Unbreakable ethnic bonds: Information-seeking behavior of Korean graduate students in the United States. *Library & Information Science Research*, *26*(3), 384–400. https://doi.org/10.1016/j.lisr.2004.04.001

Jia, R. M., Du, J. T., & Zhao, Y. C. (2022). Characteristics of the health information seeking behavior of LGBTQ+ individuals: A systematic review on information types, information sources and influencing factors. *Journal of Documentation*, *78*(2), 361–388. https://doi.org/10.1108/JD-03-2021-0069

Jiang, T., Chi, Y., & Gao, H. (2017). A clickstream data analysis of Chinese academic library OPAC users' information behavior. *Library & Information Science Research*, *39*(3), 213–223. https://doi.org/10.1016/j.lisr.2017.07.004

Jiang, T., Fu, S., Erdelez, S., & Guo, Q. (2022). Understanding the seeking-encountering tension: Roles of foreground and background task urgency. *Information Processing & Management*, *59*(3), 102910. https://doi.org/10.1016/j.ipm.2022.102910

Jiao, Q., & Onwuegbuzie, A. J. (1997). Antecedents of library anxiety. *The Library Quarterly*, *67*, 372–389. https://www.jstor.org/stable/40039590

Jia, X., Pang, Y., & Liu, S. L. (2021). Online health information seeking behavior: A systematic review. *Healthcare*, *9*(12), 1740. https://doi.org/10.3390/healthcare9121740

Johannisson, J., & Sundin, O. (2007). Putting discourse to work: Information practices and the professional project of nurses. *The Library Quarterly*, *77*(2), 199–218. https://doi.org/10.1086/517843

Johnson, C. A. (2005). Nan Lin's theory of social capital. In K. E. Fisher, S. Erdelez, & E. F. McKechnie (Eds.), *Theories of information behavior* (pp. 323–327). Information Today, Inc.

Johnson, C. A. (2007). Social capital and the search for information: Examining the role of social capital in information seeking behavior in Mongolia. *Journal of the American Society for Information Science and Technology*, *58*(6), 883–894. http://doi.org/10.1002/asi.20561

Johnson, C. A. (2012). How do public libraries create social capital? An analysis of interactions between library staff and patrons. *Library & Information Science Research*, *34*(1), 52–62. https://doi.org/10.1016/j.lisr.2011.07.009

Johnson, C. A. (2015). Social capital and library and information science research: Definitional chaos or coherent research enterprise? *Information Research*, *20*(4). http://InformationR.net/ir/20-4/paper690.html

Johnson, J. D. (1997). *Cancer-related information seeking*. Hampton Press.

Johnson, J. D. (2003). On contexts of information seeking. *Information Processing & Management*, *39*(5), 735–760. https://doi.org/10.1016/S0306-4573(02)00030-4

Johnson, J. D. (2019). Network analysis approaches to collaborative information seeking in inter-professional health care teams. *Information Research*, *24*(1). http://InformationR.net/ir/24-1/paper810.html

Johnson, J. D., & Meischke, H. (1993). A comprehensive model of cancer-related information seeking applied to magazines. *Human Communication Research*, *19*, 343–367. https://doi.org/10.1111/j.1468-2958.1993.tb00305.x

Jordan, J. L. (2013). Meta-synthesis of the research on information seeking behaviour of graduate students highlights different library resource needs across disciplines and cultures. *Evidence Based Library and Information Practice*, *8*(4), 132–135. https://doi.org/10.18438/B8MK7V

Joseph, P. (2016). Australian motor sport enthusiasts' leisure information behaviour. *Journal of Documentation*, *72*(6), 1078–1113. https://doi.org/10.1108/JD-12-2015-0150

Joyce, S. (2005). Symbolic violence. In K. E. Fisher, S. Erdelez, & E. F. McKechnie (Eds.), *Theories of information behavior* (pp. 349–353). Information Today, Inc.

Julien, H. (1996). A content analysis of the recent information needs and uses literature. *Library & Information Science Research*, *18*, 53–65. https://doi.org/10.1016/S0740-8188(96)90030-4

Julien, H. (1999). Barriers to adolescent information seeking for career decision making. *Journal of the American Society for Information Science*, *50*, 38–48. https://doi.org/10.1002/(SICI)1097-4571(1999)50:1%3C38::AID-ASI6%3E3.0.CO;2-G

Julien, H. (2004). Adolescent decision-making for careers: An exploration of information behavior. In M. Chelton & C. Cool (Eds.), *Youth information-seeking behavior: Theories, models and issues* (pp. 321–352). Scarecrow Press.

Julien, H., & Duggan, L. (2000). A longitudinal analysis of the information needs and uses literature. *Library & Information Science Research*, *22*, 291–309. https://doi.org/10.1016/S0740-8188(99)00057-2

Julien, H., & Given, L. M. (2003). Faculty-librarian relationship in the information literacy context: A content analysis of librarians' expressed attitudes and experiences. *Canadian Journal of Information and Library Science*, *27*, 65–87. https://doi.org/10.29173/cais526

Julien, H., Given, L. M., & Opryshko, A. (2013). Photovoice: A promising method for studies of individuals' information practices. *Library & Information Science Research*, *35*(4), 257–263. http://doi.org/10.1016/j.lisr.2013.04.004

Julien, H., McKechnie, L., Polkinghorne, S., & Chabot, R. (2018). The "user turn" in practice: Information behaviour researchers' constructions of information users. *Information Research*, *23*(4). http://www.informationr.net/ir/23-4/isic2018/isic1804.html

Julien, H., & Michels, D. (2004). Intra-individual information behaviour in daily life. *Information Processing & Management*, *40*(3), 547–562. https://doi.org/10.1016/S0306-4573(02)00093-6

Julien, H., & O'Brien, M. (2014). Information behavior research: Where have we been, where are we going? *Canadian Journal of Information and Library Science*, *38*(4), 239–250.

Julien, H., Pecoskie, J. L., & Reed, K. (2011). Trends in information behavior research, 1999–2008: A content analysis. *Library & Information Science Research*, *33*(1), 19–24. https://doi.org/10.1016/j.lisr.2010.07.014

Jung, J.-Y. (2012). Social media use and goals after the Great East Japan earthquake. *First Monday*, *17*(8). http://firstmonday.org/ojs/index.php/fm/article/view/4071/3285

Kahlor, L. (2010). PRISM: A planned risk information seeking model. *Health Communication*, *25*(4), 345–356. https://doi.org/10.1080/10410231003775172

Kainat, K., Eskola, E.-L., & Widén, G. (2022). Sociocultural barriers to information and integration of women refugees. *Journal of Documentation*, *78*(5), 1131–1148. https://doi.org/10.1108/JD-05-2021-0107

Kalms, B. (2008). Household information practices: How and why householders process and manage information. *Information Research*, *13*(1). http://InformationR.net/ir/13-1/paper339.html

Kane, S. K. (2007). Everyday inclusive web design: An activity perspective. *Information Research*, *12*(1). http://InformationR.net/ir/12-3/paper309.html

Kankam, P. K. (2019). The use of paradigms in information research. *Library & Information Science Research*, *41*(2), 85–92. https://doi.org/10.1016/j.lisr.2019.04.003

Karanasios, S., Thakker, D., Lau, L., Allen, D., Dimitravo, V., & Norman, A. (2013). Making sense of digital traces: An activity theory driven ontological approach. *Journal of the American Society for Information Science and Technology*, *64*(12), 2452–2467. https://doi.org/10.1002/asi.22935.

Kari, J. (2007). Conceptualizing the personal outcomes of information. *Information Research*, *12*(2). http://InformationR.net/ir/12-2/paper292.html

Kari, J. (2010). Diversity in the conceptions of information use. In *Proceedings of the Seventh International Conference on Conceptions of Library and Information Science— "Unity in Diversity"*. *15*(3). http://informationr.net/ir/15-3/colis7/colis709.html

Kari, J., & Savolainen, R. (2003). Towards a contextual model of information seeking on the Web. *New Review of Information Behaviour Research*, *4*(1), 155–175.

Karlova, N. A., & Fisher, K. E. (2013). A social diffusion model of misinformation and disinformation for understanding human information behaviour. *Information Research*, *18*(1). http://InformationR.net/ir/18-1/paper573.html

Karlsson, L., Koivula, L., Ruokonen, I., Kajaani, P., Antikainen, L., & Ruismäki, H. (2012). From novice to expert: Information seeking processes of university students and researchers. *Procedia - Social and Behavioral Sciences*, *45*, 577–587. http://doi.org/10.1016/j.sbspro.2012.06.595

Kassim, M. (2021). A qualitative study of the maternal health information-seeking behaviour of women of reproductive age in Mpwapwa district, Tanzania. *Health Information and Libraries Journal*, *38*(3), 182–193. https://doi.org/10.1111/hir.12329

Katz, E. (1989). Journalists as scientists: Notes towards an occupational classification. *American Behavioral Scientist*, *33*(2), 238–246. https://doi.org/10.1177/0002764289033002022

Kauer, S. D., Mangan, C., & Sanci, L. (2014). Do online mental health services improve help-seeking for young people? A systematic review. *Journal of Medical Internet Research*, *16*(3). https://doi.org/10.2196/jmir.3103

Kaye, B. K., & Johnson, T. J. (2003). From here to obscurity?: Media substitution theory and traditional media in an on-line world. *Journal of the American Society for Information Science and Technology*, *54*(3), 260–273. https://doi.org/10.1002/asi.10212

Keith, R. J., Given, L. M., Martin, J. M., & Hochuli, D. F. (2022). Collaborating with qualitative researchers to co-design social-ecological studies. *Austral Ecology*, *47*(4), 880–888. https://doi.org/10.1111/aec.13172

Kelly, G. (1963). *A theory of personality: The psychology of personal constructs*. Norton.

Kelly, K. M., Sturm, A., Kemp, K., Holland, J., & Ferketich, A. (2009). How can we reach them? Information seeking and preferences for a cancer family history campaign in underserved communities. *Journal of Health Communication*, *14*(6), 573–589. https://doi.org/10.1080/10810730903089580

Kelly, M. (2021). Epistemology, epistemic belief, personal epistemology, and epistemics: A review of concepts as they impact information behavior research. *Journal of the Association for Information Science and Technology*, *72*(4), 507–519. https://doi.org/10.1002/asi.24422

Kelly, W. (2019). *Navigating pathways to community: Exploring the experiences of community-engaged humanities and social sciences academics*. Unpublished dissertation, Swinburne University of Technology.

Kelly, W. (Ed.). (2022). *The impactful academic: Building a research career that makes a difference*. Emerald Publishing Limited.

Kennan, M. A., Lloyd, A., Qayyum, A., & Thompson, K. M. (2011). Settling in: The relationship between information and social inclusion. *Australian Academic and Research Libraries*, *43*(2), 191–210. https://doi.org/10.1080/00048623.2011.10722232

Kerins, G., Madden, R., & Fulton, C. (2004). Information seeking and students studying for professional careers: The cases of engineering and law students in Ireland. *Information Research*, *10*(1). http://InformationR.net/ir/10-1/paper208.html

Kerlinger, F. (1973). *Foundations of behavioral research*. Holt Rinehart & Winston.

Khan, K. S., & Eskola, E.-L. (2020). The cultural landscape of women refugees in Sweden – A road to information and integration. In *Proceedings of ISIC, the Information Behaviour Conference*, Pretoria, South Africa, 28–30 September, 2020. *Information Research*, *25*(4). http://InformationR.net/ir/25-4/isic2020/isic2033.html

Khazraee, E. (2019). Assembling narratives: Tensions in collaborative construction of knowledge. *Journal of the Association for Information Science and Technology*, *70*(4), 325–337. https://doi.org/10.1002/asi.24133

Khoir, S., Du, J. T., & Koronios, A. (2015). Everyday information behaviour of Asian immigrants in South Australia: A mixed-methods exploration. *Information Research*, *20*(3). http://InformationR.net/ir/20-3/paper687.html

Kim, K.-S., & Sin, S.-C. J. (2015). Use of social media in different contexts of information seeking: Effects of sex and problem-solving style. *Information Research*, *20*(1). http://InformationR.net/ir/20-1/isic2/isic24.html

Kim, K.-S., Sin, S.-C. J., & Yoo-Lee, E. (2021). Use and evaluation of information from social media: A longitudinal cohort study. *Library & Information Science Research*, *43*(3). https://doi.org/10.1016/j.lisr.2021.101104

Kim, S., Sinn, D., & Syn, S. Y. S. (2020). Personal health information management by college students: Patterns of inaction. *Information Research*, *25*(1). http://InformationR.net/ir/25-1/paper851.html

Kim, Y.-M. (2015). Is seeking health information online different from seeking general information online? *Journal of Information Science*, *4*(2), 228–241. https://doi.org/10.1177/0165551514561669

Kim, S., & Syn, S. Y. S. (2016). Credibility and usefulness of health information on Facebook: A survey study with U.S. college students. *Information Research*, *21*(4). http://informationr.net/ir/21-4/paper727.html

Kirk, J. (2002). *Theorising information use: Managers and their work*. Unpublished doctoral dissertation, University of Technology. https://opus.lib.uts.edu.au/bitstream/2100/309/2/02whole.pdf

Kitalong, K. S., Hoeppner, A., & Scharf, M. (2008). Making sense of an academic library web site: Toward a more useable interface for university researchers. *Journal of Web Librarianship*, *2*(2–3), 177–204. https://doi.org/10.1080/19322900802205742

Kitzie, V. L., Wagner, T. L., Lookingbill, V., & Vera, N. (2022). Advancing information practices theoretical discourses centered on marginality, community, and embodiment: Learning from the experiences of lesbian, gay, bisexual, transgender, queer, intersex, and asexual (LGBTQIA+) communities. *Journal of the Association for Information Science and Technology*, *73*(4), 495–510. https://doi.org/10.1002/asi.24594

Kitzie, V., Wagner, T., & Vera, A. N. (2021). Discursive power and resistance in the information world maps of lesbian, gay, bisexual, transgender, queer, intersex and asexual community leaders. *Journal of Documentation*, *77*(3), 638–662. https://doi.org/10.1108/JD-08-2020-0138

Knorr-Cetina, K. D. (1981). *The manufacture of knowledge: A essay on the constructivist and contextual nature of science*. Pergamon Press.

Knox, E. J. M. (2014). Society, institutions, and common sense: Themes in the discourse of book challengers in 21st century United States. *Library & Information Science Research*, *36*(3–4), 171–178. https://doi.org/10.1016/j.lisr.2014.06.003

Koh, K. (2013). Adolescents' information-creating behavior embedded in digital media practice using Scratch. *Journal of the American Society for Information Science and Technology*, *64*(9), 1826–1841. https://doi.org/10.1002/asi.22878

Koh, K., Snead, J. T., & Lu, K. (2019). The processes of maker learning and information behavior in a technology-rich high school class. *Journal of the Association for Information Science and Technology*, *70*(12), 1395–1412. https://doi.org/10.1002/asi.24197

Kostagiolas, P. A., Lavranos, C., Korfiatis, N., Papadatos, J., & Papavlasopoulos, S. (2015). Music, musicians and information seeking behaviour: A case study on a community concert band. *Journal of Documentation*, *71*(1), 3–24. https://doi.org/10.1108/JD-07-2013-0083

Kostagiolas, P., Lavranos, C., Martzoukou, K., & Papadatos, J. (2017). The role of personality in musicians' information seeking for creativity. *Information Research*, *22*(2). http://InformationR.net/ir/22-2/paper756.html

Krampen, G., Fell, C., & Schui, G. (2011). Psychologists' research activities and professional information-seeking behavior: Empirical analyses with reference to the theory of the intellectual and social organization of the sciences. *Journal of Information Science*, *37*(4), 439–450. https://doi.org/10.1177/0165551511412148

Krikelas, J. (1983). Information-seeking behavior: Patterns and concepts. *Drexel Library Quarterly*, *19*, 5–20.

Krippendorff, K. (1980). *Content analysis: An introduction to its methodology*. Sage.

Kuhlthau, C. C. (1988). Developing a model of the library search process: Cognitive and affective aspects. *Reference Quarterly*, *28*, 232–242. https://www.jstor.org/stable/25828262

Kuhlthau, C. C. (1991). Inside the search process: Information seeking from the user's perspective. *Journal of the American Society for Information Science*, *42*, 361–371. https://doi.org/10.1002/(SICI)1097-4571(199106)42:5%3C361::AID-ASI6%3E3.0.CO;2-%23

Kuhlthau, C. C. (1993a). *Seeking meaning: A process approach to library and information services*. Ablex.

Kuhlthau, C. C. (1993b). A principle of uncertainty for information seeking. *Journal of Documentation*, *49*, 339–355. https://doi.org/10.1108/eb026918

Kuhlthau, C. C. (1999). The role of experience in the information search process of an early career information worker: Perceptions of uncertainty, complexity, construction, and sources. *Journal of the American Society for Information Science*, *50*, 399–412. https://doi.org/10.1002/(SICI)1097-4571(1999)50:5%3C399::AID-ASI3%3E3.0.CO;2-L

Kuhlthau, C. C. (2004). *Seeking meaning: A process approach to library and information services* (2nd ed.). Libraries Unlimited.

Kuhlthau, C. C. (2005). Kuhlthau's information search process. In K. E. Fisher, S. Erdelez, & E. F. McKechnie (Eds.), *Theories of information behavior* (pp. 230–234). Information Today, Inc.

Kuhlthau, C. C., & Tama, S. L. (2001). Information search process of lawyers, a call for "just for me" information services. *Journal of Documentation*, *57*, 25–43. https://doi.org/10.1108/EUM0000000007076

Kuhn, T. (1962). *The structure of scientific revolutions*. University of Chicago Press.

Kundu, D. K. (2017). Models of information seeking behaviour: A comparative study. *International Journal of Library and Information Studies*, *7*(4), 393–405.

Kurbanoglu, S. S. (2003). Self-efficacy: A concept closely linked to information literacy and lifelong learning. *Journal of Documentation*, *59*(6), 635–646. https://doi.org/10.1108/00220410310506295

Kurbanoglu, S. S., Akkoyunlu, B., & Umay, A. (2006). Developing the information literacy self-efficacy scale. *Journal of Documentation*, *62*(6), 730–743. https://doi.org/10.1108/00220410610714949

Kuruppu, P. U., & Gruber, A. M. (2006). Understanding the information needs of academic scholars in agricultural and biological sciences. *The Journal of Academic Librarianship*, *32*(6), 609–623. https://doi.org/10.1016/j.acalib.2006.08.001

Kwasitsu, L. (2003). Information-seeking behavior of design, process, and manufacturing engineers. *Library & Information Science Research*, *25*(4), 459–476. https://doi.org/10.1016/S0740-8188(03)00054-9

Kwon, N. (2017). How work positions affect the research activity and information behaviour of laboratory scientists in the research lifecycle: Applying activity theory. *Information Research*, *22*(1). http://informationr.net/ir/22-1/paper744.html

Kwon, N., & Kim, K. (2009). Who goes to a library for cancer information in the e-health era? A secondary data analysis of the Health Information National Trends Survey (HINTS). *Library & Information Science Research*, *31*(3), 192–200. https://doi.org/10.1016/j.lisr.2009.01.006

Lachlan, K., Hutter, E., & Gilbert, C. (2021). COVID-19 echo chambers: Examining the impact of conservative and liberal news sources on risk perception and response. *Health Security*, *19*(1), 21–30. https://doi.org/10.1089/hs.2020.0176

Lakshminarayanan, B. (2010). *Towards developing an integrated model of information behaviour*. (Ph. D.). Queensland University of Technology.

Lambert, J. D. (2010). The information-seeking habits of Baptist ministers. *Journal of Religious & Theological Information*, *9*(1/2), 1–19. http://doi.org/10.1080/10477845.2010.508449

Landry, C. F. (2006). Work roles, tasks, and the information behavior of dentists. *Journal of the American Society for Information Science and Technology*, *57*(14), 1896–1908. http://doi.org/10.1002/asi.20385

Landry, C. F. (2021). Home buying in everyday life: How emotion and time pressure shape high-stakes deciders' information behavior. In M. G. Ocepek & W. Aspray (Eds.), *Deciding where to live: Information studies on where to live in America* (pp. 237–258). Rowman & Littlefield.

Laplante, A., & Downie, J. S. (2011). The utilitarian and hedonic outcomes of music information-seeking in everyday life. *Library & Information Science Research*, *33*(3), 202–210. http://doi.org/10.1016/j.lisr.2010.11.002

Larkin, C. (2010). Looking to the future while learning from the past: Information seeking in the visual arts. *Art Documentation*, *29*(1), 49–60. https://doi.org/10.1086/adx.29.1.27949539

Larkin-Lieffers, P. A. (2001). Informational picture books in the library: Do young children find them? *Public Library Quarterly*, *20*(3), 3–28. https://doi.org/10.1300/J118v20n03_02

Latham, K. F. (2014). Experiencing documents. *Journal of Documentation*, *70*(4), 3. http://doi.org/10.1108/JD-01-2013-0013

Latour, B. (2004). *Politics of nature: How to bring the sciences into democracy*. Harvard University Press.

Latour, B., & Woolgar, S. (1979). *Laboratory life: The social construction of scientific facts*. Sage Publications.

Laukka, E., Rantakokko, P., & Suhonen, M. (2019). Consumer-led health-related online sources and their impact on consumers: An integrative review of the literature. *Health Informatics Journal*, *25*(2), 247–266. https://doi.org/10.1177/1460458217704254

Lave, J., & Wenger, E. (1991). *Situated learning: Legitimate peripheral participation*. Cambridge University Press.

Lavranos, C., Kostagiolas, P., Korfiatis, N., & Papadatos, J. (2016). Information seeking for musical creativity: A systematic literature review. *Journal of the Association for Information Science and Technology*, *67*(9), 2105–2117. https://doi.org/10.1002/asi.23534

Layne, S. S. (1994). Artists, art historians, and visual art information. *The Reference Librarian*, *47*, 23–36. https://doi.org/10.1300/J120v22n47_03

Le Louvier, K., & Innocenti, P. (2021). Heritage as an affective and meaningful information literacy practice: An interdisciplinary approach to the integration of asylum seekers and refugees. *Journal of the Association for Information Science and Technology*, *73*(5), 687–701. https://doi.org/10.1002/asi.24572

Lechte, J. (2007). *Fifty key contemporary thinkers: From structuralism to post-humanism* (2nd ed.). Routledge.

Leckie, G. J. (1996). Female farmers and the social construction of access to agricultural information. *Library & Information Science Research*, *18*, 297–321. https://doi.org/10.1016/S0740-8188(96)90002-X

Leckie, G. J. (2005). General model of the information seeking of professionals. In K. E. Fisher, S. Erdelez, & E. F. McKechnie (Eds.), *Theories of information behavior* (pp. 158–163). Information Today, Inc.

Leckie, G. J., & Buschman, J. E. (2010). Introduction: The necessity for theoretically informed critique in library and information science (LIS). In *Critical theory for library and information science: Exploring the social from across the disciplines* (pp. vii–xxii). Libraries Unlimited.

Leckie, G. J., & Given, L. M. (2005). Understanding information-seeking: The public library context. *Advances in Librarianship*, *29*(1). https://doi.org/10.1016/S0065-2830(05)29001-3

Leckie, G. J., Pettigrew, K. E., & Sylvain, C. (1996). Modeling the information seeking of professionals: A general model derived from research on engineers, health care professionals and lawyers. *The Library Quarterly*, *66*, 161–193. https://www.jstor.org/stable/4309109

Lederer, K., Galtung, J., & Antal, D. (Eds.). (1980). *Human needs, a contribution to the current debate*. Oelgeschlagen, Gunn & Hain.

Lee, C. P., & Trace, C. B. (2009). The role of information in a community of hobbyist collectors. *Journal of the American Society for Information Science and Technology*, *60*(3), 621–637. https://doi.org/10.1002/asi.20996

Lee, H., & Pang, N. (2017). Information scent – Credibility and gaze interactions: An eye-tracking analysis in information behaviour. In *Proceedings of ISIC, the Information Behaviour Conference*, Zadar, Croatia, 20–23 September, 2016: Part 2, *22*(1). http://InformationR.net/ir/22-1/isic/isic1613.html

Lee, J., & Kang, J. H. (2018). Crying mothers mobilise for a collective action: Collaborative information behaviour in an online community. *Information Research*, *23*(2). http://InformationR.net/ir/23-2/paper792.html

Lee, J. H., & Downie, J. S. (2004). Survey of music information needs, uses, and seeking behaviours: Preliminary findings. In *ISMIR* (Vol. *2004*, p. 5).

Lee, J. Y., Paik, W., & Joo, S. (2012). Information resource selection of undergraduate students in academic search tasks. *Information Research*, *17*(1). http://InformationR.net/ir/17-1/paper511.html

Lee, L., Ocepek, M. G., & Makri, S. (2022). Information behavior patterns: A new theoretical perspective from an empirical study of naturalistic information acquisition. *Journal of the Association for Information Science and Technology*, *73*(4), 594–608. https://doi.org/10.1002/asi.24595

Lee, M., & Butler, B. S. (2018). How are information deserts created? A theory of local information landscapes. *Journal of the Association for Information Science and Technology*, *70*(2), 101–116. https://doi.org/10.1002/asi.24114

Lee, S. (2017). Implications of counter-attitudinal information exposure in further information-seeking and attitude change. *Information Research*, *22*(3). http://InformationR.net/ir/22-3/paper766.html

Lee, S. Y. (2018). Effects of relational characteristics of an answerer on perceived credibility of informational posts on social networking sites: The case of Facebook. *Information Research*, *23*(3). http://InformationR.net/ir/23-3/paper796.html

Leeder, C. (2019). How college students evaluate and share "fake news" stories. *Library & Information Science Research*, *41*(3). https://doi.org/10.1016/j.lisr.2019.100967

Leont'ev, A. N. (1978). *Activity, consciousness and personality*. Prentice-Hall.

Levitan, K. B. (1980). Applying a holistic framework to synthesize information science research. In B. Dervin & M. Voigt (Eds.), *Progress in communication sciences* (Vol. 2, pp. 241–273). Ablex.

Leydesdorff, L., & Milojevic, S. (2015). Scientometrics. In M. Lynch (Ed.), *International encyclopedia of social and behavioral sciences* (2nd ed., Vol. 21, pp. 322–327). Elsevier.

Li, X. (2021). Young people's information practices in library makerspaces. *Journal of the Association for Information Science and Technology*, *72*(6), 744–758. https://doi.org/10.1002/asi.24442

Liebnau, J., & Backhouse, J. (1990). *Understanding information*. Macmillan.

Liehr, P., & Smith, M. J. (1999). Middle range theory: Spinning research and practice to create knowledge for the new millennium. *Advances in Nursing Science*, *21*(4), 81–91. https://doi.org/10.1097/00012272-199906000-00011

Liehr, P., & Smith, M. J. (2017). Middle range theory. *Advances in Nursing Science*, *40*(1), 51–63.

Liew, C. L., & Ng, S. N. (2006). Beyond the notes: A qualitative study of the information-seeking behavior of ethnomusicologists. *The Journal of Academic Librarianship*, *32*(1), 60–68. https://doi.org/10.1016/j.acalib.2005.10.003

Li, Y., Li, Y., Pan, Y., & Han, H. (2019). Work-task types, stages, and information-seeking behavior of strategic planners. *Journal of Documentation*, *75*(1), 2–23. https://doi.org/10.1108/JD-01-2018-0015

Lilley, S. C. (2008). Information barriers and Māori secondary school students. *Information Research*, *13*(4). http://InformationR.net/ir/13-4/paper373.html

Lim, S. (2009). How and why do college students use Wikipedia? *Journal of the American Society for Information Science and Technology*, *60*(11), 2189–2202. https://doi.org/10.1002/asi.21142

Lim, S., & Kwon, N. (2010). Gender differences in information behavior concerning Wikipedia: An unorthodox information source? *Library & Information Science Research*, *32*(3), 212–220. https://doi.org/10.1016/j.lisr.2010.01.003

Limberg, L. (2017). Synthesizing or diversifying library and information science: Sketching past achievements, current happenings and future prospects, with an interest in including or excluding approaches. *Information Research*, *22*(1). http://InformationR.net/ir/22-1/colis/colis1600.html

Limberg, L., Sundin, O., & Talja, S. (2012). Three theoretical perspectives on information literacy. *Journal for Information Technology Studies as a Human Science*, *11*(2), 93–110.

Lin, N. (2001). *Social capital: A theory of social structure and action*. Cambridge University Press.

Lindau, S. T., Makelarski, J. A., Abramsohn, E., Beiser, D., Boyd, K., Huang, E., Paradise, K., & Tung, E. (2022). Sharing information about health-related resources: Observations from a community resource referral intervention trial in a predominantly African American/Black community. *Journal of the Association for Information Science and Technology*, *73*(3), 438–448. https://doi.org/10.1002/asi.24560

Lindberg, J., & Hedemark, A. (2019). Meaningful reading experiences among elderly: Some insights from a small-scale study of Swedish library outreach services. In *Proceedings of ISIC, The Information Behaviour Conference*, Krakow, Poland, 9–11 October: Part 2. *Information Research, 24*(1). http://InformationR.net/ir/24-1/isic2018/isic1836.html

Line, M. B. (1974). Draft definitions: Information and library needs, wants, demands and uses. *ASLIB Proceedings*, *27*(7), 87–97.

Lin, N., & Garvey, W. D. (1972). Information needs and uses. In C. Cuadra & A. W. Luke (Eds.), *Annual review of information science and technology* (Vol. 7, pp. 5–37). American Society for Information Science.

Lingel, J. (2015). Information practices of urban newcomers: An analysis of habits and wandering. *Journal of the Association for Information Science & Technology*, *66*(6), 1239–1251. http://doi.org/10.1002/asi.23255

Lipetz, B.-A. (1970). Information needs and uses. In C. A. Cuadra & A. W. Luke (Eds.), *Annual review of information science and technology* (Vol. 5, pp. 3–32). Encyclopaedia Brittanica.

Littlejohn, S. W. (1983). *Theories of human communication*. Wadsworth.

Little, R., Williams, C., & Yost, J. (2011). Airline travel : A history of information-seeking behavior by leisure and business passengers. In W. Aspray & B. Hayes (Eds.), *Everyday information: The evolution of information seeking in America* (pp. 121–156). MIT Press.

Livingstone, S. (2006). The influence of Personal Influence on the study of audiences. *The Annals of the American Academy of Political and Social Science*, *608*(1), 233–250. https://doi.org/10.1177/0002716206292325

Li, P., Yang, G., & Wang, C. (2019). Visual topical analysis of library and information science. *Scientometrics*, *121*(3), 1753–1791. https://doi.org/10.1007/s11192-019-03239-0

Lloyd, A. (2006). Information literacy landscapes: An emerging picture. *Journal of Documentation*, *62*(5), 570–583. https://doi.org/10.1108/00220410610688723

Lloyd, A. (2007a). Learning to put out the red stuff: Becoming information literate through discursive practice. *The Library Quarterly*, *77*(2), 181–198. https://doi.org/10.1086/517844

Lloyd, A. (2007b). Recasting information literacy as socio-cultural practice: Implications for library and information science researchers. *Information Research*, *12*(4). http://informationr.net/ir/12-4/colis/colis34.html

Lloyd, A. (2009). Informing practice: Information experiences of ambulance officers in training and on-road practice. *Journal of Documentation*, *65*(3), 396–419. http://doi.org/10.1108/00220410910952401

Lloyd, A. (2010). Corporeality and practice theory: Exploring emerging research agendas for information literacy. *Information Research*, *15*(3). http://InformationR.net/ir/15-3/colis7/colis704.html

Lloyd, A. (2014). Following the red thread of information in information literacy research: Recovering local knowledge through interview to the double. *Library & Information Science Research*, *36*(2), 99–105. https://doi.org/10.1016/j.lisr.2013.10.006

Lloyd, A. (2015). Stranger in a strange land: Enabling information resilience in the resettlement landscape. *Journal of Documentation*, *71*(5), 1029–1042. https://doi.org/10.1108/JD-04-2014-0065

Lloyd, A. (2017). Researching fractured (information) landscapes: Implications for library and information science researchers undertaking research with refugees and forced migration studies. *Journal of Documentation*, *73*(1), 35–47. https://doi.org/10.1108/JD-03-2016-0032

Lloyd, A. (2020). Shaping the contours of fractured landscapes: Extending the layering of an information perspective on refugee resettlement. *Information Processing & Management*, *57*(3), 102062. https://doi.org/10.1016/j.ipm.2019.102062

Lloyd, A. (2021). *The qualitative landscape of information literacy research: Perspectives, methods and techniques*. Facet Publishing.

Lloyd, A., & Hicks, A. (2021). Contextualising risk: The unfolding information work and practices of people during the COVID-19 pandemic. *Journal of Documentation*, *77*(5), 1052–1072. https://doi.org/10.1108/JD-11-2020-0203

Lloyd, A., Kennan, M. A., Thompson, K. M., & Qayyum, A. (2013). Connecting with new information landscapes: Information literacy practices of refugees. *Journal of Documentation*, *69*(1), 121–144. http://doi.org/10.1108/00220411311295351

Lloyd, A., Lipu, S., & Kennan, M. A. (2010). On becoming citizens: Examining social inclusion from an information perspective. *Australian Academic and Research Libraries*, *41*(1), 42–53. https://doi.org/10.1080/00048623.2016.1256806

Lloyd, A., & Olsson, M. (2019). Untangling the knot: The information practices of enthusiast car restorers. *Journal of the Association for Information Science and Technology*, *70*(12), 1311–1323. https://doi.org/10.1002/asi.24284

Lloyd, A., Pilerot, O., & Hultgren, F. (2017). The remaking of fractured landscapes: Supporting refugees in transition (SpiRiT). *Information Research*, *22*(3). http://informationr.net/ir/22-3/paper764.html

Lloyd, A., & Williamson, K. (2008). Towards an understanding of information literacy in context. *Journal of Librarianship and Information Science*, *40*(1), 3–12. https://doi.org/10.1177/0961000607086616

Longo, D. R. (2005). Understanding health information, communication, and information seeking of patients and consumers: A comprehensive and integrated model. *Health Expectations*, *8*, 189–194. https://doi.org/10.1111%2Fj.1369-7625.2005.00339.x

Loos, E., Ivan, L., & Leu, D. (2018). Save the Pacific Northwest tree octopus: A hoax revisited. Or: How vulnerable are school children to fake news? *Information and Learning Sciences*, *119*(9/10), 514–528. https://doi.org/10.1108/ILS-04-2018-0031

Lopatovska, I., & Sessions, D. (2016). Understanding academic reading in the context of information-seeking. *Library Review*, *65*(8/9), 502–518. https://doi.org/10.1108/LR-03-2016-0026

Lopatovska, I., & Smiley, B. (2014). Proposed model of information behaviour in crisis: The case of Hurricane Sandy. *Information Research*, *19*(1). http://informationr.net/ir/19-1/paper610.html

López, G. R. (2020). Information seeking patterns of psychiatrists during clinical practice. *Health Information and Libraries Journal*, *37*(1), 78–82. https://doi.org/10.1111/hir.12293

Lorigo, L., Pan, B., Hembrooke, H., Joachims, T., Granka, L., & Granka, G. (2006). The influence of task and gender on search and evaluation behavior using Google. *Information Processing & Management*, *42*(4), 1123–1131. https://doi.org/10.1016/j.ipm.2005.10.001

Loudon, K., Buchanan, S., & Ruthven, I. (2016). The everyday life information seeking behaviours of first-time mothers. *Journal of Documentation*, *72*(1), 24–46. https://doi.org/10.1108/JD-06-2014-0080

Lu, Y. (2007). The human in human information acquisition: Understanding gatekeeping and proposing new directions in scholarship. *Library & Information Science Research*, *29*(1), 103–123. https://doi.org/10.1016/j.lisr.2006.10.007

Lu, Y.-L. (2010). Children's information seeking in coping with daily-life problems: An investigation of fifth- and sixth-grade students. *Library & Information Science Research*, *32*(1), 77–88. https://doi.org/10.1016/j.lisr.2009.09.004

Lueg, C. P. (2008). Beyond FAQs: From information sharing to knowledge generation in online travel communities. In M.-L. Houtari & E. Davenport (Eds.), (pp. 105–120). Presented at *From information provision to knowledge production*, Faculty of Humanities, University of Oulu.

Lueg, C. P. (2015). The missing link: Information behavior research and its estranged relationship with embodiment. *Journal of the Association for Information Science and Technology*, *66*(12), 2704–2707. https://doi.org/10.1002/asi.23441

Luhmann, N. (1990). *Essays on self-reference*. Columbia University Press.

Lund, B. (2021). The structure of information behavior dissertations 2009–2018: Theories, methods, populations, disciplines. *Journal of Librarianship and Information Science*, *53*(2), 225–232. https://doi.org/10.1177/0961000620935499

Lund, B. D. (2019). The citation impact of information behavior theories in scholarly literature. *Library & Information Science Research*, *41*(4). https://doi.org/10.1016/j.lisr.2019.100981

Lundh, A. (2010). Studying information needs as question-negotiations in an educational context: A methodological comment. *Information Research, 15*(4). http://InformationR.net/ir/15-4/colis722.html

Lundh, A., & Alexandersson, M. (2012). Collecting and compiling: The activity of seeking pictures in primary school. *Journal of Documentation, 68*(2), 238–253. https://doi.org/10.1108/00220411211209212

Lunt, P., & Livingstone, S. (1996). Rethinking the focus group in media and communications research. *Journal of Communication, 46*(2), 79–98. https://doi.org/10.1111/j.1460-2466.1996.tb01475.x

Lu, L., & Yuan, Y. (2011). Shall I Google it or ask the competent villain down the hall? The moderating role of information need in information source selection. *Journal of the American Society for Information Science and Technology, 62*(1), 133–145. https://doi.org/10.1002/asi.21449

Ma, Y. (2021). Understanding information: Adding a non-individualistic lens. *Journal of the Association of Information Science and Technology, 72*, 1295–1305. https://doi.org/10.1002/asi.24441

Mackenzie, M. L. (2002). Information gathering: The information behaviors of line-managers within a business environment. In *Proceedings of the 65th Annual Meeting of the American Society for Information Science and Technology*, Philadelphia, PA, November 18–21, 2002 (pp. 164–170).

Mackenzie, M. L. (2003a). An exploratory study investigating the information behaviour of line managers within a business environment. *New Review of Information Behaviour Research, 4*(1), 63–78.

Mackenzie, M. L. (2003b). Information gathering: Revealed within the social network of line-managers. In R. Todd (Ed.), *Proceedings of the 66th annual meeting of the American society for information science and technology, Long beach, CA, October 19–22, 2003* (Vol. 40, pp. 85–94). Information Today.

Mackenzie, M. L. (2004). The cultural influences of information flow at work: Manager information behavior documented. In L. Schamber & C. Barry (Eds.), *Proceedings of the 67th annual meeting of the American society for information science and technology, providence, RI, November 12–17, 2004* (Vol. 41, pp. 184–190). Information Today.

Mackenzie, M. L. (2005). Managers look to the social network to seek information. *Information Research, 10*(2). http://InformationR.net/ir/10-2/paper216.html

Madden, M., Lenhart, A., Cortesi, S., Gasser, U., Duggan, M., Smith, A., & Beaton, M. (2013). *Teens, social media, and privacy*. Pew Research Center. https://www.pewresearch.org/internet/2013/05/21/teens-social-media-and-privacy/

Mahapatra, R. K., & Panda, K. C. (2001). State of information seeking and searching behaviour of working journalists in Orissa: A study. *Annals of Library and Information Studies, 48*(4), 133–138.

Mai, J.-E. (2013). The quality and qualities of information. *Journal of the American Society for Information Science and Technology, 64*(4), 675–688. https://doi.org/10.1002/asi.22783

Makri, S., & Buckley, L. (2020). Down the rabbit hole: Investigating disruption of the information encountering process. *Journal of the Association for Information Science and Technology, 71*(2), 127–142. https://doi.org/10.1002/asi.24233

Makri, S., Hsueh, T., & Jones, S. (2019). Ideation as an intellectual information acquisition and use context: Investigating game designers' information-based ideation behavior. *Journal of the Association for Information Science & Technology, 70*(8), 775–787. https://doi.org/10.1002/asi.24169

Makri, S., & Warwick, C. (2010). Information for inspiration: Understanding architects' information seeking and use behaviors to inform design. *Journal of the American Society for Information Science and Technology, 61*(9), 1745–1770. http://doi.org/10.1002/asi.21338

Ma, T.-J., Lee, G.-G., Liu, J., Lan, R., & Weng, J.-H. (2022). Bibliographic coupling: A main path analysis from 1963 to 2020. *Information Research, 27*(1). http://InformationR.net/ir/27-1/paper918.html

Mandel, L. H. (2010). Geographic information systems: Tools for displaying in-library use data. *Information Technology and Libraries, 29*(1), 47–52. https://doi.org/10.6017/ital.v29i1.3158

Manicas, P. T. (1998). *A history and philosophy of the social sciences*. Basil Blackwell.

Mansour, A. (2020). Shared information practices on Facebook: The formation and development of a sustainable online community. *Journal of Documentation*, *76*(3), 625–646. https://doi.org/10.1108/JD-10-2018-0160

Mansour, E., & Ghuloum, H. (2017). The information-seeking behaviour of Kuwaiti judges. *Journal of Librarianship and Information Science*, *49*(4), 468–485. https://doi.org/10.1177/0961000616654749

Mansourian, Y. (2020). How passionate people seek and share various forms of information in their serious leisure. *Journal of the Australian Library and Information Association*, *69*(1), 17–30. https://doi.org/10.1080/24750158.2019.1686569

Mansourian, Y. (2021). Information activities in serious leisure as a catalyst for self-actualisation and social engagement. *Journal of Documentation*, *77*(4), 887–905. https://doi.org/10.1108/JD-08-2020-0134

Marcella, R., & Baxter, G. (2000). Information need, information seeking behaviour and participation, with special reference to needs related to citizenship: Results of a national survey. *Journal of Documentation*, *56*, 136–160. https://doi.org/10.1108/EUM0000000007112

Marcella, R., & Baxter, G. (2001). A random walk around Britain: A critical assessment of the random walk sample as a method of collecting data on the public's citizenship information needs. *New Review of Information Behaviour Research*, *2*, 87–103.

Marcella, R., & Baxter, G. (2005). Information interchange. In K. E. Fisher, S. Erdelez, & E. F. McKechnie (Eds.), *Theories of information behavior* (pp. 204–209). Information Today, Inc.

Marcella, R., Pirie, T., & Rowlands, H. (2013). The information seeking behaviour of oil and gas industry workers in the context of health, safety and emergency response: A discussion of the value of models of information behaviour. *Information Research*, *18*(3). http://informationr.net/ir/18-3/paper583.html

Marchionini, G. (1995). *Information seeking in electronic environments*. Cambridge University Press.

Margree, P., Macfarlane, A., Price, L., & Robinson, L. (2014). Information behaviour of music record collectors. *Information Research*, *19*(4). http://informationr.net/ir/19-4/paper652.html

Markham, A. (2012). Fabrication as ethical practice: Qualitative inquiry in ambiguous internet contexts. *Information, Communication & Society*, *5*(3), 334–353. https://doi.org/10.1080/1369118X.2011.641993

Martinović, I., & Stričević, I. (2016). Information needs and behaviour of parents of children with autism spectrum disorders: Parents' reports on their experiences and perceptions. In *Proceedings of ISIC, the Information Behaviour Conference*, Zadar, Croatia, 20–23 September, 2016: Part 1. Information Research, 21(4). http://InformationR.net/ir/21-4/isic/isic1609.html

Martin, K., & Quan-Haase, A. (2017). "A process of controlled serendipity": An exploratory study of historians' and digital historians' experiences of serendipity in digital environments. *Proceedings of the Association for Information Science and Technology*, *54*(1), 289–297. https://doi.org/10.1002/pra2.2017.14505401032

Marton, C. (2011). *Understanding how women seek health information on the web*. PhD thesis, University of Toronto. http://hdl.handle.net/1807/29808

Martyn, J. (1974). Information needs and uses. In M. Williams (Ed.), *Annual review of information science and technology* (Vol. 9, pp. 3–23). American Society for Information Science.

Martzoukou, K. (2005). A review of web information seeking research: Considerations of method and foci of interest. *Information Research*, *10*(2). http://InformationR.net/ir/10-2/paper215.html

Martzoukou, K., & Burnett, S. (2018). Exploring the everyday life information needs and the socio-cultural adaption barriers of Syrian refugee in Scotland. *Journal of Documentation*, *74*(5), 1104–1132. https://doi.org/10.1108/JD-10-2017-0142

Maslow, A. H. (1963). The need to know and the fear of knowing. *The Journal of General Psychology*, *68*, 111–125.

Mason, D., & Lamain, C. (2007). *Nau mai haere mai ki Aotearoa: Information seeking behaviour of New Zealand immigrants*. The Centre for Applied Cross-cultural Research, Victoria University of Wellington.

Mason, H., & Robinson, L. (2011). The information-related behaviour of emerging artists and designers: Inspiration and guidance for new practitioners. *Journal of Documentation*, *67*(1), 159–180. http://doi.org/10.1108/00220411111105498

Massey, S., Druin, A., & Weeks, A. (2007). Emotion, response, and recommendation: The role of affect in children's book reviews in a digital library. In D. Nahl & D. Bilal (Eds.), *Information and emotion: The emergent affective paradigm in information behavior research and theory* (pp. 135–160). Information Today.

Massey, S., Weeks, A., & Druin, A. (2005). Initial findings from a three-year international case study exploring children's responses to literature in a digital library. *Library Trends*, *54*(3), 245–265. https://doi.org/10.1353/lib.2006.0018

Ma, J., & Stahl, L. (2017). A multimodal critical discourse analysis of anti-vaccination information on Facebook. *Library & Information Science Research*, *39*(4), 303–310. https://doi.org/10.1016/j.lisr.2017.11.005

Matusiak, K. K., Heinbach, C., Harper, A., & Bovee, M. (2019). Visual literacy in practice: Use of images in students' academic work. *College & Research Libraries*, *80*(1), 123. https://doi.org/10.5860/crl.80.1.123

Maungwa, T., & Fourie, I. (2018). Exploring and understanding the causes of competitive intelligence failures: An information behaviour lens. *Information Research*, *23*(4). http://www.informationr.net/ir/23-4/isic2018/isic1813.html

Mawby, J., Foster, A., & Ellis, D. (2015). Everyday life information seeking behaviour in relation to the environment. *Library Review*, *64*(6/7), 468–479. http://doi.org/10.1108/LR-10-2014-0120

Max-Neef, M. (1992). *From the outside looking in: Experiences in barefoot economics*. Dag Hammarskjöld Foundation.

May, F., & Black, F. (2010). The life of the space: Evidence from Nova Scotia public libraries. *Evidence Based Library and Information Practice*, *5*(2), 5–34. https://doi.org/10.18438/B8MS6J

Ma, D., Zuo, M., & Liu, L. (2021). The information needs of Chinese family members of cancer patients in the online health community: What and why? *Information Processing & Management*, *58*(3), 102517. https://doi.org/10.1016/j.ipm.2021.102517

McCaughan, E., & McKenna, H. (2007). Never-ending making sense: Towards a substantive theory of the information-seeking behaviour of newly diagnosed cancer patients. *Journal of Clinical Nursing*, *16*, 2096–2104. https://doi.org/10.1111/j.1365-2702.2006.01817.x

McKay, D., Chang, S., Smith, W., & Buchanan, G. (2019). The things we talk about when we talk about browsing: An empirical typology of library browsing behavior. *Journal of the Association for Information Science and Technology*, *70*(12), 1383–1394. https://doi.org/10.1002/asi.24200

McKechnie, E. F. (2000). Ethnographic observation of preschool children. *Library & Information Science Research*, *22*(1), 61–76. https://doi.org/10.1016/S0740-8188(99)00040-7

McKechnie, L. (2006). Observations of babies and toddlers in library settings. *Library Trends*, *55*(1), 190–201.

McKechnie, L., Baker, L., Greenwood, M., & Julien, H. (2002). Research method trends in human information behaviour literature. *New Review of Information Behaviour Research*, *3*, 113–126.

McKenzie, P. J. (2002). Connecting with information sources: How accounts of information seeking take discursive action. *New Review of Information Behaviour Research*, *3*, 161–174.

McKenzie, P. J. (2003a). Justifying cognitive authority decisions: Discursive strategies of information seekers. *The Library Quarterly*, *73*(3), 261–288. https://www.jstor.org/stable/4309663

McKenzie, P. J. (2003b). A model of information practices in accounts of everyday-life information seeking. *Journal of Documentation*, *59*, 19–40. https://doi.org/10.1108/00220410310457993

McKenzie, P. J. (2004). Positioning theory and the negotiation of information needs in a clinical midwifery setting. *Journal of the American Society for Information Science and Technology*, *55*(8), 685–694. https://doi.org/10.1002/asi.20002

McKenzie, P. J. (2005). Interpretive repertoires. In K. E. Fisher, S. Erdelez, & E. F. McKechnie (Eds.), *Theories of information behavior* (pp. 221–224). Information Today, Inc.

McKenzie, P. J. (2006). The seeking of baby-feeding information by Canadian women pregnant with twins. *Midwifery*, *22*(3), 218–227. https://doi.org/10.1016/j.midw.2005.03.006

McKenzie, P. J. (2009). Informing choice: The organization of institutional interaction in clinical midwifery care. *Library & Information Science Research*, *31*(3), 163–173. https://doi.org/10.1016/j.lisr.2009.03.006

McKenzie, P. J. (2010). Informing relationships: Small talk, informing and relationship building in midwife-woman interaction. *Information Research, 15*(1). http://InformationR.net/ir/15-1/paper423.html

McKenzie, P. J., & Dalmer, N. K. (2020). "This is really interesting. I never even though about this." Methodological strategies for studying invisible information work. *Nordic Journal of Library and Information Studies, 1*(2), 1–17. https://doi.org/10.7146/njlis.v1i2.120437

McKnight, M. (2006). The information seeking of on-duty critical care nurses: Evidence from participant observation and in-context interviews RMP. *Journal of the Medical Library Association, 94*(2), 145–151.

McKnight, M. (2007). A grounded theory model of on-duty critical care nurses' information behavior - the patient-chart cycle of informative interactions. *Journal of Documentation, 63*(1), 57–73. http://doi.org/10.1108/00220410710723885

Meho, L. I., & Tibbo, H. R. (2003). Modeling the information-seeking behavior of social scientists: Ellis's study revisited. *Journal of the American Society for Information Science and Technology, 54*(6), 570–587. https://doi.org/10.1002/asi.10244

Mehra, B. (2007). Affective factors in information seeking during the cross-cultural learning process of international doctoral students in library and information science education. In D. Nahl & D. Bilal (Eds.), *Information and emotion: The emergent affective paradigm in information behavior research and theory* (pp. 279–301). Information Today.

Mellon, C. (1986). Library anxiety: A grounded theory and its development. *College & Research Libraries, 47*, 160–165.

Menzel, H. (1960). *Review of studies in the flow of information among scientists*. Columbia University Bureau of Applied Social Research.

Menzel, H. (1964). The information needs of current scientific research. *The Library Quarterly, 34*, 4–19.

Menzel, H. (1966a). Information needs and uses in science and technology. In C. A. Cuadra & A. W. Luke (Eds.), *Annual review of information science and technology* (Vol. 1, pp. 41–69). Encyclopaedia Britannica.

Menzel, H. (1966b). Can science information needs be ascertained empirically? In L. Thayer (Ed.), *Communications: Concepts and perspectives* (pp. 279–295). Spartan Books.

Mershon, C., & Shvetova, O. (2019). *Formal modeling in social science*. University of Michigan Press.

Merton, R. K. (1968). *Social theory and social structure* (2nd ed.). Free Press.

Merton, R. K. (1972). Insiders and outsiders: A chapter in the sociology of knowledge. *American Journal of Sociology, 78*, 9–47.

Meyer, H. W. J. (2003). Information use in rural development. *New Review of Information Behaviour Research, 4*(1), 109–125.

Meyer, H. W. J. (2016). Untangling the building blocks: A generic model to explain information behaviour to novice researchers. *Information Research, 21*(4). http://InformationR.net/ir/21-4/isic/isic1602.html

Meyers, E. M. (2007). From activity to learning: Using cultural historical activity theory to model school library programmes and practices. *Information Research, 12*(3). http://InformationR.net/ir/12-3/paper313.html

Meyers, E. M., Fisher, K. E., & Marcoux, E. (2009). Making sense of an information world: The everyday-life information behavior of preteens. *The Library Quarterly, 79*(3), 301–341. https://doi.org/10.1086/599125

Middleberg, D. (2001). The seventh annual Middleberg/Ross survey of media in the wired world. www.writenews.com/2001/041301_journalists_internet.htm

Mikkonen, A., & Vakkari, P. (2016). Readers' interest criteria in fiction book search in library catalogs. *Journal of Documentation, 72*(4), 696–715. https://doi.org/10.1108/JDOC-11-2015-0142

Miller, G. A. (1983). Informavores. In F. Machlup & U. Mansfield (Eds.), *The study of information: Interdisciplinary messages* (pp. 111–113). John Wiley.

Miller, H. (2018). Veblen online: Information and the risk of commandeering the conspicuous self. *Information Research, 23*(2). http://informationr.net/ir/23-3/paper797.html

Miranda, S. V., & Tarapanoff, K. (2008). Information needs and information competencies: A case study of the off-site supervision of financial institutions in Brazil. *Information Research: An International Electronic Journal, 13*(2). http://InformationR.net/ir/13-2/paper344.html

Mishra, J., Allen, D., & Pearman, A. (2015). Information seeking, use, and decision making. *Journal of the Association for Information Science and Technology, 66*(4), 662–673. https://doi.org/10.1002/asi.23204

Mohammed, F., & Norman, A. (2017). Understanding information sharing behaviour of millennials in large multinational organizations: Research in progress. In *Proceedings of ISIC, the Information Behaviour Conference*, Zadar, Croatia, 20–23 September, 2016: Part 2. *Information Research, 22*(1). http://informationr.net/ir/22-1/isic/isics1605.html

Mokros, H., Mullins, L., & Saracevic, T. (1995). Practice and personhood in professional interaction: Social identities and information needs. *Library & Information Science Research, 17*, 237–257. https://doi.org/10.1016/0740-8188(95)90047-0

Molto, M. B. (2010). Genealogical literature and its users. In *Encyclopedia of library and information science* (pp. 1–46). Taylor & Francis.

Montesi, M. (2021). Human information behavior during the Covid-19 health crisis. *Library & Information Science Research*. https://doi.org/10.1016/j.lisr.2021.101122

Moore, M., & Singley, E. (2019). Understanding the information behaviors of doctoral students: An exploratory study. *Portal: Libraries and the Academy, 19*(2), 279–293. https://doi.org/10.1353/pla.2019.0016

Morey, O. (2007). Health information ties: Preliminary findings on the health information seeking behaviour of an African-American community. *Information Research, 12*(2). http://informationr.net/ir/12-2/paper297.html

Moring, C. (2017). Newcomer information seeking: The role of information seeking in newcomer socialization and learning in the workplace. *Information Research, 22*(1), 1–21. http://www.informationr.net/ir/22-1/isic/isic1616.html

Moring, C., & Lloyd, A. (2013). Analytical implications of using practice theory in workplace information literacy research. *Information Research, 18*(3). http://www.informationr.net/ir/18-3/colis/paperC35.html#.Vc0V_lOqqko

Morrison, K. (2012). Guided sampling using mobile electronic diaries. *International Journal of Mobile Human Computer Interaction, 4*(1), 1–24. http://doi.org/10.4018/jmhci.2012010101

Mowbray, J., & Hall, H. (2020). Networking as an information behaviour during job search: A study of active jobseekers in the Scottish youth labour market. *Journal of Documentation, 76*(2), 424–439. https://doi.org/10.1108/JD-05-2019-0086

Mowbray, J., Hall, H., Raeside, R., & Robertson, P. (2017). The role of networking and social media tools during job search: An information behaviour perspective. *Information Research, 22*(1). http://InformationR.net/ir/22-1/colis/colis1615.html

Multas, A. M., & Hirvonen, N. (2019). Employing nexus analysis in investigating information literacy. In *Proceedings of the Tenth International Conference on Conceptions of Library and Information Science*, Ljubljana, Slovenia, June 16–19, 2019. *Information Research, 24*(4). http://InformationR.net/ir/24-4/colis/colis1944.html

Munyua, H. M., & Stilwell, C. (2013). Three ways of knowing: Agricultural knowledge systems of small-scale farmers in Africa with reference to Kenya. *Library & Information Science Research, 35*(4), 326–337. http://doi.org/10.1016/j.lisr.2013.04.005

Murphy, J. (2003). Information-seeking habits of environmental scientists: A study of interdisciplinary scientists at the environmental protection agency in research Triangle Park, North Carolina. *Issues in Science and Technology Librarianship*. http://www.istl.org/03-summer/refereed.html

Murray, H. A. (1938). *Explorations in personality*. Oxford University Press.

Murthy, D., & Longwell, S. A. (2013). Twitter and disasters: The uses of twitter during the 2010 Pakistan floods. *Information, Communication & Society, 16*(6), 837–855. https://doi.org/10.1080/1369118X.2012.696123

Naeem, S. B., Bhatti, R., & Khan, A. M. (2020). An exploration of how fake news is taking over social media and putting public health at risk. *Health Information and Libraries Journal, 38*(2), 143–149. https://doi.org/10.1111/hir.12320

Nahl, D. (2001). Conceptual framework for defining information behavior. *Studies in Media and Information Literacy Education*, *1*(2), 1–15.

Nahl, D. (2005). Affective load. In K. E. Fisher, S. Erdelez, & E. F. McKechnie (Eds.), *Theories of information behavior* (pp. 39–44). Information Today, Inc.

Nahl, D. (2007a). The centrality of the affective in information behavior. In *Information and emotion: The emergent affective paradigm in information behavior research and theory* (pp. 3–37). Information Today.

Nahl, D. (2007b). Social-biological information technology: An integrated conceptual framework. *Journal of the American Society for Information Science and Technology*, *58*(13), 2021–2046. https://doi.org/10.1002/asi.20690

Nahl, D., & Bilal, D. (2007). Information and emotion: The emergent affective paradigm in information behavior research and theory. *Information Today*.

Nardi, B. (Ed.). (1996). *Context and consciousness: Activity theory and human-computer interaction*. MIT Press.

Naslund, J. A., Aschbrenner, K. A., Marsch, L. A., & Bartels, S. J. (2016). The future of mental health care: Peer-to-peer support and social media. *Epidemiology and Psychiatric Sciences*, *25*(2), 113–122. https://doi.org/10.1017/S2045796015001067

Naughtin, C., Hajkowicz, S., Schleiger, E., Bratanova, A., Cameron, A., Zamin, T., & Dutta, A. (2022). *Our future world: Global megatrends impacting the way we live over coming decades*. CSIRO. https://www.csiro.au/en/research/technology-space/data/Our-Future-World

Naveed, M. A., Batool, S. H., & Anwar, M. A. (2021). Resident university students' everyday life information seeking behaviour in Pakistan. *Information Research*, *26*(2). http://InformationR.net/ir/26-2/paper901.html

Nel, M. A. (2020). Information behaviour and information practices of academic librarians: A scoping review to guide studies on their learning in practice. In *Proceedings of ISIC, the Information Behaviour Conference*, Pretoria, South Africa, 28 September 2020 – 1 October, 2020. *Information Research, 25*(4). http://InformationR.net/ir/25-4/isic2020/isic2020.html

Nelissen, S., Van den Bulck, J., & Beullens, K. (2017). A typology of cancer information seeking, scanning and avoiding: Results from an exploratory cluster analysis. *Information Research*, *22*(2). http://InformationR.net/ir/22-2/paper747.html

Nicholas, D., & Williams, P. (1999). The changing information environment: The impact of the Internet on information seeking behavior in the media. In T. D. Wilson & D. K. Allen (Eds.), *Information behaviour: Proceedings of the second international conference on research in information needs, seeking and use in different contexts, 13/15 August 1998, Sheffield, UK* (pp. 451–462). Taylor Graham.

Nicholas, D., Williams, P., Cole, P., & Martin, H. (2000). The impact of the internet on information seeking in the Media1. *ASLIB Proceedings*, *52*(3), 98–114. https://doi.org/10.1108/EUM0000000007004

Nicholas, D., Williams, P., Smith, A., & Longbottom, P. (2005). The information needs of perioperative staff: A preparatory study for a proposed specialist library for theatres (NeLH). *Health Information and Libraries Journal*, *22*(1), 35–43. https://doi.org/10.1111/j.1471-1842.2005.00535.x

Niedwiedzka, B. (2003). A proposed general model of information behaviour. *Information Research*, *9*(1). http://informationr.net/ir/9-1/paper164.html

Nikou, S., Molinari, A., & Widén, G. (2020). The interplay between literacy and digital technology: A fuzzy-set qualitative comparative analysis approach. *Proceedings of ISIC, the Information Behaviour Conference*, Pretoria, South Africa, 28 September – 1 October, 2020, *Information Research, 25*(4). http://InformationR.net/ir/25-4/isic2020/isic2016.html

Nilsen, J. (2020). Distributed amplification: The plandemic documentary. The Media Manipulation Case Book, July 7, 2021. https://mediamanipulation.org/case-studies/distributed-amplification-plandemic-documentary

Niu, X., & Hemminger, B. M. (2012). A study of factors that affect the information-seeking behavior of academic scientists. *Journal of the American Society for Information Science and Technology*, *63*(2), 336–353. http://doi.org/10.1002/asi.21669

Niu, X., Hemminger, B. M., Lown, C., Adams, S., Brown, C., Level, A., McLure, M., Powers, A., Tennant, M., & Cataldo, T. (2010). National study of information seeking behavior of academic researchers in the United States. *Journal of the American Society for Information Science and Technology*, *61*(5), 869–890. https://doi.org/10.1002/asi.21307

Nordsteien, A. (2017). Handling inconsistencies between information modalities - workplace learning of newly qualified nurses. *Information Research*, *22*(1). CoLIS paper 1652. http://InformationR.net/ir/22-1/colis/colis1652.html

North American Aviation. (1966). *Final report DOD user-needs study, Phase II; Flow of scientific and technical information within the defense industry* (*Vols. I–III*). North American Aviation, Autonetics Division.

Nowé Hedvall, K., Gärdén, C., Ahlryd, S., Michnik, K., Carlén, U., & Byström, K. (2017). Social media in serious leisure: Themes of horse rider safety. *Information Research*, *22*(4). http://InformationR.net/ir/22-4/paper772.html

Nowé, K., Macevičiūtė, E., & Wilson, T. D. (2008). Tensions and contradictions in the information behaviour of Board members of a voluntary organization. *Information Research*, *13*(4). http://InformationR.net/ir/13-4/paper363.html

O'Brien, H., Freund, L., & Westman, S. (2014). What motivates the online news browser? News item selection in a social information seeking scenario. *Information Research*, *19*(3). http://informationr.net/ir/19-3/paper634.html

O'Brien, H., Greyson, D., Chabot, C., & Shoveller, J. (2018). Young parents' personal and social information contexts for child feeding practices: An ethnographic study in British Columbia, Canada. *Journal of Documentation*, *74*(3), 608–623. https://doi.org/10.1108/JD-09-2017-0127

Ocepek, M. G. (2018a). Bringing out the everyday in everyday information behavior. *Journal of Documentation*, *74*(2), 398–411. https://doi.org/10.1108/JD-10-2016-0119

Ocepek, M. G. (2018b). Sensible shopping: A sensory exploration of the information environment of the grocery store. *Library Trends*, *66*(3), 371–394. https://doi.org/10.1353/lib.2018.0008

Ocepek, M. G. (2021). This *Old House, Fixer Upper*, and *Better Homes and Gardens*: The housing crisis and media sources. In M. G. Ocepek & W. Aspray (Eds.), *Deciding where to live: Information studies on where to live in America* (pp. 125–150). Rowman & Littlefield.

Ocepek, M. G., & Aspray, W. (Eds.). (2021). *Deciding where to live: Information studies on where to live in America*. Rowman & Littlefield.

O'Connor, J. (1968). Some questions concerning "information need". *American Documentation*, *19*(2), 200–203.

O'Connor, L. G. (2011). Duct tape and WD-40: The information worlds of female investors. *Library & Information Science Research*, *33*, 228–235. https://doi.org/10.1016/j.lisr.2010.09.009

O'Connor, L. G. (2013). Investors' information sharing and use in virtual communities. *Journal of the American Society for Information Science and Technology*, *64*(1), 36–47. http://doi.org/10.1002/asi.22791

O'Connor, L. G., & Dillingham, L. L. (2014). Personal experience as social capital in online investor forums. *Library & Information Science Research*, *36*(1), 27–35. http://doi.org/10.1016/j.lisr.2013.10.001

Oduntan, O., & Ruthven, I. (2019). The information needs matrix: A navigational guide for refugee integration. *Information Processing & Management*, *56*(3), 791–808. https://doi.org/10.1016/j.ipm.2018.12.001

Oh, T. T., & Pham, M. T. (2022). A liberating-engagement theory of consumer fun. *Journal of Consumer Research*, *49*(1), 46–73. https://doi.org/10.1093/jcr/ucab051

Oh, S., & Worrall, A. (2013). Health answer quality evaluation by librarians, nurses, and users in social Q&A. *Library & Information Science Research*, *35*(4), 288–298. https://doi.org/10.1016/j.lisr.2013.04.007

Oh, S., Zhang, Y., & Park, M. S. (2016). Cancer information seeking in social question and answer services: Identifying health-related topics in cancer questions on Yahoo! Answers. *Information Research*, *21*(3). http://informationr.net/ir/21-3/paper718.html#.Y3AV5exBwUo

Oliveira, R. A. de, & Baracho, R. M. A. (2018). The development of tourism indicators through the use of social media data: The case of Minas Gerais. *Brazil Information Research*, *23*(4). http://informationr.net/ir/23-4/paper805.html

Olmeda-Gómez, C., Perianes-Rodríguez, A., Ovalle-Perandones, M. A., & Moya-Anegón, F. (2008). Comparative analysis of university-government-enterprise co-authorship networks in three scientific domains in the region of Madrid, 1995-2003. *Information Research*, *13*(3). http://InformationR.net/ir/13-3/paper352.html

Olsson, M. (2005). Beyond "needy" individuals: Conceptualizing information behavior. In A. Grove (Ed.), *ASIS&T '05: Proceedings of the annual meeting of the American society for information science and technology* (Vol. 42, pp. 43–55). American Society for Information Science and Technology.

Olsson, M. (2016). Making sense of the past: The embodied information practices of field archaeologists. *Journal of Information Science*, *42*(3), 410–419. https://doi.org/10.1177/0165551515621839

Olsson, M., & Lloyd, A. (2017). Being in place: Embodied information practices. *Information Research*, *22*(1). http://InformationR.net/ir/22-1/colis/colis1601.html

Olsson, M. R. (2009). Re-thinking our concept of users. *Australian Academic and Research Libraries*, *40*(1), 22–35. https://doi.org/10.1080/00048623.2016.1253426

Olsson, M. R. (2010a). All the world's a stage – The information practices and sense-making of theatre professionals. *Libri – International Journal of Libraries and Information Services*, *60*(3), 241–252. http://doi.org/10.1515/libr.2010.021

Olsson, M. R. (2010b). Michel Foucault: Discourse, power/knowledge, and the battle for truth. In G. J. Leckie, L. M. Given, & J. E. Buschman (Eds.), *Critical theory for library and information science: Exploring the social from across the disciplines* (pp. 63–74). Libraries Unlimited.

Onwuegbuzie, A. J., Johnson, R. B., & Collins, K. (2009). Call for mixed analysis: A philosophical framework for combining qualitative and quantitative approaches. *International Journal of Multiple Research Approaches*, *3*(2), 114–139. https://doi.org/10.5172/mra.3.2.114

Ooi, K. (2011). Selecting fiction as part of everyday life information seeking. *Journal of Documentation*, *67*(5), 748–772. https://doi.org/10.1108/00220411111164655

Orr, R. (1970). The scientist as information processor: A conceptual model illustrated with data on variables related to library utilization. In C. Nelson & D. Pollock (Eds.), *Communication among scientists and engineers* (pp. 143–189). D. C. Heath.

Osatuyi, B. (2013). Information sharing on social media sites. *Computers in Human Behavior*, *29*(6), 2622–2631. https://doi.org/10.1016/j.chb.2013.07.001

Otto, J., Metz, S., & Ensmenger, N. (2011). Sports fans and their information-gathering habits : How media technologies have brought fans closer to their teams over time. In W. Aspray & B. Hayes (Eds.), *Everyday information: The evolution of information seeking in America* (pp. 185–216). MIT Press.

Paisley, W. J. (1965). *The flow of (behavioral) science information – a review of the research literature*. Institute for Communication Research, Stanford University.

Paisley, W. J. (1968). Information needs and uses. In C. Cuadra (Ed.), *Annual review of information science and technology* (Vol. 3, pp. 1–30). Encyclopaedia Britannica.

Paisley, W. J. (1986). The convergence of communication and information science. In H. Edelman (Ed.), *Libraries and information science in the electronic age* (pp. 122–153). ISI Press.

Paisley, W. J. (1990). Information science as a multidiscipline. In J. Pemberton & A. Prentice (Eds.), *Information science: The interdisciplinary context* (pp. 3–24). Neal-Schuman Publishers.

Palmer, C. L., & Neumann, L. J. (2002). The information work of interdisciplinary humanities scholars: Exploration and translation. *The Library Quarterly*, *72*(1), 85–117. https://www.jstor.org/stable/4309582

Palmer, C. L., Teffeau, L. C., & Pirmann, C. M. (2009). *Scholarly information practices in the online environment: Themes from the literature and implications for library service development* (p. 59). OCLC. http://www.oclc.org/research/publications/library/2009/2009-02.pdf

Palmer, R., Lemoh, C., Tham, R., Hakim, S., & Biggs, B. A. (2009). Sudanese women living in Victoria, Australia: Health-information-seeking behaviours and the availability, effectiveness and appropriateness of HIV/AIDS information. *Diversity in Health and Care*, *6*(2), 109–120.

Pálsdóttir, Á. (2008). Information behaviour, health self-efficacy beliefs and health behaviour in Icelanders' everyday life. *Information Research*, *13*(1). http://informationr.net/ir/13-1/paper334.html

Pálsdóttir, Á. (2010). The connection between purposive information seeking and information encountering: A study of Icelanders' health and lifestyle information seeking. *Journal of Documentation*, *66*(2), 224–244. http://doi.org/10.1108/00220411011023634

Pálsdóttir, Á. (2011). Opportunistic discovery of information by elderly Icelanders and their relatives. *Information Research*, *16*(3). http://informationr.net/ir/16-3/paper485.html

Pálsdóttir, Á. (2012). Relatives as supporters of elderly peoples' information behavior. *Information Research*, *17*(4). http://InformationR.net/ir/17-4/paper546.html

Pálsdóttir, Á. (2014). Preferences in the use of social media for seeking and communicating health and lifestyle information. *Information Research*, *19*(4). http://www.informationr.net/ir/19-4/paper642.html#.VN004FOUcqY

Pang, N., Karanasios, S., & Anwar, M. (2020). Exploring the information worlds of older persons during disasters. *Journal of the Association for Information Science and Technology*, *71*(6), 619–631. https://doi.org/10.1002/asi.24294

Papen, U. (2013). Conceptualising information literacy as social practice: A study of pregnant women's information practices. *Information Research*, *18*(2). http://informationr.net/ir/18-2/paper580.html#.Y3AZjexBwUo

Park, M. S., Oh, H., & You, S. (2020). Health information seeking among people with multiple chronic conditions: Contextual factors and their associations mined from questions in social media. *Library & Information Science Research*, *42*(3). https://doi.org/10.1016/j.lisr.2020.101030

Pavitt, C. (1999). The third way: Scientific realism and communication theory. *Communication Theory*, *9*, 162–188. https://doi.org/10.1111/j.1468-2885.1999.tb00356.x

Petersen, E., Jensen, J. G., & Frandsen, T. F. (2021). Information seeking for coping with cancer: A systematic review. *Aslib Journal of Information Management*, *73*(6), 885–903. https://doi.org/10.1108/AJIM-01-2021-0004

Pettigrew, K. E., Durrance, J. C., & Unruh, K. T. (2002). Facilitating community information seeking using the Internet: Findings from three public library-community network systems. *Journal of the American Society for Information Science and Technology*, *53*(11), 894–903. https://doi.org/10.1002/asi.10120

Pham, H. T. (2019). The application of structuration theory in studying collaboration between librarians and academic staff in universities in Australia and Vietnam. *Information Research*, *24*(3). http://InformationR.net/ir/24-3/paper829.html

Pham, H. T., & Williamson, K. (2018). A two-way street: Collaboration and information sharing in academia. A theoretically-based, comparative Australian/Vietnamese study. *Information Research*, *23*(4). http://www.informationr.net/ir/23-4/isic2018/isic1810.html

Pian, W., Song, S., & Zhang, Y. (2020). Consumer health information needs: A systematic review of measures. *Information Processing & Management*, *57*(2), 102077. https://doi.org/10.1016/j.ipm.2019.102077

Pilerot, O. (2013). A practice theoretical exploration of information sharing and trust in a dispersed community of design scholars. *Information Research*, *18*(4). http://informationr.net/ir/18-4/paper595.html

Pilerot, O. (2014). Making design researchers' information sharing visible through material objects. *Journal of the American Society for Information Science and Technology*, *65*(10), 2006–2016. http://doi.org/10.1002/asi.23108

Pilerot, O. (2018). The practice of public library-work for newly arrived immigrants. *Information Research*, *23*(4). http://InformationR.net/ir/23-4/isic2018/isic1806.html

Pilerot, O., Hammarfelt, B., & Moring, C. (2017). The many faces of practice theory in library and information studies. *Information Research*, *22*(1). http://InformationR.net/ir/22-1/colis/colis1602.html

Pilerot, O., & Limberg, L. (2011). Information sharing as a means to reach collective understanding: A study of design scholars' information practices. *Journal of Documentation*, *67*(2), 312–333. https://doi.org/10.1108/00220411111109494

Pinelli, T. E. (1991). The information-seeking habits and practices of engineers. *Science & Technology Libraries*, *11*(3), 5–25. https://doi.org/10.1300/J122v11n03_02

Pinelli, T. E., Barclay, R., Glassman, N., Kennedy, J., & Demerath, L. (1991). The relationship between seven variables and the use of U.S. government technical reports by U.S. aerospace engineers and scientists. In J. Griffiths (Ed.), *ASIS '91: Proceedings of the 54th ASIS annual meeting, Washington, DC, October 27–31, 1991* (Vol. 28, pp. 313–321). Learned Information.

Pluye, P., El Sherif, R., Granikov, V., Hong, Q. N., Vedel, I., Galvao, M. C. B., Frati, F. E., Desroches, S., Repchinsky, C., Rihoux, B., Légaré, F., Burnand, B., Bujold, M., & Grad, R. (2019). Health outcomes of online consumer health information: A systematic mixed studies review with framework synthesis. *Journal of the Association for Information Science and Technology*, *70*(7), 643–659. https://doi.org/10.1002/asi.24178

Pluye, P., Grad, R., Repchinsky, C., Jovaisas, B., Johnson-Lafleur, J., Carrier, M.-E., Granikov, V., Farrell, B., Rodriguez, C., Bartlett, G., Loiselle, C., & Légaré, F. (2013). Four levels of outcomes of information-seeking: A mixed methods study in primary health care. *Journal of the American Society for Information Science and Technology*, *64*(1), 108–125. http://doi.org/10.1002/asi.22793

Polkinghorne, S. C. (2021). *Exploring everyday information practices: Embodied mutual constitution of people's complex relationships with food.* Unpublished dissertation, Swinburne University of Technology.

Polkinghorne, S., & Given, L. M. (2021). Holistic information research: From rhetoric to paradigm. *Journal of the Association for Information Science and Technology*, *72*(10), 1261–1271. https://doi.org/10.1002/asi.24450

Pontis, S., & Blandford, A. (2015). Understanding "influence:" an exploratory study of academics' processes of knowledge construction through iterative and interactive information seeking. *Journal of the Association for Information Science & Technology*, *66*(8), 1576–1593. https://doi.org/10.1002/asi.23277

Poole, A. H., & Garwood, D. A. (2018). Interdisciplinary scholarly collaboration in data-intensive, public-funded, international digital humanities project work. *Library & Information Science Research*, *40*(3–4), 184–193. https://doi.org/10.1016/j.lisr.2018.08.003

Poole, H. (1985). *Theories of the middle range.* Ablex.

Poole, M. S., & McPhee, R. D. (1994). Methodology in interpersonal communication research. In M. L. Knapp & G. R. Miller (Eds.), *Handbook of interpersonal communication* (2nd ed., pp. 42–99). Sage Publications.

Potnis, D., & Tahamtan, I. (2021). Hashtags for gatekeeping of information on social media. *Journal of the Association for Information Science & Technology*, *72*(10), 1234–1246. https://doi.org/10.1002/asi.24467

Potter, J. (1996). *Representing reality: Discourse, rhetoric and social construction.* Sage.

Prabha, C., Connaway, L. S., Olszewski, L., & Jenkins, L. R. (2007). What is enough? Satisficing information needs. *Journal of Documentation*, *63*(1), 74–89. http://doi.org/10.1108/00220410710723894

du Preez, M., & Fourie, I. (2009). The information behaviour of consulting engineers in South Africa. *Mousaion*, *27*(1), 137–158.

Price, D. (1963). *Little science, big science.* Columbia University Press.

Price, L., & Robinson, L. (2017). 'Being in a knowledge space': Information behaviour of cult media fan communities. *Journal of Information Science*, *43*(5), 649–664. https://doi.org/10.1177/0165551516658821

Prigoda, E., & McKenzie, P. J. (2007). Purls of wisdom: A collectivist study of human information behaviour in a public library knitting group. *Journal of Documentation*, *63*(1), 90–114. https://doi.org/10.1108/00220410710723902

Putnam, R. D. (2000). *Bowling alone: The collapse and revival of American community.* Simon & Schuster.

Pyati, A. (2010). Herbert Marcuse: Liberation, Utopia, and revolution. In G. J. Leckie, L. M. Given, & J. E. Buschman (Eds.), *Critical theory for library and information science: Exploring the social from across the disciplines* (pp. 237–248). Libraries Unlimited.

Pyszczynski, T., Greenberg, J., & Solomon, S. (1999). A dual-process model of defense against conscious and unconscious death-related thoughts: An extension of terror management theory. *Psychological Review*, *106*, 835–845. https://doi.org/10.1037/0033-295x.106.4.835

Qayyum, A., Thompson, K. M., Kennan, M. A., & Lloyd, A. (2014). The provision and sharing of information between service providers and settling refugees. *Information Research*, *19*(2). http://informationr.net/ir/19-2/paper616.html

Qin, H., Wang, H., & Johnson, A. (2020). Understanding the information needs and information-seeking behaviours of new-generation engineering designers for effective knowledge management. *Aslib Journal of Information Management*, *72*(6), 853–868. https://doi.org/10.1108/AJIM-04-2020-0097

Radford, M. L., Connaway, L. S., Mikitish, S., Alpert, M., Shah, C., & Cooke, N. A. (2017). Shared values, new vision: Collaboration and communities of practice in virtual reference and SQA. *Journal of the Association for Information Science and Technology*, *68*(2), 438–449. https://doi.org/10.1002/asi.23668

Rampersad, G., & Althiyabi, T. (2019). Fake news: Acceptance by demographics and culture on social media. *Journal of Information Technology & Politics*, *17*(1), 1–11. https://doi.org/10.1080/19331681.2019.1686676

Rasmussen Pennington, D., Richardson, G., Garinger, C., & Contursi, M. L. (2013). "I could be on Facebook by now": Insights from Canadian youth on online mental health information resources. *Canadian Journal of Information and Library Science*, *37*(3), 183–200.

Rawdin, E. (1975). Field survey of information needs of industry sci/tech library users. In *Information Revolution: Proceedings of the Eighth ASIS Annual Meeting. Washington (DC), American Society for Information Science, 1975*, Boston, Massachusetts, October 26–30, 1975 (Vol. 12, pp. 41–42).

Reckwitz, A. (2002). Toward a theory of social practices: A development in culturalist theorizing. *European Journal of Social Theory*, *5*(2), 243–263. https://doi.org/10.1177/13684310222225432

Reddy, M. C., & Jansen, B. J. (2008). A model for understanding collaborative information behavior in context: A study of two healthcare teams. *Information Processing & Management*, *44*, 256–273. https://doi.org/10.1016/j.ipm.2006.12.010

Reddy, M. C., & Spence, P. R. (2008). Collaborative information seeking: A field study of a multidisciplinary patient care team. *Information Processing & Management*, *44*(1), 242–255. https://doi.org/10.1016/j.ipm.2006.12.003

Reneker, M. (1993). A qualitative study of information seeking among members of an academic community: Methodological issues and problems. *The Library Quarterly*, *63*, 487–507. https://www.jstor.org/stable/4308868

Research Excellence Framework. (2011). Assessment framework and guidance on submissions. https://www.ref.ac.uk/2014/media/ref/content/pub/assessmentframeworkandguidanceonsubmissions/GOS%20including%20addendum.pdf

Reuter, K. (2007). Assessing aesthetic relevance: Children's book selection behavior in a digital library. *Journal of the American Society for Information Science and Technology*, *58*(12), 1745–1763. https://doi.org/10.1002/asi.20657

Reynolds, R. (2013). Personal construct theory. In T. Wilson (Ed.), *Theory in information behaviour research* (pp. 68–82). Eiconics.

Rich, R. F. (1975). Selective utilization of social science related information by federal policy-makers. *Inquiry: A Journal of Medical Care Organization, Provision and Financing*, *13*(3), 72–81.

Rich, R. F. (1997). Measuring knowledge utilization: Processes and outcomes. *Knowledge and Policy*, *10*(3), 11–24. https://doi.org/10.1007/BF02912504

Riley, F., Allen, D. K., & Wilson, T. D. (2022). When politicians and the experts collide: Organization and the creation of information spheres. *Journal of the American Society for Information Science and Technology*, *73*(8), 1127–1139. https://doi.org/10.1002/asi.24618

Ritzer, G. (2010). *Classical sociological theory* (6th ed.). McGraw-Hill.

Roberts, N. (1975). Draft definitions: Information and library needs, wants, demands and uses: A comment. *ASLIB Proceedings*, *27*(7), 308–313.

Robinson, M. A. (2010). An empirical analysis of engineers' information behaviors. *Journal of the American Society for Information Science and Technology*, *61*(4), 640–658. http://doi.org/10.1002/asi.21290

Robinson, J., & Yerbury, H. (2015). Re-enactment and its information practices: Tensions between the individual and the collective. *Journal of Documentation*, *71*(3), 591–608. https://doi.org/10.1108/JD-03-2014-0051

Robson, A., & Robinson, L. (2013). Building on models of information behaviour: Linking information seeking and communication. *Journal of Documentation*, *69*(2), 169–193. http://doi.org/10.1108/00220411311300039

Rogers, E. M. (2003). *Diffusion of innovations* (5th ed.). Free Press.

Rohde, N. F. (1986). Information needs. *Advances in Librarianship*, *14*, 49–73.

Rokeach, M. (1960). *The open and closed mind*. Basic Books.

Rolls, K., & Massey, D. (2021). Social media is a source of health-related misinformation. *Evidence-Based Nursing*, *24*(2), 46. http://doi.org/10.1136/ebnurs-2019-103222

Romer, D., & Jamieson, K. H. (2020). Conspiracy theories as barriers to controlling the spread of COVID-19 in the U.S. *Social Science & Medicine*, *263*(113356). https://doi.org/10.1016/j.socscimed.2020.113356

Roos, A. (2012). Activity theory as a theoretical framework in the study of information practices in molecular medicine. *Information Research*, *17*(3). http://informationr.net/ir/17-3/paper526.html

Roos, A., & Hedlund, T. (2016). Using the domain analytical approach in the study of information practices in biomedicine. *Journal of Documentation*, *72*(5), 961–986. https://doi.org/10.1108/JD-11-2015-0139

Rosch, E., & Lloyd, B. (Eds.). (1978). *Cognition and categorization*. Lawrence Erlbaum Associates.

Rose, T. (2003). Technology's impact on the information-seeking behavior of art historians. *Art Documentation*, *21*(2), 35–42. https://www.jstor.org/stable/27949206

Rosenbaum, H. (2010). Anthony Giddens' influence on library and information science. In G. J. Leckie, L. M. Given, & J. E. Buschman (Eds.), *Critical theory for library and information science: Exploring the social from across the disciplines* (pp. 119–130). Libraries Unlimited.

Rosenblatt, L. (1994). *The reader, the text, the poem: The transactional theory of the literary work* (2nd ed.). Southern Illinois Press.

Rosengren, K. (1974). Uses and gratifications: A paradigm outlined. In J. Blumler & E. Katz (Eds.), *The uses of mass communication: Current perspectives on uses and gratifications research* (pp. 269–286). Sage Publications.

Ross, C., Terras, M., Warwick, C., & Welsh, A. (2011). Enabled backchannel: Conference Twitter use by digital humanists. *Journal of Documentation*, *67*(2), 214–237. http://doi.org/10.1108/00220411111109449

Ross, C. S. (1999). Finding without seeking: The information encounter in the context of reading for pleasure. *Information Processing & Management*, *35*, 783–799. https://doi.org/10.1016/S0306-4573(99)00026-6

Ross, C. S. (2005). Reader response theory. In K. E. Fisher, S. Erdelez, & E. F. McKechnie (Eds.), *Theories of information behavior* (pp. 303–307). Information Today, Inc.

Ross, J. (1983). Observations of browsing behaviour in an academic library. *College & Research Libraries*, *44*(4).

Rothbauer, P. M. (2008). Triangulation. In L. M. Given (Ed.), *The SAGE encyclopedia of qualitative research methods* (pp. 893–894). SAGE Publications, Inc.

Rothbauer, P. (2009). Exploring the placelessness of reading among older teens in a Canadian rural municipality. *The Library Quarterly*, *79*(4), 465–483. https://doi.org/10.1086/605384

Rothschild, N., & Aharony, N. (2016). Empathetic communication among discourse participants in virtual communities of people who suffer from mental illnesses. *Information Research*, *21*(1). http://InformationR.net/ir/21-1/paper701.html

Rousi, A. M., Savolainen, R., & Vakkari, P. (2019). Adopting situationally relevant modes of music information at different stages of information-seeking processes: A longitudinal investigation among music students. *Journal of Documentation*, *75*(6), 1230–1257. https://doi.org/10.1108/JD-12-2018-0210

Rowley, J. (2007). The wisdom hierarchy: Representations of the DIKW hierarchy. *Journal of Information Science*, *33*(2), 163–180. https://doi.org/10.1177/0165551506070706

Rubenstein, E. L. (2015). "They are always there for me": The convergence of social support and information in an online breast cancer community: "They are always there for me". *Journal of the Association for Information Science and Technology*, *66*(7), 1418–1430. https://doi.org/10.1002/asi.23263

Rui, T. (2013). Farmers' reading rooms and information and communications technology in rural areas of Beijing. *Library Trends*, *62*(1), 95–104. https://doi.org/10.1353/lib.2013.0030

Ruokolainen, H., & Widén, G. (2020). Conceptualising misinformation in the context of asylum seekers. *Information Processing & Management*, *57*(3). https://doi.org/10.1016/j.ipm.2019.102127

Russell-Rose, T., Chamberlain, J., & Azzopardi, L. (2018). Information retrieval in the workplace: A comparison of professional search practices. *Information Processing & Management*, *54*(6), 1042–1057. https://doi.org/10.1016/j.ipm.2018.07.003

Ruthven, I. (2021). Resonance and the experience of relevance. *Journal of the Association for Information Science and Technology*, *72*(5), 554–569. https://doi.org/10.1002/asi.24424

Ruvane, M. B. (2005). Annotation as process: A vital information seeking activity in historical geographic research. In A. Grove (Ed.), *ASIS&T '05: Proceedings of the Annual Meeting of the American Society for Information Science and Technology*, Silver Spring, MD (Vol. 42, pp. 506–522). American Society for Information Science and Technology.

Ryan, F. V. C., Cruickshank, P., Hall, H., & Lawson, A. (2016). Managing and evaluating personal reputations on the basis of information shared on social media: A Generation X perspective. In *Proceedings of ISIC, the Information Behaviour Conference*, Zadar, Croatia, 20–23 September, 2016: Part 1. *Information Research, 21*(4). http://InformationR.net/ir/21-4/isic/isic1612.html

Saab, D. J., & Riss, U. V. (2011). Information as ontologization. *Journal of the American Society for Information Science and Technology*, *62*(11), 2236–2246. https://doi.org/10.1002/asi.21615

Saastamoinen, M., & Järvelin, K. (2018). Relationships between work task types, complexity and dwell time of information resources. *Journal of Information Science*, *44*(2), 265–284.

Saastamoinen, M., & Kumpulainen, S. (2014). Expected and materialised information source use by municipal officials: Intertwining with task complexity. *Information Research*, *19*(4). http://InformationR.net/ir/19-4/paper646.html

Sahu, H. K., & Singh, S. N. (2013). Information seeking behaviour of astronomy/astrophysics scientists. *ASLIB Proceedings*, *65*(2), 109–142. https://doi.org/10.1108/00012531311313961

Sakai, S., Awamura, N., & Ikeya, N. (2012). The practical management of information in a task management meeting: Taking "practice" seriously. *Information Research*, *17*(4). http://informationr.net/ir/17-4/paper537.html

Salzano, R., Hall, H., & Webster, G. (2020). Investigating the 'why?' rather than the 'how?': Current research priorities on the influence of culture on newcomer populations' use of public libraries. In *Proceedings of ISIC, the Information Behaviour Conference*, Pretoria, South Africa, 28 September – 1 October, 2020. *Information Research, 25*(4). http://InformationR.net/ir/25-4/isic2020/isic2032.html

Sandelowski, M., & Barroso, J. (2006). *Handbook for synthesizing qualitative research.* Springer Publishing.

Sapa, R., Krakowska, M., & Janiak, M. (2014). Information seeking behaviour of mathematicians: Scientists and students. *Information Research*, *19*(4). http://www.informationr.net/ir/19-4/paper644.html

Saumure, K., & Given, L. M. (2008). Rigor in qualitative research. In L. M. Given (Ed.), *The SAGE encyclopedia of qualitative research methods* (pp. 796–797). SAGE Publications, Inc.

Savolainen, R. (1993). The sense-making theory: Reviewing the interests of a user-centered approach to information seeking and use. *Information Processing & Management*, *29*(1), 13–28. https://doi.org/10.1016/0306-4573(93)90020-E

Savolainen, R. (1995). Everyday life information seeking: Approaching information seeking in the context of "way of life". *Library & Information Science Research*, *17*(3), 259–294. https://doi.org/10.1016/0740-8188(95)90048-9

Savolainen, R. (1999). Seeking and using information for the internet: The context of non-work use. In T. D. Wilson & D. K. Allen (Eds.), *Information behaviour: Proceedings of the second international conference on research in information needs, seeking and use in different contexts, 13/15 August 1998, Sheffield, UK* (pp. 356–370). Taylor Graham.

Savolainen, R. (2001). "Living encyclopedia" or idle talk? Seeking and providing consumer information in an internet newsgroup. *Library & Information Science Research*, *23*(1), 67–90. https://doi.org/10.1016/S0740-8188(00)00068-2

Savolainen, R. (2004). Enthusiastic, realistic and critical: Discourses of internet use in the context of everyday life information seeking. *Information Research*, *10*(1). http://InformationR.net/ir/10-1/paper198.html

Savolainen, R. (2005). Everyday life information seeking. In K. E. Fisher, S. Erdelez, & E. F. McKechnie (Eds.), *Theories of information behavior* (pp. 143–148). Information Today, Inc.

Savolainen, R. (2006). Spatial factors as contextual qualifiers of information seeking. *Information Research*, *11*(4). http://InformationR.net/ir/11-4/paper261.html

Savolainen, R. (2007a). Information behavior and information practice: Reviewing the "umbrella concepts" of information-seeking studies. *The Library Quarterly*, *77*(2), 109–132. https://doi.org/10.1086/517840

Savolainen, R. (2007b). Filtering and withdrawing: Strategies for coping with information overload in everyday contexts. *Journal of Information Science*, *33*(5), 611–621. https://doi.org./10.1177/0165551506077418

Savolainen, R. (2007c). Information source horizons and source preferences of environmental activists: A social phenomenological approach. *Journal of the American Society for Information Science and Technology*, *58*(12), 1709–1719. http://doi.org/10.1002/asi.20644

Savolainen, R. (2008a). Autonomous, controlled and half-hearted. Unemployed people's motivations to seek information about jobs. *Information Research*, *13*(4). http://informationr.net/ir/13-4/paper362.html

Savolainen, R. (2008b). *Everyday information practices: A social phenomenological perspective*. Scarecrow Press.

Savolainen, R. (2008c). Source preferences in the context of seeking problem-specific information. *Information Processing & Management*, *44*(1), 274–293. http://doi.org/10.1016/j.ipm.2007.02.008

Savolainen, R. (2009a). Information use and information processing: Comparison of conceptualizations. *Journal of Documentation*, *65*(2), 187–207. http://doi.org/10.1108/00220410910937570

Savolainen, R. (2009b). Small world and information grounds as contexts of information seeking and sharing. *Library & Information Science Research*, *31*(1), 38–45. http://doi.org/10.1016/j.lisr.2008.10.007

Savolainen, R. (2009c). Epistemic work and knowing in practice as conceptualizations of information use. *Information Research*, *14*(1). http://InformationR.net/ir/14-1/paper392.html

Savolainen, R. (2010). Source preference criteria in the context of everyday projects: Relevance judgments made by prospective home buyers. *Journal of Documentation*, *66*(2), 70–92. http://doi.org/10.1108/00220411011016371

Savolainen, R. (2012a). Conceptualizing information need in context. *Information Research*, *17*(4). http://InformationR.net/ir/17-4/paper534.html

Savolainen, R. (2012b). Elaborating the motivational attributes of information need and uncertainty. *Information Research*, *17*(2). http://InformationR.net/ir/17-2/paper516.html

Savolainen, R. (2013). Approaching the motivators for information seeking: The viewpoint of attribution theories. *Library & Information Science Research*, *35*(1), 63–68. https://doi.org/10.1016/j.lisr.2012.07.004

Savolainen, R. (2014). Emotions as motivators for information seeking: A conceptual analysis. *Library & Information Science Research*, *36*(1), 59–65. http://doi.org/10.1016/j.lisr.2013.10.004

Savolainen, R. (2015a). Expressing emotions in information sharing: A study of online discussion about immigration. *Information Research*, *20*(1). http://InformationR.net/ir/20-1/paper662.html

Savolainen, R. (2015b). The interplay of affective and cognitive factors in information seeking and use: Comparing Kuhlthau's and Nahl's models. *Journal of Documentation*, *71*(1), 175–197. http://doi.org/10.1108/JD-10-2013-0134

Savolainen, R. (2017). Contributions to conceptual growth: The elaboration of Ellis's model for information-seeking behavior. *Journal of the Association for Information Science and Technology*, *68*(3), 594–608. https://doi.org/10.1002/asi.23680

Savolainen, R. (2019). Sharing information through book reviews in blogs: The viewpoint of Rosenblatt's reader-response theory. *Journal of Documentation*, *76*(2), 440–461. https://doi.org/10.1108/JD-08-2019-0161

Savolainen, R. (2021). Levels of critique in models and concepts of human information behaviour research. *Aslib Journal of Information Management*, *73*(5), 772–791. https://doi.org/10.1108/AJIM-01-2021-0028

Savolainen, R., & Kari, J. (2004a). Conceptions of the Internet in everyday life information seeking. *Journal of Information Science*, *30*(3), 219–226. https://doi.org/10.1177/0165551504044667

Savolainen, R., & Kari, J. (2004b). Placing the internet in information source horizons. A study of information seeking by internet users in the context of self-development. *Library & Information Science Research*, *26*(4), 415–433. https://doi.org/10.1016/j.lisr.2004.04.004

Savolainen, R., & Thomson, L. (2022). Assessing the theoretical potential of an expanded model for everyday information practices. *Journal of the Association for Information Science and Technology*, *73*(4), 511–527. https://doi.org/10.1002/asi.24589

Scarton, L. A., Fiol, G. D., Oakley-Girvan, I., Gibson, B., Logan, R., & Workman, T. E. (2018). Understanding cancer survivors' information needs and information-seeking behaviors for complementary and alternative medicine from short- to long-term survival: A mixed-methods study. *Journal of the Medical Library Association*, *106*(1), 87–97. https://doi.org/10.5195/jmla.2018.200

Schatzki, T. R. (1996). *Social practices: A Wittgensteinian approach to human activity and the social*. Cambridge University Press.

Schatzki, T. R. (2002). *The site of the social: A philosophical account of the constitution of social life and change*. University of Pennsylvania Press.

Schatzki, T. R. (2019). *Social change in a material world*. Routledge.

Schement, J. R. (1993a). An etymological exploration of the links between information and communication. In J. R. Schement & B. Ruben (Eds.), *Information and behavior* (Vol. 4, pp. 173–187). Transaction Publishers.

Schement, J. R. (1993b). Communication and information. In J. R. Schement & B. Ruben (Eds.), *Information and behavior* (Vol. 4, pp. 3–33). Transaction Publishers.

Schindel, T. J., & Given, L. M. (2013). The pharmacist as prescriber: A discourse analysis of Canadian newspaper media. *Research in Social and Administrative Pharmacy*, *9*(4), 384–395. https://doi.org/10.1016/j.sapharm.2012.05.014

Schlebbe, K. (2020). Support versus restriction: Parents' influence on young children's information behaviour in connection with mobile devices. In *Proceedings of ISIC, the Information Behaviour Conference*, Pretoria, South Africa, 28 September – 1 October, 2020. *Information Research, 25*(4). http://InformationR.net/ir/25-4/isic2020/isic2006.html

Schmidt, K. (2018). 'Practice theory': A critique. In V. Wulf, V. Pipek, D. Randall, M. Rohde, K. Schmidt, & G. Stevens (Eds.), *Socio-informatics: A practice-based perspective on the design and use of IT artifacts* (pp. 105–137). Oxford University Press.

Schrader, A. (1983). *Toward a theory of library and information science*. Indiana University.

Schreiber, T. (2013). Questioning a discourse of information literacy practice in web-based tutorials. *Information Research*, *18*(3). http://InformationR.net/ir/18-3/colis/paperC36.html

Schutt, R. K. (2022). *Investigating the social world: The process and practice of research* (10th ed.). Sage Publications.

Schutz, A. (1962). *Collected papers, I: The problem of social reality*. Martinus Nijhoff.

Schutz, A. (1964). *Collected papers, II: Studies in social theory*. Martinus Nijhoff.

Schutz, A. (1967). *The phenomenology of the social world*. Northwestern University.

Schutz, A. (1970). *Alfred Schutz on phenomenology and social relations* (Vol. 360). University of Chicago Press.

Schutz, A., & Luckmann, T. (1973). *The structures of the life-world*. Northwestern University Press.

Scott, S. D., Albrecht, L., Given, L. M., Hartling, L., Johnson, D. W., Jabbour, M., & Klassen, T. P. (2017). Pediatric information seeking behaviour, information needs, and information preferences of health care professionals in general emergency departments: Results from the Translating Emergency Knowledge for Kids (TREKK) needs assessment. *Canadian Journal of Emergency Medicine*, *20*(1), 89–99. http://doi.org/10.1017/cem.2016.406

Searle, J. (1983). *Intentionality. Essays in the philosophy of mind*. Cambridge University Press.

Seldén, L. (2001). Academic information seeking – careers and capital types. *New Review of Information Behaviour Research*, *2*, 195–215.

Shah, C. (2014). Collaborative information seeking. *Journal of the American Society for Information Science and Technology*, *65*(2), 215–236. https://doi.org/10.1002/asi.22977

Shah, C., & Leeder, C. (2016). Exploring collaborative work among graduate students through the C5 model of collaboration: A diary study. *Journal of Information Science*, *42*(5), 609–629. https://doi.org/10.1177/0165551515603322

Shankar, S., O'Brien, H. L., & Absar, R. (2018). Rhythms of everyday life in mobile information seeking: Reflections on a photo-diary study. *Library Trends*, *66*(4), 535–567. https://doi.org/10.1353/lib.2018.0016

Shannon, C. (1949). The mathematical theory of communication. In C. Shannon & W. Weaver (Eds.), *The mathematical theory of communication* (pp. 31–125). University of Illinois Press.

Shen, T. S., Chen, A. Z., Bovonratwet, P., Shen, C. L., & Su, E. P. (2020). COVID-19-Related Internet search patterns among people in the United States: Exploratory analysis. *Journal of Medical Internet Research*, *22*(11), e22407. https://doi.org/10.2196/22407

Shenton, A. K., & Dixon, P. (2003). Youngsters' use of other people as an information-seeking method. *Journal of Librarianship and Information Science*, *35*(4), 219–233. https://doi.org/10.1177/0961000603035004002

Shenton, A. K., & Dixon, P. (2004). Issues arising from youngsters' information-seeking behavior. *Library & Information Science Research*, *26*(2), 177–200. https://doi.org/10.1016/j.lisr.2003.12.003

Shenton, A. K., & Hay-Gibson, N. V. (2012). Information behaviour meta-models. *Library Review*, *61*(2), 92–109. https://doi.org/10.1108/00242531211220735

Shenton, A. K., & Hayter, S. (2006). Terminology deconstructed: Phenomenographic approaches to investigating the term "information". *Library & Information Science Research*, *28*(4), 563–578. http://doi.org/10.1016/j.lisr.2006.10.003

Shenton, A. K., & Hay-Gibson, N. V. (2011). Modelling the information-seeking behaviour of children and young people: Inspiration from beyond LIS. *ASLIB Proceedings*, *63*(1), 57–75. https://doi.org/10.1108/00012531111103786

Shoham, S., & Strauss, S. (2007). Information needs of North American immigrants to Israel. *Journal of Information, Communication and Ethics in Society*, *5*(2/3), 185–205. https://doi.org/10.1108/14779960710837641

Shuker, R. (2010). *Wax trash and vinyl treasures: Record collecting as a social practice*. Ashgate.

Shuva, N. Z. (2021). Information experiences of Bangladeshi immigrants in Canada. *Journal of Documentation*, *77*(2), 479–500. https://doi.org/10.1108/JD-08-2020-0137

Sievert, D., & Sievert, M. (1989). Philosophical research: Report from the field. In *Humanists at work: Disciplinary perspectives and personal reflections* (pp. 95–99). University of Illinois at Chicago, Institute for the Humanities and the University Library.

Silvio, D. H. (2006). The information needs and information seeking behaviour of immigrant southern Sudanese youth in the city of London, Ontario: An exploratory study. *Library Review*, *55*(4), 259–266. https://doi.org/10.1108/00242530610660807

Simon, J., & Burstein, P. (1985). *Basic research methods in social science* (3rd ed.). Random House.

Sin, S.-C. J. (2011). Towards agency–structure integration: A person-in-environment (PIE) framework for modelling individual-level information behaviours and outcomes. In A. Spink & J. Heinström (Eds.), *New directions in information behaviour* (Vol. 1, pp. 181–209). Emerald Group Publishing Limited.

Sin, S.-C. J. (2016). Social media and problematic everyday life information-seeking outcomes: Differences across use frequency, gender, and problem-solving styles. *Journal of the Association for Information Science and Technology*, *67*(8), 1793–1807. https://doi.org/10.1002/asi.23509

Sin, S.-C. J., & Kim, K.-S. (2013). International students' everyday life information seeking: The informational value of social networking sites. *Library & Information Science Research*, *35*(2), 107–116. http://doi.org/10.1016/j.lisr.2012.11.006

Singh, G., & Sharma, M. (2013). Information seeking behavior of newspaper journalists. *International Journal of Library and Information Science*, *5*(7), 225–234.

Skinner, Q. (Ed.). (1985). *The return of grand theory in the human sciences*. Cambridge University Press.

Skøtt, B. (2019). Newcomers at the library: A library perspective on the integration of new citizens. In *Proceedings of the Tenth International Conference on Conceptions of Library and Information Science*, Ljubljana, Slovenia, June 16–19, 2019. *Information Research, 24*(4). http://InformationR.net/ir/24-4/colis/colis1947.html

Skov, M. (2013). Hobby-related information-seeking behaviour of highly dedicated online museum visitors. *Information Research, 18*(4). http://www.informationr.net/ir/18-4/paper597.html

Skov, M., & Ingwersen, P. (2014). Museum Web search behavior of special interest visitors. *Library & Information Science Research, 36*(2), 91–98. https://doi.org/10.1016/j.lisr.2013.11.004

Slater, M. (1988). Social scientists' information needs in the 1980's. *Journal of Documentation, 44*, 226–237. https://doi.org/10.1108/eb026827

Slife, B., & Williams, R. N. (1995). *What's behind the research?: Discovering hidden assumptions in the behavioral sciences*. Sage Publications, Inc.

Sligo, F. X., & Jameson, A. M. (2000). The knowledge-behavior gap in use of health information. *Journal of the American Society for Information Science, 51*(9), 858–869. https://doi.org/10.1002/(SICI)1097-4571(2000)51:9%3C858::AID-ASI80%3E3.0.CO;2-Q

Smith, L. N., & McMenemy, D. (2017). Young people's conceptions of political information: Insights into information experiences and implications for intervention. *Journal of Documentation, 73*(5), 877–902. https://doi.org/10.1108/JD-03-2017-0041

Søe, S. O. (2018). Algorithmic detection of misinformation and disinformation: Gricean perspectives. *Journal of Documentation, 75*(5), 1013–1034. https://doi.org/10.1108/JD-05-2017-0075

Solis, E. (2018). Information-seeking behavior of economics graduate students: If you buy it, will they come? *Journal of Business & Finance Librarianship, 23*(1), 11–25. https://doi.org/10.1080/08963568.2018.1431866

Solomon, P. (1997a). Conversation in information-seeking contexts: A test of an analytical framework. *Library & Information Science Research, 19*, 217–248. https://doi.org/10.1016/S0740-8188(97)90014-1

Solomon, P. (1997b). Discovering information behavior in sense making: I. Time and timing; II. The social; III. The person. *Journal of the American Society for Information Science, 48*(12), 1097–1138. https://doi.org/10.1002/(SICI)1097-4571(199712)48:12%3C1097::AID-ASI4%3E3.0.CO;2-P

Solomon, Y., & Bronstein, J. (2015). Serendipity in legal information seeking behavior: Chance encounters of family-law advocates with court rulings. *Aslib Journal of Information Management, 68*, 112–134. https://doi.org/10.1108/AJIM-04-2015-0056

Solomon, Y., & Bronstein, J. (2022). The information-gathering practice of liberal professionals in a workplace setting: More than just seeking information. *Journal of Librarianship and Information Science, 54*(1), 54–68. https://doi.org/10.1177/0961000621992810

Somerville, M. M., & Brar, N. (2009). A user-centered and evidence-based approach for digital library projects. *The Electronic Library, 27*(3), 409–425. https://doi.org/10.1108/02640470910966862

Song, S., Yao, X., & Wen, N. (2021). What motivates Chinese consumers to avoid information about the COVID-19 pandemic?: The perspective of the stimulus-organism-response model. *Information Processing & Management, 58*(1), 102407. https://doi.org/10.1016/j.ipm.2020.102407

Sonnenwald, D. H. (2006). Challenges in sharing information effectively: Examples from command and control. *Information Research, 11*(3). http://InformationR.net/ir/11-4/paper270.html

Sonnenwald, D. H., & Iivonen, M. (1999). An integrated human information behavior research framework for information studies. *Library & Information Science Research, 21*(4), 429–457. https://doi.org/10.1016/S0740-8188(99)00023-7

Sonnenwald, D. H., Söderholm, H. M., Welch, G. F., Cairns, B. A., Manning, J. E., & Fuchs, H. (2014). Illuminating collaboration in emergency healthcare situations: Paramedic-physician collaboration and 3D telepresence technology. *Information Research, 19*(2). http://www.informationr.net/ir/19-2/paper618.html

Sonnenwald, D. H., Wildemuth, B. M., & Harmon, G. L. (2001). A research method to investigate information seeking using the concept of information horizons: An example from a study of lower socio-economic student's information seeking behaviour. *New Review of Information Behaviour Research, 2*, 65–86.

Sormunen, E., Heinström, J., Romu, L., & Turunen, R. (2012). A method for the analysis of information use in source-based writing. *Information Research*, *17*(4). http://informationr.net/ir/17-4/paper535.html

Sormunen, E., & Lehtiö, L. (2011). Authoring Wikipedia articles as an information literacy assignment – Copy-pasting or expressing new understanding in own words ? *Information Research*, *16*(4). http://www.informationr.net/ir/16-4/paper503.html

Soroya, S. H., Farooq, A., Mahmood, K., Isoaho, J., & Zara, S. (2021). From information seeking to information avoidance: Understanding the health information behavior during a global health crisis. *Information Processing & Management*, *58*(2), 102440. https://doi.org/10.1016/j.ipm.2020.102440

Spasser, M. A. (1999). Informing information science: The case for activity theory. *Journal of the American Society for Information Science*, *50*(12), 1136–1138. https://doi.org/10.1002/(SICI)1097-4571(1999)50:12%3C1136::AID-ASI17%3E3.0.CO;2-0

Spink, A., Ozmutlu, H. C., & Lorence, D. P. (2004). Web searching for sexual information: An exploratory study. *Information Processing & Management*, *40*(1), 113–133. https://doi.org/10.1016/S0306-4573(02)00082-1

Stam, D. C. (1995). Artists and art libraries. *Art Libraries Journal*, *20*(2), 21–24. https://doi.org/10.1017/S0307472200009329

Starasts, A. (2015). Unearthing farmers' information seeking contexts and challenges in digital, local and industry environments. *Library & Information Science Research*, *37*(2), 156–163. https://doi.org/10.1016/j.lisr.2015.02.004

Stebbins, R. A. (2001). *New directions in the theory and research of serious leisure*. The Edwin Mellen Press.

Stebbins, R. A. (2009). Leisure and its relationship to library and information science: Bridging the gap. *Library Trends*, *57*(4), 618–631. https://doi.org/10.1353/lib.0.0064

Stebbins, R. A. (2018). *Social worlds and the leisure experience*. Emerald Publishing Limited.

Stefl-Mabry, J. (2005). The reality of media preferences: Do professional groups vary in awareness? *Journal of the American Society for Information Science and Technology*, *56*(13), 1419–1426. https://doi.org/10.1002/asi.20235

Steinerová, J. (2019). The societal impact of information behaviour research on developing models of academic information ecologies. In *Proceedings of CoLIS, the Tenth International Conference on Conceptions of Library and Information Science*, Ljubljana, Slovenia, June 16–19, 2019, *Information Research, 24*(4). http://InformationR.net/ir/24-4/colis/colis1905.html

Stevenson, A. (Ed.). (2015). *Oxford dictionary of English* (3rd ed.). OUP. https://doi.org/10.1093/acref/9780199571123.001.0001

Stieg, M. F. (1981). The information needs of historians. *College & Research Libraries*, *42*, 549–560.

Stilwell, C. (2002). The case for informationally based social inclusion for sex workers: A South African exploratory study. *Libri – International Journal of Libraries and Information Services*, *52*(2), 67–77. https://doi.org/10.1515/LIBR.2002.67

Stocking, S. H., & Gross, P. H. (1989). *How do journalists think? A proposal for the study of cognitive bias in newsmaking*. ERIC Clearinghouse on Reading and Communication Skills.

Stokes, P., Priharjo, R., & Urquhart, C. (2021). Validation of information-seeking behaviour of nursing students confirms most profiles but also indicates desirable changes for information literacy support. *Journal of Documentation*, *77*(3), 680–702. https://doi.org/10.1108/JD-09-2020-0158

Stokes, P., & Urquhart, C. (2011). Profiling information behaviour of nursing students: Part 1: Quantitative findings. *Journal of Documentation*, *67*(6), 908–932. https://doi.org/10.1108/00220411111183528

Stokes, P., & Urquhart, C. (2015). Profiling information behaviour of nursing students: Part 2: Derivation of profiles. *Journal of Documentation*, *71*(1), 52–79. https://doi.org/10.1108/JD-07-2013-0091

Stone, S. (1982). Humanities scholars: Information needs and uses. *Journal of Documentation*, *38*(4), 292–313. https://doi.org/10.1108/eb026734

Storer, T. (2017). Bridging the chasm: A survey of software engineering practice in scientific programming. *ACM Computing Surveys*, *50*(4), 47. https://doi.org/10.1145/3084225

Strauss, A., & Corbin, J. (1998). *Basics of qualitative research: Grounded theory procedures and techniques* (2nd ed.). Sage.

Sundin, O. (2002). Nurses' information seeking and use as participation in occupational communities. *New Review of Information Behaviour Research*, *3*, 187–202.

Sundin, O. (2003). Towards an understanding of symbolic aspects of professional information: An analysis of the nursing knowledge domain. *Knowledge Organization*, *30*, 170–181.

Sundin, O., & Hedman, J. (2005). Professions and occupational identities. In K. E. Fisher, S. Erdelez, & E. F. McKechnie (Eds.), *Theories of information behavior* (pp. 293–297). Information Today, Inc.

Suorsa, A. (2015). Knowledge creation and play – A phenomenological approach. *Journal of Documentation*, *71*(3), 503–525. https://doi.org/10.1108/JD-11-2013-0152

Suorsa, A., & Huotari, M.-L. (2014). Knowledge creation and the concept of a human being: A phenomenological approach. *Journal of the American Society for Information Science and Technology*, *65*(5), 1042–1057. https://doi.org/10.1002/asi.23035

Sutton, S. (1994). The role of attorney mental models of law in case relevance determinations: An exploratory analysis. *Journal of the American Society for Information Science*, *45*(3), 186–200. https://doi.org/10.1002/(SICI)1097-4571(199404)45:3%3C186::AID-ASI8%3E3.0.CO;2-F

Tabak, E. (2014). Jumping between context and users: A difficulty in tracing information practices. *Journal of the American Society for Information Science and Technology*, *65*(11), 2223–2232. https://doi.org/10.1002/asi.23116

Tabak, E., & Willson, M. (2012). A non-linear model of information sharing practices in academic communities. *Library & Information Science Research*, *34*(2), 110–116. http://doi.org/10.1016/j.lisr.2011.11.002

Tague-Sutcliffe, J. (1995). *Measuring information: An information services perspective*. Academic Press.

Talja, S. (1997). Constituting "information" and "user" as research objects: A theory of knowledge formations as an alternative to the information man - theory. In P. Vakkari, R. Savolainen, & B. Dervin (Eds.), *Information seeking in context: Proceedings of a meeting in Finland 14–16 August 1996* (pp. 67–80). Taylor Graham.

Talja, S. (2002). Information sharing in academic communities: Types and levels of collaboration in information seeking and use. *The New Review of Information Behaviour Research: Studies of Information Seeking in Context*, *3*, 143–160.

Talja, S. (2005). The domain analytic approach to scholars' information practices. In K. E. Fisher, S. Erdelez, & E. F. McKechnie (Eds.), *Theories of information behavior* (pp. 123–127). Information Today, Inc.

Talja, S. (2010). Jean Lave's practice theory. In G. J. Leckie, L. M. Given, & J. E. Buschman (Eds.), *Critical theory for library and information science: Exploring the social from across the disciplines* (pp. 205–220). Libraries Unlimited.

Talja, S., & Hartel, J. (2007). Revisiting the user-centred turn in information science research: An intellectual history perspective. *Information Research*, *12*(4). http://InformationR.net/ir/12-4/colis/colis04.html

Talja, S., Keso, H., & Pietiläinen, T. (1999). The production of "context" in information seeking research: A metatheoretical view. *Information Processing & Management*, *35*(6), 751–763. https://doi.org/10.1016/S0306-4573(99)00024-2

Talja, S., & Maula, H. (2003). Reasons for the use and non-use of electronic journals and databases: A domain analytic study in four scholarly disciplines. *Journal of Documentation*, *59*(6), 673–691. https://doi.org/10.1108/00220410310506312

Talja, S., & Nyce, J. M. (2015). The problem with problematic situations: Differences between practices, tasks, and situations as units of analysis. *Library & Information Science Research*, *37*(1), 61–67. https://doi.org/10.1016/j.lisr.2014.06.005

Talja, S., Tuominen, K., & Savolainen, R. (2005). "Isms" in information science: Constructivism, collectivism and constructionism. *Journal of Documentation*, *61*(1), 79–101. https://doi.org/10.1108/00220410510578023

Tandoc, E. C. (2019). The facts of fake news: A research review. *Sociology Compass*, *13*(9). https://doi.org/10.1111/soc4.12724

Tandoc, E. C., & Lee, J. C. B. (2020). When viruses and misinformation spread: How young Singaporeans navigated uncertainty in the early stages of the COVID-19 outbreak. *New Media & Society*, *24*(3), 778–796. https://doi.org/10.1177/1461444820968212

Tan, E. M.-Y., & Goh, D. H.-L. (2015). A study of social interaction during mobile information seeking. *Journal of the Association for Information Science and Technology*, *66*(10), 2031–2044. https://doi.org/10.1002/asi.23310

Tan, W.-K., & Kuo, P.-C. (2019). The consequences of online information overload confusion in tourism. *Information Research*, *24*(2). http://InformationR.net/ir/24-2/paper826.html

Taylor, M., Wells, G., Howell, G., & Raphael, B. (2012). The role of social media as psychological first aid as a support to community resilience building. *Australian Journal of Emergency Management*, *27*(1), 20–26.

Taylor, R. S. (1962). The process of asking questions. *American Documentation*, *13*(4), 391–396.

Taylor, R. S. (1968). Question-negotiation and information seeking in libraries. *College & Research Libraries*, *29*, 178–194.

Taylor, R. S. (1986). *Value-added processes in information systems*. Ablex.

Taylor, R. S. (1991). Information use environments. In B. Dervin & M. Voigt (Eds.), *Progress in communication sciences* (Vol. 10). Ablex.

Taylor-Smith, E., & Smith, C. (2019). Investigating the online and offline contexts of day-to-day democracy as participation spaces. Information. *Communication and Society*, *22*(13), 1853–1870. https://doi.org/10.1080/1369118x.2018.1469656

Tenopir, C. (2011). Beyond usage: Measuring library outcomes and value. *Library Management*, *33*(1/2), 5–13. https://doi.org/10.1108/01435121211203275

Tenopir, C., & King, D. W. (2004). *Communication patterns of engineers*. Wiley-Interscience.

ter Huurne, E. F. J., Griffen, R. J., & Gutteling, J. M. (2009). Risk information seeking among U.S. and Dutch residents: An application of the model of risk information seeking and processing. *Science Communication*, *31*(2), 215–237. http://doi.org/10.1177/1075547009332653

Thatcher, A., Vasconcelos, A. C., & Ellis, D. (2015). An investigation into the impact of information behaviour on information failure: The Fukushima Daiichi nuclear power disaster. *International Journal of Information Management*, *35*(1), 57–63. https://doi.org/10.1016/j.ijinfomgt.2014.10.002

Thivant, E. (2005). Information seeking and use behaviour of economists and business analysts. *Information Research*, *10*(4). http://informationr.net/ir/10-4/paper234.html

Thomson, L. (2018). *"'Doing' YouTube": Information creating in the context of serious beauty and lifestyle YouTube*. PhD thesis, The University of North Carolina at Chapel Hill.

Tian, Y., Gomez, R., Cifor, M., Wilson, J., & Morgan, H. (2021). The information practices of law enforcement: Passive and active collaboration and its implication for sanctuary laws in Washington state. *Journal of the Association for Information Science and Technology*, *72*(11), 1354–1366. https://doi.org/10.1002/asi.24485

Timmers, C. F., & Glas, C. A. W. (2010). Developing scales for information-seeking behaviour. *Journal of Documentation*, *66*(1), 44–69. https://doi.org/10.1108/00220411011016362

Timpka, T., & Arborlelius, E. (1990). The GP's dilemmas: A study of knowledge need and use during health care consultations. *Methods of Information in Medicine*, *29*, 23–29.

Todd, R. (1999). Back to our beginnings. Information utilization, Bertram Brookes and the fundamental equation of information science. *Information Processing & Management*, *35*(6), 851–870. https://doi.org/10.1016/S0306-4573(99)00030-8

Toms, E. G., & Duff, W. (2002). "I spent 1 1/2 hours sifting through one large box …". Diaries as information behavior of the archives user: Lessons learned. *Journal of the American Society for Information Science and Technology*, *53*(14), 1232–1238. https://doi.org/10.1002/asi.10165

Törnudd, E. (1959). Study on the use of scientific literature and references services by scandinavian scientists and engineers engaged in research and development (Vol. I). Presented at *the International Conference on Scientific Information*. National Academy of Sciences - National Research Council.

Tötterman, A., & Widén-Wulff, G. (2007). What a social capital perspective can bring to the understanding of information sharing in a university context. *Information Research*, *12*(4). http://InformationR.net/ir/12-4/colis/colis19.html

Trochim, W., & Donnelly, J. (2007). *The research methods knowledge base* (3rd ed.). Atomic Dog Publishing.
Tsai, T.-I. (2012). Social networks in the information horizons of undergraduate students. *Journal of Library and Information Studies, 10*(1), 19–45.
Tuomaala, O., Järvelin, K., & Vakkari, P. (2014). Evolution of library and information science, 1965–2005: Content analysis of journal articles. *Journal of the American Society for Information Science and Technology, 65*(7), 1446–1462. https://doi.org/10.1002/asi.23034
Tuominen, K. (2004). "Whoever increases his knowledge merely increases his heartache." Moral tensions in heart surgery patients' and their spouses' talk about information seeking. *Information Research, 10*(1). http://InformationR.net/ir/10-1/paper202.html
Tuominen, K., & Savolainen, R. (1997). A social constructionist approach to the study of information use as discursive action. In P. Vakkari, R. Savolainen, & B. Dervin (Eds.), *Information seeking in context: Proceedings of a meeting in Finland 14–16 August 1996* (pp. 81–96). Taylor Graham.
Tuominen, K., Talja, S., & Savolainen, R. (2005). The social constructionist viewpoint on information practices. In K. E. Fisher, S. Erdelez, & E. F. McKechnie (Eds.), *Theories of information behavior* (pp. 328–333). Information Today, Inc.
Turner, A. M., Stavri, Z., Revere, D., & Altamore, R. (2008). From the ground up: Information needs of nurses in a rural public health department in Oregon. *Journal of the Medical Library Association, 96*(4), 335–342. https://doi.org/10.3163/1536-5050.96.4.008
Turner, D. (2010). Orally-based information. *Journal of Documentation, 66*(3), 370–383. http://doi.org/10.1108/00220411011038458
Ujwary-Gil, A. (2019). Organizational network analysis: A study of a university library from a network efficiency perspective. *Library & Information Science Research, 41*(1), 48–57. https://doi.org/10.1016/j.lisr.2019.02.007
Urban, A. C. (2020). Narrative ephemera: Documents in storytelling worlds. *Journal of Documentation, 77*(1), 107–127. https://doi.org/10.1108/JD-04-2020-0058
Urquhart, C. (1999). Using vignettes to diagnose information seeking strategies: Opportunities and possible problems for information use studies of health professionals. In T. D. Wilson & D. K. Allen (Eds.), *Information behaviour: Proceedings of the second international conference on research in information needs, seeking and use in different contexts, 13/15 August 1998, Sheffield, UK* (pp. 277–289). Taylor Graham.
Urquhart, C., Light, A., Thomas, R., Barker, A., Yeoman, A., Cooper, J., Armstrong, C., Fenton, R., Lonsdale, R., & Spink, S. (2003). Critical incident technique and explication interviewing in studies of information behavior. *Library & Information Science Research, 25*(1), 63–88. https://doi.org/10.1016/S0740-8188(02)00166-4
Vakkari, P. (1997). Information seeking in context: A challenging metatheory. In P. Vakkari, R. Savolainen, & B. Dervin (Eds.), *Information seeking in context: Proceedings of a meeting in Finland 14–16 August 1996* (pp. 451–463). Taylor Graham.
Vakkari, P. (1999). Task complexity, problem structure and information actions. Integrating studies on information seeking and retrieval. *Information Processing & Management, 35*(6), 819–837. https://doi.org/10.1016/S0306-4573(99)00028-X
Vakkari, P. (2008). Trends and approaches in information behaviour research. *Information Research, 13*(4). http://InformationR.net/ir/13-4/paper361.html
van der Westhuizen, H.-M., Kotze, K., Tonkin-Crine, S., Gobat, N., & Greenhalgh, T. (2020). Face coverings for covid-19: From medical intervention to social practice. *British Medical Journal.* https://doi.org/10.1136/bmj.m3021
Van Rickstal, C. (2021). *American democracy under threat: Misinformation and disinformation on social media. A case study of Donald Trump's mis- and disinformation tweets in the context of the 2021 Capitol siege*. Unpublished master's thesis, Université de Liège. https://matheo.uliege.be/handle/2268.2/12157
VanScoy, A., Thomson, L., & Hartel, J. (2020). Applying theory in practice: The serious leisure perspective and public library programming. *Library & Information Science Research, 42*(3), 101034. https://doi.org/10.1016/j.lisr.2020.101034
Vardell, E., Wang, T., & Thomas, P. A. (2022). "I found what I needed, which was a supportive community": An ethnographic study of shared information practices in an online cosplay community. *Journal of Documentation, 78*(3), 564–579. https://doi.org/10.1108/JD-02-2021-0034
Vårheim, A. (2007). Social capital and public libraries: The need for research. *Library & Information Science Research, 29*(3), 416–428. https://doi.org/10.1016/j.lisr.2007.04.009.

Vårheim, A. (2011). Gracious space: Library programming strategies towards immigrants as tools in the creation of social capital. *Library & Information Science Research*, *33*(1), 12–18. https://doi.org/10.1016/j.lisr.2010.04.005

Vårheim, A. (2017). Public libraries, community resilience, and social capital. *Information Research*, *22*(1). http://InformationR.net/ir/22-1/colis/colis1642.html

Veinot, T. C. (2007). The eyes of the power company: Workplace information practices of a vault inspector. *The Library Quarterly*, *77*(2), 157–179. https://doi.org/10.1086/517842

Veinot, T. C. (2009). Interactive acquisition and sharing: Understanding the dynamics of HIV/AIDS information networks. *Journal of the American Society for Information Science and Technology*, *60*(11), 2313–2332. http://doi.org/10.1002/asi.21151

Veinot, T. C. (2010). A multilevel model of HIV/AIDS information/help network development. *Journal of Documentation*, *66*(6), 875–905. https://doi.org/10.1108/00220411011087850

Veinot, T. C., Kim, Y.-M., & Meadowbrooke, C. C. (2011). Health information behavior in families: Supportive or irritating? *Proceedings of the Association for Information Science and Technology*, *48*(1), 1–10. https://doi.org/10.1002/meet.2011.14504801070

Veinot, T. C., & Pierce, C. S. (2019). Materiality in information environments: Objects, spaces, and bodies in three outpatient hemodialysis facilities. *Journal of the Association for Information Science and Technology*, *70*(12), 1324–1339. https://doi.org/10.1002/asi.24277

Veinot, T. C., & Williams, K. (2012). Following the "community" thread from sociology to information behavior and informatics: Uncovering theoretical continuities and research opportunities. *Journal of the American Society for Information Science and Technology*, *63*(5), 847–864. https://doi.org/10.1002/asi.21653

Vergeer, M. (2015). Peers and sources as social capital in the production of news: Online social networks as communities of journalists. *Social Science Computer Review*, *33*(3), 277–297. https://doi.org/10.1177/0894439314539128

Vesga Vinchira, A. (2019). Modelling the information practices of music fans living in Medellín, Colombia. *Information Research*, *24*(3). http://InformationR.net/ir/24-3/paper833.html

Voigt, M. (1961). *Scientists' approaches to information*. American Library Association.

von Thaden, T. L. (2008). Distributed information behavior: A study of dynamic practice in a safety critical environment. *Journal of the American Society for Information Science and Technology*, *59*(10), 1555–1569. http://doi.org/10.1002/asi.20842

Vygotsky, L. (1978). *Mind in society: The development of higher psychological processes*. Harvard University Press.

Walker, C. G. (2009). Seeking information: A study of the use and understanding of information by parents of young children. *Journal of Information Literacy*, *3*(2), 53–63. https://doi.org/10.11645/3.2.214

Wall, M., Otis Campbell, M., & Janbek, D. (2017). Syrian refugees and information precarity. *New Media & Society*, *19*(2). https://doi.org/10.1177/1461444815591967

Wang, H.-J. (2020). Adoption of open government data: Perspectives of user innovators. *Information Research*, *25*(1). http://InformationR.net/ir/25-1/paper849.html

Wang, K. (2020). Information behavior of parents during COVID-19 in relation to their young school-age children's education. *The Serials Librarian*, *79*, 1–16. https://doi.org/10.1080/0361526X.2020.1806179

Wang, X., Duan, Q., & Liang, M. (2021). Understanding the process of data reuse: An extensive review. *Journal of the Association for Information Science and Technology*, *72*(9), 1161–1182. https://doi.org/10.1002/asi.24483

Wang, X., Shi, J., & Lee, K. M. (2022). The digital divide and seeking health information on smartphones in Asia: Survey study of ten countries. *Journal of Medical Internet Research*, *24*(1), e24086. https://doi.org/10.2196/24086

Ward, W. S., & Given, L. M. (2019). Assessing intercultural communication: Testing technology tools for information sharing in multinational research teams. *Journal of the Association for Information Science and Technology*, *70*(4), 338–350. https://doi.org/10.1002/asi.24159

Watson-Boone, R. (1994). The information needs and habits of humanities scholars. *RQ*, *34*, 203–216. https://www.jstor.org/stable/20862645

Webster, T., Gollner, K., & Nathan, L. (2015). Neighbourhood book exchanges: Localising information practices. *Information Research*, *20*(1). http://InformationR.net/ir/20-3/paper684.html

Wellard, J. H. (1935). State of reading among the working classes of England during the first half of the nineteenth century. *The Library Quarterly*, *5*(1), 87–100.

Wellings, S., & Casselden, B. (2019). An exploration into the information-seeking behaviours of engineers and scientists. *Journal of Librarianship and Information Science*, *51*(3), 789–800. https://doi.org/10.1177/0961000617742466

Wenger, E. (1998). *Communities of practice: Learning, meaning, and identity*. Cambridge University Press.

Wenger, E. (2010). Communities of practice and social learning systems: The career of a concept. In *Social learning systems and communities of practice* (pp. 179–198). Springer.

Wersig, G., & Windel, G. (1985). Information science needs a theory of 'information actions'. *Social Science Information Studies*, *5*, 11–23. https://doi.org/10.1016/0143-6236(85)90003-1

Westbrook, L. (2003). Information needs and experiences of scholars in women's studies: Problems and solutions. *College & Research Libraries*, *64*(3), 192–209.

Westbrook, L. (2008). E-government support for people in crisis: An evaluation of police department website support for domestic violence survivors using "person-in-situation" information needs analysis. *Library & Information Science Research*, *30*(1), 22–38. https://doi.org/10.1016/j.lisr.2007.07.004

Westbrook, L. (2009). Crisis information concerns: Information needs of domestic violence survivors. *Information Processing & Management*, *45*(1), 98–114. http://doi.org/10.1016/j.ipm.2008.05.005

Westbrook, L., & Zhang, Y. (2015). Questioning strangers about critical medical decisions: 'What happens if you have sex between the HPV shots?' *Information Research*, *20*(2). http://InformationR.net/ir/20-2/paper667.html

Westley, B. H., & Barrow, L. C. (1959). An investigation of news-seeking behavior. *Journalism Quarterly*, *36*, 431–438.

White, H. (1980). Library effectiveness—The elusive target. *American Libraries*, *11*(December), 682–683.

White, M. D. (2000). Questioning behavior on a consumer health electronic list. *The Library Quarterly*, *70*, 302–334. https://www.jstor.org/stable/4309440

White, M. D., Matteson, M., & Abels, E. G. (2008). Beyond dictionaries – Understanding information behavior of professional translators. *Journal of Documentation*, *64*(4), 576–601. http://doi.org/10.1108/00220410810884084

Whitmire, E. (2003). Epistemological beliefs and the information-seeking behavior of undergraduates. *Library & Information Science Research*, *25*(2), 127–142. https://doi.org/10.1016/S0740-8188(03)00003-3

Wiberley, S. E., & Jones, W. G. (1989). Patterns of information seeking in the humanities. *College & Research Libraries*, *50*, 638–645.

Wiberley, S. E., & Jones, W. G. (1994). Humanists revisited: A longitudinal look at the adoption of information technology. *College & Research Libraries*, *55*, 499–509.

Wiberley, S. E., & Jones, W. G. (2000). Time and technology: A decade-long look at humanists' use of electronic information technology. *College & Research Libraries*, *61*, 421–431.

Widén-Wulff, G. (2007). *Challenges of knowledge sharing in practice: A social approach*. Chandos.

Widén-Wulff, G., & Davenport, E. (2007). Activity systems, information sharing and the development of organizational knowledge in two Finnish firms: An exploratory study using activity theory. *Information Research*, *7 12*(3). http://InformationR.net/ir/12-3/paper310.html

Wiering, L. (2005). Uncertainty in the face of illness: Factors influencing patients' knowledge-related confidence. In S. Rubinelli & J. Haes (Eds.), Presented at *the Tailoring health messages: Bridging the gap between social and humanistic perspectives on health communication* (pp. 20–25). University of Lugano.

Wilkinson, M. A. (2001). Information sources used by lawyers in problem solving: An empirical exploration. *Library & Information Science Research*, *23*(3), 257–276. https://doi.org/10.1016/S0740-8188(01)00082-2

Williamson, K. (1998). Discovered by chance: The role of incidental information acquisition in an ecological model of information use. *Library & Information Science Research*, *20*, 23–40. https://doi.org/10.1016/S0740-8188(98)90004-4

Williamson, K. (2005). Ecological theory of human information behavior. In K. E. Fisher, S. Erdelez, & E. F. McKechnie (Eds.), *Theories of information behavior* (pp. 128–132). Information Today, Inc.

Williamson, K., & Manaszewicz, R. (2002). Breast cancer information needs and seeking: Towards an intelligent, user sensitive portal to breast cancer knowledge online. *New Review of Information Behaviour Research*, *3*, 203–219.

Williamson, K., & McGregor, J. (2006). Information use and secondary school students: A model for understanding plagiarism. *Information Research*, *12*(1). http://InformationR.net/ir/12-1/paper288.html

Williamson, K., Qayyum, A., Hider, P., & Liu, Y. H. (2012). Young adults and everyday-life information: The role of news media. *Library & Information Science Research*, *34*(4), 258–264. http://doi.org/10.1016/j.lisr.2012.05.001

Williamson, K., & Roberts, J. (2010). Developing and sustaining a sense of place: The role of social information. *Library & Information Science Research*, *32*(4), 281–287. https://doi.org/10.1016/j.lisr.2010.07.012

Williamson, K., & Smith, D. K. (2010). Empowered or vulnerable? The role of information for Australian online investors. *Canadian Journal of Information and Library Science*, *34*(1), 39–81. https://doi.org/10.1353/ils.0.0004

Williams, R. D., & Willett, R. (2019). Makerspaces and boundary work: The role of librarians as educators in public library makerspaces. *Journal of Librarianship and Information Science*, *51*(3), 801–813. https://doi.org/10.1177/0961000617742467

Willson, R. (2018). "Systemic managerial constraints": How universities influence the information behaviour of HSS early career academics. *Journal of Documentation*, *74*(4), 862–879. https://doi.org/10.1108/JD-07-2017-0111

Willson, R. (2022). "Bouncing ideas" as a complex information practice: Information seeking, sharing, creation, and cooperation. *Journal of Documentation*, *78*(4), 800–816. https://doi.org/10.1108/JD-03-2021-0047

Willson, R., Allen, D., Julien, H., & Burnett, K. (2020). *JASIS&T special issue on information behaviour & information practices theory: Call for papers*. Association for Information Science and Technology. https://www.asist.org/2020/02/25/jasist-special-issue-on-information-behaviour-information-practices-theory-call-for-papers/

Willson, R., & Given, L. M. (2014). Student search behaviour in an online public access catalogue: An examination of "searching mental models" and "searcher self-concept". *Information Research*, *19*(3). http://informationr.net/ir/19-3/paper640.html

Willson, R., & Given, L. M. (2020). 'I'm in sheer survival mode:' Information behaviour and affective experiences of early career academics. *Library & Information Science Research*, *42*(2). https://doi.org/10.1016/j.lisr.2020.101014

Willson, R., Greyson, D., Gibson, A. N., & Bronstein, J. (2020). Pulling back the curtain on conducting social impact research. *Proceedings of the Association for Information Science and Technology*, *57*(1). https://doi.org/10.1002/pra2.427

Willson, R., Julien, H., & Burnett, G. (Eds.). (2022). JASIS&T special issue on information behavior and information practices theory [editorial]. *Journal of the Association for Information Science and Technology*, *73*(4), 491–493. https://doi.org/10.1002/asi.24622

Wilson, T. D. (1981). On user studies and information needs. *Journal of Documentation*, *37*, 3–15. https://doi.org/10.1108/eb026702

Wilson, T. D. (1984). The cognitive approach to information seeking behavior and information use. *Social Science Information Studies*, *4*, 197–204. https://doi.org/10.1016/0143-6236(84)90076-0

Wilson, T. D. (1994). Information needs and uses: Fifty years of progress? In B. Vickery (Ed.), *Fifty years of progress: A journal of documentation review* (pp. 15–52). Aslib.

Wilson, T. D. (1997). Information behaviour: An interdisciplinary perspective. In P. Vakkari, R. Savolainen, & B. Dervin (Eds.), *Information seeking in context: Proceedings of a meeting in Finland 14–16 August 1996* (pp. 39–49). Taylor Graham.

Wilson, T. D. (1999). Models in information behaviour research. *Journal of Documentation, 55*(3), 249–270. https://doi.org/10.1108/EUM0000000007145

Wilson, T. D. (2002). Alfred Schutz, phenomenology and research methodology for information behaviour research. *New Review of Information Behaviour Research, 3*, 71–81. http://informationr.net/tdw/publ/papers/schutz02.html

Wilson, T. D. (2005). Evolution in information behavior modeling: Wilson's model. In K. E. Fisher, S. Erdelez, & L. E. F. McKechnie (Eds.), *Theories of information behavior* (pp. 31–36). Information Today, Inc.

Wilson, T. D. (2006). A re-examination of information seeking behaviour in the context of activity theory. *Information Research, 11*(4). http://InformationR.net/ir/11-4/paper260.html

Wilson, T. D. (2008a). The information user: Past, present and future. *Journal of Information Science, 34*(4), 457–464. https://doi.org/10.1177/0165551508091309

Wilson, T. D. (2008b). Activity theory and information seeking. *Annual Review of Information Science & Technology, 42*(1), 119–161. https://doi.org/10.1002/aris.2008.1440420111

Wilson, T. D. (2010a). Information sharing: An exploration of the literature and some propositions. *Information Research, 15*(4). http://InformationR.net/ir/15-4/paper440.html

Wilson, T. D. (2010b). Fifty years of information behavior research. *Bulletin of the American Society for Information Science and Technology, 36*(3), 27–34. https://doi.org/10.1002/bult.2010.1720360308

Wilson, T. D. (Ed.). (2013). *Theory in information behaviour research*. Eiconics Ltd.

Wilson, T. D. (2016). A general theory of human information behaviour. In *Proceedings of ISIC, the Information Behaviour Conference*, Zadar, Croatia, 20–23 September, 2016: Part 1. *Information Research, 21*(4). http://InformationR.net/ir/21-4/isic/isic1601.html

Wilson, T. D. (2020). The transfer of theories and models from information behaviour research into other disciplines. *Information Research, 25*(3). https://doi.org/10.47989/irpaper873

Wilson, T. D. (2022). *Exploring information behaviour: An introduction*. T.D. Wilson. http://informationr.net/ir/Exploring%20information%20behaviour.pdf

Wojciechowska, M. (2020). Social capital, trust and social activity among librarians: Results of research conducted in 20 countries across the world. *Library & Information Science Research, 42*(4). https://doi.org/10.1016/j.lisr.2020.101049

Wolf, C. T., & Veinot, T. C. (2015). Struggling for space and finding my place: An interactionist perspective on everyday use of biomedical information. *Journal of the Association for Information Science and Technology, 66*(2), 282–296. https://doi.org/10.1002/asi.23178

Wolf, F. M. (1986). *Meta-analysis: Quantitative methods for research scientists*. Sage Publications.

Wood, D. N. (1971). User studies: A review of the literature from 1966–1970. *ASLIB Proceedings, 23*(1), 11–23. https://doi.org/10.1108/eb050272

Worrall, A., & Oh, S. (2013). The place of health information and socio-emotional support in social questioning and answering. *Information Research, 18*(3). http://informationr.net/ir/18-3/paper587.html

Woudstra, L., & van den Hooff, B. (2008). Inside the source selection process: Selection criteria for human information sources. *Information Processing & Management, 44*(3), 1267–1278. https://doi.org/10.1016/j.ipm.2007.07.004

Wu, D., Dong, J., & Liu, C. (2019). Exploratory study of cross-device search tasks. *Information Processing & Management, 56*(6), 102073. https://doi.org/10.1016/j.ipm.2019.102073

Wu, D., & Li, Y. (2016). Online health information seeking behaviors among Chinese elderly. *Library & Information Science Research, 38*(3), 272–279. https://doi.org/10.1016/j.lisr.2016.08.011

Wylie Atmore, A. (2017). Just rol[l/e] with it: The sense-making practices of a tabletop roleplaying game community. In *Proceedings of RAILS - Research Applications, Information and Library Studies, 2016, School of Information Management, Victoria University of Wellington*, New Zealand, 6–8 December, 2016. *Information Research, 22*(4). http://InformationR.net/ir/22-4/rails/rails1613.html

Xia, L. (2010). An examination of consumer browsing behaviors. *Qualitative Market Research: An International Journal, 13*(2), 154–173. https://doi.org/10.1108/13522751011032593

Xie, B. (2008). The mutual shaping of online and offline social relationships. *Information Research, 13*(3). http://informationr.net/ir/13-3/paper350.html

Xie, B., He, D., Mercer, T., Wang, Y., Wu, D., Fleischmann, K. R., Zhang, Y., Yoder, L. H., Stephens, K. K., Mackert, M., & Lee, M. K. (2020). Global health crises are also information crises: A call to action. *Journal of the Association for Information Science and Technology*, *71*(12), 1419–1423. https://doi.org/10.1002/asi.24357

Yakel, E. (2004). Seeking information, seeking connections, seaking meaning: Genealogists and family historians. *Information Research*, *10*(1). http://InformationR.net/ir/10-1/paper205.html

Yakel, E. (2005). Archival intelligence. In K. E. Fisher, S. Erdelez, & E. F. McKechnie (Eds.), *Theories of information behavior* (pp. 49–53). Information Today, Inc.

Yakel, E., & Torres, D. (2007). Genealogists as a "community of records". *American Archivist*, *70*(1), 93–113. https://www.jstor.org/stable/40294451

Yang, Z. J., Aloe, A. M., & Feeley, T. H. (2014). Risk information seeking and processing model: A meta-analysis. *Journal of Communication*, *64*(1), 20–41. https://doi.org/10.1111/jcom.12071

Yates, C., & Partridge, H. (2015). Citizens and social media in times of natural disaster: Exploring information experience. *Information Research*, *20*(1). http://InformationR.net/ir/20-1/paper659.html

Ye, M. (2019, March). Collaborative information seeking in tourism: A study of young Chinese leisure tourists visiting Australia. In *Proceedings of the 2019 Conference on Human Information Interaction and Retrieval* (pp. 441–444). https://doi.org/10.1145/3295750.3298979

Ye, E. M., Du, J. T., Hansen, P., Ashman, H., Sigala, M., & Huang, S. (2021). Understanding roles in collaborative information behaviour: A case of Chinese group travelling. *Information Processing & Management*, *58*(4), 102581. https://doi.org/10.1016/j.ipm.2021.102581

Yeh, N.-C. (2008). The social constructionist viewpoint on gays and lesbians, and their information behaviour. *Information Research*, *13*(4). http://InformationR.net/ir/13-4/paper364.html

Yeoman, A. (2010). Applying McKenzie's model of information practices in everyday life information seeking in the context of menopause transition. *Information Research*, *15*(4). http://InformationR.net/ir/15-4/paper444.html

Yeon, J., & Lee, J. Y. (2021). Employment information needs and information behaviour of North Korean refugees. *Information Research*, *26*(4). https://doi.org/10.47989/irpaper914

Yerbury, H. (2015). Information practices of young activists in Rwanda. *Information Research*, *20*(1). http://InformationR.net/ir/20-1/paper656.html

Yerbury, H., & Henninger, M. (2019). Information literacy and regimes of truth: Continuity and disruption. In *Proceedings of RAILS - Research Applications, Information and Library Studies, 2018*, Australia, 28–30 November 2018. Faculty of Information Technology, Monash University. *Information Research, 24*(3). http://InformationR.net/ir/24-3/rails/rails1801.html

Yerbury, H., & Shahid, A. (2017). Social media activism in Maldives; information practices and civil society. *Information Research*, *22*(1). http://InformationR.net/ir/22-1/colis/colis1614.html

Younger, P. (2010). Internet-based information-seeking behaviour amongst doctors and nurses: A short review of the literature. *Health Information and Libraries Journal*, *27*(1), 2–10. https://doi.org/10.1111/j.1471-1842.2010.00883.x

Yu, X. (2012). Exploring visual perception and children's interpretations of picture books. *Library & Information Science Research*, *34*(4), 292–299. https://doi.org/10.1016/j.lisr.2012.06.004

Zach, L. (2005). When is "enough" enough? Modeling the information seeking and stopping behavior of senior arts administrators. *Journal of the American Society for Information Science and Technology*, *56*(1), 23–35. https://doi.org/10.1002/asi.20092

Zannettou, S., Sirivianos, M., Blackburn, J., & Kourtellis, N. (2019). The web of false information: Rumors, fake news, hoaxes, clickbait, and various other shenanigans. *Journal of Data and Information Quality*, *11*(3), 1–37. https://doi.org/10.1145/3309699

Zerbinos, E. (1990). Information seeking and information processing: Newspapers versus videotext. *Journalism Quarterly*, *67*, 920–929. https://doi.org/10.1177/107769909006700446

Zhang, G., & Jacob, E. K. (2013). Understanding boundaries: Physical, epistemological and virtual dimensions. *Information Research*, *18*(3). http://InformationR.net/ir/18-3/colis/paperC21.html

Zhang, P., & Soergel, D. (2014). Towards a comprehensive model of the cognitive process and mechanisms of individual sensemaking. *Journal of the American Society for Information Science and Technology*, *65*(9), 1733–1756. https://doi.org/10.1002/asi.23125

Zhang, Y. (2014). Beyond quality and accessibility: Source selection in consumer health information searching. *Journal of the American Society for Information Science and Technology*, *65*(5), 911–927. https://doi.org/10.1002/asi.23023

Zhang, Y., & Sun, Y. (2015). Users' link sharing behaviour in an online health community. In *Proceedings of ISIC, the Information Behaviour Conference*, Leeds, 2–5 September, 2014: Part 2. *Information Research, 20*(1). http://InformationR.net/ir/20-1/isic2/isic35.html

Zhang, Y., Sun, Y., & Xie, B. (2015). Quality of health information for consumers on the web: A systematic review of indicators, criteria, tools, and evaluation results. *Journal of the Association for Information Science and Technology*, *66*(10), 2071–2084. https://doi.org/10.1002/asi.23311

Zhao, D., & Strotmann, A. (2022). Intellectual structure of information science 2011–2020: An author co-citation analysis. *Journal of Documentation*, *78*(3), 728–744. https://doi.org/10.1108/JD-06-2021-0119

Zhao, Y., & Zhang, J. (2017). Consumer health information seeking in social media: A literature review. *Health Information and Libraries Journal*, *34*, 268–283. https://doi.org/10.1111/hir.12192

Zhao, Y., Zhang, R., & Klein, K. K. (2009). Perceived information needs and availability: Results of a survey of small dairy farmers in Inner Mongolia. *Information Research*, *14*(3). http://InformationR.net/ir/14-3/paper411.html

Zhou, J., Ghose, B., Wang, R., Wu, R., Li, Z., Huang, R., Feng, D., Feng, Z., & Tang, S. (2020). Health perceptions and misconceptions regarding COVID-19 in China: Online survey study. *Journal of Medical Internet Research*, *22*(11), e21099. https://doi.org/10.2196/21099

Zhu, C., Zeng, R., Zhang, W., Evans, R., & He, R. (2019). Pregnancy-related information seeking and sharing in the social media era among expectant mothers: Qualitative study. *Journal of Medical Internet Research*, *21*(12), e13694. https://doi.org/10.1002/asi.23023

Zigron, S., & Bronstein, J. (2019). "Help is where you find it": The role of weak ties networks as sources of information and support in virtual health communities. *Journal of the Association for Information Science and Technology*, *70*(2), 130–139. https://doi.org/10.1002/asi.24106

Zimmer, M. (2010). But the data is already public: On the ethics of research in Facebook. *Ethics and Information Technology*, *12*(4), 313–325. https://doi.org/10.1007/s10676-010-9227-5

Zimmerman, M. S. (2018). Information horizons mapping to assess the health literacy of refugee and immigrant women in the USA. *Information Research*, *23*(4). http://informationr.net/ir/23-4/paper802.html

Zimmerman, M. S., & Shaw, G. (2020). Health information seeking behaviour: A concept analysis. *Health Information and Libraries Journal*, *37*(3), 173–191. https://doi.org/10.1111/hir.12287

Zubek, J. (Ed.). (1969). *Sensory deprivation: Fifteen years of research*. Appleton-Century-Crofts.

Zweizig, D. (1977). Measuring library use. *Drexel Library Quarterly*, *13*, 2–15.

AUTHOR INDEX

SUBJECT INDEX